Applied Linguistics Research

Designed for graduate students, instructors, and seasoned researchers, this is an essential guide for robust research design and methodology in applied linguistics, covering qualitative, quantitative, and mixed methods research. It adopts a structured approach, starting with the foundational principles of research design, methodology, and data collection and analysis, and progressing to interpreting, explaining, and reporting research results, bringing together all the steps and processes of research from start to finish in one single volume in a way that is practical, easy to follow, and simple to understand. Throughout, the emphasis is on the process of research and the application of various research techniques and principles across different areas. These characteristics, coupled with numerous pedagogical features, such as key-term reviews, visuals, research scenarios, and many discussion and activity questions, make the book an indispensable reference and a valuable textbook for courses in second language and applied linguistics research.

Hossein Nassaji is Professor of Applied Linguistics at the University of Victoria, BC, Canada. He has received several prizes and awards including the Kenneth W. Mildenberger Prize from the Modern Language Association of America, the Research Excellence Award from the University of Victoria, and the BC TEAL 50 at 50 Award. He has been recently elected as a Fellow of the Royal Society of Canada.

Applied Linguistics Research

A Comprehensive Guide to Methodology, Design, Analysis, and Evaluation

Hossein Nassaji

University of Victoria, British Columbia, Canada

CAMBRIDGE
UNIVERSITY PRESS

Shaftesbury Road, Cambridge CB2 8EA, United Kingdom

One Liberty Plaza, 20th Floor, New York, NY 10006, USA

477 Williamstown Road, Port Melbourne, VIC 3207, Australia

314–321, 3rd Floor, Plot 3, Splendor Forum, Jasola District Centre, New Delhi – 110025, India

103 Penang Road, #05-06/07, Visioncrest Commercial, Singapore 238467

Cambridge University Press is part of Cambridge University Press & Assessment,
a department of the University of Cambridge.

We share the University's mission to contribute to society through the pursuit
of education, learning and research at the highest international levels of excellence.

www.cambridge.org
Information on this title: www.cambridge.org/highereducation/isbn/9781108480673

DOI: 10.1017/9781108672146

Cover illustration: Xuanyu Han/Getty Images. Cover design: Andrew Ward

When citing this work, please include a reference to the DOI 10.1017/9781108672146

First published 2026

A catalogue record for this publication is available from the British Library

A Cataloging-in-Publication data record for this book is available from the Library of Congress.

ISBN 978-1-108-48067-3 Hardback
ISBN 978-1-108-72786-0 Paperback

Contents

Figures

Tables

Preface

This book aims to provide a comprehensive guide to research and research methods in applied linguistics, and to offer practical advice on how to design and implement effective research studies. It also aims to help students develop the necessary skills and knowledge to evaluate the soundness of research designs and methods used in current research in applied linguistics and second language studies. It is based on more than two decades of my personal experience in conducting research and teaching courses on research methods, and the challenges I have seen students and researchers face when carrying out second language (L2) and applied linguistics research.

Applied linguistics is an interdisciplinary field of inquiry that embraces a wide range of disciplines and research areas, including language learning and teaching, language assessment, language policy and planning, and discourse analysis, among others. It also seeks to better understand how language is used, how it functions in various contexts, and how its use can improve practical problems and facilitate communication. As such, conducting research in applied linguistics has become paramount, requiring a diverse set of research methods that can be tailored to specific research questions and objectives. This book is designed to equip readers with the essential tools and techniques to engage in meaningful inquiry, addressing questions that matter in various applied linguistics domains, from second language acquisition and education to discourse studies, sociolinguistics, language policy, and beyond.

Doing research involves numerous decisions, ranging from determining which questions to investigate, selecting participants, and choosing an appropriate research design to procedures that ensure validity and reliability of the data and the clear and accurate presentation and interpretation of the results. In the pages ahead, we embark on a journey through this intricate process of conducting research. By breaking down the complex process and methodologies into accessible components, the book caters to both seasoned researchers seeking a refresher and newcomers eager to embark on their research journey for the first time.

The book adopts a structured approach, starting with the foundational principles of research design, methodology, and data collection and analysis, and progressing to writing and interpreting, explaining, and reporting research results. Each chapter unfolds in a progressive manner, leading readers through the intricacies of data collection, analysis, and interpretation, in qualitative, quantitative and mixed methods research. Throughout, the text emphasizes the process of research and the application of various research techniques and principles across diverse areas. As a result, it brings together all the steps and processes of applied linguistics research from start to finish in one single volume in a way that is practical, easy to follow, and simple to understand.

Many textbooks provide an overview of various research types; however, they often offer only limited guidance on practical steps for choosing the most suitable method, selecting participants and an adequate sample size, or detailing strategies to ensure the validity and reliability of research results. Few also provide learners with adequate skills to critically read, evaluate, and interpret various kinds of research conducted and reported by others. This book places particular emphasis on the skills needed to evaluate different types of research, and addresses a variety of research strategies, data collection tools, and data analysis processes, including those related to quantitative, qualitative, and mixed methods research. In doing so, the book covers all the steps and processes involved in such research from its conceptualization to its execution and the dissemination of its results. To illustrate the process, numerous practical activities and examples, both hypothetical and drawn from current research, are provided. By incorporating a mix of hypothetical situations and real-world examples, the book creates an enriching learning context that not only clarifies the complexities of the research process but also helps readers with concrete skills applicable to their own research endeavors.

Rationale and Purposes for the Book

This book is designed to fulfill several key objectives. Firstly, it aims to demystify the research process, offering a systematic guide to designing, conducting, interpreting, and evaluating research in applied linguistics and second language research. With this in mind, the book seeks to make the content accessible and comprehensible to a wide range of readers, including students, researchers, and professionals in the field. The intention is not merely to present information but to provide a structured guide that takes readers through every critical stage of research.

Secondly, the text seeks to foster an appreciation for the vibrant interplay between theory and practice. By presenting a range of research methodologies applicable to various contexts and research questions, the book seeks to provide readers with an adaptable toolkit to deal with the complexities of second language and applied linguistics research. Whether investigating language acquisition, exploring sociolinguistic phenomena, or examining other applied linguistics questions, the diverse array of methodologies discussed in these pages helps researchers tailor their approaches to the unique demands of their specific inquiries.

Thirdly, the volume not only endeavors to impart knowledge but also prioritizes readability, ensuring accessibility for learners of various backgrounds and proficiency levels. The aim has been to create a highly readable text driven by the recognition that the clear and engaging presentation of information significantly enhances the learning experience.

Furthermore, the book aspires to inspire creativity and critical reading and analysis of research in applied linguistics. It attempts to provide students and researchers with adequate skills to critically read, evaluate, and interpret various kinds of research conducted and reported by others. This book will place particular emphasis on the skills needed to evaluate the validity and reliability of different types of research designs and methodology.

Unlike most existing books, which simply describe different research methods, this book will take a process-based approach, focusing on what is actually involved in doing research and how this can be communicated to students. In doing so, it will take the reader step by step through various phases of research, from selecting the question and searching the literature to collecting, analyzing, and presenting results.

The book also goes a step further in enhancing the learning experience by incorporating practical examples that specifically utilize SPSS (Statistical Package for the Social Sciences), using version 29. The aim behind this strategic inclusion is to bridge the gap between theoretical understanding and hands-on application, providing readers with a tangible and practical grasp of the research concepts discussed. By integrating SPSS steps and examples, readers are guided through the application of statistical techniques using this widely employed software, allowing them to see how theoretical concepts manifest themselves in actual research scenarios. This approach not only reinforces comprehension but also empowers readers to gain proficiency in utilizing SPSS as a valuable tool in their own quantitative research endeavors.

Another goal of the book is to foster research skills that are both rigorous and ethically grounded. Recognizing the profound impact of research on both scholarly communities and society at large, the aim is to foster a commitment to integrity and ethical conduct in every facet of the research process. In doing so, the book discusses the importance of methodological rigor, emphasizing the significance of robust research design, data collection, and analysis. Simultaneously, it underscores the ethical dimensions inherent in research, guiding readers to navigate complex ethical considerations responsibly and with sensitivity.

In short, the book serves as a comprehensive guide for scholars, researchers, and students interested in conducting second language and applied linguistics research. It provides an in-depth coverage, enabling students, professionals, and novice researchers in the field to gain the thorough knowledge and skills that can enable them to be not just consumers of research but also producers of knowledge, by effectively conducting research in their respective fields. Whether you are a seasoned researcher or a novice entering the field, this book is designed to be a valuable resource, providing the necessary guidance and inspiration to embark on meaningful and impactful research journeys in the vibrant realm of applied linguistics.

Outstanding Features

- In-depth coverage and clear explanation of various research methods and strategies

- Focus on process and the evolving nature of research
- Numerous hypothetical examples and those from cutting-edge research in second language studies and applied linguistics
- Follow-up discussion and activity questions to keep readers actively engaged in the learning process, reinforcing their understanding of the research methods discussed
- Comprehensive exploration of qualitative and quantitative techniques for collecting, analyzing, and evaluating data
- In-depth discussion of statistical procedures, their applications, relative merits, and shortcomings
- The incorporation of examples, instruction on how to use SPSS to conduct descriptive and commonly used inferential statistics (both parametric and non-parametric), and guidance on how to interpret results
- An accessible writing style that makes complex concepts approachable for both novice and experienced researchers
- Encouragement of critical thinking by discussing the strengths and limitations of various research methods, allowing readers to make informed decisions based on their research goals
- Incorporation of pedagogical features, including summaries of key terms and visuals such as tables, charts, and diagrams to enhance learning and comprehension

Overview of the Book Content

The book consists of seven parts and twenty-five chapters. This organizational design aims to guide readers on a well-sequenced journey, progressively building their knowledge from foundational principles to more advanced concepts.

Part I, titled "Introduction to Applied Linguistics Research," discusses the foundational aspects of the discipline. It includes three chapters that define the domains, key characteristics, processes, and different methodological approaches as well as ethical considerations in applied linguistics research. Chapter 1, "Introduction: The Nature and Purpose of Research," serves as an opening, providing readers with a fundamental understanding of the nature and overarching purpose of research. It sets the stage for the subsequent exploration of applied linguistics research by introducing key concepts and the significance of research in this field. Chapter 2, "Applied Linguistics Research: Its Nature, Significance, and Scope," examines the subject in greater depth, expanding on the nature and significance of applied linguistics research. It explores the scope of research in this domain, explaining the diverse avenues and areas where applied linguistics plays an important role. This chapter aims to provide readers with a broad perspective on the multifaceted dimensions of applied linguistics research. Chapter 3, "Ethics in Applied Linguistics Research: Principles, Best Practices, and Challenges," focuses on the ethical dimensions of applied linguistics research, underscoring the importance of conducting research responsibly and with integrity. This chapter prepares readers to have the ethical framework necessary for conducting ethical research in applied linguistics.

Part II, titled "Research Process and Designing Research," provides readers with a comprehensive understanding of the foundational aspects involved in the execution and design of applied linguistics research. This part includes four chapters that address key components of the research process, offering practical guidance in designing robust linguistic studies. Chapter 4, "The Research Process: A Ten-Step Model," introduces a systematic ten-step model that serves as a guide through the entire research process. It covers the sequential stages from conceptualization to the dissemination of findings, providing a structured framework to enhance the implementation of research designs effectively and efficiently. Chapter 5, "A Framework for Understanding Research Types," focuses on the diverse research types within applied linguistics. The aim is to provide a framework for understanding different research types and the various ways in which research types can be conceptualized. Chapter 6, "Understanding and Describing Research Constructs and Variables," explores the complexities of defining, describing, and operationalizing research constructs and variables. It discusses different types of variables, such as independent, dependent, and control variables, alongside different types of measurement scales and how to use them. Chapter 7, "Review of the Literature and the Development of Research Questions," guides readers through the techniques of conducting literature reviews and also helps them to develop well-defined research questions.

Part III, titled "Quantitative Research Designs and Data Collection," is a dedicated section that explores the essential components of conducting quantitative research. It includes five chapters. Chapter 8, "Selecting Participants for Quantitative Research: Sampling Techniques and Methods," discusses the critical process of participant selection in quantitative research. It covers various sampling techniques and methods, providing readers with the knowledge to make informed decisions about sample size, representation, and generalizability. Chapter 9, "Designing Quantitative Research: Types and Techniques," focuses on the design phase, exploring the diverse design types and techniques involved in quantitative research, including various experimental, quasi-experimental, and nonexperimental designs. Chapter 10, "Collecting Quantitative Data: Tools and Techniques," addresses the practical aspects of data collection. To this end, the chapter outlines different methods for gathering quantitative data in applied linguistics research, including various tests, tasks, and measures assessing language skills, such as vocabulary, reading, writing, and speaking. It explores the design, implementation, and practical applications of these assessments. The chapter also covers the measurement of communicative skills and explains different types of communicative tasks aimed at generating research data. It also explores various tests and tasks that can measure pragmatic, cognitive, and affective domains of language research. Chapter 11, "Understanding and Assessing Reliability in Quantitative Research," focuses on the important role of reliability in quantitative research. The chapter explores various methods for ensuring the consistency and dependability of measurements, essential for establishing the rigor of research findings. Chapter 12, "Understanding and Assessing Validity in Quantitative

Research," explores the concept of validity. This chapter provides a comprehensive examination of how researchers can ensure that their measurements accurately measure the intended constructs. It discusses different types of validity, guiding readers in the critical evaluation of the soundness of their research designs and their data collection tools and measures.

Part IV, "Qualitative Research Designs, Data Collection, and Analysis," discusses the various stages of qualitative research including sampling techniques, research designs, data collection procedures, data analysis techniques and issues pertaining to reliability and validity of qualitative research. It comprises six chapters. Chapter 13, "Selecting Participants for Qualitative Research: Sampling Techniques and Methods," provides readers with the skills and knowledge necessary to select participants for qualitative research by exploring various sampling techniques and methods. Chapter 14, "Designing Qualitative Research: Types and Techniques," explores the diverse types and techniques involved in qualitative research design. The focus includes an exploration of prevalent types, such as ethnography, grounded theory, case study, and narrative inquiry, as well as a discussion of various discourse studies, examining subtypes such as conversation analysis, interaction analysis, and critical discourse analysis. Chapter 15, "Collecting Qualitative Data: Methods and Strategies," discusses the various methods and strategies employed in collecting qualitative data, including methods such as interviews, focus groups, observation, and verbal reports. The analysis extends to evaluating the strengths and weaknesses of these methods, identifying their suitability for various types of research questions. Practical considerations, such as sample selection and data analysis techniques, are thoroughly assessed. Chapter 16, "Analyzing Qualitative Data: Techniques and Strategies," provides a comprehensive exploration of qualitative data analysis, covering its definition, purpose, and the various steps involved in the process, including data preparation, transcription, data familiarization, and coding. The chapter also distinguishes between different types of qualitative analysis, such as content analysis and thematic analysis. Chapter 17, "Understanding and Establishing Reliability and Validity in Qualitative Research," focuses on the concepts of reliability and validity within the context of qualitative research. This chapter aims to guide readers in understanding and establishing the trustworthiness of qualitative research findings, and enhancing the rigor and credibility of their studies.

Part V, "Quantitative Research: Data Analysis and Interpretation," is a section dedicated to addressing the complexities involved in the analysis and interpretation of quantitative data in applied linguistics research. This part includes six chapters. Chapter 18, "Analyzing Quantitative Data: Descriptive Statistics," explores the foundational aspects of descriptive statistics, discussing essential tools for summarizing and displaying quantitative data. In Chapter 19, "Analyzing Quantitative Data: Exploring Key Concepts in Inferential Statistics," key aspects of inferential statistics are covered, from random sampling, probability distributions, and the central limit theorem to point and interval estimation. The chapter also discusses the concepts of confidence intervals, one-tailed and two-tailed tests, as well as Type I and Type II errors. In essence, the chapter covers a number of fundamental concepts in inferential statistics, providing the reader with a robust foundation to explore and apply these key principles in quantitative data analysis. Chapter 20, "Commonly Used Inferential Statistics Tests in Applied Linguistics Research: Parametric Tests," explores the parametric tests commonly used in applied linguistics research, offering insights into their applications and interpretations using various examples. Chapter 21, "Commonly Used Inferential Statistics Tests in Applied Linguistics Research: Nonparametric Tests," focuses on the nonparametric tests frequently employed in applied linguistics research, providing a thorough understanding of such alternative statistical approaches and how to use them when they are needed, supported by examples. Chapter 22 "Advanced Statistical Models: GLMs, Mixed Models, and Multivariate Analysis," discusses statistical methods that go beyond the limitations of traditional parametric and nonparametric tests. It introduces generalized linear models (GLMs) and mixed effects models, including generalized linear mixed models (GLMMs), which are powerful tools for analyzing data with complex structures. In addition, the chapter briefly overviews other advanced statistical techniques, such as factor analysis, path analysis, structural equation modeling (SEM), and Bayesian statistics, as an alternative to traditional frequentist approaches. Chapter 23, "Effect Sizes: Types, Calculations, and Interpretation," explores the important notion of effect sizes, their different types, methods of calculation, and their interpretation. Effect sizes are important in assessing the practical significance of research findings.

Part VI, "Carrying Out Mixed Methods Research," explores Mixed Methods Research. It is made up of one chapter, Chapter 24, "Mixed Methods Research: Integrating Qualitative and Quantitative Approaches," which provides an exploration of how researchers can effectively blend qualitative and quantitative methodologies to gain a more holistic understanding of their research question. It guides readers through the process of designing and conducting mixed methods studies, emphasizing the synergy between qualitative and quantitative data collection and analysis. This integration allows researchers to capitalize on the strengths of both approaches, enriching the depth and breadth of their research endeavors. Overall, Part VI provides a practical and accessible guide for researchers interested in applying mixed methods research across various areas of applied linguistics.

Part VII, titled "Dissemination of Research Findings," includes one chapter, Chapter 25, titled "Disseminating Research Findings: Writing Research Reports." This chapter specifically addresses the process of writing research reports as a means of disseminating research findings. The chapter provides a useful resource for those aiming to enhance their abilities in conveying research findings through well-crafted written reports.

Format of a Typical Chapter

Each chapter will follow a similar structure: It will begin with the chapter objectives and an introduction, followed by the presentation of its themes and ending with a summary and conclusion. Finally, there will be a set of discussion and activity questions, which are designed to encourage engagement, critical thinking, and practical application of the chapter's content. By fostering reflection and active participation, this feature aims to deepen the reader's understanding, providing an opportunity to apply the acquired knowledge in real-world scenarios. These discussion and activity questions serve as a valuable tool for self-assessment, group discussions, or classroom activities, fostering a learning experience that goes beyond the passive absorption of information. The chapters also incorporate examples from current and hypothetical research to demonstrate the concepts discussed.

Audience

The target audience for the book is diverse, including a wide range of individuals with varying levels of expertise and different interests. Primarily, it caters to graduate students and researchers in applied linguistics and L2 studies who seek a comprehensive guide to conducting research in these fields. The book's aims for this group are several: to familiarize them with the diversity of research types, methods, and approaches to research in applied linguistics; to prepare them to understand such research in depth, enabling them to develop skills in conducting original research; and to help them develop skills in critically analyzing and evaluating existing research. In doing so, the book serves as an invaluable resource, offering foundational knowledge and practical insights into qualitative, quantitative, and mixed-methods research. Its accessible language and the inclusion of numerous practical examples make the book suitable for both novices and experienced researchers. Another large part of the audience are instructors and educators who teach research methods courses and those who incorporate research methods into their curriculum. Given its comprehensive nature, the volume functions as a valuable pedagogical tool suitable for instructors guiding both beginners and more advanced-level students. To serve the needs of this group, the book provides a structured approach to teaching various research concepts and techniques. In summary, the book serves as a practical guide for L2 and applied linguistics researchers, graduate students, and instructors teaching methods courses. It is an essential resource for all these groups, facilitating and enhancing their expertise in the field.

How to Use the Book

The book is versatile in content and can be used as a comprehensive resource to guide both instructors and students through the complexities of research in applied linguistics. Given the breadth of topics covered, the following guideline provides a roadmap for both instructors and students to navigate the extensive material without feeling overwhelmed. Here is an outline of how each group can effectively use the book.

For Instructors
Course Planning and Teaching
- *Part I: Introduction to Applied Linguistics Research*
  - Chapters 1–3: Use these chapters to introduce students to the fundamental principles, significance, and ethical considerations of research in applied linguistics. This sets a strong foundation for the course.
- *Part II: Research Process and Designing Research*
  - Chapters 4–7: Structure your curriculum around the ten-step research process model. Incorporate lectures and discussions on understanding research types, constructs, variables, and literature review strategies to help students develop sound research questions.

Hands-on Activities and Assignments
- *Part III & IV: Quantitative and Qualitative Research Designs, Data Collection, and Analysis*
  - Chapters 8–17: Create assignments that require students to design both quantitative and qualitative studies, select participants, and collect data. Use the detailed explanations and examples to facilitate hands-on activities and group projects.

Data Analysis and Interpretation
- *Part V: Quantitative Research: Data Analysis and Interpretation*
  - Chapters 18–23: Guide students through the process of analyzing quantitative data using descriptive and inferential statistics. Develop practical exercises that involve using and interpreting various statistical measures so that students understand both parametric and nonparametric tests.

Mixed Methods Research
- *Part VI: Carrying Out Mixed Methods Research*
  - Chapter 24: Teach students how to integrate qualitative and quantitative approaches. Encourage them to design mixed methods research projects, highlighting the benefits and challenges of this comprehensive approach.

Reporting and Dissemination
- *Part VII: Dissemination of Research Findings*
  - Chapter 25: Focus on writing research reports and disseminating findings. Provide guidelines and templates for research reports, and have students practice writing and presenting their research.

For Students
Building a Research Foundation
- *Part I: Introduction to Applied Linguistics Research*
  - Chapters 1–3: Begin with these chapters to understand the basics of research and its importance in applied linguistics. Pay special attention to the ethical considerations to ensure responsible research practices.

Step-by-Step Research Process
- *Part II: Research Process and Designing Research*
  - Chapters 4–7: Follow the ten-step research process model to systematically plan your research project. Use the chapters on research types, constructs, variables, and literature review to develop a solid research proposal.

Designing and Conducting Research
- *Part III & IV: Quantitative and Qualitative Research Designs, Data Collection, and Analysis*
  - Chapters 8–17: Depending on your research focus, read the chapters on quantitative or qualitative research designs. Use the practical activities and examples to guide your data collection and analysis process.

Data Analysis Skills
- *Part V: Quantitative Research: Data Analysis and Interpretation*
  - Chapters 18–23: Enhance your data analysis skills by working through the chapters on descriptive and inferential statistics. Practice using statistical software and tools to analyze your data.

Combining Methods
- *Part VI: Carrying Out Mixed Methods Research*
  - Chapter 24: Learn how to combine qualitative and quantitative approaches in your research. This chapter will help you design comprehensive studies that provide richer insights.

Presenting Research Findings
- *Part VII: Dissemination of Research Findings*
  - Chapter 25: Focus on writing and presenting your research findings. Use the guidelines provided to prepare research reports and practice your presentation skills to effectively communicate your results.

General Tips for Both Instructors and Students
For a thorough understanding, follow the book sequentially, building knowledge progressively from basic principles to advanced techniques. If you have specific needs or areas of interest, target the relevant chapters directly. For example, if you are focusing on data analysis, concentrate on Parts III, IV, and V. Use the practical activities, examples, and case studies provided in each chapter to apply theoretical knowledge to real-world research scenarios. Revisit chapters on ethics, reliability, and validity regularly to ensure adherence to best practices throughout your research process.

PART I
Introduction to Applied Linguistics Research

1 | Introduction: The Nature and Purpose of Research

CHAPTER OBJECTIVES

After completing this chapter, you should be able to

- Define the nature and purpose of research.
- Understand what is meant by empirical research.
- Distinguish research from nonresearch.
- Explain different ways of obtaining an answer to a question, and describe the differences among them, as well as their strengths and shortcomings.
- Explain the value and importance of research.
- Understand the principles of the scientific method and research design.
- Identify the characteristics of good research.

Introduction

Research is an essential component of almost all graduate studies in applied linguistics. It plays an important role in advancing the field by generating new knowledge, testing theories, and developing practical applications. Both graduate students and researchers in this field are often required to both read and conduct research. This involves critically evaluating existing research studies, identifying gaps in the literature, and formulating research questions that contribute to the field. It also entails selecting appropriate research designs, collecting and analyzing data, and interpreting results. Students should also know how to use research tools, such as statistical software, to analyze data, conduct their research ethically, and then write up their findings in a clear, concise, and structured manner, adhering to academic writing standards. In short, they are expected to become proficient in the methodologies and techniques used in conducting and reporting research.

However, students and novice researchers may not always have a clear idea of the complexities involved in research. They may have some general idea of what research is, but they may be unaware of the specific processes and steps involved. Some might have a basic knowledge of different research types but not know how to design their investigations effectively, which criteria they need to meet, how to assess these criteria, or how to choose among various possibilities. They may have a research topic but experience difficulties in transforming it into a well-defined and feasible research question. Some may even face difficulties in knowing where to begin and end their research, always having a sense of uncertainty and a fear of making mistakes.

Doing research involves numerous decisions, ranging from determining which questions to investigate, selecting participants, and choosing an appropriate research design, to procedures for checking and establishing the validity and reliability of the data, and the presentation and interpretation of the results.

The aim of this chapter is to set the stage by discussing a number of key issues and foundation concepts, and their importance in research. It will examine the reasons for conducting research, various ways of knowing and answering questions, and the fundamental principles of scientific inquiry. By the end of this chapter, you will understand some of the fundamental components of research, upon which you can further build your knowledge and skills in subsequent chapters.

POINTS TO PONDER

Before reading this chapter, what is your understanding of research and how would you explain the concept to someone who is unfamiliar with research?

What Is Research?

Research is an activity conducted across a diverse range of academic fields, including the field of applied linguistics. However, we will not be able to plan and conduct research effectively if we do not know what we mean by research.

Research can be defined in different ways and can mean different things to different people. For example, for someone who is looking for information about a product, browsing the internet to find information might be considered research. For another person, reading a cookbook to find a recipe for a particular type of dish could be considered research. For an undergraduate student who has been asked to write a term paper, research might mean going to the library and collecting information related to a specific topic. A person who is looking for a job and trying to find information about the job may call it research.

In a graduate course on research methods for applied linguistics students, I asked students to write down what they thought research was. The students had different conceptions of research, ranging from finding out information to contributing new knowledge. Some have also considered some aspects of research, such as collecting data or presenting results as research itself. Here are some of their answers. For them, research:

- involves finding information about a subject matter;
- is doing an experiment to find out an answer to a question;
- involves collecting data to deal with an issue;
- involves using tests and doing statistics;
- is to test a hypothesis;
- follows objective procedures;
- is to formulate a hypothesis;
- is what is necessary;
- is to add to knowledge;
- is presenting results in a scientific manner.

It is correct that research can involve a variety of activities, such as collecting data and analyzing and presenting results. However, these activities are simply some of the components of research, and research is more than just conducting a series of individual tasks.

In a survey study with language teachers, Borg (2009) examined the English language teachers' conception of research. Collecting data from 505 teachers, he found that they held different perspectives about research. Also, more than 60 percent of them attributed the following characteristics to research:

- The researcher is objective.
- Hypotheses are tested.
- The results give teachers ideas they can use.
- Variables are controlled.
- A large number of people are studied.
- Information is analyzed statistically.
- A large volume of information is collected.

Some of the responses provided by these teachers are close to what research is. However, most of them are simply a feature of some kind of research, with none of them capturing the complexity of what is understood as academic and empirical research.

In order to see what research is, it would be helpful to make a distinction between two meanings of the term: a general meaning and a more technical meaning. A general meaning of research is searching for information. That is why we often hear the phrase "do your research" when we need to gather information about something. A more technical meaning is what is used in academic fields. In this sense, research is not simply wondering about something. It is also not a simple search for information. Rather, it is a careful inquiry or investigation to generate new knowledge or expand our understanding of a particular phenomenon. Academic research is typically conducted by researchers with specialized knowledge and expertise in their own field. To appreciate what research means in the field of academia, it would be helpful to look at some of the definitions provided by academic researchers.

> "Research is a process of steps used to collect and analyze information to increase our understanding of a topic or issue" (Creswell, 2012, p. 3).
>
> "[R]esearch is a rigorous process that involves specifying a research question, selecting a method that can best answer this question, gathering relevant data, and carefully analyzing this data" (McKay, 2006, p. ix).
>
> "Research is the *organized, systematic search* [italics in the original] for answers to the questions we ask" (Hatch & Lazaraton, 1991, p. 1).
>
> "Research comprises defining and redefining problems, formulating hypothesis or suggested solutions, collecting, organizing and evaluating data, making deductions and reaching conclusions and at last careful testing the conclusions to determine whether they fit the formulated hypothesis" (Woody, 1927, p. 172).

Although there are differences among the above definitions, they share some common elements, including systematicity, asking questions, rigor, and the generation or expansion of knowledge through a process of data gathering and analysis.

Research is careful investigation to gain new knowledge or to validate existing knowledge through a structured and rigorous inquiry into a problem or topic, using a systematic approach that involves formulating a research question, gathering, and analyzing data, and drawing conclusions based on the findings.

Systematicity means that research follows a series of planned and acceptable steps and procedures to answer a research question, including specific techniques to collect, analyze, and interpret the data. In other words, it involves a well-defined methodology with an appropriate research design including formulating a research question and reaching conclusions based on the information gathered. For example, when we say that research has shown that the child's home environment affects the development of metalinguistic skills, we are referring to this meaning of research as a systematic inquiry.

Rigor means that research is conducted using methods that are reliable, valid, and appropriate. We will define methodology later on in more detail, but for now, a methodology is a set of procedures and principles used in a given study to guide data collection, analysis, and interpretation. It is important to note that there is no one methodology and no one set of procedures and principles to follow in research. Rather, as we will see later on, there are different methodologies, including both qualitative/interpretive methodologies and quantitative methodologies, and a wide range of research designs associated with each, such as surveys, observations, descriptions, experiments, and analysis of various forms of data.

Rigor means that research is conducted using methods that are reliable, valid, and appropriate.

POINTS TO PONDER

Why is research important in applied linguistics, and what are some examples of how research has contributed to the advancement of knowledge, understanding, and practice in the field?

Why Should We Do Research?

There are many reasons why research should be conducted or why research is important. One reason is that research helps us to enhance our understanding of the world around us. By conducting research, we can learn more about the world and how it works, which can help us to better understand the problems and challenges we face, as well as potential solutions to those problems. For example, research in applied linguistics helps us understand how language works and how it is used in real-world situations. This knowledge can be used to improve language teaching and learning, language testing, language policy and planning, and issues regarding language-related technologies. Research can also help the development of new knowledge and ideas that can improve our quality of life. It can also help us to discover new knowledge and make new connections between different fields of study, which can lead to new advances and innovations that can have a positive impact on society. For example, in applied linguistics, research can help us better understand the role the language plays in different social and cultural settings, and the different social and psychological factors that influence language use and learning. It can also help us understand how first or second language acquisition takes place, which has important implications for language teaching programs and education, For example, researchers might investigate the best ways to teach grammar or vocabulary, or they might study the effectiveness of different teaching approaches such as immersion programs or online courses. Additionally, research can lead to new theories that can inspire and drive progress in many different fields. Finally, research is an essential part of the process of education, as it helps us to learn and expand our knowledge.

Research enhances our understanding of the world, fosters the development of new knowledge, facilitates the discovery of new knowledge, and can lead to new ideas and theories that can drive progress in different fields.

The Main Aims of Research

As noted above, generally, research aims to expand knowledge, solve problems, and contribute to the advancement of a particular field of study. In addition to such general objectives, there are some specific aims for any research, including research in applied linguistics. In this section, we will discuss three main aims of research.

To Explore

One of the aims of research is to explore. An exploratory study is one in which the aim is to become familiar with or further our understanding of a certain area that the researcher has just observed. Exploratory research is thus often used in the early stages of a study when the researcher is trying to gain a broad understanding of the topic before developing more focused research questions and hypotheses. This type of study is conducted when there is not yet much known about a topic. In other words, exploratory studies are often conducted when we are in the early phases of knowing about a phenomenon. For that reason, they are often more open-ended than other types of research, allowing the researcher to adapt to new information. Insights emerge as the study unfolds or during the study. With this characteristic, most exploratory studies prepare the ground for future research. That is, data are collected to discover ideas about an area that might later be subjected to more specific investigation. Since this type of research is conducted when there is limited research in the area, there may also not yet be a theory to guide the research. Thus, the purpose is not to test preexisting theories or hypotheses but rather to generate new theories or hypotheses. By generating new theories or hypotheses, researchers can generate new ideas that can be tested and evaluated in further research.

An exploratory study is one in which the aim is to become familiar with or further our understanding of a certain area that the researcher has just observed. Its aim is thus to gain insights and generate ideas rather than test specific hypotheses.

An example of an exploratory study in applied linguistics might be a research project that aims to explore the experiences and perspectives of a group of learners with respect to certain types of corrective feedback. In this study, the researcher might give students a questionnaire or conduct interviews with them to learn more about their experiences. The goal of this study would be to gain a better understanding of the learners' experiences, in order to add to our knowledge in that area and identify potential areas for further research.

Another example might be a research project that aims to explore how L2 learners learn how to make questions. This type of study could involve collecting data from a variety of sources, such as natural conversations or the elicitation of language data that include questions from learners through various forms of elicitation tasks. The goal of such a study would be to gather a representative sample of language data that could be used to gain insights into how learners use questions in different situations and the kind of developmental patterns their questions exhibit.

The following are some more examples of research objectives in different areas of applied linguistics that could be addressed through exploratory research:

- Language acquisition: To discover how and when learners use their L1 when they interact with their peers in L2 classrooms.
- Pragmatics: To explore how L2 speakers of English apologize when they feel they have misunderstood a situation.
- Sociolinguistics: To explore how L2 learners manage social roles and identity construction when they collaborate with their peers in a writing task.
- Language attitudes: To discover how L2 learners' beliefs and attitudes influence their participation in a communicative task.
- Language assessment: To find out the various roles assessment can play in a language classroom.
- Discourse analysis: To investigate how conversational structures vary between L1 and L2 speakers in different social contexts.
- Intercultural communication: To explore how cultural backgrounds impact communication strategies in multilingual settings.

To Describe

The second aim of research is to describe. Descriptive research attempts to describe what is going on or happening. It may also be used to describe the characteristics of a case, situation, or event, or to find out the relationship between them. Since the aim is to describe, descriptive research often involves observing or recording the phenomenon, and therefore it is sometimes called observational research. In language teaching, for example, you may be interested in describing what particular feedback types teachers use in the classroom or in finding out what the attitudes of learners are towards a particular classroom task. In this case, you may observe the classroom for the type of feedback, or may ask students to report their opinions or attitudes towards a classroom task.

Descriptive research seeks to describe and analyze what is occurring, providing a systematic account of the characteristics of a case, situation, or event and exploring the relationships between them.

A number of L2 studies, for instance, have aimed to describe how teachers correct learner errors in the classroom (e.g., Chaudron, 1977; Fanselow, 1977b; Lyster & Ranta, 1997). Chaudron (1977), for example, aimed to identify the various corrective feedback types teachers used in French immersion classrooms, and Fanselow (1977b) examined how teachers used corrective feedback in ESL classrooms. Several early second language researchers had also this aim, focusing on finding out and describing the developmental sequences through which L2 learners pass in order to acquire a language structure (e.g., Dulay & Burt, 1973, 1974).

The following are examples of research objectives that can be addressed through descriptive research across various domains of applied linguistics:

- Classroom interaction: To determine the kinds of questions that may be used by teachers in a language classroom.
- Second language acquisition: To describe the stages of interlanguage development in L2 learners.
- Pragmatics: To analyze the types of speech acts commonly used in L2 learner interactions.
- Language assessment: To describe the characteristics of effective formative assessments in language learning.
- Technology in language learning: To determine how different digital tools are utilized in language learning environments.
- Discourse analysis: To describe the discourse patterns in academic versus casual conversations among L2 learners.
- Lexical studies: To analyze the vocabulary acquisition patterns of L2 learners at different proficiency levels.
- Phonetics and phonology: To describe the pronunciation difficulties faced by L2 learners from various linguistic backgrounds.
- Language policy: To determine the impact of language policies on bilingual education programs.
- Corpus linguistics: To analyze the frequency and usage patterns of phrasal verbs in a spoken corpus of casual conversations across different age groups.

To Explain

The third aim of research is to explain. Explanatory research aims to understand why something is happening the way it is happening. This kind of research is often carried out when we already know about a phenomenon or when there is already a body of knowledge available on a topic to enable the researcher to make predictions. This body of knowledge is what we call a theory. As such, explanatory research aims to provide evidence to support or to reject a prediction coming from a theory or to determine the reason or causes of an event.

The explanatory objective is very common in applied linguistics studies as there has always been interest in explaining questions such as how second language is developed, how learners create a new language system with only limited exposure to a second language, or why most second language learners do not achieve the same degree of knowledge and proficiency in a second language as they do in their L1.

Here are some examples of research objectives in different areas of applied linguistics that can be addressed through explanatory research:

- Language revitalization: To investigate the effectiveness of community-based language revitalization programs in promoting intergenerational transmission of endangered languages.
- Language and identity: To investigate how language choice influences identity construction among multilingual adolescents.
- Sociolinguistics: To determine the impact of social identity on code-switching behaviors among bilingual speakers in different contexts.
- Pragmatics: To investigate the effect of explicit pragmatic instruction on the development of L2 learners' ability to perform speech acts appropriately.
- Language assessment: To determine whether formative assessment practices lead to better language learning outcomes compared to summative assessments.
- Discourse analysis: To determine the effects of discourse markers on the coherence of L2 learners' spoken narratives.
- Lexical studies: To determine the role of context in the incidental vocabulary acquisition of L2 learners.
- Translation studies: To investigate the influence of cultural context on the translation of idiomatic expressions.
- Language ideologies: To examine how language ideologies influence attitudes toward code-switching in bilingual communities.

Experimental research designs (see Chapter 9) are often used in explanatory research. In this type of research design, a particular variable is manipulated in order to assess its impact on another variable. An example is a classroom study by Doughty and Varela (1998) that used an experimental research design to investigate the effects of corrective recasting on learning English past tense (simple past and conditional past tense) in content-based classes. One of the classes was used as an experimental group, receiving corrective feedback in the form of recasts on their oral and written production of the past tense; the other class was used as a control group, receiving no recasts. The study found that the group who received recasts outperformed those who did not receive recasts.

Explanatory research seeks to understand the underlying reasons behind occurrences and is typically conducted when there is existing knowledge about a phenomenon, allowing researchers to make and test predictions based on that knowledge.

Ways of Answering Questions

When we are faced with a question, there are various approaches to finding an answer. However, a very important issue is where the answer comes from or what constitutes a good and reliable answer. For instance, when seeking ways to decrease cholesterol levels, one might consult an internet source that recommends consuming specific foods. Or a teacher aiming to engage students in a classroom task might refer to a book that suggests a particular activity. Similarly, a teacher who struggles with classroom management may seek advice from a colleague. These diverse sources all have the potential to provide answers. But the question is whether the answers acquired through these sources are reliable answers.

We often tend to place trust in expert opinions, assuming that experts' answers are good answers. However, it is important to recognize that a good answer may not always be a reliable answer. As researchers or consumers of research, we should distinguish between various sources of knowledge and understand how they differ from one another. This helps us differentiate between reliable and unreliable answers. For example, statements that are based solely on emotion or intuition may not hold the same level of reliability as those grounded in research evidence. By understanding the diverse ways of acquiring knowledge, we can effectively assess the information we receive and make well-informed decisions about its reliability. In the following sections, we discuss six primary methods through which we can obtain knowledge or find answers to questions:

- through experience
- through beliefs
- through intuition
- through experts
- through logic
- through scientific research.

Through Experience

One way of obtaining an answer to a question is through experience, including personal and professional experience. Our experience refers to the events and situations we have encountered in our lives, and the lessons and understanding we have gained from them. Our experiences can shape our perspective and the actions we take and can also influence our decisions and judgment.

If you are a language teacher, for example, one main source of information could be the experiences and knowledge you have about your students and teaching. By drawing on this information, you may be able to answer many of the questions you may have about your teaching. For example, if you have been teaching for many years, you are likely to have developed a better understanding of the dynamics of classroom interaction or of different group sizes and how they can impact the success of a particular activity. Based on this experience, you may decide that a smaller group may be more effective for some activities whereas a larger group may be better for others. You may also use your experience to decide about group composition and therefore may choose a mix of different skill levels or different learning styles in order to enhance the effectiveness of a particular group work activity. Here is an example from the literature with explicit reference to experience.

> "… in my experience, most college-level students would like to improve the grammatical accuracy of their speech and will attend to the grammatical markers in the input whenever it is possible and relatively easy to do so." (Terrell, 1991, p. 60)

While experience is a valuable source of information, it has its own limitations. First, no matter how much experience someone has, there will always be things that they do not know or have not encountered before. Second, people may have different experiences of the same event and therefore they may act differently even under the same circumstances. Also, when we use experience, we often do not scrutinize it or subject it to critical evaluation. Finally, experience is transient in nature because we often rely on our memory, which is not always reliable (Feiman-Nemser, 2013). Thus, although many of our questions can be answered through experience, we cannot rely on our experience alone to provide a valid answer to a question or a problem.

Through Beliefs

Arriving at an answer through belief is a process based on what one believes to be true. Belief is a mental state in which an individual holds a certain idea or concept to be true, without necessarily having direct evidence or proof for it. It is often based on a certain perspective or some cultural tradition. Beliefs can play a powerful role in affecting our thoughts and actions and can influence how we approach and address problems. This approach to answering questions can, however, be problematic because it can lead to incorrect or biased conclusions.

For example, if we are asked what type of transportation is best, we may use our belief and judge that planes are best. However, while planes may be the fastest mode of transportation, they may not always be the most cost-effective or convenient option, especially for shorter distances. Also, our perception of best can vary based on individual experiences and personal preferences. As another example, in response to why a particular group work activity did not work effectively in a classroom setting, a teacher might believe that it was because the task used was too difficult. However, it is possible that the task was not too difficult but that other factors, such as lack of communication or different learning styles, led to the group's struggles. Without further information or investigation, it is difficult to say for sure why the group work did not go as planned under that specific circumstance. The shortcoming of belief is that although we may think that our answer is correct, it may not necessarily be true. It is important to be open to the possibility that our beliefs may be wrong, and to be willing to revise them based on new information or evidence.

Through Experts

When we have a question, we can also ask an expert. An expert is someone who has a high level of knowledge or skill in a particular subject or field as a result of spending time studying the area. Experts are often thought to have a deep understanding of the subject and, therefore, they are typically considered authorities in their field. For that reason, their opinion or advice on a subject can be very valuable.

For example, if a teacher wanted to know what the best classroom task is, the teacher may consult a book on task-based instruction, in which the author, who has expertise in this area, has presented the idea that the most effective tasks are two-way tasks in which information goes in both directions. However, it is important to remember that although an expert is often more knowledgeable than a nonexpert, we still cannot be sure that the assertion is true. Even if they have knowledge, they can make mistakes, and their opinions are not always correct unless they are based on some evidence. Sometimes we may accept the response provided by authorities as evidence. However, evidence is the information that comes from the analysis and evaluation of some data, and it is not simply based on opinions.

Through Intuition

Another way of answering a question is through intuition. Intuition can be described as a feeling or gut instinct that comes from within. It is a way of knowing that is based on personal understanding, rather than on facts or evidence. Some people believe that intuition is a special kind of insight that allows people to understand complex ideas or situations quickly and easily. Others think of it as a subconscious process that helps people make decisions or solve problems without conscious thought. In other words, it is a type of instinctive understanding or knowledge that is often difficult to explain or justify. For example, a lot of knowledge that we have about our first language is of this type. It is tacit or implicit knowledge about how the language works.

Intuition can sometimes be a useful tool for answering a question or solving a problem, and many people rely on their intuition to guide them in their daily lives. However, intuition is not always a reliable and accurate source. It is also subjective and may differ from person to person.

Through Logic

Another way of knowing or arriving at an answer is through logic or reasoning. Logic is a method of reasoning, also called rationalism, which includes the structure and principles of arguments and their evaluation. Logic is a systematic and formal way of thinking about, analyzing, and verifying arguments and as such is an essential tool for critical thinking and effective problem solving.

There are two main types of logic, deductive and inductive. Deductive logic is a process of reasoning whereby a conclusion is reached from one or a series of general premises that are generally assumed to be true. It moves from general propositions to a specific conclusion via logical inferencing. In deductive reasoning, the conclusion is derived from the premises through the application of certain rules of logic. An important form of deductive reasoning is syllogism, which was introduced by the Ancient Greek philosopher Aristotle as a way of drawing deductions based on logic. A syllogism consists of at least two propositions, which are assumed to be true, and a conclusion. The first proposition is called the major premise, which is well-accepted. The second is called a minor premise, which introduces a particular instance. Finally, there is the conclusion. In a syllogism, the first of the two statements must be true for the conclusion to be true. The following is an example:

1. All teachers have a teaching certificate.
2. John is a teacher.
3. John has a teaching certificate.

In the above example, we assume that the first statement is true based on our previous knowledge. The second statement is also true because we know John is a teacher. Since the first two statements are true, based on a deductive logic, the third statement must be true, too.

In applied linguistics, this kind of reasoning is sometimes used. The interaction hypothesis in SLA (e.g., Long, 1996), which is about how negotiation of meaning assists language acquisition, can be a good example of deductive reasoning:

a) Negotiation of meaning makes input comprehensible.
b) Comprehensible input facilitates language acquisition.
c) Negotiation of meaning facilitates language acquisition.

In the above example, the conclusion about the contribution of negotiation of meaning to language acquisition has been arrived through deductive logical reasoning. The first two statements are considered to be true based on evidence from previous research. Since they are true, the third statement must be true too.

Deductive logic is an important tool for reasoning and problem solving. However, it has limitations. One limitation is that we have to accept that the first two premises are true in order for the third one to be true. However, this may not be always the case. Since the conclusion in deductive reasoning depends on the truth of the major premise, and since it is possible that the truth of the first one may sometimes be simply based on belief, authority, or other sources that are not necessarily valid sources, we cannot rely on deductive reasoning as a sufficient way of discovering reliable answers.

Inductive logic is the reverse of the deductive logic, in that, instead of moving from general to particular, it moves from particular to general. In other words, it is based on a number of individual observations of a particular event, which would then lead to a final generalization. An example of inductive reasoning or logic can be seen as follows:

- I parked my car near the library, and I was fined.
- I parked my car near the school, and I was fined.
- I parked my car near a community center, and I was fined.
- Thus, parking near public places is not permitted.

An example from language teaching could be as follows. In a classroom observation, the teacher noticed:

- Students made an error when saying "thin."
- Students made an error when saying "thick."
- Students made an error when saying "thunder."
- Students did not make an error when saying "cloth."
- The teacher may then conclude that students make an error when "th" occurs at the beginning of a word.

The limitation of inductive reasoning is that to be sure the conclusion is true, we need to observe all the relevant instances. For example, in the above example, for the teacher to be sure that students make an error when "th" occurs at the beginning of a word, they would have to have observed all the words that begin with "th." However, this is not feasible. For that reason, perfect induction is not possible as conclusions are often based on a sample of observations.

POINTS TO PONDER

What is your conception of scientific research? Provide examples of studies that use a scientific research approach and discuss why you consider the approach to be scientific.

Through Scientific Research

Another way of achieving an answer to a question is through scientific research. Scientific research is based on scientific method, which is a systematic approach to conducting scientific research. It involves making observations, forming hypotheses, testing hypotheses through experiments, and analyzing the results. The aim of the scientific method is to gather evidence and to use that evidence to support or refute hypotheses, with the ultimate goal of increasing our understanding of the natural world. The scientific method typically involves the following steps:

- Observation
- Hypothesis
- Experiment
- Analysis
- Conclusion.

Scientists observe the world around them and identify a problem or question that they would like to investigate. This approach is also called empiricism, which refers to gaining knowledge based on observation, and the scientific method involves learning about the world through planning, recording, and analyzing observations.

Scientific research is based on scientific method, which is a systematic approach to conducting scientific research. It involves making observations, forming hypotheses, testing hypotheses through experiments, and analyzing the results.

Based on observations, scientists form a hypothesis, which is an educated guess or prediction about the possible outcome of their investigation. For example, a scientist might be interested in knowing when birds sing. They may make many observations of a particular type of bird and notice that that bird always sings when it sits on a particular type of tree. From these observations, the scientist might form the hypothesis that all birds of that type sing when siting on that kind of tree. This hypothesis could then be tested through further observations and experiments. As another example, in the classroom, a language teacher might be interested in knowing how students participate in classroom activities. They may make some observations and notice that, as the classroom tasks become more complex, students participate less. Therefore, the teacher may hypothesize that lack of participation by students might be related to the complexity of the task. However, the teacher does not know whether that is true. This hypothesis could then be investigated through further observations and experiments.

Scientists design and conduct experiments to test their hypotheses. These experiments typically involve manipulating one or more variables and observing the effects on other variables. For example, in a quest for a reliable answer, the teacher in the above example might decide to test the hypothesis that lack of participation of those students may be related to the complexity of the task. The teacher might test this hypothesis by collecting more data through careful and systematic observation of students to see how they behave as they carry out tasks with different levels of difficulty.

Scientists analyze the results of their experiments to see if they support or refute their hypotheses. Based on their analysis, they draw conclusions. In the above example, the teacher would analyze the small group interactions and realize that the hypothesis is true. That is, as the task becomes more complex, the students participate less.

In the scientific method, we should not only follow systematic procedures to seek an answer to a question, but we also need to be convinced of the truth of the answer. Therefore, a scientific inquiry involves not only collecting and analyzing data to answer a question but also making sure that the collection and analysis of the data is valid and reliable. Furthermore, the results obtained should be further testable and verifiable by others. For the findings to be verified by others, the research findings and the processes should become public. For that reason, in scientific research, all the processes through which the research is conducted, from data collection to data analysis to interpretation, should be clearly laid out and reported. It is these characteristics that distinguish scientific research from other ways of obtaining an answer.

An Inductive and Deductive Approach to Scientific Research

We discussed earlier two logical ways of knowing: an inductive and a deductive way. An inductive approach involves using observations to make generalizations or draw conclusions about a phenomenon. This approach begins with specific observations and then uses these observations to create a more general hypothesis or theory. A deductive approach begins with a general hypothesis or theory and then uses this theory to make specific predictions. These predictions are then tested through observations and experiments. Scientific method uses both approaches.

The process of scientific research typically involves using inductive reasoning to draw conclusions from observations, and deductive reasoning to test specific predictions based on those conclusions. The overall procedure in scientific research can be as follows:

1. Making an observation
2. Asking questions
3. Forming hypotheses
4. Making predictions based on the hypotheses
5. Collecting data
6. Testing the hypotheses
7. Drawing a conclusion based on the results
8. Forming new hypotheses based on the results

As noted above, an inductive approach to scientific research begins with direct and systematic observation of a phenomenon in its naturalistic setting with the aim of understanding the phenomenon by searching and looking for patterns. The aim of an inductive approach is to gain understanding of a phenomenon about which we do not know much. Thus, it is a theory- or hypothesis-generating approach. Since it begins with the data, it is also a data-driven approach.

The process of scientific research typically involves using inductive reasoning to draw conclusions from observations, and deductive reasoning to test specific predictions based on those conclusions.

For instance, as noted earlier a language teacher might observe that certain students are not actively participating in a specific classroom activity. This raises the teacher's curiosity about the underlying reasons. The teacher therefore initiates the research process by formulating a research question: Why do students exhibit a lack of participation in classroom tasks? To address this question, the teacher engages in systematic observation of students' behavior during task performance. Through these observations, an understanding of the situation begins to emerge. The teacher observes variations in student performance across different tasks, which provides valuable insights. Further analysis reveals a consistent pattern: as tasks increase in complexity, student participation diminishes. Consequently, the teacher arrives at an inductive conclusion that the level of task complexity may be linked to the observed lack of participation.

A deductive approach begins with a general hypothesis or theory and then uses this theory to make specific predictions. These predictions are then tested through experiments.

The aim of a deductive approach is more to explain rather than to discover. As noted before, this approach is a theory- or hypothesis-testing rather than a hypothesis-generating approach. Thus, in contrast to the inductive approach, a deductive approach relies on experimentation and begins with predictions known as hypotheses. Hypotheses are often derived from existing knowledge within a specific field, such as theories. Theories include coherent bodies of knowledge that attempt to explain phenomena. Hypotheses, stemming from theories, are subject to testing in light of empirical data. The resulting data can serve to refine the theory or generate new hypotheses. This cyclical process represents an important aspect of scientific research that can ultimately foster the generation of knowledge.

For instance, in the example mentioned earlier about conducting research regarding students not actively participating in a specific classroom activity, the teacher may opt this time to investigate the question through a deductive approach. The question was: Why do students exhibit a lack of participation in classroom tasks? In the above observations, a particular focus emerged regarding the influence of task complexity on students' classroom behavior. In light of such observations and the existing knowledge in the field, the teacher may this time formulate a formal hypothesis that easier tasks may result in higher levels of student participation. To address this question, the teacher may conduct a deductive investigation aimed at testing this hypothesis. This can be achieved by comparing two groups: one receiving an easy task and the other receiving a more challenging task. The investigation involves systematic measurement of the variables and comparison of the two groups to evaluate the hypothesized effect of task complexity on student task performance.

The two scenarios presented above highlight the significance of both inductive and deductive approaches in conducting scientific research. The inductive approach, characterized by careful observation and analysis, allows the researcher to gain an initial understanding of the situation, leading to the identification of a possible relationship between variables. On the other hand, a deductive approach is based on experimentation and hypothesis testing. In this case, the researcher formulates a hypothesis based on previous observations and the knowledge emerging from them. Through a controlled investigation involving systematic measurement and comparison, the researcher tries to validate or refute the hypothesis.

It is important to note that although a deductive and an inductive approach can be used separately, studies may also combine the two approaches (this is what has been known as a mixed methods approach, see Chapter 24). For example, you may be interested in exploring or gaining an insight into an issue. This research thus moves from observation of data to drawing a conclusion or to generating an explanation or a hypothesis. Alternatively, you may be interested in testing a hypothesis based on a theory or previous research. Thus, you may move from a hypothesis, to data, to a conclusion. At another time you or another researcher may combine the two. That is, you may start inductively and end deductively or may use a cyclic procedure combining the steps of both approaches. By combining the two, you can generate valuable knowledge, refine existing theories, and generate new hypotheses, fostering a cyclical process that advances understanding of classroom dynamics and enhances educational practices.

Methodological Components of Research

Building on the foundation of scientific research discussed above, in this section, we review the methodological components of any empirical research. These include:

- research questions
- research design
- data and data collection
- data analysis
- results and findings
- conclusion and interpretation.

Research Questions

Questions are central to research, and all research begins with a question. Research questions can be defined as specific questions that the research intends to answer. However, not all questions are research questions. Research questions are empirical questions. Empirical comes from the word empiricism, which is an epistemological theory that holds that the primary source of knowledge is experience. Experience refers to what can be observed, and therefore, empirical means the information comes directly from observation. An empirical question is thus a question than can be answered by collecting and analyzing observable data rather than by theorizing or arguing.

We might sometimes ask questions that cannot be answered through collecting data or observation. These questions thus are not empirical questions. For example, a question such as "Should teachers use a particular feedback type?" is not a research question, because it is not testable; it is not possible to empirically determine whether teachers should use a particular type of feedback. However, a question such as "What type of feedback do teachers use in the classroom?" is an empirical question as we can determine the type of feedback by observing whether it is used in a language classroom. Similarly, a question such as "Why does repetition assist L2 vocabulary acquisition?" is not an empirical question as it is not testable through empirical observation. However, "Does repetition assist L2 vocabulary acquisition?" is an empirical question because it is testable through collecting and analyzing data.

In short, empirical questions are those that can be answered through observation and collecting data. Investigating a question through observation or experimentation is an important part of the scientific method and is important for our understanding the world around us. We will discuss these issues in the subsequent chapters in more detail and consider the fact that the success of any research depends on the extent to which it can answer its research question reliably. We will also examine in more detail what good research questions are and the various ways in which they can be developed and investigated.

Research questions are specific questions that the research intends to answer. They are empirical questions in that they can be answered through observation and by collecting data.

Research Design

Research design refers to the overall plan or strategy for conducting the research. It is the framework guiding the research and includes components such as identifying the research question, selecting a research method, choosing a sample or population, and determining how data will be collected and analyzed.

It is helpful to distinguish here among research design, research method, and research methodology, although these terms are sometimes used interchangeably. Research design can be understood as the specific plan for conducting research. It outlines the structure of the study, including the research questions, hypotheses, variables, and how data will be collected and analyzed. Types of research designs, for example, include experimental, quasi-experimental, and correlational designs. Research methods can be seen as the specific techniques or procedures used to collect and analyze data within the research design. Common methods, for example, include surveys, interviews, and observations. Research methodology refers to the theoretical or conceptual framework that guides the research process. It involves the rationale behind the choice of research design and methods, including the philosophical underpinnings of the study (e.g., qualitative, quantitative, or mixed methods approaches) (see Chapter 5).

Having a sound research design is important as it helps to clarify the research question and keep the study focused. A sound research design also means that that the data collection methods are appropriate and that the data are collected in a valid and reliable manner.

Research design refers to the overall plan or strategy for conducting the research. It outlines the structure of the study, including the research questions, hypotheses, variables, and how data will be collected and analyzed.

Data and Data Collection

Data is a broad term, but in research it refers to what researchers gather as part of their investigation to answer their research questions. In other words, it is the information collected or used as part of the study. Data collection refers to gathering information or data relevant to the research question or problem. This can be done through methods such as surveys, tests, observations, or interviews.

Data can be both primary and secondary. Primary data are collected specifically for the purpose of the research. Secondary data are existing data from previous studies or sources. Data can also be numerical (collected in the form of numbers) or nonnumerical (collected in the form of text, written, oral, visual, or in the form of video or audio data). Numerical data are called quantitative data and can be measured and counted. Nonnumerical data are called qualitative data and cannot be directly counted or measured.

In research, '**data**' refers to what researchers gather as part of their investigation to answer their research questions.

Examples of quantitative data include things like weight, height, temperature, age, and speed. Quantitative data also include scores on tests and exams; for example, if we measure learners' language proficiently through a language proficiency test, it will give us a score that would be a piece of quantitative data. Similarly, if you measure the amount of time the learner takes to react to a question, the time would be quantitative data. Examples of qualitative data include the written or verbal responses participants provide to questionnaires or interviews, as well as the various verbal and written texts or reports that already exist in a field. Qualitative data cannot be measured, but can be converted to quantitative data in order to perform certain types of numerical analysis or to make the data easier to understand and interpret. This can often be done through a process called coding, where the researcher assigns numerical values to different categories or attributes within the qualitative data. For example, if you are collecting demographic data, such as participants' place of birth, nationality, language background, and level of education, you may assign a numerical value of "1" to one group and "2" to another. Or if you are studying learners' attitudes towards a particular issue, you might assign "1" to those who express a positive attitude, "0" to those with a neutral attitude, and "−1" to those with a negative attitude. These procedures allow you to perform statistical analysis on the data, such as calculating the mean or comparing the attitudes of different learners. In sum, depending on the purpose of the research, you may collect and analyze either quantitative or qualitative data (see Parts III, IV, and V).

Data Analysis

Data analysis refers to the process of organizing and examining the data that have been collected as part of the research, to make sense of it. It is a process that involves detailed inspection of the data in order to answer the research question and test any possible hypotheses. It involves analyzing the collected data using an appropriate statistical or qualitative method. Researchers might use different analytical techniques or methods to understand the data, depending on the type of data they have collected. For example, if the data are quantitative, they may use various statistical techniques to understand and interpret it. If the data are qualitative, they may use qualitative data analysis techniques to understand patterns, trends, and relationships in the data. For example, if a study has collected data about a learner's ability to produce a certain linguistic feature, the researchers may analyze the data by examining how accurately or inaccurately the learner produced that feature, and create a frequency distribution of those instances for comparison. Interview data can be analyzed using a process that involves the identification of themes and patterns in the data.

Data analysis refers to the process of organizing and examining the data that have been collected as part of the research, to make sense of the data.

Results and Findings

The results of a research study are the outcomes that come from the analysis of the data. In general, results and findings are closely related and may often be used interchangeably. But they can also be considered to represent different aspects of the research process. Results can be considered as the data that have been analyzed and are often presented based on the analyses, whereas findings can be considered as the insights that emerge from those results. Results are the information discovered or obtained during the data analysis and can be the result of observations or experiments conducted by the researcher and may include a wide range of information, including patterns, trends, relationships, and anomalies. Findings are the discoveries made by the research.

Depending on the type of data and analysis, results can be presented quantitatively, through charts, graphs, or tables, or qualitatively, in the form of text. Results are used in research to support or refute a hypothesis or theory, or to provide new insights or understanding of the issues examined. It is important that both the results and the findings are presented in a clear and accurate manner, and they should be supported by the data. An example of results in a study on corrective feedback could be a higher percentage of revisions in those students who received corrective feedback compared to those who did not. The findings are the insights that emerge, which in this case, could be that corrective feedback is effective at reducing the number of errors learners produced in writing. It is important to present the results of a study in a clear and accurate manner.

Results can be considered as the data that have been analyzed. They are often presented based on the analyses, whereas **findings** can be considered as the insights that emerge from those results.

Related to the notion of data is evidence. Evidence is an important component of research and is the result of the process of evaluating data. Researchers collect, analyze, and interpret data to generate evidence that supports or refutes hypotheses, theories, or research questions. Thus, data form the building blocks of evidence, but not all data constitute evidence. It is also important to note that evidence is not assumptions, speculations, personal beliefs, guesses, or opinions. Rather, as just noted, it is information substantiated by the data. It is also helpful to note that when research provides evidence, it does not prove anything. Novice researchers may sometimes mistakenly think that research provides proof or shows that something is true. However, even the best research may only provide some tentative indication about what is true, but it cannot prove that something is definitely true.

Evidence is the information that comes from the analysis and evaluation of the data and is used to support a claim or conclusion.

Conclusion and Interpretation

The conclusion is a summary of the main findings, which may also include implications or recommendations for future research. It includes the researcher's interpretation of the data and their answer to the research question. A conclusion should be based on the analyses of data presented in the study and should provide an answer to the research question. It should be supported by the data and be clearly stated. For example, suppose you are conducting a study on the effect of explicit and implicit corrective feedback on ESL students' revision accuracy. You might conclude that, based on the results of the analysis, explicit corrective feedback is more effective for improving students' revision accuracy than implicit feedback. Such conclusions can have important implications for how language teachers can provide corrective feedback in their classroom. An implication of such findings for further research would be that future research should be conducted to investigate such effects among other learners and in other contexts.

The conclusion is a summary of the main findings, including the researcher's interpretation of the data and their answer to the research question.

POINTS TO PONDER

What is your understanding of good research? What steps do you think you should take to ensure that your own research meets the standards of good research? How could you improve the quality of a research study that you have in mind?

The Essence of Good Research

In addition to the methodological components of research discussed above, there are several characteristics that are associated with good research. When planning your research, it is important to assess it against the following features.

Significant Topic

Good research addresses a significant topic. A significant topic is one that is relevant and has the potential to contribute to new knowledge. This can be achieved by investigating a topic that has not been fully examined before, or by investigating an explored topic from a new perspective. When it comes to significance, three kinds can be distinguished: Theoretical, practical, and empirical significance (Figure 1.1).

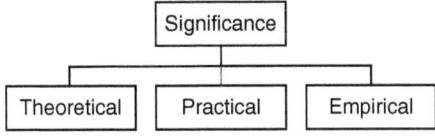

Figure 1.1 Types of significance

Theoretical significance relates to the theoretical contribution of the study, or the extent to which the study contributes to the existing theoretical knowledge in a given area. This contribution can be in the form of developing new theoretical frameworks or revising, refining, or expanding an existing theory. The theoretical contribution of a study is important because it helps advance our understanding of a particular area and can provide a basis for further research in the field. Theoretical contributions can be made, for example, by testing the predictions derived from a current theory or whether and how a theoretical concept can be applied to a new context or situation. Such an application helps us understand a phenomenon in a new light or leads to new understandings that help to see the phenomenon from a different perspective.

Practical significance has to do with the extent to which the study has relevance to – or helps to inform or improve – practice. In applied linguistics, it is expected that research has some practical significance either directly or indirectly. For example, a study that compares the relative effectiveness of different types of corrective feedback during meaning-focused interaction may make important practical contributions because it addresses a key practical concern of how corrective feedback can be provided most effectively without having the meaning-making process interrupted.

Empirical significance refers to the various ways in which the research can contribute to the already existing research. Research can be said to have empirical significance if it extends research to new domains by leading to questions that can be further examined or findings that inspire new directions for research. In other words, the research can suggest new directions for future research. A study also makes an empirical contribution if it provides new information or confirms old information through using new research approaches or through replicating previous research with new participants or in a new context.

Originality

Originality is another important characteristic of good research. However, originality does not mean that research should necessarily investigate a new area or examine a topic that other researchers have not yet researched. While originality in that sense is certainly an important aspect of good research, this is not the only meaning of originality. Originality is a broader concept and can indicate that the research is able to provide new insights or is able to extend our current state of knowledge to new domains. This can be achieved in different ways:

- by investigating new questions
- by providing new data to address a previously examined question
- by addressing a previously examined question in a new context or with new participants
- by extending research to new ideas
- by introducing or testing a new methodology (for example, a question that had been addressed quantitatively before could be approached from a qualitative perspective)
- by analyzing data in a new way.

Originality indicates that the research is able to provide new insights or is able to extend our current state of knowledge to new domains.

Interest

Before choosing any topic, we need to make sure that we are doing the research because we are interested in the topic. Research is a lengthy and time-consuming endeavor. Thus, you should have the interest and the motivation to be able to continue the research. It is essential that you stay motivated throughout the research; otherwise, you may not be able to complete the project. Of course, good research is of interest not only to us as the researcher but also to the wider research community in the field.

Clear Goal, Research Questions, and Definition of Constructs

Good research starts with a clear, manageable, and well-defined question or questions. A clear goal means that the purpose of the research is clearly articulated and justified. Good research also involves a clear definition of concepts and operationalization of variables. For example, if a research study is examining the role of classroom anxiety in students' participation in classroom interaction, the researcher should clearly define what classroom anxiety means and explain how students' participation in classroom interaction can be defined and measured (see Chapter 10 for more details).

Focusedness

Good research is focused. That is, it centers on a specific topic. It concentrates on a particular issue or area and is designed to provide a detailed understanding of the issue in question. Good research explains exactly what the researcher wants to investigate and clearly defines the scope of the research. By being focused, you can stay on topic and do not let the research wander during the course of the study.

Feasibility

Good research is feasible. That is, the research problems can be studied given the time, resources, and expertise available to the researcher. Although a research topic may be significant, data collection may or may not be possible at certain times, under certain circumstances, or given the skills the researcher has. Therefore, the researcher should consider these feasibility factors when planning a research project.

Replicability

To say good research is replicable means that the research has been designed in a way that allows other researchers to replicate the study. For a research study to be replicable, you should describe the procedure in sufficient detail that others would be able to repeat the research and verify the results. This is particularly important in applied linguistics and L2 research where the participants and the context in which the research is conducted vary, and therefore, it is important to conduct the same study across different learners and contexts to see whether we get similar or different results.

Publishability

An important characteristic of good research is that the results can be shared with others. This is what is meant by publishability (see Chapter 25). A good study is one that allows the researcher to disseminate its findings through a conference presentation or by writing an article for publication. If a research study cannot be published, this could be a sign that the research may lack sufficient quality. We publish research not only to let others know of the results of our study but also for them to be able to evaluate, confirm, and potentially replicate the findings.

Sound Methodology

Good research follows a sound and appropriate methodology. It is designed in a way that minimizes bias and maximizes the accuracy of the findings. This includes using appropriate research designs, sampling techniques, and data collection methods.

Valid and Reliable Measures

Good research uses valid and reliable measures to assess the concepts or issues being studied. Valid measures are those that accurately measure what is intended to be measured. For example, a valid measure of reading comprehension would accurately capture a learner's ability to understand a written text. Reliable measures produce consistent results. If a measure is reliable, it will produce the same results if it is administered to the same person again. Using valid and reliable measures makes the results of a study accurate, meaningful, and replicable (see Chapters 11, 12, and 17).

Adequate Sample Size

The sample size should be adequate to provide meaningful findings. If the study is quantitative, the sample size should be large enough to provide adequate statistical power to detect any differences or relationships that exist in the data (see Chapter 8). In qualitative research, sample size is also important but is determined by different criteria, such as data saturation and depth of analysis (see Chapter 13).

Conclusions Derived from the Data

In good research, conclusions are derived and supported by the data. In other words, the "data should speak"; this refers to the idea that the study provides insights and information based on the data. Good research allows the data to uncover relationships in the results without imposing preconceived ideas. To this end, it is important that the data are presented in a way that allow readers to draw conclusions from them.

Rigor

Rigor involves precision, thoroughness, and attention to detail and is an important feature of good research. Rigor should be observed during each stage of the research, including the methods used for data collection, data analysis, and even reporting the data. Good research can be shown to have rigor when there is evidence that the researcher has paid due care and attention in planning and implementing the study. For example, the methods used to develop research questions are robust; the data collected are suitable and sufficient to minimize chances of error; and the analytic techniques are sound and can detect the existence of trends and subtleties in the data. Both qualitative and quantitative research should meet these criteria.

Of course, sometimes qualitative research is criticized for lack of rigor. However, in qualitative research, rigor can be achieved by demonstrating the richness and transparency of the data, This involves providing an appropriate degree of detail in the explanation and description of the context, analytic procedures, and the methods used in selecting, organizing, sorting, and coding the data (see Part IV).

Rigor involves precision, thoroughness, and attention to detail and is an important feature of scientific research. In good research, rigor should be observed in each stage of the research, including the methods used for data collection, data analysis, and even reporting the data.

Appropriate Theoretical Framework

A theoretical framework is a conceptual framework or model that guides the study. It is a set of ideas, assumptions, concepts, and practices that provide a direction for the development of the research. In other words, it provides a lens through which the research is viewed, and thus it helps the researcher to situate the research within the existing body of knowledge in the field. It also helps the researcher to identify appropriate variables and understand the relationships between different concepts. Good research thus has an appropriate theoretical framework.

As an example, suppose you are examining the relationship between implicit and explicit interactional feedback and learning outcomes. You might use a theoretical framework, such as the interaction hypothesis that views the role of interaction as essential for language acquisition. This theoretical framework argues interaction assists learning through a process called negotiation, which is defined as the various forms of modification strategies used during interaction when learners and inter-locutors perceive difficulties in communication. Thus, according to this theory, feedback is effective when it provides opportunities for negotiation of meaning.

Of course, it is important to note that the use of a theoretical framework does not necessarily imply that the study should test a specific theory. While some studies are designed to test hypotheses derived from a theoretical model, not all research is hypothesis-testing research. However, even hypothesis-generating studies can benefit from having a theoretical framework. While this type of research focuses on exploring and generating new hypotheses, a theoretical framework can still provide a useful foundation for guiding the research process by informing initial research questions and providing guidance and direction for areas of exploration; in doing so it can serve as a starting point for hypothesis generation. A theoretical framework in a qualitative study can provide a conceptual tool that can help in organizing and understanding the emerging themes, patterns, or relationships that are discovered during the research process. Consider, for example, a qualitative study exploring how immigrant adults acquire pragmatic competence in their second language. The theoretical framework for this study might be grounded in

Sociocultural Theory (SCT), particularly Vygotsky's concept of the Zone of Proximal Development (ZPD). In this study, SCT provides the conceptual tool to understand how immigrant adults learn the social and cultural norms of interaction in their L2 through mediated activities, such as language classes, social interactions, and workplace communication. The ZPD is used to analyze how learners' pragmatic competence is co-constructed through interactions with more proficient speakers and within their social environment.

Overall, a theoretical framework can provide a useful guide and thus is essential in all good research.

Building on Past Research

Good research builds on previous research. This helps further our understanding of a particular topic and adds to the knowledge already gained. When research builds on previous research, more informed research questions can be formulated, more effective designs can be used, and more reliable conclusions can be drawn. This is why all good research begins with a review of the existing literature prior to the study, as it helps the researcher be informed about the work others have conducted in that area. However, while good research often builds on previous research, it also provides new conceptual understandings that can be used by future researchers.

Ethical Considerations

Good research is conducted in an ethical manner, respecting the rights of participants and adhering to relevant ethical norms and guidelines. Ethical research also means that the researcher is transparent about the research process, accurately reporting results and making sure that the research is conducted in a fair and responsible manner. We will discuss the ethical principles that govern research, including informed consent, confidentiality, and the protection of human subjects in Chapter 3.

Conclusion

Research is an essential component of almost all academic disciplines, including the field of applied linguistics. The methods used in research may vary depending on the nature of the study, the type of data collected, and the research questions being investigated. However, regardless of the approach taken, the principles of scientific inquiry should always be upheld. In this introductory chapter, we have provided an overview of some of the fundamental issues and concepts in research, including what is meant by research, the different ways of arriving at an answer to a question, the value and importance of research, and the characteristics of good research. As we progress to subsequent chapters, we will explore in more detail the research process and learn about the different steps and procedures involved in research. To this end, we will examine various types of research, including their strengths and limitations; the ethical principles that govern research; different approaches to research, including qualitative and quantitative, and mixed methods research; types of research design and how to select an appropriate design for different research questions; selection of participants and sampling methods; different data collection methods and how to select appropriate methods for different types of research. We will also explore different data analysis methods, including descriptive and inferential statistics, and how to analyze and interpret data in both qualitative and quantitative research. Altogether, the aim is to provide readers with a comprehensive understanding of the research process and the necessary knowledge and skills to design and conduct different types of applied linguistics research.

DISCUSSION AND ACTIVITY QUESTIONS

Discussion Questions

1. What examples might you use to illustrate what research is and what its values are? If you have seen different definitions of research in different contexts or disciplines, what commonalities have you observed among these definitions, and how have you evaluated the usefulness of each definition or perspective?
2. How can empirical research be distinguished from other forms of research?
3. What are some examples of empirical research in the field of applied linguistics?
4. What are the advantages of using a scientific research method?
5. Consider some of the specific characteristics of the scientific method, such as observation and hypothesis formation. How do these features contribute to the credibility and validity of research findings?
6. Based on your current knowledge, what steps do you think you can take to ensure that your own research meets the standards of good research? How can you improve the quality of a research study that you have in mind?

Activity Questions

1. Think about a research project you have been involved in. List at least two strengths and two limitations of the project, and explain how the strengths contributed to the quality and validity of the findings.
2. Reflect on your own experiences conducting or participating in research. Based on these experiences, create a list of at least three characteristics of good research demonstrated in the study. How do these characteristics contribute to the quality and validity of research findings? Provide examples to support your points.
3. In groups, discuss and identify examples of empirical research in applied linguistics. Reflect on and discuss the significance of those studies. Share your findings with the rest of the class.

2 | Applied Linguistics Research: Its Nature, Significance, and Scope

CHAPTER OBJECTIVES

After completing this chapter, you should be able to

- Define what is meant by "applied linguistics."
- Understand the historical development of applied linguistics as an independent research discipline.
- Identify the domains of applied linguistics research and explain why they are important and how they are interrelated.
- Develop an understanding of the benefits and values of applied linguistics research.
- Understand the key research areas of applied linguistics.
- Show an understanding of some of the key research questions in applied linguistics.

Introduction

In the previous chapter, we discussed research and its role in general. For those new to applied linguistics research, questions arising may be why we should do it and what the benefits of doing such research are. In this chapter, we will briefly discuss the role of research in applied linguistics, its nature and scope and its theoretical and practical significance. To appreciate what applied linguistics research is, it is important to know what is meant by applied linguistics. Thus, we will begin by briefly considering what applied linguistics is and then discuss the role of research in this area. By the end of the chapter, you should understand the nature and scope of applied linguistics as a discipline to address real-world language-related problems, its theoretical and practical significance, and the contributions of applied linguistics research to our understanding in areas such as language teaching, language learning, communication, and language use.

POINTS TO PONDER

How do you see applied linguistics research as relevant to your own personal or academic interests? What do you think are some of the major challenges or issues facing researchers in this field, and how can these challenges or issues be addressed?

What Is Applied Linguistics?

Applied linguistics, as it is currently understood, covers a wide range of issues related to the role of language in diverse social and cultural contexts. However, due to its expansive nature, there is some ambiguity surrounding the exact definition and disciplinary identity of applied linguistics. Cook (2015, p. 425), went as far as describing it as a field with a "chaotic history" and a discipline lacking unity. As a relatively new field of study, applied linguistics has evolved over time, with its definition adapting to the development of the field and the emergence of new research inquiries. Consequently, various scholars have expressed different perspectives on what constitutes applied linguistics, leading to multiple definitions that highlight the diverse understandings of the nature and scope of the discipline.

Corder (1974), for example, defined applied linguistics as "the utilization of the knowledge about the nature of language achieved by linguistic research for the improvement of the efficiency of some practical task in which language is a central component" (p. 24). Schmitt & Celce-Murcia (2002, p. 1) defined it as "using what we know about (a) language, (b) how it is learned, and (c) how it is used, in order to achieve some purpose or solve some problem in the real world." Brumfit (1995, p. 27) defined applied linguistics as: "The theoretical and empirical investigation of real-world problems in which language is a central issue." Grabe (2002) defined applied linguistics in terms of what the field deals with. He noted that "The focus of applied linguistics is on trying to resolve language-based problems that people encounter in the real world, whether they be learners, teachers, supervisors, academics, lawyers, service providers, those who need social services, test takers, policy developers, dictionary makers, translators, or a whole range of business clients" (p. 9).

The multiple definitions of applied linguistics reflect the diversity of the field and its multidisciplinary nature, as well as the varied contexts in which it is studied and applied. In other words, it shows the breadth and scope of applied linguistics. The breadth of applied linguistics can be seen in the expanded definition provided on the American Association for Applied Linguistics website, which defines applied linguistics as follows.

> Applied Linguistics is an interdisciplinary field of inquiry that addresses a broad range of language-related issues in order to understand their roles in the lives of individuals and conditions in society. It draws on a wide range of theoretical and methodological approaches from various disciplines – from the humanities to the social and natural sciences – as it develops its own knowledge-base about language, its users and uses, and their underlying social and material conditions. (www.aaal.org/about-applied-linguistics)

Applied Linguistics versus Linguistics Applied

Applied linguistics was initially perceived as a subdiscipline of linguistics, and hence some considered it as the application of knowledge derived from linguistics theory and research to solve practical language issues. Some of the early applied linguists emphasized this view by discussing the importance of applying principles and research results from linguistics, such as those related to phonology, syntax, and sociolinguistics, to language teaching and learning. For the same reason, most applied linguistics programs were housed in linguistics departments, and applied linguistics topics were presented and discussed at linguistically oriented organizations such as the annual meetings of the Linguistic Society of America (LSA).

However, these days, for many scholars, applied linguistics is no longer a subfield of linguistics in that sense of the term. Rather, it is a separate and independent field of study with its own missions and goals. In other words, it is no longer considered to be "applied linguistics." Instead, it is viewed as a multidisciplinary discipline that draws on knowledge from many different areas, linguistics being only one of them. This view is captured in Widdowson's distinction between applied linguistics and linguistics applied.

> The difference between these modes of intervention is that in the case of linguistics applied the assumption is that the problem can be reformulated by the direct and unilateral application of concepts and terms deriving from linguistic enquiry itself. That is to say, language problems are amenable to linguistics solutions. In the case of applied linguistics, intervention is crucially a matter of mediation. Here there is the recognition that linguistic insights are not self-evident but a matter of interpretation; that ideas and findings from linguistics can only be *made* relevant in reference to other perceptions and perspectives that define the context of the problem. Applied linguistics is in this respect a multilateral process which, of its nature, has to relate and reconcile different representations of reality, including that of linguistics, without excluding others. (Widdowson, 2000, p. 5)

Some other scholars have also adopted a similar perspective, challenging the notion of applied linguistics as linguistics applied. Kramsch (2015), for example, called applied linguistics "practical language studies" (p. 455) and argued that applied linguistics goes beyond a mere application of theory and instead focuses on the active engagement and practice of language studies. Within this perspective, applied linguistics incorporates a wide range of disciplines such as cognitive psychology, sociology, education, and anthropology. These disciplines are not only utilized for their content but also for their methodological and theoretical approaches. In addition, rather than being a mere application of these fields or a combination thereof, applied linguistics is an empirical field of research whose "object of study is the living process through which living, embodied speakers shape contexts through their grammars and are, in turn, shaped by them" (Bateson, 1979, as cited in Kramsch, 2015, pp. 455–456). This broader understanding highlights the interdisciplinary nature of applied linguistics and its emphasis on the complex interactions between language, speakers, and their environments.

POINTS TO PONDER

Looking at the history of applied linguistics, how do you think the field has evolved over time and what are some of the key changes that have shaped its development?

The Development of Applied Linguistics as an Independent Research Discipline

Interest in applied linguistics has a long history and can be traced back a few centuries. However, the recognition of applied linguistics as an independent research discipline is more recent and can in fact be traced back just a few decades. An early starting point is sometimes associated with the publication of the journal *Language* in 1925 by the Linguistics Society of America (LSA) (Tarone, 2015), and sometimes with the publication of *Language Learning: A Quarterly Journal of Applied Linguistics* in 1948. A more recent historical point would be 1964, when the International Association of Applied Linguistics (AILA) was founded.

In the early years of its development, applied linguistics was mainly concerned with activities that involved the improvement of second language teaching. This was through the development of teaching methods and materials that could be utilized in language classes. But over the years, the focus of the field expanded. Topics explored by applied linguists are now varied and extend well beyond those related to educational issues. Since applied linguistics deals with various areas of study related to language, depending on its focus, research in this domain is sometimes categorized under other names, such as second language studies, second language education, second language research, or "theory of language practice" (Kramsch, 2015, p. 455). When the focus is on practice, its goal becomes twofold "(i) to observe, explain, analyze, and interpret the practice and to communicate the results of its research to practitioners; (ii) to reflect on both the practitioner's and the researcher's practice and to develop a theory of the practice that is commensurate with its object of study" (Kramsch, 2015, p. 456).

POINTS TO PONDER

What are some of the key domains of applied linguistics research, and why do you think they are important areas of inquiry? How might these domains overlap with your own experiences or goals?

The Domain of Applied Linguistics Research

As the field of applied linguistics is broad and interdisciplinary, its research domain is vast. To have a better understanding of applied linguistics research, we can look at the major areas of research in this field listed on the American Association for Applied Linguistics website (https://www.aaal.org/about-us). The AAAL is one of the largest and most prominent research associations in the field of applied linguistics, and it has members consisting of university professors and graduate students from different areas of applied linguistics from around the world. Every year, it holds an international conference, where many attendees present the results of their latest research in their area of interest. The website has identified a number of strands as research foci represented by talks and presentations at the conference. These include:

- Assessment and evaluation
- Antiracism, decolonization, and intersectionality for systemic transformation
- Bilingual, immersion, heritage, and language minority education
- Language cognition and brain research
- Corpus linguistics
- Analysis of discourse and interaction
- Educational linguistics
- Language, culture, socialization, and pragmatics
- Language and ideology
- Language, gender, and sexuality
- Language maintenance and revitalization
- Language and the law
- Language planning and policy
- Phonology/Phonetics and oral communication

- Second and foreign language pedagogy
- Research methodology
- Reading, writing, and literacy
- Second language acquisition, language acquisition, and attrition
- Sociolinguistics
- Language and technology
- Teacher education, beliefs, and identities
- Translation and interpretation
- Text analysis (written discourse)
- Vocabulary and lexical studies.

The above list clearly shows just how broad the field of applied linguistics is. As these areas pertain to research within applied linguistics, I will briefly explain each of them below.

Assessment and Evaluation

This involves the development and administration of various forms of tests to measure different aspects of language proficiency, development, and language learning outcomes. An example of research in language assessment is examining the effectiveness or validity and reliability of different types of assessment tools in measuring second language learners' language skills such as reading, writing, listening, and speaking.

Antiracism, Decolonization, and Intersectionality for Systemic Transformation

This area focuses on addressing the systemic inequalities rooted in racism, colonialism, and the complex ways that different social identities intersect and influence experiences of oppression. Research in this area explores how language and education can challenge and disrupt structures of oppression, racism, and decolonization across various domains. It emphasizes the need for transformative practices in education and other sectors to promote inclusivity and equity.

Bilingual, Immersion, Heritage, and Language Minority Education

This refers to educational programs that teach academic content in two languages, a first language and an additional language, with the goal of promoting the ability to speak, read, and write in two languages. An example of bilingual education is immersion programs – a type of language education in which students are immersed in an environment that provides them with extensive exposure to the target language. Typically, in some models, students learn content in a language other than their L1 for a significant portion of the school day. Heritage language education aims to assist students who speak a heritage language at home to develop proficiency in their home language. Language minority education is an educational program that aims to assist students who speak a language other than English as their primary language at home to learn and maintain the home language.

In the field of applied linguistics, researchers study various aspects of bilingual, heritage, and minority education to see how they influence students' language development and academic achievement.

Bilingual, immersion, heritage, and language minority education refers to educational programs that teach academic content in two languages, a first language and an additional language, with the goal of promoting the ability to speak, read, and write in two languages.

An example of research in bilingual education would be a study investigating the effects of different bilingual programs on learners' academic achievement. For instance, you may compare the language learning outcomes of learners in full immersion, where all the instruction is in the target language, versus partial immersion, where a portion of the instruction is provided in the target language.

Language Cognition and Brain Research

Language cognition is the study of the cognitive and mental processes involved in language use and learning. It is a field of study that includes linguistics, psychology, and neuroscience. Brain research studies the structure, function, and development of the brain. Researchers in this field use a variety of techniques to study how the brain works, including neuroimaging, electrophysiology, and behavioral techniques. There is a significant overlap between language cognition and brain research. Since the brain is involved in all aspects of language processing, researchers in both fields are interested in understanding how the brain processes language and how these processes are affected by various factors.

Language cognition is the study of cognitive and mental processes involved in language use and learning.

An example of research in language cognition and brain research is a study conducted by Vogelzang et al. (2020), titled "Neural Mechanisms Underlying the Processing of Complex Sentences: An fMRI Study." The study examined whether there are distinct patterns of neural activity when participants process different complex word orders. The results showed complex sentences do indeed exhibit distinct activation patterns compared with less complex sentences.

Corpus Linguistics

Corpus linguistics refers to the study of language by examining large collections of naturally occurring written or oral texts, known as corpora. Corpus linguistics can be used to study a wide range of linguistic phenomena and how they work in context, including vocabulary, grammar, syntactic and discourse structure, as well as language change. It can also be used to determine how language is used in a given culture or to compare features of spoken and written language. An important tool commonly used in corpus linguistics is the concordance, which is a list of the occurrences of a particular word or phrase in a given text or group of texts. The study of concordances allows researchers to determine how certain words and phrases behave in a particular context and what patterns and trends can be identified in their use.

Corpus linguistics refers to the study of language by examining large collections of naturally occurring written or oral texts, known as corpora.

An example of a study in corpus linguistics would be one that examines the use of different types of formulaic constructions in a specific language context. Formulaic constructions are expressions that are composed of phrases that may be idiomatic, such as "under the weather," meaning sick, or those that are more formulaic in nature, such as "What's up?" used as a form of greeting.

Analysis of Discourse and Interaction

Discourse analysis concerns the study of how language is used in social interactions, including the analysis of written and spoken texts. Interaction analysis is a subfield of discourse analysis, focusing on how people communicate using verbal and nonverbal language, how they take turns, and how they manage social interactions. There are many different approaches to discourse and interaction, including conversation analysis, narrative analysis, and discourse analysis.

An example of research in the domain of analysis of discourse and interaction would be a study that examines different patterns of language use in a particular social context, or studies that examine how social identities and power dynamics are constructed through interaction. Classroom interaction is an important area of discourse analysis. An example of a study on classroom interaction is Nassaji and Wells (2000), which examined the use of Initiation–Response–Evaluation (IRE) in classroom interaction and discourse. This study examined how teachers initiated a question, students responded, and the teacher evaluated students' responses.

Discourse analysis concerns the study of how language is used in social interactions, including the analysis of written and spoken texts.

Educational Linguistics

Educational linguistics examines the role of language in education, including how language is used in various educational settings, how language problems can be addressed in education, and what implications these examinations can have for language teaching and learning. Educational linguistics also examines the relationship of language and culture in education, and how language is used as a tool for learning and teaching. Some areas of study relevant to educational linguistics include second language acquisition, which concerns how people learn a second or foreign language; bilingual education, which involves the use of two languages in educational settings; and language teacher education, which focuses on language teachers' professional development.

Educational linguistics examines the role of language in education, including how language is used in various educational settings.

Language, Culture, Socialization, and Pragmatics

These fields are concerned with how people use their language to communicate their particular customs, beliefs, and values, within a community or society. Socialization is the process of becoming a member of a society or community by learning their norms, values, and cultures. Pragmatics is the study of how people use language appropriately in different social settings, considering issues such as the speaker's intentions, the relationship between interlocutors, and the setting in which the communication takes place.

An example of a study in pragmatics would be one that examines how second language learners learn to make requests or apologize in certain contexts and the factors affecting their choice of strategy. The researcher may observe the learners' language use over a period of a few months, and then analyze it to see if the use of request strategies is influenced by their first language and/or the social context in which they occur.

Language and Ideology

Language and ideology are closely related because language can be used as a tool to express ideological values and beliefs. Ideology refers to a set of beliefs and values that shape an individual's perception of the world and influence their actions and behaviors. Language is a powerful means of conveying ideology, allowing people to communicate their beliefs and ideas to others. For example, certain words or phrases may be used to promote a particular ideology or to show opposing viewpoints. In this way, language can be used to influence the thoughts and actions of individuals and groups.

An example of an applied linguistics study of language ideology would be one that investigates the attitudes and beliefs about language use in a particular community. For instance, you may investigate the language ideologies attached to certain dialects or accents and how these perceptions influence language users' access to social or economic opportunities.

Language, Gender, and Sexuality

This area examines how gender and sexuality influence language use across different fields. Research in this area aims to understand and address how gendered and sexual identities shape language use, including communication patterns, perceptions, and power dynamics in diverse language contexts.

Language Maintenance and Revitalization

Language maintenance refers to efforts to support the continued use of a language so that it does not decline or become endangered. Language revitalization is the process of restoring a language that is endangered or at the risk of being lost. Revitalization of a language often takes place in a community setting using activities such as documentation, creation of teaching materials, the development of guidelines for teaching the language, and efforts to promote its use in various social settings.

An example of a study on language revitalization would be a study that investigates efforts to revive a particular endangered language and the effect of those efforts on the language community. For example, you could examine the language revitalization efforts of Cree speakers to revitalize the Cree language in Canada.

Language and the Law

This area examines how language is utilized, interpreted, and constructed within legal contexts, including courtroom discourse, legal translation, linguistic rights, and the analysis of language evidence in criminal and civil cases to support justice and legal processes.

Language Planning and Policy

Language planning concerns efforts to affect the way a language is used in a society. This can involve developing a range of activities and strategies such as setting standards for the language used, establishing guidelines, and promoting its use in various contexts. Language policy refers to the strategies adopted by governments or other organizations to guide and regulate the use of language in a society or a country. This can include policies related to the use of language in education, in official settings, and language rights.

An example of research in language planning and policy is a study examining language planning and policy in multilingual contexts. This research, for example, might explore how governments or educational institutions make decisions regarding language choices, language policies, and language planning in diverse linguistic settings. The research could be conducted using interviews or surveys with policymakers and educators to collect data on language policy decisions and practices. Researchers could also analyze government documents and educational curricula to gain insight into the motives and goals underlying language policies.

Phonology/Phonetics and Oral Communication

This area examines the study of speech sounds, including their production, perception, and role in effective spoken communication. While phonetics studies physical sound properties, phonology examines the abstract, rule-based systems that govern sound patterns.

Second and Foreign Language Pedagogy

Second language pedagogy is the study of how to teach a second or an additional language effectively. There are different approaches to second language teaching, ranging from traditional grammar-translation methods to more recent task-based and communicative language teaching. Some key factors to consider in second language pedagogy include learners' goals and objectives, age, motivation, and prior language learning experience, as well the instructional context in which the language is taught.

Second language pedagogy is the study of how to teach a second or an additional language effectively.

Research Methodology

Research methodology refers to the systematic process or framework that guides the design, execution, and analysis of data in a research project. It includes various components, including research design, sampling methods, data collection techniques, and data analysis strategies. The choice of research methodology depends on the research question, the type of data being collected, and the resources available to the researcher. In general, there are three main types of research methodology: qualitative, quantitative, and mixed methods. Qualitative research involves collecting and analyzing nonnumerical data, such as words, images, and video. Quantitative research involves collecting and analyzing numerical data. Mixed methods research involves collecting and analyzing both numerical and nonnumerical data.

Research methodology refers to the systematic process or framework that guides the design, execution, and analysis of data in a research project.

Reading, Writing, and Literacy

These are important language skills needed for effective communication. Reading has to do with understanding written materials, and writing concerns the ability to express one's meaning through written language. Literacy is the ability to both read and write. How people develop literacy skills and what factors affect their development and instruction are important questions within this area of research. Researchers in this field may use a variety of methods, including experimental studies, observations, and surveys, to investigate these questions and their implications.

Second Language Acquisition, Language Acquisition, and Attrition

Second language acquisition refers to the process of learning a second or additional language after acquiring the first language. Language acquisition refers to the process of learning any language, either as a first or a second language. Attrition refers to the loss of a language that a person has previously acquired. This can happen for a variety of reasons, such as lack of exposure to the language or a change in the language environment. It is a normal part of the language learning process, but it can be mitigated by continuing to use and practice the language.

Sociolinguistics

This involves the study of the relationship between language and society, including how language is used in society, how the use of language varies or is affected by social factors such as age, gender, and social class, and how language changes over time.

Language and Technology

This area of research examines the relationship between language as a system of communication and technology. One of its main concerns is how technology can be used to assist language teaching, learning, and processing. Examples include the development and use of computer programs that can assist language learning, machine translation (which allows computers to translate written text or speech from one language to another), or voice-recognition programs, which allow computers to recognize and interpret spoken language. Recently, artificial intelligence (AI) has emerged as a significant development in this field, influencing language-related activities by providing advanced tools that enhance interaction, personalize learning experiences, and improve accessibility for a wide range of language learners.

Translation and Interpretation

Translation is the process of converting written text or speech from one language into another. Interpretation is the process of orally translating spoken words from one language into another. Both translation and interpretation entail a deep understanding of language and culture, as well as the ability to communicate effectively in multiple languages.

Teacher Education, Beliefs, and Identities

This area examines the relationship between teacher training, personal beliefs, and professional identities. It explores how teachers' backgrounds, belief, attitudes, and values influence their teaching practices, classroom interactions, and student relationships. It also investigates the effect of teacher education programs on pedagogical beliefs and cultural awareness, highlighting how these factors can promote effective practices.

Text Analysis (Written Discourse)

Text analysis is a kind of discourse analysis and refers to the process whereby a text, written or oral, can be examined to identify its various features. This can be done either manually using close reading and annotation (in the case of written text) or using computer software that performs a variety of text analysis tasks. Some common techniques used in text analysis include word-frequency analysis, part-of-speech analysis, theme analysis (identifying main topics and themes in the text), voice and sentiment analysis (identifying the overall tone or sentiment in a text).

Text analysis is a kind of discourse analysis and refers to the process whereby a text, written or oral, can be examined to identify its various features.

Vocabulary and Lexical Studies

Vocabulary, also known as lexicon, refers to the words and phrases that a person knows and uses in their language. Lexical studies, also known as lexicology, is the scientific study of words and vocabulary, including their meanings, origins, and how they are used in a language. Lexicologists may study the vocabulary of a particular language or compare the vocabularies of different languages to understand how they work, how they have evolved, and how they are used. They may also work on creating dictionaries and other reference materials that provide definitions and information about the words in a language.

Lexical studies, also known as lexicology, is the scientific study of words and vocabulary, including their meanings, origins, and how they are used in a language.

The Values and Benefits of Applied Linguistics Research

As noted earlier, applied linguistics is a broad field that includes a wide range of subfields, such as second language acquisition, language assessment, language learning and teaching, language planning and policy, and linguistics and technology. Also, there are different approaches and research perspectives within applied linguistics, including cognitive, sociolinguistic, and educational perspectives. By using each of these perspectives and conducting research in each of its subareas, applied linguistics research can generate new knowledge and insights that can be used to improve various aspects of language studies.

Some applied linguistics research addresses questions related to language acquisition, including first and second language acquisition and how they take place. There are many social and cognitive factors that can influence an individual's ability to learn a new language. These can include their mental abilities, motivation, exposure to the language, and the learner's age and background. Through collecting and analyzing data from a variety of sources, such as various kinds of language tests, language corpora, interviews with learners and teachers, surveys, and observations of learners in different contexts, researchers in applied linguistics can study these factors and try to identify ways to optimize language learning and improve language teaching processes. This research can help us understand the underlying mechanisms of language and how it is used, which can inform the development of effective language-related interventions. It can provide information to curriculum and material developers as well as policy-makers to help them make informed policy decisions regarding second language education programs and language teaching practices in various contexts and for various purposes.

Also, as noted above, applied linguists study the role of language in society. To this end, they examine how language use varies among different social groups, how it changes over time, and how it is affected by factors such as globalization. This research can help us to better understand the complex relationships between language, culture, and society, and can inform policy decisions related to language planning and language rights. It can also have important practical implications for the fields of language education, social work, and public policy.

As indicated earlier, one area of applied linguistics concerns language and technology. As technology continues to advance and play a larger role in our daily lives, there is a growing need to understand how language and technology interact. Applied linguistics research in this area can help us gain a fuller understanding of the ways in which technology can support language learning, teaching, and communication, as well as the potential challenges and limitations of using technology in language education and use.

Research in applied linguistics also plays a very important role in examining the voices of students and teachers, including their thinking, beliefs, and attitudes. For example, it may examine why a certain group of students or teachers have certain perspectives toward an idea or their motivation. Teachers who know about the results of such research are more informed when making decisions about how and what to teach to assist their students' learning.

Last but not least, since applied linguistics research is also about solving real-world language-related problems, it helps us become better problem solvers by increasing our critical thinking and analytic skills in this area. Critical thinking refers to the ability to define problems, ask questions, and analyze, examine, and evaluate information, and then make sound judgments based on evidence coming from reliable sources, such as research, observation, or other well-supported knowledge sources.

POINTS TO PONDER

How can we use applied linguistics research to improve language teaching and learning? What specific methodologies or findings within applied linguistics research can be directly applied to enhance language learning outcomes?

Two Key Research Areas of Applied Linguistics

As previously mentioned, applied linguistics comprises a wide array of language-related issues and topics, including various subareas of research that have their own researchers and target audience. Nonetheless, within this vast field, two key areas that stand out are second language pedagogy and second language acquisition (SLA) research. These areas have been referred to as the "heartland of applied linguistics" by Cook (2015, p. 428), who argued that applied linguistics remains predominantly focused on the teaching and learning of second languages, as well as the use of research insights into practical applications. This emphasis on language instruction and learning has been recognized by other scholars as well.

Within this perspective, Kramsch (2015), for example, defined the overarching objective of applied linguistics research as being twofold. First, it aims to examine classroom practices and effectively communicate the findings to teachers. This concerns investigating the dynamics of language learning within different educational settings and providing insights to educators. Second, applied linguistics seeks to reflect upon both the practices of language practitioners and researchers, aiming to develop a theory of practice that aligns with the subject of the study. This dual perspective acknowledges the importance of understanding the experiences and challenges faced by language teachers and learners, while also attempting to establish a theoretical framework that enhances our knowledge of language learning and teaching. Such an emphasis on second language teaching and learning within applied linguistics is also influenced by the role language plays in society. The acquisition of a second language holds significant importance not only in facilitating communication and cultural exchange but also in its practical applications across various disciplines. Second language teaching and learning overlap with fields such as education, linguistics, psycholinguistics, sociolinguistics, and numerous others. The relevance of second language acquisition extends beyond the boundaries of applied linguistics, making it a subject of interest for scholars from diverse academic backgrounds. This interdisciplinary nature highlights the broader implications and impact of second language pedagogy and acquisition research, further solidifying their position as central areas of focus within the field of applied linguistics. Given its importance and their special place within applied linguistics research, it is worthwhile to explore these areas of research in more depth. In the subsequent sections, we will examine these two domains in greater detail, considering their specific features, methodologies, and contributions to the field of applied linguistics.

Second Language Acquisition and Pedagogy
Second Language Acquisition (SLA)

Second Language Acquisition is the study of how someone acquires a language after acquiring an L1. SLA researchers seek to address a wide variety of issues concerning the acquisition of an additional language in various contexts, including naturalistic and formal contexts. SLA investigates how both child and adult second language learners understand, internalize, and use a second language. Although the term includes the word "second," the focus of SLA is on any language the learner acquires after an L1, no matter whether it is their second, third, or fourth language. As a research discipline, SLA is an interdisciplinary field drawing on knowledge from a variety of disciplines, including linguistics, cognitive science, education, and educational psychology. Since language learning is a social process taking place in social contexts, it draws on the fields of social psychology and social sciences as well.

There are currently a number of theories in second language acquisition about how language is learned or how best to teach a second language; these include the interaction hypothesis, the noticing hypothesis, input processing theories, and the output hypothesis. SLA research examines the truth of these hypotheses. For example, in the SLA literature, Krashen made a distinction between learning and acquisition (e.g., Krashen, 1982, 1985). He defined acquisition as an unconscious process, happening mainly through exposure to the target language and learning as a conscious process that takes place mainly through explicit instruction and the explanation of grammatical rules and structures. In many early studies of SLA, researchers examined to what extent second language acquisition occurs through instruction versus mere exposure to the target language. This research sought to address issues concerning the acquisition of an additional language in both naturalistic and formal contexts by various learners including children, adolescents, and adults. Such research led not only to the revision of existing theories but also to the development of new theories about language learning.

The development and testing of new theories in SLA has played an important role in advancing our understanding of various aspects of this process. When new theories emerge, researchers can subject them to empirical examination to determine their validity across different conditions. This process allows for the evaluation of the theories and the potential need for revisions to enhance their explanatory power.

To illustrate this point, let us consider the comprehensible input hypothesis, which proposes that language acquisition is facilitated when learners are exposed to understandable linguistic input (e.g., Krashen, 1985). Long (1981) put forth the interaction hypothesis as an extension of this concept. The interaction hypothesis posits that language acquisition occurs through interactional exchanges. It highlights the significance of input, negotiation, and output in the language learning process. According to this hypothesis, comprehensible input is essential for L2 acquisition. Moreover, when input becomes comprehensible through interactive negotiation and modification, it assists in the process of language acquisition.

The introduction of the interaction hypothesis led to numerous inquiries and discussions among L2 researchers, raising important questions about the role of interaction, attention, feedback, and negotiation in the language learning context. Scholars have been actively investigating and addressing these questions to understand how these factors influence L2 acquisition. This ongoing research inspired by to the interaction hypothesis has contributed to the refinement and expansion of theories related to language learning and has shed light on the complex processes involved in the acquisition of a second language.

By continually analyzing and testing theories, SLA researchers have been able to refine and strengthen our knowledge of language acquisition, ensuring that theories accurately account for the acquisition of an L2 in different contexts. Through this iterative process of theory development, evaluation, and revision, applied linguistics as a discipline has continued to progress and provide valuable insights into language learning and teaching.

Language Pedagogy

Language pedagogy, as a research area closely related to language acquisition, is a field dedicated to promoting classroom teaching experiences and practices. It deals with the systematic study of how languages are taught and learned in educational settings. With an educational perspective, language pedagogy focuses on designing and implementing effective language teaching and learning materials and methodologies.

The focus of language pedagogy is to develop strategies and principles that inform the teaching of languages. Researchers in this area explore the most efficient and engaging instructional approaches and sequencing of language skills, and the incorporation of meaningful content. By examining and synthesizing research findings from language acquisition and related disciplines, language pedagogy attempts to provide evidence-based strategies for language instruction. In doing so, it aims to translate theoretical insights into tangible practical outcomes by designing language teaching programs that align with established principles and theories. It serves as a bridge between language acquisition research and classroom practice. Through the development of instructional theories, the design of teaching programs, and the evaluation of teaching methods, language pedagogy aims to optimize language education and promote effective language learning outcomes.

Examples of Research Questions in Language Acquisition and Pedagogy

As noted above, applied linguistics researchers address a wide range of questions related to second language acquisition and pedagogy. Research in the field of language pedagogy examines questions that are pedagogically motivated, and to this end it addresses questions related to classroom instruction at all levels and in all contexts. Research into language acquisition addresses issues related to how language is acquired and the various factors influen:cing this process. The goals of this research are to further our understanding of second language learning, and consequently to create knowledge that can be used to improve second language acquisition and instruction. Here are some examples of questions researchers address concerning second language acquisition:

- How do adult language learners acquire a second language?
- What kind of knowledge do learners bring to the language learning process?
- To what extent is the process of learning an L2 universal across learners?
- What role does the learner's first language play in the acquisition of a second language?
- What factors affect the acquisition of a second language, and to what extent?
- Is there a possibility for second language learners to acquire the language through mere exposure to input in naturalistic settings with no instruction?
- What are the similarities and differences between child L1 learning and adult L2 learning?
- Is there a critical period for L2 learning?
- How do the processes involved in first language learning resemble or differ from those involved in second language learning?
- Is there any order in which language learners acquire different language features?
- What role does a foreign versus a second language context play in the acquisition of a second language?

For many learners, much of second language learning occurs in the classroom. Thus, many applied linguistics studies attempt to address classroom-based questions that are highly pedagogical in nature. Some example questions include:

- How important is the role of instruction and what effects does language instruction have on language learning?
- What type of instruction is most effective?
- How effective is explicit versus implicit instruction in learning grammatical structures in a second language?
- What is the role of various individual learner differences in L2 instruction?
- Why are some classroom L2 learners more successful than others?

Studies have also been examining the role of interaction and feedback in language learning. Example questions include:

- How do language learners interact with L1 and non-L1 speakers?
- What verbal and nonverbal cues do they use, and what kind of errors do they make?
- How can language errors be corrected during interaction, and what impact does error correction have on learning?
- What types of feedback are most beneficial for students' language learning, and how can they be effectively integrated into instruction?
- Which is more effective: immediate error correction or delayed error correction?

- What variables influence the effectiveness of feedback in language learning, and how do they interact with each other?
- How do various classroom tasks facilitate interaction and feedback in language learning?

Second language acquisition research not only examines how learners learn to speak the language but also how they learn to read and write it. Issues related to the teaching and acquisition of different linguistic components, such as grammar, pronunciation, vocabulary, pragmatics, and how language is used in context, have also been important questions to examine. The area of vocabulary research, for example, focuses on the acquisition, development, and use of words and lexical items in the L2. It examines how learners expand their knowledge of vocabulary and how they effectively utilize it in various language skills, such as speaking, listening, reading, and writing. Some example questions in this area include:

- How many words do we need to know to be able to communicate effectively in a language?
- What percentage of the words in a passage do we need to know to be able understand that passage?
- What percentage of the words in a passage do we need to know to be able to guess the meaning of unfamiliar words in the text?
- What strategies and knowledge sources do learners use to guess word meanings from context?
- What are the most effective strategies for teaching vocabulary to second language learners?
- Are learners able to learn vocabulary incidentally or do they need explicit instruction?
- How does explicit vocabulary instruction impact long-term retention and the use of new vocabulary?
- What role does multimedia input (e.g., videos, audio, and images) play in enhancing vocabulary acquisition in language learners?
- How does the frequency of exposure to words influence vocabulary acquisition?
- What role do metacognitive strategies play in enhancing the effectiveness of vocabulary learning among second language learners?
- How can technology be effectively utilized to support vocabulary acquisition in second language learners?

Applied linguistics research has also examined questions related to learner and teacher beliefs, attitudes, strategies, and individual differences, such as:

- What roles do learners' beliefs and attitudes play in learning a language?
- Who is a good language learner, and what strategies do they use?
- Who is a good language teacher, and what strategies do they use?
- What roles do various individual learner differences (such as learner age, cultural and educational background, motivation, anxiety, learner styles and strategies, learner perception, etc.) play in learning a language?

As noted earlier, research in the field of applied linguistics has also examined the role and effectiveness of various assessment strategies and techniques to assess language teaching and learning. For example, there are both traditional and what are known as alternative forms of assessment, such as portfolio assessment, communicative assessment, task-based assessment, peer assessment, and so on. Applied linguistics studies frequently address issues surrounding assessment, including the use, features, and effects of various assessment strategies across different learners and contexts. Some example questions in this area are:

- What factors contribute to the effectiveness of assessment in language learning?
- What factors affect the validity and reliability of assessment tools in language learning?
- How do various test designs, development, and implementation affect assessment results?
- How can assessment be used to assist L2 learning?
- What impact does assessment training have on teachers' abilities to design effective language assessments?
- To what extent can individual differences, such as aptitude, motivation, and working memory predict L2 learners' performance on various language tests?
- To what extent do the results of teacher assessment correlate with those of self-assessment?
- How do teachers conceptualize effective assessment? What are their views of reliable and valid tests?
- How do language learners perceive effective assessment?
- What tools can be used to assess communicative competence in L2 learning?

Some Major Journals in Applied Linguistics

There are currently numerous journals as well as national and international conferences around the world at which applied linguistics research is presented.

Examples of some of the major journals in the field include:

- *Annual Review of Applied Linguistics*
- *Applied Linguistics*
- *Applied Linguistics Review*
- *Applied Psycholinguistics*
- *Bilingualism: Language and Cognition*
- *CALICO Journal*
- *Computer Assisted Language Learning*
- *ELT Journal*
- *English for Specific Purposes*
- *Foreign Language Annals*
- *Instructed Second Language Acquisition*
- *International Journal of Applied Linguistics*

- *International Review of Applied Linguistics in Language Teaching (IRAL)*
- *Journal of Applied Linguistic Studies*
- *Journal of English for Academic Purposes*
- *Journal of Language and Social Psychology*
- *Journal of Language, Identity & Education*
- *Journal of Multilingual and Multicultural Development*
- *Journal of Pragmatics*
- *Journal of Second Language Writing*
- *Language and Education*
- *Language Assessment Quarterly*
- *Language Awareness*
- *Language Learning*
- *Language Learning and Technology*
- *Language Policy*
- *Language Teaching*
- *Language Teaching Research*
- *Language Teaching Research Quarterly*
- *Language Testing*
- *Linguistics and Education*
- *ReCALL*
- *Research Methods in Applied Linguistics*
- *Second Language Research*
- *Studies in Second Language Learning and Teaching*
- *Studies in Second Language Acquisition*
- *System*
- *TESOL Quarterly*
- *The Canadian Modern Language Review*
- *The Modern Language Journal*

Examples of Some Applied Linguistics Conferences

- American Association for Applied Linguistics (AAAL)
- American Council on the Teaching of Foreign Languages (ACTFL)
- British Association for Applied Linguistics (BAAL)
- Canadian Association for Applied Linguistics (CAAL)
- Canadian Association of Second Language Teachers (CASLT)
- Canadian Linguistic Association (CLA)
- Canadian Society for the Study of Education (CSSE)
- Congress of the Humanities and Social Sciences (includes language and linguistics sections)
- European Association for Applied Linguistics Conference (EUROSLA)
- International Association for Applied Linguistics (AILA)
- International Conference on Applied Linguistics and Language Teaching (ICALLT)

- International Conference on Bilingualism (ICB)
- International Conference on Language Learning and Teaching (ICLLT)
- International Conference on Multilingualism and Multilingual Education (IMME)
- Language Testing Research Colloquium (LTRC)
- Linguistic Society of America Annual Meeting (LSA)
- Second Language Research Forum (SLRF)
- Teachers of English to Speakers of Other Languages (TESOL)

Conclusion

In this chapter, we have discussed the role of research in applied linguistics, its nature and scope as a research discipline and its theoretical and practical contributions to understanding language and language use. Applied linguistics research is a broad interdisciplinary field that has evolved over time, responding to the changing needs of society and the demands of the global community. Today, the domains of applied linguistics research are diverse, covering topics such as language teaching and learning, language policy and planning, language assessment, and discourse analysis. The importance of applied linguistics research cannot be overstated, as it has practical implications for language teaching and learning, intercultural communication, language policy and planning, and social justice. Through applied linguistics research, we gain a deeper understanding of how language is acquired and used in various contexts, and how it shapes our identities, relationships, and worldviews. In this chapter we also discussed some of the key research areas in applied linguistics, which include second language acquisition, second language pedagogy, assessment, bilingual education, corpus linguistics, and analysis of discourse and interaction, among others. There are many research questions within each area, the addressing of which necessitates the use of various research approaches and methods, ranging from experimental studies that involve the use of controlled research designs, to survey research, to case studies and ethnographic research. In the subsequent chapters, we will explore different research methods and approaches in detail, providing examples of how they can be used and implemented. But before moving forward, in the next chapter we will discuss the ethical aspects of conducting research, which must be considered before any research is carried out.

DISCUSSION AND ACTIVITY QUESTIONS

Discussion Questions

1. What was your understanding of applied linguistics research before reading this chapter, and how has it changed now that you have read it?
2. How do you think applied linguistics research can contribute to the broader social and political issues, such as language policy and planning, and intercultural communication?

3. In what ways do you think applied linguistics research may develop in the coming years, and what implications might this have for language teaching and learning?
4. In what ways can applied linguistics research contribute to the development of policies and practices related to language use and language education?
5. Why is applied linguistics research important for understanding how language is used and learned in real-world contexts, and how can this knowledge be applied to promote effective communication?

Activity Questions

1. Choose a domain of applied linguistics research that interests you, such as language teaching and learning, classroom interaction, or language assessment, and identify a few research questions or problems related to that domain. Then imagine that you have conducted a study to address those questions. Reflect on its findings and their potential implications for theory, for research, and for practice.
2. In small groups, discuss to identify some current issues or problems faced by English language teachers in their classrooms. Discuss how insights from applied linguistics and second language research can help address these challenges. Share the results of your discussion with the rest of the class.
3. As a group, think about conducting a research project that investigates a specific aspect of second language acquisition. Use insights from the chapter to develop a few research questions that you would address in that project.
4. As a group, decide on a research question about language teaching and learning that you believe is important to address. How would you go about addressing that question?

3 Ethics in Applied Linguistics Research: Principles, Best Practices, and Challenges

---

CHAPTER OBJECTIVES

After completing this chapter, you should be able to

- Understand the importance of ethics in applied linguistics research.
- Identify and explain ethical principles and codes of conduct in applied linguistics research.
- Describe and understand the concept of informed consent and its role and importance in research involving human participants.
- Recognize the ethical issues related to data collection, analysis, management, and sharing in applied linguistics research as well as those related to reporting research results.
- Understand the unique ethical considerations that may arise when conducting research involving children, including those related to informed consent, parental consent, and child protection.

Introduction

Research ethics is an essential and necessary aspect of any kind of empirical research including applied linguistics research. It involves the protection of participants' various rights and making sure that research is conducted with scientific integrity, transparency, and respect for all concerned. When planning our research, we need to be aware that, like the importance of a sound research design, ethical considerations are equally important, no matter what type of study we conduct. Also, ethical issues become relevant at every step of the research, from the research methodology and design to the implementation of research, including data collection and analysis, to the dissemination and communication of the findings.

This chapter provides an overview of the ethical principles and codes of conduct that researchers in applied linguistics should follow. The chapter considers the importance of ethical considerations and reviews guidelines to conduct research with integrity and respect for human rights and welfare.

POINTS TO PONDER

Before reading the chapter, what do you think research ethics is, and why is it important in applied linguistics research? What measures would you employ to ensure ethical conduct in your research projects?

What Is Research Ethics, and Why Should It Be Followed?

Research ethics refers to a set of principles that govern the conduct of research ensuring that research is designed and conducted in an ethical manner. It concerns a broad range of issues, including those related to informed consent, confidentiality, data management and authorship, minimization of risk and harm, conflicts of interest, plagiarism, and scientific misconduct. The overall purpose of research ethics is to make sure that research is performed in a fair and responsible manner.

Research ethics refers to a set of principles that govern the conduct of research, ensuring that research is designed and conducted in an ethical manner.

There are a number of reasons why ethics is important in research including applied linguistics research, which will be discussed in the following sections.

Protecting Research Participants

Many studies, including a great deal of applied linguistics research, involve human participants whose safety, privacy, and dignity should be protected during the research. Research ethics guidelines are essential in minimizing the risk to participants. Most major ethical codes of practice recognize several rights for research participants, including the right to privacy, anonymity, confidentiality, and protection from harm. Therefore, it is important to consider these rights when conducting research.

Research Integrity

Research integrity refers to issues such as honesty, transparency, and accountability. These require that research is free from bias, fraud, and falsification. Ethical research contributes to the integrity of the research because when research is conducted in an ethical manner, it is more likely to produce credible results. Ethical research also involves disclosing any conflicts of interest or biases that could influence the research findings. These matters should be considered at all stages of the research, from the design, to the implementation of studies, to the dissemination of findings.

Research Funding

Research ethics is also important vis-à-vis funding agencies because these agencies provide financial support for research, and therefore, would like the research they fund to be conducted ethically and with integrity. For that reason, currently, many research funding agenesis or other organizations that fund research such as universities, require that certain ethical standards should be met when a study is conducted. In addition, most professional organizations in which research is conducted with human participants require that their ethical principles be followed.

Research Collaboration

Ethical principles are also essential in research because many studies are collaborative in nature, involving more than one individual. In particular, as an interdisciplinary field, applied linguistics research often involves participation and cooperation of many individuals. In such situations, abiding by ethical standards helps protect the rights and interests of all parties while at the time making sure that the research in conducted in a fair manner. Ethical guidelines help establish and promote shared values and expectations, which are essential in collaborative research. It also helps to make sure that all the contributions are properly acknowledged and appropriately attributed and that all partners are treated with respect and dignity. In addition, ethical guidelines promote transparency, accountability, and confidentiality and thus help to promote trust and respect among collaborators, which is important for building effective teams and producing high-quality research.

Cultural Awareness

Cultural awareness refers to the understanding and skills needed to appreciate and respect cultural differences. In this context, the researcher should be able to acknowledge and respect the linguistic and cultural values and norms within which they work while avoiding cultural biases. As applied linguistics research often involves studying and analyzing language use in specific cultural contexts, it is important to be aware of and respect the cultural differences within which the research is conducted. Failure to do so can lead to stereotyping, misinterpretation, and cultural insensitivity. Research ethics guidelines assist the researcher in developing such an appreciation by providing an ethical framework for navigating cultural differences and making sure that research is conducted with respect for cultural and linguistic diversity and rights.

Researchers and Society

Researchers have a responsibility to act in the best interests of the society in which they live. Therefore, they must consider the potential social and environmental consequences of their work. Ethics plays an important role in the relationship between researchers and society. When research is conducted, its purpose is to produce new knowledge that can be used to improve the lives of the public and solve societal problems. Therefore, it is essential that researchers understand the importance of ethical conduct and adhere to ethical standards so that their work benefits the society while minimizing any potential harm. When research is conducted ethically, its findings can be better trusted by the scientific community and the public.

The Development of Research Ethics Guidelines

A Historical Perspective

Ethics in research has a long history, but its formalization and serious acknowledgement can be traced back to the mid-twentieth century when there was a growing recognition of the need for ethical guidelines in research with human participants. One of the first significant developments was the Nuremberg Code of 1947, which established ethical principles for medical research involving human participants. This code emphasized the importance of informed consent, voluntary participation, and minimizing harm to participants.

In the 1960s, social scientists began to develop ethical guidelines specific to their disciplines. For instance, the American Anthropological Association established the first code of ethics for anthropologists in 1971, which emphasized the importance of informed consent, confidentiality, and respect for cultural differences. The association adopted its formal codes of ethics in 2012, which included the following seven principles: (1) Do no harm; (2) Be open and honest regarding your work; (3) Obtain informed consent and necessary permissions; (4) Weigh competing ethical obligations due collaborators and affected parties; (5) Make your results accessible; (6) Protect and preserve your records; and (7) Maintain respectful and ethical professional relationships (https://americananthro .org/about/policies/statement-on-ethics/).

The American Psychological Association (APA) has played a significant role in the history of research ethics. The APA established the first code of ethics for psychologists in 1953, which provided a framework for ethical research. The APA developed its ethical codes according to the input solicited from psychologists regarding instances in which they encountered ethical issues, which were then analyzed by a committee who developed codes to address them. These guidelines have undergone several revisions over time to reflect changes in the field of psychology and to address new ethical issues that have emerged. The most recent version of the guidelines, the "Ethical Principles of Psychologists and Code of Conduct (2017)," elaborates on various issues related to informed consent, confidentiality, and risk reduction, and includes guidelines related to issues such as personal problems, technology-assisted services, and forensic activities. The APA Ethics Code (APA, 2017) currently includes five general principles, extracts from which are presented in Table 3.1.

Ethical guidelines have also been developed in the field of applied linguistics and its related areas. For example, in 1980, TESOL (Teaching English to Speakers of Other Languages) Quarterly published its first set of guidelines (Tarone, 1980), which

Table 3.1 APA Code of Ethics: General Principles

Principle A: Beneficence and Nonmaleficence

Psychologists strive to benefit those with whom they work and take care to do no harm ... [and] safeguard [their] welfare and rights ... When conflicts occur ... they attempt to resolve these conflicts in a responsible fashion ..., [T]hey are alert to and guard against personal, financial, social, organizational or political actors that might lead to misuse of their influence. Psychologists strive to be aware of the possible effect of their own physical and mental health on their ability to help those with whom they work.

Principle B: Fidelity and Responsibility

Psychologists establish relationships of trust with those with whom they work. They are aware of their professional and scientific responsibilities to society and to the specific communities ... Psychologists uphold professional standards of conduct ... manage conflicts of interest ... consult with, [and] refer to, or cooperate with other professionals... They are concerned about ... ethical compliance ... [and] strive to contribute a portion of their professional time for little or no compensation or personal advantage.

Principle C: Integrity

Psychologists seek to promote accuracy, honesty, and truthfulness ... do not steal, cheat, or engage in fraud ... Psychologists strive to keep their promises ... consider the need for, the possible consequences of, and their responsibility to correct any resulting mistrust or other harmful effects that arise from the use of such techniques.

Principle D: Justice

Psychologists recognize that fairness and justice entitle all persons to access to and benefit from the contributions of psychology ... Psychologists exercise reasonable judgment and take precautions to ensure that their potential biases ... do not lead to or condone unjust practices.

Principle E: Respect for People's Rights and Dignity

Psychologists respect the dignity and worth of all people ... Psychologists are aware that special safeguards may be necessary to protect ... rights and welfare ... Psychologists are aware of and respect cultural, individual, and role differences, including those based on age, gender, gender identity, race, ethnicity, culture, national origin, religion, sexual orientation, disability, language, and socioeconomic status ... Psychologists try to eliminate the effect on their work of biases based on those factors ...

Source: www.apa.org/ethics/code/ethics-code-2017.pdf

was an important landmark in the development of research ethics in the field of second language teaching. These guidelines introduced a set of principles for researchers in the field of TESOL to help them conduct their research in an ethical manner. The guidelines were developed by a committee of scholars who were concerned about ethical issues pertaining to research with human participants. This publication marked an important step forward in the development of ethical standards for research in the field of ESL. The guidelines provided a set of ethical principles aiming to protect the rights and privacy of second- and foreign-language learners who participate in research on various aspects of language teaching and its related areas. The guidelines identified six key areas that were considered important "in light of the captive nature of the population in second language learning/teaching research" (Tarone, 1980, pp. 384–386). Extracts from these guidelines are presented in Table 3.2.

Table 3.2 TESOL Research Guidelines

1. Informed Consent
All research on humans should proceed only with the uncoerced, informed consent ... With captive populations, special care must be taken to ensure that the subjects are not being subtly coerced into giving their consent... Subjects should be informed that they may withdraw from the study at any time. If research is done in the classroom ... students should be assured that the test results will not affect their grades, nor will participation/nonparticipation in the study.

2. Deception
Defined by the Canada Council as "the intentional misleading of subjects to believe that the procedures and purposes of a research project are not what they actually are" ... [D]eception is undesirable and should be avoided ... Deception is only permissible when the experimenter can show that no other method is possible, and when significant scientific advances would result. ... Withholding of a project description (for research purposes) must be at the consent of the subjects. ...

3. Consequences
... No risk should be taken unless the resultant benefits warrant it. ... No study should be allowed to consume class time unless it can be shown to be simultaneously of direct educational value to the students. ... Once the project is completed, the subjects should get an oral and/or written report or at least be given the option whether they want such a report. ... [E]very effort should be made to show the subjects that they are not being judged personally (in interviews, tests, etc.). ...

4. Privacy
Great care should be taken to preserve the subjects' sense of privacy ... [T]hey should not be required to reveal any more about themselves and their lives than they wish to. ... The cultures of people involved in our studies should be carefully considered before the research methods are chosen. This might mean having cultural representatives available to review our research methods ahead of time from the point of view of invasion of privacy.

5. Confidentiality and Anonymity
The subjects should clearly understand that the data collected will be kept confidential ... Pseudonyms, initials or numbers should be used ... We should look for efficient means of preserving anonymity ... If it is impossible to maintain confidentiality or anonymity, the subjects should be told where and to whom the information will be released and should grant consent for this release.

6. Applications of Research
Premature applications of research findings to the teaching of captive populations is also a concern. ... A researcher should not feel pressured to suggest applications in a report. It is better to simply recommend further research possibilities than to give premature recommendations...

Both the British and the American Associations for Applied Linguistics (BAAL and AAAL) have also developed a set of ethical guidelines to promote ethical research practices in the field of applied linguistics. The BAAL Ethics Guidelines were first published in 1994 (BAAL, 1994) but then were revised and updated in 2021 to reflect changes in the research landscape and address emerging ethical issues in the field of applied linguistics. The 2021 edition of the guidelines (BAAL, 2021) provides more detailed and practical guidance to help researchers navigate ethical considerations in their research, drawing on the latest insights and recommendations in the field. The guidelines covered eight areas including: responsibilities to applied linguistics, responsibilities to colleagues, responsibilities to students, responsibilities to the public, relationships in research, responsibilities to informants, relationships with sponsors, the relationship between applied linguists and their own institutions.

The American Association for Applied Linguistics (AAAL) has also developed a set of ethical guidelines for research in applied linguistics (https://www.aaal.org/ethics-guidelines). The AAAL guidelines include specific recommendations related to three important areas within applied linguistics including research, teaching, and service. These guidelines include specific recommendations for working with graduate students mentored by faculty members. To promote ethical, constructive, and transparent relations between faculty and students, the AAAL guidelines suggest ways in which ethical practices can be enacted in research, teaching, and service. Table 3.3 presents the set of guidelines recommended (p. 4) when faculty researchers work as mentors or collaborate with graduate students and other emerging scholars on research projects. In 2022, these guidelines were also endorsed by the AILA Executive Board.

Ethics Theories and Their Relevance for Research Ethics

Whenever we are concerned with ethical issues, an important question is what is ethical and what is not. Research ethics is a complex and multifaceted matter that requires a careful consideration of various ethical principles and perspectives. Two prominent ethical perspectives in research ethics are *deontological* and *teleological* ethics.

Deontology (originating from the Greek word *deon*, which means "duty") is a perspective which emphasizes moral rules and principles in research based on duties and obligations. It adheres to a view that it is the moral rules that govern researchers' action and anything different from that is not allowed. This view considers an action as inherently right and ethical or wrong and unethical, irrespective of its consequences or outcomes. While deontological rules are straightforward, they can be inflexible, and for that reason, may fail to take into account the complexities of real-world situations. They may also be difficult to apply when it comes to reconciling different perspectives.

Teleology, on the other hand, is concerned with the outcomes or consequences of an action and believes that being right or wrong depends on its consequences or outcomes. The term "teleology" comes from the Greek word *telos*, which means "purpose" or "end." Teleologists believe that the purpose or end of an action determines its morality. It judges an action as ethical based on its consequences

Table 3.3 AAAL Ethics Guidelines: Ethics in Research

- Faculty researchers should recognize that mentoring graduate students to be ethical researchers is an important component of graduate student advising and should not rely solely on the ethical education received via IRB certification, a few lessons in a research methods course, or through informal interactions (Sterling, Winke, & Gass, 2015).
- Researchers should maintain an open mind about approaches to applied linguistics that may differ from their own (Davies, 2008).
- Researchers should provide direction to graduate students; they should respect their students' scholarly interests and should not exploit students for their own personal or professional ends (MLA, 1992).
- Researchers should at no time coerce their students (or others) into participating as research subjects in any studies they are carrying out.
- Researchers should, at all times, carefully manage actual and perceived conflicts of interest, particularly in regard to their graduate students and research participants.
- Researchers should recognize that because the academic socialization process may continue well after the submission of the dissertation/thesis, former students should be provided with ongoing supported if needed.
- To avoid disagreements about which authors/co-researchers should get credit and in what order their names should be listed in co-authored publications, researchers should talk about credit for authorship and the distribution of responsibilities at the beginning of a working relationship, in keeping with conventional institutional standards (Smith, 2003).
- Researchers should consult publishing guidelines provided by Institutional [Ethical] Review Board (IRB) protocols, the American Psychological Association (2010), journals such as TESOL Quarterly (Mahboob et al., 2016), and local/national research boards (e.g. the Swedish Research Council) that provide useful guidelines on authorship.
- Researchers should inform graduate students with whom they co-author that a designated "author" on a publication has legal privileges (e.g., copyright and possible royalties) and ethical obligations regarding the acceptable conduct, representation, and/or dissemination of findings from a study (CCCC, 2015) depending on the laws of the country governing the publisher.
- Researchers should include graduate students who contribute substantively to the conceptualization, design, execution, analysis, interpretation, and editing/writing of any reported research as co-authors. However, advisors should not expect automatic co-authorship on their students' work. (Smith, 2003)
- Researchers should be aware that data collected by a graduate student in the course of their own research should not be used by their advisors in subsequent presentations and publications without the student's permission.

Source: https://bit.ly/40fkp8p

rather than based on rules or duties. Teleological rules are thus more flexible and allow for a wide range of actions based on their outcomes, which can be helpful in complex situations where following rigid rules might not be appropriate.

One disadvantage of teleological rules is that they are subjective because the evaluation of actions can be based on personal perspective and preferences, making it at times difficult to achieve consensus on what constitutes an ethical outcome.

Both deontological and teleological ethics have relevance to research ethics and play an important role in decisions about research ethics. Both of them together can provide a useful and balanced framework for making ethical decisions by emphasizing the importance of both, considering the consequences of actions as well as issues such as fairness and respect for human dignity. For example, since deontological ethics emphasizes a set of universal principles that govern ethical decision-making, it prioritizes the safety, privacy, and autonomy of research participants, and thus it requires researchers to respect participants' rights and dignity as a valued principle. In this view, avoiding harm to research participants is considered essential, regardless of the context. Applying this necessitates that the researcher considers the dignity of every human being as an important principle in themselves, rather than using it as a means to an end. However, while deontological ethics has an important place in research ethics, it places little or no emphasis on the consequences of actions, which can be problematic in situations where actions have unpredictable or unintended repercussions. That is where the teleological rules can come into play. Since teleological ethics focuses on the outcomes or consequences of research, it emphasizes issues such as the potential benefits and risks of research to individuals, communities, and society. In this view, ethical principles prioritize the overall potential benefits that research can provide, while minimizing the potential harm. Because teleological rules take into account the potential consequences of an action, it can help individuals make more informed and thoughtful decisions. Therefore, in situations where rigid rules cannot be applied and the decision needs to be made based on a balance between the potential impact of research and its benefit, the approach used could be a teleological approach.

POINTS TO PONDER

What ethical considerations should you keep in mind when collecting, analyzing, and storing data? How would you address those considerations?

Ethical Principles and Codes of Conduct

Drawing on ethical principles stipulated in various professional codes of conduct in major research organisations such as the American Educational Research Association (AERA, 1992, 2006, 2011), the American Psychological Association (APA, 2017), TESOL Quarterly Research Guidelines (Tarone, 1980), and the British and American Associations for Applied Linguistics' (BAAL, AAAL) ethical guidelines, in this section, I will discuss the ethical principles and codes of conduct that applied linguistics researchers should follow. The discussion will include critical areas of research, starting with what should be done before starting the research, such as institutional approvals, followed by ethical considerations during the planning and design phase, data collection, data management, and publication of research findings. Throughout, we will explore the ethical principles that apply to each domain and consider the challenges that researchers may encounter while adhering to them.

Ethics before Conducting the Research

As noted above, when conducting research with human participants, research ethics requires that researchers follow ethical guidelines to protect the rights and privacy of the participants, ensuring that their research does not pose serious risk and harm to participants. In this context, for all studies conducted in academic institutions and universities in North America and many other countries, one of the first and most important processes is the institutional approval, which typically happens at the beginning of the research process before any data collection or analysis has taken place.

Institutional Approval

Institutional approval refers to the process through which a researcher's proposed study or research project undergoes review by an institutional review board (IRB) or an ethics committee, so that the research is conducted in an ethical manner. It is a critical step in ensuring that research is conducted in a manner that upholds ethical principles and protects the rights of the human participants in the research. Thus, before beginning a research study, you may need to submit an ethics application, outlining your research design, methods, and procedures to the IRB or ethics committee of your institution. These committees are typically located within academic institutions, such as universities, colleges, and research organizations, where research is conducted. These boards are responsible for reviewing research proposals so that they meet the necessary ethical standards. In general, all research involving human participants and almost all data collection procedures, whether in person or via the internet or phone, should go through an IRB or ethics committee review.

Institutional approval refers to the process through which a researcher's proposed study or research project undergoes review by an institutional review board (IRB) or an ethics committee so that the research is conducted in an ethical manner.

Each institution typically has its own guidelines for conducting research involving human participants. Therefore, it is important for the researcher to become familiar with the guidelines and requirements of their own institution, and also the kind of research that needs ethics approval.

When an ethics application is submitted, the IRB or ethics committee reviews the application so that the research proposal meets their ethical standards for the protection of human participants. The committee reviews the study design, informed consent procedures, data collection methods, potential risks and benefits of participation, and other relevant aspects of the research protocol to make sure that the study is ethical and in compliance with relevant regulations and guidelines. The committee will consider factors such as the risks and benefits of the study, the recruitment and consent procedures, the privacy and confidentiality of participants, and any potential conflicts of interest. The IRB or ethics committee may also request modifications to the proposal before granting approval.

Once the IRB or ethics committee has reviewed and approved the proposal, researchers may begin recruiting participants and collecting data. It is important to note that researchers must continue to comply with ethical guidelines throughout the research process and must report any significant deviations from the approved protocol to the IRB or ethics committee. This safeguards the rights and welfare of participants throughout the research process. Because ethical considerations are important and there might not always be a straightforward answer to some of the ethical issues that may arise from our research, many universities, institutions, and colleges where research is conducted by their members are required to have an ethics review board to assess research proposals so that the research follows ethics guidelines.

Information Typically Included in a Research Ethics Application

The specific details that the IRB or ethics committee may ask for will vary depending on the institution. It typically requires information such as the study's title, background, methodology, risks and benefits, participant details, confidentiality measures, ethical considerations, funding sources, and dissemination plans. Since the specific requirements may vary depending on the study and the institutional guidelines, it is essential to carefully review the guidelines and provide all relevant information for a smooth review process.

To explain institutional ethics approval, I will use my own university's (University of Victoria (UVic)) ethics application as an example. The ethics application process at UVic is a formal procedure that upholds ethical conduct in research activities involving human or animal subjects. The process involves submitting a detailed ethics application to an ethics committee, which reviews the applications so that it meets the ethical standards of the university and adheres to relevant ethical guidelines.

The UVic ethics application (https://bit.ly/4hELNUW), for example, requires a certain amount of information including the following:

- **Research team information:**
  - Name, position, telephone number, and email address for contact
  - Affiliation and contact details of all researchers involved
- **Project information:**
  - Title, geographical location, start and end dates
- **Project funding:**
  - Details on funding received by the researcher or team

- **Approvals and consultations:**
  - Any additional permissions needed from school districts, principals, teachers, etc.
- **Scholarly review:**
  - Type of review undergone by the research project
- **Researcher(s) qualifications:**
  - Description of qualifications and relevant experience
- **Description of research project:**
  - Objectives, questions, background, justification, and contribution to knowledge
- **Recruitment:**
  - Participant details, recruitment methods, and supporting documents
- **Power relationship:**
  - Explanation of any power relationships influencing participant participation
- **Data collection methods:**
  - Procedures, locations, and time commitments for data collection
- **Data collection materials:**
  - Instruments and materials used for surveys, interviews, etc.
- **Benefits, inconveniences, and risks:**
  - Assessment of potential benefits, inconveniences, and risks to participants
- **Free and informed consent:**
  - Details on obtaining consent, including from whom, methods, and ongoing consent
- **Participants' right to withdraw:**
  - Procedures for withdrawal, compensation status, and handling of collected data
- **Anonymity and confidentiality:**
  - Measures taken to protect the anonymity and confidentiality of participants
- **Data management:**
  - How researchers handle, analyze, and store data, including commercial purposes
- **Dissemination of research results:**
  - Plans for sharing results through presentations, publications, or other means
- **Conflict of interest:**
  - Explanation of any perceived, actual, or potential conflicts of interest
- **Signatory/departmental sign-off:**
  - Endorsement from Chair/Director/Dean or designate, affirming ethical standards and research infrastructure support.

Informed Consent

Informed consent is commonly viewed as a fundamental component of ethical research. It is the process through which research participants become fully aware of the nature, purpose, and potential benefits and risks involved in their participation in the research, based on which they then either agree or disagree to participate in the research. It is a legal requirement for most studies with humans, with the aim of ascertaining that the participants are not exposed to any undue harm or compulsion in research studies. Failure to obtain informed consent can result in serious ethical consequences, including harm to participants and damage to the researcher's reputation. Informed consent is important because it allows a person to make an informed decision about their participation in the research. It is also important because it protects the participant against exploitation or coercion as it gives the participant the opportunity to fully understand the potential risks and benefits before making a decision.

In the field of applied linguistics, the importance of obtaining informed consent from participants cannot be overstated. The British and the American Associations for Applied Linguistics' (BAAL, AAAL) ethical guidelines (see above) emphasize the importance of obtaining informed consent from participants before they participate in any research study.

Typically, informed consent is provided in the form of a written information sheet, along with a consent form for informants to sign, indicating their agreement. In some circumstances, it may be more appropriate to provide this information and gain consent orally, and this must usually be agreed by an ethics committee before the study.

When conducting research, you may also come across situations where the IRB or the ethics committee need to examine pre-existing documents or records related to the participants. These documents could be, for example, test results, class performance records, or any other documents. If you plan to use these documents as part of the research, it is important to obtain consent from the participants before doing so. This means that you cannot use any individual's data without their consent, even if the data were collected for a different purpose. This also means that you must clearly explain to the participants how the existing documents will be used in the research and obtain their agreement to use them. This is because using someone's personal data without their consent is a violation of their privacy and could have legal consequences.

What Should Be Included in an Informed Consent
The APA (2017, pp. 10–11) code of conduct specifies that when obtaining informed consent, the researcher should inform the participants about:

(1) "the purpose of the research, expected duration, and procedures;
(2) their right to decline to participate and to withdraw from the research once participation has begun;
(3) the foreseeable consequences of declining or withdrawing;
(4) reasonably foreseeable factors that may be expected to influence their willingness to participate such as potential risks, discomfort, or adverse effects;
(5) any prospective research benefits;
(6) limits of confidentiality;
(7) incentives for participation; and
(8) whom to contact for questions about the research and research participants' rights. They provide opportunity for the prospective participants to ask questions and receive answers."

Although, typically, consent forms are provided in the form of written documents, in some cases, verbal consent may be sufficient in certain types of research, particularly those involving minimal risk to participants. However, for more complex or risky studies, written consent may be required so that participants fully understand the nature of the study, their rights as participants, and any potential risks or benefits. However, the use of verbal consent should be carefully considered, bearing in mind the specific requirements of the study and the ethical guidelines that govern the research. It is also important to note that some research ethics committees or IRBs may require written consent for all research projects, regardless of the level of risk involved. Therefore, you should always consult with the appropriate ethics committee or IRB to determine the best approach for obtaining consent in your specific research project.

The following is a hypothetical example of a completed consent form based on University of Victoria human research ethics applications.

EXAMPLE 3.1

Participant Consent Form

Title of the project: The Effectiveness of Corrective Feedback via Mobile Phone in Improving Second language (L2) Learners' Grammatical Accuracy

Purpose and Objectives
The purpose of this research is to investigate the effectiveness of corrective feedback via mobile phone in improving L2 learners' grammatical accuracy. Specifically, we are interested in studying different feedback types and the timing of feedback. By agreeing to participate in this study, you will be helping us to understand how mobile-assisted feedback can enhance L2 acquisition.

Importance of this Research
This study is important because it has the potential to improve teaching practices and student learning outcomes. This research is also a useful source of information for teachers as it provides insights into the most effective way of providing error correction during online language learning. Thus, by identifying the most effective feedback types and timing, we can help both educators and language teachers better support student success.

Participants Selection
You have been selected for this study because you are a learner of English as a second language. A learner of English as a second language is someone whose primary language is not English and who is learning English as an additional language. We are seeking participants who are willing to receive feedback on their written work in an online environment.

Privacy

The information collected from you for the purpose of this research study utilizes an online platform (WhatsApp) situated in the United States (US) or can be accessed from the US. Irrespective of your location, WhatsApp transfers and processes your data to the United States where they will be stored. Therefore, it is important to note that the laws, regulations, and standards of the country in which you reside may differ from those of the United States where your data are being kept. Consequently, there is a possibility that your data may be accessed by the US government without your knowledge or consent in compliance with the US Freedom Act. For more information regarding WhatsApp's privacy policy, kindly refer to their official website: https://www.whatsapp.com/legal/#privacy-policy

What Is Involved?

Your participation will involve completing a 200-word writing task on a specific topic, which should take approximately half an hour. You will then be asked to submit your work via email to the researcher and then receive feedback via the messaging app, WhatsApp. You may also be asked to complete a brief survey at the end, which should take approximately 15 minutes. Please note that the use of a mobile phone for receiving feedback may require access to a smartphone or tablet and an internet connection. So please let us know if you do not have access to a smartphone or tablet or a reliable internet connection.

Inconvenience

Participation in this study may involve some inconvenience to you such as time commitment. The writing task and survey involved in the study may take up to 1 hour and 15 minutes of your time, which could be seen as an inconvenience. Also having access to a smartphone or tablet or a reliable internet connection could also be sometimes a source of inconvenience.

Risks

There are no known risks associated with participating in this study. Please note that as part of this study, the researcher will offer corrective feedback on the language errors you make. The researcher is trained to deliver feedback in a way that minimizes inconvenience and discomfort.

Benefits

This research offers potential benefits for you as you will engage in online inter-actions with a proficient researcher, receive corrective feedback on your English errors, and improve your English skills. Additionally, the findings of this study may contribute to the development of more effective teaching practices, which could benefit future students.

Compensation

As compensation for your time and participation in this study, you will receive a $15 bookstore gift card.

Voluntary Participation

Your participation in this study is entirely voluntary. You have the right to decline to participate or to withdraw your consent at any time without any consequences.

Ongoing Consent

Your consent will be sought at every stage of the study. If at any point of the study, you decide not to participate, you can withdraw without any consequences.

Anonymity

To protect your anonymity, we will not collect any personal or identifying information from you during the research, except for the consent forms, which will be stored separately from the collected data. During the data collection, you will be assigned a unique code instead of using your name. This means that any data collected from you will not be linked to your name or any other identifiable information. Your identity will not be disclosed in any publications or presentations resulting from this study.

Confidentiality

To protect the confidentiality of both your information and the data collected, we will take the following measures: (a) your data will be stored securely in password-protected computer files, and (b) all the data will be destroyed properly after the study is completed. We will make every effort to prevent unauthorized access to the data by any third party. The data will also be collected and analysed anonymously.

Dissemination of Results

The findings of this study may be presented at conferences or published in academic journals, books, or book chapters. However, no information that could identify you will be disclosed.

Disposal of Data

The data collected from you will be securely stored for 5 years. After this time, it will be destroyed in a secure manner.

Future Use of Data

Only if you consent, the data may be used for future analyses. (You will be asked to sign a separate consent form for this.) In the future, we may reanalyze the data in terms of text features. However, note that if we decide to make future use of the data, we will do that within the 5 years of the completion of the research, after which all the data will be destroyed. If you do not consent, the data that have been collected from you will not be used for any future purposes.

Your signature below indicates that you understand the above conditions of participation in this study, that you have had the opportunity to have your questions answered by the researchers, and that you consent to participate in this research project.

Name of Participant	Signature	Date

A copy of this consent will be left with you, and a copy will be taken by the researcher.

Challenges with Informed Consent

Although informed consent is often regarded as an important aspect of ethical research, the process may not always be straightforward. As the BAAL recommendation states, in some cases, informants may not be acquainted with academic activities such as conference presentations or publications, which can make it difficult for them to provide fully informed consent. Obtaining informed consent may also not be possible or even appropriate in some situations, such as certain types of internet research where it may be unclear who the informants are or if they fall into a vulnerable category. There may also be circumstances, such as investigating criminal activities online, where seeking consent may not be appropriate or safe. In such cases, decisions must be made on a case-by-case basis with careful consideration of the informants' rights and sensitivities and with the support of a strong rationale. Additionally, any decisions made should be in accordance with the relevant ethics committee.

Informed consent requires that a person has the capacity to understand the information provided and to decide based on that information. This includes understanding the potential risks and benefits, alternative options, and any potential consequences of the decision. In some cases, a person may need additional support, such as an interpreter or a legal representative, to fully understand the information and make an informed decision.

How to Obtain Informed Consent

When obtaining informed consent, an important question is how to obtain it in a way that protects the participants' rights and privacy. Here are some guidelines that can be followed to obtain informed consent in a proper manner.

Use Clear and Understandable Language

As noted earlier, informed consent includes several types of information, including information about the purpose of the study, the methodology and procedures, the potential harms, risks and benefits, and the participant's rights to withdraw from the study at any time. When preparing a consent form, it is important to use clear and understandable language so that all potential participants can understand the relevant information. For instance, it should not include technical jargon or complex and ambiguous language that might confuse or mislead the participant.

Allow Adequate Time for Decision-Making

When obtaining consent, it is important that the participants have enough time to understand the information. Therefore, they should be given enough time to review the information provided and make an informed decision about whether to participate in the study or not. They should also be given the opportunity to ask questions and clarify any doubts they may have.

As an example, suppose you are conducting a study involving a survey, in which participants have been asked to provide consent to share their personal information such as their name, age, gender, and so on. You should give participants enough time to review the information and ask any questions they might have before giving their consent. This can be done, for instance, by providing the participants with the consent form in advance so that they can have enough time to review it before completing the form.

Respect Participant Autonomy and Privacy and Avoid Coercion

Respecting participants' autonomy and privacy means that researchers must respect the rights of participants to make their own decisions to participate in a study. This is a fundamental ethical principle in research because it is important that participants feel comfortable and safe during the study. As a researcher, you should respect the participant's autonomy and privacy throughout the consent process. You should not use coercion or pressure to obtain consent. Coercion and pressure can take many forms, including providing very large incentives such that the participants would be unduly influenced to provide consent to participate in the study. Regarding inducements for research participation, the APA Ethics Code (APA, 2017, item 8.06) states:

> (a) Psychologists make reasonable efforts to avoid offering excessive or inappropriate financial or other inducements for research participation when such inducements are likely to coerce participation. (b) When offering professional services as an inducement for research participation, psychologists clarify the nature of the services, as well as the risks, obligations, and limitations.

There are other examples of coercion that should be avoided. It could, for instance include providing incomplete or misleading information, or making promises about the outcome of the study that could unduly influence a participant's decision to participate (e.g., statements such as "this study will definitely increase your vocabulary knowledge"), time pressure, power differentials (e.g., using your position of authority or power to pressure participants to participate in the study – this includes situations where you are in a position such as a teacher or supervisor), emotional pressure (such as using emotional appeals to persuade participants to participate). As the researcher, you should be mindful of all the above and attempt to avoid them, making sure that participants provide their consent voluntarily and without any undue influence.

Obtain Written Consent

As much as possible, you should obtain written consent from the participants so that they understand the information provided and have agreed to participate voluntarily.

Provide Ongoing Information and Support

You should provide ongoing information and support to participants throughout the study. You should also inform participants of any new developments or changes that might affect their participation.

Informed Consent Involving Children

The rights mentioned so far, including privacy, anonymity, confidentiality, and safeguarding participants from harm, apply to research involving both children and adults. However, when working with children, you should pay particular attention to certain aspects of research. For example, when the research involves child participants, depending on the situation, the informed consent may be needed to be obtained from both the child and their parent or guardian. If the child is competent enough, it is important to obtain assent from the child indicating their willingness to participate in the research, in addition to informed consent from their parent or guardian. In such cases, you must make sure that the child understands what the child agrees to. In other words, the consent form should be written in age-appropriate language that is easy for children to understand. This might involve using simpler words, shorter sentences, and more visual aids to help convey the information.

The child should be given the opportunity to ask questions and have them answered in a manner that is appropriate for their developmental level. The consent process with the parent or guardian should also provide sufficient information about the research, including the potential risks and benefits, so that the parent or the guardian is able to make an informed decision on behalf of their child. It is important to explain that participation in the research is voluntary, and that they can withdraw their child from the research at any time.

According to the BAAL guidelines, in the case of children under sixteen, consent must also be obtained from parents or other adults who are authorized to act on behalf of the child. However, the age at which children can provide consent for research purposes may vary depending on the country or region, as well as the specific guidelines of the ethics committee or IRB overseeing the research.

Another important issue to consider when working with children is the power dynamic between the researcher and the child. As noted in the BAAL guidelines, to protect children participating in research, researchers must be mindful of their relatively powerless position and take steps to prevent exploitation or undue pressure. It is important to communicate clearly that participation is not linked to educational grading or assessment and that children are free to decline or withdraw from the research without consequence.

One challenge is that it is not always possible to know or determine the exact age of the participants. For example, when conducting research online, it may not be easy to accurately determine the participants' ages, or the researcher may not know whether the participant is accurately reporting their age or whether they are using a false age to gain access to the survey. In such cases, the researcher should still try to make sure that the consent is provided in an ethical manner and, when needed, they should take proactive steps so that the children's rights and privacy are maintained as far as possible.

POINTS TO PONDER

Before reading about ethics in classroom research, what specific ethical considerations do you think should be taken into account when conducting classroom research? Does classroom research involve additional considerations beyond general ethical guidelines?

Ethics in Classroom Research

Many applied linguistics studies are conducted in the classroom. Such research involves both adults and sometimes very young children. In such contexts, ethical considerations are essential to make sure that student participants are treated with respect and that their learning needs are addressed in a fair and appropriate manner. In such contexts, there are several key considerations that should be kept in mind.

Maintaining Confidentiality

Maintaining participant privacy and confidentiality is an important ethical consideration in classroom research, especially when collecting personal information about the participants. In language learning situations, researchers may collect personal information, such as students' language proficiency levels, cultural backgrounds, and learning strategies. To maintain participants' privacy and confidentiality, you must keep this information confidential and not share it with anyone who is not involved in the study.

Also, when presenting research findings, you should anonymize the data so that participants cannot be identified. As noted earlier, one way to do this is to assign each participant a unique code that can be used instead of their name or other identifiable information. This code can be used throughout the study to keep track of the data collected from each participant. When presenting research findings at conferences or other places, any identifying information should be removed so that the participants cannot be identified. Another way to maintain confidentiality is to store the data securely. This includes using password-protected files and secure servers to store the data. You must also limit access to the data by other people so that only authorized people or those who need it can have access to the data.

In addition, you should inform participants about the way their data will be collected, stored, and used in the study. Participants should be informed that their personal information will be kept confidential and that it will not be shared with anyone who is not involved in the study.

Reducing Disruption to the Learning Process

Conducting research in a classroom setting can sometimes be disruptive to the learning process. For instance, students may become distracted or disengaged during a research activity, which can negatively impact their learning outcomes. To minimize disruption, researchers may need to use research activities that are relevant to the participants' learning goals.

One way to minimize disruption is to conduct the research during designated class time or during a time when students are not actively engaged in other learning activities. Another way is to make sure that the research activities align with the students' curriculum and learning needs. For instance, you could design activities that integrate new technological tools with the existing curriculum in a way that enhances the students' language learning experiences. In addition, you may need to work closely with the classroom teacher to confirm that the research activities are appropriate and do not conflict with the regular classroom instruction. The teacher's input about the nature of the research activities can be important when conducting classroom research as it helps to make sure that the research tasks are integrated seamlessly into the classroom routine without negatively affecting the students' learning progress.

Obtaining Permission

Before conducting research in a classroom setting, you should obtain permission from both the teacher and the school director or administrator. This means that you should explain the research objectives and procedures to these parties and obtain their informed consent. You should also make sure that the research tasks comply with the school's policies and regulations.

Power Relationship

In classroom research, researchers sometimes serve as both teachers and investigators. While this offers direct observation and valuable data, ethical concerns arise. Researchers must avoid using their authority to influence students' participation decisions, ensuring students do not feel obligated due to academic consequences or grading implications.

There are some other concerns that may arise when the researcher is also the teacher, one of which is the issue of conflict of interest. For example, the researcher may prioritize their research goals over the needs and interests of their students. It may be challenging to obtain informed consent and voluntary participation because students may feel obligated to participate in the study or may be reluctant to provide any negative feedback for fear of affecting their relationship with the teacher. In addition, the researcher may have access to sensitive information about their students such as their classroom grades or information about personal learning experiences.

To address these ethical concerns, several steps can be taken. One is for the researcher to be transparent with the students about their dual role, assuring them that the research does not interfere with their teaching duties. Informed consent should also be obtained in ways that the student can be given the right to withdraw from the study at any time. Confidentiality should also always be maintained by protecting participants' personal information.

Ethics in Laboratory/Experimental Research

Ethics in experimental research concerns the principles guiding research that involves the use of experiments with human or animal subjects. Ethics in experimental research are important as they help conduct the research in a way that is ethically acceptable. The APA Ethics Code (APA, 2017) highlights that researchers conducting studies involving experimental treatments should inform the participants at the beginning of the study of the following:

(1) "the experimental nature of the treatment;
(2) the services that will or will not be available to the control group(s) if appropriate;
(3) the means by which assignment to treatment and control groups will be made;
(4) available treatment alternatives if an individual does not wish to participate in the research or wishes to withdraw once a study has begun; and
(5) compensation for or monetary costs of participating including, if appropriate, whether reimbursement from the participant or a third-party payor will be sought."
(APA, 2017, item 8.02).

Informed Consent for Recording

Ethical considerations for recording vary based on context and purpose. Recording someone without informed consent is generally unethical. Participants should be informed of the recording's purpose and usage, and should be given the option to decline. Privacy rights during recording must be respected, avoiding situations where individuals can reasonably expect privacy. Editing recordings poses ethical challenges and requires care to avoid misrepresentation. The use of recordings should adhere to ethical standards, preventing harm or exploitation of participants or others. Regarding informed consent for recording voices and images, the APA Ethics Code (APA, 2017, item 8.03) states:

> Psychologists obtain informed consent from research participants prior to recording their voices or images for data collection unless (1) the research consists solely of naturalistic observations in public places, and it is not anticipated that the recording will be used in a manner that could cause personal identification or harm, or (2) the research design includes deception, and consent for the use of the recording is obtained during debriefing.

Ethics and Rigor of the Study

Both ethics and the rigor of the study are two critical components of good research. Study rigor is essential for ensuring that research findings are valid and reliable, while ethical considerations are essential for making sure that the research is conducted in a way that respects the rights and safety of research participants. However, in some cases, study rigor can have ethical implications and therefore there is a need to find a balance between these two components so that the research can be both rigorous and ethical. To strike a balance between the two, the researcher should start by carefully considering the research question and design. They should identify potential ethical issues early in the process and consult with relevant experts, such as institutional review boards, so that the research design and methodology are ethically sound. This means that researchers should take steps to ascertain that participants fully understand the research procedures and any potential risks involved; it also means that the researcher should be willing to modify their research design or methodology if ethical concerns arise.

For example, suppose you are conducting a study examining the language development of children. You may initially plan to collect data from children over a period of two years. However, during the study, you may realise that some children may become unwilling or unable to continue participating in the study, or you may realise that some of the testing instruments might put undue pressure on the participants. For the research to be ethical, you may modify the study design to change the duration of the study or consider alternative data collection methods that are less invasive or disruptive for participants. For example, you may use video or audio recordings for data collection in a naturalistic setting, rather than requiring participants to come to a laboratory. By revising the study design and prioritizing participants' autonomy and privacy, you can conduct the research in an ethical manner.

Deception and Debriefing in Research

Deception in research refers to the situations when the researcher intentionally provides false or misleading information or withholds information from the participants for the purpose of achieving the research goal. Debriefing is when the research participants are informed about the true purpose of the study after they have completed their participation. The debriefing process is important in studies involving deception or withholding information from participants, as it helps guarantee that participants have a true understanding of the purpose and implication of their participation.

Deception in research refers to the situations when the researcher intentionally provides false or misleading information, or withholds information from the participants for the purpose of achieving the research goal.

Deception in research is a controversial practice and is generally discouraged and therefore regulated by ethical guidelines and IRBs. Deception can take various forms in research, including giving participants false information about the study's purpose, manipulating the research environment or stimuli to achieve a particular goal, or using techniques that lead participants to arrive at wrong assumptions about the study or the way the study is conducted. In applied linguistics research some examples of deception could be providing participants with false information about language ability in a study that investigates language proficiency to motivate them to participate in the study. Or participants may be given tasks, tests, or measures that appear to measure one particular aspect of language ability, but actually measure another. For example, a task that appears to measure listening comprehension may actually be meant to measure grammar knowledge.

Deception in research is not inherently acceptable and therefore organizations have established ethical guidelines that researchers must follow when using deception in their studies. For example, according to the APA Ethics Code (APA, 2017), deception can only be used in research when it is necessary to achieve the study's scientific goals and when alternative methods are not feasible. Researchers must also make sure that the potential benefits of the research outweigh any potential harm or risk to participants. To this end, the APA Ethics Code also requires that researchers obtain informed consent from participants before involving them in a study that involves deception. Participants must be fully informed about the nature of the research, including the use of deception, and must provide their voluntary and informed consent to participate. The APA Ethics Code also requires that researchers debrief participants after the completion of the study, explaining its true purpose and addressing any concerns or questions that may have arisen during the study. During the debriefing process, researchers typically provide participants with a complete explanation of the study's purpose, methods, and results. They may also address any questions or concerns that participants may have. Here is what the APA code of conduct states with regards to deception and debriefing (APA, 2017, items 8.07 and 8.08):

8.07 Deception in Research

(a) Psychologists do not conduct a study involving deception unless they have determined that the use of deceptive techniques is justified by the study's significant prospective scientific, educational, or applied value and that effective nondeceptive alternative procedures are not feasible. (b) Psychologists do not deceive prospective participants about research that is reasonably expected to cause physical pain or severe emotional distress. (c) Psychologists explain any deception that is an integral feature of the design and conduct of an experiment to participants as early as is feasible, preferably at the conclusion of their participation, but no later than at the conclusion of the data collection, and permit participants to withdraw their data.

8.08 Debriefing

(a) Psychologists provide a prompt opportunity for participants to obtain appropriate information about the nature, results, and conclusions of the research, and they take reasonable steps to correct any misconceptions that participants may have of which the psychologists are aware. (b) If scientific or humane values justify delaying or withholding this information, psychologists take reasonable measures to reduce the risk of harm. (c) When psychologists become aware that research procedures have harmed a participant, they take reasonable steps to minimize the harm.

In general, deception is often used to investigate sensitive topics or to create experimental conditions that would not be feasible otherwise. While deception can be a tool for conducting research, it raises ethical concerns about the potential harm that it may cause to participants. Deception can undermine participants' trust in the research process and damage the integrity of the study's findings. Therefore, researchers should consider it seriously to ascertain whether the risks of deception are justified by the potential benefits of the study. Deception in research should only be used when it is absolutely necessary, and it should be subject to ethical review, ensuring that the potential benefits outweigh the risks.

Ethical Issues When Managing Data

In addition to the ethical issues related to collecting data, it is also important for researchers to handle and manage the data they collect ethically. When managing data, you must consider several ethical questions, including:

- **Data security:** How can the participants' data be stored and managed securely to protect against unauthorized access or breaches of confidentiality?
- **Data accuracy and integrity:** How can you make sure that the data you are managing are accurate, reliable, and free from bias? How can you prevent the manipulation or selective reporting of data to support preconceived hypotheses or agendas?
- **Data sharing and openness:** How can you balance the benefits of data sharing and openness with the potential risks to participant privacy and confidentiality? How can you ensure that data are shared in a responsible and ethical manner that respects participant rights and welfare?
- **Data retention and disposal:** How long should data be retained after a study is completed, and how should they be disposed of to protect against unauthorized access or breaches of confidentiality?

By addressing these questions, you can maintain the integrity of the data while also protecting the rights and safety of study participants.

POINTS TO PONDER

What ethical considerations should you take into account when disseminating your research results, particularly when sharing findings with a diverse audience, including academics, practitioners, policymakers, and other stakeholders?

Ethical Issues When Publishing and Disseminating Research Results

Dissemination of research results concerns sharing the research findings with the wider community, including academics, practitioners, policymakers, and the public (see Chapter 25). When sharing your results, you have a number of options, such as presenting at conferences or scholarly meetings; publishing articles, chapters, or books; and publishing through online platforms, such as personal websites, blogs, or various social media outlets. In all these, you should consider strategies so that your work is presented ethically and responsibly. In doing so, you should maintain a strong commitment to integrity and transparency and be aware of the potential impact of your work on individuals, society, and the scientific community. When publishing and disseminating research results, there are several issues that you should consider, including the following.

Plagiarism

Plagiarism is considered unethical in academic and research publishing because it undermines the integrity of the work and violates the intellectual property rights of the original authors, and thus can have legal consequences. It can occur when someone uses another person's ideas, work, or words without proper attribution or permission. It is a form of intellectual theft that violates the code of ethical conduct. Plagiarism can take different forms such as verbatim plagiarism, which occurs when sections or sentences are copied word-for-word from another source without proper citation and attribution, or self-plagiarism, when someone reuses their own work without proper citation. Another form of plagiarism is when portions of someone else's work is taken and integrated into someone's own work without proper attribution. Plagiarism can occur accidentally or unintentionally, which happens often because of a lack of knowledge or understanding of proper citation practices.

Plagiarism is a serious ethical concern in research and publishing, and can occur when someone uses another person's ideas, work, or words without proper attribution or permission. It is a form of intellectual theft that violates the code of ethical conduct.

Data Fabrication

Data fabrication is another serious ethical issue. This means fabricating the data or creating misleading data. This also happens when the researcher intentionally manipulates the data to support their research findings or hypotheses. Data fabrication is serious because it can undermine the integrity of the research and can have serious consequences, including harming research participants and losing trust in research. In this regard the APA code of conduct states (APA, 2017, item 8.10):

(a) Psychologists do not fabricate data ... (b) If psychologists discover significant errors in their published data, they take reasonable steps to correct such errors in a correction, retraction, erratum, or other appropriate publication means.

Authorship

Another issue is authorship. Researchers must be careful when it comes to the authorship of their research paper and should make sure that it is attributed fairly and accurately, considering the contributions made by everyone to the study. In this regard, the APA code of conduct states (APA, 2017, item 8.12):

(a) Psychologists take responsibility and credit, including authorship credit, only for work they have actually performed or to which they have substantially contributed. ...
(b) Principal authorship and other publication credits accurately reflect the relative scientific or professional contributions of the individuals involved, regardless of their relative status. Mere possession of an institutional position, such as department chair, does not justify authorship credit. Minor contributions to the research or to the writing for publications are acknowledged appropriately, such as in footnotes or in an introductory statement. (c) Except under exceptional circumstances, a student is listed as principal author on any multiple-authored article that is substantially based on the student's doctoral dissertation. Faculty advisors discuss publication credit with students as early as feasible and throughout the research and publication process as appropriate.

Conclusion

This chapter has provided an overview of research ethics and its importance in applied linguistics research. Research ethics is a set of principles and guidelines that govern the behavior of researchers in conducting research with human subjects. It is an essential component of scientific inquiry, so that the research is conducted with integrity and respect for the dignity, safety, and welfare of research participants. The field of research ethics continues to evolve as new ways of collecting data and the use of various technologies in doing research come into existence. While this chapter has addressed a number of important ethical issues that researchers should consider, there are still many ethical concerns that have not been fully explored or understood, particularly those arising from advances in technology and its use in research. One such emerging ethical issue, for example, relates to the use of artificial intelligence and other new technological developments, which can raise important ethical considerations that require careful consideration. The COVID-19 pandemic also led to new concerns, underscoring the importance of research ethics in conducting research using various online data collection methods. For example, many studies had to shift to remote data collection procedures due to pandemic-related restrictions, leading to new concerns about the privacy, confidentiality, and security of participant data, particularly when researchers were collecting sensitive information from participants over the internet or through other remote means. All of these mean that as research continues to advance, researchers should remain careful and thoughtful about the ethical implications of their work, making sure that their studies remain both methodologically rigorous and ethically acceptable.

DISCUSSION AND ACTIVITY QUESTIONS

Discussion Questions

1. Why is it important to obtain informed consent from research participants even when the participants are children? In what way do you think it should be done?
2. What are the potential risks of using deception in research studies conducted by teachers using their students?
3. How can researchers make sure that the studies that they conduct do not cause harm to participants?
4. What are some of the ethical issues that may arise when using data obtained from social media or other online sources in research studies in applied linguistics? Consider issues related to privacy, informed consent, and study rigor, and discuss some of the strategies that you may use to address these ethical concerns.

Activity Questions

1. Think about a research study that you have conducted or plan to conduct in applied linguistics. What ethical issues do you think might arise in the study, and how could you address these concerns? Discuss the ethical issues involved and brainstorm potential solutions.
2. Imagine a scenario in which you as a researcher want to obtain informed consent from a participant who is hesitant to participate in the study. Discuss strategies for addressing the participant's concerns while still obtaining informed consent.
3. Analyze a research article in applied linguistics and identify any potential ethical concerns in the study design, data collection, or analysis. Discuss how these ethical concerns could have been addressed or could be addressed in future research.
4. Identify or discuss a case study in which a researcher used deception in a study. Analyze the potential risks and benefits of using deception in research and consider alternative methods that could be used to achieve the same research goals.

PART II
Research Process and Designing Research

4 The Research Process: A Ten-Step Model

CHAPTER OBJECTIVES

After completing this chapter, you should be able to

- Understand the importance of knowing about the research process and its various stages.
- Identify the key steps involved in conducting research.
- Understand the importance of determining the appropriate research design and selecting appropriate participants for a study.
- Identify different data collection methods, techniques, and tools available to applied linguistic researchers.
- Understand the importance of data processing and analysis.
- Recognize the purpose statements used in qualitative and quantitative research, and understand how to develop them.
- Understand and learn about how to identify strengths of a good study.

Introduction

In order to be able to read, understand, conduct, and evaluate applied linguistics research, it is essential to possess the knowledge of the underlying research processes. Conducting research is a significant undertaking, and its successful execution requires researchers to make various decisions, such as selecting a topic, determining the appropriate methodology, and identifying the subsequent steps to take. To make this task manageable, it is beneficial to approach these decisions as a structured process comprising several steps and substeps. This approach facilitates the organization and implementation of the research endeavor.

In this chapter, we will explore the different steps involved in conducting research, including defining the research problem, formulating research questions, selecting an appropriate research design, selecting participants, collecting data, processing and analyzing data, interpreting results, and writing research reports. Knowing the steps in research is essential as it provides a structured framework for understanding how to conduct research and in turn makes the task of doing research less formidable. By breaking down research into smaller, manageable steps, you can focus on one task at a time, which can make you feel less overwhelmed; it also allows you to assess your progress and see what needs to be done at each step.

POINTS TO PONDER

Why is it important to know about the various steps and processes involved in research? How does familiarity with these steps contribute to our understanding of research?

The Research Process

As noted earlier, research is a systematic and organized process of obtaining knowledge through careful collecting, analyzing, and interpreting data. The research process refers to the series of steps and substeps involved in planning and implementing a piece of research and communicating its findings. While there exist a range of research types and diverse questions that may necessitate various modes of investigation, the fundamental processes underpinning all forms of research remain the same. Almost every research endeavor involves the identification of a research problem, formulation of research questions, sample selection, and the collection, analysis, and reporting of the data. With this in mind, I will present and discuss a ten-step model, which involves a reasoned course of action, with each step providing the ground for the next and subsequent steps. These steps are categorized into four major stages: identification, preparation, implementation, and communication. These steps are visually presented in Figure 4.1 and consist of the following:

Identification

1. Determining what to investigate: identifying the general area of interest or a problem that warrants investigation.
2. Reviewing the relevant literature: conducting a review of existing research and literature relevant to the chosen area of investigation.
3. Identifying the research problem: narrowing down the focus to a specific research problem based on the literature review.

Preparation

4. Formulating research questions: clearly defining the questions that the research aims to answer.

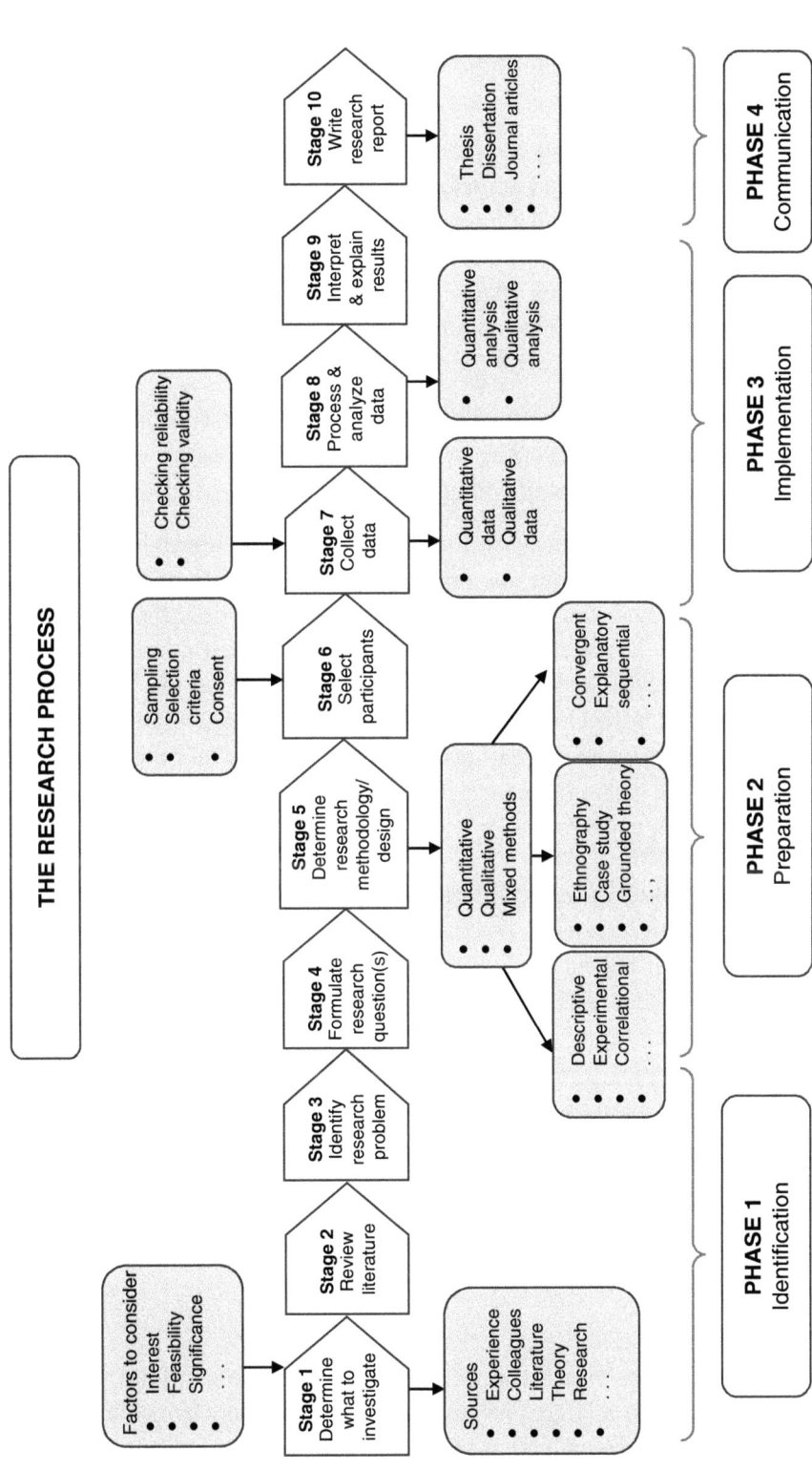

Figure 4.1 The research process

5. Determining the research methodology and the research design: developing a plan outlining the overall strategy for conducting the research, including the type of research methodology and the research design to be employed.
6. Selecting participants: choosing the appropriate individuals or entities that will be involved in the study, ensuring they align with the research objectives.

Implementation

7. Collecting data: executing the plan by gathering relevant data based on the chosen research design and participant selection.
8. Processing and analyzing data: organizing and examining the collected data to derive meaningful insights and draw conclusions.
9. Interpreting and explaining results: interpreting the analyzed data and providing explanations for the outcomes observed.

Communication

10. Writing the research report: compiling the findings, methodology, and conclusions into a comprehensive research report that can be shared with the academic community or relevant stakeholders.

Although this presentation looks linear, the process of research is not strictly linear and does not start from one point and end in another in a fixed fashion. Rather it is cyclic and can involve moving back-and-forth between steps. For example, if you are at the stage where you have formulated a research question, you may need to revise and redefine it as you read more on the topic or as the research progresses. At each stage of the research, we need to have an eye on the other stages as sometimes we may need to make changes in them. Nevertheless, thinking of research as a series of steps provides a useful framework that can make conducting research manageable.

Step 1: Determining What to Investigate

The starting point in research is determining what to study. It would be helpful to think of this stage as having two substages (Figure 4.2), the first of which would be determining the general area of investigation, and the second, selecting the topic within that area.

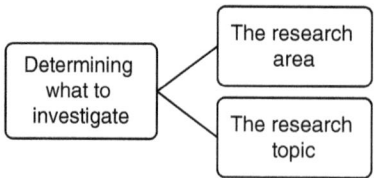

Figure 4.2 Stages involved in determining what to investigate

Research Area

A research area refers to a broad field or domain of study within a particular discipline. It represents a larger, overarching subject area that can include multiple research topics. Since research areas are broad, they can often be expressed in a few words or even just one word. Examples of research areas within applied linguistics research include: the role of interaction in language acquisition, the effectiveness of corrective feedback, various methods of classroom instruction, strategies for vocabulary learning, second language writing, language assessment, bilingualism and multilingualism, sociolinguistic factors in language use, pragmatics and inter-cultural communication, the cognitive processes involved in language learning, language policy and planning, and the impact of technology on language teaching and learning, among others. The research area is the first level of focus, which then needs to be narrowed down as you move through the process and as you read about the area.

Research Topic

A research topic refers to a specific and focused area of inquiry within a broader research area. It represents a narrower research problem that you aim to investigate. Thus, a research topic is more precise and concrete, often addressing a specific aspect or aspects of the broader research area. For example, if you decide on the role of instruction as your general research area, you may narrow it down to the differences between different types of instruction. Or, if the research area is vocabulary acquisition, your topic could be the comparison of incidental learning versus intentional learning, exploring how learners acquire vocabulary through exposure in context versus through focused, explicit instruction. What defines the topic of the project or research topic is still broad and will need to be further narrowed down to identify the research problem and then the specific research question, which is what can be addressed through collecting data.

A research area refers to a broad field or domain of study within a particular discipline. **A research topic** refers to a specific and focused area of inquiry within a broader research area.

Step 2: Reviewing the Relevant Literature

After you decide on the research topic, it is essential to find out what others have done on the topic and what remains to be done. Good research builds on previous research. Although we often want to do something that has not been done by others, strong studies are grounded in existing research and add to the current body of knowledge. Therefore, prior to conducting the study, it is essential to know what research has already been done in that area and how it can inform our research.

A literature review at the start of a study provides a valuable resource that helps you in a number of ways:

- It helps you to become familiar with the topic.
- It helps you find out what kind of research exists on the topic.

- It helps identify gaps that need addressing and a research problem that needs investigation.
- It helps you narrow down your topic and determine a problem that is specific and focused enough to be investigated.
- It helps you build your research on existing knowledge and adds to previous findings on this topic.
- It helps you to develop justification for the study (the reasons for the importance of the study).
- It allows you to become familiar with the research approaches used to investigate the topic.
- It helps you to develop a theoretical framework for the study.
- It makes you familiar with different research methods and tools used to collect data.
- It helps you to become familiar with how the findings have been validated and reported.
- It allows you to discover what issues have been raised by previous researchers and what their recommendations were about how to address them.

Therefore, the literature review performed at the start of a research project serves as a foundation for the study. It helps identify gaps, refine the research question(s), and develop a research design that builds on previous work.

The best way to understand what has been done in a given area is to examine the existing work on the topic. This means finding, reading, and evaluating the resources relevant to your research, including scholarly articles, books, reviews, conference papers, and other reliable sources related to your research topic.

In addition to individual research articles, there are now many research syntheses and meta-analyses in the field. Therefore, It is sometimes more effective to start with state-of-the-art reviews, meta-analyses, or comprehensive syntheses rather than individual studies. This approach can help identify gaps in the literature and provide a more comprehensive overview of the research landscape. Tools like the International Database of Education Systematic Reviews (IDESR; idesr.org) can be particularly useful in these initial steps to streamline the process of identifying and synthesizing relevant research (see Chapter 7).

However, although the initial literature review sets the stage for the study, it is important to note that it is a foundational element in the research process that extends beyond its initial purpose. It plays a continuous role throughout various stages of research, informing the formulation of research question(s), the development of theoretical frameworks, the design of data collection methods, the conduct of data analysis, and the reporting and discussion of findings. By reviewing existing literature, you can identify gaps, inconsistencies, or under-explored areas. However, the literature review also helps to ground all the stages of the study in existing knowledge. In terms of data collection, the literature review provides insights into effective methodologies and best practices, guiding you in designing reliable methods. During data analysis, the literature review informs the selection of appropriate analytical techniques and aids in the accurate interpretation of results by comparing them with previous findings. Furthermore, it contextualizes the study's findings within the broader body of knowledge, highlighting how the research confirms, extends, or challenges existing work, and suggests future research directions.

Thus, the literature review is not a static, one-time task but an ongoing process that informs every stage of the research, helping the study to be well-founded, methodologically sound, and meaningfully connected to existing knowledge.

Step 3: Identifying the Research Problem

After conducting the initial review of the literature, the next and very critical step is to clearly identify the research problem. This means to clarify the major goal of the study, which will be later on narrowed down to research questions and/or hypotheses. Without a clear research problem, the research cannot be effectively conducted, as it may lack focus and direction. While the research topic refers to the general area of interest that you want to explore, the research problem is a specific issue or gap within the chosen research topic that you aim to address. It identifies a specific aspect of the research topic that requires investigation. The research problem helps narrow down the focus of the study and provides a clear purpose for conducting the research. It typically emerges when a gap in the existing knowledge that needs to be addressed is identified. Examples of research areas, research topics, and research problems are provided in Table 4.1.

These examples show how a research area can be narrowed down into a research topic and then a research problem. As can be seen, the research area provides the broader context, the research topic focuses on a specific aspect within the area, and the research problem highlights the gap or issue that the study aims to address.

The Research Problem, the Problem Statement, and the Purpose Statement

A well-defined research problem is the foundation of any study. To specify the research problem, one helpful technique is to write a problem statement. A problem statement is a concise declarative statement (consisting of one or a few sentences) to capture the intent of the study as accurately and succinctly as possible. It is an important statement that identifies the gap in knowledge that the study aims to address. The problem statement can be used in the introduction and revisited toward the end of the literature review, showing that the problem is derived from and builds on previous research.

A problem statement is a concise declarative statement (consisting of one or a few sentences) to capture the intent of the study as accurately and succinctly as possible. It identifies the gap in knowledge that the study aims to address.

Table 4.1 Examples of research areas, research topics, and research problems

EXAMPLE 1
Research area: Second-language classroom instruction
Research topic: The role of input enhancement in second-language classroom instruction
Research problem: Limited understanding of the effectiveness of input enhancement techniques in promoting grammar acquisition among second-language learners

EXAMPLE 2
Research area: Language learning strategies
Research topic: Metacognitive strategies in second-language reading
Research problem: Little research into the use and impact of metacognitive strategies on second-language reading performance and development

EXAMPLE 3
Research area: Individual differences in second language acquisition
Research topic: Age-related factors in the acquisition of second language pronunciation
Research problem: Little understanding of how age influences the development of accurate pronunciation in English language learners

EXAMPLE 4
Research area: Technology and second language learning
Research topic: The effects of mobile-assisted language learning on speaking skills
Research problem: Limited research on the effectiveness of mobile-assisted language learning applications in enhancing second language learners' speaking proficiency

EXAMPLE 5
Research area: Classroom interaction in second language learning
Research topic: Teacher–student interaction patterns in content-based language classrooms
Research problem: Lack of exploration into the specific interaction patterns that occur between teachers and students in content-based language instruction and their impact on language learning outcomes

---

The problem statement can lead to a purpose statement. For example, if the research problem concerns the lack of clarity regarding the effectiveness of written corrective feedback (e.g., direct vs. indirect) across different learning contexts (e.g., EFL vs. ESL), the purpose statement could be "The purpose of this study is to examine the differential effects of direct and indirect feedback in EFL and ESL contexts."

To write an effective problem statement, it is important to provide the background context that motivates the problem and clarifies the importance of the study. Therefore, the problem statement can be proceeded by a background statement followed by a purpose statement. A purpose statement defines the specific goal of the research, clearly explaining what the study intends to accomplish. Although, there are various ways to structure a problem statement, an effective one generally includes the following three components:

1. **Background statement**: This is a succinct summary of the situation that motivates the study or contextualizes the problem.

2. **Problem/justification statement**: This central component clearly defines the research problem, identifies the gap in knowledge, and explains why it needs to be addressed.

3. **Purpose statement**: This statement specifies the exact objective of the research and is written in the form of a statement that clearly shows what the study aims to achieve, such as:
   a. The aim (purpose) of this study is to investigate . . .
   b. This study seeks to describe (explore, discover, develop) . . .
   c. This study aims to examine (understand) . . .

Examples of background statements, problem/justification statements, and purpose statements from applied linguistics research are provided in Table 4.2.

POINTS TO PONDER

When designing your research, how can you make sure that your research questions are well-defined and address a significant problem or gap in knowledge?

Step 4: Formulating the Research Question and Hypotheses

Once you have identified the research problem, you need to narrow it down into one or more specific research questions. A research question is the question that a study aims to answer, whereas a research problem is broader and specifies the issue to be investigated. More specifically, a research question is a clear, specific, and goal-oriented query related to a problem that can be addressed through systematic observation and analysis. Identifying the right research question is a very important task for the researcher and plays a very important role in conducting research. Without a clearly defined research question, research cannot accomplish its goal.

Researchable questions are those that are expressed in a way that means they can be empirically tested. That is, they can be answered by conducting the study and collecting and analyzing data. One way of doing this would be to formulate the research question in terms of single variables that can be measured. For example, you may have a problem statement such as "What is the role of recasts in learning L2 grammar?" The research question might then be "Do learners who receive recasts perform better on a grammar test compared to those who do not?" Because of the importance of formulating research questions, I will discuss this in more detail in Chapter 7.

A research question is the question that a study aims to answer, whereas **a research problem** is broader and specifies the issue to be investigated. **Researchable questions** are those that are expressed in a way that means they can be empirically tested.

Table 4.2 Examples of background statements, problem/justification statements, and purpose statements

EXAMPLE 1

Although generally supportive, most of the empirical tests of the interaction hypothesis have been conducted with adult language learners.
[Background statement]

Interestingly, however, studies of child language learners and child–adult comparisons, while generally not focusing on developmental outcomes, have indicated that the patterns and immediate outcomes of interaction may be different for children and adults.
[Problem/Justification statement]

It is therefore a crucial next step to examine if and how interaction also facilitates second language development for children, as it has been shown to do with adults.
[Purpose statement]

(Mackey & Oliver, 2002, p. 463)

EXAMPLE 2

In sum, the present review demonstrates that processing experience, orthographic knowledge, and word frequency each have empirical support, although in varying degrees.
[Background statement]

This, in turn, seems to suggest that the continual revision and fine-tuning of connections within associative networks may suggest a new lens through which L2 word recognition data can be reanalyzed and explained.
[Problem/Justification statement]

To clarify its theoretical possibilities further, we designed an experiment to examine two of the paramount factors – that is, L1–L2 orthographic distance and L2 word frequency. Specifically, the present study compared intraword structural congruity, as well as frequency, on lexical decision speed and accuracy between L2 learners from related and unrelated LI orthographic backgrounds. Four specific hypotheses were tested in a crosslinguistic experiment involving Indonesian (Roman alphabet, related) and Chinese (logographic, unrelated) ESL learners.
[Purpose statement]

(Muljani et al., 1998, p. 103)

EXAMPLE 3

Previous research on synchronous computer-mediated communication (SCMC) has shown that SCMC interaction could draw learners' attention to form in ways that are similar to face-to-face interaction.
[Background statement]

However, the role of task type in focusing learners' attention on form has not been widely researched.
[Problem statement]

In a repeated measures design, this study investigated if task type had any effect on the number and characteristics of focus-on-form instances of 54 English-as-a-foreign-language learners.
[Purpose statement]

(Yilmaz, 2011, p. 115)

While the research question takes the form of a question that can be answered, the hypothesis predicts the answer to the research question by suggesting the kind of relationship that exists between variables. Thus a hypothesis is the researcher's prediction of the findings of a study. Questions in quantitative studies such as experimental and correlational studies are often followed by a hypothesis. However, qualitative exploratory research, such as case studies or ethnographies, does not require a hypothesis as it is typically hypothesis-generating rather than hypothesis-testing.

Problem Statements and Research Questions in Quantitative and Qualitative Research

In both quantitative and qualitative research, the problem statement and the research question serve as important elements to guide the research process. However, they differ in their purpose, structure, and focus.

In most quantitative research, the aim is to explain rather than to explore or describe, and therefore the problem is very specific. Accordingly, the problem statement is focused and often identifies the research gap that the study aims to address. The literature review plays an important role in this process because the researcher often identifies the research problem based on a thorough review of the literature. In other words, the problem is derived directly from the literature, which establishes the background and rationale for the study by highlighting previous research, theories, and empirical evidence related to the topic. The research question is usually narrowly defined and often attempts to examine the effects or relationships of variables, which are measured or quantified.

The aim of qualitative research differs from that of quantitative research, focusing more on exploring or gaining a deeper understanding of an issue or a phenomenon. Thus, the problem statement, while still clarifying the intent of the research, is broader and more exploratory than in quantitative research. Similarly, the research question is typically open-ended and focuses on why or how a phenomenon occurs rather than on the effects of or relationships between variables. In qualitative research, while the problem statement and research questions can be informed by the existing literature, they are not strictly derived from it. Instead, they may emerge from various sources, including personal experiences, observations, or societal issues, allowing for a broader and more exploratory approach.

In quantitative research, the problem statement is focused and often identifies the research gap that the study aims to address. **In qualitative research**, the problem statement, while still clarifying the intent of the research, is of a broader and more exploratory nature than in quantitative research.

Step 5: Determining the Research Methodology and the Research Design

Once the research problem and questions are formulated, you need to determine how to investigate the problem. In other words, you need to determine the research methodology and then the research design. As noted before, we can make a distinction between methodology and research design. Although these may some-times be used interchangeably they can be seen as different, leading to different choices during the research process. Methodology refers to the overall approach to how the study is conducted. This is the general framework that guides the research. Research design is more specific; it connects the research question to the actual data collection procedures, the tools used to collect the data, and the conclusions drawn from the findings. Different methodologies can lead to different research designs. For example, quantitative methodology may lead to the use of experimental research designs to assess causal relationships, while qualitative methodology might lead to the use of case studies to explore individual experiences (see Parts III, IV).

When deciding on the methodology, we should consider the distinction between quantitative, qualitative, and mixed methods research. As noted earlier, qualitative research seeks to gain insight or provide an in-depth understanding of a research phenomenon in its naturalistic context through a process of collecting and analyz-ing qualitative data. For example, it explores what people feel, think, or do, or what attitudes or perspectives they hold toward a phenomenon. Qualitative data are collected through qualitative data collection tools, such as open-ended question-naires, interviews, and focus groups. Quantitative research involves selecting a set of strategies to gather quantitative or numerical data and analyzing them quantita-tively. Since such research generates numerical data, the analysis most often involves statistics. Data are collected using methods such as tests, closed-ended questionnaires, or structured interviews. A mixed methods approach involves a combination of both qualitative and quantitative approaches; in doing so it brings together the strengths of both approaches (for a more detailed discussion of mixed methods research, see Chapter 24). Since the research question(s) and the research methodology influence each other, it is important to think about the methodology when formulating the research question(s). For example, if you do not have expert-ise in a particular methodological approach, it would be advisable not to choose research questions that need that approach.

The research design refers to the specific techniques and procedures employed to address the research questions and obtain relevant evidence. It plays a critical role in determining the type and nature of data collected. The choice of research design depends on the methodology, research question(s), and study objectives. Quantitative research offers various design options, such as correlational, experi-mental, and quasi-experimental research designs (see Chapter 9 for details). Researchers select a research design based on the purpose of their study. For instance, when conducting a study that aims to test a cause and effect relationship, an appropriate research design would be one capable of testing the hypothesis that a change in one variable causes a change in another. In such cases, an experimental research design may be necessary, involving the collection of data to evaluate the validity of the hypothesis.

Research methodology refers to the overall approach to how the study is conducted. This is the general framework that guides the research. **Research design** is more specific; it connects the research question to the actual data collection procedures, the tools used to collect the data, and the conclusions drawn from the findings.

Qualitative designs aim to explore rather than to explain, seeking to get an understanding of the phenomenon under study. Many L2 studies that examine the attitudes or identities of learners might employ a descriptive qualitative research design using observation or interviews. Note that when selecting a methodology or a research design, it is very important to be able to justify your choice. An explanation of the reasons behind your choice will often go in the methods section of the research report. I will discuss this issue in more detail in Chapter 25.

POINTS TO PONDER

What should you consider when selecting participants for your study? How do these considerations influence subsequent stages of the research process, including data collection, analysis, and the interpretation of findings?

Step 6: Selecting Participants

Once the research design is established, careful consideration must be given to selecting appropriate research participants. Research participants are the individuals who take part in the research study (though not all research in applied linguistics involves human participants.). In applied linguistics research, data are most often collected from people. Depending on the research type (quantitative or qualitative) and the desired outcomes, you need to make several decisions regarding participants, including who they should be, how to select them, and how many are required.

In most cases, researchers work with a manageable group of participants from whom they collect data. The group from whom the data are collected is referred to as the sample. The sample is drawn from a larger group, known as the population. The decisions regarding participant selection and sample size are important for the study's validity and, when applicable, the generalizability of findings (see Chapters 8 and 13).

The selection of research participants depends on the specific objectives of the study. If the research focuses on EFL learners, participants should be chosen from the EFL learner population. The target population can vary in size, depending on the scope of the study. For instance, if the research aims to make claims about adult EFL learners in general, the target population would be large. However, if the goal is to make claims specifically about Chinese adult EFL learners, the target population would be smaller, limited to Chinese adult EFL learners. In cases where additional characteristics (e.g., age, language background, or language proficiency) are of interest, the target population becomes even smaller, requiring participants who possess those specific characteristics. This enables the examination of those variables in the study.

Once the target population has been identified, the next consideration is how to select a sample from this population. The selection process is guided by the nature of the research and the intended use of the findings. If the intention is to generalize the findings from the sample of EFL learners to the larger population of EFL learners, the sample should be representative of that population. However, there are instances where the focus is on studying the behavior of a particular group or on gaining insights into a specific phenomenon, without intending to generalize the findings to a broader population. In such cases, the representativeness of the sample may not be as crucial. Nevertheless, if the goal is to draw meaningful conclusions about the population using the sample, the sample selection process must be carried out in a way to enhance its representativeness. In Chapters 8 and 13, we will discuss different types of sampling methods in different types of research.

Step 7: Collecting Data

Once we have identified and selected our participants, the next step is to collect data. Data collection refers to the process through which information is gathered to answer our research questions or test our research hypotheses. It involves a number of activities including determining the data collection method, finding the data collection location, obtaining the individuals' permission to include them in the study, and collecting the data. The data collection methods are the tools used to collect data; they include various kinds of tests, tasks, questionnaires, or interviews. These methods will be discussed in Chapters 10 and 15.

Data collection refers to the process through which information is gathered to answer our research questions or test our research hypotheses.

Depending on the type of research, the data collection method can either be quantitative or qualitative. Quantitative data are numerical, such as scores, frequencies, and percentages; they are collected through methods that produce numerical data such as surveys and closed-ended or structured questionnaires, tests, exams, quizzes, or other methods that lead to numerical data. Since the purpose of collecting quantitative data is usually analyzing, comparing, and relating variables using statistical analysis, this type of data is often collected from a large number of people. While quantitative data are numerical, qualitative data are nonnumerical, such as words, texts, images, and so on; they are collected through tools such as interviews, open-ended questionnaires, observation, focus groups, and other methods that produce nonnumerical data.

The data collection phase involves not only knowing where, how, and from whom to collect data but also how to collect them in a way that is reliable and valid. We will discuss the issues relating to reliability and validity in Chapters 11, 12, and 17.

Step 8: Analyzing Data

Once the data are collected, they have to be analyzed. So, the next step in the research process is the data analysis. Data analysis refers to the process though which we make sense of the data collected and try to understand their meaning. It involves drawing useful conclusions from the data by organizing and summarizing them in ways that can help answer the research questions.

The type of analysis we do depends on the nature of the data. For example, if the data are numerical, we may analyze them statistically and summarize the results in the form of numerical tables, charts, and figures. Quantitative data analysis thus focuses on mathematical calculations, with the aim of analyzing the information objectively and with no interference from the researcher. There are different types of numerical data, each of which might need different types of statistical analysis. We will discuss these issues in detail in Part V.

Data analysis refers to the process though which we make sense of the data collected and try to understand their meaning. It involves drawing useful conclusions from the data by organizing and summarizing them in ways that can help answer the research questions.

Qualitative data analysis is subjective and involves the researchers' and the participants' subjective interpretations and judgments. It involves categorizing the data according to relevant themes and identifying patterns as a main way of organizing and reporting the data. Unlike quantitative research, where the analysis is conducted deductively after the data are fully collected, in qualitative analysis, the data are analyzed inductively, and this may occur at various stages throughout the research process. As the data analysis continues, the themes and patterns identified may be refined and reorganized in light of new themes emerging from the data. We will discuss issues regarding qualitative analysis in detail in Chapter 16.

Step 9: Interpreting and Explaining the Results

Once the data have been analyzed and the results obtained and summarized, it is important to undertake the task of interpreting and explaining the results. The purpose of this step is for the intended audience to comprehend the results and their contributions and implications. To accomplish this, you must revisit the research questions and hypotheses to assess how they have been addressed.

A critical examination of the results is essential during the process of explanation. You as the researcher should strive to explain how the data answer the research questions and whether they support the initial hypotheses, if there are any. To assist the explanation, it is beneficial to refer back to the literature review and provide an interpretation of the results within the framework of the study's theoretical and empirical background.

Once the results are examined and interpreted, they form the basis of the findings – the broader conclusions drawn from the analysis. If the research findings align with previous studies, it is important to explain how they contribute to and build upon existing knowledge. Conversely, if conflicting findings emerge, it is necessary to explore the reasons behind these disparities. This may involve discussing potential differences between the current research and previous studies, such as variations in context, participants, and research methods or tools employed.

When explaining the findings, it is also valuable to consider both the strengths and limitations of the study. By acknowledging these aspects, you can provide a balanced evaluation and suggest implications for future research. This includes outlining how future studies can address the identified shortcomings and thereby further advance the field.

Additionally, it is worthwhile to discuss other theoretical and practical implications arising from the research. This could involve exploring how the findings impact existing theories, proposing new avenues of inquiry, or offering practical applications of the research in relevant domains.

In summary, once the data analysis is complete, your role is to interpret and explain the results and the findings by connecting them to the research questions and hypotheses, highlighting the study's contributions to the field, and examining how they align or conflict with those of previous studies. You should also acknowledge the strengths and limitations of the research, and where relevant, discuss implications for future research and practice.

Data interpretation and explanation involves connecting the findings to the research questions and hypotheses, addressing both supporting and conflicting previous studies, acknowledging the strengths and limitations of the research, and discussing, where relevant, implications for future research and practice.

Step 10: Writing the Research Report

The final stage of the research process is writing the research report; this represents an important phase in which all the data and insights acquired throughout the research are synthesized and presented in an organized and understandable format. The primary purpose of the research report is to effectively communicate the research objectives and findings to fellow researchers, academic peers, or professionals and practitioners. The process of writing the research report typically follows a specific structure and format, which may vary according to the discipline or guidelines provided by the academic institution or journal. While the specific sections and organization may differ, a comprehensive research report usually includes the following core sections: introduction, methodology, data analysis and results, discussion, conclusion, and references.

The introduction provides an overview of the research topic, the research problem or questions, and the significance and objectives of the study. It often includes a literature review to situate the research within existing knowledge. The methodology section describes the research design, participants, and data collection methods and procedure used in the study. It also includes information about data analysis techniques and any other relevant methodological considerations. The data analysis and results section presents the way the data have been analyzed and the results derived from the data analysis. It may include tables, figures, or charts to present the quantitative or qualitative results. The discussion section is where you interpret the results in light of the research questions, hypotheses, and relevant theories. It involves explaining the significance and implications of the findings, comparing them to previous research, addressing any inconsistencies or limitations, and suggesting potential explanations. The conclusion section summarizes the key findings and their implications, restates the research objectives, and provides a concise response to the research questions or hypotheses. It may also suggest areas for future research based on the study's limitations or unanswered questions. Finally, the reference section includes a list of all the sources cited in the research report following a specific citation style (e.g., APA).

In addition to these core sections, a research report may also include an abstract, which provides a concise summary of the study, and an appendix at the end, which includes supplementary materials such as raw data, survey instruments, or additional analyses. Chapter 25 presents a thorough explanation of the processes and steps involved in presenting and communicating the study findings.

Conclusion

In this chapter, we have explored the process of conducting research, highlighting the importance of careful organization and planning. We discussed key steps, including defining the research problem and questions, selecting appropriate research methods and participants, collecting and processing data, and analyzing data using suitable analytic tools and techniques. When doing research, it is essential to approach each step systematically, ensuring clarity and rigor throughout the process. A well-defined research process can strengthen the reliability and validity of the findings, contributing to the advancement of the field. We also highlighted the necessity of recognizing potential limitations of our study. The next chapter provides a taxonomy and classification of different types of research and explores the various ways in which research types can be conceptualized.

DISCUSSION AND ACTIVITY QUESTIONS

Discussion Questions

1. What are some of the benefits of following a structured research process in applied linguistics research and how can it enhance the quality of the study?
2. What are some of the potential challenges that you may face in collecting any type of data, and what strategies can you use to overcome these challenges?
3. Why is it important to have a clear research design and methodology when conducting research and how does this contribute to the overall rigor of your study?
4. How does the literature review contribute to shaping your research questions and methodology, and what strategies can help make it comprehensive enough and relevant to your study?
5. How can you ensure that your research results are interpreted accurately? What potential limitations should you consider when interpreting results?

Activity Questions

1. Formulate a research question for an applied linguistic study that you are interested in and discuss how you would go about selecting an appropriate research design and data collection method.
2. Choose a research study in applied linguistics and analyze it in terms of the steps involved in the research process. Identify the research problem, research questions, research design, participants, data collection methods, data analysis procedures, and the interpretation and reporting of findings. In your analysis, identify any strengths and weaknesses in the study's research process, and reflect on how the study could have been improved.
3. Write a purpose statement for a study that you are interested in and discuss how it could be used to guide the research process.
4. Choose an article in applied linguistics that interests you and read its literature review carefully to identify previous research studies that have explored the same or related topics. Then assess how the study has built upon previous research in the field.

5 | A Framework for Understanding Research Types

CHAPTER OBJECTIVES

After completing this chapter, you should be able to

- Understand different research types.
- Understand the different dimensions or criteria according to which research types can be categorized.
- Identify the key characteristics and features of each research type.
- Understand the differences between positivist, postpositivist, interpretivist, and pragmatic research and identify the advantages and limitations of each paradigm.
- Describe the key differences between quantitative, qualitative, and mixed methods research methodologies and identify the advantages and limitations of each methodology.
- Define the main types of research designs, including experimental and non-experimental research designs, and explain the strengths and weaknesses of each research design.
- Understand the differences between basic and applied research.
- Describe the differences between cross-sectional, longitudinal, and time-series research designs.

Introduction

In previous chapters, we defined applied linguistics research and explored its fundamental characteristics. We also discussed various steps and processes involved in conducting research. These discussions laid the foundation for understanding the complexities of applied linguistics research and the factors that contribute to its success. In this chapter, we will shift our focus to an overview of different types of research. The aim is to provide a comprehensive framework for understanding the various ways in which research types can be conceptualized. By the end of this chapter, you will have a good appreciation of the different types of research available to you, which will help you to identify the most appropriate research type for your research questions and objectives.

POINTS TO PONDER

What do you know about different research types in applied linguistics? Please compile a list of those you are familiar with and identify some of their key features.

A Framework for Understanding Research Types

There are many research types and strategies discussed in the literature, sometimes termed differently and used interchangeably. This has been a source of confusion for many students and even researchers. To alleviate this confusion and foster clarity, this section aims to provide a comprehensive discussion of different research types across six key dimensions. The six dimensions used for classifying research types are as follows: paradigm, methodology, design, aim, applicability, and time frame. By exploring these dimensions, we can also effectively categorize and evaluate the various research types available to applied linguistic researchers. This framework can serve as a guide to navigate the complexities of different research types, helping to classify and compare them effectively.

The first dimension, paradigm, refers to the way research can be classified based on the researcher's philosophical stance on knowledge and reality. The second dimension, methodology, classifies research types in terms of the methods and techniques used to collect and analyze data. The design dimension refers to the overall structure of the research study, including the types of data collected and the sampling techniques used. The aim dimension classifies research in terms of its purpose, while the applicability dimension does so in terms of the research's relevance to real-world problems. Finally, the time-frame dimension conceptualizes research types in terms of the length of time over which data are collected.

Through an exploration of these dimensions, you will gain a better understanding of how research can be classified based on various criteria; as a result, you will be better able to choose the appropriate research type that best aligns with your research questions and objectives. Moreover, this chapter will highlight the strengths and weaknesses of each research type and provide examples of their practical applications.

These dimensions are graphically presented in Figure 5.1. They are discussed individually in the sections that follow.

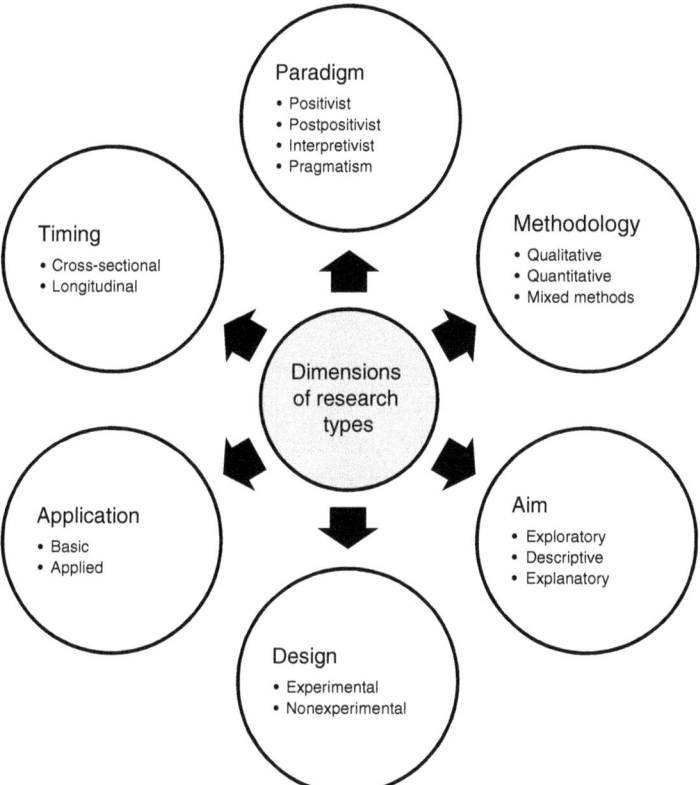

Figure 5.1 Six dimensions of research types

POINTS TO PONDER

How might the choice of research methodology and design be influenced by the overall philosophical perspective adopted by the researcher?

A Paradigm Dimension

One way of classifying research types is in terms of the overall research paradigm within which the study is conducted. The research paradigm refers to the underlying philosophy guiding the research process. It is the researcher's world view or more specifically "the set of common beliefs and agreements shared between scientists about how problems should be understood and addressed" (Kuhn, 1962). From this perspective, research can be generally classified into four broad categories: positivist research, postpositivist research, interpretivist research, and pragmatic research, as shown in Figure 5.2.

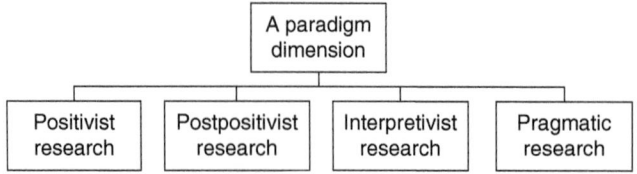

Figure 5.2 A paradigm dimension of research types

It is not my intention, and it is beyond the scope of this section, to go into detail about these perspectives and how they have come into existence. But it may suffice to say that these are different worldviews about the nature of reality and knowledge, which researchers bring to their research.

The research paradigm refers to the underlying philosophy guiding the research process. From this perspective, research can be generally classified into four broad categories: positivist research, postpositivist research, interpretivist research, and pragmatic research.

Positivist Research

What positivism means exactly and how it should be used has been the topic of much debate in the academic literature. However, positivism has long been the prevailing paradigm in most research, including applied linguistics research. Two versions of positivism can be identified: logical positivism (which is a strong form of positivism) and postpositivism (which is a weaker form). The exact meaning of logical positivism has changed over time. However, the basic assumption is that there is a single reality independent from the researcher that can be studied, understood, and verified. Objectivity is key to the pursuit of knowledge, with subjective beliefs and intuitions having no place in seeking new knowledge. In this view, naturally rooted laws and principles govern reality, and truth can be arrived at through objective procedures and logical reasoning. Scientific observation is considered a key source of reliable knowledge, and therefore the role of the researcher is to understand reality through objective inquiry. The only valid knowledge is thus knowledge obtained through careful observation, evidence, and inquiry, and the only way to verify the truth value of a statement is through empirical evidence or logical proof. According to logical positivists, all nonscientific and nonempirical knowledge is thus invalid. This view was influential in shaping the development of the social sciences, particularly in the field of psychology.

Logical positivism assumes that there is a single reality independent from the researcher that can be studied, understood, and verified.

Logical positivism is mainly associated with quantitative research methods that employ empirical observation and experimentation to establish cause-and-effect relationships. As a result, research within this paradigm typically aims to test hypotheses, formulate generalizations, and make predictions. However, logical positivism has been criticized for its overly narrow view of science and its limitations in accounting for subjective experiences.

Postpositivist Research

Postpositivism is a more modern version of logical positivism and is an approach to research that emerged in response to criticisms of positivism. Postpositivists share some common assumptions with positivists, such as the belief in empirical observation and the use of quantitative methods. A common feature of both perspectives is also their deterministic aim and their attempts to find cause and effect. They both have a strong reliance on theorization prior to research and see the role of research as testing hypotheses derived from research. However, postpositivists acknowledge the limitations of positivism and seek to address these limitations through more nuanced approaches to research. This paradigm also advocates a single reality and strives to reach knowledge though a deductive process of theorizing and testing; however, it holds that due to the limitation of human intellectual capability, reality cannot be fully discovered, and therefore, it does not consider science as an endeavor to discover absolute truth. Rather, it considers it as a progressive construction of knowledge by engaging in a continual process of conjecture and falsification (Popper, 1959). It also holds that researchers cannot be completely objective and that their biases and assumptions can influence their research. Therefore, postpositivist research aims to minimize bias and error through careful research design and analysis. This view has rejected the notion of objectivity and the pursuit of absolute and unambiguous knowledge "on the grounds that an advance in science is not a matter of scientists making a discovery and then proving it to be right but rather a matter of scientists making a guess and then finding themselves unable to prove the guess wrong, despite strenuous efforts to do so." (Nudzor, 2009, p. 114). In other words, knowledge is never certain, and all observations and measurements are subject to error and uncertainty. This is the perspective that currently underlies most quantitative approaches in research.

Postpositivism advocates a single reality and strives to reach knowledge though a deductive process of theorizing and testing. But it also holds that researchers cannot be completely objective and that their biases and assumptions can influence their research.

Interpretivist Research

Interpretivism is a philosophical orientation with an epistemology that contrasts with positivism. There are different variants of interpretivism, including constructivism, phenomenology, and hermeneutics. However, in general, while logical positivism adheres to the notion of absolute knowledge and a single reality that can be objectively observed and verified, interpretivist research assumes that there is no single reality separate from the researcher and therefore there is no single truth that can be detected in an objective manner. Reality is multiple and is constructed by individuals based on their own experiences, background, and the context in which they live. It thus emphasizes the value of subjective understanding and beliefs, and considers knowledge as essentially the product of these processes. Similarly, the role of research is to understand the reality of lived experiences. Interpretivist research typically involves the following features:

- A focus on understanding the subjective experiences and meanings of individuals and groups
- An emphasis on reflexivity and the acknowledgement and exploration of the researcher's personal perspectives, biases, and assumptions
- A recognition of the role of context and interpretation in shaping research findings.

Interpretivism underlies qualitative approaches and those that use qualitative data collection methods, such as interviews, focus groups, and observation.

While **logical positivism** adheres to the notion of absolute knowledge and a single reality, **interpretivist** research assumes that there is no single reality separate from the researcher. Reality is multiple and is constructed by individuals based on their own experiences.

Pragmatism

There are different understandings of what pragmatism is. But for most researchers, it is a paradigm that values solutions to actual problems. It seeks to move beyond the tension between positivist and interpretivist approaches and instead focuses on the practical and pragmatic roles of research and the practical outcomes of knowledge and inquiry. It holds that the value of any research approach should be judged in terms of its ability to solve the problem under investigation. Therefore, it focuses more on the research question and the efficacy of the research to address the question. Thus, for many, pragmatism is viewed as sitting between positivism and interpretivism, as it seeks to balance the importance of objective knowledge with the need for practical, context-specific solutions. Although some research questions may be addressed by using a single methodology, this paradigm allows for a combination of different methods to address complex questions. For that reason, it is the paradigm considered to underlie mixed methods research. All in all, pragmatism can be seen to have the following features:

- A focus on the importance of research questions that are relevant and meaningful to the people and communities studied
- The use for research designs that are flexible and responsive to changing needs and contexts
- Emphasis on the importance of research findings that are practical and can be used to solve real-world problems.

Pragmatists often use mixed methods research designs that combine quantitative and qualitative methods to generate a more complete understanding of the research topic.

Pragmatism is a paradigm that values solutions to actual problems. It seeks to move beyond the tension between positivist and interpretivist approaches and instead focuses on the practical and pragmatic roles of research and the practical outcomes of knowledge and inquiry.

However, although each philosophical perspective is commonly associated with certain types of research methods, it is important to note that there is no direct mapping between a particular philosophical view and a particular research method. Nowadays researchers try to draw on multiple perspectives and methods rather than a single one that may be typically associated with a certain philosophy. Furthermore, the boundaries between these perspectives are not always clear-cut. Ultimately, the choice of perspective and method should be guided by the research question and the nature of the problem being addressed.

POINTS TO PONDER

What are some of the main characteristics of qualitative research? How do they differ from quantitative research?

A Methodology Dimension

While the research paradigm refers to the overall worldview or philosophical framework the researcher brings to research, the research methodology refers to the way the research is conducted. It is what guides the specifics of an actual study in terms of its overall design and its methods of data collection and analysis.

It is important to distinguish research methodology from research methods. Although these two terms have often been used interchangeably, the two are not the same. Research methodology refers to the overall approach and includes the methods involved in identifying research questions, gathering and analyzing data, and drawing conclusions. In other words, research methodology is the overarching framework covering research design, data collection and analysis techniques, and the methods used to draw conclusions from the data. It is concerned with how the research is conducted, rather than the specific research question or topic being studied. With respect to methodology, research can be classified into three broad categories: qualitative research, quantitative research, and mixed methods research, as shown in Figure 5.3. The choice of methodology depends on the research question, the nature of the data being collected, and the goals of the research project. Research methods refer to the specific tools and techniques used for collecting and analyzing data. Research methods are often determined by the research methodology being used. Examples of research methods include questionnaires, interviews, observations, and so on.

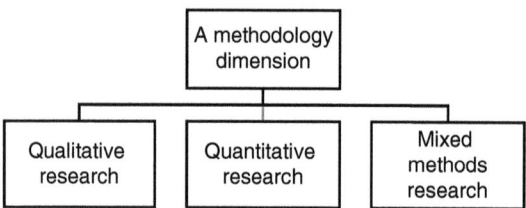

Figure 5.3 Methodology dimensions of research types

In the following chapters, I will provide a detailed explanation of these approaches. Nonetheless, I will give a brief overview of them here.

Research methodology refers to the overall approach to research, whereas **research methods** refer to the specific tools and techniques used for collecting and analyzing data.

Qualitative Research

Qualitative research refers to research that is used to gain an in-depth understanding of a research problem through exploring people's feelings, words, behavior, and experiences in their naturalistic contexts. It has been used in various academic disciplines including the social sciences and education to explore complex phenomena and generate rich, in-depth descriptions of participants' experiences. It is also widely used in applied linguistics research to explore a range of applied linguistics and language teaching and learning issues.

The main aim is to uncover the meanings that underlie human behavior and to explore how people construct and make sense of their world. It assumes that the researcher cannot be separated from the research context and therefore, instead of taking an objective position, the qualitative researcher takes a subjective stance and sees reality as subjective rather than objective. For the same reason, problems cannot be examined objectively; instead, the approach taken is more subjective. The researcher's role in qualitative research is thus to make sense of and interpret the situation by being part of it or to identify or discover patterns that emerge through the analysis of the data.

Qualitative research refers to research that is used to gain an in-depth understanding of a research problem through exploring people's feelings, words, behavior, and experiences in their naturalistic contexts.

Qualitative research typically involves collecting data using tools such as interviews, focus groups, and observations, which are then analyzed using techniques such as coding, thematic analysis, and identifying patterns and themes within the data. Since the data is collected naturalistically, the aim is not to generalize but rather to understand things as they occur in their own context. Thus, the framework is more interpretive, focusing on participants' experience from an insider's perspective.

Table 5.1 summarizes the major characteristics of qualitative research as described by Cook and Reichardt (1979, p. 10).

Table 5.1 Characteristics of qualitative research
• Advocates the use of qualitative methods
• Concerned with understanding human behavior from the actor's frame of reference
• Naturalistic and uncontrolled observation
• Subjective
• Close to the data; the "insider" perspective
• Grounded, discovery-oriented, exploratory, descriptive, inductive
• Process-oriented
• Valid: "real," "rich," and "deep" data
• Ungeneralizable: single case studies
• Holistic
• Assumes a dynamic reality

Here are some examples of situations where qualitative research may be used in applied linguistics:

- Exploring the experiences of language learners and teachers in different teaching and learning contexts, such as in the classroom, outside the classroom, or in study-abroad programs
- Investigating language use in specific contexts, such as in workplace interactions, language testing situations, or intercultural communication
- Examining language policy and planning and exploring how language policies are applied in different contexts
- Exploring learners' and teachers' attitudes, beliefs, and perspectives regarding language; how these are shaped and maintained; and how they affect language teaching and learning
- Exploring language users' – including teachers' and learners' – identity and how it is constructed, maintained, and influenced by other factors.

Qualitative research methodology has several advantages, including the following:

- **In-depth understanding:** Qualitative research is designed to explore complex phenomena in depth, allowing researchers to gain a deeper understanding of the experiences and attitudes of participants.
- **Flexibility:** Qualitative research is flexible and allows researchers to adapt their methods to fit the specific context and research question, which can lead to richer and more nuanced data.
- **Subjectivity:** Qualitative research acknowledges the subjective views and perspectives of individuals and groups, allowing for a more nuanced understanding of complex phenomena.
- **Exploration of new ideas:** Qualitative research is often used to explore new or emerging phenomena, allowing researchers to generate hypotheses and develop theories.
- **Focus on participants:** Qualitative research focuses on participants, allowing for the voices and perspectives of participants to be prioritized and heard.
- **Suitability for sensitive topics:** Qualitative research is well-suited to exploring sensitive or stigmatized topics, as it can provide a safe space for participants to share their experiences and understanding.

Qualitative research methodology also has some limitations, including the following:

- **Limited generalizability:** Qualitative research often uses small sample sizes and focuses on specific contexts, which limits the generalizability of the findings to other populations and contexts.
- **Potential for bias:** The subjective nature of qualitative research can make it more susceptible to researcher bias, which can impact the validity and reliability of the findings.
- **Time-consuming process:** Qualitative research can be time-consuming, as it involves in-depth data collection and analysis methods such as interviews, focus groups, and content analysis.
- **Lack of standardization:** Qualitative research lacks the standardization and replicability of quantitative research, which can limit its comparability across studies and contexts.
- **Analysis complexity:** The analysis of qualitative data can be complex, especially when large amounts of data are collected, which can make it difficult to draw clear and actionable conclusions.
- **Ethical concerns:** Qualitative research can raise ethical concerns, such as the need to protect the privacy and confidentiality of participants, the potential for harm to vulnerable populations, and the need to obtain informed consent.

Quantitative Methodology

Quantitative methodology refers to ways of doing research that involve collecting and analyzing numerical data. It is used to explain, describe, or examine relationships among variables or the effect of one or more variables on other variables. The assumption behind the methodology is that problems can be examined objectively with controlled measurement and without the researcher's influence and therefore the role of the researcher is to be detached from the research. One of the main aims of this kind of research is generalizing the findings beyond the study situation and context. A typical research design associated with this type of methodology is experimental research in which cause-and-effect relationships are examined. Data are typically collected through methods such as surveys, experiments, and tests and analyzed using statistical techniques such as t-tests and ANOVA to identify differences or relationships between variables.

Quantitative methodology refers to ways of doing research that involve collecting and analyzing numerical data. It is used to explain, describe, or examine relationships among variables or the effect of one or more variables on other variables.

Table 5.2 summarizes the major characteristics of quantitative research as described by Cook and Reichardt (Cook & Reichardt, 1979, p. 10).

Table 5.2 Characteristics of quantitative research

- Advocates the use of quantitative methods
- Logical positivism: seeks the "facts or causes of social phenomena with little regard for subjective states of individual"
- Obtrusive and controlled measurement
- Objective
- Removed from the data: the "outsider" perspective
- Ungrounded, verification-oriented, confirmatory, reductionist, inferential, and hypothetico-deductive
- Outcome-oriented
- Reliable: "hard" and replicable data
- Generalizable: multiple case studies
- Particularistic
- Assumes a stable reality

Quantitative research is often used when we want to test hypotheses, evaluate the effects of interventions using various outcome measures, or find out relationships among variables. Some examples of issues that can be addressed through the use of a quantitative methodology in applied linguistics include:

- Investigating how language is learned, by using various tests to measure the different aspects of language proficiency in different groups of learners and by using statistical analysis to identify factors that may influence language development

- Analyzing language use in different contexts, using corpus or text analysis or surveys
- Evaluating the effects of various instructional interventions or different language programs and comparing outcomes across groups and settings
- Examining language attitudes and beliefs by collecting numerical data and using statistical analysis to identify patterns and relationships between or among variables.

Some advantages of a quantitative methodology include the following:

- **Objectivity:** Quantitative research allows you to collect and analyze data in a more objective and systematic way, reducing the potential for bias and subjectivity in your findings.
- **Generalizability:** The use of statistical analysis in quantitative research enables you to make generalizations about a population based on a sample, increasing the external validity of your findings.
- **Precision:** Quantitative research allows you to measure and quantify the relationships between variables with a high degree of precision, providing more accurate and reliable data.
- **Replicability:** Because quantitative research involves a systematic and standardized approach to data collection and analysis, it is more easily replicable by other researchers, increasing the reliability and validity of your findings.
- **Efficiency:** Quantitative research can often yield large amounts of data quickly and efficiently, making it an effective method for studying large populations or complex phenomena.

Some of the limitations include the following:

- **Lack of depth:** Quantitative research focuses on numerical data and statistical analysis, which may not provide a detailed understanding of the complex nuances and contextual factors that influence a phenomenon.
- **Limited scope:** Quantitative research is often designed to answer specific research questions and may not be able to explore issues outside the scope of the research questions.
- **Reductionist approach:** Quantitative research often reduces complex phenomena to a set of variables, which may oversimplify the phenomenon and fail to capture its full complexity.
- **Inability to capture subjective experiences:** Quantitative research relies on objective data and may not capture the subjective experiences of individuals or groups.
- **Potential for bias:** The use of predetermined categories and numerical data can lead to biased conclusions, especially if the data collection process is not rigorous or if the research design is flawed.
- **Expensive and time-consuming:** Conducting quantitative research can sometimes be costly and time-consuming, especially if a large sample size is required or if complex data collection methods and advanced statistical analyses are needed.

Overall, while quantitative research is valuable for generating numerical data and enabling statistical analysis, it will not be the most appropriate research method for every research question or context. Furthermore, although qualitative and quantitative methodologies are often considered in the literature as opposing ways of doing research and it is sometimes suggested that, because of the epistemological reasons underlying each one, researchers should favor one over another, much recent research in the field of applied linguistics advocates the view that both are legitimate ways of conducting research and that the nature of the problem to be addressed and the purpose of the research determine which methodology is more appropriate.

Mixed Methods Research

Simply put, mixed methods research is a research approach that combines both quantitative and qualitative methods in a single study or research project. This approach involves collecting and analyzing both numerical and nonnumerical data to gain a more comprehensive understanding of a research question or phenomenon. Mixed methods research can be particularly useful for addressing complex research questions that cannot be answered through a single method or approach. For the same reason, mixed methods research has been adopted in the field of applied linguistics to examine complex issues by collecting and analyzing different types of data from different sources (see Chapter 24). A summary of the three types of research methodologies is presented in Table 5.3.

POINTS TO PONDER

How might a single research study effectively incorporate multiple methodologies, designs, and philosophical perspectives? Can you provide examples of applied linguistics studies that have successfully implemented this approach?

Qualitative/Quantitative Data Collection versus Qualitative/Quantitative Analysis

It is important to make a distinction here between qualitative/quantitative methods of data collection and qualitative/quantitative analysis, as a way of analyzing data. In research, it is possible to use a qualitative method to collect data but then use a quantitative method or a combination to analyze the data. For example, if the research purpose is to explore the kind of beliefs teachers have about certain teaching methodologies, we may use a qualitative method of data collection (e.g., interviews, focus groups, observations, etc.). Then the data collected qualitatively can be coded and converted into numerical values that can be analyzed quantitatively.

Table 5.3 A summary of the characteristics of qualitative, quantitative, and mixed methods research

	Qualitative research	Quantitative research	Mixed methods research
Objectives	▪ To gain insight into a phenomenon ▪ To uncover patterns and trends in the data	▪ Seeks explanation or causation ▪ Describes relationships	▪ Both to gain insights and seek explanation or causation
Research questions	▪ Often posed to explore the area	▪ Often posed to find explanation or describe causal relationships	▪ Both to explore or find explanation
Design	▪ Flexible, unstructured, or semistructured ▪ Uncontrolled or semicontrolled	▪ Highly structured and controlled	▪ Both a flexible and a highly structured component
Sample	▪ Typically, small with purposive or convenience samples	▪ Large, with preference for random sampling so that the sample can be representative of the population from which it is drawn	▪ A combination of both small and large samples depending on the kind of mixed methods research
Data collection tools	▪ Tools that produce qualitative data, such as interviews, observations, focus groups	▪ Tools that produce numerical data, such as various kind of tests, surveys, questionnaires	▪ Both qualitative and quantitative data collection tools
Kind of data	▪ Nonnumerical, often consisting of texts, images, or other types of qualitative data	▪ Primarily numerical	▪ Both numerical and nonnumerical
Analysis	▪ Mainly inductive and interpretive with attempts to arrive at underlying concepts by categorizing the data into themes and patterns	▪ Mainly deductive and statistical	▪ Both deductive and statistical as well as inductive and interpretive
Results	▪ Less generalizable	▪ More generalizable	▪ Both contextual and generalizable

A Design Dimension

While research methodology provides the general guiding framework for a study, research design is what translates the methodology into action. It is the specific plan used to answer the research question. It provides a blueprint or a map that serves as a guide for collecting, measuring, and analyzing data. Research can be classified in terms of design based on the specific structure used to conduct the study. From the viewpoint of research design, research can be broadly classified into two major types: experimental and nonexperimental research designs (Figure 5.4).

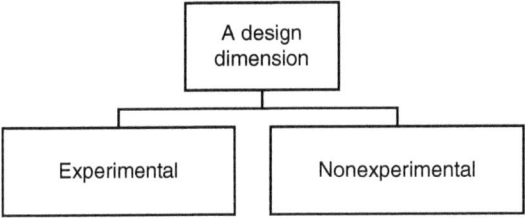

Figure 5.4 Design dimensions of research types

Experimental Research Designs

Experimental research designs aim to determine causation, and therefore the researcher systematically manipulates variables under controlled conditions in order to test the effect of one or more variables on other variables. In this design an intervention or treatment is deliberately introduced, whose outcomes are then measured. To determine the effect of a treatment, experimental research usually compares an experimental group (the group that receives the treatment) with a control group (the group that does not receive the treatment). The effect of the treatment is then measured using pretests and posttests. For example, if we want to find out which vocabulary learning strategy (contextual learning or explicit definition learning) is more effective in promoting long-term retention, we could use an experimental research design by comparing the retention rates of learners who use contextual learning with those who rely on explicit definitions.

There are various types of experimental research design, which differ from one another in important ways such as the presence of a control group, random sampling, or the degree of manipulation of a variable. These include preexperimental design, true experimental design, quasi-experimental design, and factorial design. The differences between these designs will be discussed in more detail in Chapter 9.

Experimental research designs aim to determine causation, and therefore the researcher systematically manipulates variables under controlled conditions in order to test the effect of one or more variables on other variables.

Nonexperimental Research

Nonexperimental designs are those that do not intend to determine causation. Therefore, they do not involve any manipulation of variables. Instead, they study the phenomenon as it occurs in its naturalistic context. Examples of nonexperimental research designs include various types of survey, descriptive studies, and correlational studies. A correlational study, for example, is nonexperimental as it seeks to determine the correlations between or among variables as they are observed in their natural settings. The differences between various types of nonexperimental research designs will be discussed in Chapters 9 and 14.

Nonexperimental designs are those that do not intend to determine causation. Instead, they study the phenomenon as it occurs in its naturalistic context.

An Aim Dimension

Although each research study will have its own specific objectives that will vary in terms of aims, as discussed earlier, research can be broadly categorized into three types: exploratory research, descriptive research, and explanatory research (Figure 5.5). It is important to note that while these aims differ, they are not mutually exclusive, and it is quite possible for a study to have multiple aims. It is also possible that an explanatory study may involve describing a situation.

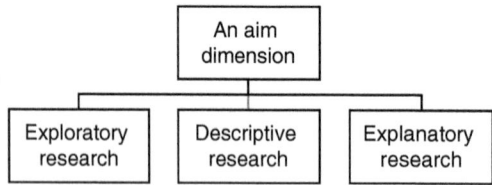

Figure 5.5 Aim dimensions of research types

Exploratory Research

An exploratory study is one in which the aim is to become familiar with or further our understanding of a certain area that the researcher has just observed. This type of study is conducted when there is not yet much known about a topic, and hence the aim is to gain new insights into the phenomenon. Therefore, exploratory research is often conducted when a topic has not yet been examined or when there is not yet much written on a given topic. Exploratory research may also be used to develop new research tools and procedure, to learn about how best to design a study, or to gain insights into the feasibility of a larger and more sophisticated study. Data are collected here to test or discover ideas about an area that might later on be subjected to more detailed investigation. Thus, it can be used as a pilot study or prepare the ground for future research. Since there is not yet much knowledge in the area, there may also not yet be a theory or hypothesis guiding the research. Therefore, exploratory research may be used to generate new hypotheses.

Because this kind of study is motivated by the data itself without any specific theory or hypothesis guiding the research, it is also described as data-driven rather than theory-driven. In L2 research, there are many exploratory data-driven studies whose aim, for example, is to discover the characteristics of L2 learners' language or the processes through which L2 learners pass to acquire a language.

Descriptive Research

Another aim of research is to describe. While exploratory research aims to discover new ideas, descriptive research attempts to describe what is happening. It is used, for example, to describe patterns, depict the characteristics of a case, or define a situation or event.

In language teaching research, descriptive research is often used to describe teaching activities. For example, you may intend to find out how a classroom event takes place, how students perform a task, or what the attitudes of learners are towards a task.

Explanatory Research

The other aim of research is to explain. Explanatory research seeks to answer the question why something is happening the way it is happening. In this case, the research is attempting to identify the cause of an event or to arrive at a causal explanation for a phenomenon. Therefore, this kind of research is also called causal research because it attempts to determine cause-and-effect relationships. Exploratory research is often carried out when we already know about a phenomenon and are also able to describe it. Therefore, exploratory research often follows descriptive research in order to determine the reason for an event. This kind of research is often based on predictions and therefore it is usually conducted when there is already a body of knowledge available on a topic to enable the researcher to make predictions. This body of knowledge is what we call a theory. As such, explanatory research aims to provide evidence to support or to reject a prediction coming from a theory. Consequently, this kind of research is also known as hypothesis-testing or theory-driven research.

An Applicability Dimension

In terms of applicability, research can be categorized into two types: basic research and applied research (Figure 5.6).

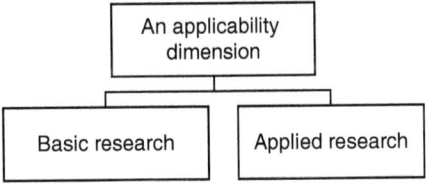

Figure 5.6 Applicability dimensions of research types

Basic Research

Basic research is conducted mainly to expand our knowledge in a given area. It is driven by intellectual curiosity and the desire to generate knowledge for the sake of knowledge. It aims primarily to achieve a theoretical understanding or to examine the processes underlying a particular situation or behavior. It does not intend to address a practical problem. Rather, it is conducted to produce knowledge that is used in building or developing a theory. For the same reason, the primary audience for basic research is researchers who are interested in the theoretical aspect of language and its use. And thus, basic research is often written in a style that is highly specialized and difficult for practitioners to access (Jakobovits, 1973).

EXAMPLE 5.1

An example of basic research is a study on the phonology of a particular language or one examining the phonological properties of two dialects. The goal of this type of research is to gain a deeper understanding of language as a system, without necessarily focusing on any practical applications. Such a study is just for the sake of understanding how similar or different the sound structures of different languages are. Here, you discover the similarities and differences between the two languages, which can then help the development of a theory about how the sound system of languages works.

Applied Research

Applied research seeks to address or find solutions to a particular real-world problem. Its aim is to develop knowledge that has immediate practical relevance; it is often conducted with the aim of informing practice. For the same reason, the primary audience for such research is often practitioners, including teachers, curriculum designers, or material developers or researchers who are interested in practical aspects of applied linguistics research. With this definition, all studies examining the effectiveness of particular instructional strategies can be classified as applied research.

EXAMPLE 5.2

An example of applied research is a classroom study that aims to identify classroom interventions that can help to teach different sound structures to different learners coming from various language backgrounds. This type of research might involve experimenting with different teaching techniques or materials, analyzing learner progress, and considering how language background influences sound-structure acquisition. By focusing on practical outcomes, this applied research addresses real classroom challenges and aims to improve instructional methods to better meet the needs of the learners.

Challenges with the Distinction between Basic and Applied Research

It is important to note that although, theoretically, a distinction can be made between basic and applied research, this distinction is not clear-cut in practice.

Many of the studies that can be classified as basic research may have important practical implications or eventually be used to address practical problems. For instance, a study that aims to examine the sound structure of a language by describing its phonetic properties might have important practical implications by suggesting how those phonetic properties could be taught in language learning contexts.

In addition, in applied linguistics, due to the nature of the field, it may be argued that studies are all applied. Basic research is more the domain of theoretical linguistics, whose aim is to develop a theoretical understanding of the nature of language, its properties, or how a language system works. Applied linguistics, by definition, is applied, as it attempts to address issues related not to the study of language per se but to the study of language to inform practice. Conversely, in applied linguistics, theory-driven research may be conducted to test a theoretical perspective. However, the ultimate aim can be to inform practice. That is why many of the theory-driven studies in applied linguistics are conducted in practical settings, such as in classroom contexts, to test theoretical models.

However, despite challenges, the distinction between basic and applied research is still useful as applied linguistics is a very broad discipline with researchers with different interest and orientations. Even if we define applied linguistics as a field that deals with practice, it can also be a field that aims to develop a theory of the practice (Kramsch, 2015).

Altogether, it might be helpful to think of basic and applied research as existing on a continuum rather than as discrete entities. At one end of the continuum, we can have studies that are very basic and, at the other end, studies that are very applied. For example, applied linguistic studies that are conducted with the aim of developing a theoretical understanding in an area of applied linguistics, such as second language acquisition, can be considered to be more basic, but those that aim to develop curriculum materials or classroom tasks can be seen as more applied. Some other examples of more basic and more applied research in applied linguistics could include the following:

- **More basic:** Examining how learners' motivations influence language learning
- **More applied:** Studying the relative effectiveness of instructional strategies to enhance learners' motivation
- **More basic:** Investigating whether age of learning is a good predictor of learners' speaking ability
- **More applied:** Examining different language programs with different age groups to determine which one is more effective
- **More basic:** Studying the relationship between attention to form and attention to content
- **More applied:** Examining what kind of focus on form strategy would help to enhance attention to both form and content.

A Time-Frame Dimension

With respect to time frame, research can be grouped into two categories: cross-sectional research and longitudinal research (Figure 5.7).

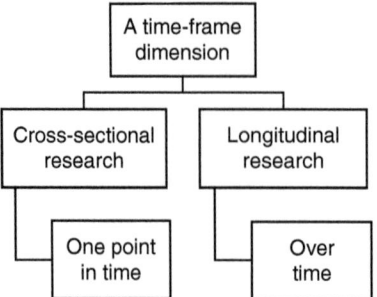

Figure 5.7 Time-frame dimensions of research types

POINTS TO PONDER

In what contexts is cross-sectional research particularly suitable, and how does this design affect the types of data collection and analysis used? For what research purposes is longitudinal research more suited, and what specific insights does it provide to enhance our understanding of language-related phenomena?

Cross-Sectional Research

Cross-sectional research, also known as one-shot studies, involves data collected at one point in time or over a short period. It gathers data from either the same or different groups of participants at a given point in time and attempts to examine what is happening at that time rather than over time. The reason it is called cross-sectional is that it examines a cross-section of the phenomenon or population. Thus, it provides a snapshot of the group's performance or characteristics at a single point in time.

EXAMPLE 5.3

An example of a cross-sectional study would be an examination of the relationship between language proficiency and pragmatic competence by collecting data from a group of English language learners at one specific point in time. These learners, who vary in proficiency levels, share similar characteristics, such as age range and educational background. By assessing their pragmatic competence in relation to their proficiency at a single time point, you can examine relationships without tracking changes over time, making this a cross-sectional approach.

Cross-sectional research is a common form of research in applied linguistics and is used to examine many issues. One common form of cross-sectional research is experimental studies that examine the effect of one variable on another at a specific point in time. Survey studies in which data are collected from a large group of participants at a given time is another popular form of cross-sectional study. In applied linguistics, survey studies can be used to examine a variety of issues, such as:

- The attitudes of a group of learners towards a particular instructional strategy
- The relationship between learners' learning styles and learning strategies
- Teachers' and students' perspectives or experiences with a particular teaching method or curriculum.

Correlational studies that collect data on multiple variables at a single point in time represent another common type of cross-sectional study. Such studies provide a snapshot of potential relationships between or among variables at a given time.

Advantages and Disadvantages of Cross-Sectional Studies

Some advantages of cross-sectional studies are that they are relatively easy to conduct and involve only one or a few data collection sessions. Therefore, they are not very time-consuming. They are also less prone to participant loss or attrition because the data are collected from participants once or only a few times (by a few times here we mean, for example, the collection of pretest and posttest data). Also, since cross-sectional studies allow for the collection of data from a large group of participants, their findings can be statistically analyzed.

However, there are also a few shortcomings. One is that cross-sectional studies cannot examine development or the degree of change in a phenomenon or a group of participants. To examine development, the data must be collected at different points in time. It is also possible that the group of participants is not representative of the population to which the conclusion is going to be extended.

Sometimes, in order to find trends in the phenomenon, several cross-sectional studies are conducted at different points in time with different groups of learners. However, one problem with this approach is that since participants are not the same, any change may not reflect development and may instead be due to the other differences that might exist between different participants.

Longitudinal Research

Longitudinal research involves data collected over a period of time (or at different points in time) with the aim of describing or tracking development or change over time. In these studies, the data can be collected from an individual participant or a group of participants representing the same population. When data are collected from the same individuals at multiple time points, you can detect any changes in their performance or characteristics over time (see Figure 5.8 for a schematic representation of a longitudinal research design).

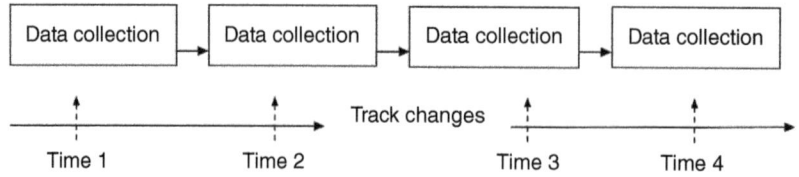

Figure 5.8 A longitudinal research design

EXAMPLE 5.4

An example of a longitudinal study would be a study examining the development of language ability in a particular group of learners over several years. For instance, a group of students could be selected in grade one, and data on their language proficiency could be collected at multiple time points – such as in grades two, three, and four. This study would allow researchers to track changes in language ability within the same individuals over time, providing insights into how language skills evolve throughout their primary education. Alternatively, the study could focus on the language development of a single individual over an extended period, examining the progression of their language abilities at various stages.

One limitation of longitudinal studies with a group of learners is that they are prone to attrition, which refers to the loss of participants over time. This may happen particularly if the study takes place over a very long period of time.

Cross-sectional research involves data collected at one point in time or over a short period from either the same group or different groups of participants, to examine what is happening at that particular time, rather than over a period of time. **Longitudinal research** involves data collected over a period of time (or at different points in time) with the aim of describing or tracking development or change over time.

Although many questions within applied linguistics can be characterized as developmental in nature, such as how L2 learners develop different L2 skills, most studies are cross-sectional rather than longitudinal, and therefore there has often been a call to conduct more longitudinal studies. An important advantage of longitudinal studies is that they allow an examination of change over time. However, they also have limitations. For example, longitudinal studies of L2 development are time-consuming. Another issue with longitudinal studies is the test–retest effect. This happens when the same learners receive the same tests at different points in time or if similar data are collected from them at multiple times. In such cases, it is possible that the participants may learn from the first instance of testing, which would then affect their performance in the second or third instance. Because of these, most studies adopt a cross-sectional research design even when addressing developmental questions. For example, if the question is how learners' understanding of a particular language concept develops over time, instead of tracking the same learner or learners over an extended period of time (which might be difficult to do), you may collect data from different groups of learners at various stages of learning and compare them to see if there are any differences that suggest development in their understanding.

Conclusion

The aim of this chapter was to provide a comprehensive overview of different types of research, using a framework that classifies research types along six dimensions: the paradigm, the methodology, the design, the aim, the applicability, and the time frame. Different classifications and terminologies are often used in the literature, which can sometimes be confusing to the reader. By exploring each of these dimensions, we have been able to provide a detailed understanding of the various research types available. Overall, the key takeaway is that there are different ways in which research types can be classified; an understanding of these can help you better decide what type of research you need. It is important that you should carefully consider your research question, aims, and objectives, as well as the advantages and limitations of each research type when deciding on the most appropriate approach for your study. Only by doing so can we achieve valid and reliable results that can contribute to our understanding of the issues examined.

DISCUSSION AND ACTIVITY QUESTIONS

Discussion Questions
1. Why is it important for researchers to consider their philosophical perspectives when designing their research studies?
2. Can researchers draw on multiple philosophical perspectives within the same study? If so, what are some examples of how this might be done?
3. In what ways do the boundaries between different research methodologies overlap or intersect?
4. What are some potential benefits of using an exploratory research design, and how might you apply this approach in your research?
5. Suppose you have a research question that you might want to address. Why might you choose to use a cross-sectional study design instead of a longitudinal study design, or vice versa?

Activity Questions
1. In small groups or pairs, discuss a research question or topic that you are currently interested in investigating. How might a mixed methods research type

help you better understand this topic? Together, identify at least one type of qualitative and one type of quantitative data that could be used to investigate the topic, and explain how each type of data would contribute to answering the research question.

2. Compare and contrast the different aims of research, including exploratory, descriptive, and explanatory. As an activity, choose a research question and identify which of these aims would be most appropriate to address the question. Then, explain your reasoning and discuss the potential benefits and limitations of using that aim.

3. Choose a research question and consider whether a cross-sectional or longitudinal study design would be more appropriate to answer the question. Then, explain your reasoning and discuss the potential benefits and limitations of using that research type. Be sure to consider factors such as the research question, the population being studied, the variables of interest, and practical considerations such as time and resources.

4. Choose a research study that you are interested in and identify its research methodology and research designs. Discuss the similarities and the differences between the two and explain how they are related.

5. Find a study that has used a longitudinal research method. Read the article carefully, paying attention to different stages of the research over time. Next take note of the research question and the specific data collection and analysis procedures for each stage. Then determine how these stages are integrated and analyzed. Share your findings and reflections with a classmate or a group of peers.

6 Understanding and Describing Research Constructs and Variables

CHAPTER OBJECTIVES

After completing this chapter, you should be able to

- Understand what is meant by a research variable.
- Define the concept of research constructs and distinguish between constructs and variables.
- Distinguish between different types of variables such as independent, dependent, and control variables.
- Describe the process of operationalizing constructs and variables, including the use of measurement tools and techniques.
- Provide examples of different types of constructs and variables used in applied linguistics research.
- Distinguish between the different types of measurement scales.

Introduction

In the previous chapters, we learned about various processes and steps involved in research, as well as the different types of research. Before moving on, we need to introduce several other concepts that we need to know. As noted earlier, research is a systematic process, and as such it has a specific language for describing research parameters. In other words, in addition to everyday language, we also need technical language for the terms that are used to define, describe, and summarize observations. Some of these terms include constructs, variables, constants, types of variables, and measurement scales. In this chapter, we will begin by defining variables and their types, look at how they differ from constructs, and examine how variables are measured and used in research.

POINTS TO PONDER

How do you differentiate between a construct and a variable? Can you provide an example of each?

Defining Variables

Research is all about variables. A variable is an attribute or characteristic that varies across people, objects, or situations. It is something that the researcher describes, observes, and measures. In research, variables are key concepts on which the research collects and analyzes data.

A variable is an attribute or characteristic that varies across people, objects, or situations.

For example, the teaching method used in a language classroom is a variable because it can vary across different classrooms or contexts (e.g., communicative language teaching, task-based language teaching, or grammar-translation method). Language proficiency of L2 learners is also a variable because learners differ in their language proficiency. Some learners may have a low level of language proficiency while others may have a higher level of language proficiency. Nationality is another example of a variable as some people may have the nationality of one country whereas others may have the nationality of another country.

The above are characteristics of people. Objects also have characteristics, such as weight, color, and length, that can vary from one object to another. We also have attributes of language, such as its sound system, its orthographic system, or its syntax. These are also variables as they vary from one language to another.

A variable has at least two observable values and in many cases more. For example, the use of multimedia in lessons can have two values: yes and no. The variable "nationality" can have two values in one study (Chinese and Japanese) and four values in another study (Chinese, Japanese, Korean, and Spanish).

Constructs and Concepts

While "variables" are characteristics that vary and can be measured, "constructs" are theoretical and abstract in nature and cannot be directly observed or measured. Notions such as intelligence, motivation, anxiety, developmental readiness, and so on can all be constructs because they are characteristics that are expressed in an abstract way and that they do not specify how they should be measured. For example, we cannot directly observe someone's level of motivation or intelligence. Therefore, we need to identify indicators that precisely show the degree to which someone possesses these characteristics. Without those indicators they remain vague as different people may have different understandings of what they are. Therefore, constructs must be operationalized into variables so that they can be measured. Operationalization involves defining the construct in terms of specific, observable, and quantifiable indicators that can be consistently measured.

Constructs are theoretical and abstract in nature and cannot be directly observed or measured.

It might be helpful here to make a further distinction between the terms "concept" and "construct". These terms have very similar meanings and are often used interchangeably too. However, there is an important difference between them. A concept is any abstract idea or notion that helps us to think, and to organize our knowledge in a productive way. It can be used to express ideas, events, objects, or any other things we are interested in. For example, self-esteem can be a concept when used to express an idea, whereas an accident is an event. Constructs are like concepts in many ways. However, they carry at least two additional meanings. One is that they are theoretical and enter into a theoretical relationship with other constructs. The other is that they are used in empirical or theoretical research for the specific purpose of investigation, including testing theories or hypotheses. For example, motivation is a concept as long as we use it to communicate the general meaning of someone's desire to do or learn something. However, it becomes a scientific construct when researchers or theoreticians use it in a scientific study to examine its properties or its theoretical or empirical relationships with other constructs. So, a construct can be said to have a theoretical purpose.

Concepts are broad and abstract ideas that offer a general understanding of phenomena. They differ from **constructs**, which are more specific, theoretical, and designed for use in research, where they can be defined by measurable indicators.

Construct Definition

When we do research that involves constructs, we need to use them in ways to avoid misunderstanding. Therefore, we need to define them precisely. There are two ways a construct can be defined. One is in terms of its general meaning, which is called constitutive definition, and the other is its operational definition.

A constitutive definition is a dictionary definition whereby other words or synonyms are used to define the concept. For example, motivation may be defined as someone's willingness or desire to do something. The constitutive definition provides theoretical clarity in common language that helps us to communicate our ideas. However, it is too broad and imprecise for scientific research because it can still be interpreted differently by different people and may be viewed from different perspectives. For example, motivation can be viewed as the desire to do something that is intrinsically or inherently satisfying (called intrinsic motivation) or as something that depends on external factors such as finding a job or getting admission to a university (called extrinsic motivation).

In addition, the terms still do not specify how the construct should be measured. When we do research that involves testing theories or hypotheses, the constructs should be measured accurately and correctly so that relationships can be tested. They should be defined in ways that allow everyone to have the same interpretation, such that if they want to replicate the study, it will be possible. This definition is called the operational definition.

Operationalization refers to a process whereby indicators are developed for measuring a construct. Therefore, the operational definition is a definition that specifies the operation or procedures the researcher uses to measure the construct for the purpose of the research. When a construct is operationally defined, it is no longer at a theoretical level and becomes empirical, thus enabling the researcher to measure the construct and examine relationships or differentiate individuals with respect to that construct. When we operationally define a construct, we are converting a construct into a variable. So, a variable is a construct defined in measurable terms.

A constitutive definition is a dictionary definition, whereby other words or synonyms are used to define the concept. **An operational definition** is a definition that specifies the operation or procedures the researcher uses to measure the construct for the purpose of the research.

For example, motivation, when generally defined, is a construct, and when it is operationally defined as scores or learners' responses to questionnaire items, it becomes a variable. As another example, intelligence is a construct; however, if someone's intelligence is measured using an IQ test, the IQ score becomes a variable. Thus, although the terms "construct" and "variable" may sometimes be used interchangeably, they are not the same. Variables are measurable forms of constructs. Some constructs are easy to measure, such as age or nationality, but others, such as motivation and intelligence, need more careful and deliberate consideration.

Table 6.1 displays examples of some more constructs and their conversion into variables in applied linguistics research.

Table 6.1 Examples of constructs and their conversion into variables in applied linguistics research

Constitutive meaning	As a construct ←	As a variable →	Operational definition
A feeling of nervousness or unease	Anxiety		Scores on an anxiety scale
The degree of competence in a language	Language proficiency		Low, high, and intermediate based on scores on a language proficiency test
The ability to understand a written text	Reading comprehension		Scores on a standardized reading comprehension test
The degree of success in producing a desired result	Effectiveness		Improved accuracy on an oral production task
A change made to one's language production	Modified output		Target-like or nontarget-like utterance following a teacher's feedback
Learners' responses following feedback	Uptake		Revised versions of the learner's original output

A construct can also be operationalized in different ways. For example, language proficiency can be operationalized as scores on a language proficiency test or as learners' self-assessment of themselves as low, intermediate, or advanced language learners. A construct can be simple and unidimensional or more complex and multidimensional. Constructs such as age are unidimensional because they can be assessed using a single measure. They are thus easy to understand and measure. Other constructs are more complex and multidimensional. They are complex in that they cannot be easily defined. They are multidimensional in that they comprise more than one dimension.

Take for example the construct of "print exposure." This construct is not as easily definable as age, as it might be difficult to come up with a definition that is identical across all studies. Here the researcher would operationalize the variable based on the purpose of the research and how this variable has been operationalized in previous research. For example, the researcher may define it as the amount of print material that a reader reads or is able to identify. For instance, a study on the contribution of different variables to reading comprehension, including exposure to print, operationally defined reading exposure as "extracurricular reading in school-aged children" (Grant, Gottardo, & Geva, 2011, p. 69) and measured it using what is called the Title Recognition Test (TRT; Stanovich & West, 1989). They explained it as follows:

> The TRT listed both real titles of popular children's books, and items that were not real book titles, the latter of which acted as foils to detect and prevent guessing. Participants were instructed to check off the names of the books that they recognized to be real titles, and to not guess names they did not recognize as being "real." The test involved a series of 40 titles, 25 of which were "real" titles, and 15 that served as foils. (p. 73)

Concepts such as intelligence, motivation, language aptitude, attention, or acquisition are also considerably difficult to operationally define and measure. When a construct is simple, a single indicator may be enough to operationalize or measure that construct. For example, it would be sufficient to simply ask people how old they are to measure their age. However, it would not be sufficient to ask only one question in order to find out how motivated someone is. When we are dealing with complex constructs, their operationalization involves many indicators so that they can cover the whole realm of the construct. As noted before, multidimensional constructs involve a number of aspects or components, making them difficult to measure. For example, the construct of language proficiency can be viewed to have at least two dimensions, including grammatical proficiency and communicative proficiency. Each of these dimensions may consist of several underlying constructs. For example, the language dimension may consist of a learner's knowledge of vocabulary, grammar, spelling, and the sound system of the language.

When we are dealing with multidimensional constructs, each underlying construct should be clearly defined for the purpose of the research, and if each dimension is complex, we need to have many indicators to specify how each dimension can be measured.

POINTS TO PONDER

What are some important variables used in applied linguistics research? Can you provide an example for each one?

Types of Variables

Understanding the notion of variables and its use in applied linguistics research also involves knowing about the different types of variables. There are several ways in which we can classify variables, depending on our focus or what the variable is used for. In what follows, we discuss four ways of classifying variables depending on the purpose for which they are used:

- Depending on the kind of data: qualitative versus quantitative variables;
- Depending on how they are measured: categorical versus continuous variables;
- Depending on their function in experimental cause-and-effect studies: dependent, independent, moderator, control, intervening, extraneous variables;
- Depending on their function in correlational studies: criterion versus predictor variables.

Depending on the Kind of Data

One way of classifying variables is with regard to the kind of data they represent. Here a distinction can be made between quantitative and qualitative variables (Figure 6.1).

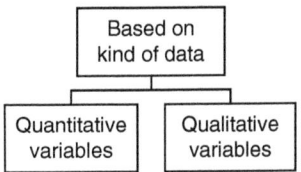

Figure 6.1 Classification of variables depending on the kind of data

Quantitative Variables

A quantitative variable is one that refers to a quantity (or represents quantitative data) and is measured quantitatively by assigning a numerical value to it. Examples of quantitative variables are the learner's age, the number of students in a class, scores on a test, and the number of yes and no responses on a questionnaire. The numerical values in quantitative variables can be subject to mathematical operations such as addition, division, or subtraction.

Qualitative Variables

A qualitative variable is one that refers to a quality and represents nonnumerical data. Qualitative variables do not possess numerical values or quantitative measurements. Instead, they represent characteristics or qualities, which can be grouped or classified into different categories. Examples of qualitative variables are first-language background, country of birth, and employment type. Employment type can be considered a qualitative variable because it is a categorical attribute that classifies individuals into distinct groups, such as full-time, part-time, self-employed, or unemployed.

For the purpose of data analysis, we may sometimes assign a numerical value to a qualitative variable. For example, we may assign 1 to part-time and 2 to full-time. However, the variable is still qualitative as the numbers assigned do not have any mathematical meaning, and we cannot perform any mathematical operations on them such as addition or subtraction. The numerical value assigned is simply a code for data classification. The level of language proficiency, such as beginner, intermediate, and advanced, can be considered as a qualitative variable as it represents qualities or characteristics that can be grouped into different categories.

However, the same variable can also become a quantitative variable if we categorize people into low, medium, and high proficiency, and assign a numerical value to each in ways that represent different levels of language proficiency, such as 1 for low, 2 for medium, and 3 for high. The variable can be considered a quantitative variable because, by assigning numerical values, we are introducing a quantitative aspect to the variable, allowing for mathematical operations and comparisons based on the assigned values. In this case, we can perform calculations such as averaging the proficiency scores or determining the difference between two individuals' proficiency levels based on the assigned values.

A quantitative variable is the one that refers to a quantity (or represents quantitative data) and is measured quantitatively by assigning a numerical value to it. **A qualitative variable** is one that refers to a quality and represents nonnumerical data.

Depending on How Variables Are Measured

Variables can also be distinguished in terms of how they are measured. In this respect, they can be classified as categorical or continuous (Figure 6.2).

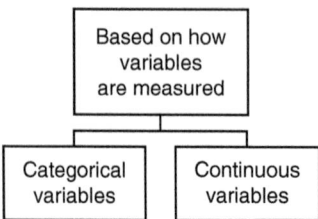

Figure 6.2 Classification of variables depending on how they are measured

Categorical Variables

Categorical variables are qualitative and consist of one or more than one category. The categories are fixed and cannot be divided or multiplied. Education level, for example, is a qualitative variable because it is a categorical attribute that classifies individuals into distinct groups, such as high school, bachelor's degree, master's degree, or doctorate. As noted above, the numerical values assigned to categorical variables can be counted, but they cannot be subject to any mathematical operation. For example, we can categorize types of feedback into (1) recasts, (2) prompts, and (3) metalinguistic feedback. Such variables are also called discrete variables.

There are several types of categorical variables as shown in Figure 6.3:

1. Nominal variables: Nominal variables represent categories that have no inherent order or ranking. Examples include occupation (e.g., doctor, engineer, lawyer), eye color (blue, brown, green), or type of feedback (oral feedback, written feedback, peer feedback).
2. Ordinal variables: Ordinal variables have categories that can be ranked or ordered, but the intervals between categories are not uniform or equal. Examples include satisfaction levels (very satisfied, satisfied, neutral, dissatisfied, very dissatisfied), or the level of language proficiency (low, medium, high).
3. Dichotomous: Dichotomous variables are categorical or nominal variables that can have two mutually exclusive categories or groups. Examples include agree/disagree, correct/incorrect.
4. Binary variables: Binary variables are a special type of dichotomous variable with two possible outcomes, typically coded as 0 or 1. Such variables are commonly used in statistical and computational contexts. Examples include yes (1) no (0), or true (1), false (0). In these examples, the variables are

dichotomous in the sense that they can be divided into two mutually exclusive categories. However, they are binary variables because they have two categories that are represented in numeric form.

5. Polytomous variables: Polytomous variables are categorical variables with more than two categories. Examples include colors (e.g., red, blue, green, yellow), types of pet (e.g., dog, cat, bird, fish), or nationality (e.g., Chinese, Spanish, Japanese, French).

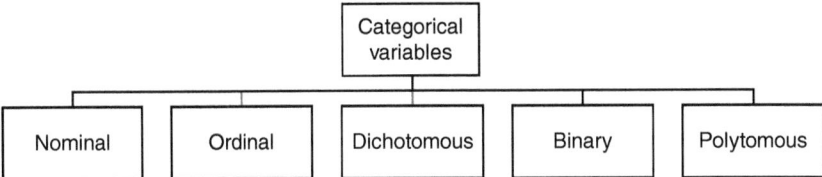

Figure 6.3 Types of categorical variables

Continuous Variables

Continuous variables are quantitative and numerical and are measured on a scale that can, in theory, have an infinite number of values. For example, weight is a continuous variable because it is measured on a scale, and the measurement can potentially have infinite values. An object can weigh 10 kilograms, 18 kilograms, 1,855 kilograms, and so on. Test scores are another example of continuous variables because we can theoretically have a score of 50, 100, or 1,099 or any other value depending on the scale. One way of testing categorical versus continuous variables is that we can do mathematical operations on continuous variables by adding or averaging them, but we cannot do so on categorical variables. In research, we can convert a continuous variable into a categorical one. For example, language proficiency can be a continuous variable if we measure it using test scores However, it can be converted into a categorical variable if we group the learners into low, mid, and high proficiency based on those test scores. As another example, you may convert age, which is a continuous variable (as it is measured on a scale), into a categorical variable by classifying the learners into young, adolescent, and old. These conversions depend on the aim of the study and how the researcher wants to analyze the data.

In truth, it is not the measurement itself but rather how the researcher chooses to look at it that is the deciding factor in whether you will call a variable continuous or categorical. For example, if you ask people about their income, they might respond in dollars (e.g., $25,000, $40,000, $100,000). This is a ratio scale because it has a true zero point (e.g., no income; see below for a discussion of different types of scales such as nominal, ordinal, interval, and ratio). But then you can classify the responses into categories such as "low income" and "high income." By doing so, you have changed a ratio scale into a nominal scale. In this case, the specific numerical income is replaced by labels that emphasize group membership rather than exact measurement. Alternatively, if you classify income into an ordered sequence such as "low," "middle," and "high," it becomes an ordinal scale, as these categories imply a natural order.

Discrete variables are also quantitative and numerical. They are numerical in the sense that they can be counted. However, the difference between a discrete variable and a continuous variable is that discrete variables cannot have an infinite number of values. They can only take specific and limited numeric values, and the number is always a whole number and cannot be divided. Examples would be the number of students in a class, the number of questionnaire items, they number of yes–no questions. In these cases, we cannot have 1.3 students in a class or 1.95 questionnaire items. When categorical variables are represented by numbers that we can count, the numbers represent a discrete variable.

Depending on Their Function in Experimental Cause-and-Effect Studies

Depending on their function and the role they play in the research design, variables can be classified into dependent, independent, moderator, control, intervening, extraneous, and confounding variables (Figure 6.4).

Such roles of variables depend on our research question and the kind of relationship we hypothesize between and among them.

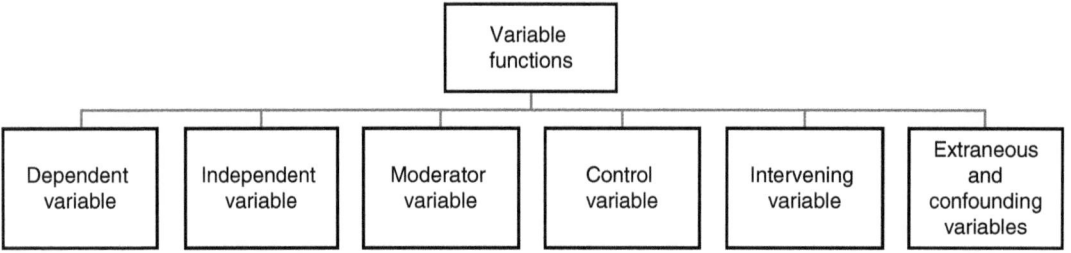

Figure 6.4 Classification of variables depending on their function

Independent and Dependent Variables

In a study, the researcher may select a variable to examine its influences or effect on another variable. The variable that is selected to examine its influence is called the independent variable, and the variable that is influenced or affected is called the dependent variable (Figure 6.5). In experimental studies, the independent variables are manipulated by the researcher in order to observe their effect on the dependent variable. The independent variable is under the control of the experimenter, and its purpose is to test the cause-and-effect relationship with the dependent variable.

EXAMPLE 6.1

Suppose you want to investigate the effect of different types of vocabulary-learning strategies on learner vocabulary retention. The independent variable would be the vocabulary learning strategies because you can manipulate it by assigning different strategies (e.g., flashcards, context-based learning, or mnemonic devices) to different groups of participants. The dependent variable would be vocabulary retention because you are interested in observing how it is influenced by the different types of vocabulary learning strategies.

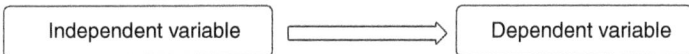

Figure 6.5 Dependent and independent variables

The independent variable refers to the variable that is manipulated or selected to examine its effect on another variable. **The dependent variable** is the one that is affected as a result of changes in the independent variable.

Manipulation of the Independent Variable

In an experimental study, manipulation means changing the value of a particular variable and measuring its effect on another variable while holding the other variables constant. Any experimental study has at least two types of variable: an independent variable and a dependent variable. As noted before, an independent variable is the one that the researcher systematically manipulates to determine its effect.

There are three techniques through which you can manipulate an independent variable: presence or absence technique, amount technique, and type technique (Johnson & Christensen, 2014).

The Presence or Absence Technique In the presence or absence technique, the independent variable is manipulated by presenting a treatment to one group, known as the experimental group, and not presenting the treatment to another group, known as the control group. By comparing the results of the two groups, researchers can determine the effect of the independent variable on the dependent variable.

EXAMPLE 6.2

Suppose you want to examine whether a writing tutorial would improve learners' writing skills. In this study, the independent variable is the writing tutorial (the intervention being tested), and the dependent variable is the writing skills of the learners. You can manipulate the independent variable by having one group that receives the tutorial and another group that does not (Figure 6.6). By comparing the writing skills of the two groups, you can determine if the tutorial has an effect on the participants' writing skills.

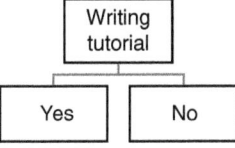

Figure 6.6 Example of the presence or absence technique

The Amount Technique In amount technique, the independent variable can be varied by changing the quantity or degree of the variable, such as increasing or decreasing the amount of a certain variable or changing its intensity. This enables you to determine whether there is any relationship between the degree of the independent variable and the dependent variable and to understand how changes in the degree affect the dependent variable.

EXAMPLE 6.3

Suppose you want to determine the effect of the amount of exposure to reading on L2 learners' reading comprehension skills. In this example, the independent variable is the "amount of exposure to reading," and the dependent variable is "L2 learners' reading comprehension skills." You can manipulate the independent variable by creating different groups of learners and providing them with varying levels of exposure to reading materials (Figure 6.7). For example, one group could be given a high amount of exposure to reading, another group could be given a medium amount of exposure, and a third group could be given a low amount of exposure. By measuring the reading comprehension skills of each group, you can determine if there is a relationship between the amount of exposure to reading and reading comprehension skills in L2 learners.

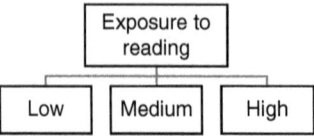

Figure 6.7 Example of the amount technique

The Type Technique A third technique through which the independent variable can be manipulated is by varying the type of condition or treatment the participants receive. Varying the type of the independent variable is a technique that is widely used in experimental applied linguistics research to manipulate the independent variable and observe its effect on the dependent variable.

EXAMPLE 6.4

Suppose you are interested in examining the effect of different types of corrective feedback on L2 learners' grammatical accuracy. You can manipulate the independent variable by varying its type. Suppose you are interested in examining the effect of three types of corrective feedback: direct feedback, indirect feedback, and metalinguistic feedback (Figure 6.8). You can manipulate the independent variable by providing direct feedback to one group, indirect feedback to another group, and metalinguistic feedback to a third group. By comparing the grammatical accuracy of the three groups, you can examine the effect of the independent variable on the dependent variable and determine which type of feedback is most effective.

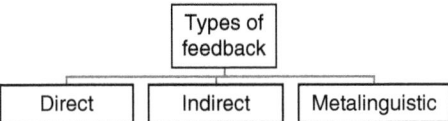

Figure 6.8 Example of the type technique

In a study, you can also use a combination of techniques to examine the effects of a particular treatment. For example, you may compare a control group (participants who do not receive the treatment) with treatment groups that receive different types of treatments (e.g., synchronous online instruction, face-to-face instruction, and blended instruction). Here you have used both the "presence and absence" technique (control and treatment groups) and the "type" technique (different types of instruction).

Moderator Variables

A moderator variable, also known as an interaction or moderating variable, is a variable that affects the relationship between an independent and a dependent variable (see Figure 6.9). In other words, it influences the strength or direction of the relationship between the two variables. Unlike independent and dependent variables, which are directly involved in studying the cause-and-effect relationship, a moderator variable comes into play when examining the conditions under which the relationship between the independent and dependent variables changes. Another way of conceptualizing a moderator variable is by seeing it as a secondary independent variable that may be considered to mediate the effect of the independent variable.

By considering moderator variables, researchers can gain a better understanding of the effect of one variable on another or identify the conditions or factors that may influence that relationship.

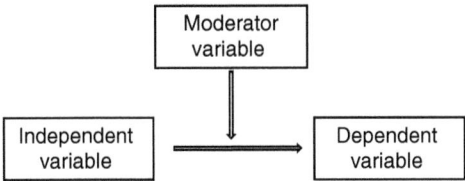

Figure 6.9 The role of the moderator variable

EXAMPLE 6.5

Let's consider an example study that examines the relationship between listening comprehension strategies (the independent variable) and listening comprehension performance (the dependent variable). In this case, the level of cognitive load can influence the strength of the relationship. If the level of cognitive load is low, the relationship between listening comprehension strategies and listening comprehension performance might be stronger, indicating that learners with a lower cognitive load are more positively affected by different listening comprehension strategies. On the other hand, if the level of cognitive load is high, the relationship between listening comprehension strategies and listening comprehension performance might be weaker, suggesting that learners with a higher cognitive load are less affected by the strategies.

A moderator variable, also known as an interaction or moderating variable, is a variable that affects the relationship between an independent and a dependent variable.

As noted earlier, the function that a variable serves in a study depends on the research question and the study design. Therefore, a variable that is an independent or a moderator variable in one study could be a dependent variable in another study. For example, type of instruction would be an independent variable in a study that examines the effect of instruction on L2 production. However, it can be a dependent variable in a study that investigates how teachers' experience influences the choice of instruction. There can be one or more than one dependent and independent variables in a study.

Control Variables

A control variable is a variable that is not in itself of interest to the researcher, in that they do not want to examine whether it affects a dependent variable or whether it is affected by a variable; however, the researcher suspects that this variable might affect the research outcome. Therefore, the researcher would control the variable by keeping it constant across groups to neutralize its effect. The variable whose effect you control in a particular study is thus called a control variable.

EXAMPLE 6.6

Suppose past research suggest that learners' first-language background may influence the effect of instruction on L2 production. In order to exclude this effect, you may exert control on the variable by selecting all your participants from the same L1 background. For example, if the study is about the effect of instruction on learning English definite articles, you may decide to include learners in your study whose first language either has or does not have definite articles.

Intervening Variables

Intervening variables are hypothetical variables that are not studied or directly observed, but they may explain the relationship between the dependent and independent variables. In a sense they are like mediating variables that come between an independent variable and a dependent variable in a causal relationship. They are called intervening because they come between the dependent and independent variable and link the two. These variables are often theoretical constructs that the researcher uses to interpret and explain their findings.

EXAMPLE 6.7

Suppose you were conducting a study examining the effect of sociolinguistic training on cross-cultural communication skills, and you found a positive effect for explicit sociolinguistic training. At first glance, this effect might be perceived as causal. However, the reason why explicit sociolinguistic training yielded better results could be attributed to the mediating role of unobservable cognitive processes. For instance, it is possible that explicit training facilitated the process of "awareness of cultural norms" and enhanced participants' ability to recognize and adapt to cultural differences more effectively compared to implicit training (Figure 6.10). In other words, the effect of explicit sociolinguistic training on cross-cultural communication skills was mediated by the intervening variable of awareness of cultural norms. Awareness of cultural norms served as the mechanism through which the independent variable (training type) influenced the dependent variable (cross-cultural communication skills).

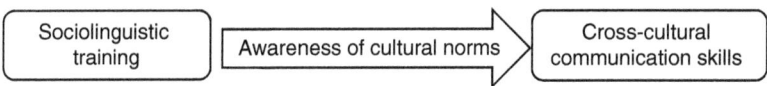

Figure 6.10 The role of the intervening variable

It might be helpful to make a distinction between intervening and moderator variables. Intervening variables explain the process of the relationship between independent and dependent variables, while moderator variables describe the conditions under which that relationship is strengthened, weakened, or changed (see Figure 6.11 for a schematic of variables in a hypothetical L2 instruction study).

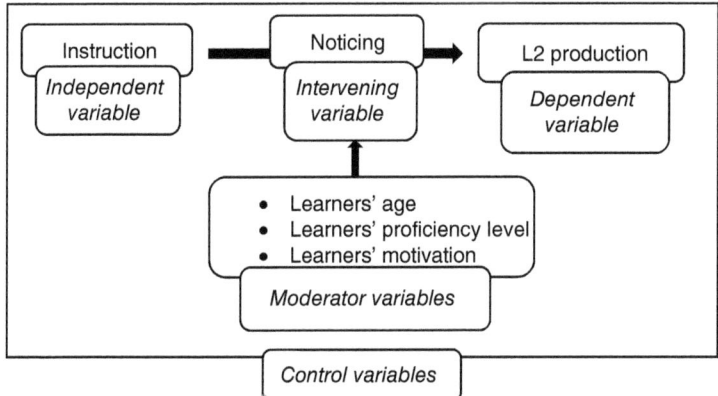

Figure 6.11 A schematic representation of independent, dependent, moderator, and control variables in a hypothetical study on the effect of instruction on L2 production

Extraneous and Confounding Variables

Extraneous variables are those that have not been controlled but may have an effect on the dependent variable. If extraneous variables are not controlled and they have an actual effect, they are called confounding variables. Therefore, extraneous variables and confounding variables are related. However, they differ in whether they systematically affect the dependent variable. An extraneous variable is any variable that is different from the independent variable and can possibly affect the dependent variable. Confounding variables are those that have confounded the results by influencing the study outcome. Confounding variables can make it difficult to determine whether the effect observed is due to the variable of interest or due to the confounding variable. Therefore, for extraneous variables not to have any confounding effect, they should be controlled as much as possible. Otherwise, they may affect the validity of the study, making it difficult to know whether the effect found in a study is because of the uncontrolled extraneous variable or because of the independent variable.

For example, if a study is examining the effect of explicit instruction on L2 learning, extraneous variables can be age, prior knowledge, motivation, and learners' learning strategies, as they can all affect the results. If these variables are not controlled for or accounted for in the study design, they can make it difficult to determine whether the effect of instruction is because of the instruction itself or because of these factors. For instance, if participants have different language proficiency levels, they may perform differently, not because of the role of instruction but because of differences in their language proficiency. If the study does not control for the level of language proficiency, it is difficult to conclude that the effect observed was solely due to instruction and not due to the differences in language proficiency level. Therefore, we must always try to identify and control for extraneous variables in our studies so that the findings can be shown to be due to the independent variable.

There are many variables that can potentially act as extraneous variables in applied linguistics and second language research. Some examples include, age, socioeconomic status, educational background, L1 background, language proficiency, cultural background, and all other affective, emotional, and cognitive individual learner differences, such as motivation, language learning styles and strategies, learner anxiety, and so on. Although there are many extraneous variables, they may not all be confounding variables in a given study. Here you should use your knowledge and also refer to theory and past research to consider what extraneous variables might become confounding variables and attempt to control them as much as possible.

When there is a confounding variable, it is difficult to determine what has caused the effect or the relationship between the variables. Thus, you as the researcher should attempt to control for as many potential confounders, particularly those for which there is a theoretical reason why they may have an effect.

There are several techniques that you can use to control for extraneous and potential confounding variables and their influence in research, which we will discuss below.

Ways to Control Extraneous and Confounding Variables

Randomization   One, and an important, solution to controlling extraneous and confounding variables, is random assignments. Random assignment refers to the process whereby participants are randomly assigned to different groups or conditions in an experiment. This helps to control for extraneous variables and makes it more likely that any differences between the groups are due to the independent variable being tested, rather than other factors. This is a critical aspect of experimental design in order to make causal inferences. Random assignment controls for unwanted variables because randomization would give an equal chance to all participants to be assigned to different groups (see also Chapter 8). In doing so, any preexisting characteristics of the participants are more likely to be distributed fairly evenly among groups, which helps selection bias and also controls for the potential confounders.

Randomization can be achieved through various methods and tools, including the following:

- **Random number generation**: This involves using a computer program to randomly generate numbers that could be assigned to each participant and then the participants selected based on those numbers. The Excel program, for example, can be used to generate such random numbers using the "= RAND ()" function. The random numbers could be used to select your sample.
- **Randomization tables**: Predetermined randomization tables with randomized numbers are often available in statistics and research methods books that focus on experimental designs.
- **Simple randomization**: This is a simple randomization method and includes techniques such as drawing names from a container. For example, if you want to select 50 participants from a list of 200, you could write all their names on a piece of paper, put them in a container, and then draw names until you have 50 participants.

Types of Randomizations   It would be helpful to distinguish between three types of randomizations (Figure 6.12):

- random selection
- random assignment
- random allocation.

Random selection: Random selection refers to the process of randomly selecting a sample from a larger population for the study. Random selection ensures that all members of a population have an equal chance of being selected to be included in the sample. This helps to minimize bias and makes the sample more representative of the population.

Random assignment: Random assignment refers to the process of randomly assigning participants to different groups in an experiment, such as a treatment group or a control group. Thus, the key difference between random selection and random assignment is that random selection is used to select a subset of a population for a study or analysis, while random assignment is used to make the groups being compared in an experiment similar, so that any differences observed between the groups can be attributed to the experimental manipulation. While random section allows for generalizability, random assignments allow for establishing cause-and-effect relationships. Random selection promotes representativeness of the sample and thus makes generalizability possible. Random assignment helps establish a cause-and-effect relationship by making it more likely that any differences observed between groups are due to the independent variable rather than to other differences between the groups. In other words, random assignment ensures that each individual has an equal chance of being assigned to any group, which helps to control for any preexisting differences between individuals.

Random allocation: Random allocation has to do with randomly allocating entire groups (rather than individuals) to conditions. For example, in a study involving two intact EFL classes, the two EFL classes can be randomly allocated to a control group and the experimental group. Random allocation might or might not involve random selection or assignment. Random allocation of groups to conditions is important as it helps to ensure that any observed differences between the experimental and control groups are not due to group selection bias.

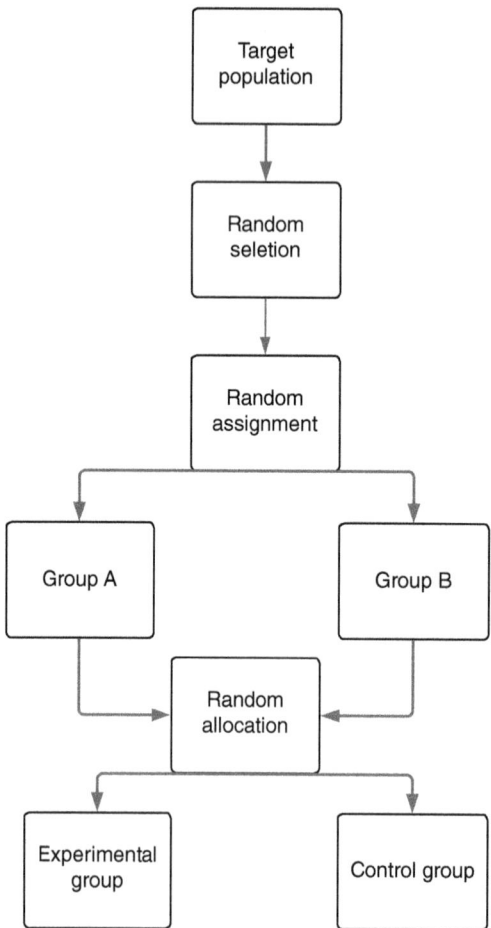

Figure 6.12 Types of randomizations

Random selection refers to the process of randomly selecting a sample from a larger population. **Random assignment** refers to the process of randomly assigning participants to different groups in an experiment, such as a treatment group or a control group. **Random allocation** has to do with randomly allocating groups to conditions.

Matching   Another way of controlling for extraneous and confounding variables is through the matching process or using a matched design. You can match participants on certain variables deemed to be important for the research to control for their potential confounding effect. Matching refers to the process whereby participants are assigned to the groups carefully based on characteristics that are considered relevant to the study. In other words, the individuals in the experimental group are matched with the individuals in the control group based on certain characteristics or factors that may affect the study outcome. To this end, the use of clear and specific inclusion and exclusion criteria can be helpful. You can then pair each participant in one of the groups with a participant from another group who has similar characteristics on the confounding variable of interest. This helps make it more likely that any observed differences in the outcome between the two groups are due to the treatments rather than preexisting differences.

EXAMPLE 6.8

Suppose you are interested in conducting a study to examine the effect of a bilingual education program on children's vocabulary development in their L2. You feel that children's age and their L1 proficiency are two important factors that should be controlled. Therefore, you decide to use a matching technique to control for these factors.

   In doing so, you form your experimental and control groups in ways that are matched on these two variables. To this end, you would give an L1 proficiency test to all participants before the study. You will then divide them into three groups: low, mid, and high L1 proficiency based on their scores. You would also assess their age and divide them into three age groups: younger, middle, and older children. You would then start to form two groups as follows: You would randomly select two children of the same age group who are classified as high L1 proficiency learners and put one of them in the experimental group and the other one in the control group. Then you would randomly select two children of the same age group who are classified as low L1 proficiency learners and put one of them in the experimental group and the other one in the control group. Similarly, you would randomly select two children of the same age group who are classified as mid L1 proficiency learners and put one of them in the experimental group and the other one in the control group.

You will use the same process to match children of different proficiency levels and age groups across the experimental and control groups until all the children are assigned. This balances each group in terms of L1 proficiency and age, allowing you to more accurately measure the effect of the bilingual education program on L2 vocabulary development.

Using Statistical Techniques   A third strategy would be to use a statistical technique, such as ANCOVA. For example, in a study on the effects of a new pronunciation strategy on student pronunciation test scores, you are aware that there are other factors that may influence the learners' performance, such as their overall language proficiency and motivation. You can control for these factors using a statistical method called ANCOVA. To do so, you collect data about the students' pronunciation and use this as the dependent variable. At the same time, you collect data on the learners' L2 proficiency and motivation for all participants and use these variables as covariates in the ANCOVA analysis. By including these two factors as covariates in the ANCOVA analysis, you are able to control for these variables and determine whether the new pronunciation strategy has a significant effect on learners' pronunciation test scores, irrespective of these other factors.

Making the Variable a Moderator Variable   Another way of controlling for a confounding variable is to make it a moderator variable. As noted earlier, a moderator variable is a secondary independent variable that is used in an experimental study to explain the relationship between a main independent variable and a dependent variable. It is a variable that is deemed to affect the relationship between the independent and the dependent variable. Therefore, you may decide to include it in the study to examine its possible effect.

For example, in a study on the relationship between corrective feedback and language learning, you may feel that learners' language proficiency would be an important variable that might affect the relationship between the feedback and learning. Therefore, you deliberately include the variable in the study to see whether it has any effect or whether the effect of the feedback would be the same irrespective of this variable. In such a study, if the moderator variable has a mediating effect, learners would benefit differently depending on the level of language proficiency. For example, you may find that those who are more proficient may benefit more from the feedback than those who are less proficient.

A moderator variable can be used to control for confounding variables in a study by allowing for the examination of how the relationship between the independent and the dependent variable may vary depending on the level of the moderator variable. This can help to determine whether the relationship between the variables is specific to the main independent variable or whether there is another variable that could potentially be influencing the results.

Often a variable would be selected as a moderator variable when there is a theoretical reason for its effect. It is selected because it is believed to have an impact on the relationship between the independent and the dependent variable.

Its selection may be based on prior research and literature in the field showing its possible impact. Since the effect of the moderator variable is going to be examined in the research, it is important to clearly define and operationalize it in the study.

Making the Variable a Control Variable Another way of controlling for the effect of a variable is to make it a control variable. A control variable is a variable that is held constant during an experiment and across the groups in the study in order to eliminate its effect on the dependent variable. Since these variables are kept constant, they are also called "constant variables." The purpose of using control variables is thus to prevent those factors from influencing the results, so that any changes observed in the dependent variable can be attributed to the independent variable not to those variables. In any educational study, including those in applied linguistics, there might be many factors that can influence the relationship between the independent and the dependent variable, and you may decide to control for many of them by keeping them constant during the study.

EXAMPLE 6.9

For example, in a study on the effect of a new pronunciation strategy on English learners' pronunciation ability, you might decide that extraneous variables such as learners' L2 proficiency and L1 background may negatively affect the results and hence that they should be controlled. These variables would be controlled by having students in both the experimental group and the control group from the same level of language proficiency and the same L1 background. You might also feel that there may be other factors that should be controlled, such as learners' educational and cultural background and the amount of time they have spent in an English-speaking environment.

It is important to note that although keeping variables constant across study groups can be a useful controlling technique, there are a number of limitations with this strategy. One is that introducing many control variables in a study can limit its generalizability. Holding certain variables constant can make it difficult to generalize the findings to a larger population or to other settings that involve those variables. Keeping many variables constant can also restrict the natural variability existing within and across groups. After all, when doing research, it is essential to weigh the potential benefits of any decisions made against the potential drawbacks of those decisions. This includes decisions relating to what variables to control as well as other design, implementation, and analysis decisions. It is also important to consider their ethical implications as they might have significant implications for or impact on the broader goals for which the study is being conducted.

Counterbalancing Counterbalancing in research refers to the process whereby the order of the presentation of different experimental conditions is systematically varied, in order to control for any order or carryover effects that the sequence of the treatment may have on the results. This can range from the order in which different treatment tasks are used, to the order in which different groups of participants are tested, to the order in which different test items are presented in a test. All these might have an effect on the relationship between the independent and the dependent variable and can hence affect the internal validity of the study. Therefore, they should be controlled as the order in which information is presented in a study can affect how participants use or understand it. One way of controlling them is through counterbalancing. If the orders are not counterbalanced, it is difficult to determine that any observed effects are actually due to the manipulation of the independent variable or are influenced by the order or sequence in which the conditions were presented in a study.

Counterbalancing refers to the process whereby the order of the presentation of different experimental conditions is systematically varied, in order to control for any order or carryover effects that the sequence of the treatment may have on the results.

EXAMPLE 6.10

Suppose you aim to examine the effects of media exposure on attitudes toward regional dialects. The study includes a sample of participants from different regions, who will be divided into two groups: an experimental group that is exposed to media content featuring regional dialects in a positive light, and a control group that is exposed to neutral media content. The study will measure the participants' attitudes toward regional dialects before and after the intervention.

Attitudes will be measured using a sociolinguistic attitude questionnaire and a matched-guise test. In this study, the order in which the participants receive the tests might influence their responses. Therefore, you may decide to counterbalance the order of the tests so that half of the participants in the experimental group will receive the questionnaire first and the matched-guise test second, and the other half, the reverse. The order in which the tests are presented to the control group would also be counterbalanced so that half of the participants would receive the questionnaire first and the matched-guise test second, and the other half would receive them in the reverse order.

This counterbalancing helps to control for any test-order effects that might influence the results of the study.

Randomization can also be used in counterbalancing so that the order of events is varied and does not introduce bias into the results. For example, in the above study, the order in which the tests are administered to each participant could be randomized to control for any order effects. This can help determine that any differences in outcomes are not due to the researcher's bias regarding who should get what test.

Depending on Their Function in Correlational Studies
Criterion versus Predictor Variables

Criterion and predictor variables are terms commonly used in correlational studies, particularly in regression analysis. A criterion variable is a kind of dependent variable that the researcher is interested in explaining or predicting. It is the outcome or the variable of interest in a study. Predictor variables are independent variables or explanatory variables, and are the variables that are hypothesized to influence the criterion variable. They are the factors being manipulated, observed, or measured to understand their relationship with the criterion variable. The researcher typically wants to understand how the criterion variable is predicted by predictor variables. For example, in a study on speaking ability, the criterion variable could be the participants' scores on an interview task, and the factors such as language proficiency and vocabulary knowledge could be the predictor variables. In such contexts, the research question can be framed in two ways: "To what extent do language proficiency and vocabulary knowledge (the predictor variables) predict or explain variance in learners' speaking ability (the criterion variable)?" or "To what extent do language proficiency and vocabulary knowledge contribute to learners' speaking ability?"

The relationship between the predictor variables and the criterion variable is typically explored using regression analysis. Regression analysis allows researchers to analyze the impact of the predictor variables on the criterion variable, assessing the strength and direction of the relationship, and making predictions or explaining variations in the criterion variable based on the values of the predictor variables (see Chapter 20).

EXAMPLE 6.11

In a study on L2 reading, Nassaji and Geva (1999) examined the contribution of phonological and orthographic processing knowledge to L2 reading skills among advanced learners of English whose L1 was Farsi. The study involved three criterion (dependent) variables:

- reading comprehension
- silent reading passage rate
- single word recognition

and six predictor (independent) variables:

- phonological processing skill, operationalized as scores on a pseudoword matching task
- orthographic processing skill, operationalized as scores on an orthographic processing task

- syntactic processing skill, operationalized as scores on a syntactic judgment task
- semantic processing skills, operationalized as scores on a sentence–semantic task and a lexical–semantic (vocabulary) task
- working memory, operationalized as recall scores on memory tasks (a simple digit-span task)
- speed of lexical access, operationalized as scores on a Rapid Automatization Naming Test (RAN).

Using hierarchical multiple regression, the study found that among the predictor variables, efficiency in phonological and orthographic processing contributed significantly to the learners' reading ability and that this contribution was over and above the contribution of syntactic and semantic knowledge.

POINTS TO PONDER

What are the different ways of measuring variables in applied linguistics research? What are the advantages and disadvantages of each method?

Levels and Measurements of Variables

Variable Levels

Since variables in research can have varying characteristics, they can have more than one level. Some variables may possess only a limited number of levels, while others may have a broader range. For instance, the variable "learning style," which is a categorical variable, can have two levels: visual and auditory. On the other hand, variables such as "nationality" can potentially have a multitude of levels, corresponding to the different national backgrounds of individuals participating in a study.

To provide another example, the variable, "language ability," can be operationalized using three distinct levels: low, medium, and high. This categorization captures the varying degrees of proficiency individuals may possess in a particular language. By employing these three levels, you can effectively differentiate between individuals who have a limited understanding or command of the language (low level), those with moderate proficiency (medium level), and those who exhibit advanced skills (high level).

The number of levels of a variable in a study is determined by the nature and scope of the phenomenon being studied. Therefore, you should carefully consider the purpose of your investigation and the specific characteristics you intend to capture when determining the appropriate number of levels for each variable.

Measurement of Variables

An important step in conducting any study, particularly a quantitative study, is measuring the study variables. Measurement is a key component of quantitative research and in essence is a process that involves converting observations into numbers. In qualitative research, variables are often represented descriptively. That is, the data is nonnumerical and is often presented using words, texts, images, and so on. In quantitative research, we first identify the variable we would like to examine, then operationally define it – which is defining a variable in a way that shows how to measure it – and finally assign a number to it.

Depending on the research, variables can be operationalized differently. For example, reading comprehension can be operationally defined as learners' scores on a multiple-choice test, in which case the number assigned would be the students' test scores. Or it could be defined in terms of the number of idea units in a summary task, in which case the number assigned would be the number of idea units recalled. Measuring variables in this way helps you to record the data in a way that is consistent and unambiguous.

Depending on the type of variable, there are different measurement scales that can be used to measure variables. In the following section, we will discuss four types of scales that have been used widely in research, including applied linguistics research. These are a nominal scale, an ordinal scale, an interval scale and a ratio scale.

A Nominal Scale

One of the basic types of measurement is the nominal scale. It is a scale used to measure variables by grouping the data into categories that has no rank order. It is called nominal because in this scale a name or a label is assigned to categories. The categories are both exhaustive and mutually exclusive. A category is exhaustive when it includes all the possible cases with that characteristic in the study. It is mutually exclusive when there is no overlap between categories, and each participant is assigned to only one category. As noted before, the number of categories in a nominal scale is called the variable level. Nominal variables can have two or more than two levels. For example, a nominal variable such as "type of language instruction" could have two levels in a study: classroom instruction and online instruction. A nominal variable such as "type of corrective feedback" could have three levels: "written feedback," "oral feedback," and "peer feedback."

After putting the data into categories, numbers can also be assigned to the categories. For example, we may assign "1" to classroom instruction and "2" to online instruction, but we can also assign "1" to online instruction and "2" to classroom instruction. The number assigned is simply a code and does not have any numerical value. For the same reason, the numbers cannot be subjected to any mathematical operations such as addition, division, or multiplication.

A nominal scale is a scale used to measure variables by grouping the data into categories that have no rank order.

Another example of a nominal variable is nationality. Learners can be classified into different categories based on their specific nationality. This variable can have two or more levels depending on the nationality of the participants in the study. We may decide to include participants from the following nationalities: Japanese, Korean, Arabic, Italian. In such a study, nationality has four levels:

- Japanese
- Korean
- Arabic
- Italian

Table 6.2 shows more examples of variables measured using a nominal scale.

Table 6.2 Examples of qualitative (categorical) variables measured on a nominal scale

Variable	Categories	Numerical code
Language proficiency	Low	Low = 1
	High	High = 2
Feedback types	Recasts	Recasts = 1
	Prompts	Prompts = 2
	Metalinguistics feedback	Metalinguistic feedback = 3
Instruction type	Explicit	Explicit = 1
	Implicit	Implicit = 2
Speaker type	Native	Native = 1
	Nonnative	Nonnative = 2
Education level	Elementary	Elementary = 1
	Secondary	Secondary = 2
	University	University = 3

As noted above, the numbers assigned to the different levels of a nominal variable have no numerical value. However, we can always count the number of people who fall into one category. For example, we can count the number of students who received classroom instruction versus those who received online instruction in a study. This would produce frequency data that can be useful in the analysis of the data when we want to know how many of people belong to a specific category. Frequency and relative frequency distributions are useful when we want to compare the number of entities in each category of a nominal variable or in different nominal variables (see Chapter 18).

An Ordinal Scale

An ordinal scale is like a nominal scale in that it groups participants, responses, or objects into categories. However, it also ranks them. The ranking may consist of three or four categories on a continuum. The scale thus has an order, and the number assigned indicates the order of the categories within the variable. For example, ranking students' performance on an achievement test into poor, fair, good, and excellent is an example of an ordinal scale. We may then assign numeric values to these categories, such as 1 = poor, 2 = fair, 3 = good, 4 = excellent. Because they are rank-ordered, ordinal scales have numerical values. Therefore, the numbers assigned in this example have numerical values in that we expect 3 to be greater than 2 and 1. However, although the numbers have numerical values, the difference between them is not the same. For example, the difference or the distance between 1 and 2, and the difference between 3 and 4 is not the same in an ordinal scale.

An ordinal scale is like a nominal scale in that it groups participants, responses, or objects into categories. However, it also ranks them.

As another example, suppose you ask students to give judgments about the helpfulness of their teacher's feedback as unhelpful, helpful, and very helpful. This is also an ordinal scale because the students have ranked the degree of helpfulness from low to high.

In research, a quantitative variable can be converted into a categorical one and measured via a nominal or an ordinal scale. For example, language proficiency can be initially represented quantitatively as test scores, and it can then be converted into a categorical or ordinal variable by grouping learners into low, mid, and high, based on those test scores. Unlike a nominal scale, subcategories in an ordinal scale are related to one another, and one is greater or smaller than the other.

In essence, an ordinal scale has three essential characteristics:

1. One category is greater or smaller than the other.
2. The number simply indicates the order and does not reflect the degree or intensity of the category. For example, if we assign "1" to "beginner," "2" to "intermediate," and "3" to "advanced" in a study, the numbers show the rank order, but they do not indicate how much more advanced "3" (advanced) is compared to "2" (intermediate) or how much greater the difference is between each level.
3. There is no equal distance or interval in an ordinal scale. In other words, we should not expect that the same difference in the degree of helpfulness that exists between 1 and 2 also exists between 2 and 3. This has important implications for analyzing data using ordinal scales.

A useful tool that has been widely used in research to measure variables on the ordinal scale is the Likert scale. A Likert scale is a rating scale used to collect data about participants' opinions, attitudes, or perspectives. It is named after its developer, an American psychologist called Rensis Likert, who used this scale to collect data about participants' attitudes toward social issues. Since then, these measurement tools have been frequently used in research including applied linguistics and L2 research when researchers have been interested in examining participants' views, beliefs, and perspectives about a learning or teaching behavior or other activities. For example, in a study on the role of teacher's comments on students' essays, a Likert scale can be used to examine the degree to which students agree or disagree with the usefulness of a particular feedback type. To that end, a questionnaire item (either a statement or a question) could be created followed by a five-point Likert scale like the one in Example 6.12. The respondents would then rate their level of agreement with the statement or provide their response to the question, using the scale provided.

EXAMPLE 6.12

How helpful is the feedback provided by the teacher?

5. Extremely helpful
4. Very helpful
3. Somewhat helpful
2. Not so helpful
1. Not at all helpful

All the categories in a Likert scale can be labeled explicitly using descriptive words or only the two ends of the scale could be explicitly labeled. The scale can have either an even or an odd number of points. A scale with an odd number of points often provides a middle or neutral response with no direction. However, a scale with an even number of points has direction. Whether to use an odd or even number of points depends on the nature of the data. However, a neutral category on the scale can lead to biased data if participants simply choose the neutral item because they do not want to provide a response that is directive.

As mentioned before, since the Likert scale is ordinal in nature, the distance between the options is not equal. For example, if you have used options such as "not useful," "quite useful," and "very useful," the difference between the magnitude of usefulness is not the same between "not useful" and "quite useful," or between "quite useful" and "very useful."

As just noted, one issue that may arise when developing Likert scale items is the number of categories or options in a Likert scale. This issue depends on the nature of the research and the type of question the participants are asked. However, research seems to suggest that if an item has fewer than five categories, its reliability might be negatively affected (McKelvie, 1978).

From a data analysis perspective, the more categories a Likert scale has, the closer it becomes to an interval scale (see below). Therefore, sometimes Likert scale data can be treated as interval data in applied linguistics research. However, we can do so only when the number of options or categories within the scale is great enough.

In this respect, it would be problematic to treat scales involving four or five categories as an interval scale, but if there are more categories, we may be able to treat them as interval data.

For example, it would not be advisable to treat "usefulness" with the following options as an interval variable: Very useful, Somewhat useful, Not so useful, Not at all useful. However, we can treat the following seven-point agreement scale as an interval scale: 1 = Strongly disagree, 2 = Disagree, 3 = Somewhat disagree, 4 = Neither agree nor disagree, 5 = Somewhat agree, 6 = Agree, 7 = Strongly agree.

Even if we treat an ordinal scale as an interval scale, it is not still a true interval scale, and the finding simply shows general tendencies regarding the issue measured. For that reason, we should be careful when using statistical analysis that requires interval scales (such as parametric tests); in such cases, we should use statistical analysis that does not require interval data, such as nonparametric tests. If you are going to use the Likert scale data with parametric tests, you should make sure that the data meet the assumptions of parametric tests, such as normality of distribution and equality of intervals (see Chapters 20 and 21).

Issues to Consider When Developing Likert Scale Items When developing Likert scale items, you need to be mindful of the following. Since L2 research mostly involves participants who are L2 learners, you should make sure that learners understand the language of the items. Otherwise, the validity of the responses will be negatively affected. In cases where the participants are from one language background and it is not easy to develop items that are easy for them to understand, the items could be presented in the L1.

Another issue to consider is the cultural background of the learners. As Turner (1993) pointed out, it is possible that learners from different cultures might approach the task differently. For example, in some cultures, participants might tend to be more open to expressing their opinions or perspective than others. In such cases it is always good to pilot the scale or the questionnaire with similar learners and use that information to develop the items for the main study.

An Interval Scale

An interval scale is frequently used in applied linguistics and L2 research. It is a scale that has the following characteristics. There is order from low to high. In that sense, an interval scale is like an ordinal scale. However, the distance between the numbers on the scale is assumed to be equal. The numbers on interval scales also have arithmetic value, which can be subjected to mathematical operations such as addition, subtraction, or division. In addition, there is no absolute zero on the scale, and the presence of the zero is arbitrary.

For example, test scores are interval scale measurements. If a student receives 60 on a test and another student receives 61, the difference between 60 and 61 is the same as the difference between 70 and 71. However, if a student gets 0 on the test, it does not mean that the student has zero knowledge of what was measured.

As noted before, we can sometimes convert an interval scale into an ordinal one. For example, the data from a language proficiency test measured via an interval scale (represented by scores) can be grouped into low, mid, and high proficiency learners, which is an ordinal scale. When doing research, we should always use the type of scale that is more appropriate to our research and address the research question in the best way possible.

An interval scale is a scale with equal distances between values, allowing for arithmetic operations such as addition and subtraction.

As stated earlier, sometimes the Likert scale data may be treated as interval data. In doing so we should make sure that the response choices on the scale have nearly equal distance. Also, if we want to use parametric tests, such as *t*-tests, ANOVA, or correlations with such scales, we should either make sure that the data meet the assumption of these tests, or we should use nonparametric tests (see Chapters 20 and 21).

Among the nominal, ordinal, and interval scales, the latter provides the most precise measurement. Therefore, there are a variety of statistical procedures available for analyzing variables that are measured using this scale.

A Ratio Scale

A ratio scale is an interval scale that has an absolute zero. An absolute zero means there is a complete absence of the variable that is measured. For example, a scale that measures length is a ratio scale because it has a true zero, meaning that the zero on the scale indicates the absence of length. For instance, 0 meters means there is no physical length present. Other examples of ratio scales are height, weight and income. Income is a ratio scale because this variable has an absolute zero point in that we can have someone with zero income. While it is theoretically possible for height to be zero, in practical terms, people, for example, always have some measurable height. Nevertheless, height is still a ratio scale because it includes a true zero point.

The distance between points is equal in a ratio scale. For example, someone who earns $11 per hour earns $1 more than someone who earns $10, and someone who earn $21 earns $1 dollar more than someone who earns $20. In both cases the difference is equal and is $1.

A ratio scale is an interval scale that has an absolute zero. An absolute zero means there is a complete absence of the variable that is measured.

Ratio variables can be discrete or continuous. They are discrete when they are expressed in whole numbers, and they are continuous when they can have an infinite number of values. The number of students in a class is an example of a discrete ratio scale because we can have no students in the class (absolute zero), the difference between points is equal (two students are twice as many as one student), and we can take on only whole numbers (we cannot have 1.5 students). Income measured in dollars is an example of a continuous ratio scale because we can have someone with no income, someone who earns $10, and we can have someone earning $10.5 dollars.

Ratio scales are rarely used in applied linguistics and L2 research because there are few cases where the researcher uses a scale that has an absolute zero (see Table 6.3 for a summary of different measurement scales).

Table 6.3 A summary of different measurement scales

Type of scale	Definition	Example
Nominal	A scale that groups data (participants, responses, events, or objects) into categories that are discrete and have no rank order	Nationality
Ordinal	A scale that groups data (participants, responses, events, objects) into categories that are rank ordered in terms of the degree of the attribute in the category	Language proficiency operationalized as low, medium, and high
Interval	A scale that has the characteristics of an ordinal scale but also assumes an equal distance between the points on the scale	Test scores
Ratio	An interval scale with an absolute zero	Income

The Role of Measurement Scales in Research

Now that we have learned about the different variables and measurement scales, the question may arise as to what role they play in research. Knowing the type of variables and measurement is important for several reasons. One reason is that different types of variables and scales provide different types of information. For example, when a variable is measured using a nominal scale, the scale provides information about the categories in the variable, which does not involve ranking. However, when the variable is measured using an ordinal scale, the scale provides information about the ranking of the category. When a variable is measured using an interval scale, it provides information about the ranking and also tells us that the distance between the categories is equal. It also tells us that the scale has arithmetic properties and can be subjected to addition, subtraction, and division.

In addition to the above information, knowing the type of variable and scale of measurement also helps us determine what kind of statistical analysis to use. We will discuss these issues in more detail in Chapters 20 and 21. For now, it may suffice to say that if, for example, we have nominal data, we are unable to calculate the mean (average) of the variable; however, if we have interval data, we can do so. Table 6.4 presents examples of the relationship between scales of measurement for the dependent and independent variables and the kind of statistical analysis to use.

Table 6.4 Examples of the relationship between scales of measurement and the kind of statistical analysis to use

Independent variable	Dependent variable	Analysis	Example
Type of discourse marker (Nominal: 2 levels: hedging vs. boosting)	Perceived credibility of the speaker (Interval: rating score)	Independent samples t-test	A study examines the effect of different types of discourse markers on the perceived credibility of a speaker. Participants listen to recorded speeches and rate the credibility based on the type of discourse marker used.
Type of language policy (nominal: 3 levels: immersion, bilingual, heritage language)	Students' proficiency in their heritage language (interval: test scores)	ANOVA	A study examines how three different language policies affect students' proficiency in their heritage language, measured by test scores.
Time spent studying (interval: hours per week)	Academic performance (interval: GPA or test scores)	Pearson correlation	A study explores the relationship between time spent studying and academic performance. Both variables are interval, with time measured in hours per week and academic performance measured by GPA or test scores.
Regional background (nominal: 2 levels: urban vs. rural)	Intonation pattern used (nominal: 2 levels: rising and falling)	Chi-square	A study examines whether speakers' regional background (urban vs. rural) influences their use of intonation patterns.
Age (interval), socioeconomic status (ordinal: measured on a scale from 1 to 5), education (interval: measured in years of formal education)	Language variation (interval: frequency of specific linguistic features)	Multiple regression	A study investigates the relationship between social factors (age, socioeconomic status, education) and language variation in a community. Multiple regression analysis predicts language variation based on these social factors.

Conclusion

Variables play a crucial role in research as they allow researchers to measure the different aspects of an issue that they are interested in studying. Therefore, understanding them and also the different ways of measuring them are critical for conducting valid and reliable research. By selecting the appropriate type of variable and measurement method, you can accurately measure the construct of interest and draw valid conclusions based on the findings. This chapter has covered the basics of defining constructs and variables, discussing different types of variables such as dependent, independent, and moderator variables. We have also explored the different types of measurement scales, including nominal, ordinal, interval, and ratio, and how they are used in research. Each type of measurement scale has its own characteristics and has implications for research design, data analysis, and interpretation of results. Understanding these issues and the differences in variables are important for selecting appropriate statistical tests for data analysis and drawing accurate conclusions from the data analysis.

DISCUSSION AND ACTIVITY QUESTIONS

Discussion Questions

1. Why is it important to clearly define constructs and variables in research? What are the potential consequences of not defining constructs and variables in the proper way?
2. What is the meaning of operationalization? Why is it important in research? Can you provide an example of how to operationalize a construct or a variable in applied linguistics research?
3. Why is it important to distinguish between different variable types? Could you identify several variable types along with their distinctive characteristics?

Activity Questions

1. In groups of two or three, choose a different type of variable (nominal, ordinal, interval, etc.). Brainstorm examples and explain why the examples fit that type of variable. Share your ideas with the rest of the class and discuss key takeaways from the process.
2. Work individually or in pairs with a list of constructs provided by the teacher to operationalize each construct by identifying appropriate variables and measurement methods. Share your ideas with the rest of the class and discuss any discrepancies or challenges that arose in the process.
3. Select a research topic of your choice. Select appropriate measurement scales and explain why you have chosen those measures. Share your research designs with the rest of the class and discuss any feedback or suggestions for improvement.
4. Choose and read a research article that uses a specific type of variable and measurement scale. Critically evaluate the article's use of the variable and measurement tools and explain any potential strengths or weaknesses. Share your findings with the rest of the class and invite feedback to further refine your analysis.
5. Identify a research question in applied linguistics that you are interested in. Then, working individually or in pairs, brainstorm the possible independent and dependent variables that could be used to answer your research question. After identifying your variables, discuss with your partner how you would go about measuring and manipulating the variables in your study.

7

Review of the Literature and the Development of Research Questions

CHAPTER OBJECTIVES

After completing this chapter, you should be able to

- Define the concept of the literature review and explain its aim and importance in the research process.
- Understand the steps involved in conducting an effective literature review.
- Distinguish between various types of literature review, identifying their characteristics and purposes.
- Identify the key features that define a high-quality literature review.
- Explore the different sources of research questions.
- Develop clear, concise, and effective research questions.
- Recognize the differences between research questions for qualitative and quantitative research.
- Understand the criteria for assessing good research questions.

Introduction

One of the most important and challenging processes in conducting research is the review of the relevant literature. In the context of research, "the literature" refers to the body of knowledge currently available on the topic. This can be found in journal articles, books, review articles, and any other sources that report the past and current state of knowledge on the topic of your research. Irrespective of the type of research, all research involves a literature review as an important step in the research process. Once we decide on our general topic, it is essential know what others have already done on that topic. The best way to do so is to examine the literature relating to it. This means finding the resources relevant to your research and reading and evaluating them. Without doing an effective literature review, it is not possible to conduct an effective study. However, doing and writing an effective literature review is not an easy task. Given the importance of literature reviews, "it may be surprising that so many of them are faulty" (Randolph, 2009, p. 1).

The purpose of this chapter is to provide a detailed overview of the review of literature and the development of research questions. It will begin by defining the concept of the literature review and discussing its importance in the research process. The chapter will then provide guidance on how to conduct a thorough review of the literature, including the identification of relevant sources, the evaluation of the quality of studies, and the synthesis of the findings. The chapter will also discuss the process of developing research questions, including their importance and characteristics, along with examples of good research questions.

POINTS TO PONDER

What is a literature review? Why is doing a literature review important for a research study? What are the key benefits of conducting a literature review?

What Is a Literature Review, and Why Does It Need to Be Done?

A literature review refers to a thorough and critical examination of the existing theory and research on a particular topic. The process typically involves identifying the relevant sources and databases, including books, book chapters, and journal articles; selecting and screening them based on predetermined criteria; critically appraising the quality of the selected studies; and synthesizing their findings into a cohesive narrative.

As briefly discussed in Chapter 4, there are a number of reasons why we conduct a literature review. The first is to be familiar with the existing body of knowledge related to the issue we want to investigate.

The second reason is to identify gaps and limitations in the existing knowledge. Conducting a literature review will help us to identify the deficiency of past research, showing us what needs to be done and why it needs to be done. In other words, it helps develop a rationale or justification for our research.

A literature review can also inform the methodology and design of our research. It helps identify methods for data collection, analysis, and interpretation.

Another important reason is that it allows us to develop research questions that are built upon previous research. When we review the literature and identify gaps in knowledge on that topic, we can develop research questions and hypotheses that are grounded in existing knowledge, which can therefore contribute to the advancement of the field.

Doing a literature review can also help us to identify and select appropriate theoretical frameworks for our study. When we examine past research, we can become familiar with the theoretical frameworks that have been used successfully before, and can determine their relevance to our research.

Finally, doing a literature review can make us familiar with how to write our own. When we read research articles or reports of past research, we can see how others have summarized, synthesized, and evaluated research relevant to their topic. In other words, it helps us enhance our skill in writing a literature review.

A literature review refers to a thorough and critical examination of the existing theory and research on a particular topic.

Types of Literature

In order to be able to produce an effective literature review, it is important to know the different types of literature review. There are different taxonomies or classifications of literature reviews. One classification is based on the sources used. In this respect, we can distinguish between two general types: empirical and theoretical (Figure 7.1).

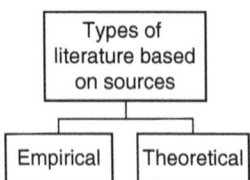

Figure 7.1 Types of literature based on sources used

Empirical Literature

Empirical literature consists of reports of previous empirical studies conducted in a given area. This could be reports that present the results of individual studies, as well as review articles that have reviewed groups of studies. Empirical literature helps us to know not only what has already been done on the topic, but also what kind of findings have been achieved, what discrepancies exist in the research findings, if any, and what issues need further research. It also shows what research methods have been used to investigate the issue, and even how the past research has analyzed, reported, and interpreted data. It also provides information about how and whether your study adds to the existing literature.

The best source for empirical literature is research that has been published in academic journals, scholarly books, and monographs. Although sources such as the internet can also sometimes provide useful information, many webpages may not be reliable sources, and it is advisable not to use them unless their credibility, such as the expertise of the author or the reliability of the website, is confirmed. Also, many such sources do not have a known author, and therefore, it would be difficult to cite them. Studies published in academic journals, however, have gone through a peer review process whereby the article has been examined by qualified researchers before it is published. This then means that the study has a good degree of rigor, meets a high standard of quality, and hence can be considered a reliable source.

It is also good practice to examine studies that are recent, and there are two reasons for that. First, recent studies make reference to older studies. Therefore, by consulting recent studies you also become familiar with older studies. A second reason is that you come to know what has been done recently on the topic and what still needs to be done.

Empirical literature consists of reports of previous empirical studies conducted in a given area.

Theoretical Literature

Theoretical literature refers to scholarly work that provides the foundational concepts, theories, models, and frameworks within a particular field of study. It involves the exploration and discussion of existing theoretical models, perspectives, and principles that explain a phenomenon or guide research in that field. Theoretical literature serves to provide a foundation for understanding a topic, identifying gaps in knowledge, and framing research questions.

Theoretical literature can be found in a variety of academic sources. It is often present in studies that report research findings, where researchers discuss and apply theoretical frameworks to interpret their data, explain their results, or support their hypotheses. These studies may involve theoretical models that guide the research or offer new perspectives on existing theories. It can also be found in other scholarly works, such as books, which aim to explore and analyze specific theoretical perspectives. These books often provide a review of key theories, concepts, and debates within a field, and may propose new theoretical models or frameworks. Theoretical literature may also appear in other sources, including review articles, theoretical papers, and conference proceedings, which focus on the development, refinement, or critique of theories.

Examining the theoretical literature can contribute to a study in many ways. Theories provide a conceptual framework that can help relate the different facets of a study. A theory can help focus the study on a particular aspect of the phenomenon that needs more understanding. It will thus help explain the need for the study. A theory also helps narrow down the focus of a study, as there are many issues that can be examined related to any topic. A theory can limit the range of possibilities to be examined. It can also help in the formation of a hypothesis that can be further tested in a study. For example, a theory might propose that interaction assists language acquisition. From this, we can predict that if a teacher uses interactional strategies in their classroom, learning will be enhanced. Finally, a theory can help explain and understand the findings. For example, in SLA, the input processing model (VanPatten, 1996, 2004) provides a framework for understanding findings from studies on the effectiveness of processing instruction, an approach that encourages learners to process linguistic input more accurately within meaningful contexts. The model hypothesizes that structured input activities can help learners notice and interpret specific grammatical features, reducing their reliance on default strategies that often lead to errors.

Theoretical literature refers to the body of scholarly work that provides the foundational concepts, theories, models, and frameworks within a particular field of study.

Another type of classification for literature reviews is based on the methodology and approach used in conducting them. Here we can distinguish four main types of reviews: a traditional – or narrative – review, a systematic review, a meta-analysis, and a meta-synthesis (Figure 7.2).

Traditional or Narrative Review

A traditional or narrative literature review summarizes and synthesizes the existing literature on a specific topic or research question in a narrative format. Its aim is to provide a broad overview and find out what exists in an area of research, often without adhering to any systematic procedure. In this kind of review, the reviewer analyzes and interprets the literature and draws conclusions by highlighting the main findings and identifying any gaps, using a descriptive approach. A narrative literature review does not usually involve statistical analysis of quantitative data but rather relies on a qualitative synthesis of the available literature. Since it is not systematic, it does not have the rigorous criteria of exclusion and inclusion of studies, and the reviews are often written in a more accessible style compared to more technical research reviews, such as meta-analyses of statistical studies.

One limitation of narrative reviews is their subjectivity and reliance on the author's interpretation. This can introduce bias into the review, potentially affecting the conclusions drawn. Also, since there is often a wide range of literature available on any given topic, it can be difficult for the reviewer to identify and review all relevant studies, which can lead to an incomplete analysis. The range of material

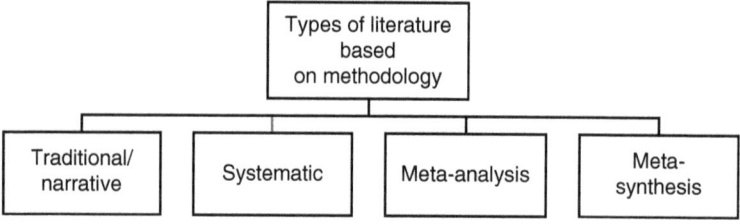

Figure 7.2 Types of literature review based on methodology

available may also lead to studies being selected subjectively, or if reviewers have preexisting views, they might select studies that support their own perspective or conclusions. Despite these issues, narrative reviews provide a valuable way of reviewing the literature and identifying areas where further research is needed.

A traditional or narrative literature review summarizes and synthesizes the existing literature on a specific topic or research question in a narrative format.

Systematic Review

A systematic literature review is a rigorous and structured approach to identifying, selecting, and evaluating the relevant literature on a specific topic or research question. The goal is to provide a more objective way of analyzing the available literature than the narrative review to identify key findings, gaps, and areas for further research. This type of review typically includes a formal search of multiple databases and a detailed screening process according to some predetermined inclusion and exclusion criteria. This systematicity in the process allows the author to minimize subjectivity, adding rigor to the evaluation of the relevant studies in the analysis.

One limitation of systematic reviews can be the difficulty in synthesizing studies that may come from divergent areas, as differences in study design, population, and intervention may make it challenging to draw objective conclusions.

A systematic literature review is a rigorous and structured approach to identifying, selecting, and evaluating the relevant literature on a specific topic or research question.

Meta-Analysis

A meta-analysis is a quantitative approach to synthesizing data from multiple studies to estimate the overall effect or relationship. This type of review often investigates the literature on the same or a similar research question. It uses statistical procedures to combine the results from multiple studies with the aim of drawing more robust and reliable conclusions. To this end, the analysis generates a summary estimate of the effect sizes of the studies reviewed to identify sources of similarities and variation across studies. The effect-size estimate provides a more objective approach to data analysis because it provides a standardized measure by considering the size and variability of the effects observed in each individual study. By pooling data from multiple studies, meta-analyses can provide more accurate estimates of the true effect and can also identify sources of heterogeneity across studies.

A meta-analysis is conducted through the following steps:

1. **Define the research question**: Start by clearly stating the research question or hypothesis to guide the review and identify which studies are relevant.
2. **Develop inclusion and exclusion criteria**: Establish specific criteria for selecting studies, such as the study design, population, intervention, and outcome measures. Studies that meet these criteria are included while those that do not are excluded.
3. **Conduct a literature search**: Perform a thorough search of the literature to find relevant studies. This search may also include unpublished studies to reduce publication bias.
4. **Select relevant studies**: Based on the inclusion and exclusion criteria, screen the identified studies and select those that are most relevant to the research question.
5. **Extract relevant data**: Collect relevant data from each selected study, such as effect sizes, sample sizes, and outcome measures, as well as study characteristics such as design and participant demographics.
6. **Conduct statistical analysis**: Use statistical methods to combine the data from the selected studies, calculating a pooled effect size (e.g., mean differences, correlation coefficients, odds ratios). Depending on the study characteristics, apply either a fixed-effects model, which assumes a constant effect size across studies, or a random-effects model, which accounts for potential variability in effect sizes across studies due to differences in populations or study conditions (see Chapter 23 for a discussion of different effect sizes).
7. **Interpret and report results**: Analyze the combined results, draw conclusions based on the overall effect size, and discuss the implications. Also, address the limitations of the meta-analysis, such as the quality of the studies or potential biases in the selection process.

To conduct a meta-analysis, you can use a variety of software tools specifically designed to handle statistical data, effect sizes, and the aggregation of study results. One widely used option is Comprehensive Meta-Analysis (CMA), which supports a range of statistical models (e.g., fixed-effects, random-effects). It also offers features for calculating effect sizes, performing subgroup analyses, and assessing publication bias. CMA offers detailed tutorials to help users understand how to use the software effectively.

In the field of applied linguistics, meta-analyses have been frequently used to synthesize research evidence in various areas, answering a wide range of questions, from those related to the efficacy of a particular instructional intervention or treatment, to the association between different variables. Like any research method, meta-analyses also have their own limitations, such as the potential for publication bias or the challenges of synthesizing studies coming from divergent areas.

A meta-analysis is a quantitative approach to synthesizing data from multiple studies to estimate the overall effect or relationship.

Meta-Synthesis

A meta-synthesis is a qualitative nonstatistical synthesis of data from multiple studies that have investigated the same or a similar research question. It is a research technique that synthesizes qualitative research studies to develop a new interpretation or understanding of a particular research problem. The difference between a meta-analysis and a meta-synthesis is that the former combines numerical data from multiple studies; a meta-synthesis, however, analyzes and synthesizes textual data from qualitative studies. Thus, this type of review typically involves a thematic analysis of the data to identify common themes or patterns across studies. Meta-synthesis is also distinct from meta-analysis in that the latter often aims to test hypotheses based on an analysis of quantitative data. Instead, meta-synthesis is often used to generate new theories or develop hypotheses for future testing, rather than testing hypotheses.

A meta-synthesis is a qualitative nonstatistical synthesis of data from multiple studies that have investigated the same or a similar research question.

Primary versus Secondary Sources

The main places where the relevant literature can be found are the library and various online databases. Thus, it is important to familiarize yourself with these resources. In this respect, it might be useful to distinguish between primary and secondary sources.

Primary sources are the original sources, which provide a direct and firsthand account of a study. This includes articles and manuscripts in which the original study is reported. They can also be conference proceedings, the publication of papers presented at a conference. Since these sources provide a firsthand report of a study, they are considered primary sources.

Secondary sources are those that provide a review, synthesis, or summary of the primary sources by another author. This includes, for example, books (both monographs and edited volumes), review articles, and various forms of commentaries based on a primary source. Primary and secondary sources are both useful resources.

While secondary sources can provide valuable information, it is advisable to use more primary sources for your research, as secondary sources are often based on another author's analysis and interpretation of a primary source. Therefore, they are one step away from the original source. For that reason, any time you decide to include information from secondary sources in your review, it is essential to check the accuracy of the information provided by looking at the primary source.

As for primary sources, journal articles may sometimes be very technical, but they are the best resources as they can also provide a guide as to the style and other information you may need for your research, such as matters relating to the research methods, data collection procedures, and data collection tools. The reference list at the end of research articles can also provide information on other related studies, which can be reviewed. Reviewing all the relevant sources can sometimes be overwhelming as you may realize that there are a huge number of sources that could potentially be reviewed.

Primary sources are the original sources, which provide a direct and firsthand account of a study. **Secondary sources** are those that provide a review, synthesis, or summary of the primary sources by another author.

POINTS TO PONDER

What strategies would you use to effectively conduct a literature review? Discuss specific situations where each strategy would be most appropriate and explain the rationale behind your choices, considering the goals and scope of your research.

How to Conduct a Literature Review

The process of conducting a literature review can involve several stages. Drawing on Cooper (1984), Randolph (2009), as can be seen in Figure 7.3, discussed five key stages deemed to be essential for a successful literature review. These stages seem very much like those involved in conducting research and include problem formulation, data collection, data evaluation, and data analysis and interpretation. The fifth stage is presenting the findings of the literature review to the intended audience. When doing a literature review for a thesis or a dissertation, another stage would be how the literature review contributes to the identification of the research problem and the development of the research question.

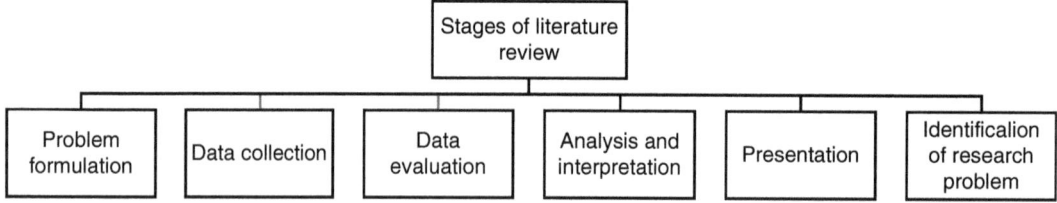

Figure 7.3 Stages of literature review

Problem Formulation

As discussed by Randolph (2009), the first stage of a literature review involves identifying and formulating the research question or problem that the review will address. This stage involves defining the scope of the review, identifying the key concepts and keywords, and developing a search strategy to identify relevant literature. The identification of the research problem should also include a justification for the review and the presentation of its main objectives. A well-articulated literature review question provides a framework that informs the entire review process, guiding the type of information needed, the selection of relevant literature, and the subsequent analysis. As Randolph noted, it is important to make a distinction here between an empirical research question, which is the question addressed by the study, and a literature review question, which determines the approach to conducting the literature review. Criteria for the inclusion or exclusion of the studies and data sources should also be established at this stage.

Data Collection

Once the literature review question has been defined, the next stage is to search for and collect the relevant literature. This involves conducting a comprehensive and systematic search of multiple databases, journals, and other sources to identify all relevant literature on the topic. Depending on the aim of the literature review, you can include a comprehensive, partially comprehensive, representative, or important group of pertinent articles in the literature review. Like primary research, you should have a systematic plan for data collection as well as a detailed description of the data collection process. To collect data, you can start with an electronic search of academic databases. The electronic search of academic databases is a common and widely used method for identifying relevant sources. This method involves conducting keyword searches within academic databases. Key databases for applied linguistics include Google Scholar, JSTOR, ERIC (Education Resources Information Center), Linguistics and Language Behavior Abstracts (LLBA), MLA International Bibliography, and Scopus, which provide a wealth of peer-reviewed content specifically related to language acquisition, second language learning, teaching methods, sociolinguistics, and other subfields of applied linguistics. ProQuest Dissertations & Theses Global is also an invaluable database for accessing dissertations and theses, many of which feature cutting-edge research in applied linguistics.

As discussed in Chapter 4, in addition to identifying, reading, and evaluating individual research reports and articles, it is important to examine previous synthetic work, such as research syntheses, state-of-the-art reviews, and meta-analyses. Consulting synthetic works is important in a literature review process because it provides a comprehensive overview of existing research, highlights consensus and discrepancies in the field, and identifies gaps that need further exploration. As mentioned earlier, tools such as IDESR can be particularly useful in these initial steps to identify relevant synthetic and meta-analytic reviews.

IDESR (idesr.org) is a comprehensive online resource that aggregates systematic reviews and meta-analyses in the field of education. This tool allows you to quickly locate existing syntheses on various topics, helping to avoid duplication of effort and build on a solid foundation of existing knowledge. By using IDESR, you can quickly find systematic reviews and meta-analyses related to your research topic, which will provide a broad overview of what has already been studied and synthesized.

Data Evaluation

The third stage of a literature review involves critically evaluating the quality and relevance of the identified literature. This involves assessing the credibility and reliability of the sources and selecting the most relevant and appropriate ones for inclusion in the review. During the data evaluation stage, the reviewer extracts and assesses the information in the articles based on the goal of the literature review. For instance, as noted by Randolph, if the goal is to integrate research outcomes, the reviewer will extract research outcome data from each article and develop a plan for integrating those outcomes.

Analysis and Interpretation

The fourth stage of a literature review involves synthesizing and analyzing the findings of the included studies to answer the literature review question. This involves identifying the key themes and concepts and drawing conclusions based on the analysis. In doing the analysis and the interpretation, the reviewer should have the goal of the literature review in mind. As noted before, if the goal is integration, the data collected will be integrated. The type of synthesis to be performed (quantitative or qualitative) depends on the type of data that has been collected and extracted.

Presentation

Another stage of the literature review involves selecting the most relevant infomation and presenting the findings to the intended audience. This may also involve writing a review report, or even presenting the findings at a conference or seminar, or publishing the review in a peer-reviewed journal.

Identification of the Research Problem

As noted earlier, an important aim of the literature review for a study is to facilitate the development of a research question to examine. To that end, the reviewer should use the evidence from the review to determine how the study will contribute to knowledge in the field. As explained by Randolph (2009), the American Education Research Association (2006) provides guidelines for how new research can contribute to existing research. If the study contributes to an established line of theory and empirical research, it should explain how it enriches that theoretical perspective. If it establishes a new line of theory, it should clarify the new theory, how it relates to existing theories and evidence, and why it is needed. If the study is motivated by practical concerns, it should explain the importance of those concerns and how the investigation can address them. If the study is motivated by a lack of information about a problem or issue, the problem formation should explain what information is lacking, why it is important, and how the investigation will address the need for information.

A Preliminary versus a More Comprehensive Literature Review

When we are at the beginning stage of a research study and our aim is to review the literature to decide on a particular research question or to decide whether the research area we have in mind is a worthwhile area to pursue, we often start by conducting a literature review, which is usually considered a preliminary literature review or an exploratory literature review. Preliminary literature reviews are often conducted at the beginning of the research process to identify and gain a general understanding of the existing literature on a topic. The review can have a narrative focus with the goal of helping you identify gaps or inconsistencies in the literature, to inform the development of a research question or the identification of an empirical or theoretical framework for the investigation.

During a preliminary literature review, you may read through relevant studies and articles, take notes, and begin to organize your thoughts and ideas. This process can help identify gaps in the literature as well as potential areas for further research. It is important to remain open-minded and flexible during the process, as the research question or projected areas for study can evolve or change based on the literature review findings. For the same reason, it is also important to critically evaluate the quality and relevance of the literature, and to avoid preconceptions that may influence the interpretation of the results.

As the study progresses, you may conduct a more comprehensive literature review to refine and clearly define the research question and focus.

Preliminary literature reviews are often conducted at the beginning of the research process to identify and gain a general understanding of the existing literature on a topic.

Characteristics of a Good Literature Review

Conducting an effective literature review can be challenging for many novice researchers. Doing a good literature review does not only need a considerable amount of time and research to locate and select the relevant information, but it also needs the skill to integrate, synthesize, and evaluate the sources.

According to Copper (1988, p. 106), a literature review has at least two elements. First, it "uses as its database reports of primary or original scholarship and does not report new primary scholarship itself." While the primary reports may be verbal, most are written documents. The second is that "a literature review seeks to describe, summarize, evaluate, clarify, and/or integrate the content of the primary reports."

This means the effective literature review requires reading the sources reflectively and analytically, evaluating the relevance of the information to your study.

Also, you may need to be selective. For some research topics, the literature might be small, but for others it might be so large that a thorough literature review is not possible. You may also come across some material that might be directly related to your study and other knowledge that, while important, might not. You should be able to distinguish between the two and be able to select the body of knowledge that is most relevant. Given the easy access afforded by the internet to many different sources these days, it is also important that you pay attention to the type of sources you use and consider their quality, reliability, and credibility.

A good literature review is not a chronological summary of what has been done by previous researchers. It analyzes and synthesizes information in a coherent and integrated text that is thematically organized and attempts to contextualize your study and provide a conceptual background for it. In essence, instead of simply listing studies, it does the following:

- Evaluates the related sources and synthesizes information in ways that can inform the study
- Presents an argument and discusses the debate and controversies around the issue, instead of summarizing each individual study
- Connects the studies to each other and identifies emerging trends
- Identifies the gap or problems that needs to be addressed
- Shows convincingly that there is still research that needs to be conducted in the area
- Highlights the contribution of your work and how it extends our knowledge in that area
- Reviews key sources or the most relevant studies and does not attempt to include every possible study.

A good literature review is not a chronological summary of what has been done by previous researchers. It analyzes and synthesizes information in a coherent and integrated text that is thematically organized and attempts to contextualize your study and provide a conceptual background for it.

The following suggestions made by Roudertan and Newtom (2007 cited in Starfield 2018, p. 189) can also be helpful when organizing and writing the literature review:

- Try to avoid beginning your sentences with "Jones said . . .;" "Smith found . . ." – this shifts the focus of your reviews from your own argument to the work of others.
- Try to "develop a theme and then cite work of relevant authors" (p. 65) to support your arguments or to provide examples or counterexamples of your point.

- Try to limit excessive quoting. This can also lessen your authority and control.
- Try to avoid reporting everything. Be selective – "build an argument not a library" (p. 66).

The Literature Review in Qualitative and Quantitative Studies

While many of the issues discussed above are relevant to all research, there are some additional issues to consider when writing a literature review within a particular research paradigm.

In a quantitative study, the literature review may focus on and be framed around a specific research problem or question. To this end, the literature review may move from general to specific with an attempt to identify the gap in knowledge and to present an argument justifying both the research question and the theoretical and methodological approaches used to address it. It should also show that you have a solid understanding of the previous work in the area by comparing and contrasting previous studies and connecting them with your own research.

Qualitative research may not start with a specific research question in the same way that a quantitative study does. However, a literature review is still a key component of any qualitative study and should be able to contextualize and provide a conceptual framework for the study. It should identify and discuss the key concepts, ideas, and constructs that inform the study and analyze the previous work in that domain. Because qualitative studies are exploratory, there may not be as much previous research on the topic as there is when conducting quantitative research. Therefore, the literature review might be shorter, particularly the one that comes at the beginning of the study. However, it might be integrated into other sections or chapters.

POINTS TO PONDER

What makes a research question effective, and what criteria would you use to assess the effectiveness of your research question?

The Development of the Research Question

Developing a clear and effective research question is a critical component of any good research project. A well-defined research question not only helps to guide the research process but also makes the study focused and produces results that are meaningful and contribute to the field.

Effective research questions are those that are explicitly stated and operationalized in terms of the variables measured, implying the type of data that needs to be collected (particularly in quantitative research).

Effective research questions are those that are explicitly stated and operationalized in terms of the variables measured, implying the type of data that needs to be collected, particularly in quantitative research.

The process of reviewing the literature is an important step towards the development of the research questions and hypotheses. The review of the literature leads to the identification of the gap in knowledge and the need for further research. However, while the research literature is an essential source of information for the development of research questions, there are many sources that can provide important direction and guidance, particularly when researchers are at the beginning stages of their research. In the following section, we will discuss some of the sources of research questions and explore strategies for incorporating multiple sources of information into the development of research question and hypotheses.

Sources of Research Questions

There are several sources for research questions, including personal observation, theories, study limitations, practical concerns, experts and other researchers, research literature, colleagues, and your own research. These are shown in Figure 7.4.

Figure 7.4 Sources of research questions

Personal Observation/Experience

One possible source of research questions is our own personal observation or experience. This includes our observation of various phenomena and their characteristics in different contexts. It could also be the observations made by others that we have been informed about through reading books, articles, or other sources.

An example of a personal observation or experience that could lead to a research question is observing that L2 international students in a particular university struggle with academic listening in English, despite having met the English language proficiency requirements of that university for admission. This observation could prompt you to wonder why. You may start thinking about the possible factors that could have contributed to this situation. You may then decide to empirically investigate this issue by exploring the listening strategies that students use or by examining instructional strategies that could help them improve their listening skills. Such an observation could thus serve as a good starting point for developing a research question that can be further refined and that allows for systematic exploration of the issue.

Many of the questions that applied linguists ask are inspired by or come from formal or informal observations of themselves or others. However, it is important to note that research questions derived from personal observation or experience should still be approached with a critical mindset to make sure that the questions are significant and framed in a way that promotes rigorous inquiry and analysis.

One source of research questions is our **personal observation** of various phenomena in different contexts, as well as observations made by others.

Theories

Another source for research questions could be theories and concepts in the field. Theories can provide a framework for understanding and explaining issues and can be used to guide the development of research questions by providing opportunities for testing or refining the theory. Research that is inspired by a theoretical perspective can test existing theories or hypotheses as the theory that inspires research questions can lead to predictions about a phenomenon.

For example, a theory in the field of language acquisition might suggest that individuals who are extroverted are more successful in learning a new language. You could develop research questions to investigate this theory by, for example, exploring whether there is any relationship between extroversion and language acquisition.

Similarly, a theoretical perspective might hold that language acquisition is a social process and that its success might be linked to social interaction. Therefore, there is a possibility that those who engage more in social interaction are more successful in their language learning than those who do not.

Study Limitations

Another source of research questions is study limitations. As noted earlier, good research is research that is built on the work conducted by others. This is how scientific knowledge grows. One way to locate research ideas is by reading research reports in a particular area that you are interested in. Journal articles that report research results have different sections, and one important section to look at would be the discussion section where the researcher discusses, evaluates, and explains their findings. This section often includes a discussion of the findings' implications for future research in which the researcher identifies the shortcomings of their research and provides suggestions for future research. You can then consider conducting a study that can address the shortcomings, which could be methodological or theoretical. Since these implications are drawn from a study already published, they can provide a good source of research questions. For example, a corrective feedback study may note a limitation in sample size, which a follow-up study could address.

Even if a question has been previously addressed, it does not mean that we cannot address it again. We can always conduct replication studies to find out whether the results of a previous study can be confirmed. We can also modify the question so that it can still contribute to the literature. A previous study can also be extended in a new direction by identifying variables that have not been addressed in the study.

Pedagogical Concerns

Pedagogical concerns can be an important source for research questions. Pedagogy refers to the theory and practice of teaching, and one aim of applied linguistics research has often been investigating and improving language teaching methods and materials. Pedagogical concerns may arise from a variety of factors, such as changes in curriculum, student needs, or new technologies. Pedagogical concerns may also be related to how different learner variables or individual learner differences, such as age, language proficiency, learning styles, and strategies or motivation, may affect classroom language learning or how particular language teaching methods and materials may be adjusted to the needs of different language learners. Of course, we may have some initial ideas about these issues, which will need to be fine-tuned through reading further on the topic, before being developed into a question that needs to be investigated.

Colleagues

Colleagues can also be a source of research questions. Through interaction with them, you may hear about their own research interests, research findings, experiences, and observations, which might also interest you. For example, they may share their experiences of working with specific learner populations or in a certain educational context, which could inspire interesting research questions.

Experts or Other Experienced Researchers

Another important source for research questions could be experts or experienced researchers. For graduate students, this could be their supervisors or other faculty members. These individuals may have conducted many studies; therefore, they may well be familiar with the field and the topics and hence may know what questions are significant and should be addressed. These people are often familiar with the latest developments, debates, and research findings in the field, which can be helpful in developing questions that are significant and worth addressing. Experts also have specialized knowledge, skills, and experience in a specific area of research and therefore can provide insight into important research questions that need further research. One way to benefit from experts in generating research questions is to interact with them; this may happen through going to conferences and networking with them. During these interactions, you can ask them questions about current research, issues, trends, and the current challenges in the field. You can ask them about the emerging research gaps that need to be addressed or the new research questions that are important to the field.

Research Literature

The research literature can be an important source for research questions as the literature review can reveal ideas to examine. As discussed earlier, reviewing the literature means examining the literature available on a topic by examining the existing published works, including books, research articles, and research reports. By reviewing the literature, you can generate new research questions or refine existing ones. For example, when you read the literature, you may encounter a question that has not been investigated or suggestions about what needs to be examined. Sometimes even reading the abstract of an article in a journal can provide an idea, which can then be followed up by further reading on the topic and narrowing down the idea to develop research questions.

Your Own Research

Another source for research questions could be your own study or the findings that come from the research that you have conducted. When we do research, our findings may answer the question that we have formulated for that study. However, the study might also lead to other questions. Additionally, you may reflect on your own research process, methods, and outcomes, which can then lead you to consider new questions for further research or even refine your current questions. Therefore, your own study can serve as an important source of inspiration and lead you to develop new research questions that can guide future investigations in your field.

Wording Research Questions

Research questions should not only be specific, but they should also be appropriately worded. There are many ways we can formulate a research question, but certain language and particular wording are commonly associated with research questions. Questions are interrogative sentences that can take a variety of forms. Depending on the exact purpose of the study, they may take the form of simple yes/no questions or start with question words such as what, how, which, when, to what extent, who, where, etc.

Sometimes we may have several research questions; the answer to one may lead to another question. In this case they can be sequenced accordingly. In such cases, we may have one main research question followed by a few subquestions related to the main question. For example:

- Are there any differential effects of explicit versus implicit instruction on L2 learners' acquisition of English articles?
  - If so, does the effect depend on learners' level of language proficiency?

When formulating research questions, we should avoid questions that are judgmental or evaluative. The aim of research is not to make a value judgment but to seek an answer to a research question. For the same reason, questions that ask how the world should be must be avoided. For example, if our research is about corrective feedback, we should not use questions such as "What is the best way of providing corrective feedback?". We should also avoid asking questions containing the word "should," or those that suggest solutions to problems, as research is not about finding solutions or dictating what should be done; it is about answering a specific question that might further our understanding of an issue. For example, if our research addresses a pedagogical issue, such as the use of L1 in L2 learning, we should avoid questions such as "Should teachers use L1 in their L2 classrooms?". A much better question would be "What uses do experienced teachers make of L1 in their L2 classrooms?".

Characteristics of Good Research Questions

Good research questions have a number of characteristics; these are considered below.

Focusedness

Good research questions are focused enough. They focus on a single dimension, factor, or characteristic that can be examined in a single study. For example, they address the relationship of one factor with another factor, or the effect of one factor on another factor. A question cannot be answered successfully if it is too broad or focuses on too many variables at the same time. However, the question should not be too narrow, otherwise it may not be worth investigating, given the time and resources involved in research. By narrowing down the focus, you can maintain clarity and precision in your study and can generate meaningful findings. Therefore, although the more specific the question, the easier it is to address that question, striking the right balance in focus is essential for conducting effective research. Here are examples of a focused and a broad research question:

Focused Research Question: What are the effects of explicit grammar instruction on the acquisition of English articles among adult ESL learners in a classroom setting?

This research question specifies the population (adult ESL learners), the variable of interest (effects of explicit grammar instruction), and the context (classroom setting). It focuses on a specific aspect of language acquisition (English articles) and allows for a targeted investigation into the impact of explicit grammar instruction on adult learners in a particular learning environment.

Broad Research Question: How does instruction affect language acquisition?

The above research question is too broad and lacks specificity. It does not define the specific language, population, or outcomes of interest. It leaves room for multiple interpretations and could include various aspects of language learning and its effects on diverse individuals. To make it more focused, the question would need to be narrowed down by specifying the language, population, and specific outcomes or variables under investigation.

In applied linguistics research, like in any other field, it is important to formulate focused research questions that clearly define the variables, population, and context of interest. This specificity allows you to conduct targeted investigations, obtain meaningful findings, and contribute to existing knowledge in the field.

Feasibility

Good research questions are feasible. This means that they are manageable within the constraints of the research project and can be addressed given the researcher's resources. For example, if you have developed a research question that requires participants that you do not have access to or that needs resources that you think may be hard to obtain, it is advisable to revise the research question to make it more feasible.

Clarity and Reasonable Scope

Good research questions are clearly articulated and easily understood. They also have reasonable scope and do not expect to achieve more than what is likely. A research question with a reasonable scope allows for in-depth investigation and analysis without becoming overwhelming.

Not Being Too Obvious

Good research questions should not be too obvious. This means that they should go beyond what is already known or readily apparent in the field. Asking obvious questions may not contribute significantly to the existing knowledge or generate new insights. Instead, good research questions should examine unexplored areas, challenge existing assumptions, or provide novel perspectives. An example of a research question that is too obvious could be:

"What are the values of learning vocabulary for L2 learners?"

This research question is too obvious because the values and benefits of vocabulary learning for language learners are well-established and widely recognized. Therefore, asking such a question would not contribute significantly to the existing knowledge. A more effective question could be:

"What are the effects of using dictionaries versus traditional flashcards on the retention of vocabulary knowledge among intermediate-level L2 learners?"

This refined research question explores a less obvious aspect of vocabulary learning by comparing the effects of using dictionaries with using traditional flashcards. By investigating the effectiveness of these two methods specifically for intermediate-level language learners, the research question probes a less obvious area of inquiry, and thus the findings could shed new light on the optimal instructional strategies for enhancing vocabulary acquisition.

Being Well Defined and Operationalizable

Good research questions have key terms or concepts that are clearly defined and operationalized. As noted earlier, operationalization refers to the process whereby an abstract concept or construct is defined in terms of measurable indicators. For example, in a study on the effects of explicit and implicit instruction on the acquisition of simple and complex target structures, Spada and Tomita (2010, p. 4) addressed the following two questions:

- Do the effects of explicit and implicit instruction vary with simple and complex features in the short and long term?
- Do the effects of explicit and implicit instruction lead to similar types of language ability for complex and simple forms?

Spada and Tomita (2010, p. 10) then operationalized the term "complex structure" as follows:

> [W]e used the number of linguistic transformation rules as the basis for distinguishing between simple and complex forms. . . . For example, "Wh-question as object of preposition" is described as a complex feature because in order to arrive at the sample sentence "Who did you talk to?" seven transformations need to be fulfilled. On the other hand, the past tense of regular verbs is defined as simple because only one criterion needs to be met in order to arrive at the target form: suppliance of the "ed" inflection.

Being Empirically Testable

Good research questions are formulated in ways that can be answered through empirical research or data analysis and by using a given research design. For example, a question like the following by VanPatten and Cadierno (1993) clearly shows what research design is needed to answer the question:

- "Is PI more effective than output-oriented instruction at promoting the development of learners' abilities to interpret the subjunctive?"

The question shows that the study needs a comparative experimental research design. It also shows that the effects should be measured in terms of the development of learners' abilities to interpret the subjunctive. Both PI (processing instruction) and output-based instruction have also been clearly defined in the study.

Significance

Good research questions are significant. That is, they should contribute to the existing body of knowledge and have potential practical implications. Contribution to the existing body of knowledge occurs when the question expands upon or challenges current theories, concepts, or established knowledge within the field or when it seeks to provide new insights that can deepen our understanding of the phenomenon under investigation.

Table 7.1 provides examples of poor research questions along with improved versions. The revised versions allow for more refined investigations and offer opportunities for more meaningful insights. The table also provides reasons for weakness and improvement. By knowing the reasons, we can better understand the rationale behind transforming weak research questions into stronger ones.

Table 7.1 Examples of poor and good research questions

	Research question	Reason
Poor	What effect does corrective feedback have on students' learning?	This question is not focused enough and is too general. It is unclear what type of corrective feedback with what kind of learners is being examined.
Better	What effect does written corrective feedback have on EFL learners' acquisition of the simple past tense?	This question is more focused and can be answered through collecting data.
Poor	What factors influence the effectiveness of incidental learning?	This question is vague and unfocused. "What factors" shows that there are many possible factors, which would make the question difficult to answer.
Better	How do ESL learners' attitudes toward reading affect their reading comprehension?	Focusing on only one factor and using more specific terms makes the question more focused and easier to answer.
Poor	Does type of task planning lead to better L2 learners' production?	This question is too broad, and it is unclear what is meant by "better."
Better	Do intermediate EFL learners produce more fluent speech when they have opportunities to plan?	The second question is much more researchable. It uses clearly defined terms and narrows its focus to a specific population.
Poor	Are there any advantages of using L1 in L2 classrooms?	The question is not focused enough. The question seems to be too obvious as this issue has been researched before. Also, it is framed in a way that is not easy to answer.
Better	What effect does using L1 in L2 classrooms have on learners' comprehension and production?	This question narrows the focus to specific outcomes (comprehension and production) while addressing the role of L1 in the classroom.

Research Questions in Qualitative versus Quantitative Research

The way research questions are formulated depends on the aim of the research and the approach within which the research is conducted. Therefore, they should be stated in ways that align with the aim of the study. Thus, the differences between research questions for qualitative and quantitative research relate to the nature of the research design and the type of data that will be collected. In quantitative research, the research questions are typically framed to test a specific hypothesis or to answer a specific research question using numerical data. In other words, the questions are defined in terms of measurable data and involve a methodology that focuses on sampling, measurement, and statistical analysis.

In contrast, qualitative research questions are usually open-ended and exploratory in nature, seeking to understand the complexity of a phenomenon through detailed analysis of qualitative data such as interviews, observations, and textual analysis. Qualitative research questions are not only broader and more general, but they are also often developed iteratively throughout the research process. The research design for qualitative research is often flexible and responsive to the research context, and the methods used to collect and analyze data are more varied and may be adapted to suit the needs of the research question.

For the reasons mentioned above, qualitative research questions are often worded in an exploratory and open-ended manner. They often begin with phrases like "How do people perceive ... ?", "What are the experiences of ... ?", and "What is the process of ... ?".

In contrast, quantitative research questions are typically worded in a more precise and specific manner, as they seek to measure and quantify relationships between variables. They often include words like "effect," "relationship," "difference," "correlation," and "association." Quantitative research questions are usually structured to generate hypotheses that can be tested through statistical analysis.

Quantitative research questions are typically framed to test a specific hypothesis or to answer a specific research question using numerical data. **Qualitative research questions** are usually open-ended and exploratory in nature, seeking to understand the complexity of a phenomenon through detailed analysis of qualitative data such as interviews, observations, and textual analysis.

Here are some examples of quantitative research questions in various areas of applied linguistics:

- **Language Acquisition:** What is the relationship between input frequency and the acquisition of grammatical structures in young L2 learners?
- **Lexical Studies:** What is the differential effect of word lists versus context-based learning on vocabulary acquisition in adult language learners?
- **Multilingualism and Multiculturalism:** What is the impact of multilingualism on cognitive ability of children?
- **Translation:** What are the effects of different translation techniques on the accuracy and readability of translated texts?
- **Language and Identity:** Is there any relationship between language choice and identity perception in multilingual individuals?

- **ESP (English for Specific Purposes):** What is the impact of specialized vocabulary instruction on the language proficiency of learners in a specific field (e.g., medical English)?

All these research questions are measurable and can be addressed by collecting and analyzing numerical data.

Here are some examples of qualitative research questions in different domains of applied linguistics:

- **Computer-Assisted Language Learning (CALL):** How do English language learners perceive the effectiveness of computer-assisted language learning in improving their pragmatic skills?
- **Identity and Sociolinguistics:** How do ESL learners negotiate their identity in the context of English language learning in a new country, and what factors influence this process?
- **Language Teaching Methodology:** What are the challenges and opportunities in implementing task-based language instruction in Chinese EFL classrooms?
- **Code-Switching and Multilingualism:** What are the attitudes of advanced-level English language learners towards code-switching in communication contexts?
- **Intercultural Competence:** How do English language learners develop intercultural competence through study-abroad programs?
- **Academic Literacy and Writing:** What are the experiences of international students in adapting to academic writing conventions in English-speaking universities?
- **Interpreting Studies:** How do sign language interpreters navigate cultural nuances in legal interpreting scenarios?
- **Digital Language Learning:** What are the impacts of social media usage on the language learning strategies of adolescents learning Spanish as a second language?
- **Heritage Language Maintenance:** How do heritage speakers of Spanish maintain their language proficiency across generations in a predominantly English-speaking environment?
- **Teacher Identity and Classroom Management:** What are the strategies used by nonnative English-speaking teachers to assert authority and maintain classroom management in diverse EFL settings?
- **Pragmatics:** How do learners of Japanese as a foreign language use politeness strategies in different social contexts?
- **Phonetics and Pronunciation Training:** How do teachers view the role of pronunciation training tools in the phonetic development of Arabic learners of English?

These research questions are all open-ended and exploratory and can be addressed by collecting and analyzing nonnumerical data through interviews, focus groups, or observations. For example, interviews can be used to gather learners' perceptions and experiences regarding the effectiveness of CALL in improving pragmatic skills. Or, for the heritage language maintenance question, an ethnographic study using interviews and family language-use diaries can explore how heritage language proficiency is maintained across generations.

It is important to note that some research questions can be approached through various methodological frameworks, including quantitative research, qualitative research, or a combination of both, known as mixed methods research (see Chapter 24).

For example, to address a question like "What role does socioeconomic status play in the language learning experiences of refugees learning English in resettlement programs?", you can employ qualitative, quantitative, or mixed methods research. Using qualitative research, you can conduct interviews with refugees to explore their personal experiences, challenges, and perspectives on learning English in resettlement programs. These interviews can provide detailed insights into how socioeconomic status influences their language learning journey. Alternatively, you may organize focus-group discussions with refugees to facilitate conversations about their collective experiences. This method can reveal common themes and diverse viewpoints on the impact of socioeconomic status. Or, you can employ a quantitative research methodology by designing and distributing surveys to refugees to collect data on their language learning experiences. Surveys can include Likert scale questions to measure attitudes, challenges, and perceptions related to socioeconomic status and language learning. You can then analyze the survey data using statistical techniques to identify patterns, correlations, and significant factors that relate to the impact of socioeconomic status on language learning outcomes. As a third option, you may employ mixed methods research. To this end, you can start with quantitative methods by administering surveys and conducting statistical analyses to identify general trends. Then you can follow up with qualitative methods, such as interviews or focus groups, to explore these trends in more depth and understand the underlying reasons and experiences.

Of course, deciding on the research methods to use depends on several key factors, including not only the nature of the research question and the objectives of the study but also the context, resources, and constraints, as well as ethical considerations.

The Difference between Research Questions and Hypotheses

Research questions and hypotheses are closely related. However, they are not the same. While research questions are worded as interrogative statements, hypotheses are noninterrogative predictions about the results that the researcher attempts to confirm or disconfirm through data.

According to *The American Heritage Dictionary* a hypothesis is "a tentative explanation for an observation, phenomenon, or scientific problem that can be tested by further investigation." Hypotheses are more characteristic of deductive studies and seek to test either casual effects or whether a relationship exists between or among variables.

When formulating a hypothesis, it is essential to distinguish between causal and associative relationships, as well as to consider the study aim and design, whether it is explanatory (as in experimental studies) or descriptive (as in correlational studies).

In some studies, such as in experimental studies, research questions are followed by hypotheses that are often derived from a theory or past research. Such hypotheses often test a causal effect. To write such a hypothesis, we often state the independent and the dependent variables or the groups we are comparing and the kind of prediction in terms of the effect.

As an example, suppose in a study the research question is "Does language proficiency affect the effectiveness of explicit instruction?". After reviewing the literature, you may find out that most studies have shown a mediating role for language proficiency. A hypothesis might then be formulated that predicts that students who have a higher level of language proficiency benefit more from instruction than those who have a lower level of language proficiency.

As noted above, hypotheses can also indicate a relationship or association. The hypothesis that motivation is positively associated with the rate of learning an L2 is an example of a relationship hypothesis, as it indicates that two variables are interrelated without indicating that one variable is causing or affecting the other.

Research questions are worded as interrogative statements. **Hypotheses**, however, are noninterrogative predictions about the results that the researcher attempts to confirm or disconfirm through data.

Hypotheses can be alternative or null. A null hypothesis predicts no relationship, change, or difference. An alternative hypothesis, on the other hand, predicts a change or relationship. The alternative hypothesis can be either directional or nondirectional. If the hypothesis predicts a change and shows the direction of the change or the study results, it will be a directional hypothesis. A nondirectional hypothesis simply states that there is a difference between two groups or that there is a relationship between two variables without stating the direction of the relationship (e.g., positive, or negative)

A null hypothesis predicts no relationship, change, or difference. **An alternative hypothesis,** on the other hand, predicts a change or relationship. The alternative hypothesis can be either directional or nondirectional.

As noted above, a null hypothesis predicts no relationship. The hypothesis that "Motivation is positively associated with the rate of learning an L2" can be turned into a null hypothesis by rewriting it as "There is no relationship between motivation and rate of L2 learning." A null hypothesis is formulated mostly for statistical testing purposes. However, it is the directional hypothesis that the researcher is interested in, and it is often derived from a theory and used in a study when the researcher presents the research problem or discusses their findings.

Conclusion

In this chapter, we have discussed the importance of conducting a literature review, the different types of literature reviews, the essential characteristics of a good literature review, and the sources and criteria for developing research questions. We have also discussed specific criteria that can be used to assess the value of a research question, including its clarity, specificity, and measurability, and provided examples of good research questions for both qualitative and quantitative research. By learning and applying the concepts and skills explored in this chapter, we hope you will be able to conduct an effective literature review and develop research questions for studies that can contribute to the advancement of the field. In Chapters 8 and 13, we will discuss the process of selecting participants for qualitative and quantitative research studies and learn about the various methods for identifying and recruiting participants.

DISCUSSION AND ACTIVITY QUESTIONS

Discussion Questions

1. What are the different types of literature reviews, and what are their unique features? How do you decide which type of literature review is appropriate for your research question?
2. What are the key steps involved in conducting an effective literature review? Are there any steps you find particularly challenging or crucial for success?
3. What are the important characteristics of a good literature review, and how can you make sure that your literature review meets these criteria?
4. What type of literature review would be most suitable for a large-scale quantitative study, and why? How might this differ from the type needed for a smaller, exploratory study?
5. What are the advantages and disadvantages of narrative reviews compared to systematic reviews? Which do you think is more challenging to conduct?
6. How can you determine that your research question is specific, measurable, and achievable? What steps can you take to refine and improve your research question?

Activity Questions

1. Conduct a literature review on a topic of interest. Identify at least five recent sources and evaluate them based on their relevance to your research. Write a summary of the key findings and highlight the gaps in the literature.
2. Identify two potential sources of research questions in your field of interest. How might these sources inspire research ideas?

3. Rewrite the following vague research question into a clear and focused one: "How does technology affect education?" What challenges might arise in narrowing the scope, and how would you address them?

4. Identify a research question that interests you and assess it based on the criteria for good research questions discussed in this chapter. Refine your research question as necessary so that it can be appropriate and effective.

5. Select a published research study. Analyze its research question and determine whether and how it meets the criteria for assessing good research questions. Would you revise the research question? If so, explain why.

6. Decide on a research topic of interest and develop two research questions for that study: one that is appropriate for a qualitative research study, and another that is appropriate for a quantitative research study. Identify the key differences between the two and explain the type of data that will be collected for each.

PART III
Quantitative Research Designs and Data Collection

8 Selecting Participants for Quantitative Research: Sampling Techniques and Methods

---

CHAPTER OBJECTIVES

After completing this chapter, you should be able to

- Understand the concept of sampling in quantitative research and explain its value and importance.
- Define sampling frame and population and explain their role in selecting a representative sample from a larger population.
- Identify the different types of sampling strategies used in quantitative research, including probability and nonprobability sampling, and understand the advantages and disadvantages of each.
- Determine the required sample sizes for quantitative research and the factors that influence the size of a sample.

Introduction

Selecting participants and determining an adequate sample size are important considerations and steps in conducting research. Sampling procedures are methods or strategies used to select participants. Sample size refers to the number of observations or participants in a sample selected. The accuracy and reliability of the results of any study depend heavily on the quality and nature of the sample selected. Adequate and appropriately selected participants allow you to collect data that are meaningful and can be used as the basis of valid conclusions.

Researchers frequently face the challenge of determining what constitutes an adequate sample size and how many participants are required to fulfill the study's objectives. There is no easy answer to the question of sample size, as it will depend on several factors, including the type, goal, and scope of the research; the nature of the topic; the kind of research questions; and the methods of analysis to be used. There are different sampling procedures that can be used in both quantitative and qualitative research to select participants. Quantitative researchers often seek to recruit participants in ways that allow them to conduct statistical analysis and generalize findings from the sample to the broader population. Therefore, they need to select the sample carefully and explain the procedures used to do so. Qualitative research aims to gain a rich insight into the phenomenon of interest. Therefore, participants are selected in ways that will provide an in-depth understanding of the issue under investigation.

In this chapter, we will discuss the importance of selecting an appropriate sample, the different sampling procedures, and the factors that researchers must consider when selecting a sampling procedure and determining an appropriate sample size in quantitative research. Since the choice of a sampling procedure depends on the research questions and the population being studied, we will first consider issues related to sample and population and then how to select participants by discussing different types of sampling methods and their use in quantitative research.

Sampling procedures are the methods used to select participants from a population. There are several different sampling procedures available, each with its own strengths and weaknesses. The most common ones include random sampling, stratified sampling, systematic sampling, and cluster sampling. While some of these techniques are also useful for qualitative research, they are more useful for studies that involve statistical analyses or aim to make inferences about the population. In quantitative research, once the population has been identified, depending on the purpose of the research, we need to not only decide on the sampling procedure to use to select our sample but also determine how many participants we need in our study. The issue of sample size is an important factor in quantitative research and in statistical analysis, as it affects the accuracy and precision of the results. Therefore, in this chapter, we will also consider the issue of sample size and how to determine the number of participants in a given study.

Sampling procedures are methods or strategies used to select participants. **Sample size** refers to the number of observations or participants in a sample selected.

POINTS TO PONDER

How do you distinguish between a sample and a population, and how important is their role in quantitative research?

The Study Sample and Population

In quantitative studies, the concepts of sample and population are fundamental to understanding how data are collected and analyzed. In a study, we often deal with a group of participants from whom we collect our data. This group of participants is called a study sample, and the entire group who share similar characteristics and from which we have drawn our sample is called the study population. For example, a population could be all the adult intermediate L2 learners in an EFL context. In quantitative research, we would often like to know the behavior of a particular population. However, we cannot examine the behavior of all the members of the population. Instead, we select and study only a sample. However, to be able to generalize inferences from the sample to the population, we need to carefully select our sample so that it is representative of the population. If a sample is not representative, the results may not accurately reflect the characteristics or the behavior of the population. Therefore, it is important to carefully select samples using appropriate sampling methods so that they are representative of the population of interest.

The group of participants from whom we collect data is called **a study sample.** The entire group who share similar characteristics and from which we have drawn our sample is called the **study population.**

The goal of sampling is to obtain a sample that reflects the characteristics of the population. Representativeness means that the sample and the population have similar characteristics in the areas that pertain to the research. These characteristics could include their age, level of language proficiency, educational, cultural, and first language background, or any other characteristics that pertain to the study. It is important to specify these characteristics before selecting a sample so that the population from which the sample is drawn is appropriately defined. For example, if our sample is going to be a group of experienced English L1 teachers, everyone in the population should have the same characteristics. That is, they should be experienced English teachers who speak English as their L1. If that is the case, we can select an adequate number of those teachers in order to be able to generalize from the sample to the population.

Representativeness means that the sample and the population have similar characteristics in the areas that pertain to the research.

Sampling Frame

The term population is often used to refer to the entire group of individuals, objects, or events that share a common characteristic of interest. It is the complete set of all those under consideration. However, in research we rarely deal with the entire population, but we often have a particular population of interest in mind. This could be, for example, L2 beginner-level learners or adult L2 learners with a particular first language in a university context, or the population of interest may be first-year undergraduate students.

A sampling frame is thus a list of the individuals from which a sample is drawn. The sampling frame serves as the basis for selecting the sample from the population. For example, if the population of interest is all the experienced ESL teachers in a university context, the sampling frame would be a list of those teachers in that university. If the population of interest is all the students in a university, the sampling frame could be a list of the students currently enrolled in that university. The accuracy and representativeness of the sampling frame are important to the validity of any quantitative analysis. If the sampling frame does not accurately represent the population, the sample drawn from it will also be biased and may not accurately reflect the characteristics of the population. Therefore, it is important to make sure that the sampling frame is as comprehensive and accurate as possible when selecting a sample for a statistical analysis.

A **sampling frame** is a list of the individuals from which a sample is drawn and serves as the basis for selecting the sample from the population.

Depending on the study, sometimes the sampling frame is big and sometimes it is smaller. For instance, in the above examples, if the research is to make a claim about adult EFL learners, the sampling frame is a large group. However, if we want to make a claim about Chinese adult EFL learners in a particular school district, then our sampling frame is smaller, as it would include only Chinese adult EFL learners in that district. If there are other characteristics that we want to examine in our study – such as the role of age, language proficiency, and so on – our target population becomes smaller, and we should select the participants from a population that has these characteristics. This would then allow us to examine these variables.

In selecting a sample for a study, it is essential to define both the target population and the sampling frame. The choice of participants depends on the research nature and the intended use of the findings. If the goal is to generalize from a sample of English as a Foreign Language (EFL) learners to the entire EFL learner population, the sample must be representative. However, if the focus is on studying a specific group's behavior and gaining insights into a phenomenon without intending to make a population-wide generalization, representativeness may be less important. Nonetheless, when aiming to draw conclusions from the sample to the population, careful and representative sample selection becomes imperative.

The fact that a sample comes from a population does not indicate that the sample is representative of the population. A sample can be either biased or representative. A biased sample is not representative and happens, for example, when some participants have a higher chance of being selected as the sample. This can happen when you select those who are easy to select or those who volunteer in a study. In a representative sample, all members of the target population have an equal chance of being selected.

In what follows, we will discuss different types of sampling methods, some of which enable you to select representative samples, in which case you can draw inferences from the sample to the population. Others allow you to select a sample, but the sample may not be representative, and therefore, you may make claims only about the sample and not about the larger population.

If we want to make inferences about the population based on our sample, we need to select our sample very carefully so that it can **represent** the population. In a representative sample, all members of the target population have an equal chance of being selected.

POINTS TO PONDER

How do you ensure that your sample is representative of the larger population? What are some of the sampling techniques that you will use?

Sampling and Sampling Types

Sampling refers to the process by which we select the participants from whom we collect our data. In research, most of the time it is not possible to select data from the population of interest, therefore, we collect data from a sample. As can be seen in Figure 8.1, in general, there are two main types of sampling techniques: probability sampling and nonprobability sampling.

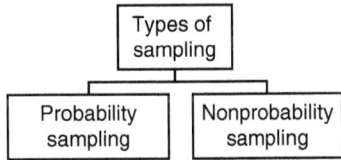

Figure 8.1 Types of sampling

Probability sampling is a kind of sampling in which each member of the population has an equal chance of being selected as participants. That is, each participant has the same probability of being selected and this selection is not affected by other extraneous factors, including the researcher's or the participants' preferences. What is sought in probability sampling is to have a sample that is representative of the population.

Probability sampling addresses the issue of sampling bias, which can occur if our sample is selected in ways that favor certain characteristics or groups of participants. Therefore, this method enables you to select a sample that is representative of the population. Since it allows you to obtain a representative sample, it is used mainly in quantitative research that aims for generalizability, which refers to drawing inferences from the sample to the larger population from which the sample has selected. Therefore, if your intention is to generalize from the sample to the population, this is the appropriate method to use.

Probability sampling is not used in qualitative research, whose aim is not to generalize in the same way as in quantitative research. However, it is important to note that although random sampling is an ideal form of sampling in research that aims to generalize, it is a sophisticated and time-consuming procedure, and hence may not always be possible to use.

Nonprobability sampling refers to the type of sampling in which you do not select the participants based on their probability of selection, because this probability is unknown. Therefore, participants do not have an equal chance of being selected. Nonprobability sampling can be used in both quantitative and qualitative research. However, because, the participants do not have an equal chance of being selected, the sample will not be representative of the population. Therefore, this kind of sampling cannot be used in research whose aim is to generalize, which might be the case in some quantitative studies. However, it can still allow testing theoretical claims, research hypotheses, or predictions based on a theory. It is also a method to use in small-scale studies or in the early stages of larger quantitative studies to get some idea about how things will work in a subsequent quantitative study. Nonprobability sampling is an appropriate method for qualitative research which is exploratory and whose aim is to gain a deeper understanding of the group under study.

In **probability sampling**, each member of the population has an equal chance to be selected as a participant. In **nonprobability sampling**, participants are not selected based on their probability of selection as this probability is unknown. Probability sampling is used in **quantitative research**. Nonprobability sampling is used in both **qualitative** and **quantitative** research.

Types of Probability Sampling

There are a number of probability sampling procedures that you can use. These are shown in Figure 8.2 and discussed briefly in this section (see Table 8.1 for a summary).

Simple Random Sampling

As noted earlier, to be able to generalize from the sample to the population, the sample should be representative of the population, and for that purpose, we need to

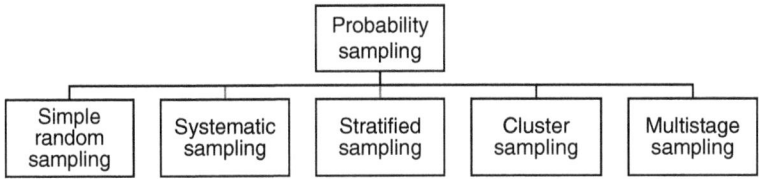

Figure 8.2 Probability sampling techniques

randomly select our participants. One type of probability sampling that helps promote representativeness is simple random sampling. This is a kind of sampling that allows each member of the population an equal probability or chance of being selected. The assumption behind random sampling is that through random sampling, any characteristic of the population relevant to the study will be similarly represented in the sample, particularly if the sample is large enough. When we use random sampling, we minimize other subjective influences and therefore can argue that our sample is representative of the population. This then allows us to generalize from the sample to the target population.

Drawing a random sample involves having or creating a list of all the members of the population of interest (which was called a sampling frame in the previous section) and then drawing the sample from that list. An easy way to do this, when the population is small enough, would be to write the names of those in the target population on a piece of paper and then put those names in a container, mix the names up, and then draw out each participant one at a time until we have the required number of participants for the study. We could also assign numbers to individuals and then, using random number tables, select the individuals randomly. Such tables of random number are handy and can be found in some books on statistics or research methods. These procedures can be feasible if the target population is not large. If we are dealing with a bigger population, we could use a computer to assign and generate random numbers. Currently, there are online sources that can be used to create a list of random numbers. One of these sources is Stat Trek (https://stattrek.com/statistics/random-number-gener ator) and another is Randomizer.org (https://randomizer.org). There is also a tutorial on the latter that helps you to use the program to generate random numbers (https://www.randomizer.org/tutorial).

The assumption behind **random sampling** is that through random sampling any characteristic of the population relevant to the study will be similarly represented in the sample, particularly if the sample is large enough.

Random sampling occurs in two ways: with replacement and without replacement. In sampling with replacement, each chosen population member is returned to the pool before the next selection. For example, if you need to select five participants from a pool of twenty, you randomly pick one participant, record the selection, return that participant to the pool, and then randomly select again. This process is repeated until all five participants are chosen. In sampling without replacement, once a participant is selected, that participant is not returned to the pool before the next selection. This gives each participant an equal chance of being chosen only once.

Generally, random sampling without replacement is preferred for its unbiased representation of the population. In contrast, sampling with replacement introduces the possibility of selecting the same member multiple times, potentially leading to bias and a less accurate portrayal of the population. However, in certain scenarios with small populations or repeated sampling, sampling with replacement might be considered.

While random participant selection is desirable for generalizability, it is not always feasible, due to the absence of a complete list of the target population. This poses a challenge for researchers aiming to generalize findings. However, in experimental research, especially when comparing groups, random assignment becomes important. Though random participant selection might be impractical, random assignment allows any observed differences between groups to be attributed to the treatment rather than preexisting differences among participants. While generalizations often assume random sampling, this is less problematic if the focus is on testing theories rather than population-wide generalization. However, random assignment "is an important assumption of several statistical procedures" (Evans & Rooney, 2008, p. 121; see Chapter 20).

In addition to simple random sampling, there are other types of probability sampling, such as systematic sampling, stratified sampling, cluster sampling, and multistage sampling.

Systematic Sampling

In systematic sampling, we first create a list of the target population members and then choose every nth participant in the target population until we have all the participants needed for the study.

EXAMPLE 8.1

For example, if you have a population of 200 immigrant students who you want to study, and you want to select 40 of them, you would prepare a list of the 200 individuals and then select every fifth student on the list. This type of sampling is easier than real random sampling and can provide a representative sample given that our population is rather uniform in the characteristics we intend to examine.

Stratified Sampling

In stratified sampling you would divide the target population into subgroups (or strata) based on similar characteristics that need to be studied and then select randomly within those subgroups. This strategy would allow subgroup generalizations. Stratified sampling is a useful technique when we are dealing with a population that is rather heterogenous. It is also useful when the subgroups make up a smaller or bigger percentage of the population. In this case, we would then need to stratify the population in such a way that each subgroup could be more homogenous with respect to a certain characteristic that we intended to examine.

EXAMPLE 8.2

Take for example, the above scenario in which you have a population of 200 immigrant students to examine, but at the same time you want to examine the role of a particular variable such as first language background. If you have enough learners from different language backgrounds, you first divide your population into subgroups based on their language backgrounds and then select randomly from each subgroup the number you need for your study.

In the above example, stratified random sampling would give each learner from each language background an equal chance to be selected, and this allows the required participants from each subgroup to be included in your sample. On the other hand, if you use simple random sampling, you may have fewer or more participants from one language background in one group compared to another.

In **stratified sampling**, you would divide the target population into subgroups (or strata) based on similar characteristics that need to be studied, and then select randomly within those subgroups.

In stratified sampling technique, there are two ways of selecting the number of participants. One is to select the number of participants irrespective of the size or the subgroup or stratum. This technique is called disproportionate stratified sampling. Another method is to consider the size of the subgroup and then select the number of participants in each subgroup in relation to the size or proportion of each subgroup or stratum in the total target population. This is called proportionate stratified sampling.

EXAMPLE 8.3

Suppose we need a sample of 30 students from a target population of 100. We have divided the 100 students into three subgroups. The first subgroup includes 10 Chinese students, the second subgroup includes 30 Japanese students, the third subgroup includes 60 Korean students. If we use the disproportionate stratified sample, we randomly select 10 students from each subgroup irrespective of the number of students in each of the population subgroups. However, if we use the proportionate stratified sampling, we first calculate the proportion of the stratum in relation to the population and then we include the same proportion in our sample. In the above scenario, the total number of Chinese students in the Chinese stratum is 0.1 of the total population. Therefore, the number of Chinese students in our sample should also be 0.1 of the sample which would be ($30 \times 0.1 = 3$). As for the Japanese students, the number of them in the Japanese stratum would be 0.3 of the population. Therefore, we should have the same proportion of Japanese students in our sample, which means 9 students ($30 \times 0.3 = 9$). As for Korean students the number of them in the Korean stratum is 0.6 of the population. Therefore, their number in the sample should be in proportion to the size of that stratum, which would be 18 ($30 \times 0.6 = 18$).

In **disproportionate stratified sampling**, participants are selected in each subgroup irrespective of the size of the subgroup. In **proportionate stratified sampling**, participants in each subgroup are selected in relation to the size or proportion of each subgroup in the total target population.

Cluster Sampling

Cluster sampling refers to a kind of sampling in which we randomly select larger subgroups (or clusters) within our target population and then study the members of those subgroups. We use this technique when we do not have access to all the population but can identify groups of them in certain places or geographical locations. Suppose we want to examine reading strategies among intermediate ESL learners in Canada. We may not have access to all the ESL learners in Canada, but we know that there are twenty schools in town that teach intermediate ESL classes. We first randomly select some of those schools (for example three) and then include either all the ESL students studying in those schools in our research or select randomly from the students in each of those selected schools, depending on the number of participants needed.

Cluster sampling refers to a kind of sampling in which we randomly select larger subgroups (or clusters) within our target population and then study the members of those subgroups.

Multistage Sampling

Multistage sampling involves selecting samples through a series of stages. For example, in the above example about cluster sampling, suppose the population of ESL learners is so large that they are distributed across a number of school districts,

Table 8.1 A summary of the main probability sampling types, their aims, and characteristics

Sampling type	Aim	Characteristics
Simple random sampling	To obtain a representative sample in a way that every member of the population has an equal chance of being selected	Each member of the population has an equal probability of being selected.
Stratified random sampling	To obtain a representative sample by dividing the population into similar subgroups (strata) and selecting randomly from each subgroup (or stratum)	The population is divided into strata based on relevant characteristics such as age or language proficiency, and participants are selected from each stratum using simple random sampling.
Systematic sampling	To obtain a representative sample by selecting every nth member of the population	Members of the population are listed in a random order, and every nth member is selected. The value of n is determined by dividing the population size by the desired sample size.
Cluster sampling	To obtain a representative sample by dividing the population into clusters and randomly selecting the entire clusters	The population is divided into clusters based on geographic locations, organizational structures, or other relevant characteristics. Clusters are randomly selected.
Multistage sampling	To have a representative sample by selecting the samples in several stages	The first stage involves selecting clusters of the population. The second stage is selecting smaller clusters. The third stage is selecting participants randomly from that third cluster.

each containing multiple schools and classes. In this case, we might begin by selecting several school districts at random (the first stage). Then, within those selected districts, we would randomly choose a few schools (the second stage). Finally, within those schools, we would randomly select the number of participants we need for our study (third stage).

Multistage sampling involves selecting samples through a series of stages.

Table 8.1 provides a summary of the main probability sampling types. It is important to note that all of the above probability sampling methods involve randomly selecting participants from the population. This helps to make the sample representative of the population.

Types of Nonprobability Sampling

It is not always feasible or easy to use probability sampling in applied linguistics or L2 research. In addition, although we would ideally like to have a sample that is representative of the population, achieving true representativeness may not be possible even when we use random sampling. Therefore, although nonprobability sampling is much less rigorous than probability sampling, due to the constraints that exist in most applied linguistics research, researchers use what is called non-probability sampling. We will discuss some commonly used types of nonprobability sampling used in quantitative research in the following section. As can be seen in Figure 8.3 and Table 8.2, these include purposive sampling, convenience sampling, snowball sampling, quota sampling, and expert sampling. (Other nonprobability sampling methods used in qualitative research are discussed in Chapter 13.)

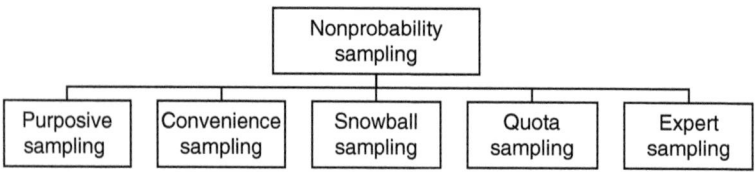

Figure 8.3 Nonprobability sampling techniques

Purposive Sampling

Purposive sampling is a kind of nonprobability sampling in which you choose a sample based on your knowledge of the participants and their specific characteristics that are relevant to the study. It is also known as judgmental or selective sampling because, as the researcher, you make a judgment to select participants who are suitable for the study. Since in this kind of sampling the selection is done based on some criteria, the sample's characteristics, while not being representative of the population, can be close to those of the population. However, one problem with this kind of sampling is that it is highly subjective and therefore very liable to researcher bias. In this kind of sampling, the more prior knowledge you have about the participants and the clearer the criteria for selection, the more effective the sample will be.

In the literature, another term used for purposive sampling is purposeful sampling; these terms are often used interchangeably. In general, both purposive and purposeful sampling refer to a type of nonprobability sampling method in which you select participants based on specific criteria relevant to the research question. However, some researchers may use the term purposive sampling to refer specifically to selecting participants based on predefined criteria, such as age, education level, or occupation, and purposeful sampling as a way of selecting participants based on the researcher's judgment and the research question rather than pre-defined criteria. In essence, both purposive and purposeful sampling mean that the participants are selected with a specific purpose in mind, but the criteria used to select participants may differ depending on the research approach and the context of the study.

Purposive sampling is a kind of nonprobability sampling in which you choose a sample based on your knowledge of the participants and their specific characteristics that are relevant to the study.

Convenience Sampling

Convenience sampling refers to a sampling procedure in which participants are selected based on availability or ease of access. These participants are selected because they are easily reachable due to factors such as time, location, or other circumstances that make them convenient to select.

Although convenience sampling is not a very rigorous method of selecting study samples, many research studies in applied linguistics use this kind of sampling approach in both qualitative and quantitative research, and the reason for this is that it is convenient to use participants who are available for the study. For example, a graduate student who in interested in examining the effect of explicit instruction on learning an L2 among beginner-level learners of English may go to an ESL school on campus to recruit their participants; this is because that student has access to that school and the participants are available.

Using convenience sampling is a common practice in most qualitative research in which there is no intention to generalize. It can also provide informative data in studies that examine a hypothesis or the effect of one variable on another. However, it is less suitable for research focused on understanding the characteristics of an entire population, as it may introduce sampling bias.

The terms "convenience sampling" and "purposive sampling" are sometimes used interchangeably, but they refer to different sampling methods. In purposive sampling the researcher makes a judgment about the characteristics of the sample and, as noted above, attempts to choose a sample that is as close as possible to the population even if it is not representative of the population. Convenience sampling, however, is simply based on availability.

Convenience sampling refers to a sampling procedure in which participants are selected based on availability or convenience.

Snowball Sampling

Snowball (or referral) sampling is when the recruitment of the participants happens through others or when a group of participants helps to identify other participants.

Since the sample becomes larger as participants introduce others, the sample gets larger and larger as the study progresses like a snowball that grows as it rolls through the snow. Also, since in this procedure the study sample is made through referrals among those who know others, this method of sampling is also called referral sampling.

For example, if you are interested in conducting a study with English language teachers, you might contact the directors of the schools to help you to identify or recruit participants. Or you might first select a few participants and then ask them to identity and introduce other participants. This is a useful procedure when the research cannot locate the participants or when a large sample is needed. However, since the participants are not drawn from an identified target population, the drawback is that it can lead to biases, as those who help with participant recruitment might suggest their friends or only people they know. Therefore, the sample selection is influenced by the choice of others. In this type of sampling, the identity of the participants might be hidden to the researcher, which, in one sense, can be useful when the data must be collected from anonymous participants.

Snowball (or referral) sampling is when the recruitment of the participants happens through others or when a group of participants helps to identify other participants.

Quota Sampling

Quota sampling is a nonprobability sampling method similar to stratified sampling used when the researcher selects participants based on certain characteristics or quota. However, the participants within each quota are often selected in a nonrandom manner, similar to convenience sampling or purposive sampling.

Quota sampling can be used in both qualitative and quantitative research. One difference between quota sampling and stratified sampling is that stratified sampling is a kind of probability sampling. Therefore, you use probability methods, such as random sampling, to select your sample from the subgroup, but in quota sampling such probability sampling methods are not used. Another difference is that in quota sampling, you decide on a quota or proportion for the sample subgroups. This can be either an equal or different proportion depending on the needs of the study. For example, if a study wants to examine the difference between three first language backgrounds (e.g., Chinese, Japanese, and Korean) and needs a certain proportion of participants to be from each background (for example 30% Chinese, 30% Japanese, and 40% Korean). You would first divide the target population into three subgroups (as in stratified sampling) and then recruit the required proportion or quota within each subgroup with no random selection.

Quota sampling is a nonprobability sampling method similar to stratified sampling used when the researcher selects participants based on certain characteristics or quota.

Expert Sampling

Expert sampling is a type of nonprobability sampling method in which you select participants who are experts or have certain skills or knowledge in a particular field or area of study. You may use your own judgment to select the participants or may consult other experts to identify individuals who have specialized knowledge or expertise relevant to the research question or objective. Expert sampling can be a useful technique when you are interested in gaining insight into or understanding of a particular phenomenon or detailed and knowledge-based perspectives on the topic of interest. However, since the sample is not randomly selected, it is not representative of the larger population.

Expert sampling is a type of nonprobability sampling method in which you select participants who are experts or have certain skills or knowledge in a particular field or area of study.

Table 8.2 provides a summary of the main probability sampling types. It is important to note that nonprobability sampling methods do not involve random selection and therefore have the limitation of not being appropriate for studies that intend to generalize from the sample to the population. Therefore, when using these techniques, you should carefully consider the purpose of the study, including the research question and study design.

Table 8.2 A summary of the main nonprobability sampling types, their aims, and characteristics

Sampling type	Aim	Characteristics
Purposive sampling	To select participants based on specific criteria or characteristics relevant to the research	Useful for studying participants with certain characteristics, but it can be subject to researcher selective bias
Convenience sampling	To select participants who are available	Easy to find participants, but they may not be representative of the population
Quota sampling	To select participants based on predetermined quotas for certain characteristics	Does not involve random selection, so it may be subject to researcher selection bias
Snowball sampling	To select participants based on referrals from other participants	Useful when it is hard to find participants, but can be subject to selection bias and may not be representative of the population
Expert sampling	To select participants who are considered to have specialized knowledge or be experts in a particular area	Useful for collecting information from knowledgeable participants, but the sample may not be representative of the population

POINTS TO PONDER

How do you determine the appropriate sample size for your study? What factors influence the size of the sample you need?

The Size of the Sample

A question that is asked by many students or novice researchers when they are selecting research participants is how many participants they need for their study or how big their sample should be. The answer to this question depends on the type and purpose of the study. It also depends on the level of precision required in the findings. In the above section, we discussed two major types of sampling: probability and nonprobability. When you are making a decision about a sampling method, you should also ensure that the sampling technique is consistent with the type of methodology used. A quantitative research design, rather than a qualitative one, is used when you are interested in making generalizations from the sample to the population. Therefore, although there are cases where quantitative researchers use nonprobability sampling, probability sampling should be used when generalizability is the goal. Qualitative research, on the other hand makes use of nonprobability sampling. The reason for this is that in probability sampling, the goal is to have a sample that is representative of the population. This, however, is not the goal of qualitative research. As noted earlier, in qualitative research, the aim is to further our understanding of the phenomenon under investigation; therefore, the sampling strategies used should enable the researcher to do so. The issue of sample size becomes important in quantitative research if you intend to determine cause and effect, find relationships among variables, test hypotheses, or generalize from the sample to the population. In the following section we will discuss how to determine sample size in quantitative research.

The issue of **sample size** becomes important in quantitative research if you intend to determine cause and effect, find relationships among variables, test hypotheses, or generalize from the sample to the population.

The Required Sample Size in Quantitative Research

In quantitative research, when the intention is to have a sample representative of the population, the general rule is that the larger the sample size, the better. The reason for this is that the larger the sample, the more representative it can be of the population. In statistical terms, the larger the sample, the closer its statistics value will be to the population value. In other words, the results we get from our sample will be closer to what we get in the population. The smaller the sample size, the less close the sample will be to the population, and therefore the sample estimate will be more different from the population estimate. The difference between the sample statistics and the population statistics is called sampling error, which becomes greater as the sample becomes less representative of the population.

However, the size of our sample also depends on other considerations. One consideration is the type of statistical analysis used. From a statistical point of view, depending on the type of analysis, we need to have enough participants to have statistically significant results. If the sample size is too small, chances are that we may not get a statistical significance even if that exists. This is what is called a Type II error in statistics. A Type II error differs from a Type I error, which involves rejecting a true null hypothesis.

Scholars have suggested some sample sizes for different types of studies, which although not precise could be considered as good suggestion. For example, Creswell (2012, p. 146) suggested the following for conducting educational research:

- Approximately 15 participants in each group in an experiment
- Approximately 30 participants for a correlational study that relates variables
- Approximately 350 individuals for a survey study, but this size will vary depending on several factors.

For L2 studies, Dörnyei (2007) pointed out that the literature usually suggests a sample size of between 1 percent and 10 percent of the population for survey research. To have a normal distribution, as required by some statistical tests, a sample size of at least 30 is suggested by some researchers (e.g., Hatch & Lazaraton, 1991). Dörnyei also suggested about 50 participants in correlational analysis in applied linguistics, and with some statistical analysis, such as factor analysis or structural equation modeling, that we need more – sometimes a minimum of 100.

However, it is important to note that these numbers are rough and are not precise. If we need a more precise number, we need to systematically compute the sample size required. To this end, there are formulas we can use that calculate the sample size based on a number of criteria, including the precision we want to have in our findings, the confidence in the data produced, and the error that can be tolerated in rejecting our null hypothesis. One statistical technique is power analysis. Power analysis is used in hypothesis-testing studies to determine the sample size needed to detect a statistically significant effect given a specific level of power. In the following section, we will briefly discuss the notion of power and power analysis, what it means, and how it works for determining sample size.

Power analysis is a statistical technique used in hypothesis-testing studies to determine the sample size needed to detect a statistically significant effect given a specific level of power.

Sample Size, Power, and Power Analysis

The Importance of Sample Size

Many quantitative applied linguistics studies involve hypothesis testing, and to this end they use inferential statistics. Inferential statistics is a kind of statistical analysis that is used to draw inferences from the sample to the population. It involves testing what is called a null hypothesis, which expresses the notion that there is no effect of a variable on another one in the population or no correlation exists between two variables. Researchers often hope to reject the null hypothesis. In statistical analysis, the ability to reject the null hypothesis depends on various factors, and one important factor is the sample size. The larger the sample size, the greater the possibility of rejecting the null hypothesis as a larger sample size generally provides more information about the population and reduces the impact of random variation or chance on the results.

In statistical analysis, the ability to reject the null hypothesis depends on various factors, and **one important factor** is the **sample size**.

When rejecting the null hypothesis, two errors might take place. First, it is possible that the null hypothesis is actually true but is falsely rejected. For example, we may wrongly reject the hypothesis that there is no effect of X on Y and then claim that there is an effect whereas there is actually no effect. As noted above, this is called a Type I error. The probability of making a Type I error is indicated by the level of significance, or the p value. Researchers commonly set the significance level at 0.05, meaning that if the p value is less than or equal to 0.05, the null hypothesis is rejected in favor of the research hypothesis. The p value or significance level refers to the probability of wrongly rejecting a true null hypothesis, which is known as a Type I error. If you increase the significance level from, for example, 0.05 to 0.001 to decrease the chance of making a Type I error, you would increase the likelihood of making a Type II error. A Type II error occurs when a false null hypothesis is not rejected. For example, you may wrongly accept the null hypothesis that there is no effect of X on Y and then wrongly claim that there is no effect whereas actually there is an effect (see Chapter 19 for a discussion of Type I and Type II errors).

When the sample size is small, there is a higher likelihood of making a Type II error. This means that even if there is a true difference or relationship in the population, the number of participants or the observed data may not be sufficient to detect it. As the sample size increases, even minimal effects can become statistically significant. The probability of making Type I and Type II errors is inversely related. Therefore, in research we should try to find a balance between the two by having enough participants, but not too many, to generate meaningful results.

When the sample size is **small**, there is a higher likelihood of making a **Type II error**. If the sample size is **very large**, even small effects may become statistically significant.

Statistical Power and Power Analysis

Statistical power refers to the ability of the study to reject the null hypothesis truly. In other words, it refers to the ability of a test to detect a true effect or relationship when it exists. Power analysis is a statistical technique used to determine the likelihood that a study will detect an effect of a certain size (if it exists) in a given dataset. It is an essential step in research planning, particularly when designing experiments or studies that involve hypothesis testing.

As the sample size increases, the statistical power of a statistical test improves. Power analysis helps determine the appropriate sample size needed for a desired level of statistical power. It enables a balance between having a sample size large enough to detect an effect and avoiding both excessively small and excessively large samples. Therefore, when we do our research, we always want our statistical test to have enough power to minimize the likelihood of making an error in our evaluation of the null hypothesis. A high-power study is more likely to be able to reject a null hypothesis correctly than a low-power study. In other words, when the statistical power is high, the chance of a Type II error is low; that is, the probability of incorrectly accepting a false null hypothesis is low, and the chances of detecting an effect when the effect actually exists are high.

Statistical power refers to the ability of the study to reject the null hypothesis truly. In other words, it refers to the ability of a test to detect a true effect or relationship when it exists. As the sample size increases, the statistical power of the test improves.

The power of a statistical test depends on the sample size as sample size is an important factor in reducing the variability in our sample. The larger the sample, the closer the sample to the population, and therefore the smaller the variance within the sampling distribution. Since the power of a test depends on the sample size, conducting a power analysis before doing our study can help to decide on the number of participants needed to achieve the desired level of power.

Power analysis helps determine the appropriate sample size needed for a desired level of statistical power. It enables a balance between having a sample size large enough to detect an effect and avoiding both excessively small and excessively large samples.

How to Do Power Analysis to Determine Sample Size

In the past, power analysis was determined by using tables that were published in statistical books. Cohen (1988), for example, provided several tables organized around finding sample size given the desired power, effect size, and significance level. The main aims of these tables were to determine the power of a statistical test after the study was conducted. However, the tables could also be used to plan experiments by changing the sample size or other values. These days, however, there are different computer programs that can be used to do power analysis. These include commercial software such as PASS (sample size and power) which provides sample size analysis for many statistical tests (https://www.ncss.com/software/pass/). There is also currently a free computer program called G*Power that can be used to conduct statistical power analyses for many different statistical tests, such as *t*-tests, ANOVA, and the chi-square test. This program can also calculate effect sizes if we have the other parameters mentioned before, such as sample size, significance level, the kind of test and its power. It also produces graphs showing the result of the power analysis. G*Power is available for free download at the following website: https://bit.ly/4cJeRJc.

To use G*Power for determining sample size, we need to know the type of statistical test used as well as the following three pieces of information:

- **Effect size:** This is the magnitude of the effect we wish to detect in our analysis.
- **Statistical power:** This is the probability of detecting an effect when it actually exists.
- **Significance level or alpha (α):** This is a predetermined threshold used to determine the statistical significance of a statistical test. It shows the maximum acceptable probability of rejecting the null hypothesis when it is actually true. Significance level is different from power. While power shows the probability of avoiding a Type II error, significance level shows the probability of committing a Type I error. In research, we usually set the significance level at 0.05, showing the likelihood of erroneously rejecting a true null hypothesis.

G*Power is a computer program that can be used to conduct statistical power analyses for many different statistical tests, such as *t*-tests, ANOVA, and the chi-square test.

Power analysis helps determine various study elements based on available information. For instance, if we know the effect size, sample size, and significance level, we can estimate the power of our study. Similarly, knowing the kind of statistical test, the effect size to be detected, significance level, and the desired power allows us to estimate the required number of participants.

Effect Size

One piece of information needed for doing power analysis in G*Power is the effect size. Effect sizes provide important information in addition to the significance level, or the *p* value, and are often reported in research results. Effect size refers to the magnitude of an effect or the strength of the association between two variables in the population. Determining the effect size we expect to detect is an important consideration when it comes to power analysis. We will discuss the notion of effect size, how it is calculated, and what it means in detail in Chapter 23. However, it will be useful to briefly explain it here for our purpose of power analysis.

In applied linguistics studies that compare group performance, effect size refers to the size of the difference between the groups. Statistically, this is calculated by computing the difference between the groups while taking account of variability in the data. Cohen's *d* is often used to measure the effect size in a study with two groups. Cohen's *d* is a standardized measure of the difference between two means coming from the two groups. In a study with an experimental group and a control group, Cohen's *d* is calculated by subtracting the mean of the control group from the mean of the experimental group. The result is then divided by the pooled standard deviation, which is a weighted average of the standard deviations of both groups. This provides a standardized measure of the difference, enabling comparisons of effect sizes across studies with different units of measurement (see Chapter 23).

As an example, let's assume that we are interested in comparing an experimental group that receives instruction and a control group that does not. Suppose that after the intervention the experimental group has a mean of 55 on a posttest, the control group has a mean of 35, and the standard deviation of both groups is 15. The Cohen's *d* effect size would be $[55-35]/15 = 1.33$. A Cohen's *d* of 1.33 indicates that the difference between the means of the two groups is 1.33 times the pooled standard deviation. This is conceptually similar to a *z* score in a normal distribution, where a *z* score indicates how many standard deviations a score is from the mean. In this case, a Cohen's *d* of 1.33 suggests that the mean score of the experimental group is 1.33 pooled standard deviations larger than the mean score of the control group.

Determining the effect size we expect to detect in our research is an important consideration when it comes to power analysis.

Effect size is often interpreted as small, medium, or large depending on the type of effect size measure being used. For example, according to Cohen's guidelines for Cohen's *d*, a small effect size is 0.2, a medium effect size is 0.5, and a large effect size is 0.8 (Cohen, 1988). An effect size of 1.33, calculated using Cohen's *d* above indicates a very large effect size, suggesting that the difference between the two groups is substantial, as it exceeds the threshold for a large effect size (0.8), based on Cohen's guidelines.

We are always able to calculate an effect size after we conduct a study based on the data. However, in power analysis, we must define the magnitude of the effect we wish to detect beforehand to determine the sample size needed for the study. Several approaches can be used to estimate this effect size. One method involves reviewing the existing literature or an analysis of a group of studies addressing similar questions (such as a meta-analysis) to determine the effect sizes found. Another approach is conducting a pilot study, which can then provide insight into the potential effect size of the variable under investigation. The third approach would be to make an educated guess.

One method to determine the effect size when using G*Power for sample size involves reviewing the **existing literature** or a group of studies addressing similar questions (such as a meta-analysis) to determine the effect sizes found. Another approach is conducting **a pilot study**, which can then provide insight into the potential effect size of the variable under investigation.

Statistical Power

When using G*Power for determining sample size, another piece of information we need is the desired power that we would like to have in our statistical test. Power is typically denoted as $1 - \beta$, where β is the probability of committing a Type II error. To find the Type II error rate (β), we subtract the power from 1. So, if the power is 0.80, then the probability of committing Type II error is 0.20 ($\beta = 1 - 0.80 = 0.20$). How much power we need in a study depends on a number of factors, including not only the aim of the research but also other practical constraints.

For example, if you are conducting a study in which committing a Type II error would be costly, it is advisable to go for a high power such as 90 percent or 95 percent. This would then mean the chances of making a Type II error would be much less. But the drawback of this is that we need a large sample size. However, if you are conducting a study where the consequences of failing to detect an effect are less critical, you might choose to accept a lower power. So, the decision of the desired effect size should be made based on the trade-off between the cost and effort of obtaining a larger sample size and the importance of avoiding a Type II error.

Having said that, for most studies in the field of psychology and social sciences, scholars suggest a minimum statistical power of 80 percent, and this can also be applicable to most applied linguistics and L2 research studies. As noted before, this suggests that there is a 20 percent chance of committing a Type II error, or failing to detect the effect if it exists. This degree of power (i.e., 80 percent) may seem low on the surface as it suggests that we still accept a 20 percent chance of committing a Type II error. But as just mentioned, to gain more power, we need to increase our sample size. For example, to increase our power from 80 percent to 90 percent, in some cases, we need an increase in our sample size by about one third. Thus, if we need 72 participants to have a power of 80 percent for a t-test, we may need to have around 96 participants to have a power of 90 percent. However, it is important to note that the relationship between power and sample size is not linear, and the exact sample size increase depends on the specifics of the statistical test, the effect size, and the desired power level. Given these considerations and the practical constraints of recruiting a large sample, a power of 80 percent seems to be a reasonable compromise between power and sample size.

For most studies in the field of psychology and social sciences, scholars suggest a minimum **statistical power of 80 percent**, and this can also be applicable to most applied linguistics and L2 research studies. This suggests that there is a **20 percent chance of committing a Type II error**, or failing to detect the effect if it exists.

Significance Level

In order to determine the adequate sample size through power analysis, in addition to knowing the level of power we expect, we also need another piece of information, which is the significance level. The significance level indicates the probability of rejecting the null hypothesis when it is true. More specifically, it assesses the probability of Type I error; that is, the probability of incorrectly rejecting a true null hypothesis. Power assesses the probability of Type II error, which occurs when the research fails to reject a false null hypothesis. As we said, there are common criteria for power (80% or sometimes 90%). For significance level, there is also a common standard which is 0.05. So, when doing power analysis using G*Power, we can choose a significance level of 0.05, which is the common norm.

The significance level indicates the probability of incorrectly rejecting the null hypothesis when it is true. A widely used standard for this level is 0.05. Hence, when doing power analysis using G*Power, it is typical to use a significance level of 0.05, which is the common norm.

Running Power Analysis: An Example

Now let's give an example of how to run power analysis using G*Power for determining sample sizes.

EXAMPLE 8.4

Suppose you are interested in examining the role of language proficiency in the effectiveness of recast. You might hypothesize that higher language proficiency leads to greater learning from recasts among EFL students. To test this, you plan to recruit two groups – one with low language proficiency and another with higher proficiency – to compare the effects of recasts. Before proceeding, it is essential to determine the required number of learners in each group for a robust hypothesis testing procedure. To do so, we can use the G*Power program.

Figure 8.4 shows what the G*Power program will look like once you download it.

To run the analysis, first you need to choose the kind of statistical test that you want to use under "Test family." For the example we provided above, the statistical test will be a *t*-test since we are comparing two independent groups. Similarly, for the type of *t*-test under "Statistical test," we will choose "Means: Difference between two independent means (two groups)." We will then need to choose the type of power analysis. The statistical power of a study can be determined both before the study and after the study. When it is conducted before the study it is called an "a priori power analysis," and when it is conducted after the study it is called a "post hoc power analysis." To determine the sample size for a given study, we use an a priori power analysis since we are conducting it before we collect our data. So, for our purposes, we will choose "A priori: Compute required sample size – given α, power, and effect size."

We need to decide whether our test is a two-tailed test or a one-tailed test. This depends on the kind of hypothesis we have for the study. If we are simply hypothesizing that there will be a difference between the two groups without knowing the direction of the difference, we will choose a two-tailed test. However, if we know from the literature that one of the groups may perform better than the other group, then we can choose a one-tailed test (see Chapter 19 for a discussion of one-tailed vs. two-tailed tests). In applied linguistics research, the type of test we use is often a two-tailed test because we often hypothesize that a difference might exist in general without specifying the direction. So, we will choose a two-tailed test for our example too.

We will then go to the input parameters and enter the values required. First, the window asks for the *effect size*. If we hover our cursor over the box, it gives us Cohen's conversion for small ($d = 0.20$), medium ($d = 0.50$) and large effect sizes ($d = 0.80$). In order to decide the effect size, as noted earlier, we can make some educated guesses based on the literature. Again, if previous literature suggests a large effect size, we can choose a large one, but most often we may not exactly know what effect size to expect, in which case we can choose a medium effect size. For our example, we can define a large effect size of 0.80, assuming that past research indicates a large effect for language proficiency.

For the alpha (α) or the significance level, we set it at the conventional level of 0.05 which is also a program default.

We will then need the power. As explained before, we often expect a power of 0.80. The default is 0.95, but we can change it to 0.80.

Then we need to decide on the allocation ratio. In G*Power, the allocation ratio refers to the proportion of participants allocated to different groups. An allocation ratio of 1 means equal sample sizes for each group, while an allocation ratio of 2 means one group will have twice as many participants as the other. For example, if you have 10 participants in one group, the other group will have 20 participants. For our purpose, we will keep the allocation ratio at 1 (the default value).

That is all we need. We will then hit the "calculate" button, and the program will generate the number of participants we need, given the parameters we entered. For

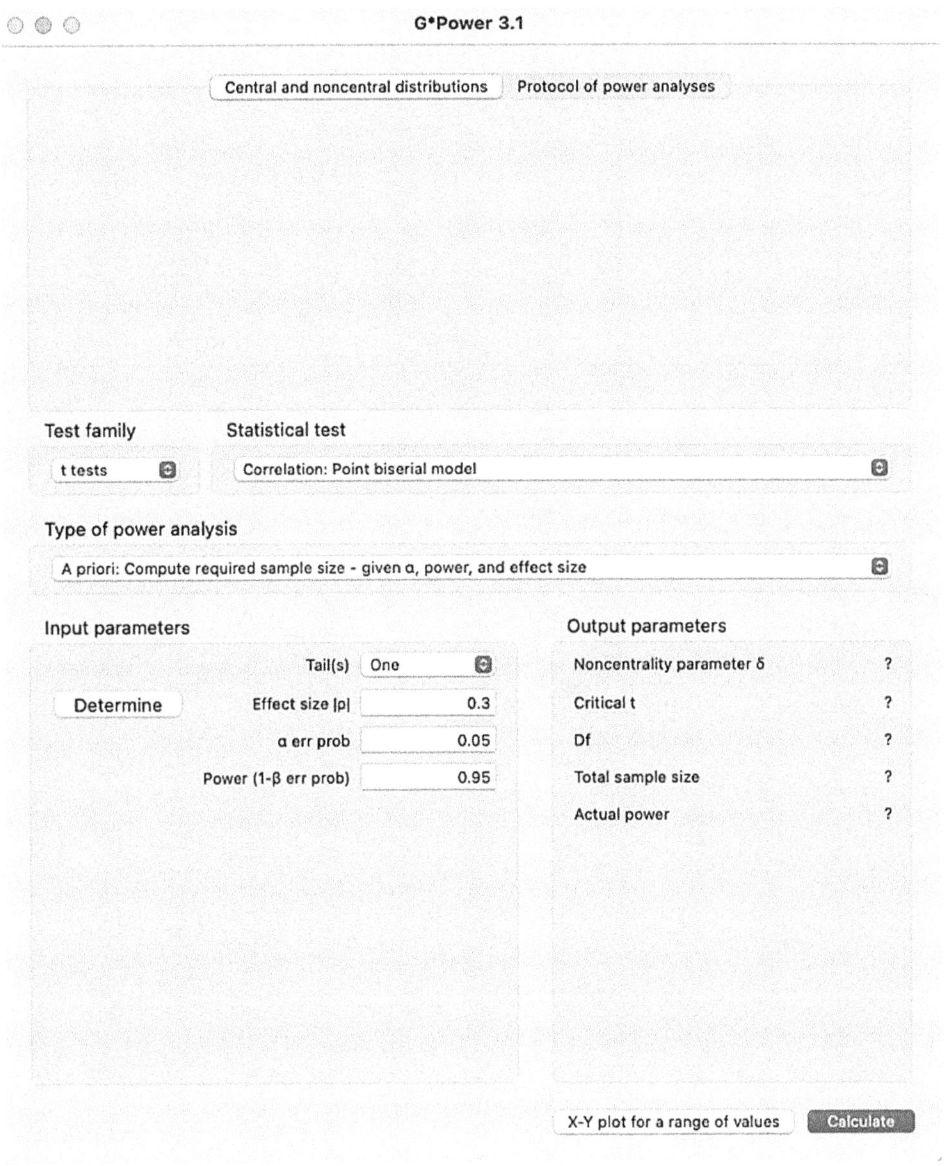

Figure 8.4 G*Power main window

this example, it gives us a total sample size of 52, with 26 participants per group (see Figure 8.5).

Please note that the larger the effect size we anticipate from the literature, the smaller the sample size we need to test our hypothesis. This is because a larger effect size means the effect is more pronounced and easier to detect. In other words, if the effect size of an intervention is large, an effect can be detected in smaller sample sizes. However, if the effect size is small, there is a need for a larger sample size to detect it.

In this example, we calculated the number of participants for an independent *t*-test; we can use the same procedure for calculating the number of participants for other statistical tests, such as ANOVA, correlation, regression, and so on.

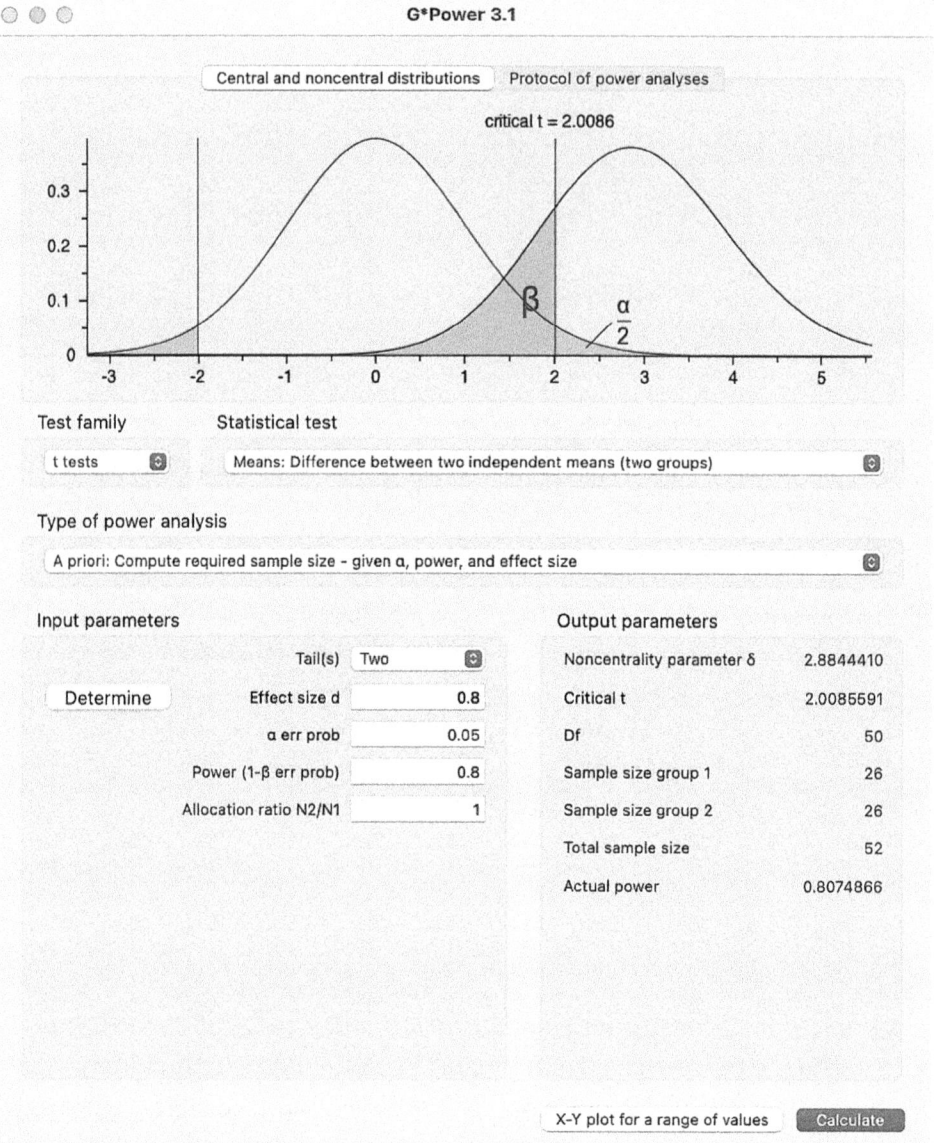

Figure 8.5 G*Power test selection window

Conclusion

In this chapter, we discussed the issues of sampling and sampling procedures in quantitative research. Sampling is an important component of any research that involves selecting a subset of individuals or entities from a larger population to study. As discussed, there are different types of sampling strategies, including probability and nonprobability sampling, each with their own characteristics, aims, advantages, and disadvantages. Selecting an appropriate sampling method depends on the research question, the characteristics of the population, and the availability of the resources. For our sample to be representative of the population, it is important to use an appropriate sampling procedure and also to make sure that the sample that is selected is sufficient. If the aim is to generalize, we need to make sure that the sample is representative of the population. Randomization is an important method used to increase the representativeness of the sample. In the next chapter, we will discuss issues related to sampling in qualitative research.

DISCUSSION AND ACTIVITY QUESTIONS

Discussion Questions

1. What is the difference between probability and nonprobability sampling techniques? When might you use each of them?
2. Can you provide an example of a study where randomization was used to select the sample? What impact did this have on the study results?
3. Discuss the advantages and disadvantages of using random sampling compared to convenience sampling in quantitative research. In what situations might convenience sampling still be appropriate?
4. How can you balance the need for a large sample with the practical constraints of time, cost, and resources in your research study?
5. Give an example of a situation where stratified sampling is appropriate. How will you determine that the sample includes an appropriate representation of different subgroups within the population?
6. What are some potential challenges for conducting random sampling in quantitative research? How might you address these challenges in your own research?
7. How might you use the knowledge gained from this chapter to design a study with an appropriate and adequate sample? What sampling procedures would you use, and why?

Activity Questions

1. Imagine you are conducting a study on the effectiveness of an instructional intervention in the classroom. What sampling technique would you use and why? How would you determine that your sample is representative of the population?
2. Identify a study that used stratified sampling. What was the research question? How did the researchers use stratified sampling to make the sample appropriate and also representative of different subgroups within the population?
3. Choose a study that used a particular kind of nonprobability sampling technique. What were the strengths and limitations of the technique used, and why were these considered strengths or limitations in the context of the study? How might you have used a different sampling technique to address the same question?
4. In groups, design a sampling procedure for a research study on a topic of your choice. What sampling technique would you use, and why? What challenges

might you face in selecting a representative sample, and how would you address these challenges?

5. In pairs, analyze and interpret data from a sample used in a study. What are the limitations of generalizing the results to the larger population? What biases might have influenced the sample, and how could you have minimized these biases?

6. Choose a research question in applied linguistics and identify the relevant statistical test to analyze your data. Use G*Power to determine the appropriate sample size for your study with the desired level of statistical power and effect size. What was the result of your power analysis?

7. Identify a study that has issues with sampling and sample size. What steps could the researchers have taken to minimize the issues, and how might the study results have been different if the researcher had used a different sampling procedure or a different sample size?

9 | Designing Quantitative Research: Types and Techniques

CHAPTER OBJECTIVES

After completing this chapter, you should be able to

- Understand and distinguish between different types of quantitative research designs in applied linguistics.
- Explore various subtypes of each research design and identify their key characteristics.
- Understand the limitations and advantages of different types of quantitative research designs.
- Critically evaluate different quantitative research designs used in applied linguistics research.
- Apply different quantitative research designs.

Introduction

In the previous chapter, we discussed issues surrounding selecting participants and the various sampling methods used in quantitative research. In this chapter, we focus on quantitative research design. Quantitative research design plays an important role in applied linguistics, as it allows researchers to gather data and analyze it in a systematic and rigorous manner. By using quantitative research designs, researchers can measure variables and the relationships between them, test hypotheses, and make predictions. This chapter will explore different types of quantitative research designs commonly used in applied linguistics, including experimental, quasi-experimental, correlational, and survey research designs. Understanding the different types of quantitative research design is essential for being able to choose the most appropriate research design for our research question. We will also discuss the characteristics of each design and explore their advantages and limitations.

Types of Quantitative Research Designs

When conducting quantitative research, one of the key decisions is what type of research design should be used. As shown in Figure 9.1, in general, quantitative research designs can be classified into the two broad categories:

- experimental
- nonexperimental.

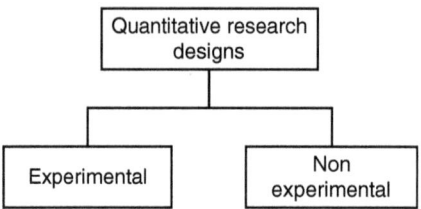

Figure 9.1 Types of quantitative research designs

Experimental designs are research designs in which the researcher manipulates one or more independent variables to determine the effects on a dependent variable. Nonexperimental quantitative research designs are those that do not manipulate a variable to determine its effect. Instead, they observe and describe relationships among variables as they exist. They typically involve collecting data from existing sources or observing a phenomenon as it naturally occurs. They also do not involve random assignments. Therefore, they do not examine cause-and-effect relationships, or if they do, the evidence is not very strong or at least not as strong as that in experimental research that involves random assignments. Understanding the differences between these two types of research designs and their subtypes is essential in choosing the appropriate design to address research questions in applied linguistics.

Quantitative research designs can be classified into the two broad categories: experimental and nonexperimental designs.

Experimental Research Design

Experimental research is a very commonly used research design in the field of applied linguistics. An experimental research design is one in which the researcher is interested in examining the effect of one or more independent variables on dependent variables. It is deductive and theory-driven in nature and often attempts to test a hypothesis. The design is explanatory rather than exploratory in terms of aim. That is, it attempts to explain relationships (which may often entail causality) rather than describing or exploring relationships (which is often the aim of non-experimental research). It is quantitative in nature, involving collecting quantitative numerical data and conducting statistical analysis to analyze the data. They are interventional; that is, they concern measuring the effects of an experimental intervention or treatment on the performance of the participants.

An **experimental research design** is one in which the researcher is interested in examining the effect of one or more independent variables on dependent variables.

In experimental research design, answers are sought through the following sequence: first, questions are posed, and then predictions are made about the possible outcome; data are then collected to test the prediction. Predictions, technically called hypotheses, are tentative statements that describe the relationship between variables. Hypotheses are often grounded in previous research within a specific area or in a particular theory, which is a well-established body of knowledge in the field that attempts to explain a phenomenon. Theories give rise to hypotheses, which can be tested in light of empirical evidence. This process can refine the theory or generate new questions.

The experimental research design is commonly employed in applied linguistics to study the impact of various interventions on learning outcomes. Example 9.1 presents a hypothetical scenario.

EXAMPLE 9.1

Suppose you are conducting a study that aims to explore the impact of two language revitalization strategies (community-based immersion programs and digital language learning platforms) on the fluency of ninety speakers of an endangered language. Participants with similar initial proficiency levels will be randomly assigned to Group A (community-based immersion program), Group B (digital language learning platform), or Group C (no intervention).

The study includes pretests to assess initial fluency and posttests to measure potential improvements after the intervention. Participants will undergo a series of assessments designed to measure their spoken and written proficiency in the endangered language, including conversational skills, comprehension, and vocabulary use, both before and after the intervention.

By comparing the performance of the three groups, the study aims to determine which strategy is more effective in enhancing and maintaining the fluency of speakers in the endangered language, contributing to efforts in language maintenance and revitalization.

Characteristics of Experimental Research Designs

Experimental research designs have a number of key characteristics, some of which apply more strongly to certain types of experimental designs, such as true experimental designs. Some of the main characteristics include:

- **Control:** Experimental research takes place in a controlled environment, managing extraneous variables to isolate and examine the effects of the independent variable, and attributing observed changes in the dependent variable to the independent variable.
- **Manipulation of variables:** This involves intentionally varying the levels of the independent variable to examine its effect on another variable, enabling comparisons or causal inferences.
- **Random assignment:** In true experimental research, participants are randomly assigned to different groups (e.g., experimental and control), ensuring that any differences between groups are due to the treatment rather than other factors.
- **Replicability:** Another characteristic of experimental research design is replicability. That is, the experiment is designed in such a way that it can be replicated by other researchers to test or confirm the validity of the results.
- **Hypothesis testing:** Experimental studies aim to test specific hypotheses or predictions about the relationship between dependent and independent variables.
- **Quantitative data:** Experimental research employs quantitative data collection tools, generating numerical data.
- **Use of statistical analysis:** To analysis the data, experimental research uses statistical methods to describe the relationship among variables or to determine the significant effect of the independent variable on the dependent variable.
- **Cause-and-effect relationships:** The primary goal of experimental research is to establish cause-and-effect relationships among variables.
- **Explanatory:** Experimental research is considered as explanatory research as the aim is to explain the causal relations among variables rather than simply describing relationships.

Types of Experimental Research Designs

There are three main types of experimental research designs (Figure 9.2):

- preexperimental design
- quasi-experimental design
- true experimental design.

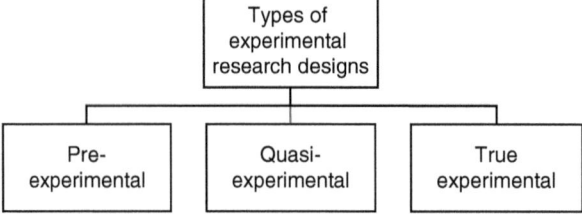

Figure 9.2 Types of experimental research designs

Preexperimental Designs

Preexperimental research designs are the most basic and weakest forms of research design. This type of design may include only one treatment group and no control group; in cases where there are control groups, there are no pretests and participants are not randomly assigned to groups. It typically involves a group of participants who have received treatment. The lack of a control group is a big limitation in such a design because it means that it is not possible to determine if any effects shown for the treatment are actually because of the treatment. Therefore, such designs are considered to be the least rigorous of the experimental designs and are prone to have higher chances of bias.

However, such designs are easy to use, and therefore they can be used for generating preliminary findings, testing procedures in pilot studies, or conducting exploratory research where the goal is not to establish causality.

Preexperimental research designs may include only one treatment group and no control group; in cases where there are control groups, there are no pretests and no random assignments.

Types of Preexperimental Research Designs There are several types of preexperimental research designs (Figure 9.3). These include

- one-shot case study (one group)
- one-group pre- and posttest design
- static-group comparison design.

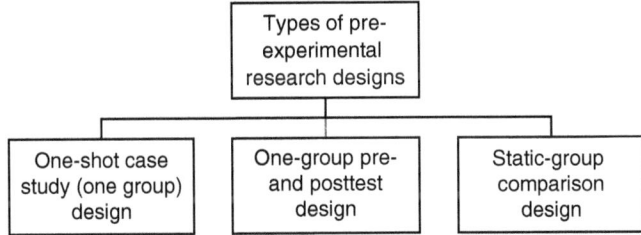

Figure 9.3 Types of preexperimental research designs

One-Shot Case Study The one-shot case study, also known as one-group posttest study, is a research design that involves a single treatment group and one posttest. It does not include a control group, and it does not involve random assignment of participants to the group. Although it includes a posttest, the posttest does not need to be a formal test. It can take various forms such as a questionnaire, interview, or checklist, used to observe or evaluate the participants' performance following the treatment. Figure 9.4 shows a schematic representation of this design.

Figure 9.4 A one-shot case study

For the sake of simplicity, the following notation is used in this representation and the others throughout the chapter:

$X_{Treatment}$ = Treatment group
$X_{Control}$ = Control group
0 = Observation or measurement

One-shot case study, also known as one-group posttest study, involves a single treatment group and one posttest, with no control group or random assignment of participants to the group.

Example 9.2 presents a hypothetical study.

EXAMPLE 9.2

Suppose you are conducting a study to investigate the impact of using a language learning app on the acquisition of collocations among thirty intermediate-level English learners. The research question is whether the use of the app influences learners' ability to use collocations correctly in spontaneous speech and writing. The study employs the app as the instructional tool, providing interactive exercises and feedback on colloca-tion usage. Using a one-group posttest design, the participants engage with the app for a set period, followed by a posttest measuring their ability to use collocations accur-ately and fluently in spoken tasks. By analyzing the results, the study aims to determine the effectiveness of the language learning app in enhancing learners' collocation knowledge.

There are important limitations of the above design which can make the results not very dependable. Since the study does not have a control or a comparison group, it is difficult to conclude that any effect shown is because of the treatment. For that same reason, it is difficult to establish a causal relationship between the independent and dependent variables. Because the study does not involve any pretesting, it is challenging to determine if any effects shown are due to the treatment or due to the initial knowledge of the participants.

The limitations of a one-group posttest study include the **lack of a control group**, **pretest**, and **random** participant assignments, making it difficult to **establish causality** or account for potential confounding variables.

Having said that, this design may be used to provide a preliminary examination of a research question. It could also be used as a pilot design to test the feasibility of a study and the procedures.

One-Group Pretest–Posttest Design This design includes a pretest, a treatment or intervention applied to a single group, and a posttest. Figure 9.5 provides a schematic representation of this design.

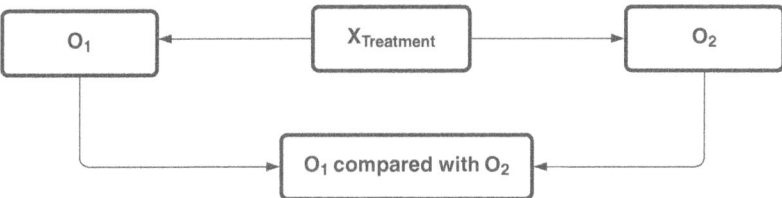

Figure 9.5 A one-group pretest–posttest design

Example 9.3 presents a hypothetical study.

EXAMPLE 9.3

Suppose you are conducting a study to assess the impact of a two-week extensive reading program on intermediate ESL vocabulary knowledge. Thirty volunteer participants from a specific language course will receive a pretest to measure their initial vocabulary proficiency. Subsequently, they will participate in the extensive reading program, engaging in regular reading sessions over the two weeks. After the program concludes, the same participants will take a posttest to measure changes in English vocabulary knowledge.

One advantage of this design over the previous one is the administration of both a pretest and a posttest. This is an improvement upon the previous design, in which participants are tested only once, after the treatment. In this design, participants are tested twice: once before the treatment and once after the treatment. This allows you to compare the scores on the pretest with those on the posttest and determine whether there has been any change or improvement.

However, this design also has notable limitations. The absence of a control group makes it challenging to attribute changes from the pretest to the posttest solely to the treatment. Without a control group, we do not know whether the observed effects result from the treatment, from normal learner progress, from test–retest effects, or from exposure to other similar situations during the study. These factors collectively impact the internal validity of the research (see Chapter 12).

Static-Group Comparison Design Static-group comparison design, also known as posttest-only comparison group design, involves two or more intact or existing groups (hence static), a treatment, and posttests after the treatment. One of the two groups can be an experimental group that receives treatment, and another group, a comparison or control group that receives no treatment. A static group design does not usually involve a pretest, and the study typically focuses on comparing the groups at posttest point only. Figure 9.6 shows a schematic representation of this design.

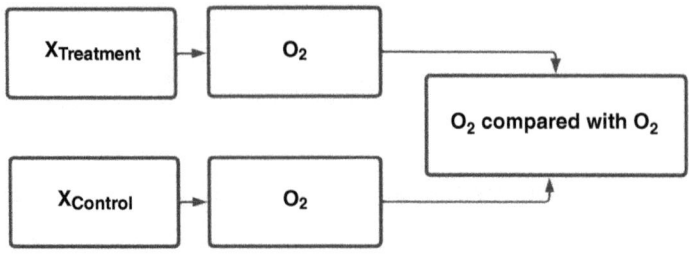

Figure 9.6 Static-group comparison design

Example 9.4 presents a hypothetical scenario.

EXAMPLE 9.4

Suppose you are conducting a study to compare language proficiency gains in English writing skills between two groups of learners: one undergoing a writing course and the other without such an intervention. Both groups have similar initial proficiency levels and consist of English language learners from intact classes. The experimental group receives the writing course, including various activities, lessons, assignments, and feedback to enhance writing abilities, while the control group has no specific writing instruction. After the intervention, both groups receive a posttest to evaluate their writing skills.

The fact that this design can have an experimental and a comparison group could be an improvement upon a design that does not. However, the design is still flawed as it does not have some of the important features of experimental research. First, it does not have a pretest. A lack of a pretest can lead to a number of problems, including the inability to establish a baseline measure of the variable examined. This would also make it difficult to attribute any changes or differences observed in the posttests to the treatment, as an increase could have been likely due to the initial differences. Additionally, a lack of a pretest can make it difficult to determine the effectiveness of an intervention or treatment, as it is not possible to compare the participants' performance before and after an intervention. When there are no pretests, we do not know whether the two groups are the same at the outset of the study with respect to the dependent variable.

There is no random assignment of the participants to groups. This then leads to a bias in sample selection. In other words, since the design uses an intact group, it is difficult to to know whether the two groups are similar in terms of their characteristics, including their level of language proficiency, background knowledge, motivation, and learning styles and strategies. These would make comparison difficult.

However, although this design has the above problems, it may still be a useful one in situations where the researcher is simply interested in getting some overall understanding of the effect of an instructional strategy in two intact classes. Thus, it may be used as a preliminary study before conducting the main study.

POINTS TO PONDER

How can you determine which research design is most appropriate for your research question, and what are the factors that you would consider when making your decision about what research design to use?

Quasi-Experimental Research Designs

Quasi-experimental research designs aim to establish cause-and-effect relationships by examining or comparing the effect of an independent variable on a dependent variable (Figure 9.7). These designs do not involve random assignments. Instead, they involve intact groups, which are naturally pre-existing. Researchers can manipulate the different levels of an independent variable to study their effects on the dependent variable. Pretest–posttest designs are commonly used in quasi-experimental research to establish a baseline and measure changes after an intervention (Figure 9.7). For example, if the independent variable is instruction with two levels, explicit and implicit, the researcher can create one group that receives implicit instruction and another group that receives explicit instruction. Using a pretest–posttest design, this helps evaluate which type of instruction is more effective.

Quasi-experimental research designs aim to establish cause-and-effect relationships by examining or comparing the effects of an independent variable on a dependent variable without using random assignments.

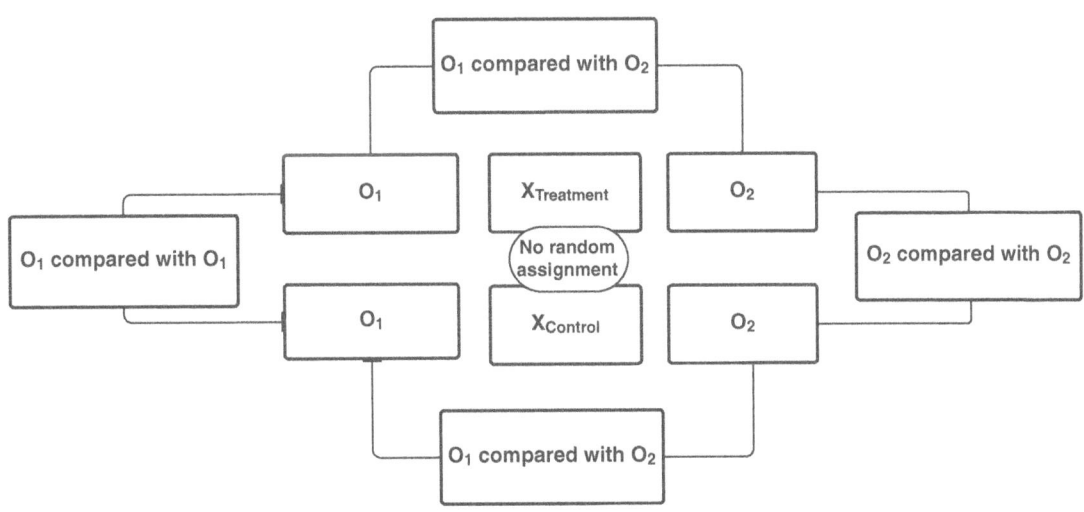

Figure 9.7 Quasi-experimental research design

Example 9.5 presents a hypothetical scenario.

EXAMPLE 9.5

This study aims to compare the use of native-speaker corpora and conventional teaching materials in improving ESL students' writing proficiency. Two groups (Group A and Group B) with similar language proficiency levels from the same school will participate. Due to challenges in random assignment, a quasi-experimental design will be used, with Group A as the experimental group and Group B as the control group. Both groups will receive a pretest to assess their initial writing proficiency. Group A will be taught using materials developed from native-speaker corpora, which include examples of authentic language use, common collocations, and discourse patterns. Group B will continue with conventional instruction, using materials not specifically derived from corpus data. After one semester, a posttest will be administered to both groups, and the results will be compared to assess their writing proficiency improvement.

One drawback of quasi-experimental research is lack of randomization; that is, the participants are not randomly selected or assigned to groups. Instead, groups are formed based on preexisting characteristics, or the researcher might use intact groups or classes. This means that any preexisting characteristics of the participants may affect the results. Since the researcher selects intact groups, even if the study has a control group, it cannot rule out the effect of extraneous variables, Therefore, any effect shown for the independent variable could also be due to other uncontrolled factors. These would then affect the internal validity of the results, making it difficult to establish causality.

One **drawback** of quasi-experimental research is lack of randomization. This affects the internal validity of the study, making it difficult to establish causality.

To improve the validity of quasi-experimental research designs, you could try to use strategies to control or minimize such threats to internal validity. We will discuss some of these strategies as we discuss the different types of quasi-experimental design. However, it should be noted that although you may use strategies, there might still be variables that are not controlled for. Nonrandom selection and assignment would also limit the generalizability of the findings because when the sample is not randomly selected, it is not representative of the population, and therefore it is hard to generalize inferences from the sample to the population.

Having said that, quasi-experimental designs are very useful when you cannot randomly assign participants or when random assignment is not necessary. Indeed, quasi-experimental design is one of the most frequently used research designs in applied linguistics because it allows the researcher to examine the effect of an independent variable on a dependent variable (or the effectiveness of a treatment or intervention) among existing groups or intact classes, which are also much easier to access. Because quasi-experimental design often involves using intact groups, this can increase the ecological validity of the study. Ecological validity is the degree to which the conclusions of a study can be applied to contexts similar to those in which the study was conducted (see Chapter 12). For example, the results of studies conducted in intact classes can be more easily applied to other intact classes.

Types of Quasi-Experimental Research Designs As shown in Figure 9.8, there are several types of quasi-experimental designs, including:

- nonequivalent control-group design
- matched-groups design
- time-series design
- repeated-measures design.

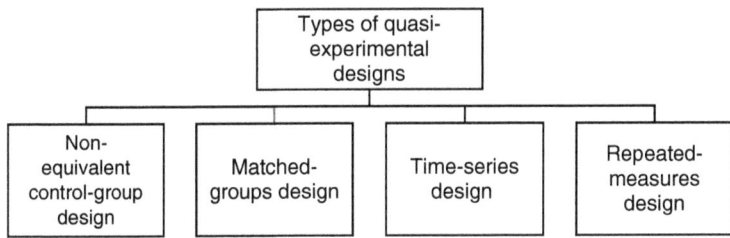

Figure 9.8 Types of quasi-experimental designs

Nonequivalent Control-Group Design This is a type of quasi-experimental design that compares two or more groups (such as the experimental and the control group) that are not equivalent in terms of characteristics. The experimental group receives the treatment whereas the control group does not. In this design, the groups selected are often intact, and thus they may have their own preexisting characteristics, which might affect the result of the study. All the groups are both pretested and posttested, but participants are not randomly assigned to groups.

A **nonequivalent quasi-experimental** design compares two or more groups (such as the experimental and the control group) that are not equivalent in terms of characteristics.

Figure 9.9 presents a schematic representation of a nonequivalent control-group design.

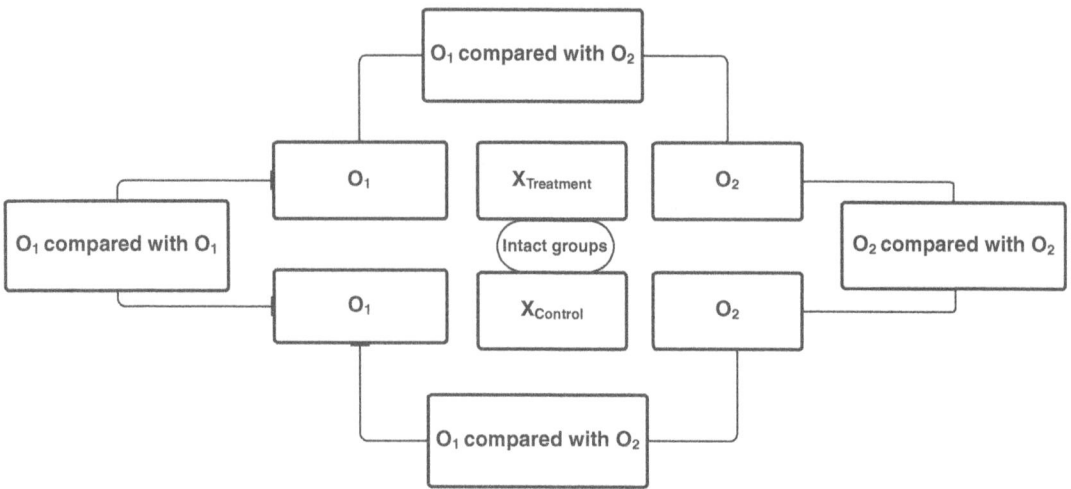

Figure 9.9 Nonequivalent control-group design

Example 9.6 illustrates a nonequivalent control-group study.

EXAMPLE 9.6

Hartshorn et al. (2010) conducted a nonequivalent control-group study examining dynamic written corrective feedback's impact on writing skills. The study compared two groups: one receiving conventional writing instruction (comparison group), and the other, dynamic feedback (treatment group). The participants were 47 ESL students at Brigham Young University's English Language Center (ELC) in the United States with advanced-low to advanced-mid levels of language proficiency. Test results showed no significant impact on rhetorical competence, fluency, and complexity but a notable effect on writing accuracy. The nonequivalent control-group design stems from the fact that the study used existing groups who were not equivalent in terms of their prior language proficiency, L1 background, age, and possibly other educational backgrounds.

To improve the design, you may try to select groups that are comparable on some characteristics. However, because there are no random assignments, the two groups still cannot be assumed to be equivalent in the same way as when random assignments are used. As a result, the internal validity of the research is limited compared to a study where participants are randomly assigned to groups. However, as noted before, this design is useful for situations where it is not possible or practical to randomly assign participants to the experimental or control group. It is also used when the groups being compared are not similar in terms of their characteristics.

Matched-Groups Design This design matches individuals in the treatment group with individuals in the control group, based on certain characteristics. This is an improvement on the nonequivalent control-group design as the participants in each group have been closely matched before assignment to the groups by creating pairs of similar participants in each group. The design is still quasi-experimental because it does not involve random assignment. But matching participants in each condition on important characteristics improves the internal validity of the research and the ability to identify the effect of the independent variable on the dependent variable. Thus, this design can be used when random assignment of participants to the experimental and control groups is not possible but you are interested in eliminating the effects of preexisting characteristics as far as possible.

Time-Series Design This is a type of quasi-experimental research design that involves pretesting and posttesting participants multiple times before and after the treatment. There are at least two types of such a design: one-group time-series (or simple interrupted time-series) and two- or multiple-group time-series.

ONE–GROUP TIME–SERIES DESIGN   In a one-group time-series design, also called a simple interrupted time-series design, one group of participants will receive multiple measurements over a series of time points before a treatment and then multiple measurements over a series of time points after the treatment. The purpose is to examine changes or trends over time rather than comparing different groups. In many ways this type of time-series design is very similar to the pretest–posttest one-group design discussed earlier, with the difference that it involves multiple pretests and multiple posttests.

The number of pretests and posttests can vary depending on the research question and the specific objectives of the study. The pretests provide a baseline measurement before any intervention, and the posttests measure the outcome after the intervention. Multiple pretests also allow you to control any preexisting differences or trends among participants, providing a more robust baseline for comparison than only one pretest does. This design allows you to observe how the variable of interest changes over time in response to the intervention.

In a **one-group time-series design**, also called a simple interrupted time-series design, one group of participants will receive multiple measurements over a series of time points before a treatment **and** then after the treatment.

Figure 9.10 shows a schematic representation of a one-group time-series design.

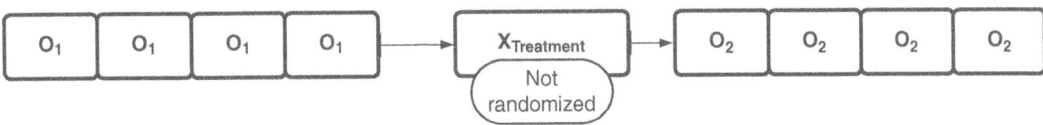

Figure 9.10 A one-group time-series design

Example 9.7 presents a hypothetical study.

EXAMPLE 9.7

This one-group time-series study aims to examine the impact of a culturally relevant literacy program on the reading skills of heritage language learners. Participants, who voluntarily enrolled in the program, receive a series of pretests and posttests (pretests 1–4, posttests 1–4) with the literacy training in between. The study uses a repeated-measures design to track changes in participants' reading proficiency over time. The training program, spanning four weeks, involves targeted exercises, culturally relevant reading materials, and feedback. Data analysis examines participants' reading scores at each time point to identify significant changes or trends. Results may indicate immediate improvements after the intervention (posttest 1) and the durability of these enhancements over subsequent posttests (2–4). However, if consistent improvement occurs after each pretest when students are not receiving any treatment, this may indicate that the improvement could have occurred without the intervention and that the intervention had little effect.

A one-group time-series design does not involve random assignments. So, this can be a limitation that can affect the generalizability or external validity of the results. The design does not have an actual control group either (as it consists of only one group), which makes it different from other longitudinal designs that may have a control group. But in a time-series design, the presence of multiple pretests and posttests can somewhat address the limitation of not having a control group.

In a time-series design, multiple pretests can act as controls. The pretest data establish a baseline pattern, allowing for comparison with posttests. Plotting the pretest and posttest data over time reveals trends. As noted before, a sudden change in the posttest pattern after treatment, not observed during pretests without treatment, indicates the potential effect of the intervention. This change may be reflected in the steeper slope or direction of the posttest plot, as depicted in the schematic representation shown in Figure 9.11, with the axis line indicating the points of pretests and posttests. Therefore, you may use this design when you do not have access to control groups.

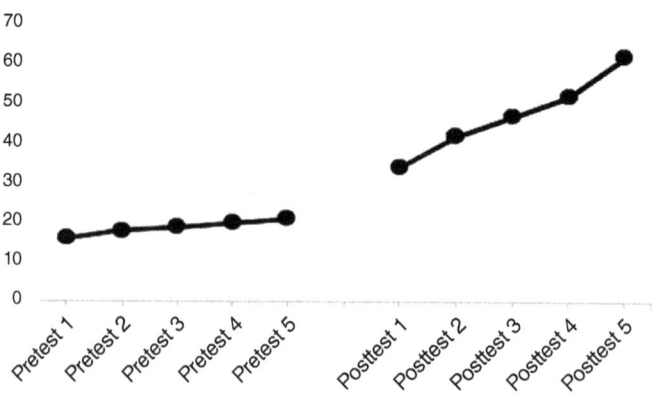

Figure 9.11 A schematic representation of a possible trend in a time-series design

Control-Group Time-Series Design Another type of time-series design is a control-group time-series design. This design is like the one-group time-series design, with the difference that that it has both a treatment group and a control group. Both groups are intact groups (i.e., not randomly assigned) and are both pretested and posttested at multiple time points. While the design includes pretesting and posttesting at multiple time points, which helps to compare the effects of the treatment over time, the lack of random assignments means it does not meet the criteria of a true experimental research design. Figure 9.12 shows a schematic representation of this design.

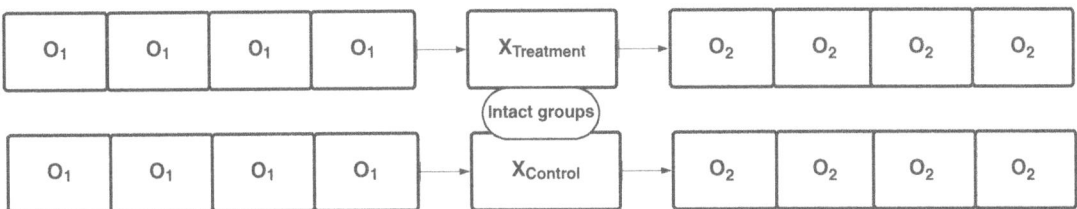

Figure 9.12 A schematic representation of a control-group time-series design

One improvement of this design over the one-group time-series design is that it has an actual control group, which then allows for comparison. That is, if you observe a gain in the posttests in the treatment group and not in the control group, you may conclude that the treatment has had an effect. The control group can reduce the effect of extraneous variables that may have affected the outcome, including the threats that may come from history or maturation, because any history events or maturation that may have affected the results would have affected both the experimental group and the control group in similar ways. Another advantage of this design is that, in addition to allowing for the examination of the trend in the data over time, it also allows for both within-group and between-group comparisons. That is, you can compare the pretest and posttest scores within the treatment group and between the treatment and the control groups. This can increase the robustness of the findings.

A control-group time-series design is like the one-group time-series design with the difference that that it has both a treatment group and a control group. Both groups are intact groups, and they are both pretested and posttested at multiple time points.

Repeated-Measures Designs Repeated-measures designs are another type of quasi-experimental research design. It is called a repeated-measures design because the same participants participate in all conditions and/or are measured or tested repeatedly or multiple times. For example, a study that examines the effectiveness of a particular instruction strategy by testing the same learners' language learning before and after the instruction is an example of a repeated-measures design because the same participants are tested before and after the treatment.

Repeated-measures designs are often classified as a type of quasi-experimental design because they involve observing the same participants under different conditions, rather than randomly assigning participants to different groups. However, they can also be used in true experimental research if participants are randomly assigned to conditions and counterbalancing is used to control for order effects. As noted in Chapter 6, counterbalancing is a method used in experimental research to minimize the influence of order effects by systematically varying the order in which participants experience conditions. For example, if there are two conditions (Condition A and Condition B), half of the participants can experience Condition A first, followed by Condition B, while the other half experience Condition B first, followed by Condition A. In studies with more conditions, such as four (A, B, C, D), participants can be randomly assigned to different sequences (e.g., A-B-C-D or C-D-A-B) to control for potential order effects while maintaining randomization within the sequence.

In cases where a repeated-measures design incorporates a mixed-model design, involving both within-subjects and between-subjects variables (see below), participants can be randomly assigned to groups that experience different orders of the treatment. For instance, participants in Group 1 might receive Treatment A first followed by Treatment B, while participants in Group 2 receive the treatments in the reverse order (Treatment B first followed by Treatment A). This method helps control for order effects across groups while maintaining the rigor of random assignment.

There are several types of repeated-measures designs (Figure 9.13) including:

- one-way within-subjects design
- two-way/*n*-way within-subjects design
- mixed-model design
- Latin square design.

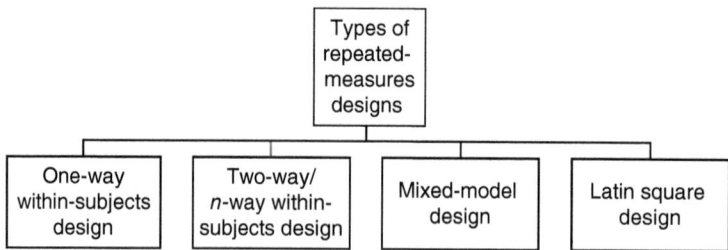

Figure 9.13 Types of repeated-measures designs

ONE–WAY WITHIN–SUBJECTS DESIGN Within-subjects designs are a type of design in which the same participants are measured at different points of time or under multiple conditions. Such designs are called within-subjects designs because the comparison is within the same group of participants. They are different from between-subjects designs, which involve comparing different independent groups. Since the same participants are repeatedly measured, the design is called a repeated-measures design. A one-way within-subjects design is a specific type of within-subjects design in which there is only one independent variable, and the participants are tested under different levels or conditions of that variable. Figure 9.14 shows a schematic representation of a one-way within-subjects design.

Participants		Condition 1		Posttest 1		Condition 2		Posttest 2		Condition 3		Posttest 3
P1	→	A	→	PT1	→	B	→	PT2	→	C	→	PT3
P2	→	A	→	PT1	→	B	→	PT2	→	C	→	PT3
P3	→	A	→	PT1	→	B	→	PT2	→	C	→	PT3
---	→	---	→	---	→	---	→	---	→	---	→	---

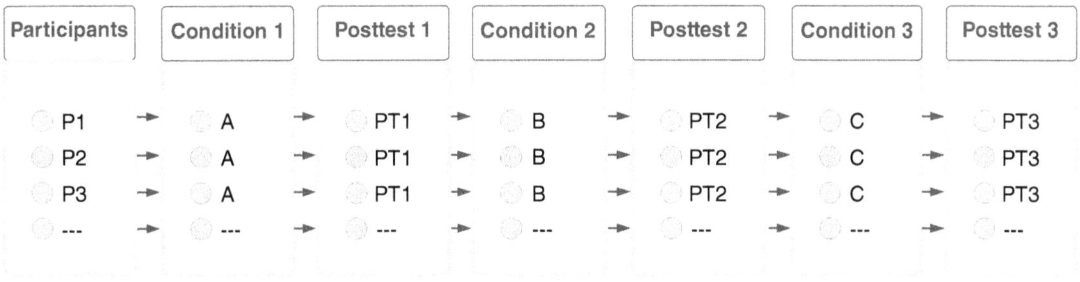

Figure 9.14 A one-way within-subjects design

In Figure 9.14, each row under participants corresponds to a different participant (P1, P2, P3, . . .), and each column marked as "condition" corresponds to a different condition (Condition 1, Condition 2, Condition 3, etc.). Each participant experiences all the conditions. For instance, Participant P1 goes through condition A, then condition B, and condition C, and so on. The same applies to the other participants (P2, P3, . . .). This design includes posttests after each condition, allowing the researcher to examine changes within participants over time. Example 9.8 presents a hypothetical scenario for the use of such a design.

EXAMPLE 9.8

This study explores how different ideological perspectives presented in reading materials affect critical thinking among adult L2 learners, utilizing a one-way within-subjects design. Participants are adult ESL learners with similar language proficiency who engage with texts representing varying ideological perspectives. The independent variable is the ideological perspective of the texts (e.g., liberal, conservative, neutral), and the dependent variable is the frequency and depth of critical thinking responses.

The design of the study in Example 9.8 is a within-subjects design because each participant will engage with multiple texts representing different ideological perspectives. Since there is one independent variable (ideological perspective) with multiple levels, it is called a one-way design, and since there is no random assignment of participants, the study is a quasi-experimental study.

Within-subjects designs are useful designs in that they help eliminate within-group individual differences, which can be a source of extraneous variance. Since the same participants are tested or introduced to different levels of the independent variable, it makes it easier to attribute any observed effects to the manipulation of the independent variable rather than the differences between participants. Also, it allows for the comparison of results across different levels of the independent variable within the same participants, which can increase the statistical power of the study.

Within-subjects designs are useful in that they help eliminate within-group individual differences, which can be a source of extraneous variance.

However, repeated-measures designs are subject to a few limitations. Generalizability can be limited if the study involves nonrandomly selected participants. Therefore, it is important to consider the specific characteristics of the participants when interpreting the results and to exercise caution when making inferences about the populations or about other context based on the results. In repeated-measures designs, the control and the experimental groups are merged into the same group of participants. This reduces the number of participants needed, which could help in situations where recruiting participants is difficult.

Another limitation is the possibility of carryover effects. A carryover effect occurs when performance in one condition affects the performance in the subsequent condition. Carryover effects can be positive (e.g., exposure improving performance) or negative (e.g., fatigue or one condition negatively affecting the next). It is applicable to designs where different treatments or conditions are tested with the same participants over time.

In a repeated-measures design, the effects of one level of the independent variable may carry over to the next level. For example, in the repeated-measures study in Example 9.8, since participants are engaging with multiple texts that represent different ideological perspectives, their responses to one text could influence how they respond to the next one. For example, exposure to a liberal text might influence how participants engage with a conservative or neutral text later on, either by priming certain ideas or by causing fatigue or mental overload.

A practice effect may also occur in repeated-measures designs. This effect refers specifically to the improvement in performance that occurs due to repeated performance or exposure to the same task. As participants practice a task over time, they may get better at it because they become more familiar with it. This effect is common in experiments where the same participants perform a task multiple times.

Another limitation of repeated-measures designs is the order effect. This refers to the influence that the sequence in which conditions or tasks are presented has on participants' performance. For example, an order effect might occur if participants are required to read an essay before writing their own. This sequence might make participants approach the writing task differently compared to when they write before they read a text.

It is important to note that carryover, practice, and order effects are related, as they all arise from the arrangement of tasks in within-subjects designs. However, their focus differs: order effects broadly concern how the order of conditions influences performance; carryover effects concern how specific aspects of one task affect another task, and practice effects refer to improvements due to repeated practice of similar tasks. These problems, which can exist in any repeated-measures design, can often be mitigated through counterbalancing.

Repeated-measures designs are subject to **carryover**, **practice**, and **order effects**, which occur because the same participants are exposed to multiple conditions or measurements over time.

TWO–WAY/N–WAY WITHIN–SUBJECTS REPEATED–MEASURES DESIGNS   Depending on the number of independent variables, within-subjects repeated-measures designs can range from one-way to n-way. A one-way repeated-measures design involves a single within-subjects independent variable. A two-way repeated-measures design involves two within-subjects independent variables, while a three-way repeated-measures design involves three independent variables. These designs are useful for studying how the different levels of different within-subjects variables affect the dependent or outcome measures and their interaction.

In a two-way within-subjects repeated-measures design, for example, the same participants are subjected to all levels of both variables. The two independent variables in this design are both within-subjects variables because each participant experiences every condition of both variables. Example 9.9 provides a hypothetical scenario.

EXAMPLE 9.9

This study investigates the impact of various vocabulary exercises on immediate and delayed vocabulary learning using a two-way repeated-measures design. The exercises include multiple-choice, flashcards, and sentence translation, with a single intact group of EFL students ($n = 30$). Participants with similar language proficiency are tested on their vocabulary learning at three time points: before the exercises (pretest), immediately after the exercises (posttest), and two weeks later (delayed posttest). Each participant engages in all exercises across four sessions. The analysis examines the effects of exercise type (multiple-choice, flashcards, and sentence translation), testing time (pretest, posttest, and delayed posttest), and their inter-action on vocabulary learning and retention.

The study in Example 9.9 uses a two-way repeated-measures design because it involves two independent variables (exercise and time). It is a repeated-measures or within-subjects design because each participant is presented with the levels of each of the two variables, that is, the same participants are asked to do the three types of exercises and the same participants are also tested three times.

One advantage of the above design is that it allows for the examination of the interactions between the two within-subjects independent variables. It also increases the robustness of the study by eliminating the effects of individual differences as the same participants participate in all tasks and conditions. However, as noted earlier, this design can be subject to both carryover and order effects, which must be controlled for or considered when interpreting the results.

One advantage of a two-way repeated-measures design is that it allows for the examination of the **interactions** between the two within-subjects independent variables.

In a repeated-measures design, as the number of within-subjects factors increases, the complexity of the design also increases. This can make it more difficult to disentangle the effects of the different factors and to understand the interactions between them. Additionally, multiple comparisons can increase the likelihood of Type I errors as it can be more challenging to control for potential confounding variables. A Type I error, also known as a false positive, is a type of error that occurs when a statistical study concludes that a difference or association exists between or among variables when in reality such relationships or differences do not exist (see Chapter 19). In other words, it is the probability of rejecting the null hypothesis when it is true. It is important to minimize the Type I error rate when conducting statistical research tests to reduce the risk of drawing incorrect conclusions.

MIXED–MODEL DESIGNS   A mixed-model design is a design that examines the effects of a within-subjects independent variable and a between-subjects independent variable. As noted above, a within-subjects variable, also known as a repeated-measures variable, is a variable that is measured more than once on the same participants. A between-subjects (or a between-groups) variable is a type of independent variable that differs between participants who are exposed to different levels or conditions of the variable. For example, in a study investigating the immediate and delayed effects of a new instructional strategy, the between-subjects variable would be the new instructional strategy (with one group receiving the new strategies and another group receiving no strategies), and time would be the within-subjects variable.

A **mixed-model design** examines the effects of a within-subjects independent variable and a between-subjects independent variable.

A mixed-model within-and-between-subjects design combines the advantages of both a within-subjects and a between-subjects design. For example, within-subjects comparisons can be used to examine the effects within participants while controlling for individual differences, whereas the between-subjects comparisons can be used to examine the effects of the variable between groups while controlling for the within-subjects effect. Overall, this is a useful design if you are interested in examining the main and interaction effects of two independent variables when one of them is manipulated within subjects and the other one between subjects. Example 9.10 presents a hypothetical scenario.

EXAMPLE 9.10

This study investigates how task complexity influences negotiation strategies among language learners and also explores the moderating role of language proficiency. The independent variables are task complexity (within-subjects) and language proficiency (between-subjects), with negotiation strategies as the dependent variable. The study includes language learners from three proficiency levels (beginner, intermediate, advanced) in intact classes. Due to practical constraints, a quasi-experimental design is used, and participants engage in communicative tasks of low, medium, and high complexity. Task complexity is treated as a within-subjects variable because all participants within each proficiency group experience all complexity levels.

As noted above, the benefit of a mixed-model design is that it allows the examination of the main and interaction effects of both a within- and a between-subjects variable. One limitation is that it lacks random assignment. Without random assignment, the groups may differ systematically on certain variables, which can introduce potential confounding factors and threaten the internal validity of the study. Other limitations are that the study is subject to both order effects and practice effects, which must be controlled for or considered when interpreting the results. One solution, therefore, could be counterbalancing, in which the participants are presented with the tasks in a different order to eliminate the order effect. This can be achieved by using a design called the Latin square design, which will be explained below.

LATIN SQUARE DESIGN   A Latin square design is a type of design used to control for unwanted variation coming from the order or carryover effects discussed earlier. A Latin square is a table consisting of several rows and columns that should be filled with letters and numbers. The name comes from an ancient Roman puzzle that requires the letters or numbers to be arranged in such a way that each one appears once in each row and each column. This leads to a different order for the arrangement of the letters and numbers in the table. Figure 9.15 is a schematic representation of a Latin square design.

As can be seen, the arrangement illustrated meets the criteria of the Latin square in that each letter appears once in each row and column. If there are different levels of different variables, such a Latin square design can be used to counterbalance the order of the treatments and condition. Thus, in a Latin square design, each treatment

A	B	C	D
B	C	D	A
C	D	A	B
D	A	B	C

Figure 9.15 A Latin square design

is applied to participants in a different order. This helps to counterbalance the design and control for any effects that may be caused by the order in which the treatments are applied.

For example, in the study mentioned earlier about the effect of task complexity (Example 9.10), a Latin square design can be used to counterbalance the order and carryover effect, as in Figure 9.16.

Beginner	Simple	Medium	Complex
Intermediate	Medium	Complex	Simple
Advanced	Complex	Simple	Medium

Figure 9.16 An example of a Latin square design

A **Latin square design** is a type of design used to control for unwanted variation coming from the order or carryover effects discussed earlier. It is a table consisting of several rows and columns that should be filled with letters and numbers.

In a Latin square design (Figure 9.16), the tasks are applied to the participants in a different order. This helps to control for order effects by ensuring that any differences in the results of the experiment are due to the treatment itself rather than the order in which the treatment was used.

POINTS TO PONDER

What are some examples of research questions in applied linguistics that would be best addressed through an experimental research design, and what are some questions that would be best addressed through a nonexperimental research design?

True Experimental Research Designs

True experimental research designs aim to establish cause-and-effect relationships between variables by using random assignment to control for extraneous variables. Participants are randomly assigned to different groups, such as the treatment group and the control group. True experimental designs are considered an improvement on quasi-experimental research designs because they involve random assignments.

True experimental research designs aim to establish cause-and-effect relationships between variables by using random assignment to control for extraneous variables.

The characteristics of true experimental research include:

- manipulation of the independent variable
- control of extraneous and confounding variables
- random assignment of participants
- use of a control group
- use of a pretest and a posttest.

The above components are important in true experimental research as they allow you to establish causality and make it more likely that any differences observed are due to the manipulation of the independent variable. Because of them, true experimental research designs are considered the strongest type of research design for determining causality. In other words, they have high degree of internal validity in that that any observed differences between groups can be attributed to the manipulation of the independent variable. Because of randomization, they also have a high degree of external validity, and in particular, sample-to-population external validity. However, they may not have high ecological validity, which is the extent to which findings from a study can be generalized to other real-world settings.

True experimental research may have limited ecological validity because the controlled settings often do not reflect real-world conditions, making it difficult to generalize findings to everyday situations.

Because of the above features, true experimental research designs are used frequently in hard science because it deals with the physical world where the researcher is better able to control and manipulate variables. However, they are not used as frequently in applied linguistics research because applied linguistics research occurs most often in practical settings where the researcher is not able to control all the variables and therefore is unable to establish a cause-and-effect relationship. Also, random assignment of participants to control and experimental groups is not often possible in applied linguistics research. Many studies in this field may occur in naturalistic settings, such as classrooms, making random assignments and full control over variables difficult. Applied linguistics often involves complex language learning and teaching scenarios, defying reduction to a single easily manipulable variable. Moreover, conducting true experimental research with tight control may be ethically questionable in certain teaching and learning contexts.

Types of True Experimental Research Designs   There are several types of true experimental research designs, as can be seen in Figure 9.17, including:

- pretest–posttest control-group design
- Solomon four-group design
- factorial design.

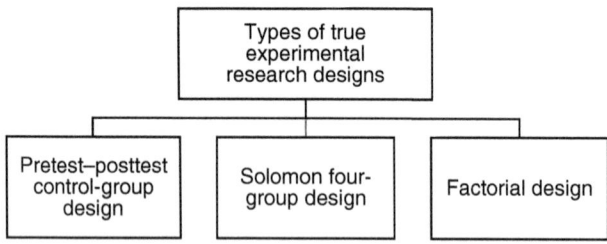

Figure 9.17 Types of true experimental research designs

Pretest–Posttest Control-Group Design   Pretest–posttest control-group design is a type of true experimental research design, which in its simplest form involves two randomly assigned groups: an experimental group and a control group (Figure 9.18). The experimental group receives a treatment or intervention while the control group does not. Both groups are assessed using a pretest before the treatment and a posttest after the treatment. This enables you to determine whether the treatment has an effect by comparing the results of the two groups. The difference between a quasi-experimental and a true experimental research design is that in the latter you randomly assign participants to different groups (i.e., the treatment and the control groups). This allows for a high degree of control over extraneous variables and the ability to make causal inferences. Therefore, such a design has a high degree of internal validity.

Pretest–posttest control-group design is a type of true experimental research design, which in its simplest form involves two randomly assigned groups (an experimental group and a control group), a pretest and a posttest, and the random assignment of participants to groups.

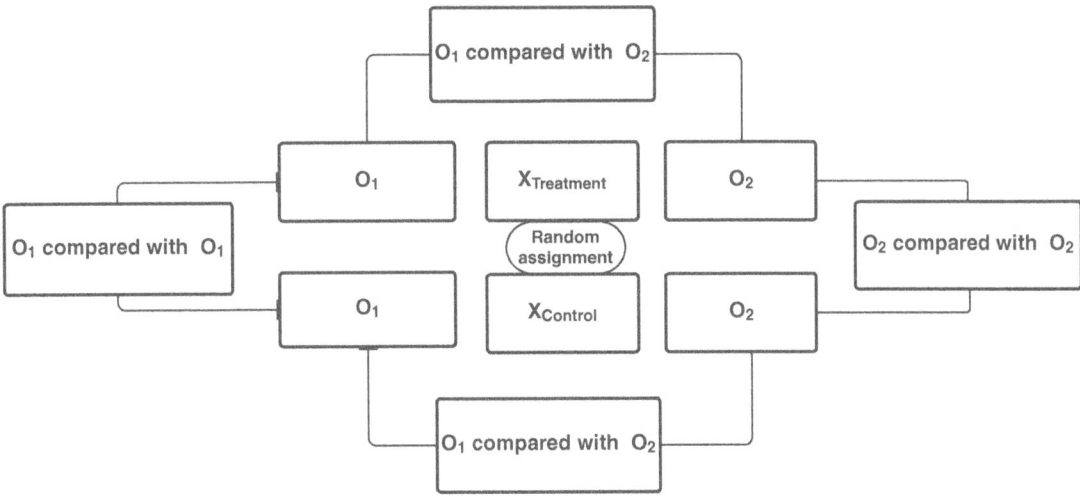

Figure 9.18 Pretest–posttest control-group design

Example 9.11 presents a hypothetical scenario.

EXAMPLE 9.11

This true experimental research investigates the effect of two metaphor instruction methods on adult EFL learners' understanding and use of metaphors. Sixty participants aged 18 to 35, with similar language proficiency and no prior exposure to the study metaphors, will be recruited from a local EFL language institute. Participants will be randomly assigned to three groups:

Group A (Control): No metaphor instruction
Group B (Comparison): Traditional instruction with lists of metaphors and their meanings
Group C (Experimental): Cognitive linguistic method involving conceptual metaphor theory and contextual learning through interactive activities

The experiment will be conducted over a ten-week period, with the comparison and experimental groups receiving instruction twice a week for 1.5 hours each session. The study will employ pretest and posttest measures to assess participants' understanding and use of metaphors. The pretest and posttest scores for all groups will be compared using appropriate statistical tests to determine whether there are significant differences in metaphor acquisition and usage between the two instruction methods.

Solomon Four-Group Design The Solomon four-group design is an experimental research design that is used to assess the effects of pretesting on the dependent variable in an experiment. The design contains four groups: two experimental groups and two control groups, with the participants being randomly assigned to each group. One of the experimental groups is pretested before receiving the treatment, and the other is not. Similarly, one of the control groups is pretested, and the other is not. All four groups are posttested. Figure 9.19 shows how the design will look.

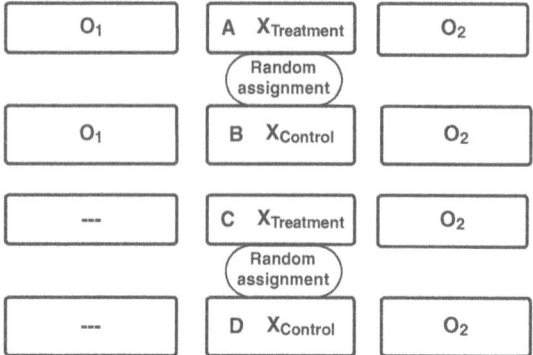

Figure 9.19 Solomon four-group design

The **Solomon four-group design** is an experimental research design that is used to assess the effects of pretesting on the dependent variable.

This design allows you to compare the results of the pretests and the posttests among the four groups and their interaction. The analysis of the results of the first two groups (A and B) are the same as the standard pretest–posttest control-group design mentioned earlier. However, the following additional comparisons can be made:

- One comparison could be the difference between the posttests of groups C and D (who did not receive a pretest) compared to the difference between the posttests of groups A and B (who received a pretest). If the difference between the posttests of Groups C and D is different from that between Groups A and B, it can be concluded that the pretest has had an effect on the study outcome.
- A comparison between the pretest of Group B and the posttest of Group D assesses natural changes over time or effects unrelated to the treatment or the pretest. Similar scores suggest no significant time-related or extraneous effects, showing that differences in treated groups (A and C) could be due to the treatment. Differences indicate the presence of extraneous factors influencing the outcomes independently of the treatment or the pretest.
- We can compare the posttest of Group B and the posttest of Group D. This comparison shows whether the pretest itself has had an effect, irrespective of the treatment. If there is a difference, we can conclude that pretesting has had an effect in the study results overall, and therefore the study design should be revised.
- Another comparison could be between the posttest of Group A and the posttest of Group C. This can help determine whether the pretest has had an effect. If there is a difference in the posttests of the two groups, we can conclude that the pretest

has had an effect on the treatment and the results cannot be attributed to the treatment.

Altogether, the Solomon four-group design offers a comprehensive approach to experimental research by simultaneously assessing the impact of pretesting, treatment, and their interaction. By combining a standard pretest–posttest control-group design with a variant, where the treatment and control groups are not pretested, the design can evaluate pretest sensitization, an issue arising when participants in the experimental group may become sensitive to the test content, potentially affecting internal validity. This sensitization may occur when participants learn from the pretest itself, which can influence their performance on subsequent measures. While the design does not directly address threats to external validity, controlling confounding variables enhances generalizability. By establishing a causal relationship between treatment and dependent variables, the design contributes to a more generalizable study.

However, although the Solomon four-group design is effective for controlling threats to validity, its complexity, resource demands, and logistical constraints make its implementation and data analysis challenging for many researchers. Interpreting results can also be challenging due to the potential influence of pretest effects and interactions between groups, and random assignment does not always guarantee group equivalence. Furthermore, ethical concerns may arise when control groups are denied potentially beneficial treatments. These challenges make the design less practical for studies with limited resources or small populations, despite its strengths in addressing validity threats.

Pretest sensitization occurs when the effect of the independent variable on the dependent variable can be partly due to the fact that the participants are pretested.

A Factorial Design A factorial design is any experimental research design that investigates the effects of two or more independent variables (factors) and their interactions on a dependent variable. It qualifies as a true experimental design when participants are randomly assigned to groups. However, it can also be used in quasi-experimental research if random assignments are not employed,

In a factorial design, each independent variable is manipulated at two or more levels, resulting in a combination of levels within each variable. For example, in a 2×2 factorial design, there are two independent variables, each with two levels. This results in four different experimental conditions or cells, created by the combination of the levels of the two independent variables.

A **factorial design** investigates the effects of two or more independent variables (factors) and their interactions on a dependent variable.

Figure 9.20 is a schematic representation of a 2 × 2 factorial design.

Variable 1	Variable 2	
	Level 1	Level 2
Level 1	X	X
Level 2	X	X

Figure 9.20 A 2 × 2 factorial design

In this 2 × 2 factorial design, there are two independent variables, each with two levels. Independent variable 1 has Level 1 and Level 2, and independent variable 2 has Level 1 and Level 2. The resulting factorial design has four cells, representing the different combinations of levels of the two independent variables. Each cell represents a unique experimental condition, and the dependent variable is measured for each condition. Example 9.12 provides a hypothetical scenario.

EXAMPLE 9.12

This study explores the joint effects of two independent variables, "instruction type" (formal sociolinguistic lessons vs. informal community-based lessons) and "socio-economic status" (high vs. low), on participants' sociolinguistic awareness, using a 2 × 2 factorial experimental design (Table 9.1). Equal numbers of participants from different socioeconomic status (high and low) are randomly assigned to four groups, as shown in Table 9.1:

1. Formal sociolinguistic lessons – High socioeconomic status
2. Formal sociolinguistic lessons – Low socioeconomic status
3. Informal community-based lessons – High socioeconomic status
4. Informal community-based lessons – Low socioeconomic status

The study manipulates these variables to examine their individual and interactive effects on sociolinguistic awareness. Formal sociolinguistic lessons involves structured lessons on language variation, identity, and power, while informal community-based lessons focuses on engaging with sociolinguistic phenomena through community interactions and participatory activities. All participants will receive a pretest before the intervention to assess their initial sociolinguistic awareness and then a posttest to measure changes after the intervention. This 2 × 2 factorial analysis will help determine the main effects of instruction type and socioeconomic status as well as their interaction effect on participants' sociolinguistic awareness.

Table 9.1 The design of the study

Socioeconomic status	Education	
High	Formal sociolinguistic lessons	Informal community-based lessons
Low	Formal sociolinguistic lessons	Informal community-based lessons

Nonexperimental Research Designs

Nonexperimental research designs are those in which there is no manipulation of the independent variable. Instead, you observe relationships among variables as they exist. Therefore, they are not often used to examine cause-and-effect relationships, and if they are, the evidence is suggestive and is not as strong as in experimental research that involves manipulation of variables. Nonexperimental research does not involve random assignment to experimental and control groups. It typically involves collecting data from existing sources or observing a phenomenon as it naturally occurs.

Nonexperimental research designs are those in which there is no manipulation of the independent variable. Instead, the researcher observes relationships among variables as they exist.

Researchers conduct nonexperimental research because they are either simply interested in the relationship among variables, with no aim to make causal inferences, or because in certain circumstances it is not possible to conduct experimental research by controlling or manipulating the independent variable. Indeed, many questions in applied linguistics and L2 research may not be amenable to experimental research.

One example of a situation where experimental research may not be feasible is the study of child language acquisition in naturalistic settings. Because the process of language acquisition occurs over a long period of time and is affected by many variables, it would be difficult to control all variables and conduct experiments in a controlled environment. Also, it may be unethical to manipulate the child's linguistic environment in order to study language acquisition. In this case, you may need to rely on nonexperimental research, including observational or descriptive methods to study language acquisition.

It is important to note that nonexperimental research is an important type of scientific research involving systematic empirical investigations in which you collect and analyze data in order to answer a specific research question. Similar to experimental research, nonexperimental research can also involve hypotheses and testing hypotheses. However, the methods used to test hypotheses in nonexperimental research are different from those used in experimental research. Nonexperimental research often relies on correlation and association rather than manipulation of the independent variable and assigning groups to experimental and control groups. As a result, the results gained through nonexperimental research are less decisive than those obtained through experimental research.

Types of Nonexperimental Research

There are a number of nonexperimental research designs, including correlational research, comparative research, and survey research. We will discuss each of them below with examples.

Correlational Research

Correlational research involves measuring two or more variables of interest and assessing their relationship or association. It is nonexperimental because it involves no manipulation of variables and no random assignment. Therefore, it does not control extraneous variables and hence cannot establish cause-and-effect relationships. Correlation is a term that refers to the association between two variables and how they change together. Correlations are positive or negative. A positive correlation means that as one variable increases, the other variable also increases, whereas a negative correlation means that as one variable increases, the other variable decreases.

Correlational research involves measuring two or more variables of interest and assessing their relationship or association.

In correlational research, correlations are statistically shown by a correlation coefficient, which is a numerical index varying between -1 and 1, showing the strength and direction of the correlation. A coefficient of 1 indicates a perfect positive correlation, a coefficient of -1 indicates a perfect negative correlation, and a coefficient of 0 indicates no correlation. Thus, any correlation coefficient greater that 0 indicates a positive correlation, and any number less than 0 indicates a negative correlation. Again, correlations indicate the degree of association and not causation.

Because correlational research does not involve cause-and-effect relationships, we usually do not talk about dependent and independent variables unless we are interested in examining whether two groups are different in the level of an independent variable, in which case the design of the nonexperimental research will be comparative rather than correlational; we will discuss that later.

In some other cases, the independent variable will be called the predictor variable. A predictor variable is a kind of independent variable that is used to predict an outcome or a dependent variable. In the same context, the dependent variable may be called the response or criterion variable. The criterion variable is a dependent variable that is predicted and is often used in regression analysis, which is a more robust subset of correlational analysis, commonly used to predict the value of one variable based on the other.

For example, in a study examining the relationship between reading and vocabulary learning, the researcher may intend to examine to what extent the amount of reading would predict vocabulary learning, in which case the amount of reading would be the predictor variable (the independent variable that predicts) and vocabulary learning would be the criterion variable (a dependent variable that is predicted; see Chapter 6). As shown in Figure 9.21, there are two types of correlational research: simple and multivariate.

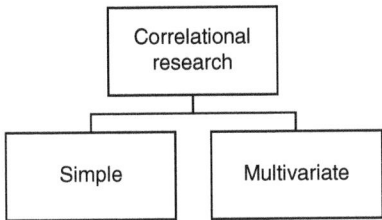

Figure 9.21 Types of correlational research

Simple Correlational Research In the case of simple correlational research, you examine the relationship between two variables that are quantitatively measured using either a continuous scale of measurement or a rank-order (ordinal) scale of measurement. Continuous scales provide data that can take any value within a certain range, such as scores on a test. Rank-order scales provide data that can be ordered by magnitude. For example, participants may be asked to indicate their level of agreement or disagreement with a statement, such as "Strongly Agree, Agree, Neutral, Disagree, Strongly Disagree." These responses are ordinal because they indicate the relative order of agreement or disagreement.

In the case of **simple correlational research**, you examine the relationship between two variables that are quantitatively measured using either a continuous scale of measurement or a rank-order (ordinal) scale of measurement.

Depending on the type of data, you may use different types of correlational analyses and different correlation coefficients, such as Pearson's correlation coefficient, Spearman's rank correlation coefficient, or Kendall's tau correlation coefficient.

Pearson's correlation is used to measure the linear relationship between two continuous variables. Spearman's rank correlation, also known as Spearman's rho, and Kendall's tau correlation coefficient are both used to measure the strength and direction of a monotonic relationship between two ordinal variables or when the assumption of Pearson's correlation, which is that the data should be normally distributed, is not met (see Chapter 20). The difference between a linear relationship and a monotonic relationship is that in the former, the change in one variable is proportional to the change in the other variable. In other words, the rate of change is constant and the two move together like a straight line. In a monotonic relationship, the change in one variable is not proportional to the change in the other variable.

The focus is on the consistent direction of change, whether it is increasing or decreasing, although the rate of change may not be constant.

In strongly increasing monotonic relationships, as the values of one variable increase, the values of the other variable consistently increase as well. The overall trend is upward, even though the rate of change might not be constant; for example, the more hours a student studies, the higher their exam scores tend to be. In strongly decreasing monotonic relationships, as the values of one variable increase, the values of the other variable consistently decrease. The overall trend is downward, even though the rate of change might vary; for example, as students' anxiety goes up, their exam scores tend to go down. Nonmonotonic relationships can be u-shaped, inverted u-shaped, or scattered. In u-shaped relationships, the relationship starts by increasing, then reaches a peak, and then decreases. The trend is not consistently upward or downward. In scattered relationships, the relationship does not show any consistent trend in a particular direction.

Figure 9.22 illustrates various patterns of relationships between variables, both monotonic and nonmonotonic. It is important to note that real-world relationships can be complex and might not always fit perfectly into simple patterns.

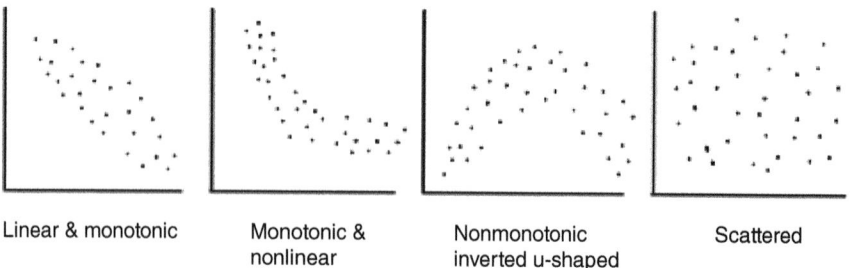

Linear & monotonic   Monotonic & nonlinear   Nonmonotonic inverted u-shaped   Scattered

Figure 9.22 Types of relationships between variables

Example 9.13 illustrates a hypothetical study using a simple correlational design.

EXAMPLE 9.13

This study aims to explore the correlation between English vocabulary size and reading comprehension skills among 100 intermediate-level ESL learners (aged 18–30). Participants enrolled in an English language program will receive the Vocabulary Levels Test (VLT) and a standardized reading comprehension test. Statistical analysis, using Pearson's correlation coefficient, examines the strength and direction of the relationship between vocabulary size and reading comprehension. A positive correlation would imply that learners with a larger vocabulary tend to exhibit stronger reading comprehension skills.

Multivariate Correlational Research Multivariate correlational research refers to the relationship between three or more variables. It is used to determine the degree to which more than two variables are related or associated with each other (see the hypothetical Example 9.14). Like simple correlation, in this design there is no manipulation of the independent variables, and there is no random assignment of participants to experimental and control groups. Therefore, the design cannot examine causality.

To analyze the data, you can use statistical methods such as multiple regression (see Chapter 20) to examine how multiple independent variables predict a single dependent variable, or other more advanced analysis such as factor analysis to identify underlying factors that explain the patterns of correlations among multiple variables, or structural equation modeling (SEM) to test complex relationships among multiple variables, including direct and indirect effects (see Chapter 22).

Multivariate correlational research is a research design used to determine the degree to which more than two variables are related or associated with each other.

EXAMPLE 9.14

This study explores the interrelationships among language anxiety, motivation, L2 proficiency, and additional contextual factors such as cultural background and language learning environment in 200 adult bilingual participants (aged 18–30). Standardized tests are used to measure language proficiency, including vocabulary, grammar, speaking, and listening skills. To assess language anxiety, intrinsic and extrinsic motivation, and cultural background, questionnaires such as the Foreign Language Classroom Anxiety Scale, the Language Learning Orientations Scale, and the Cultural Background Questionnaire are employed. Additionally, semistructured oral interviews are conducted to gather qualitative data on participants' language learning environments and personal experiences. Multiple regression analysis, structural equation modeling, or factor analysis can be used to examine the inter-correlation of these variables.

Comparative Nonexperimental Designs

Comparative nonexperimental research designs are those in which you compare two or more groups or individuals without manipulating the independent variable or randomly assigning participants to groups. Although an independent variable exists in such designs, you do not directly manipulate them, either because it is not possible to manipulate them, the aim of the research is not to manipulate them, or there might be some ethical reasons preventing you from doing so. These designs rely on existing data or preexisting conditions, rather than experimental manipulation, with the aim of examining how variables affect each other as they exist.

Comparative nonexperimental research designs are those in which you compare two or more groups or individuals without manipulating the independent variable or randomly assigning participants to groups.

As previously noted, in correlational research designs, both independent and dependent variables are quantitative. Comparative research designs involve a categorical independent variable, such as nationality. Categorical variables can be identified with numbers, but the number does not have an inherent quantitative value and serves only as a label. Nonexperimental comparative research designs do not manipulate the categorical independent variable. The dependent variable, however, can be quantitative, including continuous variables. When the independent variable is categorical, it means that the variable can be divided into distinct categories or groups. As a result, the analysis can involve comparing the groups to each other. Example 9.15 shows a hypothetical nonexperimental comparative design with a categorical independent variable and a continuous dependent variable.

EXAMPLE 9.15

The aim of this study is to compare the speech intelligibility of advanced English as a Second Language (ESL) learners with two different language backgrounds: Mandarin Chinese and Spanish. It aims to investigate how the phonological characteristics of their L1s influence their English speech intelligibility. Using a nonexperimental comparative design, 60 participants (30 Mandarin Chinese, 30 Spanish speakers), aged 20–30, will read a standardized English passage including sentences that contain sounds and phonological features that are known to be challenging for speakers of Mandarin Chinese and Spanish. The speech samples from both groups will be recorded and presented to a panel of L1 English speakers who are experienced in assessing the intelligibility of nonnative English speech. The panelists will rate the intelligibility of the speech samples on a scale, where higher scores indicate greater intelligibility. The speech intelligibility scores of both groups will be statistically analyzed to compare the intelligibility of the two groups.

The study described in Example 9.15 is nonexperimental because it does not involve manipulating any independent variables or using an intervention or treatment in any way. It simply involves observing and comparing the speech intelligibility of two groups.

Survey Research

Survey research involves collecting data using self-report measures, such as questionnaires. Surveys are a type of descriptive research study that is used to describe characteristics of a population or phenomenon being studied. Surveys, which involve collecting quantitative data through closed-ended questionnaires, are a common method of quantitative research in applied linguistics to gather information about a specific language-related issue. Example 9.16 illustrates a hypothetical study using a survey research design.

EXAMPLE 9.16

This survey investigates undergraduate students' attitudes and perceptions regarding the effectiveness of an intermediate-level Spanish language course. The study aims to understand the impact on language skills, motivation, and overall learning experience. The participants are 150 students aged 18–35 with diverse academic majors and language backgrounds. The study will employ a survey research design in which participants will be asked to complete a Likert-scale questionnaire that assesses their attitudes and perceptions related to the effectiveness of the course. Participants will receive the questionnaire in either printed or online format, based on their preference. The completed questionnaires will be analyzed to determine the distribution of responses and the overall student perceptions of the effectiveness of the course.

The above example is a nonexperimental study because the research involves gathering descriptive information from a sample without manipulating a variable and measuring its effect on another variable. It is simply used to gather data about a preexisting phenomenon and is not designed to establish cause-and-effect relationships.

Conclusion

In this chapter, we have discussed the different types of quantitative research designs, including experimental and nonexperimental designs, along with their key characteristics, different subtypes, and examples of studies where they might be used. Quantitative research designs are those that involve the collection and analysis of numerical data to study the effects of variables on one another or to examine the relationships between them. They are commonly used in applied linguistics research to examine the role of various variables or the cause-and-effect relationships between them. In the next two chapters, we will focus on how to collect data in quantitative and qualitative research.

DISCUSSION AND ACTIVITY QUESTIONS

Discussion Questions

1. What are the key differences between experimental and nonexperimental research designs? What are some advantages and limitations of each?
2. How do you determine the appropriate design for an experimental study, and what factors should be considered when choosing between a within-subjects design and a between-subjects design?
3. Why is it important to carefully select a research design that is appropriate for your research question and research purpose?
4. What are the different types of nonexperimental research designs, and what are some advantages and limitations of each?
5. What are factorial research designs in quantitative research, and what are some advantages and limitations of such designs in applied linguistics?
6. What is correlational research, how can it be used, and what are some advantages and limitations of such a research design?
7. Why might you decide to use a quasi-experimental research design instead of a true experimental design? How can a quasi-experimental design be used to evaluate the effectiveness of an instructional strategy?

Activity Questions

1. Consider a research question that can be addressed using a quantitative research design. What type of design would you use? Develop a hypothetical design for this study, including the independent variables, dependent variable, or any control variables.
2. Consider a research question that might be best investigated using a correlational research design, identify the variables, and explain why you would use that design.
3. Develop a hypothetical study design that uses a specific subtype of experimental research design. Identify the independent and dependent variables and any potential confounding variables that might need to be accounted for, and explain how you would account for those variables.
4. Design a study that involves a survey research design on a topic of interest to you. Identify the key variables you want to measure and create appropriate questions or items to assess these variables.
5. Find a research article on a study that has used a pretest–posttest control-group research design. Identify the key variables and research question or hypothesis that the study addresses and assess the strengths and limitations of that study design. What would you do to address any limitations that you have found?
6. Consider a research question in your area of interest that can be addressed through a quasi-experimental research design. What are the procedures in conducting this research? What are the advantages and disadvantages of using this type of design for your research question?

10 Collecting Quantitative Data: Tools and Techniques

CHAPTER OBJECTIVES

After completing this chapter, you should be able to

- Identify and describe different methods for collecting quantitative data in applied linguistics research, including the use of various tests, tasks, and measures.
- Identify and explain different types of tests used to assess specific language skills, affective factors, and cognitive variables in applied linguistics.
- Understand the design, implementation, and practical use of these tests in research.
- Evaluate the strengths and limitations of different quantitative data collection methods and their suitability for various research goals.

Introduction

In the previous chapter, we discussed quantitative research designs. In this chapter, we will focus on quantitative data collection methods, particularly those used in applied linguistics research. As noted earlier, quantitative data are numerical data that can be analyzed statistically. This type of data is different from qualitative data that are nonnumerical and are often in the form of text (written or oral) or visual data such as pictures and audio and video data.

In applied linguistics research, various quantitative data collection tools are used, including language tests and oral or written tasks that assess comprehension and production. These tools provide important data on learners' language abilities. There are also various types of communicative/interaction tasks that learners participate in. Structured questionnaires using closed-ended questions or response scales in which participants rate their responses are often used to collect quantitative data about learners' opinions, beliefs, attitudes, motivation, or anxiety. In this chapter, we will provide an overview, with examples, of the most common types of quantitative data collection tools. However, before doing so, it might be helpful to make a distinction between two general categories of data collection tools: naturalistic and elicited data collection tools.

Naturalistic versus Elicited Data Collection Tools

In research, data collection tools can be either naturalistic or elicited. Naturalistic data collection methods are those that involve collecting data as they occur naturally in their real-world contexts. This can include observing classroom interactions, collecting spontaneous conversations, or recording authentic language use in social settings. The goal of naturalistic data collection is to capture the phenomena and their characteristics in their natural settings, without the influence of any intervention. For that reason, naturalistic data collection can provide a more authentic understanding of the participants' behavior and characteristics.

Elicited data collection tools attempt to actively elicit the data from the participants. These methods are often more structured and collect data in a more predetermined manner than naturalistic data collection tools. The aim of elicited data collection is to provide data that can be used to investigate specific hypotheses under more controlled conditions or when there is a need to control for extraneous variables, allowing the researcher to examine issues more directly.

Naturalistic data collection methods involve collecting data as they occur naturally in their real-world contexts. **Elicited** data collection tools attempt to actively elicit the data from the participants, using a more structured format and collecting data in a more predetermined manner.

Quantitative research most often uses elicited data, but naturalistic qualitative data can also be collected and analyzed quantitatively by coding and converting them into numerical form. In the following section I will discuss some of the most common types of data collection methods used in quantitative applied linguistics research. These tools gather quantifiable data related to various domains including linguistic, cognitive, affective, and pragmatic domains. I will describe them under the following seven categories:

- Tools for collecting survey data
- Tools for measuring language proficiency and skill-specific abilities

- Tools for measuring explicit and implicit knowledge
- Tools for measuring communicative and interactive skills
- Tools for measuring affective variables
- Tools for measuring cognitive variables
- Tools for measuring pragmatic skills.

Tools for Collecting Survey Data

Surveys are tools used in quantitative research to collect data, often from a large sample of research participants. They aim to capture opinions, attitudes, perspectives, and characteristics. A specific type of survey is questionnaires, which consist of questions designed to measure specific constructs (e.g., attitudes, behaviors) or traits (e.g., personality characteristics).

Questionnaires range from structured to unstructured. In this section, I will briefly go over structured questionnaires, as they are the most commonly used in survey-based research. A more detailed discussion of types of questionnaires will be provided in Chapter 15. Structured questionnaires are especially suited to quantitative research because they allow for the collection of measurable data. These questionnaires often include closed-ended questions, which limit respondents to predefined answers. This format is particularly effective in large-scale surveys where the goal is to gather data that can be easily compared and analyzed across different participants. Structured questionnaires often include a variety of question types, such as multiple-choice questions or those that ask respondents to provide ratings.

One common approach to gathering rating data is through the use of Likert scales, which are frequently employed in closed-ended questionnaires. Developed by American psychologist Rensis Likert, this scale consists of a rating with two opposing ends, such as "strongly agree" and "strongly disagree," or "always" and "never," with several points in between to capture varying degrees of agreement, frequency, or intensity. Respondents select the option that best represents their view or experience.

Surveys are tools to collect data, often from a large sample of research participants, in order to learn about their opinions, attitudes, perspectives, and characteristics.

Questionnaires can be administered using various methods. The most traditional is the pen-and-paper format. However, there are also a number of online and web-based tools available that can help create and distribute surveys to a large group of participants; these include Google Forms (which is a free online tool to create forms and surveys), Typeform (another online platform that creates online forms including surveys), and SurveyMonkey (a popular online survey platform). The kind of format you choose depends on your needs and also other factors such as the number of questions that need to be asked, the number of respondents, and the nature of analysis that needs to be conducted.

Closed-ended questionnaires can be used to collect a wide range of data, including:

- learners' attitudes, opinions, motivation, and beliefs about second language learning and use (see the section on affective variables)
- self-reported language ability and skills in a second language
- demographic information about the participants, such as age, gender, nationality, and language background
- information about language learners' or teachers' experiences, such as how long they have been studying or teaching a second language, and how often, where, and when they use it.

As noted before, closed-ended questionnaires are useful data collection tools when the goal is to gather data from a large number of participants in an efficient manner. They can be administered easily, and the responses can be quickly analyzed using quantitative analyses. However, it is important to carefully design questionnaires to ensure that they are clear, concise, and relevant to the research questions being addressed. It is also important to consider the limitations of questionnaires, such as the potential for response bias and the inability to probe or follow up on responses to gain more in-depth information (see Chapter 15 for more details).

Tools for Measuring Language Proficiency and Skill-Specific Abilities

Measuring language knowledge is a key aspect of second language acquisition research. Various tools are used to assess different aspects of language knowledge, from language proficiency to specific language skills. These tools are typically designed to elicit data that provide insight into how learners use and understand the target language. The choice of the tool depends on the research question and the purpose of the assessment. Tools to measure linguistic knowledge can be broadly categorized into two groups:

- **Language proficiency measures:** These tools assess the overall language ability, including vocabulary, grammar, reading, writing, and speaking, in a single integrated test. Examples include TOEFL and IELTS.
- **Skill-specific measures:** These tools are focused instruments that evaluate particular skills or components, such as speaking or writing (production), listening or reading (comprehension), vocabulary, or grammar, often in isolation to target specific areas of proficiency.

Language knowledge can be measured using various tools, with the choice of the tool depending on the research question and the purpose of the assessment.

Language Proficiency Measures

Language proficiency measures assess individuals' language ability, often in a nonnative language. They can be formal and standardized or informally developed by researchers or teachers for specific contexts or purposes.

Standardized language proficiency tools are designed by testing agencies to evaluate learners' overall level of proficiency in a language. These measures are typically designed to be objective, reliable, and valid. To achieve this, they are developed through rigorous test development processes, including piloting and testing and retesting, to make sure that they are accurate and valid measures. Examples of standardized English proficiency tests include TOEFL (Test of English as a Foreign Language), IELTS (International English Language Testing System), PTE (Pearson Test of English), and CEFR (Common European Framework of Reference for Languages).

Standardized English language proficiency tests serve various purposes, such as assessing proficiency for study or work in English-speaking countries. TOEFL and IELTS scores, for instance, are often required for admission to colleges in the United States and Canada. PTE is an English language proficiency test designed to assess the speaking, listening, reading, and writing skills of nonnative English speakers and is accepted by many universities and employers in the United Kingdom, Australia, and other English-speaking countries. CEFR was developed by the Council of Europe and describes language proficiency by dividing it into six levels of competence in an increasing order: A1, A2, B1, B2, C1, and C2. A1/A2 represents beginner user, B1/B2 represents independent user, and C1/C2 represents proficient user. Standardized tests are widely used in language education, assessment, and policy to provide a consistent framework for evaluation. They are also used in research to assess participants' language skills and general proficiency levels.

Nonstandardized assessment tools are informal data-collection instruments developed without the formal rigor of standardized tests. They are typically developed and used locally by the researcher, tailored to the specific purpose of the research. These measures can be used to assess learners' overall language ability as well as specific language skills such as grammar, vocabulary, reading, writing, speaking, and listening. Examples of nonstandardized measures include:

- **Informal tests and quizzes:** These assessment tools are less structured than standardized tests and come in various forms, such as multiple-choice, true/false, or short-answer questions. Teachers use them for tracking students' progress, and researchers can use them to assess participants' skills.

- **Self-assessment measures:** Participants rate their own language proficiency, offering a subjective perspective. Although these measures can be useful, they may not always be accurate, due to bias or the individual's self-perception. Applied linguistics studies sometimes use self-assessment tools for participants to rate their proficiency in a second language.
- **Proficiency scales:** These scales, commonly used by schools, teachers, or researchers, assess progress or competence using level indicators. Ranging from low beginner to advanced, each level includes criteria and descriptors. Proficiency scales can be used for both self-assessment and assessment conducted by others. Below is an example of a proficiency scale that outlines different ability levels, with corresponding indicators:
  - **Low beginner:** At this level, the learner has limited knowledge of the target language and may only be able to understand and use very basic language including simple phrases.
  - **Beginner:** The learner can understand and use simple phrases as well as sentences but may not be able to use complex sentences or complex grammar and vocabulary.
  - **Intermediate:** The learner can hold a conversation on a variety of topics and can understand more complex language but may still make mistakes when using the language.
  - **Advanced:** The learner can speak and write the language fluently in a variety of contexts, using a wide range of vocabulary and grammatical structures.

Standardized language proficiency tools are developed through formalized test design procedures to achieve objectivity, reliability, and broad applicability. **Nonstandardized measures** lack formal testing procedures and are created and used to fit specific research goals and contexts.

In applied linguistics research, language proficiency measures, including standardized and nonstandardized ones, are used for several purposes. Some common ways of using them could be as follows:

- **Determining participant proficiency prior to a study:** Before a study, language proficiency tests can be used to screen participants, ensuring they meet the required language proficiency or skill level.
- **Establishing baseline data:** Language proficiency tests can be used to establish baseline data in longitudinal studies. Participants can take a test before a study to create a reference point, enabling the tracking of language proficiency changes over time, comparing groups across different contexts.
- **Establishing group similarity:** Prior to a study, language proficiency tests can assess participants' skills, ensuring similar proficiency levels among groups. This is crucial in studies examining the effects of language learning programs.

- **Pretest and posttest comparison:** Language proficiency tests can function as pretests and posttests in studies assessing the effect of instructional interventions or teaching materials. Changes in language proficiency before and after the study can be compared.
- **Identifying factors influencing proficiency:** Language proficiency tests can be used to examine factors influencing language proficiency, such as motivation, age, and language learning styles. Proficiency can become the dependent variable, while other factors can serve as independent variables.
- **Using proficiency as a moderator variable:** Language proficiency may act as a moderator variable, affecting the relationship between the variables being studied. For instance, in examining the link between language instruction and student motivation, language proficiency can be considered as a potential moderator.
- **Other uses:** Language proficiency tests can identify strengths and weaknesses in learners' language skills, compare proficiency levels between L1 and L2 speakers, or serve various other purposes in applied linguistics research.

Skill-Specific Linguistic Measures

Skill-specific language assessment tools are those that are designed to assess an individual's ability or knowledge in a particular language skill or area. In applied linguistics research, depending on the research question, sometimes you may want to measure the participants' skill in specific areas of language such as grammar, vocabulary, pronunciation, speaking, reading, or writing.

Data about specific skills can be collected through the specific sections of standardized tests such as the TOEFL or IELTS. For example, the listening section of the TOEFL test can be used to assess learners' ability in listening. The advantage of using standardized tests is that they can provide an objective measure, whose reliability and validity have been previously examined. However, they may not be tailored to the specific strengths and weaknesses of individual participants or may not include the relevant content intended by the researcher. Therefore, in some contexts, non-standardized tools may be more suitable to collect data concerning specific language skills. These tools offer flexibility and can be tailored to the particular skills or competencies being studied. Below are examples of such tools categorized into production measures and comprehension measures.

Production Measures

Various production tests can be developed and used to measure participants' oral or written skills. Examples of oral production tests include tasks such as conversations, interviews, and presentations. These tasks can be used to measure participants' overall skills in speaking but can also provide insights into other aspects of language proficiency such as pronunciation, fluency, and overall coherence. For instance, analyzing an oral presentation can reveal whether learners are able to use accurate grammar, appropriate vocabulary, correct pronunciation, and even effective communication strategies.

Production tasks can also evaluate writing abilities, through tasks such as writing a short text based on a topic or prompt. Evaluation can be done using holistic rubrics, considering overall impressions, or analytic rubrics, assessing individual elements such as grammar, spelling, and punctuation. Writing tasks can also be used to assess various aspects of vocabulary skills, including richness (range and sophistication of words), diversity (variety and avoidance of repetition), and accuracy (correct use in meaning, context, and word form).

Production measures assess learners' ability to produce language through speaking or writing. **Comprehension measures** evaluate understanding of written or spoken texts through tasks such as answering questions or summarizing the content.

Comprehension Measures

Comprehension measures assess an individual's ability to understand, interpret, and process information. These tests typically involve presenting learners with a text (written or oral) and evaluating their understanding through tasks such as responding to questions about the information in the text or summarizing the content. Questions typically fall into two categories: selected-response items like multiple-choice and true/false, and constructed-response items where learners provide written or visual responses, ranging from specific information to summarizing main ideas. Responses may involve verbal explanations or the completion of charts, graphs, or figures related to the text. For instance, participants might be tasked with creating a visual representation of a text's main ideas and relationships to evaluate their comprehension.

Measuring Reading Skills Reading is a comprehension skill that involves actively engaging with a written text to understand its meaning, purpose, and implications. This process requires decoding words, recognizing sentence structures, and interpreting the text's content in light of its context. Comprehension goes beyond merely understanding the literal meaning of the words; it involves making inferences, identifying themes, and evaluating the author's intent or argument. Some common ways of assessing reading comprehension might include reading a passage and answering questions to evaluate the reader's ability to understand details or infer meaning. Another approach is summarizing the main ideas of a written text, which requires identifying and understanding its central points and overarching message. Other techniques include comparing and contrasting different texts or parts of a text to evaluate readers' ability to identify similarities, differences, and relationships.

Measuring Listening Skills Listening is a comprehension skill that involves comprehending spoken language. The same methods mentioned above about assessing reading could also be used for assessing listening, with the difference that the text will be delivered orally. The participants listen to an oral passage and answer questions about it, summarizing its main ideas, or comparing and contrasting different passages or parts of a passage. Other tasks to assess listening include:

- **Dictation tasks:** These tasks involve listening to a spoken passage and writing it down word-for-word. They can measure participants' ability to both understand spoken language and reproduce it in written form. Therefore, they can be used to collect data about participants' comprehension and production skills.
- **Note-taking tasks:** These tasks involve listening to a spoken text, such as a lecture or presentation, and taking notes on the content. They can measure the ability to understand spoken language, retain information, and reproduce it in writing.

A reading or listening task may also be used to assess pronunciation. For example, you may ask participants to read a passage that involves certain words to sound out loud. Then you can listen and note the learners' accuracy in producing those sounds; these may be vowel sounds, consonant sounds, or even stress patterns.

Grammatical Ability Measures

Grammatical ability refers to a person's ability to use and understand the rules and structures of a language correctly. Learners' grammatical ability can be measured in different ways and through different tasks, each measuring a particular aspect of grammatical knowledge, depending on the focus of the research. For instance, researchers have differentiated between explicit and implicit knowledge of grammar. Therefore, an assessment measure to assess learners' explicit knowledge of third-person singular -s would not be the same as one measuring learner's implicit knowledge. The distinction between explicit and implicit knowledge is important for understanding how different aspects of grammar are acquired and processed. Therefore, I will discuss this distinction and related assessment methods in greater detail later under the section on tools for measuring explicit and implicit knowledge.

However, there are scenarios where the researcher aims to assess learners' overall grammar knowledge, disregarding the explicit and implicit knowledge dimensions. In such cases, it is essential to adopt broader approaches that assess general grammatical ability. Both traditional grammar tests, such as discrete point tests, and more integrative tests can be used to assess the participants' grammatical ability.

- **Discrete point tests:** These assess specific knowledge or skills, often focusing on a single grammatical point, such as subject–verb agreement or verb tenses. Typically, they take the form of multiple-choice or fill-in-the-blank questions.
- **Integrative tests:** Integrative tests are those that assess a student's ability to integrate and apply multiple skills such as grammar and vocabulary combined with other language skills such as speaking and writing abilities.

Discrete point tests evaluate specific skills irrespective of the context, while **integrative tests** evaluate overall understanding of the grammatical points and the learners' using and understanding them in context.

Vocabulary Skills Measures

Vocabulary plays a crucial role in language learning, influencing effective communication and understanding written and spoken language. Assessing vocabulary is vital for learners, teachers, and researchers. Teachers assess students' vocabulary to identify strengths and weaknesses, enabling tailored lesson planning. Researchers examine vocabulary knowledge to study acquisition, evaluating the impact of instructional methods or materials and comparing vocabulary across participants or contexts. Thus, reliable data collection tools are essential for measuring learners' vocabulary knowledge.

In the literature, two dimensions of vocabulary knowledge have been distinguished: breadth or size of vocabulary knowledge and depth of vocabulary knowledge. Size of vocabulary knowledge refers to the number of words a learner knows, whereas depth of vocabulary knowledge indicates the quality or how well an individual knows a word. Therefore, tests have been designed to measure both dimensions.

Size of vocabulary knowledge refers to the number of words a learner knows, whereas **depth of vocabulary knowledge** indicates the quality or how well an individual knows a word.

Measuring Size of Vocabulary Knowledge Vocabulary size tests include a relatively large sample of words using various response formats, including yes/no format, definition- or synonym-matching format, and multiple choice. Commonly used word lists for these tests include West's General Service List (GSL) and Coxhead's (2000) Academic Word List (AWL), which includes a set of 570 word families frequently used in written academic English texts. Examples of vocabulary size tests include:

- Vocabulary Levels Test (VLT): Developed by Paul Nation, VLT measures receptive knowledge by requiring learners to match words with their definitions. It assesses vocabulary quantity at different frequency levels, including 2,000, 3,000, 5,000, and 10,000 word levels, along with academic level words.
- X-Lex and Y-Lex measures: Developed by Meara and colleagues, these tests use a yes/no format to assess learners' ability to recognize words. X-Lex covers the most frequent 5,000 vocabulary items across languages, while Y-Lex focuses on the 6,000–10,000 word range in English. Aural_Lex is a spoken vocabulary measure, similar to X-Lex but with participants hearing the words instead of reading them.

Measuring Depth of Vocabulary Knowledge Depth of vocabulary knowledge refers to how well a learner understands and uses a word in various contexts. Because of its multidimensionality, depth of vocabulary knowledge is not easy to assess reliably and in a valid manner. But currently there are several such tests in the literature that have been used in applied linguistics research. Some include the Word Associates Test (WAT), the Vocabulary Knowledge Scale (VKS), and the Peabody Picture Vocabulary Test (PPVT).

- **Word Associates Test (WAT):** Developed by John Read, this test assesses receptive vocabulary knowledge based on word associations and semantic relationships. Learners are presented with a target word followed by associated and nonassociated words to gauge their depth of knowledge.
- **Vocabulary Knowledge Scale (VKS):** Developed by Paribakht and Wesche (1997), VKS uses a self-report format to measure partial to full knowledge of a target word on a six-point scale. While assessing both receptive and productive knowledge, it has limitations, testing proficiency in only one meaning of the target word. Example 10.1 shows the VKS format.

EXAMPLE 10.1

Target word X

1. I don't remember having seen this word before.
2. I have seen this word before, but I don't know what it means.
3. I have seen this word before, and I think it means _____ (synonym or translation).
4. I know this word. It means _____ (synonym or translation).
5. I can use this word in a sentence: _____.

Tools for Measuring Explicit and Implicit Knowledge

In the field of second language acquisition (SLA) and applied linguistics, a distinction has been made between explicit and implicit knowledge. Explicit knowledge is defined as a kind of knowledge that is conscious and declarative whereas implicit knowledge is considered to be unconscious and procedural. In applied linguistics research, an important question has been how these different kinds of knowledge are developed and used, and how they affect each other, Therefore, a variety of tests have been developed and administered to collect data about these different types of knowledge. In the following sections, I will provide an overview of various measures to assess explicit and implicit knowledge.

Explicit knowledge is conscious and declarative whereas **implicit knowledge** is unconscious and procedural.

Measuring Explicit Knowledge

Tools to measure explicit knowledge vary depending on the context and the specific type of knowledge being assessed. A variety of tests can be developed and/or used to assess explicit knowledge. These include:

- metalinguistic knowledge tests
- untimed grammaticality judgment tests
- error correction/ identification tests.

Metalinguistic Knowledge Tests

Metalinguistic knowledge tests assess learners' metalinguistic knowledge, which is knowledge of how language works. The operationalization of metalinguistic knowledge varies in studies, often defined as learners' ability to describe and explain errors using their understanding of grammatical rules. Analytic ability is a significant component of this knowledge. Tasks for assessing metalinguistic knowledge involve presenting learners with ungrammatical sentences, asking them to explain errors using metalinguistic terms and to correct the mistakes.

Metalinguistic knowledge tests assess learners' metalinguistic knowledge, which is knowledge of how language works.

Example 10.2 illustrates sample items for a metalinguistic knowledge test.

EXAMPLE 10.2

Instruction: These sentences contain an error. The error has been underlined. Please (a) correct the error; (b) explain why it is wrong.

1. We get a lot of snows in the winter.
2. Five car were damaged in the accident.
3. She wake up early and drove to work.
4. She left me message when I was at school.

Untimed Grammaticality Judgment Tests

Untimed grammaticality judgment tests are tools used to assess a learner's ability to evaluate the grammaticality of sentences when no time pressure is imposed. Administered in written, oral, or computerized formats, participants judge sentences as grammatically correct or incorrect. Learners' responses are often in the form of categorical judgments, but learners may also sometimes be given choices such as "clearly grammatical," "probably grammatical," "probably ungrammatical," and "clearly ungrammatical" (Ellis & Barkhuizen, 2005).

Because learners have time to reflect on their responses, untimed grammaticality judgment tasks are generally considered to measure explicit knowledge, allowing learners to draw on their conscious understanding of language.

Untimed grammaticality judgment tests are data collection tools used to assess a learner's ability to evaluate the grammaticality of a sentence without time pressure.

Example 10.3 illustrates sample items for an untimed grammaticality judgment test.

EXAMPLE 10.3

Instruction: Please read the following sentences at your own pace and decide whether the underlined parts of each sentence contain an error. Check the "Correct" box if you think the underlined part is correct and check the "Incorrect" box if you think the underlined part is wrong. If the section contains an error, please correct the error. See the following example. The first sentence provides an example. (There are no spelling mistakes.)

Example		
I go to school yesterday. went	☐ Correct	☒ Incorrect
1.	Go to the kitchen and bring me <u>a glass</u> of water. ☐ Correct ☐ Incorrect	
2.	This painting did not sell well although <u>painter</u> was well known. ☐ Correct ☐ Incorrect	
3.	Tokyo is the capital of Japan. <u>City</u> is famous for its shopping malls. ☐ Correct ☐ Incorrect	

Error Correction/Identification Tests

Error correction/identification tests measure learners' accuracy in using grammatical structures. Unlike grammaticality judgment tests, where learners judge sentence correctness, error correction tests involve identifying and correcting errors in written sentences or passages. These tests push learners to focus on language structure, utilizing conscious language knowledge. Since there is no time pressure, learners can monitor their performance, applying explicit analytic knowledge.

In a study of the relationship between recasts and learner anxiety, Sheen (2008) used an error correction/identification test consisting of two related statements, one of which contained an error, which had been underlined. The learners were required to correct the underlined erroneous part. Sample items from the test are shown in Example 10.4.

EXAMPLE 10.4

Error Correction Test

(Instruction)

Please read each statement. Each statement has two sentences that are related. One of the sentences is underlined. The underlined sentence contains at least one error. There may be more than one error in each underlined sentence. Write out the underlined sentence correcting all the errors. (Note: There are no punctuation or spelling errors.)

Example 1: Gloria have lived in New York during 2001. She really enjoys living in New York.

Answer: Gloria has lived in New York since 2001.

Example 2: John got a cold. He couldn't went to school yesterday.

Answer: He couldn't go to school yesterday.

1. Mary used to living in Chicago. She lives in New York now.
2. I look after a little girl and a little boy on Saturday. A little girl was smart but the boy isn't.
3. I took three tests yesterday. Tests was so difficult.
4. Tom quits smoking last week. He started smoking again because he is too stressed out.

(Sheen, 2008, p. 873)

Measuring Implicit Knowledge

As noted earlier, explicit knowledge is declarative and involves conscious awareness. Implicit knowledge, on the other hand, involves little conscious awareness, is proceduralized, and can be accessed fluently and spontaneously. It has been argued that the goal of language instruction should be the development of implicit knowledge, and therefore, research in this area should include measures that tap into implicit knowledge. To assess implicit knowledge, several assessment tools have been developed and used in applied linguistics research. Four of the most widely used ones are:

- timed grammaticality judgment tasks
- oral elicited imitation tasks
- speeded dictation tasks
- free oral production tasks.

Timed Grammaticality Judgment Tasks

As discussed previously, untimed grammaticality judgment tasks are assumed to assess explicit knowledge. Timed grammaticality judgment tasks, however, are assumed to measure implicit knowledge because the time pressure in such tests is assumed to give the learner little opportunity to rely on explicit knowledge. Responses to grammatical sentences of grammaticality judgment tasks are considered to tap into implicit knowledge, whereas responses to ungrammatical sentences tap into explicit knowledge (e.g., Ellis, 2004, 2005; Ellis, Loewen, & Erlam, 2006). Grammaticality judgment tasks can be written or aural. Aural grammaticality judgment tasks are more cognitively demanding than written tests as the learners need to process the language under real operating conditions. Therefore, they might provide a better measurement of implicit knowledge.

In **timed grammaticality judgment tasks,** participants are required to quickly decide whether sentences are grammatically correct or not. The time constraints in these tasks are assumed to push learners to rely on their implicit grammatical knowledge by limiting the time available for conscious analysis.

Oral Elicited Imitation Tasks

Oral elicited imitation tasks, initially used in L1 acquisition research, have gained attention in L2 learning and applied linguistics research for assessing general proficiency and implicit knowledge. In these tasks, learners are required to listen to an utterance, usually containing a target structure, and repeat it accurately. The assumption is that correct repetition indicates internalized grammar and lexicon. These tasks are constructive, requiring learners to process and reconstruct input using their grammatical knowledge. Research, such as Ellis et al. (2006), has employed these tasks to explore the impact of feedback on implicit knowledge development, revealing advantages for metalinguistic feedback over recasts.

Oral elicited imitation tasks require learners to listen to an utterance containing a target structure and repeat it accurately. Correct repetition is assumed to require learners to process and reconstruct input using their implicit grammatical knowledge.

Speeded Dictation Tasks

Speeded dictation tasks involve presenting learners with a series of sentences containing the target structure and asking them to write down the sentences read to them by the researcher (see Example 10.5). Because of the time pressure and their reconstructive nature, these tasks are also assumed to minimize learners' ability to use their explicit knowledge and therefore are considered to tap into implicit knowledge.

Speeded dictation tasks ask participants to write down sentences read to them at a normal pace, but under time pressure, which is assumed to push learners to rely on their implicit language knowledge.

EXAMPLE 10.5

Sheen (2008) used a speeded dictation task to examine the effects of recasts among low- and high-anxiety learners. The test consisted of fifteen sentences containing the target structure (English definite and indefinite articles). Learners were asked to listen to each sentence and write it down as quickly as they could and exactly as they heard it.

Example

You will hear: "Money cannot buy love." Then write, "Money cannot buy love."
   . . .

Example 1: I feel good when I speak English.
Example 2: Tom speaks many languages. He's very talented.

1. I know the man who runs this college.
2. The red car across the road looks suspicious.
3. Do you know the pilot who flies this airplane?
4. I saw a movie last night. The movie made me sad.

Free Production Tasks

Free production tasks include various kinds of unplanned oral or written tasks that provide opportunities for free and meaningful language production, such as storytelling tasks, picture-description tasks, narrative tasks (e.g., Ellis, 2005; Nassaji, 2009; Yang & Lyster, 2010), and story-retelling tasks, in which students read and rewrite a story (e.g., Sheen, 2008) or retell a story orally (e.g., Yang & Lyster, 2010). Since free production tasks require learners to produce the language without any preplanning while their focus is on meaning, they are considered to tap into implicit knowledge. The assumption is that the lack of planning time will prevent the activation of explicit knowledge and will trigger implicit knowledge.

POINTS TO PONDER

What factors should we consider when selecting the appropriate quantitative data collection tool for our research project?

Tools for Measuring Communicative and Interactive Skills

Learners' communicative and interactive abilities can be assessed through a variety of activities such as role plays, conversations, or interviews. In applied linguistics research, these tools can serve as treatment tasks to collect production data or as pre- and posttest measures to evaluate treatment effects on language use. Communicative tasks can be one-way or two-way; one-way tasks involve information flow from one participant to another, while two-way tasks simulate interactive communication scenarios, requiring participants to exchange information and collaborate to complete the task.

A variety of one-way tasks have been used in applied linguistics research. These tasks can be categorized into distinct types, each focusing on specific aspects of language use and comprehension. Below are several examples, organized by task type.

Picture-Cued or Picture-Description Tasks

Picture-cued tasks, specifically picture-description tasks, involve presenting participants with images to elicit spoken or written data. Responding to one or more images, participants answer questions, complete sentences, or produce spoken or written paragraphs/dialogues related to the image content. Administered via paper-and-pencil, audio-recordings, or computer-based tasks, learners describe the image details, including objects, people, and settings. The aim is to convey a clear and accurate representation of the image content through words (see Example 10.6).

EXAMPLE 10.6

A picture-description task might involve presenting the participants with a photograph or drawing of a scene and asking them to describe the contents of the image in as much detail as possible. The participant might be asked to describe the location depicted in the image, the actions taking place, the appearance and characteristics of the people or objects depicted, and any other relevant details. For example, if you are interested in measuring learners' knowledge of English articles, you might present the participants with a photograph of a beach scene and ask them to describe it in writing. One of the participants might write something like the following (with some sentences containing errors):

> The picture shows a beach with a few boys and girls playing and relaxing on sand. There are several other people in the picture, including a woman in blue swimsuit and a man with a red shirt and shorts on a beach towel. The beach has also a number of umbrellas under which the boys and the girls are relaxing. In distance, a boat can also be seen on the water, or a number of seagulls are flying. In the background, there is a palm tree and a small building.

Storytelling or Story-Description Tasks

Storytelling or story-description tasks are one-way tasks in which learners are asked to tell a story orally or in a written form, based on a series of prompts. In an oral storytelling task participants tell the story using the spoken language whereas in the written task, they write it down. A storytelling task can be used as a treatment task to collect data about learners' production or as a pre- and posttest measure to examine the effect of a treatment on the participants' correct use of language, including grammar and vocabulary, or other aspects of the story, such as its narrative structure. An example of a storytelling task is given in Example 10.7.

EXAMPLE 10.7

Suppose you are studying what effects corrective feedback has on learners' production of definite and indefinite articles. To gather data for your study, you might design a storytelling task where you may ask each participant to tell a story based on what they see in a series of pictures. If the storytelling task is oral, you can record the participants' storytelling and transcribe it for analysis. If it is written, you can collect the participants' writing production. The data can then be analyzed with respect to the correct use of the target structure, which in this case is the correct use of definite and indefinite articles.

Information-Gap Tasks

An information-gap task is a type of communicative task designed to encourage interaction and communication between participants by creating a situation where one person has information that the other(s) do(es) not. The goal is for participants to exchange information in order to complete the task. This type of task is often used in language learning and applied linguistics research to study how learners use language to communicate and negotiate meaning. Information-gap tasks are typically considered two-way communicative tasks. However, they can also be designed to be one-way tasks. In two-way tasks, the participants have different pieces of information, and they need to communicate to fill in the gaps in each other's knowledge. In one-way tasks, one participant possesses the information and the other participant (s) do(es) not, and the goal is for the person with the information to effectively convey it. There are different types of information-gap tasks that can be used in applied linguistics research to elicit language features and use. Some examples include:

- picture-drawing tasks
- role plays
- spot-the-difference tasks
- story-completion tasks
- picture-sequencing/ordering tasks
- jigsaw tasks
- decision-making/problem-solving tasks.

An information-gap task is a type of communicative task designed to encourage interaction and communication between participants by creating a situation where one person has information that the other(s) do(es) not.

Picture-Drawing Tasks A picture-drawing task is a data collection technique in which participants are asked to create a drawing based on a given prompt, such as an object, an image, or a scene. They work in pairs, with one participant describing the object to the other person, who tries to draw it based on the description provided by their partner (see Example 10.8)

EXAMPLE 10.8

In this task, students should work in pairs. Each student in the pair receives a different description of a scene, such as a park, a city street, or a beach. One student (Student A) has a detailed image of the scene that they cannot show to their partner, while the other student (Student B) has a blank sheet of paper and needs to draw the scene based on the description provided by Student A. Student A describes the scene to Student B in the target language, using specific vocabulary and phrases. For example, Student A might say, "There is a big tree on the left side, and a bench near the center. A dog is running next to the fountain." Student B listens carefully, asks questions if necessary or seeks clarification if something is unclear, and then draws the picture based on the understanding of the description.

Role Plays In role plays, one person assumes the role of a character who has certain information, while the other takes on the role of someone who needs to ask questions or gather information in order to complete a task (see Example 10.9). The focus of role play is often on communication, negotiation, and interaction rather than on exchanging specific pieces of missing information, which is a defining characteristic of information-gap tasks. However, role plays can become an information-gap task if participants need to share information to accomplish a goal or solve a problem.

EXAMPLE 10.9

In this role play, one participant plays the role of a patient and the other a doctor. The patient has specific information that the doctor does not have, and the doctor must gather that information through questioning and asking for information, such as "What symptoms are you experiencing?" or "Have you had any previous medical conditions?" The patient provides the necessary information, and the doctor uses it to diagnose the issue and recommend treatment.

Spot-the-Difference Tasks These are two-way tasks in which participants are presented with two seemingly identical pictures and are asked to work together to identify the differences between them. These differences are often small and need careful attention to find (see Example 10.10).

EXAMPLE 10.10

You and your partner each have a picture (Picture A) and (Picture B) with subtle differences. Without seeing each other's pictures, verbally communicate to identify and find the differences in your respective images.

Story-Completion Tasks These are tasks in which the participants work in pairs to complete a story by asking each other questions. In such tasks, each participant is provided with a different part of a story that the participants are required to communicate to complete. To this end, they can also fill in missing information by asking each other questions (see Example 10.11).

EXAMPLE 10.11

You and your partner will each receive different parts of a story, and your goal is to communicate to complete the story. Additionally, you can fill in the missing information by asking each other questions.

Participant A:
You have the beginning of the story, which provides the setting and introduces the main characters. You will start the storytelling. Begin by describing the setting and introducing the main characters.

Participant B:
You have the middle section of the story, which includes the plot development and conflicts. Your task is to continue the story from where Participant A left off. Listen carefully to Participant A's description and continue the story. If you need more information, ask Participant A to clarify and gather the missing details.

Picture-Sequencing/Ordering Tasks In picture-sequencing tasks, participants are usually provided with a set of images or pictures that depict a sequence of events. They are asked to arrange these pictures in the correct order to represent the chronological flow of the story or process (see Example 10.12). Such tasks can be completed without requiring the participants to exchange specific missing information. However, these tasks can also become an information-gap task if participants have different pieces of information and they need to interact with each other to fill in the gaps in their knowledge.

EXAMPLE 10.12

In this picture-sequencing task, each participant is given a set of images representing different activities involved in a typical morning routine. However, one participant's set contains half of the activities, such as brushing teeth, eating breakfast, and leaving the house, but these activities are out of order. The other participant has a different set of images that completes the routine, containing the other half of the activities (e.g., getting dressed, packing a bag, or preparing a coffee), but again, these images are also out of sequence. The participants must work together to arrange the activities in the correct order. They will need to communicate with each other, describing their images, asking questions, and helping each other piece together the sequence of events. For example, one participant might say, "I have an image of a person brushing their teeth. Do you have the image where they eat breakfast?" By sharing descriptions and using their knowledge of typical routines, they will collaboratively organize the images into the proper sequence.

Jigsaw Tasks Jigsaw tasks are a particular type of information-gap task. They are two-way tasks in which the participants are required to exchange information in order to complete the task (see Example 10.13). In a jigsaw task, each student has only a portion of the information, and they have to share that information to complete the task.

EXAMPLE 10.13

An example of a jigsaw task is a pair work activity where students are required to give directions in a city. In this task, each student receives a different map of the city, with various landmarks marked on it. For example, Student A may have a map with landmarks like a museum, a park, and a hotel, while Student B's map includes a train station, a library, and a shopping mall. The task is for each student to ask and answer questions in the target language to help the other person find specific landmarks.

- Student A might ask, "How do I get to the library?" and Student B would respond with directions, like "Go straight, turn left at the second intersection, and it's on your right."
- Student B could ask, "Where is the nearest hotel?" and Student A would give directions, such as "Walk past the park, turn right, and you'll see it on the left."

Decision-Making/Problem-Solving Tasks These are two-way tasks that require participants to work together to decide on one outcome among many possible outcomes or to solve a problem. They require making choices or decisions based on a set of options, information, or criteria. In such tasks, participants are presented with a scenario or a problem and must analyze the available information to arrive at a decision or solution (see Example 10.14). These tasks can vary widely in complexity and may range from simple everyday decisions, such as choosing what to have for lunch, to complex strategic decisions in business.

EXAMPLE 10.14

An example of a decision-making tasks is "hire a qualified applicant task" used in Hawkes and Nassaji's (2016) study on interactional feedback. In this task, students were told that their school needs to hire a new English teacher. As a group, they needed to decide which applicant to hire. In doing the task, participants were divided into groups of three or four. Each student was given a different (fictional) CV and was required to read the information and then share it with the other students in the group. The participants discussed the candidates and came to a consensus about which applicant was the best person to hire.

POINTS TO PONDER

What assessment tools are often used to collect data about learners' attitudes, beliefs, and motivations? Can you provide some examples? Share your personal experience if you have used any of them.

Tools for Measuring Affective Variables

Affective measures are tools that assess affective factors. Affective factors are variables such as attitude, motivation, or anxiety, which can positively or negatively affect a learner's second language acquisition success. There are different ways to measure affective variables, but in applied linguistics research the most common data collection method has been surveys involving structured questionnaires asking learners to report their responses. The scale used in such questionnaires often has a Likert scale format. These scales have been frequently used to assess affective factors. The following sections explain how some key affective variables can be measured.

Affective measures assess affective factors, such as attitude, motivation, or anxiety, which can affect a learner's success in learning a language, either positively or negatively.

Measuring Attitude

An attitude is a mental and emotional state of readiness. It is a psychological construct that represents an individual's perspectives, feelings, and beliefs towards a particular topic or phenomenon. Attitudes could be positive, neutral, or negative and can be influenced by a person's past experiences. A positive attitude towards a language can be a key factor in the learner's success. A learner with a positive attitude may learn a language more effectively than a person with a negative attitude. Attitudes can be measured with an attitude questionnaire.

Example 10.15 provides sample items from an attitude questionnaire from the test battery developed by Gardner (1985, p. 178; i.e., Attitude/ Motivation Test Battery). The items are intended to measure participants' attitudes towards European French people.

EXAMPLE 10.15

Attitudes toward European French People

1. The European French are considerate of the feelings of others.
2. I have a favourable attitude towards the European French.
3. The more I learn about the European French, the more I like them.
4. The European French are trustworthy and dependable.
5. I have always admired the European French people.
6. The European French are very friendly and hospitable.
7. The European French are cheerful, agreeable and good humoured.
8. I would like to get to know the European French people better.
9. The European French are a very kind and generous people.
10. For the most part, the European French are sincere and honest.

Participants have to provide their responses on a scale of 1 to 7: Strongly Disagree, Moderately Disagree, Slightly Disagree, Neutral, Slightly Agree, Moderately Agree, Strongly Agree.

Measuring Motivation

Motivation is the general desire that inspires someone to act in a particular way. It is the driving force to act towards a specific goal. Motivation is a key factor in language learning, as it can affect how much effort a learner might put into learning the language. Learners who are highly motivated to learn a language may put more effort into learning it, and therefore they may be more likely to be successful than those who are not as motivated.

There are different types of motivation in the context of language learning, including:

- integrative motivation, which refers to a desire to learn a new language to connect and identify with a new language and culture
- instrumental motivation, which refers to a willingness to learn a new language to achieve a specific goal, such as getting a job, entering university, etc.
- intrinsic motivation, which is a kind of motivation that comes from within. It involves a personal desire to learn an additional language for its own sake.

One of the first tools that was developed to measure language motivation was Gardner's Attitude/Motivation Test Battery (AMTB) (Gardner, 1985). Initially designed for English-speaking Canadians learning French, it has been adapted for various settings. The questionnaire covers multiple subscales, exploring attitudes towards language learning as well as integrative and instrumental motivation. The Attitude/Motivation Test Battery has been used in different forms, and its structure varies depending on the form and the purpose for which the form is used. Example 10.16 from Gardner (1985, p. 178) provides some sample items from this questionnaire related to interest in foreign languages.

EXAMPLE 10.16

Interest in Foreign Languages

1. If I were visiting a foreign country, I would like to be able to speak the language of the people.
2. Even though Canada is relatively far from countries speaking other languages, it is important for Canadians to learn foreign languages.
3. I wish I could speak another language perfectly.
4. I want to read the literature of a foreign language in the original language rather than a translation.
5. I often wish I could read newspapers and magazines in another language.
6. I would really like to learn a lot of foreign languages.
7. If I planned to stay in another country, I would make a great effort to learn the language even though I could get along in English.
8. I would study a foreign language in school even if it were not required.
9. I enjoy meeting and listening to people who speak other languages.
10. Studying a foreign language is an enjoyable experience.

Participants have to provide their responses on a scale of 1 to 7: Strongly Disagree, Moderately Disagree, Slightly Disagree, Neutral, Slightly Agree, Moderately Agree, Strongly Agree.

Although the AMTB is still in use, some recent studies of motivation have adopted Dörnyei's (2005) L2 Motivational Self System (L2MSS) and have incorporated aspects from this theory into their motivation questionnaire. L2MSS highlights the role of three factors in motivation, including language-learning environment and two self-related factors: the ideal L2 self and the ought-to L2 self. The ideal L2 self is an image of oneself as a proficient speaker of an L2, and the ought-to L2 self is the qualities one desires to possess.

An example of a questionnaire including this conceptualization of motivation is the one used by Taguchi, Magid, and Papi (2009). The questionnaire included two types of items. One type measured motivation through six-point Likert scales in which participants had to mark their responses on a scale from 1 (strongly disagree) to 6 (strongly agree). The second type were questions where participants had to respond through a six-point rating scale with "not at all" at one end and "very much" at the other end. Example 10.17 provides sample items taken from their questionnaire (Taguchi et al., 2009, pp. 90-97).

EXAMPLE 10.17

- If an English course was offered at university or somewhere else in the future, I would like to take it.
- I am working hard at learning English.
- I am prepared to expend a lot of effort in learning English.
- I can imagine myself living abroad and having a discussion in English.
- I study English because close friends of mine think it is important.
- Do you like meeting people from English-speaking countries?
- I have to learn English because without passing the English course I cannot graduate.
- I find learning English really interesting.
- Do you like to travel to English speaking countries?
- How much do you like English?

Scales for statement-type items:
1 (Strongly disagree), 2 (Disagree), 3 (Slightly disagree), 4 (Slightly agree), 5 (Agree), and 6 (Strongly agree)

   Scales for question-type items:
   1 (not at all), 2 (not so much), 3 (so-so), 4 (a little), 5 (quite a lot), and 6 (very much)

Several other motivation instruments have been developed to capture the dimensions of Dörnyei's L2 Motivational Self System model. For instance, Hessel (2015) introduced an 8-item scale designed to measure aspects of the ideal L2 self using a series of Likert-scale items. Similarly, Teimouri (2017) developed a motivation questionnaire that differentiated and measured various dimensions of L2 selves, including the ideal L2 self, ought-to L2 self/own, and ought-to L2 self/others, along with other motivational dimensions. This questionnaire used a six-point Likert scale, ranging from strongly disagree to strongly agree, and is available in the IRIS digital repository (http://www.iris-database.org).

Measuring Anxiety

Anxiety is a feeling of nervousness, fear, or unease about something that has an uncertain outcome. It can be a normal and sometimes healthy state of mind. However, when a person regularly feels disproportionate levels of anxiety, it might become a problem. In language learning, we are often dealing with a particular type of anxiety, which is referred to as language anxiety, which has been defined as "the worry and negative emotional reaction aroused when learning or using a second language" (MacIntyre, 1999, p. 27). High levels of language anxiety can interfere with language learning as it might lead to over self-consciousness about possible mistakes and less confidence when interacting or speaking with people. Indeed, anxiety has been considered as "the affective factor that most disrupts the learning process" (Arnold & Brown, 1999, p. 8). Students who are too anxious may participate less in classroom activities, which can negatively affect their success.

There are several tests that are commonly used to measure anxiety in applied linguistics research, including:

- **The State-Trait Anxiety Inventory (STAI):** This is a self-report questionnaire that measures both state anxiety (anxiety in response to a specific situation) and trait anxiety (a general tendency to experience anxiety).
- **The Foreign Language Classroom Anxiety Scale (FLCAS):** Developed by Horwitz, Horwitz, & Cope (1986), this is a self-report measure that assesses anxiety specifically related to learning a foreign language in the classroom setting. The FLCAS contains thirty-three items using the following five-point Likert scale: "Strongly agree," "Agree," "Neither agree nor disagree," "Disagree," "Strongly disagree." The FLCAS includes such questions as:
  - I get nervous when I don't understand every word the language teacher says.
  - I feel overwhelmed by the number of rules you have to learn to speak a foreign language.
  - I am afraid that the other students will laugh at me when I speak the foreign language.
  - I would probably feel comfortable around L1 speakers of the foreign language.
  - I get nervous when the language teacher asks questions which I haven't prepared in advance.
- **The Test Anxiety Inventory (TAI):** This is a self-report questionnaire that measures anxiety specifically related to taking tests.
- **The State-Trait Anger Expression Inventory (STAXI):** This self-report questionnaire (e.g., Spielberger, 1988) measures both state and trait anger, as well as the tendency to express anger outwardly or inwardly. Some researchers have used this test to measure anxiety indirectly, as anxiety and anger can be closely related.

Measuring Willingness to Communicate

Willingness to communicate is a psychological construct that refers to the desire or motivation to engage in communication and interaction with others. Willingness to communicate has been assumed to play an important part in effective communication, as it affects the degree of participation and engagement in a conversation.

Research on willingness to communicate (WTC) in applied linguistics has received much attention in recent years, with this factor being considered an important factor in language learning success. The concept was originally defined as an important personality trait in the study of first language (L1) communication by McCroskey and Baer (1985) and was then applied to the L2 context by applied linguistics researchers (e.g., Gregersen & MacIntyre, 2014; MacIntyre et al., 1998). It has been suggested that someone who is more willing to communicate may try to find more opportunities for interaction and communication, which can help the person to receive more input to the language and also practice his or her speaking and listening.

One of the first measures of willingness to communicate was in the L1 literature developed by McCroskey and Baer (1985). This was a twenty-item probability-estimate scale, with eight of the items being fillers, and the other twelve part of the scale. The scale was designed to measure respondents' willingness to initiate or desire to avoid communication, representing three types of receivers (friends, acquaintances, and strangers) in four communication contexts (dyads, small groups, meetings, and public speaking). Responses are measured on a scale of 0–100 percent, based on how willing the person would be to communicate in each context. Example 10.18 provides sample items from the Willingness to Communicate Scale (WTC) from McCroskey (1992, p. 18).

EXAMPLE 10.18

Directions: Below are twenty situations in which a person might choose to communicate or not to communicate. Presume you have completely free choice. Indicate the percentage of times you would choose to communicate in each type of situation. Indicate in the space at the left what percent of the time you would choose to communicate.

0 = never, 100 = always

— 1. *Talk with a service station attendant.
— 2. *Talk with a physician.
— 3. Present a talk to a group of strangers.
— 4. Talk with an acquaintance while standing in line.
— 5. *Talk with a salesperson in a store.
— 6. Talk in a large meeting of friends.
— 7. *Talk with a police officer.
— 8. Talk in a small group of strangers.
— 9. Talk with a friend while standing In line.
— 10. *Talk with a waiter/waitress in a restaurant.
— 11. Talk in a large meeting of acquaintances.
— 12. Talk with a stranger while standing in line.
— 13. *Talk with a secretary.
— 14. Present a talk to a group of friends.
— 15. Talk in a small group of acquaintances.
— 16. *Talk with a garbage collector.
— 17. Talk in a large meeting of strangers.
— 18. *Talk with a spouse (or girl/boy friend).
— 19. Talk in a small group of friends.
— 20. Present a talk to a group of acquaintances.

*Filler item

Measuring Personality Traits

Personality refers to the person's characteristics that "account for consistent patterns of feeling, thinking, and behaving" (Pervin & John, 2021, p. 4). It can be considered a factor that includes the combination of an individual's emotions, attitudes, behaviors, and values that makes them different from others. It can be referred to as an affective factor because it influences how someone feels and expresses their emotions.

Psychologists have identified several different personality types, and there are many different personality typologies that have been proposed over the years. Two of the most well-known and widely used personality typologies include the Five Factor Model and the Myers-Briggs Type Indicator (MBTI). The Five Factor Model is composed of the following five factors: neuroticism, extroversion, openness, agreeableness, and conscientiousness. A total of thirty facets make up the Five Factor Model, which is used in various personality tests and assessments. The MBTI is a personality test that is based on the theories of Carl Jung and is designed to measure personality along four dimensions: extroversion vs. introversion, sensing vs. intuition, thinking vs. feeling, and judging vs. perceiving. It assigns individuals to one of sixteen personality types derived from the combination of the above four dimensions. There are different forms and versions of this instrument with a different number of tests items and scoring formats.

There are other commonly used personality traits assessment tools that measure an individual's personality based on the five-factor model (FFM) of personality; these include the NEO Five-Factor Inventory (NEO-FFI) and the NEO Personality Inventory Revised (NEO-PI-R). The NEO-FFI is a sixty-item self-report inventory that asks individuals to rate how well certain statements describe their personality. The NEO-PI-R is a longer inventory, with 240 items that measure 30 narrower facets of personality traits.

Many studies in applied linguistics have examined the relationship between various aspects of learners' personalities and second language learning success, and in particular the link between Myers-Briggs personality types and second language learning success. One frequently studied trait is extroversion, characterized by being sociable, outgoing and enjoying being around other people. Extroverts tend to be more expressive and draw energy from engaging with others. In contrast, introverts are generally more inwardly focused and prefer solitary activities. However, these tendencies exist on a spectrum, with most individuals exhibiting varying degrees of extroversion and introversion rather than being entirely one or the other.

Kim and Nassaji (2018) investigated the role of extroversion in second language learning by examining how introversion, a key dimension of personality, affects learners' attention to form in second language classrooms. Data on extroversion were collected using a personality trait questionnaire adapted from the Big Five Inventory (BFI) (John, Robins, & Pervin, 2008). Example 10.19 illustrates sample items taken from this questionnaire.

EXAMPLE 10.19

Instructions: Below are several characteristics that may or may not describe you. For example, do you agree that you enjoy spending time with others? For each statement, tick the response in the table that best reflects your level of agreement, ranging from disagree strongly to agree strongly.

	Disagree strongly	Disagree a little	Neither agree nor disagree	Agree a little	Agree strongly
Is talkative					
Is reserved					
Is full of energy					
Generates a lot of enthusiasm					
Tends to be quiet					
Has an assertive personality					
Is sometimes shy, inhibited					
Is outgoing, sociable					

POINTS TO PONDER

What assessment tools are often used to collect data about cognitive factors in applied linguistics? Can you provide some examples? Share your personal experience if you have used any of them.

Tools for Measuring Cognitive Variables

Cognitive factors refer to the mental processes involved in learning a language. There are many cognitive variables that can significantly influence language learning, including attention, noticing, working memory, processing speed, aptitude, and language analytic ability. Measuring these cognitive variables is crucial for understanding their impact on language acquisition. These, along with how they can be measured, will be briefly discussed below.

Cognitive factors are mental processes like attention, noticing, working memory, processing speed, aptitude, and language analytic ability that influence language learning.

Measuring Attention

Attention is a complex cognitive process, and in language learning it can refer to the process of attending to specific aspects of language input in order to understand and remember it. When learners pay attention to linguistic input, they are more likely to notice and process relevant language features, such as vocabulary, grammar, and pronunciation.

Attention can be measured in second language research through various methods, depending on the specific research objectives and the aspects of attention being studied. Here we will discuss some common methods for doing so.

Eye Tracking

One way of measuring attention is through eye tracking. Eye tracking is a technology that uses a device that records eye movements. It can measure either the point of gaze (where the eye is focused) or the motion of an eye relative to the head. This can be used to examine what learners are looking at, how long they focus on specific elements (e.g., words, grammar structures), and patterns of gaze to understand visual attention.

An example of eye tracking for measuring attention might be a study in which participants are asked to read a sentence and their eye movements tracked as they read the content. The tracking of the eye can be used to understand what and how much the reader attends to the different parts of the sentence as they read; this is possible by analyzing the learners' eye movements and gaze patterns.

Reaction Time

Reaction time (RT) is a measure used to assess how quickly an individual responds to a stimulus. In applied linguistics research, it can be used to measure the speed of learners' responses to language stimuli. Faster response times may indicate quicker attentional processing. Thus, it can provide insights into attention, cognitive processing, and language learning. For example, you might measure the time it takes for participants to identify and understand words or sentences in the target language, to reveal differences in language processing among them. Typically, advanced learners have faster reaction times, reflecting quicker and more automatic processing.

Error Rates

Assessing learners' error rates in language tasks can provide insights into attention. Frequent errors or inconsistent performance may suggest attentional issues. They can also provide valuable insights into attention by revealing how learners allocate and sustain their attention during language processing tasks. For example, if a learner makes errors that are unrelated to the task or linguistic context, it may indicate an issue in their selective attention or a lack of attention to linguistics items.

Neuroimaging Techniques

Neuroimaging techniques such as Functional Magnetic Resonance Imaging (fMRI) or Electroencephalography (EEG) can also provide insights into learners' attention and cognitive processing. fMRI scans, for example, can reveal brain activity patterns associated with attention during language processing tasks; you can examine which brain regions are active when learners pay attention to specific language features and which brain regions are not. Electroencephalography (EEG) can measure electrical activity in the brain, providing real-time information about cognitive processes. Researchers can analyze event-related potentials (ERPs) obtained through EEG to study how attention operates during language tasks.

Measuring Noticing

Mental activities including noticing or L2 processing are not subject to direct observation. It is impossible to directly observe what goes on in a learner's mind when performing a task. However, there are indirect ways of getting some evidence. To this end, research has used a number of tools, including the following.

Immediate Recall

Immediate recall is a retrospective technique in which learners are asked immediately after an event to recall what they noticed (see also Chapter 15); one of the studies that used immediate recall is Philp (2003), which examined learners' noticing of recasts in dyadic task-based interaction. Noticing was operationalized as remembering recasts following the feedback and was measured by cued immediate recall, where, after each recast, the learner's response was interrupted by the sound of two knocks to cue the learner to recall the feedback. The results showed that learners were able to notice a substantial proportion of the recasts (60–70%).

Stimulated Recall

Another research tool used to collect noticing or processing data is stimulated recall (e.g., Egi, 2007, 2010; Mackey, Gass, & McDonough, 2000). Stimulated recall (see also Chapter 15) is a retrospective method in which learners are required to recall their thought processes after a task is completed. It is called stimulated recall because learners are presented, after the task, with a clue or stimulus to recall their thoughts at the time they were doing the task. One of the studies using such a method is Mackey et al. (2000), which examined learners' noticing of corrective feedback in task-based dyadic interaction. The researchers found that the learners perceived the target of the feedback differently depending on error types and feedback types.

Think Aloud

The think aloud is a concurrent strategy used to capture learners' thoughts when completing a task. When doing a think aloud, learners are often asked to verbalize their thought processes while completing the task. The think-aloud reports are then recorded, transcribed, and coded. Think alouds might be difficult to use at the time of some events such as oral feedback. In such cases, they can be used during a subsequent task. Nipaspong and Chinokul (2010), for example, employed think-aloud protocols during a follow-up discussion task to examine the effect of explicit and implicit feedback on learners' noticing of a pragmatic feature (English refusals). Their results showed an advantage for implicit over explicit feedback.

Retrospective Questionnaires and Interviews

Retrospective questionnaires and interviews are other means that can gather information about learners' perception, though very indirectly. In a classroom study of interactional feedback, Fu and Nassaji (2016), for example, used a retrospective questionnaire in which students were asked to indicate how often they received such feedback. The findings showed that the perception of the feedback frequency reported was very close to the actual frequency of the feedback.

Measuring Working Memory

Memory is the ability to store, retain, and recall information. In language learning, memory plays an important role as it allows learners to retain and recall what they hear, including grammar rules, vocabulary, and pronunciation. There are different types of memory, including short-term memory, long-term memory, and working memory. Working memory is the ability to hold and manipulate information in the mind for a short period of time for further processing. Research has shown that the ability to learn new words or comprehend language is greatly influenced by a learner's working memory capacity.

There are several tests that have been used in applied linguistics research to measure memory, depending on the goals and purpose of the research. Some of these include the following.

The Digit Span Test

This test measures the ability to remember and repeat sequences of numbers, which requires attention and working memory. The test involves hearing a series of numbers and trying to repeat them back in the same order. The number of digits in the series gradually increases until the participant is no longer able to accurately repeat them back. The test is typically scored based on the number of digits accurately repeated.

Word Span Test

This test is similar to the digit span test with the difference that it involves recalling a list of words instead of numbers.

The Digit Span Backward Test

This is a memory test that involves recalling a string of digits in reverse order. For example, if the string presented is "9, 2, 1, 7, 5" the learner should say "5, 7, 1, 2, 9." This task is often used to assess working memory, as it requires the learner to hold the digits and manipulate them in the memory in order to be able to repeat them in the correct order. As the length increases, the test becomes more challenging.

The Reading Span Task (RST)

One of the most widely used working memory tasks that investigate working memory is the reading span task (RST). Developed by Daneman and Carpenter (1980), this is a complex verbal task measuring both storage and processing components of working memory. The task involves asking participants to read aloud sets of sentences that increase in length as the test goes on and to then recall the final words of the sentences in the same order presented. Various versions of this task can be used to measure learners' working memory.

Letter–Number Ordering Task

The letter–number ordering task involves hearing a series of letters and numbers. The participants should reorder and repeat the characters, and also repeat the numbers in numerical order and the letters in alphabetical order. For example, they may be presented with "B-8" and they should repeat "8-B." Then they may hear "V-1-S-3," and should repeat "1-3-S-V." If the participant misses three series in a row, the task would be discontinued.

Operation Span Task

Developed by Turner and Engle (1989), the operation span task is a memory task that involves presenting participants with a series of mathematical equations followed by a target word ("$2 \times 7 = 14$, pen"). Participants must read the operation out loud, say whether it is correct or incorrect, and then read the target word (there is no time limit for responses). After a series of operations such as these, participants are asked to recall the target words in the order presented.

Measuring Processing Speed

Processing speed refers to how quickly an individual can perform cognitive tasks, including learning and processing new information. This factor is crucial in cognitive functioning and has implications for language learning, influencing the speed at which someone can process, understand, and produce language.

Studies often measure processing speed through reaction time (as mentioned before), which can be assessed in various ways. One common method is the simple reaction time task, where participants read a presented sentence at their own pace and press a button when finished. The time between stimulus presentation and the participant's response is recorded as a measure of reaction time. Other methods involve tasks requiring a choice or decision, where reaction time is defined as the time between stimulus presentation and the decision response.

Measuring Aptitude

Aptitude is a complex cognitive construct that refers to people's inherent talents and natural ability to learn a new skill. Some examples of aptitude include verbal aptitude, numerical aptitude, spatial aptitude, and language aptitude. Carroll (1981) identified the following four components as being involved in aptitude for language learning:

- **phonemic coding ability**: recognizing and distinguishing between different sounds in a language
- **grammatical sensitivity**: understanding and processing the rules of grammar in a language
- **inductive language learning ability**: learning a language through making inferences and generalizations based on examples and patterns
- **rote learning ability**: learning and remembering information through repetition and memorization.

There are several tests that have been used to measure learners' aptitude in applied linguistics research. Two widely used measures include the Modern Language Aptitude Test (MLAT) and the LLAMA Language Aptitude Test.

Modern Language Aptitude Test (MLAT)

The MLAT, developed by Carroll and Sapon (1959), is a widely used test for language aptitude, specifically designed to assess an individual's ability to learn English as a foreign language. It measures various abilities related to foreign language learning, such as memory, auditory discrimination, and grammatical sensitivity. The MLAT consists of five subtests: (1) Number Learning (memory), (2) Phonetic Script (sound–symbol association), (3) Spelling Clues (English vocabulary and sound–symbol association), (4) Words in Sentences (grammatical structure), and (5) Paired Associates (rote memory). These subtests aim to measure three essential aptitude components: phonetic coding, memory, and language analytic ability. Example 10.20 provides a practice item with an example from part 4 of the test.

EXAMPLE 10.20

Instruction: In each of the following questions, we will call the first sentence the key sentence. One word in the key sentence will be underlined and printed in capital letters. Your task is to select the letter of the word in the second sentence that plays the same role in that sentence as the underlined word in the key sentence.

Look at the following sample question:

Sample: JOHN took a long walk in the woods.

<u>Children</u> *in blue*	*jeans were*	*singing and*	*dancing in the*	*park.*
A	B	C	D	E

You would select "A," because the key sentence is about "John" and the second sentence is about "children."

NOW GO RIGHT AHEAD WITH THESE SAMPLE QUESTIONS.

Write down your answers so that you can check them when you are finished.

1. MARY is happy.

From the	look on your	face,	I can tell that you	must have had a bad	day.
	A	B	C	D	E

From: https://lltf.net/mlat-sample-items/mlat-part-iv/

The LLAMA Language Aptitude Test

The LLAMA Language Aptitude Test was developed by Paul Meara (2005) and is to some degree based on MLAT. The LLAMA is a computer test used for adult language learners, including four components: LLAMA B (a vocabulary measure) LLAMA D (a sound recognition measure), LLAMA E (a sound–symbol correspondence measure), and LLAMA F (a measure of grammatical inferencing). Example 10.21 demonstrates the use of LLAMA B.

EXAMPLE 10.21

LLAMA B presents test-takers with a set of twenty images whose names they do not know (see Figure 10.1 for examples). The images are all displayed on the computer screen, and by clicking on the image, learners can see its name. They have two minutes to study and learn the names of all the images.

After this learning phase, the program goes into a testing phase where it displays the name of each object, and learners should correctly identify the image by clicking on the image.

Figure 10.1 Some of the images used in LLAMA B

Measuring Language Analytic Ability

An important dimension of language aptitude is language analytic ability, which is defined as the ability to analyze language. Sheen (2007) used a language analytic measure in her study on the role of language analytic ability in focused written corrective feedback. The measure was based on the subtest of another commonly used aptitude test, the Hungarian language aptitude test (HUNLAT) developed by Ottó (2002). The test consists of four sets of twenty items intending to measure the four components of language aptitude proposed by Carroll (1981) mentioned above, namely phonetic coding ability, language analytical ability, grammatical sensitivity, and rote memory. Although the test was originally developed for first-language Hungarian speakers, the test, particularly its language analytic subtest, has been adapted to evaluate learners of other languages including English. Sheen (2007) adapted a version of this test to examine the role of language analytic ability. She described the test as follows.

> The test consisted of 14 multiple choice items. The learners were given a glossary consisting of words and sentences from an artificial language and their English translations (see Figure 1 [here Figure 10.2]). They were then given 14 English sentences and for each sentence were asked to choose the correct translation from the four choices provided. To make the correct choice, the learners needed to analyze grammatical markers supplied in the glossary and apply these to the multiple-choice translations. Figure 1 [here Figure 10.2] contains an example question. To choose the correct translation in Example 1, the student had to first deduce the rule that "i" is a past (progressive) marker and "o" is a present (progressive) marker and then apply that rule to the translated choices ... The language analysis test was scored on a discrete item basis with 14 points being the perfect score. Students' final scores were calculated as percentages.

Imaginary language	English translation
Kau	Dog
Meu	Cat
kau meud bi	The dog was chasing the cat.
kau meud bo	The dog is chasing the cat.
So	Watch
Ciu	Mouse

Example 1
The dog is watching the cat.
a. kau meud so   b. kau meud si
c. meu kaud so   d. meu kaud si

Figure 10.2 Language analysis test examples
(Sheen, 2007, pp. 267–268)

Tools for Measuring Pragmatic Skills

Previously we discussed data collection tools used to measure various linguistic knowledge. Even when communicative tasks are used, their scoring typically focuses on linguistic accuracy. Pragmatic tests emphasize not only learners' ability to produce grammatically accurate sentences but also utterances that are contextually or pragmatically appropriate. These tests are usually context specific, and their scoring considers both accuracy and contextual appropriacy. They have often been used in pragmatics research to assess learners' pragmatic ability.

Examples of such tests include role plays designed to examine how learners understand and produce language appropriately in social interaction. Examples of more controlled forms of such tasks are dialogues and what is known as discourse completion tasks (DCTs) used to examine learners' ability to use a particular speech act, such as requests, refusals, apologies, and so on, in simulated communicative contexts. In the following section, we will briefly describe the different tools through which pragmatic skills can be measured.

Pragmatic tests assess learners' ability to produce not only grammatically correct sentences but also contextually and pragmatically appropriate utterances.

Role Plays

Role plays have been widely used as a data collection method in pragmatics research. Their aim is to elicit oral data in which two interlocutors are given certain roles to play. They can be either closed or open role plays. Closed role plays involve only one single turn in response to what the other character would say. Open role plays, however, are interactive and can include as many turns as needed in order to complete the interaction. Example 10.22 provides a hypothetical scenario of a role play item about requests and apology.

EXAMPLE 10.22

Instruction: Role-play this situation with a partner.
Student A: You are the project manager. Ask one of your team members to stay later today and finish preparing the presentation for tomorrow's meeting.
Student B: Politely decline your project manager's request and offer a different solution.
Student A: Politely decline Student B's suggestion and explain your reasoning.
Both: Discuss until you find a mutual agreement.

Discourse Completion Tasks

In discourse completion tasks (DCTs), learners are provided with a description of a situation and are asked to describe what they would say in that situation. These tasks can be both written and oral and can be in the form of a single situation, multiple situations, or even a dialogue. In a dialogue completion task, participants are presented with an incomplete dialogue and are asked to complete it. Their oral form may tap more into implicit knowledge whereas their written form may encourage explicit knowledge. Example 10.23 provides a sample written DCT item where participants have to provide their response to a discourse situation.

EXAMPLE 10.23

Sample DCT item

- Your term paper is due, but you haven't finished it yet. You want to ask the professor for an extension. What would you say?
- A professor wants a student to present a paper in class a week earlier than scheduled. What would the professor say?

(Billmyer & Varghese, 2000, p. 548)

Discourse completion tasks can be used to measure both comprehension and production pragmatics and may also differ in the degree of control, ranging from those that are closed-ended, such as multiple-choice DCTs, to those that require learners to say whatever they would say in a specific situation.

Comprehension DCTs

Multiple-choice DCTs are a kind of DCT that involves only recognition and therefore can be used for measuring pragmatic comprehension. In a multiple-choice DCT, learners are presented with a discourse scenario to read, followed by multiple-choice responses, which include one target or correct option and a few distractors or incorrect options. Learners should choose what they think would be the best response in that situation. Example 10.24 provides a hypothetical scenario of a multiple-choice DCT item related to apology and requests.

EXAMPLE 10.24

Instruction: Please read the following scenario. Then, review the three possible responses and choose the one that is most appropriate for the situation.

You are a new employee at a company, and you have been working on an important project. However, you realize that one of your colleagues has been playing loud music in the shared workspace, making it difficult for you to concentrate. You decide to ask your colleague to lower the volume. What would you say?

A. "Hey, I like your music taste! But do you think you could keep it down a bit so I can focus?"
B. "Excuse me, can you please turn the music down? Some of us are trying to work."
C. "Can you shut that music off? It's really annoying when I'm trying to get things done."

Production DCTs

Pragmatic production refers to the ability to respond to communicative situations productively and appropriately. Such abilities can be measured via production DCT. Production DCTs are those in which learners are presented with a discourse scenario and are asked to say either orally or in written form what they would say in that situation. Example 10.23 given earlier is an example item of a production DCT where the learners are asked to indicate what they would say in the situation presented in the item.

Pragmatic Judgment Tasks

Another method for measuring pragmatic skills is through pragmatic judgment tasks. In these tasks, participants are presented with a scenario involving communication between two interlocutors. After reading the scenario, participants are asked to rate the appropriateness of the response using a provided scale (see Example 10.25 and Figure 10.3).

EXAMPLE 10.25

Your friend, Maria, is struggling with her math homework. She has a test coming up and is having a hard time understanding the material. She comes to you and says, "Can you help me with my homework because you are good at math." But you say "No, I can't."

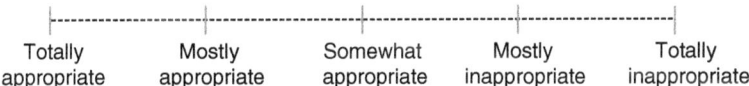

| Totally | Mostly | Somewhat | Mostly | Totally |
| appropriate | appropriate | appropriate | inappropriate | inappropriate |

Figure 10.3 A pragmatic judgment task

It is important to note that although pragmatic tests such as DCTs might be an effective way of gathering socially appropriate responses from the learner, one limitation is that they do not elicit naturally occurring speech. Another is the difficulty of designing such tests in ways that can elicit only the speech act targeted.

Conclusion

This chapter has explored various quantitative data collection tools commonly used in applied linguistics research. Understanding the purpose and application of these tools is essential for researchers, as it helps in selecting the most appropriate methods that align with their specific research goals. In applied linguistics, research often involves assessing language abilities, affective factors (such as motivation and attitudes), and cognitive variables (such as memory and processing skills). This chapter has provided an overview of different quantitative measures that can be used to collect data in these areas, demonstrating how they can be applied to evaluate learners' language abilities and related variables.

While it is important to be familiar with a wide range of quantitative tools, it is equally vital that the tools used in research are reliable and valid. In the following chapters, we will discuss the concepts of reliability and validity in quantitative research, offering strategies and guidelines for assessing and enhancing the quality of the data collection tools you choose to use in your research.

DISCUSSION AND ACTIVITY QUESTIONS

Discussion Questions

1. Why is it important to know about various quantitative data collection tools in the field of applied linguistics research?
2. What are the different types of tests to measure language proficiency? Can you provide examples and explain their differences?
3. To what extent can explicit and implicit language knowledge be accurately measured in research, and what challenges might arise in this process? Do you believe the distinction between explicit and implicit knowledge is meaningful in language acquisition research? Why or why not?
4. How are affective factors such as motivation and anxiety measured in language learning, and what are some examples of tests used to assess these factors?
5. Which tests are commonly used to evaluate cognitive variables such as working memory or language processing in language research and what are the advantages and limitations of these tests?
6. Consider a scenario where a researcher uses a multiple-choice grammar test to assess learners' writing ability. What are the potential strengths and limitations of this approach?

Activity Questions

1. Locate an applied linguistics study that has used measures of specific language skills, such as vocabulary or grammar, to collect data about the participants' abilities in these areas. Explain the rationale behind the use of such tests and discuss their strengths and limitations.
2. Develop and administer a structured questionnaire to collect data on learners' attitudes towards learning a second language. Analyze the data collected and draw conclusions based on the results.
3. Suppose you are designing a study to investigate the relationship between memory and perception in second language learning. Identify the measures and procedures for data collection and discuss potential limitations of those measures for the study.
4. Locate a research study that has used a structured questionnaire to collect quantitative data about learners' beliefs, attitudes, or motivation towards

language learning. Describe the questionnaire and explain how the researcher used the data to draw conclusions about the learners' attitudes or motivation.

5. Suppose you are planning to conduct a research study that involves collecting data on learners' pragmatic skills. What specific pragmatic skills will you assess (e.g., ability to use appropriate apology strategies in different social situations)? What types of data collection tools will you use, and why?

6. Imagine you are designing a study to measure learners' speaking proficiency. What data collection tool would you use, and why?

Understanding and Assessing Reliability in Quantitative Research

CHAPTER OBJECTIVES

After completing this chapter, you should be able to

- Understand the concept of reliability and its importance in quantitative research.
- Evaluate different types of reliability, including test–retest, interrater, and internal consistency.
- Develop skills to conduct and calculate reliability estimates for a given measure or instrument such as Cronbach's alpha, Cohen's kappa, correlation coefficients, and intraclass correlations.
- Understand how to interpret reliability estimates with examples.
- Examine the pros and cons of different types of reliability and the implications for research.

Introduction

Two key elements of quantitative research designs are reliability and validity. Reliability has to do with consistency of the research results. In other words, it addresses the question of whether the research results can be replicated or consistently reproduced over time. In quantitative research, by checking the reliability, we measure the degree to which a measurement instrument, such as a questionnaire or a test, consistently produces the same results when we use it to measure a concept. Validity has to do with how accurately our measures reflect the concept being studied. Both reliability and validity are important in applied linguistics research as they directly affect the accuracy and credibility of research findings. In this chapter, we will discuss the concept of reliability and its role in applied linguistics research. We will explore various types and methods for assessing reliability in quantitative research, along with examples. We will also explore strategies for improving reliability in ways that can increase the rigor of data collection procedures.

POINTS TO PONDER

What does reliability mean to you, and why is it important in applied linguistics research?

The Notion of Reliability

Research is multifaceted, and measurement is an important aspect of empirical research, particularly in quantitative studies. In quantitative research, variables are systematically measured to explore their relationships or impacts. While measurement is less central in qualitative research, it can still play a role, for example, in coding or categorizing data to analyze themes and patterns.

In applied linguistics quantitative research, we always quantify and measure abstract language-related variables and phenomena. As discussed earlier, this can include measures of language proficiency, vocabulary size, grammatical knowledge, motivation, reading comprehension, and more. For example, to study the impact of a particular instructional strategy on students' motivation, we need to measure the participants' level of motivation through an assessment method such as a questionnaire. Measurement is widely used in many contexts outside of research as well. For example, language teachers and educators often use various types of tests to measure a student's knowledge and skill in a specific area, such as reading, writing, or speaking. Given the widespread use and crucial role of measurement in research, it is important to evaluate the accuracy of the measurement tools. One important aspect of measurement accuracy is its reliability. This chapter will explore various ways in which reliability can be established in quantitative research. The overall goal is to provide a comprehensive understanding of reliability in quantitative research, and of how it can be used to enhance the consistency of research findings.

The Importance of Reliability in Quantitative Research

As noted above, reliability refers to the consistency and dependability of the study findings, as well the way they are measured. It is the ability of a test or a study to produce consistent and stable results over time. Reliability in research is important because it indicates that the findings are consistent and that the results can be replicated. This helps to build trust in the research and increases the chances that the findings will be useful and applicable to real-world situations. If a study does not have good reliability, we cannot trust that the data provided are an accurate reflection of the participants' performance. In applied linguistics research, researchers often assess the effect of an intervention such as that of a teaching method on learners' performance to see whether it enhances language teaching and learning, or they may want to determine how different knowledge, skills, and other learning and teaching characteristics are related. Without confidence in the measure used to examine these, it is difficult to conclude whether the relationship found, or the changes shown in the learners' performance, are due to the intervention itself or due to measurement errors. In short, reliability helps to minimize the potential for errors in research, which is important for ensuring the credibility of the research findings.

Reliability refers to the ability of a test or a study to produce consistent and stable results over time.

It is also important to report reliability estimates in research publications because they provide information about the consistency or stability of a measurement. Reporting reliability estimates allows readers to evaluate the quality of the measurement used in a study and the extent to which the findings can be replicated. Without this information, it is difficult to determine the credibility and generalizability of the research findings.

Reliability and Reliability Coefficient

Any tools we use to measure should be able to be relied upon to produce accurate and dependable results. Let's give an example outside research. Suppose you want to measure the temperature of a glass of water. You would use a thermometer to do so. The thermometer that you use should be reliable. That is, it should consistently measure the temperature in the same way, even when used multiple times or by your friend. Now suppose you measure the temperature of a cup of water three times in a row, and the thermometer gives the following readings:

- first measurement: 40 degrees Celsius
- second measurement: 43 degrees Celsius
- third measurement: 53 degrees Celsius.

In this case, the thermometer is considered unreliable because it gives you different results each time you use it, and the three measurements are far from each other in value and the deviation is high. Now let's consider another scenario, where you use another thermometer to measure the temperature of the same cup of water three times in a row; this thermometer gives these readings:

- first measurement: 40 degrees Celsius
- second measurement: 41 degrees Celsius
- third measurement: 42 degrees Celsius.

In this case, the thermometer is considered more reliable because it gives more consistent results over time. The three readings are close to each other, and the deviation is minimal. We have the same situation in research. In research, we measure variables to determine if they are related or if they affect each other. Therefore, the assessment tool or the instrument that we use to measure the variable should produce accurate and consistent results. If the tool used produces similar results whenever it is used, the assessment tool is fairly reliable. If not, it is not reliable.

Suppose you are interested in examining the role of a spelling instruction program on the spelling ability of beginner-level learners. Here you need to use measures that reliably distinguish beginners from advanced-level learners. You also need to have a reliable test of spelling. If you design the test, it should be designed in a way that is reasonably reliable, meaning that if the participants take the test multiple times, they should receive similar scores each time. This allows you to assess the effectiveness of the program more accurately.

In quantitative research, the reliability of a measurement can be determined quantitatively and is presented in the form of an index called the reliability coefficient.

The reliability coefficient is a statistical measure, which is often calculated using a formula. It shows the consistency of a test or a measurement tool. It is often expressed as a value between 0 and 1, with 1 indicating perfect reliability (i.e., 100% agreement between the two times of testing) and 0 indicating no reliability at all. It is uncommon for a test to have perfect reliability, as most tests will have some degree of error or variability. A value between 0.80 or 0.90 is generally considered to be good reliability with 0.90 and above considered to be excellent. A reliability between 0.80 and 0.70 is also considered acceptable, but anything below 0.60 is either questionable or unacceptable.

The reliability coefficient is a statistical measure that shows the consistency of a test or a measurement tool. It is often expressed as a value between 0 and 1, with 1 indicating perfect reliability and 0 indicating no reliability.

The reliability coefficient is important because it allows you to evaluate, report, and compare the consistency and stability of your data, and to determine whether tests or measurement tools are suitable for particular purposes. Depending on the type of data, there are different types of reliability coefficients, including Cronbach's alpha, test–retest reliability, split-half reliability, and inter-rater reliability. These coefficients are commonly used in the field of applied linguistics to measure the reliability of a test or a measurement used in the study. Overall, a high reliability coefficient indicates that a test or measurement is producing consistent results, and a low reliability coefficient suggests that the test or measurement tool is producing inconsistent results and is not suitable for use procedures.

POINTS TO PONDER

Can a study be considered a robust study if it is reliable but not replicable, or replicable but not reliable? How do these concepts work together to shape the rigor of a study?

Reliability and Replicability

There are two conceptions of reliability. One has to do with the reliability of the instruments of data collection, and the other, the study. In the former sense, it refers to the consistency and stability of the measurements obtained when a particular instrument such as a test or a questionnaire is used. If an instrument is reliable, it should produce similar results when used by different researchers or when administered to the same participants at different times. The consistency and stability of the findings and conclusions of a study are more related to the replicability of the study. Thus, although reliability and replicability are related, they are distinct concepts in research. Reliability refers to the consistency or stability of a measure or a study, meaning that if the study were repeated multiple times, the results would be similar. Replicability refers to the possibility for other researchers to replicate or reproduce the results of a study using the same methods and procedures. Since reliability and replicability are closely related, if the tests or instruments are reliable, the results could be better replicable by other researchers using similar methods. If the findings are replicable and the study were to be repeated, the test results would be consistent and similar. Altogether these confirm that the findings can be trusted.

While **reliability** refers to the consistency of a measure or a study, **replicability** refers to the possibility for other researchers to reproduce the results of a study using the same methods and procedures.

POINTS TO PONDER

What types of reliability measures have you heard about or come across? How do these measures differ from one another, and when should each one be used?

Methods to Determine Reliability

There are different ways to check the reliability of a test or an assessment tool in applied linguistics research. These include:

- test–retest reliability
- equivalent-form (or parallel form) reliability
- internal consistency
  - Cronbach's alpha
  - split-half reliability
- interrater or intercoder reliability
  - percent agreement
  - kappa coefficient
  - intraclass correlation (ICC)
- intrarater or intracoder reliability.

The use of these various methods of calculating reliability depends on the type of measure and the goal of the study. We will discuss each of these in more detail below.

Test–Retest Reliability

Test–retest reliability is a very common measure of reliability in applied linguistics research. It is a statistical measure that assesses the degree to which the same test produces similar results when administered to the same group of individuals at different points in time. Thus, test–retest reliability assesses the stability of a test or assessment measure over time. Test–retest reliability is checked by giving the same assessment tool to a group of participants on two or more occasions and comparing their results (Figure 11.1). If a test has a high test-retest reliability, it will produce similar results at different points in time, indicating that it is measuring the construct consistently. If it has low test-retest reliability, it will produce different results at different points in time, indicating that it is not measuring the construct consistently.

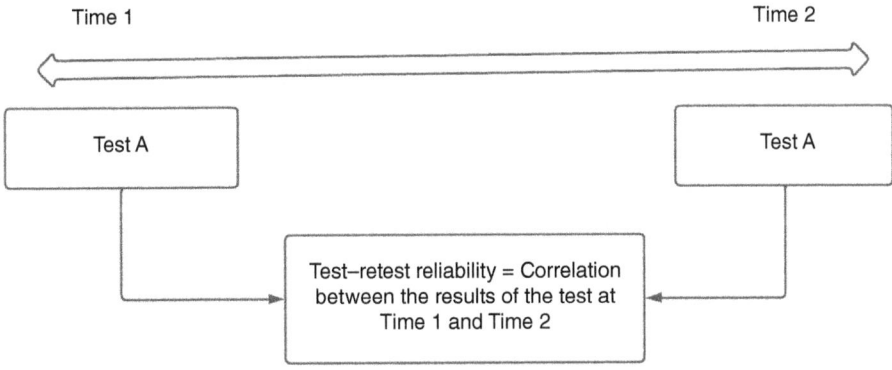

Figure 11.1 Test–retest reliability

Test–retest reliability is a measure that assesses the degree to which the same test produces similar results when administered to the same group of individuals at different points in time.

As for calculating the reliability, the most commonly used correlation coefficient for measuring test–retest reliability is Pearson's correlation coefficient for continuous scores and Spearman's rank correlation coefficient for ordinal measures. This correlation coefficient is called the reliability coefficient. Usually, a coefficient of 0.70 is generally considered acceptable, and over 0.80 is good for test–retest reliability. However, the interpretation of the values often depends on the test characteristics and its aim.

The Use of Test–Retest Reliability

This measure of reliability is particularly important for assessments that are intended to be stable over time, and the goal is to determine whether the results are consistent across multiple test administrations. This method is particularly useful when measuring cognitive abilities and personality traits, which tend to be relatively stable over time, or educational tests of knowledge, which should have consistent results over time. It is important to note that test–retest reliability is not appropriate for all types of measurement. For example, if the measure is intended to capture a current state or a one-time event, test–retest reliability would not be an appropriate measure of reliability.

Research in second language acquisition and applied linguistics frequently uses measures to assess constructs such as language proficiency, aptitude, attitude, motivation, learning strategies, and other personality traits. The reliability and stability of these measures over time is important for researchers and practitioners to make accurate inferences. Therefore, test–retest reliability can be used as an important method to assess the consistency of results obtained from these measures over time.

The steps involved in calculating test–retest reliability are as follows:

- Select the test or measure that will be used in the study;
- Administer the test to the study participants or a sample similar to them on two separate occasions, with an appropriate time interval between test administrations;
- Calculate the correlation coefficient (such as Pearson's correlation coefficient or Spearman's rank correlation coefficient) between the scores for the two occasions;
- Examine the correlation coefficient to determine the level of test–retest reliability. A coefficient of 0.70 or higher is generally considered acceptable for test–retest reliability.

Example 11.1 presents a hypothetical scenario.

EXAMPLE 11.1

Suppose you want to conduct a study to examine the effect of an intensive reading program on L2 learners' language proficiency. But before the study, you want to make sure that your tests reliably measure language proficiency. To assess this, you conduct a test–retest reliability by administering the test to a group of learners at two different time points (e.g., with a two-week interval). The resulting correlation coefficient ($r = 0.89$) indicates strong test–retest reliability, affirming that the test consistently measures language proficiency over time.

Assumptions Underlying Test–Retest Reliability

Test–retest reliability is based on a few assumptions.

Assumption 1: The first assumption is that the test is measuring a construct that is stable and does not change over time, meaning that the scores on the test will be consistent if the test is administered again. For example, intelligence or other personality traits such as field dependence–field independence or extroversion–introversion are examples of those characteristics that can be assumed to be stable over time. However, test–retest reliability may not be an appropriate measure for calculating reliability when assessing mood or other characteristics that may fluctuate over time, such as stress. This is because the scores obtained on the test or measure may be affected by changes in the individual's mood or stress, making it difficult to determine if any observed changes in scores are due to changes in the individual or to measurement error. Alternative methods, such as internal consistency, may be more appropriate for assessing the reliability of measures of mood or other characteristics that can fluctuate over time.

Assumption 2: Test–retest reliability is also based on the assumption that the ability, skill, or knowledge the test measures does not change from time 1 to time 2. This then suggests that the testing and retesting should not be conducted when people are exposed to a treatment or a situation where their knowledge has increased.

Assumption 3: Test–retest reliability also assumes that the test-taking conditions are consistent and the same, including the testing environment and the instructions given to the test-taker. This suggests that to have an accurate reliable measure, the testing should be conducted in the same environment, if possible.

Assumption 4: Test–retest reliability assumes that there are no memory effects (recalling responses from the previous occasion) or practice and test–retest effects, which refers to the changes in the test scores as a result of taking the test multiple times.

If the above assumptions are met, consistent scores across administrations indicate that the test is reliable, while any inconsistencies suggest potential problems with the test's reliability. It is important to note that it is not possible for a test to have 100 percent reliability. Even if a test is well-designed and administered properly, there will always be some degree of error or variability in the results. It is possible for a test to have a high level of reliability, but it is not possible for a test to be 100 percent reliable. That is also why the reliability coefficient is always considered to be an estimate.

The test–retest effect or the practice effect mentioned earlier suggests that when doing test–retest reliability, we should always consider the interval between the two occasions on which the test is administered. This should not be too short nor too long. If it is too short, the learners may remember their responses, which can occur because of "practice effects." Thus, we should wait a sufficient length of time to make sure that any change in scores from one time to another is not due to practice or learning effects. However, if the interval is too long, the results can be affected by extraneous variables such as maturation or history, which happens due to the learners' natural growth over time, or because there are other history events, such as being exposed to situations that help learners to learn about the content of the test. These can lead to improved scores on the retest. However, since the learners' growth or improvement as a result of history is not often the same and varies among individuals, this can lead to a lower reliability score (or an underestimation of the reliability). How long we should wait often depends on the type of measure used and the sample being studied. However, in general, an interval of two to three weeks is suggested to be an optimal amount of time. Again, it is important to consider the goal of the research, the specific characteristics of the measure, and the reason for which the reliability is being used.

In doing **test–retest reliability,** we should always consider the interval between the two occasions on which the test is administered. A short interval may affect reliability due to memory effects, while a long interval can introduce external factors that impact consistency.

Advantages and Limitations of Test–Retest Reliability

There are several advantages and limitations of test–retest reliability Some of the advantages include the following:

- It provides a straightforward and simple method for measuring the consistency of a measurement;
- It provides an estimate of the stability of a measure over time, which is important for long-term research studies or those that need to use a test in different occasions;
- It can be used to assess the reliability of a wide range of measures, including self-report measures, behavioral measures, and physiological measures.

However, there are also some limitations or disadvantages of test–retest reliability. These include the following:

- The potential for practice effects or changes in the test-taker's circumstances to influence test scores, as well as the need for an optimal amount of time between test administrations;
- Test–retest reliability might be more difficult to obtain in certain circumstances or with certain participants such as children (or it may be hard to convince people to take a test twice);

- It may not accurately reflect the true reliability of a measure if there is significant change in the construct being measured between the administration of the two tests;
- It may not be appropriate for measures that are expected to change over time, such as measures of growth or development;
- It can be time-consuming and costly to administer the same measure twice to a large sample;
- Not only practice effects but other factors such as maturation and history can also affect the test–retest reliability results.

Despite limitations, test–retest reliability is a **useful measure** that can provide valuable information about the stability of test scores over time. This can be useful for researchers, practitioners, and test developers as it helps them to interpret test results accurately and make informed decisions based on those results.

Equivalent-Form (Parallel-Form) Reliability

Equivalent-form reliability measures the consistency of results when different versions of a test are used to measure the same construct. In other words, it is a measure of the degree to which different versions or parallel forms of a test or an assessment tool produce similar results for a given population.

In research, sometimes there is a need to create two or more versions of a test that are different but the same in terms of content and what they measure. This may be needed for several reasons. One reason is to control for practice effects, where participants may perform better on a test after having taken it previously. For example, if a study is using a pretest–posttest design, you may use different versions of a test as a pre- and posttest to prevent practice and memory effect. Memory effect occurs when the participants remember some of the test items from the previous administration. To control for both effects, you may create two different forms of the test (such as Form A and Form B), which are considered parallel forms. Then you can administer Form A as the pretest and Form B as the posttest.

Different versions of a test may also need to be created when a test is going to be used in different cultures or languages. Using different versions of a test can help to confirm that any differences in scores are due to true changes in the construct being measured, rather than simply to familiarity with the test. However, when different versions of a test are used, you should make sure that they are measuring the same construct and are comparable with one another.

Additionally, you may administer multiple versions of a test to the same group of participants just to confirm their reliability. By comparing the results, you can establish the test's consistency in measuring the same construct.

To create equivalent versions of the same test, it is important that the tests measure the same skill and knowledge and are also the same in terms of the number of items and difficulty level. We should also make sure that all the versions are administered in the same way and with the same instructions and time limit. The tests should also be scored in the same way, using the same scoring rubric, instructions, and procedure. Finally, it is important to consider pilot testing each version to identify any issues or problems before administering the tests.

Once the two versions are created, they can be administered to the same group of participants to determine their equivalent-form reliability. They can be administered at the same time, immediately one after the other, or with a very short interval.

The equivalent-form reliability can be determined by calculating the correlation between the two forms and then using the correlation coefficient of the scores as the equivalent-form reliability coefficient, as was done for test–retest reliability above. If the score on the first and second form of the test are highly correlated, the two versions can be considered to have high equivalent-form reliability.

EXAMPLE 11.2

Suppose you are interested in examining the effect of corrective feedback on learners' implicit knowledge. You are thinking of using a timed grammaticality judgment test as a pretest and posttest. To mitigate practice effects, you create two versions of the test by randomly assigning eighty items into two sets of forty. These versions are administered to the same group a few days apart. You use correlational analysis, the Pearson correlation coefficient, to compare the scores. A high correlation (above 0.70, preferably 0.80) suggests a strong relationship between the two versions, indicating that they likely measure the same construct consistently.

Equivalent-form reliability has advantages, such as minimizing the test–retest effect. However, it is challenging to develop parallel forms with identical content, format, and difficulty. Creating two versions requires a substantial question pool, making the test development complex. Administration may also pose challenges due to time constraints and potential participant fatigue.

Internal Consistency

Another commonly used and very important method of determining reliability in applied linguistics research is internal consistency reliability. This kind of reliability refers to the degree to which different items within a test consistently measure the same construct. Therefore, it is a within-test measure. High internal consistency reliability indicates that the items on a test or questionnaire are highly correlated and measure the same construct, whereas low internal consistency reliability indicates that the test items are not very closely related to one another and thus they may not measure the same trait or construct. What is good about measuring internal consistency is that it does not need different groups of participants. You only need one group to take the test. This makes it much easier than test–retest or equivalent-form reliability, which need different forms of the test and different groups of participants.

Internal consistency reliability refers to the degree to which different items within a test consistently measure the same construct.

The Importance of Internal Consistency Reliability

Checking internal consistency within a test is important for accurate and valid measurements of the intended construct. It helps identify and correct any issues with test items before administering the test to participants. In applied linguistics research, where complex concepts are common, calculating and reporting internal consistency is important. For instance, when using a questionnaire on anxiety, it is essential to make sure that all items measure the anxiety construct. Similarly, if you are using a multicomponent test that has different components, you should check the items for each of its components so that they reliably test the construct underlying each one. For example, if you plan to use a language aptitude test that includes items related to phonetic coding ability, grammatical sensitivity, and rote learning ability, you will need to check the test items to make sure they consistently measure each of those components.

Methods to Calculate Internal Consistency Reliability

There are several methods to calculate internal consistency reliability. Two widely used ones are Cronbach's alpha and split-half reliability. We will discuss these below, with examples.

POINTS TO PONDER

In what contexts are measures like Cronbach's alpha and Cohen's kappa used, and what do their results reveal about data reliability?

Cronbach's Alpha Cronbach's alpha is a measure of internal consistency developed by Lee Cronbach (1951). This method of checking internal consistency assesses the reliability of a test or questionnaire by calculating the correlation between all items that make up the test or questionnaire. This method is widely used in the field of applied linguistics and second language research to assess the internal consistency of assessment tools.

One of the advantages of Cronbach's alpha is that it can be applied to a wide range of response types, including multiple-choice questions, Likert scale (ordinal) items, and categorical (nominal) items. For example, if a questionnaire includes a seven-point Likert scale (e.g. Strongly Disagree, Disagree, Somewhat Disagree,

Neutral, Somewhat Agree, Agree, Strongly Agree), Cronbach's alpha can be used for those responses. Or if a test includes true/false questions, yes/no questions, or any question that involves a dichotomous response, Cronbach's alpha is appropriate. This flexibility makes it a widely used measure of reliability in both research and practice. Equation 11.1 shows the formula for Cronbach's alpha.

Equation 11.1
$$\alpha = \frac{K}{K-1}\left[\frac{Sy^2 - Sum\ Si^2}{Sy^2}\right]$$

where

α = Cronbach's alpha
K = the number of items in the scale
Si^2 = the variance of individual items
Sy^2 = the variance of the total scores for all items

While it might be helpful to know how Cronbach's alpha is calculated, because of the availability of statistical software such as R or SPSS, you do not need to manually calculate it. For example, you can calculate Cronbach's alpha in SPSS (version: 29.0) by following the steps set out in SPSS Steps 11.1.

SPSS STEPS 11.1

- Open the data file in SPSS.
- Select "Analyze" > "Scale" > "Reliability Analysis."
- In the "Reliability Analysis" dialog box, choose the responses to be analyzed and transfer them to the "Items" box.
- Under "Model," select "Alpha" for reliability coefficient.
- Click "OK."

You will get a table showing the result of the analysis with the Cronbach's alpha coefficient for the selected variables. A coefficient of 0.7 or higher is generally considered acceptable, while a coefficient below 0.6 is considered low. Table 11.1 shows the Cronbach's alpha values and their general interpretation in the field.

Table 11.1 Cronbach's alpha values and their general interpretation

Reliability	Cronbach's alpha
Excellent	$\alpha \geq 0.9$
Good	$\alpha \geq 0.8 < 0.9$
Acceptable	$\alpha \geq 0.7 < 0.8$
Questionable	$\alpha \geq 0.6 < 0.7$
Poor	$\alpha \geq 0.5 < 0.6$
Unacceptable	$\alpha < 0.5$

Example 11.3 provides a hypothetical scenario.

EXAMPLE 11.3

Suppose you have developed a questionnaire on anxiety with the following six items (please note, this is a hypothetical example and often a questionnaire with six items is too short to be able to assess the construct of anxiety).

1. I feel nervous when I have to speak in a foreign language.

    1) Strongly Disagree   2) Disagree   3) Neutral   4) Agree   5) Strongly Agree

2. I worry about making mistakes when speaking in a foreign language.

    1) Strongly Disagree   2) Disagree   3) Neutral   4) Agree   5) Strongly Agree

3. I feel self-conscious when I have to speak in a foreign language.

    1) Strongly Disagree   2) Disagree   3) Neutral   4) Agree   5) Strongly Agree

4. I get anxious when I have to listen to others speak in a foreign language.

    1) Strongly Disagree   2) Disagree   3) Neutral   4) Agree   5) Strongly Agree

5. I feel nervous when I have to read or write in a foreign language.

    1) Strongly Disagree   2) Disagree   3) Neutral   4) Agree   5) Strongly Agree

6. I feel comfortable participating in class discussions in a foreign language.

    1) Strongly Disagree   2) Disagree   3) Neutral   4) Agree   5) Strongly Agree

Now suppose that you have administered this questionnaire to ten participants; Table 11.2 shows their responses.

Table 11.2 Example data for Cronbach's alpha reliability

	Questions (test items)					
Participants	Q 1	Q 2	Q 3	Q 4	Q 5	Q 6
1	2	3	3	2	2	2
1	3	4	4	3	4	3
3	3	4	4	4	4	5
4	2	1	2	2	1	2
5	1	2	3	2	2	4
6	3	4	3	3	2	2
7	3	4	3	3	3	2
8	1	3	2	2	1	4
9	3	3	2	3	3	2
10	4	4	5	4	4	5

Using SPSS Steps 11.1, you can calculate Cronbach's alpha for the data. The output displays the overall alpha coefficient for the scale and the number of items contributing to reliability. In our hypothetical questionnaire, Cronbach's alpha is 0.888, showing high internal consistency.

SPSS OUTPUT 11.1

Reliability Statistics

Cronbach's alpha	N of items
.888	6

Split-Half Reliability Split-half reliability is a statistical technique to estimate the internal consistency or reliability of a test or a questionnaire. It is an important aspect of research in applied linguistics, and researchers commonly use it as a method to measure the reliability of their data collection tools. The method involves dividing a test into two equal halves. The scores on the two halves are then correlated to determine the degree of consistency between the two halves. A high correlation between the scores on the two halves indicates a high level of internal consistency or reliability for the test. A low correlation suggests a low split-half reliability, which indicates that the test may not be consistent in measuring what it is intended to measure.

Split-half reliability estimates the internal consistency or reliability of a test or a questionnaire by dividing a test into two equal halves and correlating the scores of the two halves.

To divide a test into two halves, you can use the odd–even split method, where you assign odd-numbered items to one half of the test and even-numbered items to the other half. Another method is the random split method, where you randomly assign items to each half of the test. It is important to note that the test should be divided into two equal halves in terms of the number of items, difficulty level, and content.

The odd–even split method in split-half reliability has a few drawbacks. One drawback is that it may not accurately represent the true reliability of a test if the items in the test are not randomly distributed. For example, If the odd-numbered items are more difficult than the even-numbered items, the split-half reliability will be negatively affected. Another drawback is that it is sensitive to the number of items in the test.

The following are steps in conducting split-half reliability:

1. Administer the test or instrument to a group of participates.
2. Divide the test into two equal subtests using an odd–even number method or a random method.
3. Score each item for each participant on each of the two subtests.
4. Calculate the reliability coefficients to determine the split-half reliability of the test or measure.

Please note that the Pearson correlation is one way to calculate reliability, and there is also the Spearman–Brown coefficient, which can be used when we want to check whether the length of the test has any impact on its reliability. Example 11.4 provides a hypothetical scenario.

EXAMPLE 11.4

Let's look at the example that we had in the previous section about Cronbach's alpha reliability, in which you had developed a questionnaire on anxiety with six items. You can use the split-half method of estimating reliability for the question-naire. Table 11.3 shows the data again in addition to dividing the data into two subsets. You correlate the two sets using the Pearson correlation, and the coeffi-cient is 0.799.

Table 11.3 Example data for split-half reliability

Participants	Q 1	Q 2	Q 3	Q 4	Q 5	Q 6	Subtest 1 Sum of Q1,3,5	Subtest 2 Sum of Q2,4,6
1	2	3	3	2	2	2	7	7
1	3	4	4	3	4	3	11	10
3	3	4	4	4	4	5	11	13
4	2	1	2	2	1	2	5	5
5	1	2	3	2	2	4	6	8
6	3	4	3	3	2	2	8	9
7	3	4	3	3	3	2	9	9
8	1	3	2	2	1	4	4	9
9	3	3	2	3	3	2	8	8
10	4	4	5	4	4	5	13	13
							$r = 0.799$	

You can also conduct the analysis using statistical software such as R or SPSS. SPSS has an option that calculate split-half reliability using the raw data. To use SPSS, follow the steps laid out in SPSS Steps 11.2.

SPSS STEPS 11.2

- Open the data file in SPSS.
- Click "Analyze" > "Scale" > "Reliability Analysis."
- In the "Reliability Analysis" dialog box, select the variables and move them to the "Items" box.
- Under "Model," choose "Split-half" for reliability estimate.
- Click "OK."

SPSS OUTPUT 11.2

Reliability Statistics			
Cronbach's Alpha	Part 1	Value	.843
		N of Items	3[a]
	Part 2	Value	.758
		N of Items	3[b]
	Total N of Items		6
Correlation Between Forms			.797
Spearman–Brown Coefficient	Equal Length		.887
	Unequal Length		.887
Guttman Split-Half Coefficient			.887

a. The items are: Q1, Q2, Q3.
b. The items are: Q4, Q5, Q6.

The output displays split-half reliability coefficients, such as the Pearson correlation coefficient (0.797), along with other indexes like Cronbach's alpha, the Spearman–Brown correlation coefficient (0.887), and Guttman Split-half coefficient (0.887). The Spearman–Brown and Guttman coefficients closely represent the split-half reliability of the test. The Spearman–Brown formula adjusts for test length, providing a more accurate measure when a test is split into halves and administered multiple times or to a larger sample size. The Spearman–Brown coefficient provides an estimate of the reliability based on the full length of the test. Equation 11.2 gives the formula.

Equation 11.2
$$\text{Spearman–Brown} = \frac{2\left(r_{half}\right)}{1 + r_{half}}$$

r_{half} is the Pearson correlation between the two subtests. If you use this formula, you will get the Spearman–Brown estimate shown in the output:

$$\text{Spearman–Brown} = \frac{2\,(.799)}{1 + .799} = .887$$

As noted above, the Spearman–Brown formula helps adjust for the length. The formula can also be used to estimate the correlation coefficient that would be obtained if the test or questionnaire were made longer, which is then called the predicted reliability. This can be useful in situations where a test or questionnaire is being developed and you want to know what the reliability would be if the test or questionnaire became longer. To predict the reliability of a test if the length increases, we can use the following Spearman–Brown predicted reliability formula (Equation 11.3).

Equation 11.3 $$\text{Predicted reliability} = \frac{K\,(r)}{1 + (K - 1)\,(r)}$$

where

- r is the original reliability
- K is the degree by which the length of the test is changed. For example, if the original test consists of 10 items and the new test is 25 items, $K = 25/10 = 2.5$.

Suppose in Example 11.3 above, where we have a six-item questionnaire, you want to know what the reliability would be if you increase the length to ten items. If we assume that the reliability of the previous test was 0.887 (based on the Spearman–Brown coefficient), you can use the above formula to calculate the predicted reliability.

- $K = 10/6 = 1.66$.

$$\text{Predicted reliability} = \frac{1.66\,(0.887)}{1 + (1.66 - 1)\,(0.887)} = 0.929$$

So, if we increase the length of the questionnaire from six to ten items, its internal split-half reliability increases from 0.887 to 0.929.

Pros and Cons of Split-Half Reliability One advantage of split-half reliability is that it is relatively easy to perform, as it only requires the test or measurement to be split into two halves and the scores on each half to be correlated. It can be used with all kinds of test, including various types of item responses including Likert scale and multiple-choice items.

However, the estimate of split-half reliability may be influenced by the specific items that are included in each half of the test or measurement. For example, if the items are not randomly distributed within the test and most of the easier items appear at the beginning of the test and the more difficult ones towards the end, this can negatively affect the accuracy of the internal consistency. Relatedly, split-half reliability does not take into account the fact that some items may be more difficult or easier than others, which can influence the correlation between the two halves of the test. Split-half reliability estimates are also influenced by the length of the test, with longer tests tending to have higher reliability coefficients than shorter tests. Of course, that might be true with other methods of reliability as well.

Additionally, the way the test is divided into halves may create different reliability coefficients. As noted earlier, subtests can be formed by separating odd and even numbers or by randomly choosing items. The subtests can also be formed by having the first half of the test items in one subtest and the second half of the items in the second subtest. These different techniques can produce different reliability results.

Split-half reliability assumes that the two subtests have similar within-item variance, although that might not be true, particularly if the different sections of the test differ on their difficulty level. In addition, although split-half reliability may account for the errors associated with the nature of the items (i.e., errors that may occur because an item does not measure an intended construct or because it does not correlate well with other items), it does not consider performance error that might originate from learners' random responses to items because of lack of attention or because they may get bored as they reach the end of the test.

In short, split-half reliability, while easy to calculate, may not provide an accurate estimate of a test or measurement's reliability. As a result, researchers may prefer to use other methods, such as Cronbach's alpha, which may not have some of issues mentioned above. Cronbach's alpha is considered to be a more robust measure than the split-half method because the latter simply calculates the correlation between two halves of a scale. Cronbach's alpha, however, takes into account the correlation between all items on a scale, rather than just two halves, making it less susceptible to some of the sampling errors mentioned earlier. Additionally, Cronbach's alpha can be calculated for scales with both an odd and an even number of items, whereas the split-half method can only be applied to tests or scales with an even number of items. Despite these limitations, split-half reliability is still widely used in research and practice because it is relatively easy to calculate and interpret.

POINTS TO PONDER

What are interrater and intracoder reliability? Why do you think they are important, and how might inconsistencies in these measures influence the overall findings of a study?

Interrater (Intercoder) Reliability

Interrater reliability (used here to also refer to intercoder reliability in coding contexts) assesses the consistency of results when different raters evaluate the same responses or performances. It measures the degree of agreement among raters. High interrater reliability implies that different raters are likely to have similar judgments, while low reliability suggests potential variation in results. In research and assessment, interrater reliability is important for ensuring accuracy and fairness when multiple individuals are involved in evaluating a construct or phenomenon.

Interrater reliability refers to the level of agreement between two or multiple raters or evaluators in their assessment or measurement of a particular phenomenon.

Interrater reliability is used in second language and applied linguistics research when the research requires multiple raters to independently evaluate the same data or performance. This includes, for example, evaluating learners' language proficiency, their fluency or pronunciation, or their performance in oral presentations. The data can be nominal or ordinal. For example, two or more raters can assess whether a learner's responses in a test are correct or incorrect, or whether the level of anxiety is high, low, or medium. The goal is for the raters to provide consistent and accurate evaluations of the data or performance being assessed. This type of reliability is used to assess the consistency and agreement among the raters in their evaluations.

Things to Consider When Doing Interrater Reliability
When doing interrater reliability, the following should be considered:

- **Clear guidelines and rating criteria:** Provide clear instructions and scoring criteria to enhance agreement. Provide practice opportunities for familiarity.
- **Training:** Properly train raters to achieve consistency in assessments.
- **Manageable task:** The task should be manageable for raters to maintain consistency in scores.
- **Similar conditions:** Conduct ratings under similar conditions to avoid potential inconsistencies.
- **Independence:** Raters or coders should work independently without collaboration during rating or coding.
- **Representative sample:** Make sure the rated or coded sample is representative, considering size, complexity, and variability.
- **Adequate definition:** Clearly define preexisting criteria or codes and their usage if employed.

How to Calculate Interrater Reliability
There are different ways to calculate interrater reliability, and therefore there are different types of interrater reliability. Some of the most commonly used methods are

- percentage agreement
- Cohen's kappa
- intraclass correlation coefficient (ICC).

Each of the above has its own pros and cons, and some of them are more appropriate depending on the type of data and the number of raters. (These methods also apply to intercoder reliability.)

Percentage Agreement

Percentage agreement is the simplest form of calculating interrater reliability. As the name suggests, it provides a measure of interrater reliability based on the proportion of agreements among raters. It is used for interrater reliability when the data being coded or categorized is nominal or ordinal in nature. It measures how often two raters agree on a category or code that they have assigned to a particular item. It is calculated by dividing the number of agreements by the total number of agreements plus disagreements, and then multiplying the result by 100. It is a simple way to measure the consistency of ratings across two raters.

When there are three or more raters, we calculate the agreement among them by pairing raters and then adding up and averaging their level of agreement (for example rater1/rater 2, then rater 1/rater 3, etc.). However, when there are multiple raters, the process becomes a bit complicated, so there are other procedures such as the intraclass correlation coefficient (see below), which can be used.

Percentage agreement provides a measure of interrater reliability based on the proportion of agreements among raters.

Percentage agreement does not take into account the possibility of chance agreement and does not account for the severity of disagreements. However, it is still widely used in the fields of applied linguistics and second language research to assess the level of agreement between multiple raters when they are coding data. Example 11.5 is a hypothetical scenario.

EXAMPLE 11.5

Take the example of a study on L2 pragmatics. Two raters are asked to independently rate the pragmatic appropriacy of learners' utterances on a two-point scale (e.g., Acceptable, Unacceptable) based on their performance. Let's assume that there are ten learners in the group and the raters rate the learners as shown in Table 11.4.

To calculate percentage agreement, count the instances of agreement and divide them by the total (agreements + disagreements) multiplied by 100. In the example, seven out of ten cases resulted in agreement (Participants 1, 2, 3, 4, 5, 7, and 8), producing a percentage agreement of 70 percent. This indicates an acceptable level of agreement between the raters.

Table 11.4 Example data for percentage agreement reliability

Participants	Rater 1	Rater 2	Agreement/Disagreement
1	Acceptable	Acceptable	Agreement
2	Unacceptable	Unacceptable	Agreement
3	Acceptable	Acceptable	Agreement
4	Acceptable	Acceptable	Agreement
5	Unacceptable	Unacceptable	Agreement
6	Acceptable	Unacceptable	Disagreement
7	Acceptable	Acceptable	Agreement
8	Acceptable	Acceptable	Agreement
9	Acceptable	Unacceptable	Disagreement
10	Acceptable	Unacceptable	Disagreement

Cohen's Kappa

Cohen's kappa is a method used to measure interrater reliability when there are two raters coding the same data and the data is categorical (nominal) or ordinal in nature, as in the percentage agreement method. In was introduced by Jacob Cohen (1960) in response to a problem he identified with percentage agreement. He argued that percentage agreement does not account for chance agreement and the possibility that raters might guess on some of the items because they are uncertain.

Cohen's Kappa is considered a more robust measure of agreement than simple percentage agreement because it takes into account the possibility of chance agreement. It thus provides a statistic that takes into account both the proportion of agreement and the proportion of expected agreement by chance. The value of Cohen's kappa ranges from -1 to 1, with values close to 1 indicating almost perfect agreement and values close to 0 indicating little or no agreement (Cohen's kappa is shown with the lower case Greek κ).

Cohen's Kappa is a method used to measure interrater reliability when there are two raters coding the same data and the data is categorical (nominal) or ordinal in nature.

In applied linguistics, Cohen's kappa (often referred to simply as kappa) is widely used as a measure of interrater reliability to assess the degree of agreement between two raters who code the data or rate participants on a variable. Example 11.6 provides a hypothetical scenario.

EXAMPLE 11.6

In the previously mentioned pragmatics study (Example 11.5), where raters assessed students' utterances as acceptable or unacceptable, the string variable is converted to nominal. Unacceptable is coded as 0, and acceptable as 1. Table 11.5 displays the ratings provided by Rater 1 and Rater 2 for the ten learners.

Five participants were rated as "Acceptable" by both raters.

Two participants were rated as "Unacceptable" by both raters.

Overall, Rater 1 rated eight participants as "Acceptable" and two participants as "Unacceptable."

Overall, Rater 2 rated five participants as "Acceptable" and five participants as "Unacceptable."

Equation 11.4 shows the formula to calculate Cohen's kappa for these two raters.

Equation 11.4
$$\kappa = \frac{P_o - P_e}{1 - P_e}$$

where

p_o = the percentage of agreement among both raters.
p_e = the probability of chance agreement

To calculate Cohen's kappa for our example data, follow these five steps:

1. **Calculate p_o:** This represents the percentage of agreement between the two raters. In this example, there are 7 agreements out of 10 cases, resulting in a p_o of 70% (7/10 × 100).
2. **Calculate the probability that both raters would randomly rate participants as Acceptable:** Determine the individual probabilities that each rater assigns an "Acceptable" rating and then multiply these probabilities together. In this case, Rater A rated 8 out of 10 as "Acceptable" (80% or 0.8), and Rater B rated 5 out of 10 as "Acceptable" (50% or 0.5). The product is 0.8 × 0.5 = 0.40.
3. **Calculate the probability that both raters would randomly rate participants as Unacceptable:** Given that Rater A rated 2 out of 10 participants as Unacceptable (20% or 0.2) and Rater B rated 5 out of 10 participants as Unacceptable (50% or 0.5), the total probability of both raters rating participants as Unacceptable randomly is: 0.2 × 0.5 = 0.10.
4. **Calculate p_e:** Adding the answers from Step 2 and 3 gives the overall probability that raters would randomly agree: p_e = .40 + .10 = .50
5. **Apply the formula:**

$$\kappa = \frac{0.70 - 0.50}{1 - 0.50} = 0.40$$

$kappa = 0.40.$

Table 11.5 Example data for Cohen's kappa reliability

Participants	Rater 1	Rater 2
1	1	1
2	0	0
3	1	1
4	1	1
5	0	0
6	1	0
7	1	1
8	1	1
9	1	0
10	1	0

Kappa values, as noted earlier, range from -1 to 1, with values close to 1 indicating high agreement and values close to -1 indicating high disagreement. As you can see, this is different from simple percentage agreement as it takes into account chance agreement. Cohen suggested the following interpretations of kappa values:

- Less than 0 = poor agreement
- 0 to 0.20 = slight agreement
- 0.21 to 0.40 = fair agreement
- 0.41 to 0.60 = moderate agreement
- 0.61 to 0.80 = substantial agreement
- 0.81 to 1.00 = almost perfect agreement.

Kappa for our above example = 0.40, which according to Cohen's guidelines indicates fair agreement.

While it might be helpful to know the kappa formula, calculating kappa by hand can be difficult, especially if the dataset is large or if there are multiple categories. This process can also be time-consuming and error-prone if done manually. It is recommended to use a statistical software or package to calculate kappa. SPSS can calculate kappa easily. To do so, you can follow the steps shown in SPSS Steps 11.3.

SPSS STEPS 11.3

- Open the data file in SPSS.
- Click "Analyze" > "Descriptive Statistics" > "Crosstabs."
- In the Crosstabs dialog box, move the variables to the "Row(s)" and "Column(s)" boxes.
- Click "Statistics" > select "Kappa."
- Click "Continue" > "OK."

The kappa coefficient will be reported in the output, along with a *p* value for the test of significance. The following is the kappa output generated by SPSS. As you see, the kappa calculated for our example data above is the same as we found by calculating it manually using the formula (see the value under the "Value" column).

SPSS OUTPUT 11.3

Symmetric Measures		Value	Asymptotic Standard Error[a]	Approximate T[b]	Approximate Significance
Nominal by Nominal	Contingency Coefficient	.447			.114
Interval by Interval	Pearson's R	.500	.181	1.633	.141[c]
Ordinal by Ordinal	Spearman Correlation	.500	.181	1.633	.141[c]
Measure of Agreement	Kappa	.400	.232	1.581	.114
N of Valid Cases		10			

a. Not assuming the null hypothesis.
b. Using the asymptotic standard error assuming the null hypothesis.
c. Based on normal approximation.

Please note that Cohen's kappa is a measure of agreement between two raters with categorical data and is calculated based on a 2×2 contingency table. When there are more than two raters, there is a possibility for calculating kappa but it has to be calculated first on a 2×2 basis for each pair of raters, and then the resulting estimates have to be averaged across coder pairs. For example, if there are three coders, there would be three coder pairs: coders 1 and 2, coders 2 and 3, and coders 1 and 3. If the coder pair kappa estimate is 0.65 for coders 1 and 2, 0.67 for coders 2 and 3, and 0.81 for coders 1 and 3, the average kappa estimate would be 0.78. Another possibility is to use Fleiss's kappa which is an extension of Cohen's kappa for multirater and multi-item data.

POINTS TO PONDER

How do you evaluate reliability when multiple raters are involved in your research? What challenges arise when assessing reliability with multiple raters, and how might these challenges impact the rigor of your research conclusions?

Intraclass Correlation

Another type of interrater reliability is intraclass correlation (ICC). ICC is a statistical measure of the reliability of ratings or measurements made by multiple raters or assessors (two or more). It is typically used with continuous data or measures the consistency and reliability of observations on a scale close to a continuous scale. It is calculated as the ratio of the between-rater variance to the total variance, and ranges from 0 to 1, with higher values indicating greater agreement or consistency between the ratings or measurements provided by different raters or assessors.

ICC is widely used in applied linguistics research to measure the degree of agreement among multiple raters or assessments of a given language ability or performance. It is used when measuring the same construct, such as language proficiency, speaking fluency, or pronunciation.

Intraclass correlation (ICC) is a statistical measure of the reliability of ratings made by multiple raters or assessors and is typically used with continuous data or measures the consistency and reliability of observations on a scale close to a continuous scale.

There are three models of ICC which can be used, depending on the type of data and the raters: Model 1, Model 2, and Model 3.

Model 1: This is called the one-way random effect model. This model assumes that each participant is rated by a different set of randomly selected raters. In other words, it is used when participants are rated by different pairs or groups of raters; that is, each pair or group of raters have rated a subset of the data.

An example of a study that uses this model of intraclass correlation would be a study in which the performance of participants is evaluated on a given construct, with each participant being evaluated by a different set of randomly selected raters. In the example, "different set" refers to the fact that the group of raters who evaluate each participant is unique and not the same as the group of raters who evaluate any other participants. For example, if there are ten participants being rated, participants 1–3 may be rated by a group of randomly selected raters, participants 4–7 may be rated by another group of randomly selected raters, and participants 8–10 may be rated by a third group of randomly selected raters. Each group of students evaluating each participant is a different set, meaning they are not the same group of raters. This model is rarely used in applied linguistics research because often in applied linguistics research the same set of raters evaluate all participants.

Model 2: This model is the two-way random effect model. This model assumes that each subject is randomly selected for the study and is rated by each rater, and the raters are randomly selected. In other words, in this model each participant is rated by all raters randomly selected from a larger population or group of potential raters. This model is used when we plan to generalize the reliability of the raters to the general population of raters or to any raters who possess the same characteristics as the selected raters.

Imagine a study in which you want to assess the interrater reliability of a test used to measure anxiety levels in participants. There are ten participants and ten raters randomly selected. Each participant is rated by all ten raters on a scale of 0 to 10.

Model 3: This is the two-way mixed effects model. It assumes that each participant is assessed by each rater, but the raters are fixed and not randomly selected. In other words, they are the only raters of interest. Put differently, a pair or group of raters have rated all the participants, and the raters are not randomly selected from a larger population. In this model, conclusions relate only to the raters participating in the study. In other words, the results of this model only represent the reliability of the specific raters selected and cannot be generalized to other raters.

An example would be a study in which ten participants are each assessed by five different raters on a scale measuring their level of anxiety. The raters are trained professionals, and a standardized questionnaire has been used. In this case, each participant is assessed by all five raters, and the goal is to determine the reliability of the ratings provided by the raters. A high ICC value would indicate that the raters are providing highly consistent ratings, while a low ICC value would indicate that the raters are providing less consistent ratings. This information could also be used to improve the training of the raters or to select a subset of raters whose ratings are most reliable for use in future studies.

In applied linguistics research, we use either Model 2 or Model 3, depending on the type of raters. In cases when we have randomly selected the raters, we use the two-way random model. If the raters are not randomly selected (for example, if they are trained raters who are trained for the purpose of the study), we use Model 3 or the two-way mixed model.

Table 11.6 provides a summary of when we use each model of intraclass correlation.

Table 11.6 When to use each model of intraclass correction

Type of intraclass correlation	When we use it
One-way random effects model	Participants are rated by different sets of randomly selected raters. Each set of raters rates a different group of participants.
Two-way random effects model	All participants are rated by a set of raters who are randomly selected from a larger population of raters.
Two-way mixed effects model	All participants are rated by a set of raters who are not randomly selected from a larger population of raters.

The flowchart shown in Figure 11.2 summarizes the decisions we need to make when conducting ICC.

To calculate intraclass correlation for interrater reliability, you can follow these steps:

1. Gather data from multiple raters on the same set of items and participants.
2. Make sure that your data is in the appropriate format for ICC analysis, which typically means continuous data and multiple measurements of the same variable from each participant.
3. Compute the intraclass correlation either manually (for which there is a formula for each of the models) or use the computer. It is not advised to calculate it

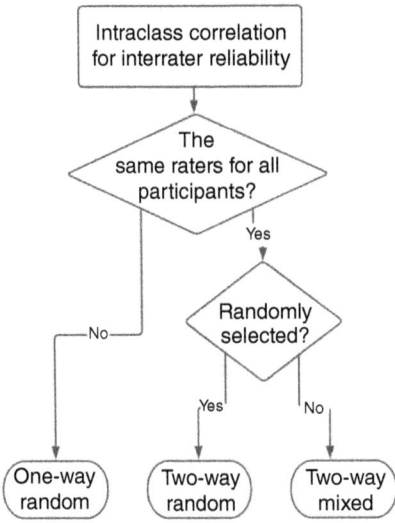

Figure 11.2 A flowchart of how to use ICC

manually as it is complicated and there are statistical software packages such as SPSS, SAS, or R that can do it for you easily.

If you use SPSS, you can follow the steps outlined in SPSS Steps 11.4.

SPSS STEPS 11.4

- Open the data file in SPSS.
- Select "Analyze" > "Scale" > "Reliability Analysis."
- In the "Reliability Analysis" dialog box, choose and move the variables representing the ratings (columns with rater scores) to the "Items" box.
- Select "Statistics" > "Intraclass correlation coefficient."
- In "Model," choose "Two-Way Mixed." Under type, select "Absolute agreement."
- Click "Continue" > "OK."

There are two choices that you need to make when conducting ICC. One choice is whether you are interested in reliability in the form of a simple correlation coefficient or in the form of agreement among raters. If you use SPSS to calculate the reliability, these two are under ICC "Type" and are labelled as "Consistency" and "Absolute Agreement." If you choose "Consistency" the analysis simply calculates the correlation between raters, similar to Pearson correlation. This tells us how the two variables are related to one another but does not show the degree of agreement. For example, there is a perfect correlation between these two sets of scores (2, 4, 6, 8) and (10, 12, 14, 16). However, there is no agreement. In reliability analysis, we are often interested in agreement rather than correlation. Therefore, we choose the "Absolute Agreement" option. In all these cases, ICC can provide a single value that quantifies the degree of similarity or agreement between the observations and can be used to determine whether the measurements are reliable and consistent.

Another choice is an interpretation choice in the analysis output. This relates to whether you want to use the mean value of the raters as an assessment basis for reliability or whether the reliability is going to be based on the measurement from a single rater. When calculating ICC using SPSS, the two indexes are shown in the output table as "Single measure" and "Average measures." Most often in applied linguistics research, we are interested in the average ratings of all raters rather than the reliability of a single rater (see Figure 11.3 for a flowchart of these choices). In such cases we use the value for "Average measures."

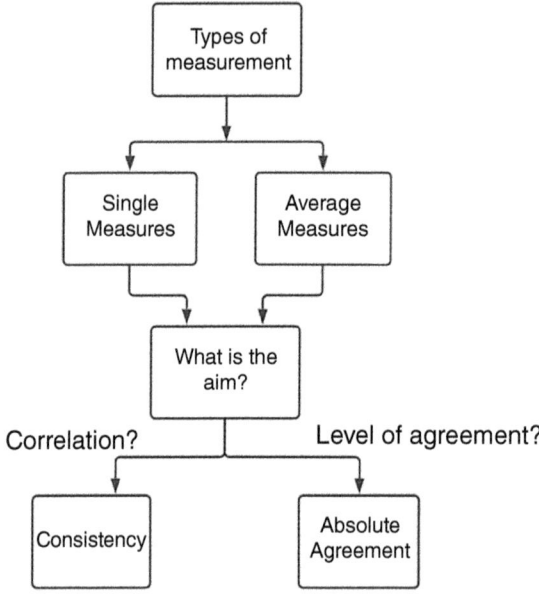

Figure 11.3 A flowchart of SPSS options for ICC

Once you have the ICC, you can use the following thresholds to evaluate the level of agreement among raters:

- ICC values between 0.75 and 1.00 indicate excellent agreement
- ICC values between 0.60 and 0.75 indicate good agreement
- ICC values between 0.40 and 0.60 indicate fair agreement
- ICC values below 0.40 indicate poor agreement.

It is worth noting that when interpreting the output of ICC, it is important to consider the design of the study, the number of raters and participants, and the specific research question.

Example 11.7 provides a hypothetical scenario with a dataset and SPSS output.

EXAMPLE 11.7

Suppose in a study you want to assess the consistency of ratings provided by a group of trained raters of an oral presentation given by a group of participants. The study aims to assess the consistency of ratings provided on their intelligibility of speech on a ten-point scale (from highly intelligible to not intelligible at all). The data is collected from ten participants, each of whom is rated by three raters. Table 11.7 gives a sample of the data for the ten participants.

Table 11.7 Example data for ICC reliability

Participants	Rater 1	Rater 2	Rater 3
1	8	7	7
2	7	7	6
3	5	4	3
4	9	8	9
5	7	9	7
6	8	8	8
7	6	7	6
8	9	9	8
9	6	7	8
10	6	7	6

To calculate ICC, you go to SPSS and follow the steps explained earlier. As noted, before, there are different models for ICC: one-way random, two-way random, and two-way mixed. For our example, we use the two-way mixed model because we have trained raters and have not selected them randomly form the population of raters. We also use "Absolute agreement" as the type because we are interested in the level of agreement.

SPSS Output 11.4 shows the output.

SPSS OUTPUT 11.4

Intraclass Correlation Coefficient

	Intraclass Correlation[b]	95% Confidence Interval		F Test with True Value 0			
		Lower Bound	Upper Bound	Value	df1	df2	Sig
Single Measures	.764[a]	.481	.927	10.894	9	18	.000
Average Measures	.906[c]	.735	.974	10.894	9	18	.000

Two-way mixed effects model where people effects are random and measures effects are fixed.

a. The estimator is the same, whether the interaction effect is present or not.

b. Type A intraclass correlation coefficients using an absolute agreement definition.

c. This estimate is computed assuming the interaction effect is absent, because it is not estimable otherwise.

SPSS Output 11.4 shows the ICC coefficient values under the Intraclass Correlation column. There are two values "Single Measures" (0.764) and "Average Measures" (0.906). The Single Measures value is used when we are interested in the reliability of an individual rating. The Average Measures is used when we are interested in the reliability of all measures combined, which is most often the case.

As noted earlier, the ICC value can range from 0 to 1, with higher values indicating greater reliability. ICC values of 0.75 or higher are generally considered to be acceptable levels of reliability. So, in this study, the ICC for both measures is fairly high. In addition to the ICC reliability, the SPSS output for ICC also includes other statistics such as the p value, the 95 percent confidence intervals, and the F value. These statistics can provide additional information about the reliability of the ratings. Among them, the ICC coefficient and p value are the most important for interpreting the results. A p value of less than 0.05 indicates that the ICC coefficient is statistically significant and that there is a high degree of agreement across the ratings, which is the case in the current example (i.e., $p < 0.001$).

Intrarater Reliability

Intrarater or intracoder reliability refers to the consistency of coding decisions made by a single coder or rater. It measures the degree to which the coder consistently applies a set of coding rubrics or guidelines to a set of data. High intracoder reliability indicates that the coder is consistent in coding and applying the rubrics, while low intracoder reliability suggests that the coder is making inconsistent or arbitrary coding decisions. It is important to have a high intracoder reliability so that the data are being coded accurately and consistently.

For example, you may code a set of data and then leave it for some time, and then go back to that data and recode all or a randomly selected portion of the data. The two sets of data can then be compared to establish the degree of agreement.

Intrarater or intracoder reliability refers to the consistency of coding decisions made by a single rater or coder. It measures the degree to which the coder consistently applies a set of coding rubrics or guidelines to a set of data.

To calculate intracoder reliability, the same procedures we discussed earlier such as Cohen's kappa or the intraclass correlation coefficient (ICC) can be used, depending on the type and nature of the data. To increase the intrarater reliability, it is important to have clear and specific rating criteria and to provide training and practice opportunities for the rater so that they are familiar with the criteria and apply them consistently.

The Pros and Cons of Intrarater (Intracoder) Reliability

Intrarater reliability has both advantages and disadvantages. One advantage is that it only needs one rater, which can be more cost-effective and logistically simpler than having multiple raters. This can also make data collection and analysis more efficient by reducing the need for multiple raters.

However, there are several drawbacks with this procedure. One is limited generalizability. The scores obtained from intrarater reliability may only be generalizable to that specific rater and not to other raters. The second is bias. The rater may have their own biases that can influence their scoring, which can affect the reliability of the measure or assessment. The third is lack of objectivity. Having a single rater to rate or code some data cannot be considered the same as when two independent raters code the data.

For these reasons, intrarater reliability is not very common in applied linguistics research unless it is needed and it is the only option because of the constraints. However, intrarater reliability is useful when we want to know the consistency of a single rater's scores or judgments. Consider a study, for example, whose aim is to assess the consistency of a language teacher's scoring when they rate their students' oral presentations. In such cases, you may ask the same teacher to listen to each student's presentation a few times and score their presentation according to a set rubric. You would then calculate the intrarater reliability by comparing the scores given by that teacher on different occasions, to see if they are consistent. If the scores are highly consistent, the teacher's scoring would be considered reliable.

Conclusion

Reliability is an important aspect of quantitative research. Reliability refers to the consistency and stability of a measure or instrument used in research. When conducting research, it is essential to use measures or instruments that are able to obtain accurate and reliable results. If measures are unreliable, the results will be inconsistent, leading to incorrect conclusions. In this chapter, we have discussed the concept of reliability and its importance in quantitative research within applied linguistics. We have explored the different types of reliability measures, including test–retest, interrater, and internal consistency, and discussed how to conduct and calculate reliability estimates using measures such as Cronbach's alpha, Cohen's kappa, correlation coefficients, and intraclass correlations. We learned how to interpret reliability estimates and make decisions about using measures or instruments that are reliable. We also examined the strengths and limitations of different types of reliability measures. Throughout, we provided examples to illustrate how to assess and interpret reliability measures. We will discuss reliability and validity in qualitative research in Chapter 17.

DISCUSSION AND ACTIVITY QUESTION

Discussion Questions

1. What is reliability and why is it important in quantitative research? How does it impact the conclusion of our research findings?
2. What are the different types of reliability measures that can be used in applied linguistics research? How do these measures differ from one another, and when should each one be used?

3. When should we calculate correlation coefficients and intraclass correlations, and how do we interpret the results? What are the key factors to consider when conducting and interpreting such reliability measures?
4. What are some of the general considerations that you should bear in mind when trying to enhance the consistency and reliability of your measures or instruments?
5. How can you choose the most appropriate type of reliability measure for your study? What are the factors that you will consider when making such a decision?
6. What are some strategies that can be used to enhance the accuracy of interrater reliability or to minimize the impact of rater variability?
7. What does it mean for the robustness of your research if multiple raters show low agreement, and how can you address the underlying causes of this variability?

Activity Questions

1. Choose a research question that you are interested in that can be addressed using quantitative research methods. Identify the measures that you would use and the type of reliability estimate that would be most appropriate for your study. Explain why you would use those methods.
2. Collect some data using a measure or instrument that you have developed or have used in a previous study. Calculate the reliability estimates for the measure and interpret the reliability estimate.
3. Locate a published study in applied linguistics that has used a quantitative research design. Find out if any reliability has been calculated for the measures used in the study and discuss the implications of those estimates for the accuracy of the study's findings and conclusions.
4. Choose a language proficiency or any other language test that you have access to and evaluate its reliability using one or more of the reliability measures discussed in this chapter. Discuss the strengths and limitations of the assessment's reliability and suggest ways to improve it.
5. Think of a research project that involves multiple raters or observers. Develop a strategy for checking interrater reliability and minimizing the impact of rater variability. Explain your strategy and discuss the potential challenges or limitations that you may encounter.
6. Collaborate with a peer and do the following: (a) Choose a specific research question related to applied linguistics that requires the use of multiple raters or observers. (b) Select a measure or instrument that will be used to collect data. (c) Develop a strategy for estimating interrater reliability among the raters or observers. (d) Identify the potential challenges or limitations that you may encounter and discuss how you plan to address these challenges. (e) Write up your strategy in detail, including specific steps that will be taken to determine interrater reliability. (f) Present the results to your classmates.

Understanding and Assessing Validity in Quantitative Research

---

CHAPTER OBJECTIVES

After completing this chapter, you should be able to

- Define and explain the concept of internal and external validity and their importance in quantitative applied linguistics research.
- Describe the different types of validity, including face validity, content validity, and construct validity, and explain how they can be measured.
- Understand the different types of external validity and how to measure them.
- Describe the potential threats to external and internal validity in quantitative research, including selection bias, maturation, history, and testing effects.
- Identify strategies for addressing and mitigating these threats to increase the internal and external validity of a study.

Introduction

In the previous chapter, we discussed the concept of reliability in quantitative research. In this chapter, we will focus on validity. Like reliability, validity is an important concept in quantitative research, as it determines whether a study accurately measures what it intends to measure. In applied linguistics research, validity is particularly important because in this field we often deal with complex concepts and constructs, such as language proficiency, literacy, and language acquisition. All quantitative studies including experimental studies should attempt to meet the criterion of validity. If a study is not valid, it is flawed and may have poor methodology or inaccurate measurements, which can lead to inaccurate or invalid conclusions. Thus, it is important to make sure that a study is valid so that its findings and conclusions can be trusted. This chapter will discuss the concept of validity in quantitative research. It will discuss the different types of validity, including face validity, content validity, construct validity, criterion validity, and predictive validity. It will also discuss the notions of internal and external validity and explore various strategies and techniques that can be used to establish validity in quantitative studies, including the use of appropriate and careful sampling and recruitment procedures, and the use of statistical methods to assess the validity of a study.

By the end of this chapter, you will have a solid understanding of the concept of validity in quantitative research and will be equipped with the knowledge and tools needed to design and conduct valid research studies in applied linguistics.

POINTS TO PONDER

What does validity mean to you and how do you distinguish it from reliability, discussed earlier? Why is it important to consider validity in quantitative research?

The Concept of Validity

Validity refers to the extent to which a study measures what it is intended to measure. In other words, it is a measure of how accurately the study, including its design, data collection tools, and tests or other measures used, can assess the construct or variable under investigation. So the question basically is, "Am I measuring what I want to measure?" The answer might seem obvious, and many may not question it, as they may assume that they always measure something with an appropriate instrument. For example, when we want to measure weight, we always use a weighing scale, which we believe is appropriate for that purpose. We never use a thermometer. When we want to measure temperature, we often use a thermometer, and we never use a weighing scale. However, when it comes to research, things are not that obvious, and there is a possibility that we will not use the appropriate tool. The reason for that is that in research we often deal with abstract concepts that are difficult to define and not easy to measure. For example, if we want to examine the effect of motivation, we need to first define motivation and then make sure that the instrument that we use to measure motivation really does measure motivation. To this end, we may develop a questionnaire to measure motivation. However, if most of the questions are about the learners' aptitudes instead of motivation, the instrument is not measuring motivation. As another example, when measuring language proficiency, we often use tests that are assumed to measure learners' level of language proficiency. But the question is whether the test really measures language proficiency, and whether it measures it accurately. In other words, is the test used a valid test? The validity of any research depends on the validity of the measures used. If the measures are not valid, the results are invalid too.

Validity refers to the extent to which a study measures what it is intended to measure.

Types of Validity

There are different types of validity pertaining to quantitative research including the following:

- face validity
- content validity
- construct validity
- criterion validity.

Face Validity

Face validity concerns the extent to which the instrument looks like it is measuring what it is supposed to measure. In other words, an instrument or test has face validity when it appears to be a sensible measure of the variable in question. Therefore, it is a type of validity that is based on the researcher's or the participants' subjective judgments rather than any objective analysis. For example, a short ten-item questionnaire on learner motivation would look as though it has lower face validity as a measure of motivation than a longer fifty-item questionnaire. Face validity can be assessed by consulting experts or asking the participants who take the test to judge the extent to which the instrument looks like it is measuring what it is supposed to measure. For example, if you are interested in measuring language proficiency, you might develop a test that includes questions related to grammar, vocabulary, and reading comprehension. You could then ask a group of language teachers or experts to review the test and judge whether the questions appear to be relevant to measuring language proficiency.

Although face validity is an important matter to consider in research, the fact that a measure looks like a valid measure is not a guarantee of validity. Therefore, it is essential to use other measures of validity, such as content, construct, or criterion validity, to establish the validity of the measures or instruments used.

Face validity concerns the extent to which the instrument looks like it is measuring what it is supposed to measure.

Content Validity

Content validity concerns the extent to which the contents of the instrument adequately cover the content or the domain it is intended to measure. It involves examining whether the items or questions in a research questionnaire or instrument represent a comprehensive and representative sample of the content being measured.

For example, if we are trying to measure motivation, the question is how well the questions or the items in the questionnaire cover the various aspects of that concept. If the questions do not represent that domain, the instrument does not have content validity.

To determine whether the measure has content validity, one strategy is to use expert judgment and feedback to evaluate the coverage, relevance, and representativeness of the items or questions. For example, if you are developing a test to measure language proficiency, you might ask a group of language teachers or experts to review the test items and provide feedback on whether the items are representative of the various aspects of language proficiency, such as grammar, vocabulary, and reading comprehension.

Content validity concerns the extent to which the contents of the instrument correctly measure the variable under investigation.

Thus, if you are trying to measure language proficiency and all the test items are about vocabulary and grammar, that test does not have content validity, as language proficiency is far more than knowing the meaning of words or knowing the grammar of a language.

Overall, content validity is an important concept in research because if a measure or instrument does not adequately cover the various aspects of a construct, the measure cannot accurately measure the construct. As such, this type of validity should be considered when designing research in a field such as applied linguistics, where constructs that are studied are often complex and multifaceted.

Construct Validity

Construct validity is one of the most important types of validity. It refers to the extent to which an instrument measures accurately the theoretical construct that it is intended to measure. Thus, while content validity assesses the degree to which the instrument covers the content, construct validity assesses whether the instrument measures the theoretical construct it is intended to measure. Therefore, it goes beyond content and explores the underlying theoretical framework that defines the construct.

For example, if a study has been designed to examine students' classroom anxiety, you might use a questionnaire to measure that construct. In this context, construct validity would be concerned with how accurately the questionnaire measures language anxiety rather than some other constructs. To determine construct validity, we need to first define the construct operationally and then determine the degree to which the instrument represents the operational definition of the variable.

Construct validity refers to the extent to which an instrument measures accurately the theoretical construct that it is intended to measure.

There are several ways in which construct validity can be assessed. One way is by conducting factor analysis. For example, to measure the construct of motivation, you can develop a questionnaire measuring motivation and administer it to a group of participants. Then you can analyze the results using factor analysis to determine whether the test items cluster together to form a coherent construct of motivation.

There are also other ways of establishing construct validity. Three common ways are through determining convergent validity, discriminant validity, and known-groups validity.

Convergent validity is a kind of construct validity that concerns the degree to which different measures of the same construct are correlated with each other. In other words, it concerns whether different measures of the same construct are consistent with each other, and thus whether they measure the same construct. A high degree of consistency between or among them indicates that they all tap into the same construct. For example, if you are developing a cloze test to measure language proficiency of the participants in a second language study, you can determine the convergent validity of that test by comparing the scores on the test with another well-established test such as the TOEFL test. If the scores on the two tests are highly correlated, this can indicate that both tests measure the same construct, otherwise they may assess different constructs.

Discriminant validity concerns the degree to which different measures of different constructs are not correlated with each other. In other words, it examines whether different measures assess different constructs. For example, if you are developing a new vocabulary test in a second language study, you can determine discriminant validity by comparing the scores on this test with scores on a test of grammar knowledge. If the scores on the two tests are not correlated, this can indicate that the two tests are measuring different constructs, otherwise, they may be testing the same construct.

Known-group validity refers to the extent to which a measure can discriminate between two groups that are known to differ on the construct of interest. For example, if you are developing an English listening test for a study, you can use known-group validity to evaluate whether the test can distinguish between the listening comprehension of L1 speakers and non-L1 speakers of English. To this end, you can administer your test to both groups and compare their scores. If the test has good known-group validity, then the scores of the L1 speakers should be significantly higher than those of the non-L1 speakers. This would then indicate that the test has construct validity.

Construct validity can be assessed through factor analysis or by determining convergent validity, discriminant validity, or known-group validity.

Criterion Validity

Criterion validity refers to the extent to which the performance of a test is related to an external criterion. It involves comparing the results of a measure or test of interest with those of an established criterion. If there is a high correlation between the scores of the two measures, it indicates that the test has a high degree of criterion validity. There are two types of criterion validity:

- concurrent validity
- predictive validity.

Concurrent validity involves comparing the results of a measure with those of an external criterion that has been administered simultaneously to see how well they are correlated. In other words, it refers to the degree to which a measure is related to an external criterion that is measured at the same time. This will be done by examining the correlation between scores on the measure and scores on an external criterion that is concurrently measured. For example, if you have developed a new language proficiency test and you want to assess its concurrent validity, you would compare the scores on this new test with scores on an established language proficiency test that is known to be a valid test, and thus serves as a criterion.

Concurrent validity can be used in applied linguistics research to establish the validity of new tests or assessments. It is important to note, however, that although high concurrent validity can be an important indicator of the quality of a new measure, it does not necessarily mean that the two tests measure the same construct or that the new test is accurately measuring the construct that is intended to measure. Therefore, to make sure that our test is valid, other types of validity, such as construct validity, must also be checked.

Criterion validity refers to the extent to which the performance of a test is related to an external criterion. There are two types of criterion validity: concurrent validity and predictive validity.

Predictive validity refers to the extent to which the instrument predicts the results of another instrument that measures the same variable. In other words, it is a type of validity that concerns the ability of a research measure or instrument to forecast a future outcome related to the construct being measured. This type of validity is often used in educational or occupational contexts to assess how well a particular measure or instrument predicts a future performance or outcome.

An example of predictive validity could be a study that aims to investigate the effectiveness of an English language proficiency test in predicting the academic success of international students at an English-speaking university. You can administer the proficiency test to a group of international students before they begin their studies at the university. Their test scores can then be compared to their academic performance during their first year of studies to determine whether the language proficiency test has predictive validity. If the results show a strong correlation between the test scores and the students' academic performance, then the test can be considered to have high predictive validity, otherwise the test can be considered to have low predictive validity. This kind of information would be useful for the university administration when deciding on the language requirement criteria for international students and determining whether the test they use predicts students' academic success.

Altogether, predictive validity is an important consideration in research design because it enables researchers to evaluate the practical usefulness of their research measures. If a research measure has high predictive validity, it can be considered to be a useful tool to make accurate predictions about future outcomes. However, if it has low predictive validity, it may be limited in its utility for making accurate predictions.

POINTS TO PONDER

How can you measure validity types such as content validity, criterion validity, and construct validity? Can you provide specific examples to illustrate the application of each type in practical research scenarios?

Internal and External Validity

External and internal validity are two other important types of validity in research that are closely related to the types of validity discussed, including face validity, content validity, construct validity, and criterion validity. Internal validity refers to the extent to which a research study can accurately establish cause-and-effect relationships between variables. It has to do with to the extent to which the results of a study are due only to the effect of the independent variable and not to any other variables.

For example, a study claims to be measuring the impact of a new instructional strategy on students' language proficiency. This study can be said to have internal validity if it is designed in such a way that it accurately establishes a cause-and-effect relationship between the new instructional strategy and the changes in students' language proficiency.

A study does not have internal validity if the findings can be explained by factors other than the independent variable. The accuracy of the conclusions drawn from the data depends on the degree to which changes in the dependent variable can be related to the independent variable and not to other explanations, possibilities, or extraneous factors.

Internal validity refers to the extent to which a research study can accurately establish cause-and-effect relationships between variables or the extent to which the results are due only to the effect of the independent variable and not to any other variables.

Since internal validity has to do with cause-and-effect relationship, it is also called causal validity. Two types of causal relationships can be distinguished: causal description and causal explanation (Shadish, Cook, & Campbell, 2002). Causal description refers to describing the effect resulting from manipulating the independent variable. In other words, it identifies a cause-and-effect relationship between two or more variables. For example, "exercise causes weight loss" is a causal description because it describes the relationship between the two variables. A causal explanation, however, provides an explanation of how and why a causal relationship exists. This can involve identifying the underlying mechanisms through which the observed cause-and-effects are produced. For example, in applied linguistics research, if we see a cause-and-effect relationship between feedback explicitness and language learning, a causal explanation could be that the explicitness of feedback helps learners notice the feedback. In the context of a single study, internal validity often has more to do with a causal description, as it concerns establishing a cause-and-effect relationship rather than explaining it. Many studies might be needed to explain why a cause-and-effect relationship exists among variables.

Causal description refers to describing a causal relationship, whereas a **causal explanation** provides an explanation of how and why a causal relationship exists.

Internal validity can be affected by several factors, such as problems with the study design, issues with measurement or instruments used, or other unintended variables that may influence the results. Additionally, bias in sample selection or lack of randomization can affect the internal validity of a study. We will discuss the various threats to internal validity in more detail in the next section.

External validity concerns the generalizability of the study and refers to the extent to which the results of a study can be applied beyond the context in which the study was conducted or to individuals other than those participating in the study. It is the ability of the results to be applied to other similar groups, populations, settings, or measures outside those studied. This is important because if a study does not have external validity, it is difficult to determine its potential theoretical and practical implications.

Several types of external validity can be distinguished including:

- sample-to-population validity
- ecological validity
- temporal validly
- external construct validity
- treatment variation validity
- outcome validity.

Sample-to-population validity refers to the extent to which the findings for a sample in a study can be generalized to the population from which the sample is drawn. For example, a study with a small sample size or one that includes participants from a very specific group without random selection can have limited sample-to-population external validity. Unfortunately, many studies in applied linguistics may fall short with regard to this type of validity as it is often difficult to have large groups of participants or to use random selection due to various constraints. This highlights the importance of replication in applied linguistics research. When a study is replicated and similar results are obtained, the validity of the research and the confidence in the original findings can be increased. Replication also tests whether the findings can be generalizable across different groups and settings.

Ecological validity is the extent to which the results of a study can be generalized to other contexts or environments. For example, if findings from a study that is conducted in one setting can be applied to another setting, the study can be said to have ecological validity. To have ecological validity, the study should consider and include in the research the specific factors and the characteristics of the situation to which the study is going to be applied. In applied linguistics or second language research, there are many studies that are conducted in lab settings. These studies may have limited ecological external validity if their findings cannot be applied to classroom settings or to naturalistic real-world situations.

Temporal validity refers to the extent to which the results of a study can be generalized across different time periods. For example, a study that is conducted at a specific point in time may have limited temporal external validity if the findings cannot be applied to other time periods. This is important because factors such as societal transformation and changes, cultural shifts, technological advancements, or other significant changes over time can influence the results of a study and make it challenging to generalize the findings to other time periods. For example, an applied linguistics study using an old way of presenting materials can have limited temporal validity for a time when more advanced technologies are used for presentation. To help determine the temporal external validity of their study, researchers should report the specific time period during which the study is conducted and also replicate the study at different points in time to evaluate whether the findings still apply.

As noted earlier, construct validity refers to the extent to which a tool used in a study accurately measures the theoretical construct it is supposed to measure. External construct validity shows the extent to which the results of a test measuring a specific construct in a study can be generalized to other measures of the same construct in other studies or contexts. For example, an applied linguistics study that measures reading comprehension using a specific multiple-choice test may have limited external construct validity if the findings cannot be generalized to other tests of reading comprehension used in other studies, such as summary or recall tasks. Therefore, this type of validity is related to the broader category of construct validity.

Treatment variation validity refers to the degree to which the results of a study can be generalized beyond the specific treatment used in the study to other variations of that treatment. For example, if an applied linguistics study examines the effectiveness of communicative language teaching, the question becomes to what extent the findings from this study can apply to other variations of communicative language teaching, as there are different variations of this methodology. This is important because when an instructional strategy is used by teachers, it is unlikely that all teachers will use it in the same way. So, we do want to have our research to have some level of treatment variation validity.

Outcome validity refers to the extent to which the results of a study can be generalized across related dependent variables. Experimental studies investigate the effect of one or more independent variables on one or more dependent variables. For example, they may investigate the effect of computer-assisted language learning (CALL) on students' motivation. If the study shows a positive effect of CALL on instrumental motivation, it can be said to have outcome validity if the findings are also applicable to other, conceptually related measures of motivation, such as integrative motivation, and if CALL similarly shows a positive effect on that measure.

Outcome validity can also be taken to refer to the extent to which the results of a study using a particular outcome measure can be generalized to situations when other similar outcome measures are used. This type of validity can be demonstrated by showing that one measure of the same or a related variable yields similar results to those of another measure of the same variable. For example, a multiple-choice measure of reading comprehension should show similar effects of an independent variable when compared to another measure of reading comprehension, such as short-answer questions.

External validity concerns the generalizability of the study. Several types of external validity can be distinguished, including sample-to-population validity, ecological validity, temporal validly, external construct validity, treatment variation validity, and outcome validity.

It should be noted that although internal and external validity are related, having internal validity does not necessarily mean that the study also has external validity. For example, a study that only includes a small group of participants may have a high degree of internal validity because the findings obtained in the study could be due to the independent variable, but because the sample size is small, it may have low external validity as it may be difficult to generalize the results to the larger population. Additionally, a second language acquisition study that is conducted in a laboratory setting may have high internal validity because it has been able to tightly control the extraneous variables, but it may have low external validity when trying to generalize the results to real-classroom or naturalistic settings.

POINTS TO PONDER

What are some common threats to internal and external validity, and how can you address or mitigate some of these threats?

Threats to Internal and External Validity

As noted above, a study can be said to be valid depending on the extent to which it can establish cause-and-effect relationships (what was called internal validity: that is the effects observed are only due to the independent variable) and the findings are generalizable across samples, contexts, measures, or groups beyond the experimental research (what was called external validity). There are several threats to internal and external validity, which you should be aware of.

Threats to internal validly refer to factors that limit drawing cause-and-effect conclusions. Threats to external validity are those factors that can limit the generalizability of study findings to the population (population validity), settings (ecological validity), measures (outcome validity), or time periods (temporal validity). In the following section, we will discuss threats to internal validity, but many of the factors that threaten internal validity also provide a threat to external validity. Some of these common threats include:

- selection bias
- maturation
- history
- instrumentation
- regression to the mean
- mortality
- interaction of selection and treatment.

Selection Bias (Differential Selection of Participants)

Selection bias occurs when the way in which participants are selected or assigned to groups in a study leads to differences between those groups that could affect the study's findings. This is also called differential selection of participants, which refers to the problem of selecting and assigning participants with different characteristics to the study groups. For example, when, we compare two groups (such as an experimental and a control group), the two groups might differ in several factors, such as demographic variables, including age, gender, nationality, and L1 background, as well as in other cognitive, affective, and personality factors. When an experimental and a control group in a study are different in various factors, it is difficult to attribute any observed effect to the independent or the treatment variable. A cause-and-effect relationship can be made only when the two groups are the same or similar on all relevant variables.

Selection bias occurs when the way in which participants are selected or assigned to groups in a study leads to differences between those groups that could affect the study's findings.

Selection bias is also a threat to external validity, as it can lead to a sample of participants that is not representative of the population from which the sample is drawn. This can lead to findings that cannot be generalized to the larger population. Additionally, if a study includes participants only from a specific group, or if it is conducted in a specific context, the findings may not be generalizable to other groups or contexts. In other words, the study may have limited ecological validity. Example 12.1 presents a hypothetical situation.

EXAMPLE 12.1

Suppose you aim to investigate whether a particular instructional strategy, such as translation into L2, can lead to improvement in learners' accuracy of the use of English articles. You design a study with two groups of L1 Spanish and L2 English learner volunteers: an experimental group that receives a set passage to read and translate from L1 to L2, and a control group that is asked to read the passage in the L1 without translating it into the L2. You give both groups a pretest and a posttest and then compare the results of the two groups to determine if there are any significant differences in their accuracy in using the target structure. You then observe an improvement in the experimental group's performance and conclude that translation has a positive effect on learning English articles. This study is susceptible to selection bias or differential selection of participants due to non-random participant selection. Volunteers, not randomly chosen, may differ in motivation or language proficiency, affecting internal validity. To address this, you should carefully select a representative sample using random sampling techniques, such as simple or stratified sampling, to enhance external and internal validity and reduce bias.

In applied linguistics research, particularly in classroom studies, intact groups are commonly compared, posing a threat to internal validity through selection bias. While random selection or assignment may be impractical in classroom settings, minimizing selection bias is essential for internal validity. There are alternative strategies, including matched-groups design, where participants are paired based on relevant characteristics, a process that can address confounding variables. Employing pretest–posttest designs with a control group can also capture initial differences and mitigate selection bias by comparing treatment and nontreatment groups. Additionally, statistical techniques such as ANCOVA can be used to control for important confounding variables, contributing to the validity of the findings.

Maturation

Maturation refers to the changes in the participants' knowledge, performance, experience, and so on that naturally occur over time and that are not related to the independent variable. These changes can happen physically, cognitively, emotionally, and intellectually, as well as linguistically. For example, the participants may get older, tired, or bored during the study. They may become more motivated, more experienced, or more knowledgeable as time goes on. These all act as extraneous variables not related to the effect of the independent variable and thus can threaten the internal validity of a study. Thus, any effect observed in the dependent variable could also be attributed to these factors in addition to or instead of the effect of the independent variable.

Maturation refers to the changes in the participants' knowledge, performance, experience, and so on that naturally occur over time and that are not related to the independent variable.

The maturation threat becomes a real threat in longitudinal studies or those conducted over an extended period of time, as it is possible that during the course of the study, the participants' experience, knowledge, or other attributes may grow too, irrespective of the independent variable. To address this, you can include a control group without the treatment to make sure any maturation effects are consistent across both groups. Another strategy is measuring the same variable at multiple time points to track natural growth changes. Random assignment of participants to experimental or control groups is also an effective strategy. This helps determine that any effects observed are likely due to the treatment and not maturation. Example 12.2 presents a hypothetical scenario.

EXAMPLE 12.2

Suppose you are conducting a classroom study on the effect of corrective feedback on learners' accuracy in past tense usage. The study uses a pretest–posttest–delayed posttest design, in which the groups receive a pretest before the treatment and two posttests, with one administered immediately after the treatment and the other two weeks later. Based on the difference between their pretest and posttest performance, you conclude that corrective feedback has a significant effect on students' accuracy of past test usage. However, the study is subject to the maturation threat, as learners' accuracy may naturally develop during posttest intervals. While a control group is utilized, strategies such as time-matched controls and detailed recordkeeping can minimize the risk of maturation effects and enhance the study's validity.

History

History refers to the events that occur during the study that are not related to the independent variable but can affect the results of the study. History becomes a threat if the study participants are exposed to situations that can have a similar effect as the independent variable. This can become even more acute if the two groups go through two different concurrent events and the results of the study are affected differently by these events. The effect of history as a threat becomes stronger as the study period is extended. Therefore, the risk of this threat is higher in studies that are longitudinal or are conducted over an extended period of time. Example 12.3 presents a hypothetical scenario.

EXAMPLE 12.3

Suppose you are conducting a study that seeks to investigate the effectiveness of dyadic interaction on students' negotiation strategies such as clarification requests and confirmation checks in the classroom. You use a treatment group that participates in dyadic interaction and a control group that does not. Using a pretest-posttest design, you conclude that dyadic interaction improves negotiation strategies. However, the study faces a history threat, as students may also have dyadic interactions outside the classroom, making it difficult to solely attribute improvements to classroom interaction.

One way to minimize the threat of history in the study in Example 12.3 or other similar studies is to randomly assign the participants to the treatment and the control groups. This helps to control for any history factors that may affect the results. It is also important to clearly document any events that may have occurred during the study that could potentially affect the results. You can then consider their potential effect when explaining or interpreting the findings and drawing conclusions.

History refers to the events that occur during the study that are not related to the independent variable but can affect the results of the study.

Testing or Measurement Effect

Testing is another threat to internal validity. It refers to the potential changes in the participants' performance on a test as a result of their prior experience with the test. In other words, it is the effect of prior test exposure on subsequent test performance. This threat suggests that if there is an improvement on a posttest, it could also be partly due to the fact that the students have taken a pretest. The likelihood of testing as a threat increases when the same pretest and posttest are used or when the time between the pretest and posttest is short. One reason for the testing effect could be because when the participants take a test for the second time, they might have become more familiar with the test or its format. They may also develop strategies to perform better in the test. If the two tests are the same, it is also possible that the participants may remember some of the items, particularly if the interval between the two tests is short.

Testing or measurement effect refers to the potential changes in the participants' performance on a test as a result of their prior experience with the test.

To control for this threat, you could use several strategies, such as counterbalancing the order of tests if there are multiple pretests and posttests. Another possibility is to use a control group that is not pretested, to control for the effects of testing. Additionally, you could use different versions of a test as the pretest and the posttest. This can reduce the effect of testing. Overall, it is important to consider the potential effects of testing on internal validity and to use appropriate design and data analysis and data collection strategies to control for these effects. Example 12.4 presents a hypothetical scenario.

EXAMPLE 12.4

Suppose you are conducting a study on students' attitudes towards English language learning after they have been through a semester of computer-assisted language learning (CALL) program. You give the students an attitude questionnaire before the program and the same questionnaire after the program. You then compare the results of the two questionnaires and conclude that the CALL program had a positive effect on the students' attitudes towards English language learning. This study faces a testing threat, which should be addressed or considered when interpreting the results.

The study is subject to the testing threat because the act of responding to the questionnaire before the program can influence the participants' responses on the same questionnaire after the program. The participants may reflect on their initial responses or become more attentive to issues raised in the questionnaire and then change their responses in the second instance of the questionnaire. To control for this, you may use multiple data sources or methods to gather information about the students' attitudes to triangulate the findings from the attitude questionnaire. This can include using other questionnaires as well as interviews and, if possible, observing the learners to see if there have been any changes in their learning behavior.

Instrumentation

Instrumentation refers to the tools or techniques that are used to measure variables in a research study. It can be a threat to internal validity if the way the measurement has been used affects the results. This can also be a threat if the measurement tools or techniques are not reliable or valid or if they do not accurately measure what they are supposed to measure. Example 12.5 presents a hypothetical scenario.

EXAMPLE 12.5

Suppose you are conducting a study that has used observation as a data collection method to examine classroom interaction in two ESL classrooms: Class A and Class B. In this study, you have observed and taken field notes about the interactions between teachers and students in the two classroom settings. You have coded the data focusing on specific communication patterns and strategies employed by the teachers and students during the interaction, with a focus on the types of inter-actions (e.g., teacher–student, student–student interaction) and who initiates and who responds to interaction. After calculating the frequency of these patterns, you conclude that there are differences in the patterns of interaction in the two classes, with class A using more student–student interaction than class B. However, the study is subject to an instrumentation threat, given potential limitations of field notes such as subjectivity, inaccuracy, and lack of detail. Additionally, the fact that data were coded by the researcher with no mention of interrater reliability raises concerns about the consistency and reliability of the conclusions drawn from the data.

In Example 12.5, to ensure the internal validity of the study, field notes could be accompanied by audio and/or video recordings of the classrooms because audio and video recordings can provide a more complete and accurate record of observations. Additionally, instead of taking field notes, you could have used observation check lists or schemes, as they can provide a more consistent way to collect data. Also, when coding the data, you could have used a second trained coder to independently code all or part of the data and interrater reliability could have been calculated. Good interrater reliability is essential in a study such as this because it shows the degree to which the results are influenced by the biases or personal perspectives of the researcher.

Instrumentation refers to the tools or techniques that are used to measure variables in a research study and can be a threat to internal validity if the way the measurement has been used affects the results.

Statistical Regression

Statistical regression (or regression toward the mean) refers to a statistical phenom-enon where extreme values in an observation tend to be followed by more moderate values in the second observation. In the context of applied linguistics research, this means that the study participants who score extremely high or extremely low on an initial language ability test are likely to move toward the mean in the second or subsequent measurements. In other words, those very high or very low scores tend to get closer to the mean or the average score the next time they are tested, irrespective of the independent variable. Regression toward the mean can be a threat to internal validity because it can lead to inaccurate conclusions about the effect of the independent variable. Example 12.6 provides a hypothetical illustration.

EXAMPLE 12.6

Suppose you are conducting a study to examine the effect of a reading program on the spelling performance of a group of learners who are poor spellers. You measure the spelling ability of the participants using a spelling test before and after the intervention and then compare the scores of the two tests to determine the effectiveness of the program. You observe an increase from the pretest to the posttest and conclude that the reading program has a positive effect on the learners' spelling ability.

However, this study is subject to the statistical regression threat because there is a high likelihood that the students with low spelling scores improved even without the intervention due to regression toward the mean. This is because learners who score low on an initial test have a greater potential for improvement than those who score high, and thus their scores are more likely to move closer to the mean or average score on posttest. This would make it difficult to determine if the improvement is the result of the reading program or just an effect of regression toward the mean. This is then a threat to the internal validity of the study, as the results may not accurately reflect the true effectiveness of the program.

To avoid or minimize a threat such as the above, you could use a variety of strategies, such as using a control group and random assignment of participants to groups. In many cases, using a large sample size would also be very helpful. A large sample size can help reduce the effects of regression towards the mean because it reduces the chance of some extreme scores drastically changing the overall mean of the groups. It also increases the chance that the sample represents the population more closely.

Statistical regression refers to a statistical phenomenon where extreme values in an observation tend to be followed by more moderate values in the second observation.

Mortality

Mortality (attrition) in a study occurs when recruited participants drop out. Reasons include moving away, loss of motivation, negative effects, health issues, time constraints, or study-related factors. High attrition rates can bias results, leading to unbalanced groups and making comparisons challenging. Factors including poor study design and communication may contribute to attrition, influencing the study's validity and outcomes.

Mortality refers to losing the participants in a study and happens when participants who have been recruited to participate in the study drop out in a way that can affect the results.

EXAMPLE 12.7

Suppose you are conducting a study that aims to investigate longitudinally the development of second language literacy skills of two groups of low- and high-proficiency adult L2 learners who are taking intensive English courses over a period of four semesters. You select the two groups based on the results of a reading and writing proficiency test before the study. Data are collected at two points in time, at the beginning of the program and at the end of the two semesters. The data include several measures of the participants' second language literacy skills, such as reading comprehension tests, language awareness tests, and writing ability measures. The study begins with a group of eighty participants, but by the end of the study, only fifty participants remain. The students who do not complete the study all belong to one of the low-proficiency classes. The remaining data are compared across the two groups of learners to examine any differences in their language development. You observe a more positive trend in the development of the high-proficiency learners.

The above study shows a high attrition rate, leading to an imbalanced and biased sample, compromising the accuracy of the conclusions. The reduced number in the low-proficiency group may also weaken the study's power to detect true effects.

You can use a number of strategies in such cases to minimize attrition, including:

a) Clearly communicating the purpose and expectations of the study to the participants so that they can make an informed decision at the start of the study.

b) Offering incentives, when possible, to encourage participants to remain in the study.

c) Keeping participants informed about the study's progress and providing feedback on their contributions to maintain their interest and increase retention.

d) Being mindful of the time commitment required for participants, including the time needed to complete various study tasks, and attempting to minimize any unnecessary demands or inconvenience placed on them.

e) Providing regular updates, following up with participants, and making necessary adjustments to the study design when needed.

Analyzing the reasons for attrition and making appropriate adjustments to your
data analysis can also be effective strategies to address attrition effects. For
instance, you can compare the characteristics and performance of participants
who dropped out with those who completed the study. This comparison may reveal
factors such as demographic differences, baseline data, or initial performance
metrics that can help identify patterns and underlying causes of non-participation.
Once the reasons for attrition are identified, you can adjust your data analysis
procedures to minimize its effects. For example, you might modify your statistical
methods to better account for the missing data.

Selection Interaction Effects

Another threat to internal validity is the interaction of some of the threats discussed
above with the participant selection, which can lead to an effect that confounds the
effect of the independent variable. For example, it is possible that differential
participant selection may interact with maturation or history in ways that can
create a combined effect that appears to result from the treatment. Therefore, you
may wrongly attribute the results to the effect of the independent variable whereas
the effect is because of the interaction of the threats.

Selection by maturation occurs if the groups in the study mature at different rates.
For example, if you have two groups of learners, beginner-level learners and advanced-
level learners, and want to examine the effect of a reading program over the course of a
semester on their reading ability, the students who are beginner-level learners may tend
to naturally improve more than advanced-level learners, and therefore, any differences
in their reading ability on the posttest may be partly due to the groups' differing
developmental rates rather than the reading program. Example 12.8 provides another
hypothetical example of selection by maturation interaction.

EXAMPLE 12.8

Suppose you are conducting a study that aims to investigate the effects of a tutoring
program on student writing achievement. The study includes a sample of 100 volunteer undergraduate students from an English language center. The students will
be divided into two groups: an experimental group and a control group. The
experimental group will receive the tutoring program whereas the control group
will not. The tutoring program will consist of weekly one-on-one sessions with a
trained tutor. The sessions will focus on writing skills such as organization, grammar, and style. Writing achievement will be measured using pre- and posttest
writing assessments. You compare the pretest and the posttest performance of the
two groups and observe a difference, with the experimental group performing better
than the control group. You conclude that the tutoring program has a positive effect
on students' writing achievement.

The study in Example 12.8 is subject to the selection by maturation interaction. Since the above study is using volunteers, it is possible that the groups will include disproportionate number of students who are more or less motivated to improve their writing skills. If so, and if there are more motivated students in the experimental group than the control group, any improvement in their writing skill may be because of the interaction between motivation and maturation rather than due to the effect of the tutoring program.

There are several ways to minimize the effect of the maturation by selection effect in the above research or similar research. One is by using a matched control group in which the control group is matched with the experimental group in terms of their characteristics. For example, the research can match the two groups in the study in terms of their motivation and interest. This means that you as the researcher need to collect information regarding their interest and motivation before the study. Another solution is randomly assigning participants to the two groups. By doing so, you can control for the effects of maturation and other extraneous variables. Additionally, by having information about the participants' motivation, the study can use appropriate statistical methods to control or account for the possible effects of differences in motivation levels. It is important to note that no single method can completely eliminate the effects of selection interaction, but by using a combination of methods, the effects can be minimized.

Selection interaction effects refer to the interaction of the threats discussed above with the participant selection.

Selection can also interact with other threats such as testing (when the testing affects the groups in the study differently), instrumentation (when the validity and reliability of a data collection tool affects the groups differently), or regression toward the mean (when the groups' scores regress toward the mean differently).

Selection can also interact with history when an event that occurs during the study (in addition to the treatment) affects the study groups differently. Take for example, a study that is examining the effect of a classroom reading program on students' literacy when participants in one group are exposed to additional reading opportunity at home during the study and the other group is not. This can lead to selection by history interaction. In such situations, if there are changes in the variables being studied, you may attribute them to the intervention being studied, whereas in fact they can be due to the effects resulting from the history–selection interaction.

Conclusion

Validity is an important aspect of quantitative research in applied linguistics, as it contributes to the accuracy and credibility of research findings. In this chapter, we have discussed the importance of validity and explored how it enhances the accuracy of the research findings and conclusions. We have examined the different types of validity, including face validity, content, criterion, and construct validity, and explored how they can be measured. We have also discussed the concepts of internal and external validity, their various types, and their importance in quantitative research. In Part IV, we will consider issues related to qualitative research including research designs, data collection, and analysis.

DISCUSSION AND ACTIVITY QUESTIONS

Discussion Questions

1. What are the different types of validity in quantitative research, and how do they contribute to ensuring the accuracy of the research findings?
2. What are some ways in which you can establish construct validity in your research?
3. How do you distinguish between internal and external validity, and how important are they in applied linguistics research?
4. How can you balance the need for internal validity with the need for external validity or generalizability of research results?
5. What are some potential challenges in achieving high levels of internal validity in quantitative research, and how can you address these challenges?
6. What are some potential threats to internal validity and how can they affect the results of a study?
7. What are some effective strategies to address threats to internal validity, such as maturation or testing effects, and how can these strategies improve the validity of the study findings?
8. As a researcher, how would you determine which types of validity are most relevant to your study and what strategies would you use to enhance each type of validity?

Activity Questions

1. Find a quantitative research study in applied linguistics and determine how the researcher(s) addressed validity in their study. Which types of validity were considered, and what strategies were used to assess and improve each type of validity?
2. Analyze a published research article and critically evaluate the evidence provided for the construct validity of the research measures used. Identify any potential limitations of the measures and explain what you would do differently.
3. In small groups, consider a research study in applied linguistics that is of interest to you. Then brainstorm potential threats to the internal and external validity of that research. Discuss strategies that you would use to address those threats. Share the results of your discussion with the rest of the class.
4. Do a literature review of at least five recent studies on a topic of interest to you. Identify and compare the approaches and methods they have used to establish

validity in different studies. Reflect on the strengths and limitations of these approaches and propose alternative strategies.

5. Consider a research project that involves multiple measures and constructs. Identify the types of validity that would be most relevant to that study. Then explain how you would assess and demonstrate the validity of the measures used. Justify the choices made based on the research goals and the expected findings.

PART IV
Qualitative Research Designs, Data Collection, and Analysis

13 Selecting Participants for Qualitative Research: Sampling Techniques and Methods

```
┌─────────────────────────────────────────────────────────────────┐
│ CHAPTER OBJECTIVES                                               │
│                                                                 │
│ After completing this chapter, you should be able to            │
└─────────────────────────────────────────────────────────────────┘
```

CHAPTER OBJECTIVES

After completing this chapter, you should be able to

- Understand the difference between qualitative and quantitative sampling procedures.
- Describe different types of sampling techniques used in qualitative research, including maximum variation sampling, theoretical sampling, extreme case sampling, homogeneous sampling, criterion sampling, and confirming and disconfirming cases sampling.
- Recognize the importance of identifying a sampling strategy that is suitable for the research question and purpose.
- Understand the strengths and limitations of different sampling techniques and how they may impact the study's findings and conclusions.
- Identify techniques to determine sample size in qualitative research.
- Understand the concept of generalization in qualitative research and how it differs from generalization in quantitative research.

Introduction

Qualitative research methods are widely used in the field of applied linguistics to explore language learners' and teachers' experiences, behaviors, and attitudes. Like quantitative research, one of the key aspects of conducting qualitative research is the process of sampling, which involves selecting participants, settings, and events that are relevant to the research question. However, the issue of sample size is contentious in qualitative research. Many may argue that the consideration of sample size is a matter more relevant to quantitative research than qualitative research. In quantitative research, since the goal is to make statistical generalizations, sample size and sampling considerations become highly important. However, most qualitative research is context dependent and does not intend to generalize findings from the sample to the population from which the sample has been selected. For the same reason, the issue of sample size has not received as much attention in qualitative research as it has in quantitative research.

However, although qualitative and quantitative research have different goals, many qualitative researchers argue that selecting participants in qualitative research is as important as it is in quantitative research (Morse, 2015a, 2015b). Since in qualitative studies the sample size is often much smaller, cases must be selected judiciously so that they can provide the best data and insight into the phenomenon.

In Chapter 8, we discussed sampling and sampling procedures in quantitative research, including nonprobability sampling strategies. While these methods can also be used in qualitative research, there are several sampling methods that are specific to qualitative research. In this chapter, we will explore the principles of sampling in qualitative research. We will first discuss different types of sampling methods and their use in qualitative research and then consider the issue of sample size and how to determine the number of participants in a qualitative study. We will also discuss issues regarding generalizability in qualitative research.

POINTS TO PONDER

How do you differentiate between qualitative and quantitative sampling procedures? What specific criteria or characteristics do you consider when selecting participants in qualitative research, and how does this differ from the criteria used in quantitative research?

Sampling Methods in Qualitative Research

Although different from quantitative research, sampling methods are also a crucial component of qualitative research, as they determine the participants, events, or settings that will be included in the study. As noted earlier, unlike quantitative research, qualitative research aims to explore the depth and complexity of human experiences, meanings, and behaviors, without aiming to generalize findings to a larger population. As a result, sampling in qualitative research is different and often involves selecting participants that are relevant to the purpose of the research and the research question.

Before considering sampling procedures in qualitative research, it may be helpful to discuss some of the key differences in sampling in the two types of research methods. While both types of research involve selecting participants or cases for study, the aims, techniques, and ethical considerations in sampling differ significantly.

The first difference is that qualitative research typically aims to explore a specific phenomenon in depth, without being concerned with generalizability. As a result,

qualitative researchers may use sampling methods that allow them to select participants, events, or settings that are most relevant to the research purpose and the
research question. For that reason, sampling methods in qualitative research are
mainly purposive in nature. That is, you make a judgment about what kind of
participant and how many of them are needed according to the purpose of the study.
As Lincoln and Guba (1985) noted, "In purposeful sampling the size of the sample is
determined by informational considerations. If the purpose is to maximize information, the sampling is terminated when no new information is forthcoming from
new sampled units; thus, redundancy is the primary criterion" (p. 202). There are a
number of purposive sampling strategies that qualitative researchers can use,
depending on the aim and scope of the research. These strategies, which can be
used alone or in combination and technically belong to the nonprobability sampling
method, help you to select their participants in ways that are suitable for your study.
We will provide a summary of some of the most common ones in the sections
that follow.

Sampling methods in qualitative research are mainly purposive in nature.

The second difference is that since qualitative research is often ongoing, it makes
use of sampling techniques that involve selecting new participants or cases based on
the emerging data. Thus, in contrast to quantitative research, where researchers may
use participants at the beginning of the study, in qualitative research, there is
sometimes a need to identify cases or participants that can provide information as
the study evolves.

Since **qualitative research** is often **ongoing,** it makes use of sampling techniques
that involve selecting new participants or cases based on the emerging data.

The third difference is that, in qualitative research, the sample size is often smaller
than in quantitative research, as the focus is on exploring experiences, beliefs, and
perspectives rather than analyzing large numerical datasets. Therefore, while the
quantitative researcher uses generalizability as a criterion for sample size and
sample selection, qualitative researchers may use data saturation as a criterion,
which means that they continue to collect data until no additional insights are
obtained from the new data or information.

Finally, ethical considerations in sampling are also different in qualitative and
quantitative research. While both types of research must adhere to ethical principles
and guidelines, qualitative research may need to consider unique ethical factors due
to the nature of the data collected. For example, in qualitative research, researchers
often collect detailed personal information about participants through interviews,
observations, or other methods. This can create a potential for harm, as participants

may reveal sensitive personal information that could be used against them, or they may feel uncomfortable sharing their experiences. To address these ethical concerns, you must take steps to protect the confidentiality and privacy of participants, obtain informed consent, and confirm that participants understand the purpose and scope of the research (see Chapter 3).

While the quantitative researcher uses **generalizability** as a criterion for sample size and sample selection, qualitative researchers may use **data saturation** as a criterion, which means that they continue to collect data until no additional insights are obtained from the new data or information. Qualitative studies are designed to provide **rich and in-depth** insights into the phenomenon being studied.

Altogether, although sampling and sampling procedures are important in both qualitative and qualitative research, they are not the same. The sampling methods in quantitative research aim toward generalizable findings, whereas in qualitative research they are designed to provide rich and in-depth insights into the phenomenon being studied. While some sampling techniques, particularly nonprobability techniques, may be used in both quantitative and qualitative research, qualitative research also employs specific sampling methods tailored to its goals, which emphasize in-depth understanding and context-specific insights rather than generalizability. In the following section, we will discuss a number of these techniques that have been discussed in publications on qualitative research (e.g., Onwuegbuzie & Leech, 2005, 2007b; Patton, 1990; Patton, 2015).

POINTS TO PONDER

What types of qualitative sampling methods are you familiar with or have you come across in research? Do you find certain sampling methods preferable or more effective in some context than others? If so, explain why.

Types of Sampling in Qualitative Research

Like quantitative research, there are also a number of sampling procedures used in qualitative research. While the nonprobability sampling techniques used in quantitative research, such as convenience sampling, snowball sampling, and quota sampling, can also be used in qualitative research, there are also some techniques that are unique to qualitative research. These techniques, which are purposive in nature, allow you to intentionally select participants who have specific characteristics that are relevant to the research question.

In this section, we will discuss some of the common sampling methods used in qualitative research. These methods differ in their underlying assumptions, purposes, and procedures, and each has its own strengths and limitations. Understanding the different types of sampling methods available in qualitative research can help us make informed decisions about selecting participants and generating insights from our data.

While the **nonprobability sampling techniques** used in quantitative research, such as convenience sampling, snowball sampling, and quota sampling, can also be used in qualitative research, there are also some techniques that are unique to qualitative research.

Maximum Variation Sampling

One of the purposive sample strategies used in qualitative research is maximum variation sampling. In this kind of sampling, a wide variety of participants are selected in ways that maximize variation in the sample, in terms of characteristics to be studied. This technique is particularly useful when you want to understand the different perspectives and experiences of individuals related to a phenomenon. According to Patton (1990) this kind of sampling provides: "(1) high-quality, detailed descriptions of each case, which are useful for documenting uniqueness, and (2) important shared patterns that cut across cases and derive their significance from having emerged out of heterogeneity" (p. 172).

The assumption behind this technique is that a wide range of participants would better reflect the diversity of the cases and perspective examined. The use of this technique allows you to have participants who represent a wide range of variations with regard to a particular phenomenon and therefore you can examine the phenomenon from multiple perspectives, which is needed when the aim is to gain a full picture of the issue examined.

EXAMPLE 13.1

Suppose you are conducting a study investigating language attitudes towards L2 speakers of English in various communities. You might purposively select participants who differ in education, gender, ethnicity, socioeconomic status, and geographic location to capture a broader perspective on this issue. By selecting participants who vary in such important characteristics, you can gain a more comprehensive understanding of people's attitudes towards L2 speakers across different sociolinguistic contexts.

Maximum variation sampling refers to a kind of purposive sampling in which a wide variety of participants are selected in ways that maximize variation in the sample in terms of characteristics to be studied.

Extreme Case (or Unique Deviant Case) Sampling

In extreme case sampling, the sample is selected because they have characteristics that are unique or extreme in some way, by having experienced an unusual event or having special perspectives deviant from the norm. This technique is useful when the aim is to explore the boundaries or limits of a particular issue or phenomenon. The assumption here is that cases that are extreme can provide insights that may not be obtainable through examining normal cases. It also assumes that by studying cases that are unusual or deviant, you can gain a deeper understanding of the underlying processes and factors that are at play in a given situation.

EXAMPLE 13.2

As an example, take a study that aims to explore various factors that contribute to success in language learning. To that end, you might decide to interview individuals who have shown exceptionally high levels of motivation and those who are not very motivated. By selecting these extreme cases, you can gain insights into the specific strategies and motivations that lead to success in language learning, which may not be evident from studying more typical language learners.

Extreme case sampling can also be used to challenge or test dominant theories or assumptions in a related area. By identifying cases that do not fit the expected pattern or norm defined by that theory, you can gain a better understanding of the limits and boundaries of that framework or model.

EXAMPLE 13.3

For example, in a study investigating the effectiveness of implicit and explicit instruction, extreme case sampling can be used to gain insights into the factors that contribute to successful language learning and to challenge the assumption that all students learn best when language rules are explicitly taught. As the researcher, you might identify two extreme cases: one group of students who have successfully learned the language with little or no explicit instruction and another group who, despite extensive explicit teaching, have struggled to acquire the language. By examining these unique extreme cases, you can gain a deeper understanding of the factors that influence the effectiveness of implicit versus explicit instruction and uncover variables that contribute to language learning success.

In **extreme case sampling,** the sample is selected because they have characteristics that are unique or extreme in some way, by having experienced an unusual event or having special perspectives deviant from the norm.

Homogeneous Sampling

Homogeneous sampling is a type of purposive sampling in which participants are selected based on their similarity with each other in terms of certain characteristics. This method, thus, is in contrast to maximum variation sampling and "is the strategy of picking a small, homogenous sample" (Patton, 2015, p. 429). We use this method when we want the sample to be as homogeneous as possible, reducing the potential variability in the data and increasing the chances of finding patterns or themes that are specific to the population being studied. Therefore, when selecting the participants or cases, the focus is on how similar they are in their characteristics. In such cases, the homogeneity in the sample not only minimizes variation but also leads to simpler analysis and the provision of more consistent data.

For example, suppose you are studying the language learning experiences of refugees in a particular country. For that purpose, you might use homogeneous sampling to select participants who are all from the same country, speak the same language, and have similar migration experiences. You may then conduct a focus group with these participants. The homogeneous approach used in such a study can help you to make sure that the data collected is specific to the viewpoints and experiences of that particular group of participants rather than being influenced by other factors, such as cultural differences, language differences, and other different characteristics.

Homogeneous sampling is a type of purposive sampling in which participants are selected based on their similarity with each other in terms of certain characteristics.

Critical Case Sampling

Critical case sampling is a sampling method in which you select participants or cases that provide the most critical information or, as (Patton, 2015) pointed out, those that "yield the most information and have the greatest impact on the development of knowledge" (p. 508). This technique is important when only a small sample can be selected. The assumption is that those few cases provide the most essential insight or information that you are seeking. For example, suppose you are interested in examining whether a particular language teaching method can be successfully implemented in a particular region. You may consider interviewing only those who have knowledge about the implementation of similar language programs in that region. These would be the participants that can provide the most vital information. One thing that is important in this technique is defining critical cases and using measures to determine their significance.

Critical case sampling is a sampling method in which you select participants or cases that provide the most critical information.

Criterion Sampling

Criterion sampling is a kind of sampling in which you identify and select cases based on some predetermined criteria. The criteria are based on the purpose of the study and could be related to the participants' experience, knowledge, or behavior, in relation to the research question or the research topic. The aim of criterion sampling is to select participants that have a particular characteristic or experience relevant to the research question or topic under investigation.

EXAMPLE 13.4

Suppose you want to study the challenges encountered by international students in adapting to a new cultural and academic environment. You may use criterion sampling by selecting students who have just arrived in a new country or been in a new country for less than a year. Or you may select those who have limited language proficiency or come from countries that have different cultural norms. This criterion for selection helps select the participants who have the necessary characteristics or experiences that are relevant to the research purpose and the research question.

Criterion Sampling is a kind of purposive sampling in which you identify and select cases based on some predetermined criteria.

Theoretical Sampling

Theoretical sampling is a kind of sampling in which cases are selected because of their potential contribution to developing or expanding a theory, or participants are chosen based on theoretical insights emerging from the data. This technique is often used in grounded theory research, whose purpose is the development of theory from the data. In grounded theory research, data collection and analysis often occur concurrently. In these studies, the theory also emerges from the data, and the theoretical sampling helps to collect additional data as the study progresses to refine or expand the concepts that have emerged from the initial data. The goal then is to select participants to provide data that can help develop or refine the emerging theoretical concepts. You select new participants or cases based on the analysis of previously collected data, and continue the process until theoretical saturation is reached, meaning that no new themes or categories are emerging from the data.

EXAMPLE 13.5

Suppose you are interested in understanding students' conceptions of self-assessment among advanced L2 learners. In this study, you aim to contribute to a theory of self-assessment by exploring students' perspectives on its usefulness. You may start by interviewing a small number of participants who meet the required language proficiency level. As you analyze the data and identify the emerging concepts, you will adjust your sampling strategy by selecting additional participants or data based on the evolving insights and theories that arise from the data analysis. For example, you might include students from different instructional contexts or revise the interview questions. Through this iterative process of adding participants and refining your approach based on the emerging concepts, you can develop a better understanding of students' views on self-assessment and build a grounded theory to explain their conceptions.

Theoretical sampling is a kind of sampling in which cases are selected because of their potential contribution to developing or expanding a theory, or participants are chosen based on emerging theoretical insights from the data.

Confirming and Disconfirming Cases Sampling

Confirming and disconfirming cases sampling is a qualitative sampling strategy used to help confirm and disconfirm the findings during data collection. Confirming sampling is used to collect data from additional cases that support or enrich previous findings or assist in understanding the patterns emerging from initial analyses. This would then add to the credibility of the findings. Disconfirming sampling is used to discover cases that do not fit the emerging findings and therefore allow you to test the limitation of the findings: "They are a source of rival interpretations as well as a way of placing boundaries around confirmed findings" (Patton, 2015, p. 457).

EXAMPLE 13.6

Suppose you are conducting a study exploring the relationship between student classroom participation and students' perception of language learning success. You may use confirming and disconfirming cases sampling to examine whether high levels of participation lead to higher levels of learning outcome. You may select cases of high-achieving students with low levels of classroom participation and low-achieving students with high levels of participation and conduct in-depth interviews focusing on the students' perceptions of the role of classroom participation and language development. You may then analyze these cases, through which you can either confirm or disconfirm the assumption about the relationship between classroom participation and students' perception about language success.

Confirming and Disconfirming Cases Sampling is a qualitative sampling strategy used to help you to confirm and disconfirm the findings during data collection.

Random Purposeful Sampling

Random purposeful sampling involves selecting cases randomly from a previously selected purposive sample. This method is used when the potential purposive sample for the study is too large (Miles, Huberman,& Johnny, 1994). The participants are randomly selected but are still chosen from a purposive sample. This allows you to select randomly a smaller number from the first sample. This method combines the strengths of both random sampling and purposive sampling, allowing for a more representative sample while still making sure that the sample is relevant to the research purpose and the research question.

EXAMPLE 13.7

For example, in a study exploring the experiences of L2 learners with a new instructional strategy, you may use random purposeful sampling to randomly select students from a purposive sample that comes from different language levels and first language background, while still selecting students who have experienced the new instructional strategy. By doing so, you can compare the perceptions of students with different language ability and first language backgrounds to gain a better understanding of the effectiveness of the new instructional strategy.

Random purposeful sampling involves selecting cases randomly from a previously selected purposive sample.

Opportunistic Sampling

Opportunistic sampling is a strategy in which you take advantage of the participant selection opportunities that occur during data collection. As pointed out by Onwuegbuzie and Leech (2007a, p. 114), "This form of sampling is particularly useful when you are unable or unwilling to declare in advance of the inquiry every case that will be included in the investigation." For example, in a qualitative study on students' interest in reading, you might initially select a group of students who vary in their motivation. However, during the study, you might encounter a student who is highly interested in reading extensively. You may take advantage of this opportunity and collect data for this individual. The additional data from this participant would provide new insights into how students become interested in reading.

Opportunistic sampling is a strategy in which you take advantage of the participant selection opportunities that occur during data collection.

Mixed Purposeful Sampling

In mixed purposeful sampling, you may use a combination of different sampling strategies. For example, you may select a sample through convenience sampling and another sample through extreme case sampling and then compare the results. This would then help the triangulation of the findings across samples. For instance, in a study on teachers' perceptions of translanguaging, you may initially use convenience sampling to recruit teachers who are readily available and easily accessible. After collecting data from these participants, you may then use extreme case sampling to identify and study the cases that deviate from others in their attitude and perception or those whose beliefs challenge prevailing assumptions about translanguaging. This combination of sampling techniques can help you obtain a broader and more detailed understanding of the issue under investigation.

In **mixed purposeful sampling**, you may use a combination of different sampling strategies.

Table 13.1 briefly describes the aims and characteristics of the qualitative sampling methods discussed so far.

POINTS TO PONDER

How would you determine an appropriate sample size in your qualitative research, and what factors would influence your decision?

Sample Size in Qualitative Research

Although the sample size is smaller in qualitative research than in quantitative research, the question that qualitative researchers still ask is what their size should be in order to be able to answer their research question adequately. There is no easy answer to this question, except that the size of the sample should be such that it allows you to have sufficient information to capture an accurate and complete picture of the phenomenon under study. It is thus suggested that sample sizes in qualitative research should neither be too small nor too large. Morse (2015a) pointed out, "[w]ith too few participants or too little data, analysis is more difficult as patterns are more difficult to identify. With too little data, replication may not occur: Variation is scattered, and important features in these data may be missing or overlooked. So, with a small sample, what have you got? Not very much interesting to write about" (p. 1317). So, if the sample size is too small, it will be difficult to achieve data saturation, and if it is too large it will be hard to carry out an in-depth analysis.

Table 13.1 A summary of the aims and characteristics of qualitative sampling methods

Sampling method	Aim	Characteristics
Purposive sampling	To select participants based on specific criteria that align with the research question and objectives (this approach includes those described below)	Nonrandom and subjective selection of participants
Maximum variation sampling	To select a diverse range of participants who exhibit maximum variation in the phenomenon under study	Nonrandom and subjective selection of participants
Homogeneous sampling	To select participants who share common characteristics or experiences related to the phenomenon under study	Nonrandom and subjective selection of participants
Extreme/unique deviant case sampling	To select participants who represent an extreme or deviant case in relation to the phenomenon under study.	Nonrandom and subjective selection of participants
Critical case sampling	To select participants who are crucial to understanding the phenomenon under study.	Nonrandom and subjective selection of participants
Theoretical sampling	To select participants based on emerging concepts and theories as they arise during data collection	Nonrandom and subjective selection of participants
Confirming and disconfirming cases sampling	To select participants who either support or challenge prevailing theories or assumptions about the phenomenon under study	Nonrandom subjective selection of participants
Random purposeful sampling	To select participants randomly from a purposively chosen group of individuals	Combination of random and purposive sampling
Opportunistic sampling	To select participants based on the opportunities that arise during data collection	Nonrandom and subjective selection of participants
Mixed purposeful sampling	To select participants based on a combination of sampling methods	Nonrandom and subjective selection of participants

The number of participants in qualitative research depends on many factors, including the theoretical background of the study, its purpose, the kind of data, the method used, the researcher's background and expertise, the nature and kind of analysis used as well as the various practical and methodological constraints. As Patten (1990, p. 184) pointed out, in a qualitative study "Sample size depends on what you want to know, the purpose of the inquiry, what's at stake, what will be useful, what will have credibility, and what can be done with available time and resources."

The richness of information is an important consideration in determining the sample size in qualitative research. With too little data or information, it is hardly possible to obtain a reliable answer to the research question. With regard to the richness of information, Lincoln and Guba (1985) suggested redundancy of information as the primary criterion. They suggested that if the purpose is to maximize information, sampling should stop when the research reaches a point where no new information or insights can be provided by the data analysis. This is what is called data saturation. Data saturation would tell you that there is no need for more data. Glaser and Strauss (1967) referred to this as theoretical saturation. This suggests that the question regarding sample size for a qualitative researcher is always whether new cases would add any useful insight to what has already been gained. For example, in an interview study, the number of participants would be decided on by whether interviewing additional participants would add any new information or simply repeat the previous information.

Morse (2015a) suggested that sample sizes in qualitative research also depend on the nature of the analytic strategies used. Two basic analytic techniques often used in qualitative research are the development of categories and themes (see Chapter 17). Although these two might seem similar and are often used interchangeably, they are not the same and indeed they "are two different cognitive and mechanical operations" that may require differences in sample size (Morse, 2015a, p. 1317). Categorical analysis is a process in which you separate the text data into related segments and then analyze it to identify commonalities, including descriptors. The most representative descriptor is often used to name the category. Many categories can be identified in the data you are working on, which can then be compared and contrasted. Thematic analysis differs from categorical analysis in that while the former involves identifying the meanings that are in a segment, the latter involves identifying the meaning that runs through the whole text or data. In other words, a theme is "the basic topic that the narrative is about, overall" (Morse, 2008, p. 727).

According to Morse (2015a), these two different analytic strategies have implications for sample size. When identifying categories, sometimes the content or the examples representing them are clear, but depending on the nature of the data, sometimes they are more difficult to identify. When the data are not very clear and the content is more varied and complicated, we need either more extended data or a larger sample size, as a larger sample size can provide more data, which can then help us to recognize and understand the subtleties within the data better. In thematic analysis, the amount of data is also important. Since the method of analysis is interpretive, more data are needed so that the research is able to run through the data and identify the gist or overall themes. Thus, "the more interpretative, thematic the method, the larger the sample required" (Morse, 2015a, p. 1318).

The number of participants also depends on the method of data collection. Semistructured interviews that ask the same question of all participants are more restricted than unstructured interviews. Therefore, they may require more participants than unstructured interviews, and the latter would produce longer interviews that allow you to identify the categories or themes that you are looking for. According to Morse (2015a), if such data are going to be analyzed quantitatively and statically, "a sample large enough to conduct nonparametric statistics should be used – ideally 30 to 60 participants" (p. 1318).

The number of participants in a qualitative research study depends on many factors, including the theoretical background of the study, its purpose, the kind of data, the method used, the researchers' background and expertise, and the nature and kind of analysis used, as well as the various practical and methodological constraints.

Longer interviews, or when a participant is interviewed more than once, may require fewer participants. In thematic analysis, the amount of data is important. The more data there are, the more able the researcher will be to run through the data and identify the gist or overall themes. Studies such as grounded theory that uses both a categorical analysis and a thematic analysis may need a good number of participants. According to Morse (2015a), depending on the purpose and scope of the research, a good, grounded theory may need a sample size of about thirty to fifty participants. There are a number of other suggestions depending on the type and aim of research. For example, as cited in Omona (2013, p. 175):

> Creswell (2002) has recommended that qualitative researchers should, (a) study one cultural-sharing group in ethnography, (b) examine three to five cases in a case study, (c) Interview 15–20 people during a grounded theory study, (d) explore the narrative stories of one individual in narrative research. In addition, Creswell (1998) recommended interviews with up to 10 people in phenomenological research and interviews with 20–30 people in grounded theory. Johnson & Christensen (2004) surmise that focus groups usually contain 6–12 persons, whereas Langford et al., (2002) and Morgan (1997) recommend 6–10 individuals. Krueger (2000) recommends 6–9 focus group members, and groups with more than 12 participants tend to "limit each person's opportunity to share insights and observations" (p. 78).

However, although these recommendations exist, we do not know on what basis the suggestions have been made. In some qualitative research such as grounded theory studies, data saturation is often suggested as a criterion. However, deciding whether data saturation has occurred is not an easy task. Sometimes, you might simply claim that saturation has occurred without specifying how it was assessed (Malterud, Siersma, & Guassora, 2016). Therefore, there is a need for more explicit procedures that can guide the selection and evaluation of an adequate sample size in qualitative research.

Techniques to Determine Sample Size in Qualitative Research

As noted earlier, one technique in determining sample size in quantitative research is to conduct a power analysis, which calculates the sample size for the research. In qualitative research, such quantitative procedures cannot be used. However, a few parallel suggestions have been made for qualitative research. Onwuegbuzie and Leech (2007a), for example, argued that the determination of sample size in qualitative research should be evidence-based. They then suggested what they called a qualitative power analysis for determining sample size in qualitative research. Such analyses, they argued, should be conducted through a qualitative meta-syntheses and meta-summaries, involving a systematic review of previous similar qualitative research designs, samples, and findings in a particular domain. They described the qualitative power analysis procedure as follows.

[B]efore deciding on an appropriate sample size, qualitative researchers should consider identifying a corpus of interpretive studies that used the same design as in the proposed study (e.g., grounded theory, ethnography) and wherein data saturation was reached. The researcher then could examine the sample sizes used in these studies with a view to selecting a sample size that is within the range used in these investigations. In addition, when observations or interviews are the data collection methods of choice, researchers should consider using the extant literature to determine an appropriate number of observations/interviews and an adequate length of time for each observation/interview that are consistent with Lincoln and Guba's (1985) recommendations of persistent observation and prolonged engagement, respectively, as well as allow the researcher to reach data saturation, theoretical saturation, and/or informational redundancy. (p. 118)

Onwuegbuzie and Leech also highlighted the importance of an audit trail when making decisions about sample size, which is documenting and keeping track of all the decisions made regarding sample size during the research and also providing such methodological information in research reports. Such audit trails are essential as they help the readers to evaluate the rigor of the study and the trustworthiness of its findings and interpretations.

Malterud et al. (2016) proposed the notion of "information power" as a guiding principle for determining adequate sample size for qualitative studies. "Information power indicates that the more information the sample holds, relevant for the actual study, the lower amount of participants is needed" (p. 1753). They suggested that the adequacy of the sample size and its information power depends on a number of factors, including the study aim, the specificity of the sample, the use of established theory, dialogue quality, and the analysis strategies. These factors suggest that the sample should be selected purposefully to collect data from information-rich cases that provide detailed information related to the purpose of the study.

The first factor influencing sample size is the aim of the study. A study with a broader aim requires a larger sample than a study with a narrower aim, as the issue under investigation in the former needs more comprehensive information than in the latter. Malterud et al. (2016) suggested that "A study *will need the least amount of participants* [italics in the original] when the study aim is narrow, if the combination of participants is highly specific for the study aim, if it is supported by established theory, if the interview dialogue is strong, and if the analysis includes longitudinal in-depth exploration of narratives or discourse details" (p. 1756). As an example, an L2 researcher aiming to qualitatively examine low-proficiency L2 learners' perception of the usefulness of explicit instruction would need fewer participants than a study examining the perception of L2 learners with different proficiency levels.

The second factor is sample specificity. This refers to "the specificity of experiences, knowledge, or properties among the participants included in the sample" (Malterud et al. 2016, p. 1755). The information power of the sample increases when the participants have characteristics specific to the focus of the study, and it would have less power as those characteristics diverge from what the study has intended to examine. Since in qualitative research a purposeful sample is often selected based on convenience, sometimes it may not be possible to recruit specific participants or even predict whether their characteristics are specific enough. In such cases, either more data should be collected from the participants or the number of participants should increase so that the study can obtain sufficient data to cover the scope of the study.

The **information power** of the sample increases when the participants have characteristics specific to the focus of the study, and it would have less power as those characteristics diverge from what the study has intended to examine.

Established theory is the next factor guiding sample size. This has to do with the theoretical background of the study and the extent to which the study is supported by previous theoretical perspectives. The more limited the theoretical background of the study, the more participants are needed to provide adequate information to draw the theoretical conclusion needed. On the other hand, if a study is supported by a clear and strong theoretical framework, a smaller number might be enough as the "frameworks offer models and concepts that may explain relations between different aspects of the empirical data in a coherent way" (Malterud et al. 2016, p. 1755). Conversely, if either the theoretical foundation of the study or the phenomenon under investigation is less clear and more ambiguous, a larger sample size is required (Morse, 2015a).

The **more limited** the theoretical background of the study, the **more participants** are needed to provide adequate information to draw the theoretical conclusion needed.

The next factor affecting the information power of the sample is the quality of the dialogue. In a qualitative study, the degree and richness of information gathered depends on the communication between the researcher and the participant (Malterud et al. 2016). Thus, the clearer this channel of communication, the fewer participants are needed to provide sufficient data. Or as Malterud et al. (2016, p. 1755) pointed out, "A study with strong and clear communication between researcher and participants requires fewer participants to offer sufficient information power than a study with ambiguous or unfocused dialogues." The clarity of communication depends not only on the participants but also on the expertise of the researcher and how theoretically and empirically knowledgeable the researcher is (Morse, 2015a). For example, if you know your area of research well and have strong experience in conducting interview studies, you would be able to gather data with a higher information power. However, a less experienced researcher may need to collect more data or from a larger sample size to obtain the same amount of information because their lesser experience may lead to obtaining more ambiguous and less focused data; this can be compensated for by collecting more data.

Finally, the adequacy of sample size depends on the kind of strategies or methods used to analyze the data. A cross-case analysis of individuals "requires more participants to offer sufficient information power compared with a project heading for in-depth analysis of narratives or discourse details from a few, selected participants" (Malterud et al. 2016, p. 1756). For example, an L2 study whose aim is to analyze similarities and differences regarding attitudes and beliefs of L2 learners and teachers about the use of computers in L2 classrooms will need a larger group of participants than a study whose aim is to provide an in-depth analysis of a few beginner-level learners' needs and difficulties in reading English. In a case study, the intention is to provide an understanding of particular case(s) or process(es) and not to cover a whole range of experiences. Therefore, a few carefully selected participants can provide sufficient information. However, for a study that aims to explore variations in experiences, two participants may not be enough to provide adequate information, and we need a much larger group to be able to gather sufficient data for analysis.

In a qualitative study, the adequacy of sample size also depends on the kind of **strategies or methods** used to **analyze** the data.

Generalization in Qualitative Research

An important consideration related to sample size in qualitative research is the extent to which the investigator is interested in making inferences beyond the data collected and the sample in the study; in other words, the extent to which the aim is to generalize. Generalization is often considered an important aim of quantitative research, but its role in qualitative research is considered contentious as qualitative studies are mostly context-specific, and instead of making generalizations beyond their context, they aim to provide a deep understanding of a phenomenon through collecting rich data from specific cases. However, as Polit and Beck (2010) pointed out, "in an environment where evidence for improving practice is held in high esteem, generalization in relation to knowledge claims merits careful attention by both qualitative and quantitative researchers" (p. 1451). Therefore, although the issue of generalization is a thorny issue in qualitative research, many qualitative researchers have argued that generalization is also a very important concept in qualitative research. Polit and Beck (2010) argued that "without generalization, there would be no evidence-based practice: research evidence can be used only if it has some relevance to settings and people outside of the contexts studied" (p. 1452). Ayres et al. (2003, cited in Polit and Beck, 2010, p. 1452) stated that, "Just as with statistical analysis, the end product of qualitative analysis is a generalization, regardless of the language used to describe it (p. 881)."

Although the issue of **generalization** is a thorny issue in qualitative research, many qualitative researchers have argued that generalization is also a very **important concept** in qualitative research.

Generalization in quantitative research often involves making inferences from a sample to a population. This type of generalization, also known as statistical generalization, aims to select a sample that is representative of the population to which the researcher intends to generalize. Inferential statistics are commonly used in such research to determine whether the results found in the sample can be applied to the bigger population. The appropriate sampling method for this kind of generalization is probability sampling.

However, in addition to statistical generalizations, there is another type of generalization called analytic or theoretical generalization. Analytic generalization aims to draw inferences from cases or observations to constructs or theories. This is a common type of generalization in theory-driven qualitative studies whose aim is to develop a theory such as grounded theory. It is also relevant to other qualitative studies that collect data from a small sample to gain an understanding of the general phenomenon investigated, or to situations when qualitative data are inductively analyzed in ways that contribute to the identification and development of overall themes or constructs. By doing so, along with processes that the qualitative researcher uses to establish the credibility of their findings, the qualitative researcher arrives at a kind of inductive generalization. Theoretical sampling, which is a sampling method used in grounded theory research, serves to collect and analyze data through coding to inductively develop a theory through generalization.

Generalization in quantitative research is **statistical generalization** and often involves making inferences from a sample to a population. Generalization relevant to some qualitative research, such as grounded theory, is analytic or **theoretical generalization**, which aims to draw inferences from cases or observations to constructs or theories.

When discussing the notion of trustworthiness in qualitative research, Lincoln and Guba (1985) introduced four criteria (credibility, transferability, dependability, and confirmability) considered to parallel the commonly used assessment principles in quantitative research: internal validity, external validity, reliability, and objectivity. The criterion of credibility in qualitative research concerns the extent to which the results can be viewed as credible or plausible by the participants under investigation and others. Dependability is similar to the notion of reliability in quantitative research, which is concerned with the extent to which you can obtain similar results if the study is repeated. In qualitative research, this principle entails clear explanation of the research strategies employed and also justification and assessment of their effectiveness against the data. Confirmability concerns the extent to which others agree with or confirm the interpretations made by the researcher. This notion is parallel to the notion of objectivity in quantitative research, with the difference that in quantitative research the research seeks to be objective, whereas in qualitative research you admit that the research is not objective. Transferability, however, looks analogous to external validity or generalizability in quantitative research. Other researchers have referred to this notion as case-to-case transfer (Tobin & Begley, 2004) or case-to-case translation (Firestone, 1993).

Transferability involves the application of the findings from a qualitative study to a different setting or group of people not participating in the study. If that is the case, some degree of representativeness is also needed in qualitative research. However, there is a difference between transferability in qualitative research and generalizability in quantitative research. Since qualitative research is interpretive and the participants are often small in number and hence not representative of the population, the findings may not be generalizable in the sense used in quantitative research. Therefore, as Lincoln and Guba (1985) noted, by transferability, it is not meant that you should make generalizable claims but instead provide sufficient details that make transfer possible in case the reader desires to do so. This can happen by providing detailed and thick description of the study (see Chapter 17), including its setting, participants, and the data collection and analysis. Such descriptions enable the reader to understand the study and make a judgment about the credibility of its finding and its transferability to their own or another context. Therefore, transferability is not done by the researcher but is judged by the reader.

Transferability in qualitative research is parallel to **generalizability** in quantitative research and involves the application of the findings to different settings or groups of people not participating in the study.

Similarly, Onwuegbuzie and Leech (2007a) argued that qualitative studies always involve some kind of generalization. In quantitative research, the goal is to generalize findings beyond the sample. However, it is difficult not to see cases where qualitative researchers also try to generalize their findings beyond the context of their own study. Thus, qualitative research whose aim is to develop a theory tries to transfer the knowledge gained from particular cases, experiences, and contexts to multiple situations. A theory is in fact a generalization or a set of generalizations through which we attempt to explain and understand how and why things happened the way they did. This thus necessitates attention to the issue of sample size in qualitative research.

Onwuegbuzie and Leech (2007a) discussed several generalizations that are often made in every qualitative study including:

> (a) from the sample of words to the voice; (b) from the sample of observations to the truth space; (c) from the words of key informants to the voice of the other sample members; (d) from the words of sample members to those of one or more individuals not selected for the study. (p. 107)

The first generalization is the kind of generalization that a qualitative researcher makes from the words that research participants have used to describe a situation to capture the voice in the data. For example, in an interview, the opinions expressed by the participants may not always capture the whole insight, and therefore to have a true picture of the phenomenon, you should collect a sufficient number of words from the participants to be able to understand the experiences under study. Therefore, the quantity of the spoken text gathered from the participants serves here as a sample and becomes crucial. This then suggests that when doing a qualitative study that involves interviews, attention should be paid to the number of words collected and the length of the interviews.

The second generalization is from the sample of observations to the truth space. This suggests that not only a sufficient sample of words is needed in qualitative research, a sufficient sample of observations is also needed. Qualitative research should then pay attention to "how much data should be sampled until data saturation ... or informational redundancy is reached" (Onwuegbuzie and Leech, 2007a, p. 109).

The third generalization is from the words of key informants to the voice of the other sample members. This occurs when a qualitative researcher collects data from a subsample of the participants in the study. For example, suppose you have collected questionnaire data from a larger group. You may interview a smaller group to gain more in-depth insight. However, by doing so the research also makes a generalization to the whole sample. This generalization is only valid when the subsample is representative of the study participants and also the sample of words collected is representative of the voice of each of the subsample members. Therefore, you must pay attention to both sampling units; that is, the participant subgroup and their words.

The next generalization involves extending from the words of the sample to those of other individuals who are not part of the study. It occurs when you apply observations from the study to those outside it. As noted earlier, a qualitative researcher may not always be interested in the traditional sense of sample to population generalization. However, sometimes, "interpretations and theories emerging from the findings might be expected to be generalized to individuals or groups outside the sample" (Onwuegbuzie & Leech, 2007a, p. 110). In such cases, attention must be paid to how the participants are selected for the study.

Conclusion

In this chapter, we began by discussing the importance of sampling in qualitative research and how it differs from quantitative research. Qualitative research relies heavily on purposive sampling procedures to select participants for data collection. It aims to identify participants who can provide rich, in-depth information that is relevant to the research question. Sampling procedures discussed in this chapter include theoretical sampling, extreme case sampling, homogenous sampling, criterion sampling, opportunistic sampling, mixed purposeful sampling, maximum variation sampling, and confirming and disconfirming cases sampling. Each of these procedures has its own unique characteristics, strengths, and limitations, which should be considered in relation to the research question and context. We also discussed how to determine sample size for qualitative research and issues regarding generalizability in qualitative research. Throughout the chapter, we also provided examples of how these sampling methods can be used in applied linguistics research. We hope that by understanding the various sampling methods, you can now make informed decisions about which techniques to use in your studies so that your sampling strategies align with the research questions and ethical considerations at hand.

DISCUSSION AND ACTIVITY QUESTIONS

Discussion Questions

1. What are some of the possible advantages and disadvantages of using purposive sampling techniques in qualitative research?
2. In what situations would you choose to use extreme case sampling rather than theoretical sampling? What factors might influence this decision?
3. When would you use confirming and disconfirming cases sampling? What are some potential challenges of this approach?
4. Can you combine convenience sampling and extreme case sampling? When, and why? What are some potential benefits and drawbacks of this combination?
5. Why is generalization not a primary goal in qualitative research? Do you think generalizability can still be obtained in qualitative research? If so, how?
6. What does the concept of data saturation mean in qualitative research? How can data saturation be used to determine sample size in qualitative research? What are the advantages and disadvantages of using this approach?
7. How do considerations of sample size and generalization differ between qualitative and quantitative research?

Activity Questions

1. Imagine you are conducting a study using extreme case sampling. Identify a phenomenon you would like to investigate, and identify two extreme cases that

represent opposite ends of the spectrum. What data collection methods would you use to study these cases, and how would you compare and contrast them?

2. In groups, design a study using theoretical sampling. Choose a research question and identify the key concepts that you will study. Then explain how you will select cases for analysis based on the emerging themes or patterns in the data.

3. Think about a research question that you would like to explore qualitatively. Select the sampling method that you think would be most appropriate for your research question and explain why. Describe the benefits and limitations of using this sampling method, and explain how it might affect the findings of your study.

4. Select a published qualitative study. What sampling method did the authors use, and how well did it address the research question? Were there any limitations or potential issues in the sampling procedure? How might you address those issues?

5. Review a qualitative research study in applied linguistics and discuss the generalizability of its findings. What aspects of the study design or sampling procedure may affect the generalizability of the results?

6. Conduct a literature review on the topic of generalization in qualitative research and present your findings to the class. What are some common strategies for enhancing the generalizability of qualitative research, and what are the limitations of these approaches?

14 Designing Qualitative Research: Types and Techniques

CHAPTER OBJECTIVES

After completing this chapter, you should be able to

- Understand the role of various qualitative research designs in applied linguistics research, and how they can be applied to real-world research contexts.
- Identify the main types of qualitative research designs in applied linguistics, including ethnography, grounded theory, case study, narrative inquiry, and discourse studies.
- Understand the defining features of each design and how they differ from one another.
- Critically evaluate different qualitative research designs and identify potential strengths and limitations.

Introduction

In Chapter 13, we discussed different types of sampling techniques used in qualitative research. In this chapter, we focus on qualitative research design; we will discuss various types of qualitative research designs that are commonly used in applied linguistics research. The chapter focuses on the exploration of prevalent types such as ethnography, grounded theory, case study, narrative inquiry, and discourse studies. It also discusses the various types of discourse studies, such as conversation analysis, interaction analysis, and critical discourse analysis.

Key objectives involve understanding the distinctive features of each design, discerning their differences, and developing the capability to identify situations where specific qualitative research designs are most appropriate.

Types of Qualitative Research Designs

For the research to be successful, it is important to follow a procedure that directly addresses the research question. Therefore, identifying an appropriate research design is of paramount importance. As a researcher, you must carefully select the research design that best aligns with your research topic and the specific question you aim to answer. This process involves initially choosing an overarching research methodology, followed by a suitable research design. In the following sections, we will discuss five main types of qualitative research designs commonly used in applied linguistics, including ethnography, grounded theory, case study, narrative inquiry, and discourse studies with its four main subtypes: conversation analysis, interaction analysis, discourse analysis, and critical discourse analysis (see Figure 14.1).

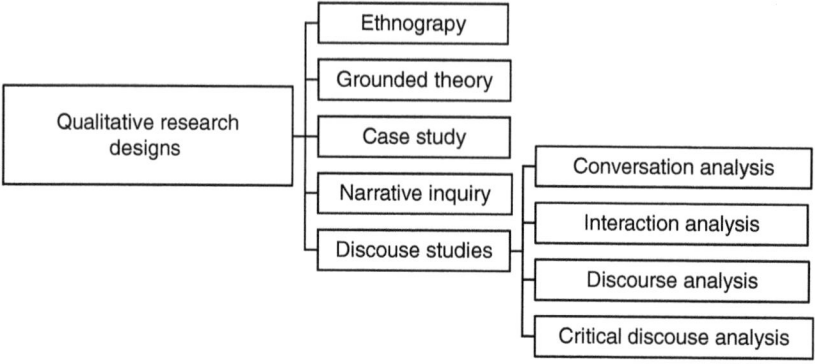

Figure 14.1 Types of qualitative research design

Ethnography

Ethnography, a qualitative research design rooted in anthropology and sociology, involves a systematic study of a cultural group within their real-life contexts. It employs immersive fieldwork and observation to understand patterns of behavior, language use, and beliefs. In applied linguistics, ethnography provides insights into the differences between students' cultural backgrounds and the culture in educational settings, exploring the impact of these variations on second language acquisition and cultural understanding (Johnson, 1992). The holistic approach aims to uncover how participants create, experience, and contribute to the culture in which they live.

In ethnography, you observe the behavior of a group in their natural social settings with no intervention. Taking an interpretive approach, you interact with participants to learn about them and the community in which they live. The focus is on how the participants behave or perform as members of the community to which they belong.

The notions of culture and cultural groups are important in ethnography, and this is one of the features that distinguishes an ethnography from other qualitative research designs. Because the focus of ethnography is on cultural behavior, it is essential to know what culture means in ethnography. Culture is usually defined as "an abstract concept used to account for the beliefs, values, and behaviors of cohesive groups of people" (Richards & Morse, 2007, p. 53). However, the scope of culture is broad and diverse and can include any aspect of peoples' behavior within a community or group of people who share the same culture, including their aims, purposes, and motives. In this respect a school, or even a classroom, can also be a cultural group or community. A classroom, for example, is a community of learners who have gathered to pursue a collective goal. A classroom can be considered a community, with learners' collective goals and motives as their shared culture. An applied linguistics researcher interested in exploring the learning behavior of a group of students in the classroom can conduct an ethnography to develop an understanding of the cultural world that the students build in the classroom. They may explore questions about ways in which learners participate in classroom activities, such as class discussion, interaction with the teacher or other students, and student behavior in group work activities.

Ethnography is a qualitative research design rooted in anthropology and sociology. It involves systematically studying participants in their real-life contexts, focusing on a group that shares the same culture, with the aim of providing an in-depth exploration of their culture and behavior.

In ethnography, as in other types of qualitative studies, the method of data collection is mainly qualitative and occurs through a variety of means, such as interviews, field notes, diaries, participant observation, and the collection of documents and artifacts. Since the cultural context of the phenomenon is important in ethnography, the site and location where participants live become important as well. For this reason, traditionally, ethnographic research has taken place on a particular site. The researcher enters this site and lives there in order to observe the group for an extended period of time in an attempt to develop an understanding of their cultural behavior and patterns.

The type of observation in ethnography is often participant observation, in which the researcher not only watches but also becomes part of the research community by participating in the activities of the group. To this end, "Ethnographers should be able to listen, show interest in what people do and what they say, so that they may carry out data collection" (Hughes & Sharrock 2002 in Nixon & Odoyo, 2020, p. 51). To explore cultural behaviors, researchers try to immerse themselves in the cultural events and activities, in order to examine how they are created and shared and how they change over time.

The method of analysis in ethnography is inductive, iterative, and open-ended, and the researcher might start to analyze the data as they are collected. The information collected and the descriptions of events are categorized, and patterns are identified. The data are then interpreted, and the participants' meanings are inferred from the categories, meanings, and patterns that often emerge from the data rather than being imposed from outside sources.

Key Characteristics of Ethnography

- Studies people within their natural social environments, such as classrooms, homes, schools, or communities.
- Focuses on participants' behavior and performance within a specific cultural group.
- Takes place in a natural setting, emphasizing prolonged observation for a first-hand account of experiences and actions.
- Involves data collection through direct observation, field notes, interviews, diaries, and archival materials.
- Adopts a holistic and contextual approach.
- Aims to understand meaning and functions from participants' perspectives, utilizing an emic (insider's) rather than an etic (outsider's) viewpoint.
- Analyzes data inductively, interpretively, and emically, prioritizing understanding from the participants' standpoint.

Steps in Conducting Ethnography

1. Decide on the research question or the problem to explore.
2. Decide on the research site(s).
3. Seek permission to access the site.
4. Plan to visit the site.
5. Determine the methods of data collection and collect the data.
6. Organize the data.
7. Code and analyze the data.
8. Interpret and present the findings.

Ethnographic research has not received the same degree of attention in L2 and in applied linguistics as other types of research designs. However, this research design has been used in a number of studies that have aimed to provide an in-depth understanding of the various cultures or cultural behaviors in a language learning and teaching context. Example 14.1 illustrates the use of ethnographic research in applied linguistics by presenting the abstract from a study entitled "Understanding the Learning Process of Peer Feedback Activity: An Ethnographic Study of Exploratory Practice" (Zheng, 2012, p. 109).

EXAMPLE 14.1

Abstract

This ethnographic study attempts to find, reveal and understand the learning possibilities, from the social learning perspective, in the process of peer feedback activity in a college English classroom for non-English majors in China. The study reveals the nature of Exploratory Practice (EP), and the investigation is guided by EP principles, aiming at exploring the viability of the practice in this specific teaching and learning context. Through classroom observation, discourse analysis, discussion, interviews and drafts of students' writing, the study finds five group cooperative patterns, represented by the five patterns of discursive interaction: collaborative, expert–novice, dominant–dominant, dominant–passive and passive–passive. Wherein the former two patterns witness the obvious reciprocal nature, the latter three seem not to. The subsequent classroom discussion reveals a general conformability of the teacher and students' understanding of the virtues and problems of the activity, and the broadening of the teacher's understanding in this social process. Meanwhile through discussion and interview, the practitioners reached a consensus that the teacher's tutoring is necessary to turn the problems into possible learning opportunities where the learners act as the learning agents. The study also discussed the possible ways of the teacher's tutoring in the activity in a specific context.

Strengths and Limitations of Ethnography

Like any other type of research, ethnography has its strengths, limitations, and challenges. One of the strengths is that it provides an in-depth approach to carrying out research. Therefore, it gives you an opportunity to gain a rich insight into the participants' own community and culture.

On the weakness side, however, conducting an ethnographic study can be time-consuming as it is longitudinal in nature. The data collection requires the ethnographer to be with and observe the participant for an extended period of time. Another weakness is that the data are often unstructured and disorganized, and the analysis is also often time-consuming, requiring careful data sorting, exploring, and cross checking. Furthermore, since ethnography often explores a small group, generalizing the findings to a bigger population is problematic although theoretical or analytic generalization is possible, which refers to the contribution of a study to the development of a new theory.

Case Study

A case study is a type of qualitative inquiry that follows an interpretive approach to research with the main purpose of providing an in-depth exploration of one or more cases. It is one of the earliest types of qualitative research, which has long been used in social sciences and has also been frequently used in applied linguistics and L2 research. A case study does not intend to generalize to the larger population. However, case studies can facilitate theoretical generalizability (Yin, 2003), which is to generalize from a case study's findings to theory. The aim here is to construct or expand theories instead of testing theories.

Examples of early case studies in applied linguistics include Shapira's (1978) study of Zoila, an adult Spanish speaker with slow progress in learning English; Schumann's (1978) case study of Alberto, an adult Costa Rican as a second language learner in the US; Kessler and Idar's (1979) study of a Vietnamese mother and child; Schmidt's (1983) study of Wes, a Japanese learner of English in the US; and Schmidt and Frota's (1986) case study of Schmidt learning Portuguese. There are many other case studies in different areas of SLA and applied linguistics that have been published in recent years.

However, despite its frequent use, a case study is not an easy research design to define. Thus, it has remained an ambiguous term, and many students and researchers may not have a good understanding of what it is and how it can be used in research. There are a number of definitions of a case study. While they differ in certain respects, a key common feature of them all is an in-depth exploration of a particular case or cases. Sturman (1997, p. 61) defined case study as "a general term for the exploration of an individual, group or phenomenon." Gall, Borg, & Gall (2002, p. 545) defined it as "the in-depth study of instances of a phenomenon in its natural context and from the perspective of the participants involved in the phenomenon." Yin (2003, p. 13) described a case study as "an empirical inquiry that investigates a contemporary phenomenon within its real-life context, especially when the boundaries between phenomenon and context are not clearly evident". Creswell (2007) provided a more detailed description defining a case study as a study "in which the investigator explores a bounded system (a case) or multiple bounded systems (cases) over time, through detailed, in-depth data collection involving multiple sources of information (e.g., observations, interviews, audiovisual material, and documents and reports), and reports a case description and case-based themes. For example, several programs (a multi-site study) or a single program (a within-site study) may be selected for study" (p. 73). Bounded means "the case is separated out for research in terms of time, place, or some physical boundaries" (p. 465).

A case study is a qualitative inquiry that follows an interpretive approach to research with the main aim of providing an in-depth exploration of one or more cases.

The difference between an ethnographic study and a case study is that in an ethnographic study, the focus is on understanding the culture of a group or case, but in a case study the focus is more on understanding the case itself. Therefore, case study research explores one or more cases within a particular social setting or context. Also, as Stake (2008) pointed out, a case study "is defined by interest in an individual case, not by the methods of inquiry used" (p. 443).

In conceptualizing a case study, the question that might arise is what a case is and how to define it. Miles and Huberman (1994, p. 25) provided a general definition, defining a case as "a unit of analysis" or "a phenomenon of some sort occurring in a bounded context." Patton (2015, p. 121) made it more specific, defining a case as "a person, an event, a program, an organization, a time period, a critical incident, or a community," which can be studied "in detail holistically, and in context." In applied linguistics, a case thus can be a language learner or a group of learners, a teacher or a group of teachers, or a language teaching school or program.

When a case involves a group, the case study primarily aims to describe and understand the activities of the group in their specific context, rather than seeking to identify broader trends or patterns. This approach involves a detailed examination of the group's interactions, processes, and behaviors to build a contextually grounded understanding of the case itself. The focus is on exploring how the group functions, what it does, and how its members interact within their particular environment.

In contrast to quantitative research, where the goal is often to make generalizable conclusions that can apply beyond the study's context (e.g., to a larger population), case studies of groups are more concerned with the unique characteristics and experiences of the specific group being studied. The aim is not to extend the findings to other groups or settings but to gain rich insights into the particular case in its own context.

The case can also be a process. A process refers to a series of activities or steps that need to be taken to achieve an outcome or accomplish a goal. In applied linguistics, it can be the process of teaching or learning a language, the process of developing a curriculum, a lesson plan, or other teaching materials. When the case is a process, to gain a detailed understanding, a case study may also explore the various factors that contribute to the process.

A case in a case study can be an individual, a group, an organization, or a process.

A case study can investigate either a single case or multiple cases. When focusing on a single individual, it attempts to provide detailed exploration of experiences, perspectives, and behaviors. Examining multiple cases involves describing and comparing them to unveil insights into a shared phenomenon. Data collection in case studies primarily employs qualitative methods such as interviews, artifacts, observation, archival records, and documentation. Among these, interviews, participant observation, and documentation are three commonly used sources. An artifact refers to an object or item that has significance for the research. It can be physical or cultural and can include a "technological device, a tool or instrument, a work of art, or some other physical evidence. Such artifacts may be collected or observed as part of a case study and have been used extensively in anthropological research" (Yin, 2003, p. 113). Observation occurs in naturalistic settings, in which the researcher has a chance to directly observe the case during the research.

An artifact refers to an object or item that has significance for the research and can include a "technological device, a tool or instrument, a work of art, or some other physical evidence" (Yin, 2003, p. 113).

Observation can be unstructured, where the observer records observations without a specific framework, or more structured, using codes or schemes. It may also be either participant or nonparticipant, the latter involving the researcher observing without actively participating in the event. Nonparticipant observation can occur covertly or overtly.

In a case study, documentation can be used to collect evidence for triangulation, which is the use of multiple data sources to gain a more comprehensive understanding of the research issue. In case studies, documentation supports triangulation, which enhances understanding by using multiple data sources.

A case study design does not involve sophisticated statistical data analysis since the focus is more on exploration. However, to examine a case in detail, the researcher may use a mixed methods approach combining both qualitative and quantitative data collection and analysis procedures (see Chapter 24).

Key Characteristics of a Case Study

- It analyses the case as "an integrated system" (Stake, 1995, p. 2) with the focus on a holistic understanding of an entity as a unit. In that sense, a case study is like an ethnography, and for this reason, some consider a case study as a kind of an ethnographic study. The difference, however, is that an ethnography focuses on exploring the behavior of a cultural group, whereas in a case study, the focus is on specific cases or individuals.
- It examines the case within a particular boundary, which can be a particular time, place, or context (Miles & Huberman, 1994). Knowing the boundary of the case is important in a case study as it helps maintain the focus on the case as a unit.
- Like ethnography, case studies are often longitudinal in nature, in that the case is studied deeply for an extended period of time.

Steps in Conducting a Case Study

1. Define the research question.
2. Conduct a literature review to establish a theoretical framework.
3. Choose and justify the selection of relevant cases.
4. Select cases and obtain necessary permissions or informed consent.
5. Determine data collection methods (e.g., interviews, observations, document analysis).

6. Collect and organize data, scheduling interviews if applicable.
7. Adhere to ethical guidelines during data collection.
8. Decide on data analysis methods.
9. Describe and analyze the chosen cases.
10. Interpret and present the findings.
11. Write the research report.

Strength and Limitations of Case Studies

Case studies have several strengths and limitations. Their strength lies in the ability to gather in-depth, context-specific data, providing profound insights into a particular case. Unlike group studies, case studies allow detailed analysis, offering crucial understanding of complex phenomena. They enable data collection from various sources, supporting comparison and theory building across multiple cases.

However, case studies face challenges in managing and analyzing data from multiple sources, potentially becoming complex and time-consuming. The detailed information may overwhelm researchers, diverting focus from the study's main objectives. Moreover, case studies are primarily descriptive and lack cause-and-effect explanations, making them appear less rigorous than experimental studies. External validity is limited, as generalization to a population is not feasible due to the focus on specific cases. While theoretical or analytical generalizability is possible, case study replications can be challenging. Using a strong theoretical framework may enhance external validity in case studies, according to Yin (2003).

The issue of subjectivity is another concern, particularly for those who believe that a scientific study must be objective. Case studies are considered subjective because the interpretations of the findings are much affected by the researcher's own judgments, perspectives, and points of view. Of course, to what extent a study is subjective or objective is not easy to determine. Although quantitative measures are often regarded as more objective, as Berg and Lune (2012) pointed out, this objectivity holds only if we refrain from questioning the origin and nature of the data. Absolute objectivity becomes questionable when dealing with phenomena that are difficult to define, as their meaning is inherently shaped by our interpretations.

A case study does not allow sample-to-population generalizability. However, it can facilitate **theoretical** or **analytical generalizability.**

Furthermore, unlike some quantitative studies, such as experimental studies that have a well-established procedure for data collection and data analysis, there are no established guidelines and procedures for conducting and reporting a case study. Although many researchers have attempted these days to develop standard procedures and guidelines, still case studies do not have as strict methodological principles as their more quantitative counterparts. Maoz (2002, pp. 164–165) argued that "the use of the case study absolves the author from any kind of methodological considerations. Case studies have become in many cases a synonym for freeform research where anything goes."

Validity and Reliability of Case Studies

Like any other research, reliability and validity are important considerations in case studies. Regardless of the research type, meticulous attention to data collection and analysis processes is essential for ensuring reliability and validity.

As noted earlier, the reliability and validity of a study depend on how the data have been collected. One way to enhance the reliability of a case study is to make the data collection more structured. For example, when collecting interview data, interview guides can be developed and used. Having an interview guide can enhance the reliability of the data as it allows you to collect the same data. An interview guide is "a list of questions or issues that are to be explored in the course of an interview" (Patton, 1990, p. 283). As Patton pointed out, the benefit of an interview guide is that it draws the researcher's attention to the areas or topics of importance, while at the same time allowing the researcher to build a free conversation with the interviewee by freely asking and probing other questions that can further illuminate the issue.

Another strategy is to critically examine the questions before they are asked so that they can be well aligned with the theoretical framework used in the research. The interview transcript can also be carefully examined and reviewed by independent reviewers. The researcher must also be aware of potential biases and either attempt to minimize them or take them into account when interpreting the data.

An important factor that can affect the reliability and validity of a case study is the researcher himself. As Patton (1990) noted, "the quality of the information obtained during an interview is largely dependent on the interviewer," as "the task for the interviewer is to make it possible for the person being interviewed to bring the interviewer into his or her world." (Patton, 1990, p. 279). Thus, the more skillful the interviewer is, the better they can collect the data needed. The choice of the case to study is still another factor that can affect the validity of a case study. Dobbert (1982) highlighted the importance of "good informants":

> They appear comfortable and unstrained in interactions with the researcher; they are not hurried; they are generally open and truthful although they may have certain areas about which they will not speak or where they will cover up; they stay on the topic or related important issues; they are thoughtful and willing to reflect on what they say." (p. 263)

Example 14.2 shows the use of a case study in applied linguistics.

EXAMPLE 14.2

A well-known early study is Schmidt (1983), which examined the role of social and psychological factors in acquiring communicative competence in English. Schmidt's case study focused on Wes, a 33-year-old Japanese learner of English, navigating English communication in the US. Wes, an extrovert, predominantly used English

(75–60 percent of the time) and had a low social and psychological distance from the target language. The study spanned three years and involved informal data collection, primarily from 18 one-hour audio tape recordings of Wes's monologues and various informal conversations. Schmidt used Canale and Swain's (1980) model of communicative competence as a guiding theoretical framework to analyze and interpret the findings. One issue noted was Wes's limited interest in classroom instruction and correction, prioritizing communication over formal learning. Data analysis revealed a significant improvement in Wes's discourse and strategic competence during the study period. However, there was limited progress in his linguistic competence, as he communicated using various words and chunks without strict adherence to correct grammar.

POINTS TO PONDER

What do you think grounded theory is? Can you list some of the characteristics? Can you give an example of a research question in applied linguistics that might be addressed using a grounded theory approach?

Grounded Theory

Grounded theory is a qualitative research design to generate theoretical explanations about social phenomena based on data collected. The main goal is to develop theories that are "grounded" in the data rather than being based on preconceived notions or existing theories. It involves systematic and rigorous data collection and analysis to derive theoretical concepts, categories, and relationships directly from the data.

Grounded theory is widely used in various fields, including sociology, anthropology, psychology, and education. It has also become an important research type in applied linguistics. This research design was first developed by Glaser and Strauss (1967) and since then has been expanded or adapted in other works such as Strauss and Corbin (1990), Charmaz (2006), and Glaser (1992). It is called grounded theory because the development of the theory is grounded in the data. In other words, the theory emerges from the data. In this type of research, a corpus of qualitative data is collected and analyzed inductively, based on which concepts are constructed and relationships among them are identified, which contributes to the development of a theory.

Grounded theory is a qualitative research design to generate theoretical explanations about social phenomena based on the data collected. The main goal is to develop theories that are "grounded" in the data rather than being based on preconceived notions or existing theories.

Grounded theory research is a useful procedure when there is no existing theory to explain the issue the researcher is interested in. For example, if you are interested in classroom management and do not find a theory that can explain the process of L2 classroom management, you may then conduct a grounded theory study by observing a number of classrooms with students and by interviewing teachers and students. Analysis of the data could lead to a theory about L2 classroom management.

Although grounded theory is generally viewed as one research design, several versions have been distinguished and discussed in the literature. These include, for example, the traditional or classic version rooted in the work of its early developers (e.g., Glaser & Strausss 1967); the Straussian version, which was a slightly modified version (e.g., Strauss, 1987); and the constructivist version (e.g., Charmaz, 2000, 2006). A full discussion of these versions is beyond the scope of this chapter, but there are a number of works that have discussed these differences (see Sebastian, 2019, for a useful discussion).

Suffice to say that what distinguishes these different versions are some of their underlying assumptions and how they approach data. For example, while the traditional version takes a more positivistic approach, advocating a distant position for the researcher, the Straussian one takes an interpretive approach, advocating the researcher's active engagement and interpretation of the data. The traditional version argues that the researcher should have no preconceived notions about the concepts or categories when beginning the studies; therefore, it does not encourage a literature review prior to the study. The Straussian version, on the other hand, allows for some background knowledge and a prior literature review to enhance the researcher's theoretical ability. The traditional version is more unstructured, encouraging the researcher to be completely open and allowing the theory to emerge from the data without much interference from the researcher, whereas the Straussian version is more structured with more complex coding procedures. In its classic form, the process of discovering the theory is inductive and iterative. The researcher "generates conceptual categories or their properties from evidence, then the evidence from which the category emerged is used to illustrate the concept" (Glaser & Strauss, 1967, p. 23). "During the research the emergent categories will begin to form patterns and interrelations which will ultimately form the core of the emerging theory" (Glaser & Strauss, 1967, p. 40). The hypotheses or theory derived can be refined by the researcher by collecting more data from the same group or different groups, or be further explored in other studies, which can suggest modifications to the theory or the concepts to make them fit the data better. In its more modified version, categorization can also occur following a preestablished paradigm, which Glaser described as "systematic generating of theory from data that itself is systematically obtained from social research" (Glaser, 1978, p. 2). Strauss and Corbin (1990, p. 24) expressed a similar position by defining grounded theory as "a qualitative research method that uses a systematized set of procedures to develop and inductively derive [grounded theory] about a phenomenon." Also, in Straussian grounded theory, a a general purposive sampling can also be used, particularly at the early stages. Strauss and Corbin (1998, p. 210) argued: "The ideal form of theoretical sampling might be difficult to carry out if the researcher does not have unlimited access to persons or sites or does not know where to go to maximize similarities and differences. Realistically, the researcher might have to sample on the basis of what is available."

However, although there are different versions and interpretations of grounded theory, the overall purpose is the same across all versions, which is to reveal a theory using data. This research design contrasts with other types of design, such as experimental research, which aims to verify a theory or a hypothesis through logical deduction.

In grounded theory, the data are collected mainly through interviews and focus groups. Data collection is open-ended and flexible, and it continues until theoretical data saturation occurs. Theoretical saturation of data used in grounded theory refers to the point in data collection and analysis when no new information or data are needed, and when any additional data do not contribute to the theory. This happens when the researcher notices that the same categories, themes, or ideas are occurring in the data repeatedly. At this point, the researcher realizes that the themes and categories are saturated and can decide to stop collecting new data and conducting new analysis.

Theoretical saturation of data refers to the point in data collection and analysis where no new information or data are needed, and any additional data do not contribute to the theory.

Key Characteristics of Grounded Theory

- Grounded theory focuses on theory development.
- Open, axial, and selective coding are important procedures in grounded theory (see Chapter 16).
- Data analysis is heuristic and inductive, moving from specific situations to general concepts.
- Constant comparative methods are essential, involving continuous comparison of data, situations, and codes to verify interpretations and introduce new categories for theory development.
- Memoing, an active note-taking process during data collection and analysis, is a key feature.
- Data analysis and collection are simultaneous, allowing adaptation of data collection to emerging theories.
- Theoretical sampling and theoretical saturation are key features of grounded theory research.
- Grounded theory often results in substantive theories, derived from data about concepts and their relationships, which may contribute to the development of formal theories in applied linguistics or other fields.

A substantive theory refers to a set of propositions derived from the data about the concepts and their relationship. It is a cohesive account and explanation of the phenomenon studied.

Steps in Conducting Grounded Theory

1. Identify and define the research problem.
2. Conduct a literature review or consult the sources related to your topic to develop a theoretical framework to guide the research.
3. Collect and organize data.
4. Categorize and code the data, extract themes and concepts.
5. Compare themes, concepts, and categories.
6. Develop taxonomies.
7. Arrive at generalizations.
8. Develop the initial explanatory theory.
9. Collect more data if needed.
10. Go back to developing and comparing themes, concepts, and categories.
11. Elaborate on themes and extract patterns.
12. Refine the explanatory theory based on the data collected.
13. Repeat the above data collection and theme extraction as needed.
14. Interpret and present the findings.
15. Write the research report.

Strengths and Limitations of Grounded Theory

One of the strengths of grounded theory is that the approach is heuristic and flexible, allowing you to understand the phenomena as they exist without any preconceived assumption of how they should be. It allows you to discover concepts by sifting through naturalistic data and derive concepts as they emerge in the data. As such, it is a useful design for studying and understanding issues we know little about or issues that cannot be explained through existing theories or principles.

Grounded theory offers a principled approach to data collection and analysis, using systematic procedures to develop theories about a phenomenon. This involves comparative and inductive logic, systematic comparison, coding, recoding, and memoing (writing reflective notes on the data and emerging codes or concepts to facilitate theory development). These procedures contribute to the trustworthiness of the emerging theory through rigorous data collection and analysis.

However, grounded theory research presents challenges, such as generating large amounts of data that can be time-consuming and demanding of analytical skills, particularly for novice researchers. The subjective nature of grounded theory makes it susceptible to researcher biases and preconceived notions, potentially impacting the study's rigor and credibility. Example 14.3 demonstrates how grounded theory research is used in applied linguistics by presenting the abstract of a study titled "Exploring Inner Speech as a Psycho-educational Resource for Language Learning Advisors" (McCarthy, 2018, p. 159).

EXAMPLE 14.3

Abstract

The analysis of advising sessions has recognized common standards of the profession in areas such as advising skills employed and non-verbal communicative practices. There are however numerous variations in advisor behavior due to differences in cognitive processes. This study used a stimulated recall approach to identify the content of inner thought categories of eight learning advisors-in-action during individual advising sessions. A grounded theory analysis of 800 thought units revealed a hierarchical structure of five main and 16 sub-categories. By tapping into the cognitive processes of advisors, a descriptive framework of advisors' inner speech was created and a more complete picture of advising emerged. This led to an appreciation of the wealth of information advisors held and applied during their sessions and provided empirical evidence which could possibly influence changes in the current method of advisor training.

POINTS TO PONDER

What is narrative inquiry? Can you list some of the characteristics? Can you give examples of research questions in applied linguistics that might be addressed using narrative inquiry?

Narrative Inquiry

Narrative inquiry is a qualitative research design that focuses on understanding individuals' experiences and stories as a means of generating knowledge, with an emphasis on the power of narratives, storytelling, and personal accounts to reveal insights into people's lives, perspectives, and the meaning they attach to events. Narratives are a kind of textual discourse that brings together diverse events and experiences "into thematically unified goal-directed processes" (Polkinghorne, 1995, p. 5). They can be either spoken or written, "giving an account of an event/action or series of events/actions, chronologically connected" (Czarniawska, 2004, p. 17). Thus, in narrative inquiry, you collect and analyze individuals' stories, whether they are in the form of interviews, diaries, autobiographies, or other narrative expressions. These stories are considered valuable sources of data, as they provide rich and detailed information about the complexities of human experiences and emotions.

Narrative inquiry is a qualitative research design that focuses on understanding individuals' experiences and stories as a means of generating knowledge, with an emphasis on the power of narratives, storytelling, and personal accounts to reveal insights into people's lives, perspectives, and the meaning they attach to events.

Narrative inquiry has been frequently used in applied linguistics to study a variety of issues, such as individual differences, motivation, agency, identity, learning strategies, and emotional expressions (see Benson, 2014 for a review). Using various sources of data such as autobiographies, life histories, journals, diaries, memoirs, language learning histories, and interviews, narrative inquiry has provided important information to inform both L2 theory and practice in various areas. The significance of narrative inquiry as a research design lies in the ability of stories to provide a powerful window into understanding participants' experiences and actions (see Clandinin & Connelly, 2000). Those advocating this research design believe that we not only "achieve our personal identities and self-concept through the use of the narrative configuration" but that we also "make our existence into a whole by understanding it as an expression of a single unfolding and developing story" (Polkinghorne, 1995, p. 105).

According to Pavlenko (2007), three types of autobiographic narratives are commonly studied in sociolinguistics of bilingualism and SLA. The first type includes diaries and journals by L2 learners, capturing their beliefs and experiences. The second type consists of linguistic biographies, focusing on how and why languages were acquired, used, or abandoned, often collected through interviews. The third type is published linguistic autobiographies, or language memoirs, written by individuals about their experiences with language learning and use.

Given the variety of narrative genres and data sources in narrative inquiry, in applied linguistics such studies are also sometimes referred to as life histories, language learning histories, diary studies, autoethnography, and so on (Barkhuizen, 2014). Stories reveal the meaning attached to peoples' experiences and actions at every stage of their lives, and as such studying them has been used as an accepted form of inquiry in many disciplines including applied linguistics.

Narrative inquiry has been frequently used in applied linguistics to study a variety of issues, such as individual differences, motivation, agency, identity, learning strategies, and emotional expressions.

Types of Narrative Inquiry

There are different types of narrative inquiry, depending on the method of analysis and the nature of narratives collected. Polkinghorne (1995) distinguished between two types, according to the type of analysis: paradigmatic analysis of narratives and narrative analysis.

In paradigmatic narrative analysis, which is a more common type of analysis, you collect narratives or stories as data and then analyze them paradigmatically by identifying common themes and categories or classifying different types of stories. This kind of analysis results in concepts that run through stories and produce knowledge that helps us understand participants' experiences. The identification of the meanings and concepts can be conducted in two ways. The first is inductively; it is like other types of qualitative research in which you read through the stories and arrive at meanings and concepts as they emerge through stories. The second is deductively, in which you attempt to make sense of the stories by interpreting them in light of preexisting theories or hypotheses.

The second type of narrative inquiry is narrative analysis. This type is different from the analysis of narratives in that it uses other sources of data to arrive at a narrative, including descriptions of events, occurrences, and actions. You then create a story based on these data using a plot line. Therefore, while the paradigmatic analysis of narratives moves from stories or elements of separate stories into parts, narrative analysis synthesizes events and descriptions into a coherent narrative or story.

There are different types of narrative inquiry depending on the method of analysis and the nature of the narratives collected. Two main types of analysis are **paradigmatic analysis** and **narrative analysis**.

For example, an applied linguistic researcher may collect data about a classroom or students' learning experiences through conversations, interviews and journals, diaries, and other forms of qualitative data, and then construct a narrative or story based on all these sources. The story created would link the different pieces of information in these multiple sources, leading to a coherent understanding in the form of an overarching story that connects the elements in the individual data sources. Thus, while paradigmatic analysis moves from stories to common themes and concepts, narrative analysis moves from multiple sources of data to the construction of a narrative or story.

As noted above, most narrative enquiries studies have used the first approach as it is easier because the research can use qualitative methods of analysis that have been used in other types of qualitative research, such as coding the data into common themes and concepts. The second approach is more difficult because you need to not only reproduce a coherent narrative based on a number of other sources, which requires a particular skill, but also be able to draw out meanings that cut across the various forms of data collected.

Narrative Inquiry and Story Types

Narrative inquiry brings together several story types. The following four story conceptions have been prevalent in applied linguistics: the canonical story, life histories and autobiographies, grand narratives, and narratives-in-interaction (Benson, 2014). All these different story genres reveal important insights into the participants' experiences and actions by the way they are described in the narrative. As discussed by Benson (2014), the canonical story, as presented, by Labov (1972), for example, includes six parts in a fully formed oral narrative: an abstract (what the story is about), orientation (who, when, where, and what), complicating action (then what), resolution (what happened finally), evaluation (why it is interesting), and coda (the final stage of the narrative, when it is finished). Life histories can provide important insights into the participants' life. They can provide information about not only the learners' experience and assumptions but also how these experiences and assumptions are shaped by the broader context, including the social, cultural, political, educational, and even economic contexts. Grand narrative, as described by Lyotard (1984), is a kind of meta-narrative that attempts to provide an overarching and comprehensive account of various cultural and historical experience and events. This type of narrative is often used to legitimize or validate certain historical or social events by explaining the various events and connecting them into a meaningful whole. Narratives-in-interaction are those that are related to integrative accounts of experiences in the form of everyday talks or small stories.

Therefore, narrative inquiry is not only using stories that are told to study a phenomenon but also using stories to create a coherent understanding of other sources of data. Benson (2014) provided a detailed review of narrative studies in applied linguistics that have used the latter approach, producing autobiographical reflection or retelling learners' personal accounts related to their learning experiences.

Narrative inquiry brings together several story types in applied linguistics including the **canonical story, life histories and autobiographies, grand narratives,** and **narratives-in-interaction**.

Key Characteristics of Narrative Inquiry

- Focus on stories and narratives.
- Emphasis on meaning-making.
- Qualitative data collection and analysis.
- Subjectivity: Researchers recognize and embrace subjectivity in narrative inquiry, acknowledging that the process of data collection, analysis, and interpretation is influenced by their own perspectives and biases.
- Reflexivity: Researchers conducting narrative inquiry engage in reflexivity, which involves critically reflecting on their own biases, assumptions, and influence on the research process.

- Contextuality.
- Holistic understanding.
- Longitudinality.
- Multiplicity of voices: Narrative inquiry aims to give voice to a diverse range of experiences and outlooks.
- Flexibility: Narrative inquiry does not follow a rigid set of procedures.

Steps in Conducting Narrative Inquiries

1. Identify the research problem.
2. Select the individual(s) to study.
3. Collect stories from the individual(s).
4. Examine the stories, identify key elements, themes, and concepts.
5. If experiences are collected, write the individual's experiences into a story.
6. Retell the story in a way that describes the individual's experiences.
7. Validate the accuracy of the story told.

Strengths and Limitations of Narrative Inquiry

One of the strengths of narrative inquiry is its naturalistic approach to data collection and the fact that stories provide an authentic description of what people have experienced. The fact that this research design focuses on stories reveals significant information about how people make sense of their experiences through stories. One of the limitations is that stories can be interpreted and analyzed differently by different researchers.

Most narrative inquiry studies are longitudinal, and therefore they are time-consuming. The confidentiality of the stories is another challenge that should be considered.

As noted earlier, most narrative inquiries adopt a paradigmatic approach to data analysis, in which stories are analyzed to generate themes and concepts. While the advantage of this type of narrative inquiry is the development of common knowledge, it heavily relies on the researchers' preconceived notions of what the categories or themes should be. This reliance limits the ability of narrative inquiry to capture its unique potential, namely, the richness that comes from examining stories as cohesive, meaningful accounts (Polkinghorne, 1995). By focusing on predefined themes, this approach also overlooks the deeper insights and nuanced understanding that emerge when stories are heard or told in their entirety.

Numerous narrative studies are currently available in applied linguistics, and their number continues to grow; however, when reviewing these studies, it is often difficult to find clear-cut results or summarize precisely what the findings are (Benson, 2014). This difficulty may stem from the fact that narrative inquiry addresses complex issues, leading to complex results. However, despite this, the value of narrative inquiry lies in its ability to provide rich insights into the issues under investigation. Even if these insights do not always lend themselves to clear-cut conclusions, such studies are still highly significant as they offer a deeper understanding of the complexities involved.

In applied linguistics, narrative inquiry has been used to gain insights into a variety of areas, including language learners' and teachers' experiences, classroom practices, students' and teachers' identity, emotion, agency, and motivation. It has also been a major research design for exploring how language learners and teachers develop new identities by studying them in various formal and informal teaching contexts. Example 14.4 illustrates the use of narrative inquiry in applied linguistics research by presenting the abstract of a study titled "Complexities of Identity Formation: A Narrative Inquiry of an EFL Teacher" (Tsui, 2007, p. 657), which examines how an EFL teacher navigates identity formation while addressing challenges and negotiating meaning in professional contexts.

EXAMPLE 14.4

Abstract

This article explores teachers' identity formation through a narrative inquiry of the professional identity of an EFL teacher, Minfang, in the People's Republic of China. Drawing on Wenger's (1998) social theory of identity formation as a dual process of identification and negotiation of meanings, it examines the lived experience of Minfang as an EFL learner and EFL teacher throughout his 6 years of teaching, the processes that were involved as he struggled with multiple identities, the interplay between reification and negotiation of meanings, and the institutional construction and his personal reconstruction of identities. The stories of Minfang highlighted the complex relationships between membership, competence, and legitimacy of access to practice, between the appropriation and ownership of meanings, the centrality of participation, and the mediating role of power relationships in the processes of identity formation.

POINTS TO PONDER

Can you identify and explain the key features of conversation analysis, interaction analysis, and critical discourse analysis? How do these features distinguish each subtype from one another?

Discourse Studies

Discourse studies are a group of research designs focusing on the study of discourse in its different manifestations. They are like other types of qualitative research in that the data are qualitative in nature, and the approach to data analysis is mainly inductive and discovery oriented. However, unlike some qualitative research designs, such as grounded theory, they do not rule out the use of previous theory or literature in guiding the research and the research question (Giles, 2002). Another difference between discourse studies and other types of qualitative studies is that in discourse studies the focus is less on the content of the data collected than on its structure. For example, when verbal data are collected from the participants, through interviews or focus groups, the focus is less on what is said but more on how it is said or how a certain event or phenomenon is constructed through language.

Discourse studies are a group of research designs focusing on the study of discourse in its different manifestations, with the focus being less on the content of the data collected than on its structure.

Discourse can be defined in various ways, capturing its multifaceted nature. A linguistic definition views discourse as language extending beyond a sentence, involving a coherent and cohesive sequence of sentences and utterances. However, discourse studies go beyond the linguistic aspects of text; they focus on how text contributes to the construction or reflection of social reality through language. This perspective highlights the role of language as a means through which we perceive and act toward reality, rather than merely a tool to talk about it.

Widdowson (1984, p. 100) defines discourse as "a communicative process by means of interaction," emphasizing the interactive nature of communication, whether oral or written. Celce-Murcia and Olshtain (2000) describe discourse as an instance of language with internal relationships of form and meaning, highlighting both linguistic aspects and functional purposes, emphasizing the rule-based relationship between the two. Gumperz (1977) sees discourse as communication routines distinguished by special rules, emphasizing its rule-based nature and specific structure. Fairclough (2012) views discourse as semiotic ways of construing aspects of the world, emphasizing its social role in establishing and maintaining social relationships. This perspective focuses on the relationship between language and its social context, exploring how language influences social reality, power dynamics, authority, and ideology.

In the following section, we will discuss four types of discourse study designs that reflect the above perspectives on discourse and are widely used in applied linguistics. These are conversation analysis, interaction analysis, discourse analysis, and critical discourse analysis (Figure 14.2).

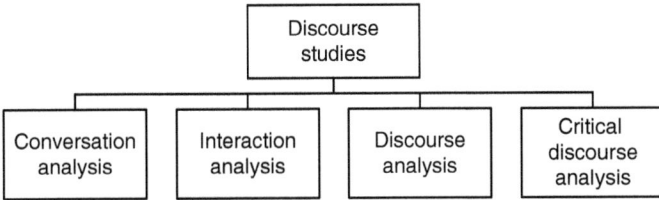

Figure 14.2 Types of discourse studies

Conversation Analysis (CA)

Conversation analysis (CA) is a qualitative research design used to examine the structure and organization of naturally occurring conversations in everyday social interactions. In other words, it is an approach to studying discourse that examines conversation. Conversation is a daily activity that takes place everywhere – at home, in school, between students and teachers, over the telephone, in the office, and so on. One of the earliest developers of CA was Harvey Sacks (Sacks, 1984a, 1984b), a sociologist who started by investigating tape-recorded phone call interactions and how people engaged in such conversations. This approach was further developed in subsequent works by Sacks, Schegloff, and Jefferson (e.g., Schegloff, 1982, 2000; Schegloff, Sacks, & Jefferson, 1992) and has been increasingly used as a research design for examining the characteristics of conversational interaction in applied linguistics (e.g., Kasper, 1985; Kasper & Wagner, 2014; Markee, 2000; Seedhouse, 1994, 2004).

Conversation analysis (CA) is a qualitative research design used to examine the structure and organization of naturally occurring conversations in everyday social interactions.

Methodologically, conversation analysis is related to and derived from ethnomethodology, an interpretive method of analysis focusing on how people conduct social interaction, including conversation. The focus of conversation analysis is on ordinary and naturally occurring conversation. It assumes that conversation is an orderly social act that is systematically organized and has specific characteristics. The aim is to explore the interactional organization of conversation, including its various linguistic and nonlinguistic features in different social settings. As Lazaraton (2002, p. 29) pointed out, CA "attempts to uncover the systematic properties of sequential organization of talk and the social practices that are displayed by and embodied in talk-in-interaction."

The primary data for CA often involve recordings of authentic conversation. A conversation analysis does not simply listen to the tapes but transcribes it using detailed CA transcription conventions, providing detailed information about the interaction.

Transcription is a key component of CA. The transcription allows a meticulous analysis to identify systematically the recurrence of patterns and features. This notion is captured in the following, where Sacks (1984b) describes his work in conversation analysis:

> The idea is to take singular sequences of conversation and tear them apart in such a way as to find rules, techniques, procedures, methods, maxims (a collection of terms that more or less relate to each other and that I use somewhat interchangeably) that can be used to generate the orderly features we find in the conversations we examine (p. 411).

Methodologically, conversation analysis is related to and derived from **ethno-methodology,** an interpretive method of analysis focusing on how people conduct social interaction, including conversation.

Key Characteristics of Conversation Analysis

- Sequential organization: CA emphasizes the systematic nature of conversational interaction, examining the ordered arrangement of moves that interlocutors make during a conversation.
- Turn taking: Turn-taking is an important aspect studied in CA, exploring how interlocutors manage speaking and listening turns, deciding when and how each person should contribute to the conversation.
- Adjacency pairs: CA scrutinizes adjacency pairs, where two turns from different interlocutors occur consecutively. This includes initiation and response sequences as well as repair sequences.
- Repairs: Repairs are an important aspect of CA. They refer to the ways in which speakers resolve issues that arise during a conversation, such as misunderstandings, unclear expressions, or misstatements. These strategies help participants clarify meaning, correct errors, or rephrase their words to keep the conversation flowing smoothly and maintain mutual understanding.
- Nonverbal language: While CA primarily examines spoken language, it acknowledges the significance of nonverbal cues, such as gestures and facial expressions, in the overall interaction.
- Naturalistic conversation: CA relies on the collection of data through audio or video recordings of naturalistic conversations, ensuring that the interactions studied occur in authentic settings.
- Thorough transcription: Detailed and thorough transcription of recorded data is an important aspect of CA, aiming to achieve a deep and accurate understanding of interaction patterns. Transcription often employs a specific notation system. One frequently used is the Jefferson Transcription System or its modified version, which is a series of notations capturing how interaction takes place through various verbal, nonverbal and paralinguistic means (e.g., Jefferson, 1984).
- Microanalytical approach: In conversation analysis, the approach to the analysis of discourse is microanalytical, involving breaking down the conversation into sequences and examining the sequences turn by turn.

As noted earlier, repairs are a significant aspect of CA. According to Seedhouse (2004), CA identifies four types of repairs based on who initiates and who performs the repair:

1. **Self-initiated self-repair:** The speaker identifies a problem in their own speech and resolves it without prompting from others. For example, a speaker might say, "I'll call you tomorrow–uh, I mean Friday."

2. **Other-initiated self-repair:** Another participant highlights a problem in the speaker's speech, prompting the speaker to resolve it themselves. For instance:
   ○ Speaker 1: "I met Jack's brother yesterday."
   ○ Speaker 2: "His brother?"
   ○ Speaker 1: "Oh, I mean his cousin."
3. **Self-initiated other-repair:** The speaker identifies a problem but invites another participant to help resolve it. For example:
   ○ Speaker 1: "I can't remember the name of that movie . . . you know, the one we saw last week?"
   ○ Speaker 2: "Oh, you mean *Inception*?"
4. **Other-initiated other-repair:** Another participant identifies and corrects the speaker's mistake directly. For example:
   ○ Speaker 1: "We went to Paris last summer."
   ○ Speaker 2: "Actually, it was Rome, not Paris."

These distinctions are important because they highlight how communication is a collaborative process, with participants working together to address and resolve issues to maintain understanding and coherence in interaction. As previously noted, transcription of recorded data is also an important component of CA. It often relies on a specialized notation system designed to capture the intricate details of verbal, nonverbal, and paralinguistic features of interaction. Table 14.1 provides a simplified version of this notation from Baxter (2010, p. 174).

A CA design is widely used in applied linguistics to investigate the dynamics of L2 interaction. Example 14.5 shows the use of CA by presenting the abstract of a study titled "What's the Problem? L2 Learners' Use of the L1 during Consciousness-Raising, Form-Focused Tasks" (Scott & de la Fuente, 2008, p. 100).

Table 14.1 Transcription notation

(1.0)	Timed pause (in tenths of seconds)
(.)	Micropause (i.e. too short to time)
No=	Indicates the absence of a discernible gap between the end of one
=gap	speaker's utterance and the beginning of the next
Wh	Marks overlap between speakers. The left bracket indicates the beginning of
[en] [No]	the overlap while the right bracket indicates its end
No::w	One or more colons indicate the extension of the previous sound
> <	Indicate talk produced more quickly than surrounding talk
text	Word(s) emphasized
CAPITAL	Noticeably louder talk
hush	Noticeably quieter talk
↑↓	Rising and falling intonation
?	Indicates rising inflection (but not necessarily a question)
.	Indicates a stopping fall in tone (but not necessarily the end of a turn)
hh	Indicates an audible out-breath (the more 'h's the longer the breath)
.hh	Indicates an audible intake of breath (the more 'h's the longer the breath)
(())	Nonverbal activity (e.g. Banging)
[text]	Clarificatory information

EXAMPLE 14.5

Abstract

This qualitative study provides preliminary insight into the role of the first language (L1) when pairs of intermediate-level college learners of French and Spanish are engaged in consciousness-raising, form-focused grammar tasks. Using conversation analysis of audiotaped interactions and stimulated recall sessions, we explored the ways students used the L1 and their second language (L2) to solve a grammar problem. Students who were allowed to use the L1 (Group 1) worked collaboratively in a balanced and coherent manner; students who were required to use the L2 (Group 2) exhibited fragmented interaction and little evidence of collaboration. Findings from the stimulated recall sessions suggested that reading, thinking, and talking appeared to be simultaneous and integrated processes for the students in Group 1, whereas these processes appeared to be sequential and competing for the students in Group 2. In addition to suggesting that using the L1 for these kinds of tasks reduces cognitive over-load, these findings invite teachers to tackle the "problem" of the L1 in the foreign language classroom.

Interaction Analysis

Interaction analysis is a subbranch of conversation analysis with many of its principles having roots in conversation analysis. Both deal with naturalistic inter-action and also consider interaction as a social and situated activity co-constructed by participants in social settings. In both, data collection consists of audio or video recordings of naturalistic interaction, which will be then transcribed for analysis. The analysis in both is data-driven and inductive, and categories emerge from the data rather than from the researcher or an external theory. Methodologically both focus on the structural characteristic of interaction and pay attention to how interaction is constructed and organized. Issues such as turn-taking, the interaction structure, and repair are central to both.

However, there are some differences between the two. One difference is that the method of transcription in interaction analysis is not as detailed as in conversation analysis. For CA, "the degree of detail of the transcript plays an enormous role" (Ayaå, 2015, p. 509). Therefore, the transcription is conducted in such a way as to reflect as many nuances of the interaction as possible, includ-ing characteristics such as pauses, silence, contractions, emphases, simultaneous talking, intonation, and so on. In interaction analysis, however, a simpler form of transcription may be used. In conversation analysis, it is often the organiza-tion of interaction that the researcher is interested in. In interaction analysis, the emphasis is more on how meaning is negotiated between and among interlocu-ters. For example, many studies of interactional feedback in applied linguistics have used interaction analysis with a focus on the different interactional feed-back moves, such as student's initiation, teacher's feedback, and the student's response to the feedback.

Another difference is that while the focus of conversation analysis is on spoken conversation, interaction analysis includes both spoken and written interaction. In applied linguistics, interaction analysis has mainly been used in classroom research to analyze classroom interaction (Chaudron, 1988), including student–teacher interaction, peer interaction, and feedback. In classroom research, the use of this design has led to the development of observation and interaction analytic schemes to study interaction and how it influences language acquisition.

An example of such an interaction scheme is the FLint (Foreign Language Interaction Analysis) system reported by Moskowitz (1971), which is a modified version of Flanders Interaction Analysis system. Using real-time coding, FLint attempts to capture various interactional behaviors commonly observed in a foreign language classroom. It does so by coding the classroom interaction data (observed for example for a period of 20 to 30 minutes in length) into three main categories: teacher talk, student talk, and other categories. Teacher talk, for example, includes six categories named "indirect influence," related to behaviors such as praising, complementing, accepting and verifying students' ideas, asking questions, and so on, and six categories named "direct influence" attempting to code behaviors such as giving information, correcting without rejection, giving direction, or directing pattern drills. Student talk includes categories that attempt to code various student responses to the teacher, including both predictable responses, such as responses to known questions, and unpredictable responses, when the student responds to the teacher with their own ideas and opinion. Other categories include matters such as silence and pauses in interaction, confusion, and laughter. This approach was used in the work of Allen, Fröhlich, and Spada (1984), which looked into how various learning outcomes were impacted by classroom activities and their communicative features. Example 14.6 shows the use of interaction analysis by presenting the abstract of a study titled "The Role of NS Personality and Experience in NS–NNS Interaction" (Derwing, 1991, p. 9).

EXAMPLE 14.6

Abstract

This study investigates the relationship of native speakers' (NSs) personality traits and experience interacting with non-native speakers (NNSs) to the use of conversational adjustments and differences in word frequency and speech rate. Eight ESL instructors and eight persons who had no regular contact with NNSs were asked to view a film, then tell a NS and a NNS partner its story. Transcripts of the subjects' film narratives to the listeners were examined for differences in word frequency, rate, and conversational adjustments. Although the ESL instructors used certain conversational adjustments significantly more with NNSs than did the inexperienced subjects, the two groups did not differ in terms of word frequency or rate. When subjects were grouped according to the personality traits of interpersonal affect and social participation, they did not differ in overall usage of conversational adjustments, but significant differences were found in both word frequency and speech rate.

Discourse Analysis

Like conversation analysis, discourse analysis considers language as a social action and seeks to explore how language contributes to people's social reality. Both of them "reject the representational model of language, whereby statements are held to correspond to phenomena that exist independently of them" (Hammersley, 2003, p. 756). In terms of their principles, they both draw on ethnomethodology, and the primary data for both are transcribed audio- or video- recordings of data.

However, while conversation analysis studies conversation when two or more people talk, discourse analysis studies the interpretation and production of discourse in a broader sense. It studies written or oral text or any other semiotic tools that are used as discourse in a variety of social and linguistics contexts. This includes different types of text: formal or informal, academic or nonacademic, monologues and dialogues, lectures, discussions, interviews, news accounts, and media reports. Each of these would provide suitable data for discourse analysis.

In applied linguistics, the use of discourse analysis has made important contributions to understanding how language is used in context and how or what social actions are performed by language. For example, rather than treating the learners' language as a set of linguistic elements governed by and represented by an inner cognitive system to be explored through experimental research, in which the researcher attempts to control many context factors, a discourse analyst treats language as a discursive social practice.

Like conversation analysis, **discourse analysis** considers language as a social action and seeks to explore how language contributes to people's social reality.

An influential work relevant to discourse analysis is Austin and Searle's speech act theory (Austin, 1962; Searle, 1969), which argues that the function of language is not just to describe facts or transmit some information. We use language to do things. For example, we use language to give orders, to make requests, to give advice, to complain. Language in this view is not just to convey information. There are many times that differences exist between what a person says and what the person intends to say. In this respect, a discourse analysis is interested in the relationship between the two. For example, if someone says, "It is hot in here," the person is not just talking about the temperature but may intend to make a request to open the window.

In speech act theory, the literal or propositional meaning is called the locutionary meaning, and what we intend to say is called the illocutionary meaning. According to Austin (1962) there are three kinds of acts which happen when we say something. One is the locutionary act, which refers to the literal meaning of an utterance; the second is the illocutionary act, which refers to the speakers' intention; and the third is the perlocutionary act, which is the effect of the statement on the receiver or the listener. For example, if someone says, "It is hot in here," the locutionary act is that it is hot, the illocutionary act is, please open the window, and the perlocutionary act is the opening of the window performed by the person hearing the utterance.

The locutionary act refers to the literal meaning of an utterance, while **the illocutionary act** refers to the speaker's intention. **The perlocutionary act** is the effect of the statement on the receiver or the listener.

Critical Discourse Analysis (CDA)

Critical discourse analysis (CDA) is a research design to study ways in which social power and structure are established and influenced by language and through language. It is "a qualitative analytical approach for critically describing, interpreting, and explaining the ways in which discourses construct, maintain, and legitimize social inequalities" (Mullet, 2018, p. 116). In CDA, discourse is defined as the use of language as a type of social practice (Fairclough, 2001, 2012). It is not only an essential component of social interaction and communication but also a tool to shape and influence social relationships (Van Dijk, 1993). It can take different forms, including oral, written, verbal and nonverbal texts, or any other ways of expressing meaning, experiences, and events (Mullet, 2018).

Because of the strong concern of critical discourse analysis with the relation between language and social reality, issues of ideology and power, and their realizations in and through language become central to critical discourse analysis. In this respect, one of the main concerns of CDA is the issue of injustice, power imbalance, and abuse as relates to language and discourse. CDA addresses these issues by analyzing and attempting to understand their relationships.

Critical discourse analysis (CDA) examines language use to uncover **power structures, ideologies, and social inequalities**, with the aim of analyzing how language shapes and reflects social, political, and cultural realities.

Critical discourse analysis may use the same data collation tools and analysis as discourse analysis, but it rests on the premise that language plays a key role in how social relationships and hierarchies are constructed and how they can be legitimized and normalized in society. Since CDA deals with complex societal problems, it uses both an inductive and deductive approach in data analysis. In critical discourse analysis, language is viewed as a powerful medium through which social reality and power are maintained, and hence it seeks to explain the relationship between language and social power. Therefore, CDA does not limit itself to simply describing discourse but also examines how discourse shapes social values.

Critical discourse analysis has been used in studying a wide range of topics, such as media representation, political propaganda, gender and race ideologies, educational practices, and environmental discourse. In educational research, this method has been employed to investigate connections among teaching, learning, and curricula: issues related to students' identities in different contexts and timeframes, as well as analysis of cultural representations in textbooks and exploring how teachers' ideological perspectives impact their teaching approach (Mullet, 2018).

Those interested in classroom discourse have sometimes used CDA as a framework to examine how language is used in the classroom as a way of enacting and reinforcing power relations (see Pennycook, 2021). With the advent of digital and social media, there is a need to understand how different media as a type of discourse influence power relationships and structure and how they reinforce certain cultural and political assumptions in society.

Key Characteristics of CDA

- Focuses on power and ideology.
- Studies language as a social and cultural phenomenon.
- Emphasizes social context.
- Examines how language is used in various discursive practices.
- Explores domination and resistance: CDA explores how dominant ideologies are maintained through language and how marginalized groups may resist and subvert these ideologies through their discourse.
- Considers multimodality: CDA recognizes that meaning is not solely constructed through words but also through images, gestures, and other forms of communication.
- Is interdisciplinary.

Steps in Conducting CDA

1. Define the research question.
2. Identify specific discursive practices.
3. Choose data for analysis, such as written texts, spoken transcripts, audio, video, or a combination.
4. Contextualize the data within its social, historical, and cultural context.
5. Transcribe the data (if necessary).
6. Conduct textual analysis.
7. Identify discursive strategies.
8. Uncover ideologies and power relations within language use.
9. Interpret and critically reflect on findings, considering implications for social practices and power dynamics.
10. Write up the analysis.

Conclusion

Understanding qualitative research designs and their various types is important as it provides a valuable approach to gaining insights into complex research issues and generating rich, contextually grounded data. In this chapter, we have explored several key qualitative research designs, including ethnography, grounded theory, case study, narrative inquiry, and discourse studies. We have discussed their characteristics, examined the strengths and limitations of each design, and discussed their applications in applied linguistics research, along with examples. We have also discussed the steps involved in conducting such research. It is important to note that no single qualitative research design is superior to others, and each has its own unique strengths and limitations. You should select the qualitative research design that is best suited to your research questions, context, and data sources. Moreover, conducting high-quality qualitative research requires commitment to rigor and transparency, and validity and reliability, which we will cover in subsequent chapters. In the next chapter, we will explore issues pertaining to collecting qualitative data.

DISCUSSION AND ACTIVITY QUESTIONS

Discussion Questions

1. What are the different types of qualitative research designs, and how do they differ from one another?
2. What is ethnography, and what are some of the key characteristics of this research design?
3. What are some of the challenges you might face when collecting data in an ethnographic study, particularly in terms of access to participants and cultural sensitivity?
4. What are the key differences between ethnography and grounded theory and in what ways do their methodologies and outcomes differ?
5. What are discourse studies, and what are the different subtypes of this research design?
6. What are the steps involved in conducting grounded theory in applied linguistics? How does that design differ from a cases study design?
7. What are the defining features of case study research, and how can it be applied to a specific language-related issue or an individual case? What are some of the potential challenges of using this design?
8. How can you determine which qualitative research design is most appropriate for a particular research question? What factors influence this decision?
9. How are the data analyzed in narrative inquiry, and what challenges arise when interpreting the stories of language learners?

Activity Questions

1. In groups, select a study in applied linguistics that has used one of the qualitative research designs discussed in this chapter. Then, discuss the benefits and limitations of using that design to address the study's research question.
2. Read and analyze a published qualitative research study in an area of your interest. Identify the research design used and evaluate the study's strengths and weaknesses, as well as the implications of the study's findings for the field.

3. In groups, select a case study related to an issue in applied linguistics. Discuss the research question and objectives of the study and how they align with the research design used.

4. In pairs or small groups, design a research study using an ethnographic research design to investigate a specific language-related research question in a particular context. Develop research questions and data collection methods and discuss the ethical considerations involved in collecting and analyzing data in that context.

5. Consider a small-scale study using grounded theory to explore a specific phenomenon in language teaching and learning, such as learner motivation, teacher beliefs, or classroom discourse. What are the steps in conducting that research?

15 | Collecting Qualitative Data: Methods and Strategies

Introduction

When doing research, after deciding what research methodology and research design to use, we should next decide what would be the most appropriate tools for data collection. If we have decided to use qualitative research, the data would be collected through qualitative data collection tools. As noted earlier, qualitative research attempts to provide an in-depth understanding of the issues investigated. Unlike quantitative research, which focuses on numerical data and statistical analysis, qualitative research relies on nonnumerical data such as words, texts (spoken or written) images, or any other verbal or nonverbal observations. Qualitative research is particularly useful in applied linguistics research, as it allows researchers to gain a deeper understanding of the complex linguistic, social, and cultural factors that shape language use, teaching, and acquisition. To collect such data, you use various data collection methods that allow you to engage with the research participants in a meaningful way and elicit rich and detailed information. In this chapter we will discuss some of the most common qualitative data collection tools that are frequently used in applied linguistics research including:

- interviews
- focus groups
- observation
- questionnaires
- verbal reports (introspective and retrospective methods)
- field notes
- journals and diaries.

Each data collection method will be discussed in terms of its strengths and weaknesses and the types of research questions it can address as well as practical considerations for its implementation. Throughout the chapter, examples will be provided to illustrate how different methods can be used to investigate various aspects of language use, teaching, and learning.

It is important to note that although each of the tools is discussed separately, they are rarely used alone, as qualitative researchers often use multiple ways of collecting data in order to provide a deeper understanding through triangulation of the data across sources.

POINTS TO PONDER

To what extent are you familiar with qualitative data collection methods? Have you used any of them in any research? What challenges have you encountered when applying these methods?

Interviews

Interviews are frequently used in applied linguistics research. In interviews, you gather information from the participant either in face-to-face conversation or through a telephone call or via other electronic platforms. The nature of the data collected depends on the purpose of the study and can range from factual information to information about participants' beliefs, opinions, attitudes, and experiences. There are different types of interviews, which can be classified in terms of the degree of structure and the kind of data they provide. The most common ones are shown in Figure 15.1:

- unstructured interviews
- structured interviews
- semistructured interviews.

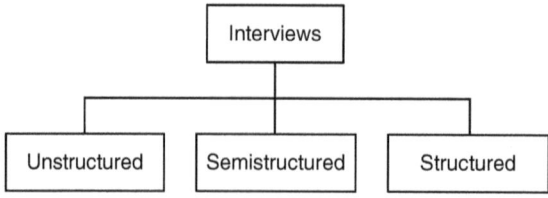

Figure 15.1 Types of interviews

Interviews are used to gather information from the participant either in face-to-face conversation or through a telephone call or via other electronic platforms.

Unstructured Interviews

Unstructured interviews are a type of qualitative data collection tool that elicits information from the participants in the form of informal open-ended conversations without using any predetermined questions. Instead, the interviewer relies on their own judgment and experience to guide the conversation, allowing for a more open-ended and spontaneous conversation to take place.

The aim is to obtain an in-depth and holistic understanding of the interviewees' opinions, behaviors, or attitudes, and the interview is done in such a way as to allow participants to express their opinion freely and as they wish without much interference from the researcher. Therefore, questions are broad and not prepared in advance, and play the role of triggers. The format is loose, and the aim is to gain a deeper perspective on the interviewee's opinion without interrupting the natural flow of the conversation. Such interviews are useful when you aim to gain in-depth data to explore an unfamiliar topic or experience without having much knowledge about the issue. For example, if you want to find out about a learner's experiences of learning a second language, you may use an unstructured interview. Since you may not know a lot about their experiences, you would like to allow the participant to talk freely and provide as much information as they can. Since participants can say whatever they like, without much direction and interruption from the researcher, such an interview is called an unstructured interview.

Unstructured interviews elicit information from the participants in the form of informal open-ended conversations without using any predetermined questions.

Unstructured interviews often produce lengthy texts that need to be analyzed qualitatively, through one or a combination of qualitative data analysis procedures such as content and thematic analysis (see Chapter 16). However, although unstructured interviews are qualitative in nature, they can also be analyzed quantitatively when the data gathered through the interview are categorized, coded, and quantified. Example 15.1 demonstrates how an unstructured interview can be conducted.

EXAMPLE 15.1

Suppose you, as the researcher, are interested in exploring the research question: "What are the experiences of adult language learners with learning English as a foreign language?" You recruit a small group of participants (perhaps ten) who are adults and currently learning English as a foreign language. You invite them to participate in individual interview sessions, which might proceed as follows:

You: Thank you for agreeing to participate in this interview. I'm interested in hearing about your experiences with learning English. Could you start by telling me a bit about your background and how you began learning the language?

Learner: I learned English as a foreign language in my country, mostly as a school subject. We had three hours of English per week, but I also studied on my own because I was eager to learn to speak the language.

You: That's really interesting. Could you tell me more about what learning English was like for you, both in the classroom and outside it?

Learner: Classroom learning was challenging. Three hours a week wasn't enough, and the large class size limited opportunities to speak and practice. At home, I listened to tapes and watched movies, which helped me improve.

You: That's great. Can you share how practicing outside the classroom influenced your ability to communicate, especially with native speakers?

Learner: It made a significant difference. Watching movies, for example, taught me not just language rules but also communication strategies. It improved my understanding of spoken English and my ability to interact. I realized language learning goes beyond grammar and vocabulary. It's also about understanding the culture, which wasn't emphasized much in class.

As the above example demonstrates, an unstructured interview begins with a broad, open-ended question that encourages the learner to share their experiences freely. The learner has the freedom to provide any information they consider relevant, without being guided by a predetermined set of questions. While the interviewer may ask questions, they are driven by the participant's responses and not pre-planned. The key feature of this approach is thus flexibility. The interviewer does not interrupt or steer the conversation but instead allows it to flow naturally. When relevant issues arise, follow-up questions can be used to gain deeper insights into the learner's thoughts and experiences.

Advantages and Limitations of Unstructured Interviews

- They allow for a more natural conversation and a more relaxed and genuine exchange of ideas.
- They allow participants to express their thoughts and opinions freely and fully, leading to a better sense of their experiences and behavior.
- They can be more flexible and hence more adaptable to the needs of the interviewee.

- They allow the interviewer to get to know the participants better and engage in deeper discussion with them.
- They can help build rapport between the interviewer and the interviewee, as they allow for more real-life and natural conversation.
- They can provide a more in-depth understanding of the interviewee's experiences, thoughts, and feelings.
- They can be more engaging and enjoyable for both the interviewer and the interviewee.
- Since they are open-ended and not constrained by a set of predetermined questions, they can provide more information and allow the interviewer to explore in more detail an area of interest.

Unstructured interviews have limitations, such as difficulty in maintaining focus, potential for irrelevant information, and challenges in covering all relevant topics. Probing is essential to extract the necessary details. These interviews can be time-consuming, requiring expert interviewer skills for effective management. Unstructured interviews yield unorganized data, demanding experienced interviewers for analysis. Varied participant responses may complicate group evaluation and comparison too.

Considerations to Keep in Mind When Conducting Unstructured Interviews

- Clearly define interview goals and understand the nature of the data to be collected.
- Select suitable participants and establish a positive rapport.
- Use open-ended questions for detailed responses.
- Be adaptable during the interview process.
- Consider recording or take thorough notes.
- Respect participants' time, privacy, and confidentiality.
- Plan ahead for data analysis.
- Actively listen and ask follow-up questions when necessary.

Semistructured Interviews

A semistructured interview involves a mix of pre-planned, open-ended questions with room for improvisation based on participants' responses. While providing a general outline, this approach allows for flexibility, enabling the conversation to flow naturally. By striking a balance between structure and adaptability, it covers key topics while remaining responsive to participants' unique perspectives. The questions are designed to be clear and unbiased, and they may be piloted for clarity before the actual interviews. These interviews can be conducted face-to-face, by telephone, or using electronic means. The interviewer guides the conversation, incorporating follow-up questions based on responses. Clear goals and attentive listening are essential for effective data collection.

A semistructured interview involves a researcher using a predefined set of topics and questions, ensuring consistency across participants.

The following provides an example of a semistructured interview (Han & Hyland, 2015, p. 42). The study explored how learners engage with written corrective feedback. Four non-English major Chinese EFL learners and their teacher were interviewed twice (once at the beginning and once at the end of the research). Example 15.2 shows the questions that guided the first semistructured interviews with the students.

EXAMPLE 15.2

1. Tell me about your learning experiences of English writing.
2. How did your former teachers help with the grammatical problems in your English writing?
3. Share your experiences with me of the level-three English course so far.
4. In your opinion, what is the role of English writing in English learning?
5. What is the role of language accuracy in English writing?
6. Teachers may give feedback on linguistic errors in your writing. In general, what do you think of teacher feedback on these errors?
7. There are many types of feedback on linguistic errors, such as underlining, correction, giving clues or codes, and comments in the margin. What type of feedback do you prefer? Why?"
8. To what extent do you understand the teacher's feedback on linguistic errors?
9. How do you usually use teacher's feedback on linguistic errors to revise your draft?
10. How do you feel when you receive feedback from your teacher on linguistic errors in your writing?
11. If your teacher intends to improve the way she offers feedback to you, what advice or suggestions would you give her?
12. Do you have further comments or reflections on English learning and English writing?

The above interview is semistructured because although it includes pre-planned, open-ended questions, there is flexibility for the interviewer to explore responses further, enabling follow-up questions. Thus, there is a balance between structure and adaptability. This distinguishes it from a structured interview (see below), where questions are more rigid with little room for elaboration or exploration.

Advantages and Limitations of Semistructured Interviews
- Semistructured interviews allow the interviewer to ask both specific and follow-up questions to explore topics in more depth. This creates a more natural and

flexible conversation while allowing the interviewer to seek the information desired.

- Since the interview is not fully structured, the interviewer can tailor the questions to fit the specific needs and goals of the study or research project.
- Semistructured interviews can produce rich, detailed data because the interviewer can probe for more information and ask open-ended questions.
- Since the interviewer can ask follow-up questions, topics can be explored in more depth. The questions also allow the interviewer to gather more consistent information, which can be compared across participants. Therefore, semistructured interviews can be more reliable than unstructured interviews.
- The fact that the interviewer follows a set of questions helps cover important and specific topics.

There are, however, several limitations of semistructured interviews. First, such interviews can produce more subjective information, as the interviewer may have preconceived notions about the area and may ask leading questions. In addition, although there is some direction, there is no fixed format, so the questions may vary from participant to participant. This may negatively affect the reliability of the findings. Semistructured interviews can also be time-consuming as the interviewer may need to probe for more information. The analysis of the data can be challenging, as the interviewer may use more open-ended questions, and the responses to these questions may be difficult to code and categorize.

Structured Interviews

Structured interviews are interviews in which the interviewer follows a predetermined set of questions that are asked in the same format and order. These types of interviews are designed to collect data in a consistent manner across participants. Since the format is structured and relatively fixed, they are called structured interviews.

The questions can be open-ended or closed-ended, and like the unstructured and semistructured interviews, they can be conducted in-person, over the phone, or even online via video conferencing software.

The difference between semistructured and structured interviews is that although both involve a set of predetermined questions in semistructured interviews, the questions serve as a guide, and the interview may involve a mix of predetermined and spontaneous questions. Structured interviews are more controlled and do not allow for a personalized open conversation. The aim is to collect more controlled data.

Structured interviews are interviews in which the interviewer follows a predetermined set of questions that are asked in the same format and order.

Structured interviews can be used in both qualitative and quantitative research based on their usage and analysis. In qualitative research, predetermined questions are used to gather detailed information about participants' experiences, presented as textual evidence. In quantitative research, structured interviews also have predetermined questions, but responses are coded numerically for statistical analysis, with the aim of collecting numerical data for quantitative purposes. Example 15.3 demonstrates how a structured interview can be conducted.

EXAMPLE 15.3

Suppose you intend to address the research question, "What are the experiences of adult language learners with learning English as a foreign language?" Previously, this question was addressed using an unstructured interview, where the conversation flowed naturally, with the interviewer following up on topics as they arose. Now you decide to use a structured interview approach.

You recruit a group of participants (e.g., N=15) who are adult foreign language learners currently learning English. For the structured interview, you prepare a set of specific questions in advance and ask each participant the same questions in the same order. For example, you might ask:

1. Can you please tell me a little bit about your background and language learning experience?
2. How long have you been learning English?
3. What motivated you to start learning English?
4. What strategies do you typically use to learn the language?
5. What have been some of the challenges you have faced in learning the language?
6. How do you feel about your progress in learning the language so far?
7. How do you characterize your level of proficiency and why?
8. Do you feel you can use English comfortably in your daily life?
9. Do you have any advice for those learning English as a second language?

The above interview is structured because it follows a strict set of pre-determined questions that are asked in the same order, with limited opportunities for the interviewer to deviate from the script. Prompts are typically minimal or absent, and if used, they are brief and intended solely for clarification when necessary.

Advantages and Limitations of Structured Interviews

- They are more reliable than unstructured interviews. This is because they are based on a predetermined set of questions that all participants are asked. This allows all participants to be evaluated and compared on the same criteria, reducing subjectivity throughout the interview process.
- They are more efficient, as they allow the interviewer to cover a set of predetermined questions in a shorter length of time and in a systematic way.
- They are easier to code as the interviewer follows a set format and the responses are more uniform.

- They elicit the same information, which can make analysis and comparison easier.
- They require fewer interviewing skills than unstructured interviews.
- They are more objective as they rely less on the subjective judgment of the researcher than the other two types of interviews.

However, structured interviews also have some limitations. They may be less effective at assessing certain characteristics, such as personality or communication skills, and may be less engaging for the interviewee. In addition, they may be less flexible and adaptable to the needs of the interviewee. Structured interviews can be effective at gathering a lot of information in a short period of time. However, they may not provide as much insight into the learners' perspectives.

Focus Groups

A focus group is a qualitative data collection method involving a small group of participants (usually 8–19) discussing a specific topic. It aims to gather insights into their attitudes, opinions, and experiences, focusing on qualitative data rather than numerical information. In applied linguistics, focus groups are commonly employed to explore participants' beliefs on language-related issues. The researcher, acting as a facilitator, guides the discussion with prompts. This method can be conducted in person or online, with discussions recorded and transcribed for later analysis. To collect meaningful data, careful planning is essential. Focus groups can be conducted in person or online and the discussion is typically recorded and transcribed so that the researcher can review and analyze the data later. For the focus group to provide accurate and meaningful data, the discussion should be carefully planned so that the information gathered is accurate and meaningful.

A focus group is a qualitative data collection method involving a small group of participants (usually 8–19) discussing a specific topic.

Example 15.4 demonstrates how to conduct a focus group.

EXAMPLE 15.4

Suppose you want to explore the same research question as in Example 15.3: "What are the experiences of adult language learners with learning English as a foreign language?". This time, however, you decide to conduct a focus group. To carry out the focus group, you can follow these steps:

1. You recruit a group of adults who are currently learning English as a foreign language.
2. You invite the participants to a focus group discussion. You facilitate and lead the discussion, using open-ended questions and prompts to encourage the

participants to share their thoughts, feelings, and experiences related to their experiences of second language learning.

3. During the group discussion, participants may talk about their motivations for learning a second language, their challenges and successes, and any strategies they have used or found helpful when learning the language.

4. You observe and record the discussion, by taking notes and/or making an audio/ video recording.

In the above example, you may transcribe the discussion and then analyze the data using qualitative analysis techniques, such as thematic analysis, to identify and interpret the themes and patterns emerging from the data. For example, you might look for common strategies used and their reported impact on the learners' language learning. You may report the findings in a research paper or present them at an academic conference.

Advantages and Limitations of Focus Groups
Some of the advantages of focus groups are the following:

- They allow the researcher to gather in-depth and detailed data about a specific topic or issue under investigation.
- They allow for the exploration of a broad range of diverse perspectives on a topic by providing a rich source of data.
- They provide an opportunity for participants to interact with one another, which can lead to a more in-depth and dynamic discussion.
- They can be conducted relatively quickly. They can also be an inexpensive way to gather a large amount of rich information.
- In focus groups, participants share their thoughts and experiences in an open and interactive setting. This helps researchers uncover new and rich insights and ideas that might not be discovered through more traditional research methods.

However, focus groups do have limitations. First, the data from a small, nonrepresentative group are not generalizable to the wider population. Second, findings are context-specific and reliant on specific participants, introducing subjectivity. The data may be influenced by leading questions, the group setting, and the presence of dominant members. Relatedly, since a focus group involves a public discussion, it is possible that some of the members may not express their personal opinions or beliefs, particularly when they feel that their ideas are opposed to others'; some people may be shy or not feel comfortable talking in groups.

Observation

Observation is a qualitative data collection method frequently used in applied linguistics research. It is used to observe and record the behavior and interactions of participants in their own natural language learning and teaching settings. The goal of observation is to gain a deep understanding of the sociolinguistic processes and dynamics at play within the group by systematically watching their action and behavior in a naturalistic setting, with the aim of gaining insights into their language use, communication patterns, and social interactions. In applied linguistics research, observation can be used to study a wide range of language-related phenomena, such as language learning in the classroom, communication between teachers and learners, and how language is used in various settings.

Observation is often combined with other data collection tools, such as interviews and field notes for more in-depth data, and the data are often audio or video recorded, so that they can be transcribed for later analysis. For example, during the observation, the researcher typically takes detailed field notes, describing what is happening, who is involved, and what is being said. These notes may include both objective observations of behavior and subjective impressions and interpretations. The researcher may also make an audio or video recording of the observation, to aid in the analysis process. The analysis often involves identifying patterns and themes in the data collected through coding the data using a set of predefined categories or developing new categories based on emergent themes. The researcher may also use more analytical tools, such as conversation analysis, to examine the structure and organization of language use, interaction, and conversation in the observed data.

Observation is a qualitative data collection method frequently used to observe and record the behavior and interactions of participants in their own natural language learning and teaching settings.

POINTS TO PONDER

What data collection method would you use to explore language learning strategies among second language learners, and why? What advantages or challenges do you foresee in using this data collection method?

Classroom Observation

Classroom observation is a kind of observation in which you observe and/or record classroom interactions, behaviors, and teaching practices of a teacher as well as the learning behaviors of students in a classroom setting. Classroom observation is frequently used as a data collection tool in applied linguistics research to examine what goes on in language classroom instruction. For example, there are many observational studies on corrective feedback or learner–learner interaction that have documented teachers' feedback or interaction strategies and students' responses. Classroom observation is also often used in research on teachers' professional development or as a part of teacher-training activities. One of the benefits of classroom observation in such contexts is that it enables you to observe what teachers do directly and closely in naturalistic settings, including their manner of teaching verbal and nonverbal communication with the students. As such, it can provide a valuable tool for identifying areas of strength and areas for improvement in a teacher's instruction and can also provide important feedback to teachers in professional development courses. The types of activities and behaviors you watch will depend on your research goals and questions.

Classroom observation is a kind of observation in which you observe and/or record classroom interactions, behaviors, and teaching practices of a teacher as well as the learning behaviors of students in a classroom setting.

There are both advantages and limitations to using observation as a research method in applied linguistics. One advantage is that observation allows you to study language use in naturalistic contexts, rather than in controlled laboratory settings. It also allows you to collect rich and detailed data on language-related matters, which can be analyzed and interpreted in a variety of ways.

However, there are also some limitations. For example, it can be difficult to determine the reliability and validity of the data collected through observation, as you may not be able to control all the variables that may affect language use. Additionally, there maybe be ethical issues when using observation as a data collection tool, particularly when you are participating in the activities being observed or when the participants do not know that they are being observed (see below).

Types of Classroom Observation
There are different types of classroom observation, including:

- structured observation
- unstructured observation
- participant observation
- nonparticipant observation
  - covert nonparticipant observation
  - overt nonparticipant observation.

Structured Observation There are different approaches to observation. One is structured or systematic observation. This involves using a specific set of criteria or checklists to guide the observation process. The aim is to produce more objective data on particular predetermined behaviors or features in interaction. You then look for those specific behaviors or actions and record them using a rubric, checklists, or other structured observation systems that are related to the research goal and the purpose of the study. Classroom observation checklists, for example, help record instances of teaching and learning in a classroom and facilitate the further analysis of the data collected. In the field of applied linguistics, such checklists may focus on specific aspects of language teaching and learning. Depending on the research goals and questions, here are some example items that might be included on a classroom observation checklist:

- The type of materials, tasks, and exercises the teacher uses (e.g. authentic versus simplified or teacher-made materials, rote versus meaningful exercises, fluency versus accuracy-based practices, etc.).
- The types of teaching methods and strategies used (e.g., communicative activities, task-based materials, grammar-based activities, etc.).
- The teacher's assessment techniques (e.g., formative quizzes, self-assessment, peer assessment, etc.).
- The teacher's classroom management behaviors.
- The teacher's techniques to engage and motivate students (e.g. group work, real-life scenarios, etc.).
- The teacher's use of technology (e.g., online resources, language learning software, etc.).

Structured or systematic observation involves using a specific set of criteria or checklists to guide the observation process.

An example of an influential structured observation system frequently used in applied linguistics research is Flanders Interaction Analysis Categories (FIAC) (Flanders, 1970), which focuses on teacher talk with ten categories. There are other examples of observation schemes similar to and based on Flanders's scheme with various categories, such as the FLint interaction analysis scheme by Moskowitz (1976), which is a modified version of FIAC with a focus on teacher–student interaction; Allwright's (1980) observational scheme; the FOCUS (Foci for Observing Communication Used in Setting) scheme by Fanselow (1977a), with a focus on classroom communication with categories related to purpose, medium, use, and content; and also Communicative Orientation of Language Teaching (COLT) designed by Allen, Fröhlich, and Spada (1984), which is divided into two parts with one part describing classroom activities and the second part focusing on communicative features of interactional exchange.

It is important to note that classroom observation checklists are just one tool among many that can be used to assess teaching and learning in the classroom, and they should be used in conjunction with other methods, such as teacher and student interviews, focus groups, and lesson plans.

Structured observation can be used both as a qualitative and a quantitative data collection method based on how it is used and the data being analyzed. When used as a qualitative data collection method, the observation involves a set of predetermined and specific means to guide the observation. However, the goal is still to gain a rich understanding of the issues being observed and to identify patterns and themes emerging from the data. When being used as a quantitative data collection method, structured observation also contains predetermined specific means to guide the observation, such as a checklist or the use of predetermined categories. However, the focus is on having numerical data to be analyzed quantitatively later on, using frequencies and percentages, for example.

Unstructured Observation Unstructured observation involves allowing the observer to observe the setting more naturally, without a specific set of criteria to follow. During an unstructured observation, you observe and record what is happening without trying to impose a preconceived structure or framework on the data. The goal is to gain an in-depth understanding of the issue being observed by identifying themes and patterns that emerge from the data.

One of the advantages of unstructured observation is that it is flexible and can be easily adapted to the needs of the situation. For example, you can easily adjust your focus and your documentation methods based on what occurs in the context, enabling you to detect unpredicted issues or aspects related to nonverbal communication, such as body language and facial expressions, which can be important in understanding language use in social settings but may not be captured through highly structured observations. One limitation, of course, is that it is time-consuming and also highly subjective, making it prone to the researcher's biases, personal impressions, and interpretations.

Unstructured observation involves allowing the observer to observe the setting more naturally without a specific set of criteria to follow.

In applied linguistics research, classroom observation, whether structured or unstructured, can be used to examine a wide range of language-related issues. Here are a few examples of research questions that could be examined through classroom observation:

- What instructional strategies do teachers use in the classroom, and how do they affect student learning?
- What kind of group-work activities are used in language classrooms, and what impact do they have on students' collaborative efforts?
- How do teacher–student interactions influence student motivation and achievement?
- How do teachers use technology in the classroom, and how does that affect student engagement and learning?
- How do teachers track student progress and adjust their instruction accordingly?
- How and to what extent do teachers incorporate cultural content into their language lessons?

Types of Observation Based on Researcher Involvement There are two main types of observations based on the researcher involvement:

- participant observation
- nonparticipant observation.

Participant Observation Participant observation involves actively participating in the group or community under investigation. This can include participating in group activities and interacting with members of the group and/or engaging in informal conversations with them. Participant observation is often used as the main method of data collection in ethnographic research, where your goal is to study a group of participants or their community's culture, values, and belief systems.

Nonparticipant Observation Nonparticipant observation happens when you simply observe the group from the outside without actively participating in their activities. This kind of observation allows you to gain an outsider perspective of the group's actions and behavior. In this type of observation, you may record the activities and interactions of the group or take field notes about their behavior, which can be later analyzed.

Both participant observation and nonparticipant observation have their advantages and limitations, which you should consider when choosing the approach. For example, one of the advantages of nonparticipant observation is that it allows you to remain more objective and unbiased; on the other hand, it may also prevent you from achieving the depth of understanding that could be gained by participating in the group's culture and dynamics.

Participant observation involves actively participating in the group or community under investigation. **Nonparticipant observation** happens when you simply observe the group from the outside without actively participating in their activities.

COVERT AND OVERT NONPARTICIPANT OBSERVATION   Nonparticipant observation can be done either covertly or overtly. Overt observation is when the participant knows or is aware that they are being observed. This type of observation is often used in naturalistic settings, where you want to observe subjects in their natural environment without altering their behavior.

Covert observation is when the participants are not aware that they are being observed. This type of observation is often used when you believe that the participants' behavior may be negatively affected if they are aware that they are being observed. Therefore, you hide yourself from the participants, and the participants do not know that they are being studied. Covert observation can be considered to be ethically problematic and should only be used when the study requires it.

As noted earlier, observation is a common data collection tool in applied linguistics research, where it is used to collect data about language-related issues in naturalistic settings. Example 15.5 illustrates how observation can be used to examine an instructional issue.

EXAMPLE 15.5

Suppose you are interested in studying aspects of language instruction in classroom settings. You may take the following steps:

1. You identify a research question, such as "How do teachers use corrective feedback in intermediate adult English classrooms, and what effects does it have on student engagement?"
2. You select one or a few language classroom(s) and observe them when the teacher provides feedback.
3. You may take detailed notes on the feedback strategies the teachers use or audio/video record the interactions between teachers and students in order to have a more complete record of the feedback strategies used in the classroom.
4. You might also closely observe the nature of classroom tasks used, the questions the teacher asks, the responses students provide, or any other instructional activities used. Such an observation can provide insights into how students engage with feedback and how it can affect their learning outcomes.
5. Once the observations are complete, you can analyze the data in order to understand how teachers provide feedback and how students respond to it.

POINTS TO PONDER

Based on your experiences, if you have any, what criteria should be considered when designing and administering questionnaires for applied linguistics research? How do you evaluate and address potential biases, ensuring the reliability and validity of questionnaire data?

Questionnaire

Another data collection tool used in in applied linguistics research is the questionnaire. A questionnaire is a data collection tool that consists of a list of questions, items or other prompts used to gather information from a group of participants. Questionnaires are useful tools as they allow researchers to collect data both quickly and efficiently. They can take different forms and can be used to collect a wide range of data, including demographic data as well as data about opinions, attitudes, behaviors, knowledge, and experiences. They can be administered in various ways, including online, by phone, by mail, or face to face, and can also be designed to be used as web-based tools accessed through a browser. The way a questionnaire is administered and how it is responded to depend on the research goals and questions. Questionnaires can be used in both qualitative and quantitative research.

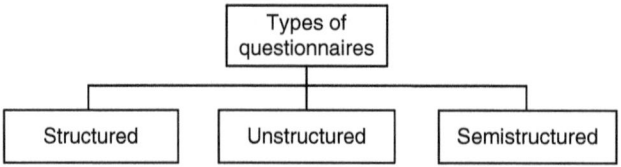

Figure 15.2 Types of questionnaires

A questionnaire is a data collection tool that consists of a list of questions, items, or other prompts used to gather information from a group of participants.

Questionnaires can be closed-ended, open-ended, or a combination (see Figure 15.2 and the following section for the types of questionnaires). When used in qualitative research, the questions are often open-ended, and the aim is to collect detailed information from a smaller number of participants. In quantitative research, the questions are often closed-ended, administered in the form of survey research, and the aim is to gather data from a large number of participants.

Types of Questionnaires

There are three main types of questionnaires (Figure 15.2), including

- structured questionnaires
- unstructured questionnaires
- semistructured questionnaires.

Structured Questionnaires

Structured questionnaires are data collection tools that include a series of fixed questions or items designed to elicit specific responses from participants. The questions are closed-ended, that is they are followed by a specific response. This type of question may take the form of yes/no or multiple-choice questions, or use rating scales, such as the Likert scale. Likert-scale items use a scale to elicit participants' responses. For example, they may elicit the participant's agreement or disagreement on an issue, with a statement on a five-point scale such as "Strongly agree," "Somewhat agree," "Neither agree nor disagree," "Somewhat disagree," and "Strongly disagree."

Structured questionnaires are data collection tools that include a series of fixed questions or items designed to elicit specific responses from participants. The questions are closed-ended; that is, they are followed by a specific response.

Structured questionnaires can be administered online, over the phone, or face-to face. It is important to carefully design and pilot the questionnaire to make sure that it is both valid and reliable. Some examples of structured questionnaire questions are given in Example 15.6.

EXAMPLE 15.6

1. Do you use L1 in your classes?   Yes ☐   No ☐

2. What age groups have you taught?   Children ☐   Adults ☐

3. What language levels have you taught?

    Beginner ☐   Low intermediate ☐   High intermediate ☐   Advanced ☐   Other _____

4. On a scale of 1 to 5, (1, 2, 3, 4, or 5), do you agree or disagree with the following statement: "Vocabulary is the most important aspect of language learning"?
    (1 agree ————5 disagree).

Structured questionnaires are often used in quantitative research because they can be easily administered to a large group of participants, and the data collected can be analyzed quickly, as the responses can be coded and quantified. A structured questionnaire has both advantages and limitations. The advantages include:

- ease of administration with fixed questions and response options
- efficiency of administration for large participant numbers
- facilitation of straightforward analysis through scoring and statistical software
- provision of more reliable data with consistent, predetermined questions
- potential for valid data collection with carefully designed questions.

Structured questionnaires have some limitations. Closed-ended questions, while efficient for gathering information, provide a limited range of responses. Participants may feel constrained and unable to express their exact thoughts or diverse perspectives. Additionally, the fixed format and numerous questions may lead to lengthy surveys, potentially affecting response rates or causing incomplete submissions. Overall, these constraints can limit the depth of understanding of participants' perspectives and hinder the identification of their true meanings and responses.

Unstructured Questionnaires

Unstructured questionnaires are those that do not include closed-ended questions with fixed responses. Rather, they include open-ended questions that allow participants to answer in their own words. Unstructured questionnaires usually provide a space for the participants to answer in as much detail as they wish or to elaborate on their responses to the questions. Such questionnaires collect qualitative data, and as such they are typically used in qualitative research. Because the questions are open-ended, unstructured questionnaires provide a deeper understanding and insight into the experiences, thoughts, opinions, and attitudes of the participants.

Unstructured questionnaires do not include closed-ended questions with fixed responses. Rather, they include open-ended questions that allow participants to answer in their own words.

Semistructured Questionnaires

A semistructured questionnaire is a data collection tool that combines elements of both structured and unstructured questionnaires. That is, they include a combination of both closed and open-ended questions. Closed-ended questions are used to gather specific and fixed responses, whereas open-ended questions allow respondents to provide their own answers, which can be more in-depth. As such, semistructured questionnaires allow researchers to collect both qualitative and quantitative data.

Because semistructured questionnaires include both closed and open-ended questions, they can have the advantages of both structured and unstructured questionnaires. The closed-ended questions allow you to collect and analyze a large amount of data efficiently. The open-ended questions allow participants to provide more detailed responses or to elaborate on the responses they have provided to closed-ended questions.

Example 15.7 illustrates sample items of a semistructured questionnaire. Suppose you want to investigate students' perceptions and preferences regarding corrective feedback in second language writing. A semistructured questionnaire, like the following, can be designed to explore this issue.

EXAMPLE 15.7

Instruction: Please indicate your preferred type of corrective feedback by checking the appropriate box. Choose the option that best reflects your preference. For the open-ended questions, please provide your responses.

1. Which type of corrective feedback do you prefer the most?
   [ ] Direct feedback (e.g., the teacher provides the correct answer)
   [ ] Indirect feedback (e.g., the teacher highlights the error but does not provide the correct answer)
   [ ] Peer feedback (e.g., feedback from classmates)
   [ ] None of the above
2. How often do you act on the feedback you receive from your teacher?
   [ ] Always
   [ ] Often
   [ ] Sometimes
   [ ] Rarely
   [ ] Never

3. Can you describe an example when feedback helped you understand a grammatical issue in your writing? ....

4. Do you think written corrective feedback should focus more on linguistic errors or on other issues such as organization and ideas? Why? ....

The above is considered a semistructured questionnaire because it includes both closed-ended questions (the first two questions) and open-ended questions (the last two questions).

What to Consider When Creating a Questionnaire

To create a questionnaire, you should first determine your research goals and the type of data you wish to collect. You should then consider the types of questionnaire items that will best help you achieve your goals, and whether those items should be structured or open-ended. Once the items have been determined, they should be organized in a logical order and the questionnaire should be pilot-tested to be effective and reliable. A good questionnaire has the following characteristics:

1. The questionnaire items should be clear. Here is an example of an ambiguous questionnaire item:

   "How often do you use group-work activities in your classroom?"

   This question is ambiguous because it does not specify the exact timeline, so the participants will not know exactly what "often" means in this context: Does it mean once a week, once a month, or every day? To make the question less ambiguous, it could be revised by providing a clear time frame, such as in the following:

   "In the past week, how many times did you use group-work activities in your classroom?"

2. The questionnaire items should be unbiased and should not include leading questions. Here is an example of a leading question:

   "Do you believe that teachers should always follow the textbook in their instruction?"

   The above question may guide the participants towards a particular answer and suggests that the participants should agree that the teachers should follow textbooks even if they may not actually believe that teachers should do so. A more neutral version of this question could be:

   "What is your opinion about teachers following textbooks in their instruction?"

3. The questionnaire items should be relevant and appropriate for the purpose of the research.

4. The questionnaire items should be piloted. Piloting the questionnaire before it is being used is essential as it can help identify any potential problems, which can then be addressed before using the questionnaire.

POINTS TO PONDER

How do you define a verbal report as a qualitative data collection tool in applied linguistics research? What are the different types of verbal reports? Can you provide examples of situations or studies where any kind of verbal reports can be effectively used to gather data? Can you think of any other qualitative data collection tools in addition to what we have discussed so far?

Verbal Reports

Verbal reports are qualitative data collection tools that are used to collect data about participants' mental processes. Since it is not possible to directly observe mental processes, researchers use verbal reports to collect such data. Language learning often involves cognitive processes not directly and easily observable. Therefore, verbal reports have been frequently used in applied linguistics and second language research to gather data on the cognitive processes used in language acquisition. There are different types of verbal reports (Figure 15.3):

- retrospective verbal reports
  - ◦ immediate recall
  - ◦ stimulated recall
- introspective verbal reports
  - ◦ think alouds.

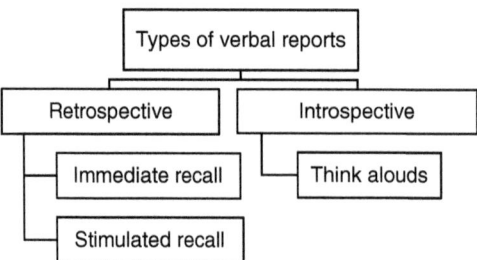

Figure 15.3 Types of verbal reports

Retrospective Verbal Reports

Retrospective verbal reports are those in which the participants are asked to recall and describe past experiences or events. They are called retrospective because the reports are obtained after a given task has been completed. Thus, in retrospective reports, participants are asked to think about a specific event that happened before and recount their memories of it through talking or writing about it.

Two types of retrospective reports commonly used in applied linguistics research are:

- immediate recall
- stimulated recall.

Immediate Recall

Retrospective recalls can either be immediate or delayed. Immediate recall is used to assess recall performance immediately after the information has been presented to the participants. This type of recall is commonly used in applied linguistics research, particularly in studies of language acquisition and memory as it can provide insight into how learners process and store new linguistic information and can also be used to compare memory performance across different groups or conditions. For example, in an applied linguistics study, participants might be asked to repeat back a list of words or sentences that they have just listened to, and their memory performances can be compared.

Immediate recall is used to assess recall performance immediately after the information has been presented to the participants.

Immediate recall is often used as a qualitative method, particularly for gathering data on learners' subjective interpretations. In this context, it can provide rich insights into how learners process new linguistic information by revealing, for example, the strategies they use to retain what they have learned. The resulting data are typically analyzed qualitatively. However, immediate recall can also be used as a quantitative method, depending on the analytic approach. For instance, you may quantify responses or assign numerical codes, enabling statistical analysis. Therefore, immediate recall can serve as both a qualitative and a quantitative data collection method, depending on the research goals and how the data are analyzed.

As noted before, Philp (2003), for example, used the immediate recall technique to examine learners' noticing of recasts in task-based interaction. Noticing was operationalized as remembering recasts following the feedback and was measured by cued immediate recall, where the learners were asked to verbalize their thoughts immediately after they received the feedback. The procedure was like this: After each recast, the learner's response was interrupted by the sound of two knocks to cue the learner to recall the feedback. The noticing of the feedback was then calculated and compared numerically using percentages and frequencies.

Stimulated Recall

Recalls can be conducted with or without some stimulus to help the participants to recall. Stimulated recall is a data collection technique used to gain insights into the thought processes when the recall is used with a stimulus. In this technique, the participants are asked to recall an event or information while at the same time they are presented with the original material or event as a stimulus. The stimulus could be a video or audio recording of an activity that the participant took part in or a written document that the learner produced.

The goal of stimulated recall is to get the individual to think about and remember what they did, which can in turn help the researcher understand their thought processes at the time they were doing the task. Like immediate recall, stimulated recall is inherently a qualitative data collection method because the data that are collected are initially nonnumerical. When used as qualitative research, the focus is on understanding the learners' subjective experiences, attitudes, and beliefs, and the data can be analyzed qualitatively using themes and patterns. However, the data collected through stimulated recall can also be analyzed quantitatively. For instance, if you use stimulated recall to identify patterns or trends in learners' cognitive processes or strategies, you may then quantify those patterns or themes using coding schemes or other analytical techniques. This allows you to conduct statistical analyses using frequencies and percentages to determine what cognitive processes or strategies occur more frequently or how learners compare with respect to the frequency of certain strategies.

Stimulated recall is a data collection technique used to gain insights into thought processes when the recall is used with a stimulus.

Example 15.8 shows the use of stimulated recall in a study on recasts by Sakai (2011). The stimulated recall was used to collect data about noticing recasts (an implicit corrective feedback strategy in which a learner's utterance is reformulated into a correct form). After the interaction, the students listened to the audio-taped interactions in which they had received recasts and were asked to report what they were thinking about at that time.

EXAMPLE 15.8

Recast episode:

Momo: He dro.. drinken coffee. He have a coffee. [an erroneous utterance]
Researcher: He drank coffee? [a recast]
Momo: Yes.
Researcher: OK.

Stimulated Recall:

Momo: Well, about this, I stopped because I was thinking of what the past form of the word drink was. Actually, I wanted to say a cup, full of coffee, but I did not know the expression. That was before speaking. Yes. I did not know the past form of the word drink before starting to speak.

(Sakai, 2011, p. 369)

The data collected was qualitative. However, it was then coded and categorized and analyzed quantitatively through frequencies and percentages to determine the extent to which learners noticed recasts.

Steps in Conducting a Stimulated Recall

1. Decide on the purpose and goals of the stimulated recall by clearly defining what you want to achieve by conducting the recall.
2. Identify the event or activity that you want to study.
3. If using stimulated recall, determine the nature of the prompts that should be used to stimulate the participant's recall.
4. Decide on an appropriate recording device.
5. Explain the process and the purpose of the retrospective recall to the participants and provide clear instruction.
6. Have a training session with the participants in which you show the participants how the verbal reports work.
7. Start the retrospective recall process.
8. If using stimulated recall, present the stimulus to the participant and ask them to describe what they recall or their experiences related to the event in as much detail as possible. Ask them to explain their thoughts and feelings relevant to the task.
9. Record and transcribe the session.
10. Analyze the data by reviewing the transcript in relation to the goals of the study.
11. Report and disseminate the findings in an appropriate form.

Advantages and Limitations of Retrospective Verbal Reports

There are several advantages of retrospective verbal reports. First, they can provide insights into the thought processes of participants when they were doing the tasks, which may not be possible to capture through other data collection methods. The data can also be collected relatively easily. In applied linguistics research, retrospective verbal reports can be used as a tool to gain insights into the learners' mental processes of a past language-related activity or the challenges they may have faced when doing the task.

There are, however, several limitations. First, since they rely on memory, they are affected by the limitations of memory. They may also be influenced by other factors such as the passage of time, personal biases, and the individual's mood or state of mind at the time of recall. In addition, people may be reluctant to report certain events or experiences if they are sensitive or embarrassing, leading to a potentially inaccurate report.

Introspective Verbal Reports

Introspective verbal reports are qualitative research methods used to gain insight into participants' subjective experiences or mental processes by having them verbalize their thoughts, feelings, and perceptions as they engage in a particular task or activity. In contrast to retrospective techniques, such as immediate recall or stimulated recall, which ask participants to recall and describe their thoughts or experiences after completing a task or activity, introspective techniques ask learners to report their thought processes or strategies during a task. Like retrospective techniques, introspective techniques can provide insight into the participants' mental processes. Introspective techniques enable the researcher to capture participants' cognitive processes as they occur, providing a more direct understanding of how they process or approach a task.

Introspective verbal reports are qualitative research methods used to gain insight into participants' subjective experiences or mental processes by having them verbalize their thoughts, feelings, and perceptions as they engage in a particular task or activity.

An example of introspective self-report is when the learners are asked to report what they do when they guess the meaning of a word from context while reading. They might, for example, provide the report in Example 15.9.

EXAMPLE 15.9

While I am reading and encounter a new word, I try to look for clues in the immediate context that can help me to guess the meaning of the words such as whether it is verb, an adverb or an adjective.

Think Alouds

Think alouds are a particular type of introspective research technique during which participants are asked to verbalize their thoughts as they complete a task or an activity. They are called think alouds because participants are essentially thinking out loud or provide a verbalization of their thoughts in real time as they do the task. This allows you to gain insights into how participants approach the task or activity, and what cognitive processes and strategies they use to complete it.

Think alouds are widely used in applied linguistics research, particularly in studies of language learning and language processing. Researchers use think alouds to investigate a range of topics, including learners' comprehension and interpretation of written or spoken texts, their use of language learning strategies, and their development of metalinguistic awareness.

While think alouds are primarily a qualitative research technique, they can be used in combination with other qualitative and quantitative research techniques to provide a more comprehensive understanding of participants' experiences and ideas. By combining multiple sources of data, researchers can gain a rich and detailed understanding of how learners approach language learning and use language in real-world contexts.

Think alouds are a particular type of introspective research technique during which participants are asked to verbalize their thoughts as they complete a task or activity.

Steps in Conducting Think Alouds

1. Select the participant and explain clearly what they need to do.
2. Provide necessary background information.
3. Choose an appropriate setting for the think-aloud session.
4. Give clear instructions on verbalizing thoughts during the task.
5. Demonstrate think-aloud process through modeling.
6. Initiate the think-aloud session, prompting when needed. Here are some examples of prompts that can be used during think alouds.
   a. "What are you thinking about right now?"
   b. "Why are you saying this?"
   c. "Why are you making this decision?"
   d. "What strategies are you using now?"
   e. "What information are you using now?"
7. Record the session and take additional notes if necessary.
8. Transcribe the recording for further analysis.
9. Analyze data through techniques like coding and categorization.

Example 15.10 illustrates data from a think-aloud protocol conducted by a Spanish language learner, as reported by Leow (1998). The learner worked through a crossword puzzle, verbalizing their thought process while addressing a grammar issue.

EXAMPLE 15.10

Vertical now ... 2 down, OK I have an *o* here but I don't know why because in 1 across I have *se morio* but I guess it has to be **murio** because 2 down has to be *un* [changes *o* to *u*] ... OK I have *to* but it must be *tu* so it means that 7 across for the past tense of *dormirse* must be **durmio** instead of *dormio* [changes *o* to *u*] ... OK third person plural form of the verb *pedir* they asked for, 5 down ... *pedieron* [pause] OK I am wondering whether because I have **pidieron** [spells out] and I am thinking it should be *pe-* but that would make it *dormeo* with an e instead of *i*, ... I guess I will see how the other ones go and take a look at that one again ... OK, the opposite of *no* is *si* which means that for 11 across I have *mentieron* but it should be *mintieron* for the third person plural past tense of *mentir*, *mintieron* [changes e to i] which makes me now realize that **pidieron** with an *i* is probably right since the *e* in *mentir* changes to an *i* so the *e* in *pedir* is also going to change to an *i* as well ... OK 12 down, the opposite of *no* is *si*, which means that where I have *corregio* it becomes **corrigio** corrigio so the third person singular of past tense *corregir* is *corrigio* [changes *e* to an *i*] ... looks like all the *e*'s are becoming *i*'s in the stems ...

OK, third person singular form of *descubrir* discovered OK it is *descubrio*, OK 17 down possessive adjective in Spanish OK now here yet again I have *to* because I have *se dormieron* and that must become *tu* so it becomes *se **durmieron*** [changes *o* to *u*] OK third person singular form of *preferir* preferred, OK now here yet again *prefe-* [spells out] is going to change to *prefi-* [spells out] ***prefirio*** [changes *e* to *i*] ... OK 25 down, the verb to go in Spanish which is *ir* and I have *er* [spells out] because with 24 across I have *repetieron* but I guess now that *e* becomes an *i* becomes ***repitieron*** ... [changes *e* to *i*] ... and 25 down is *ir*, so now I am going to go back and change any other ones where I have *e* in the stem that should become an *i*, like 1 down, I believe would become se ***divirtieron***, it becomes an *i* and – everything else looks OK so I guess that's it [9 Minutes].

(Leow, 1998, p. 146)

Advantages and Limitations of Think Alouds   There are several advantages for think alouds, such as the following:

- They can provide insights into unobservable mental processes, which cannot be collected otherwise.
- They can help understand how participants approach a task, which can then provide insight into what strategies they use when doing the tasks.
- They can help with the identification of problems or difficulties participants have in completing a task. This can then help identify areas for improvement.
- By asking learners to verbalize their thoughts at the time of doing a language task, second language acquisition researchers have been able to get insights into learners' attention distribution and whether and how they notice a language form, a process considered to be essential for language learning.
- They can be used with a wide range of participants in a variety of settings (e.g., both lab and naturalistic settings) and can study a wide range of tasks and behaviors).

Think alouds have some limitations. First, participants may struggle to accurately express their thoughts, potentially compromising data validity. Second, the act of verbalizing thoughts may interfere with task performance, known as the reactivity effect. Third, verbalization may not capture all cognitive processes, particularly implicit or complex ones. Additionally, some tasks may be too difficult for effective verbalization. Also, think-aloud protocols require trained researchers for facilitation, transcription, and analysis. Participants may also be limited by working memory capacity, verbalizing only immediately available information.

Field Notes

Field notes are qualitative data collection tools through which written records are made while observing and studying a particular phenomenon. They are used to document and record observations, thoughts, and ideas and insights during the research and are commonly used in observational research when you are collecting data in naturalistic rather than controlled laboratory settings. Field notes can be written by hand on paper or typed into a computer. They can be the main source of data or they can be used to complement and triangulate data from other sources of data collection, such as interviews, surveys, or questionnaires, to provide a more in-depth understanding of the research issue.

Field notes are qualitative data collection tools through which written records are made while observing and studying a particular phenomenon.

Field notes are an important data collection tool because they allow researchers to capture rich and detailed data about participants. They provide a documented record of the research process and also descriptions of the observations made, quotes from participants, and the researcher's own thoughts and interpretations. They can be used to study a phenomenon or to verify and validate findings collected through other means. Field notes are often qualitative and are gathered in the forms of text, but they can be analyzed quantitatively or qualitatively, depending on the nature of the research and its goals. When analyzing them qualitatively, the data can be coded to identify themes and patterns and trends in the data. The themes identified can also be quantified for any statistical analysis if needed.

What to Consider When Taking Field Notes

1. Take accurate and detailed notes containing essential information about the studied phenomenon.
2. Write notes in clear language for easy readability.
3. Organize notes with clear headings, subheadings, and numbered or bulleted points for accessibility.
4. Maintain unbiased language, avoiding subjective judgments or personal opinions.
5. Provide detailed information about the research process and context, including location, conditions, and individuals present.
6. Use abbreviations and codes for efficiency and streamlining the note-taking process.
7. Store notes securely and confidentially, recognizing their value for future research and analysis.

Example 15.11 illustrates a hypothetical field note in an applied linguistics study on a teacher's use of communicative language teaching in the classroom.

EXAMPLE 15.11

Observation date: February 15, 2022,
Location: English Language Centre, University of Victoria
Time: 10 am.

The class observed was at an intermediate level in the English Language Center at the University of Victoria. The lesson was about practicing the simple past tense, and the teacher seemed to approach this task within a communicative language teaching framework. The teacher did little talking or explaining in front of the classroom, and students worked in small groups most of the time, either exchanging information, problem solving, or discussing. The bulk of the lesson consisted of a discussion of what students did in the past.

The teacher began by asking the students the date, the time, and the current weather conditions, all of which she recorded on a whiteboard at the side of the classroom. For the first activity, the instructor went through the class asking everyone about their yesterday. The students all knew that they would be asked, so they all had their answers at least somewhat prepared. This routine activity affords the students preparation time, allowing them to feel safe and comfortable responding in front of their peers. The instructor then asked each of the students to read a few lines from a story and asked them questions related to that story. The instructor encouraged students to ask questions also. At the end of the activity, which took approximately 35 minutes, the instructor wrote on the board a few sentences in the past with some of the sentences being correct and some incorrect. The students were asked to work in groups and identify which sentence was correct and which sentence was wrong and why.

Journals and Diaries

Journals and diaries are written records of personal thoughts and experiences. While the words "journal" and "diary" are often used interchangeably, a distinction can be made between them, with a diary being seen mainly as a record of personal daily experiences and a journal providing a broader concept, not only recording events but also expanding on them. Both provide a way of reflecting on and documenting thoughts and feelings on a regular basis. Entries can be written in a notebook by hand or recorded using an electronic device such as an app on a computer.

Journals and **diaries** are written records of personal thoughts and experiences.

Collecting data through journals and diaries can be a useful method for gathering information about a particular case and individual phenomena. They can provide a rich source of data, which can be analyzed and interpreted in different ways. For example, you can use both qualitative and quantitative data analysis techniques to identify and examine patterns and themes in the data.

Ways in Which Journals and Diaries Can Be Used in Research

Journals and diaries can be utilized in research in two main ways. First, existing journals and diaries can be reviewed and analyzed, providing insights into the personal accounts and perceptions of specific individuals or groups. This approach is commonly employed in biographic research across various disciplines, including applied linguistics, to understand the life experiences and influences shaping an individual. Second, participants can be asked to keep journals or diaries about their experiences and views related to a specific research issue. These collected writings serve as valuable data for in-depth analysis, either as the primary focus of a study or as part of a larger research endeavor. For instance, in a study on classroom instruction, language teachers or learners may be prompted to document their thoughts and opinions on a given lesson, offering detailed insights into their experiences and reflections.

Advantages and Limitations of Journals and Diaries

There are several advantages to using journals and diaries in research.

- They provide a first-hand and authentic record of the participants' perspectives, thoughts, and feelings. Because journals and diaries document the experiences of individuals in their own words, they can provide valuable insights that may not be possible to collect through other research tools.
- They are a useful method of collecting data in longitudinal research whose aim is to track changes and developments in a person's thoughts, behaviors, or experiences over time. In this way, the information collected through journals and diaries can be useful for understanding how the participants' experiences or perspectives evolve or change over time.
- Journals and diaries can be used to study issues about which individuals may not be willing to share information in a face-to-face interview or survey. The participants can share any information they want to share without the researcher being physically present during the data collection.

However, it is also important to consider the limitations of using journals and diaries as a data source. Journals and diaries are about the personal experiences and viewpoints of the participants. Therefore, in that sense, they may be considered biased. Additionally, it may be difficult to use journals and diaries to collect data from a large group of participants. They are usually used in case studies or qualitative research with a small number of participants. As such, the generalizability of the findings of such research will be limited as the individual or group examined, and so may not be a representative sample of a larger population. Journals or diaries may also involve inaccuracies or omissions that need to be considered when using them as a source of data.

Conclusion

This chapter has discussed a variety of qualitative data collection tools commonly used in applied linguistics research, such as interviews, focus groups, observations, questionnaires, verbal reports, and field notes. Each data collection method was discussed with examples highlighting its unique features, advantages, and limitations. By understanding the strengths, limitations, and practical applications of these tools, you can make informed decisions about which methods to use for your own research. Choosing the right tool is essential for making the findings rigorous, relevant, and meaningful. Altogether, the chapter has aimed to provide a solid understanding of qualitative data collection tools and their application in applied linguistics research. The next chapter will focus on the analysis of qualitative data.

DISCUSSION AND ACTIVITY QUESTIONS

Discussion Questions

1. What are the advantages and disadvantages of using interviews as a data collection method in applied linguistics research?
2. What are the advantages and limitations of structured and unstructured classroom observation methods in applied linguistics research, and how can you choose the most appropriate method(s) for your research questions?
3. How might focus groups be used to explore language-related issues in research? What are the challenges associated with the use of this method?
4. What considerations should you take into account when selecting participants for interviews, focus groups, or observations in a study?
5. Are there specific challenges associated with eliciting and interpreting verbal reports, and how can you address these challenges in your research practice?
6. What are the key features that distinguish interviews and verbal reports as qualitative data collection tools?
7. What limitations might you encounter when using think alouds in your research? How could these be mitigated?
8. Share an example of a qualitative research study that you have read or are familiar with. Which data collection method(s) did the researchers use, and were they effective in addressing the research questions?

Activity Questions

1. Choose a research question related to language learning or teaching and identify which qualitative data collection method(s) would be most appropriate for answering your research question. Justify your choices.
2. Choose a research study in applied linguistics that has used qualitative data collection methods. Read the study carefully and identify which methods were used, and determine why and how they were applied. Describe the strengths and

limitations of the methods used, and explain how they contributed to the research findings.

3. Conduct an unstructured observation of a language learning classroom, taking detailed notes. What challenges did you face when doing so?

4. Conduct a think-aloud protocol with a fellow student, asking the student to verbalize their thought processes while completing a language learning task. Identify any challenges that emerged and explain how you addressed those challenges.

16 | Analyzing Qualitative Data: Techniques and Strategies

CHAPTER OBJECTIVES

After completing this chapter, you should be able to

- Define qualitative data analysis and explain its purpose.
- Understand the process of doing qualitative data analysis, including data preparation, transcription, data familiarization, and coding.
- Understand the steps involved in transcribing data, including issues that may arise during transcription and the different types of transcription.
- Explain the concept of coding and distinguish between different types of coding.
- Understand and apply qualitative data analysis methods, such as content analysis, thematic analysis, discourse analysis, and grounded theory.
- Critically evaluate the strengths and limitations of different qualitative data analysis techniques and choose the most suitable approach for specific research questions.

Introduction

Qualitative data analysis is an approach used in qualitative research to analyze, interpret, and understand qualitative nonnumerical data such as text, images, video, and audio. As noted before, qualitative research is a type of research method that attempts to explore and understand participants' experiences, beliefs, perspectives, and behaviors through collecting nonnumerical data using methods such as observations, open-ended interviews, and focus groups. It is naturalistic, interpretive, and contextual, aiming to provide an in-depth understanding of the problem under investigation. It is an essential method for understanding complex and often very unstructured data based on subjective perspectives and experiences. The goal of qualitative data analysis is to search and sort through such data in order to understand the complexity of participants' behaviors and perspectives embedded in the data.

Qualitative data analysis can involve a variety of strategies and techniques, but typically it includes stages such as transcription, data coding, categorization, data display, presentation of results, interpretation, and drawing conclusions. The process is often inductive and iterative, with researchers revisiting the data multiple times as new patterns and insights emerge. The choice of technique used depends on the aim of the research, the research question, the nature of data, and the researcher's perspective and approach.

In this chapter, we will discuss the various strategies involved in qualitative research data analysis and how to conduct it effectively. We begin by explaining key steps, such as data preparation, data familiarization, coding, and interpretation, and emphasize the importance of rigor throughout the analysis process. We also provide an overview of the analytic methods commonly used in qualitative data analysis, including content analysis, thematic analysis, discourse analysis, and grounded theory.

POINTS TO PONDER

How do you think qualitative data analysis is different from quantitative data analysis? What are some of the key steps involved in qualitative data analysis?

When to Start the Analysis

One question that we may have when dealing with qualitative research is how and when we should start analyzing our data. In quantitative research, data analysis usually begins after the data collection phase is completed because quantitative research is often more controlled and structured and follows a set of standard research designs, in which the phases of data collection and data analysis are separate phases. The data are usually numerical and analyzed through statistical procedures, which should be used after the data collection is completed. In contrast, qualitative research is often exploratory and more open-ended, and the data are usually nonnumerical. Because of this and also because the research process is more of an iterative and cyclical process, in qualitative research, data analysis can begin while the data collection is still in progress. The aim is to identify emerging themes and patterns in the data, which can inform the direction of the study. The simultaneous data collection and data analysis also enables you to gain insights into the data early on and to make modifications to the data collection as the study evolves.

Simultaneous data collection and analysis can be particularly useful in studies in which data are collected over an extended period of time, from several sites, or from multiple sources. It is also helpful in studies with evolving data. In all these circumstances, concurrent analysis enables you to gain insights into the data as they are being collected and to make any necessary changes to the research design or the data collection tool as the study goes on. It is important to note that although in some cases such interim and concurrent data analysis can be more thorough, most often it might be preliminary, and the purpose might be to identify preliminary patterns and themes, which can help with refining the research design or data collection methods. The focus could be on gaining insights into the data. Thus, if any coding happens it involves open coding, where you generate preliminary codes or categories which can be later refined or recategorized. Having said that, when exactly to begin the data analysis depends on the research question, the research goal, and the researcher's perspective. For some studies, you may even prefer to wait until the data collection is completed because you believe that it would be helpful to consider all the data at the same time, as it helps identify patterns more effectively and also makes the analysis more efficient.

Steps in Analyzing Qualitative Data

The ultimate goal of qualitative data analysis is to explore and understand participants' underlying meanings, attitudes, or what has shaped their behaviors, beliefs, and perspectives. This is typically done by a series of analytic activities that are used to examine the data and uncover the relevant and meaningful patterns, themes, and insights. There are several steps common to analyzing almost all qualitative data, including:

- data preparation
- data transcription
- data familiarization
- coding.

Data Preparation

The initial phase of qualitative data analysis involves data preparation, where raw data from various sources are organized, cleaned, and transformed into a suitable format. For example, if the raw data come from field notes, they may contain abbreviations or incomplete information. Therefore, you might need to clean them up by expanding or adding the missing details from your recollection. Starting this process soon after data collection enhances the readiness for analysis, enabling easier identification of patterns, themes, and relationships within the data.

Data preparation refers to the process through which the raw data, collected through various qualitative sources, are organized, cleaned, and changed to a form suitable for analysis.

POINTS TO PONDER

What are some of the limitations and issues that you may encounter when transcribing qualitative data, and what are some strategies that you can use to address those issues?

Data Transcription

In applied linguistics, transcription is important in most qualitative data analyses, especially for spoken data such as interviews and focus groups recorded in audio or video formats. Transcription transforms spoken text into a written form, facilitating analysis by identifying patterns and relationships.

Transcription is a process in analyzing data through which audio and video data are converted into written text, keeping its original meaning and the context in which it occurred as accurately as possible.

Of course, it is also possible to analyze qualitative data without transcription by analyzing it directly from observation or by simply listening to audio data or watching video recordings. Depending on the research purpose, some data, such as images, photographs, or other forms of non-verbal data, may not be transcribable. However, transcription remains beneficial in many cases.

There are a number of benefits for transcription. First and foremost, it offers a written representation of spoken data, making analysis more systematic and controlled. Transcribed data are also easier to process, especially when dealing with initially unstructured data, as it facilitates coding, categorization, and in-depth analysis.

In addition, there are a number of other advantages, including:

- **Improving accuracy:** Transcribing qualitative data can improve its accuracy in several ways. First, transcription provides a written record of the data that can be reviewed, edited, and corrected if needed, hence eliminating any possible errors that may have occurred during data collection.
- **Improving validity:** Transcription helps maintain accuracy in the representation of spoken language data, reducing the possibility of errors in coding and analysis. Because it is written, it can provide a more objective and reliable record of the data that can be used to validate findings and conclusions. It can also make it easier for other researchers to review and analyze the data, as they have a written record of the data that can be used to validate findings and conclusions. It can also be stored, shared, and compared with other datasets. These can all help to increase the validity of the results.

- **Improving consistency in the data:** Transcription can help maintain consistency in the data as you can review and edit the transcription to verify that all relevant information is captured and recorded in a consistent manner.
- **Increasing ease of accessibility and collaboration:** Transcription makes the data more accessible to a wider range of researchers, analysts, and stakeholders. It also makes it easier to share the data with other researchers and to work collaboratively on projects.

Steps in Transcribing Data

Data transcription typically involves the following steps:

- **Preparation:** The initial step in transcribing spoken data involves setting up essential equipment such as a computer, audio recording device, and, if available, transcription software. It is also important to check that the equipment functions properly. This stage also requires decisions on transcription specifics, including whether it will be verbatim, capture nonverbal cues, or adopt a normal orthography. Familiarizing yourself with the nature of the speech and its various aspects, such as accent, terminology, and topic, enhances the accuracy and ease of transcription.
- **Listening and transcribing:** At this stage you will listen to the audio or video data and transcribe them. For transcription, you can either listen and transcribe directly, or, if needed, you can listen first and take some notes and then transcribe them. When transcribing, it might be helpful or more efficient sometimes to use abbreviations, symbols, or keywords. But if you do so, it will be easier to understand them later if you turn them into meaningful representations immediately after the transcription.
- **Verifying:** The next step is verification, which is verifying the transcription against the spoken data. This is an important step, which entails comparing the transcribed text with the original audio or video recording and checking for accuracy to identify any errors or discrepancies.
- **Reviewing, editing, and finalizing:** The next stage is reviewing, editing, and cleaning up the transcribed data. At this stage, you will check the transcription for accuracy, clarity, and consistency. During this step, you review the transcribed data and make any necessary formatting corrections or clarifications. For example, if necessary, you can check any abbreviations, symbols, or keywords used to make sure that they are meaningfully represented in the data.

Limitations and Issues with Transcription

While transcribing data for analysis offers advantages, it comes with inherent challenges. Notably, transcription is a time-consuming and labor-intensive process. How long it will take depends on factors such as recording length and audio quality; large amounts of qualitative data or poor-quality audio will potentially take many hours or days. A fast transcriber may complete one hour of high-quality audio in two to three hours, but challenging content or technical language may extend this to four to six hours or more.

Transcription can involve some subjectivity, especially when the speech is unclear or requires interpretation. This influence can impact data accuracy. Additionally, the change in medium from spoken to written data during transcription may result in the loss of information relating to tone of voice, body language, and nonverbal cues, potentially leading to incomplete or inaccurate data. Strategies, such as checking, revising, and verifying transcripts against the original data, can help address some of these limitations.

If you need to transcribe, a few pieces of advice here would be:

a) Plan ahead and start transcribing the data as they come in, rather than letting them pile up.

b) Make sure that the audio is of high quality, as the quality of the audio can significantly impact the transcription time.

c) If needed, consider the help of a professional transcriber if that is possible and does not impact your data negatively. However, you should make sure that the transcriber is sufficiently trained in the topic and the goal of the research.

d) Consider collaborating with others by dividing the workload, particularly if you have a large amount of qualitative data to transcribe.

e) Consider using transcription software. There are currently various pieces of transcription software available that can automate the transcription process and reduce the time required. However, it is important to choose a software program that meets the specific needs of your project.

Selective Transcription

Sometimes you feel that you do not need to transcribe all your data in order to be able to answer your research questions. Selective transcription is a strategy in analyzing qualitative data whereby only a selected part of the data is transcribed and analyzed. This approach focuses on specific segments of the data that are deemed most relevant or important to the research question or objective. This means that you do not always need to transcribe all the data, and depending on the purpose of your research, you can choose to transcribe only certain parts of the video or audio data that are relevant and can exclude those that are irrelevant. The goal of selective transcription is to save time and resources while at the same time providing data that can be analyzed for meaningful insights. It can also be used to analyze specific themes or features that emerge while the data are being collected.

Selective transcription can be a useful strategy in many applied linguistics studies when the focus is on certain language features or aspects of interest. For example, in a study examining classroom discourse, you might be interested in the use of discourse markers by the students and the teacher, such as "*you know*," "*well*," "*so*," "*I mean*," or "*anyway*." You may choose to transcribe only instances of the use of such discourse features and exclude other parts of the conversation that do not contain those markers.

> **Selective transcription** is a strategy in analyzing qualitative data whereby only a selected part of the data is transcribed and analyzed.

Some Useful Transcription Programs

Transcription software programs are computer applications designed to transcribe audio or video recordings into written or typed text. There are several such programs available. Some popular ones include:

- **Express Scribe** (https://www.nch.com.au/scribe/): A professional transcription tool that supports various file formats (e.g., WAV, MP3) and features playback controls, foot pedal support, timestamps, and speaker identification. It integrates with speech recognition programs, though transcription still requires manual typing.
- **InqScribe** (https://www.inqscribe.com/): A user-friendly tool for transcribing audio and video files. It allows for easy playback control, time coding, and exporting in formats like PDF, HTML, and Microsoft Word. It also includes a built-in spell checker and speaker identification.
- **Transana** (https://www.transana.com/): A software program for organizing and analyzing qualitative data, including video and audio data. It supports transcription, coding, memo writing, and data visualization, making it useful for researchers in fields like sociology, anthropology, and applied linguistics.
- **Otter** (https://otter.ai/): A cloud-based tool that transcribes audio in real-time using AI. It provides accurate transcriptions with speaker identification and timestamps and allows for file export and collaboration. Otter also offers live captions and searchable transcripts.
- **Sonix** (https://sonix.ai/features): A cloud-based AI transcription tool supporting multiple languages. It provides accurate transcriptions with editing features and search functionality, making it ideal for transcribing diverse audio and video content.

These tools vary in features, but all enhance transcription efficiency, depending on your needs.

Data Familiarization

Once the data are transcribed, they can be analyzed. An important step before doing any systemic analysis would be data familiarization, also known as data immersion, which refers to familiarizing yourself with the data. This is an essential step as it helps to gain a general understanding of the data, which can be useful for the later identification of any initial patterns or themes. The aim at this stage is to develop an overall sense of the data and what it can tell us. This stage begins with reading and rereading through the data, including transcripts, field notes, or other qualitative data that have been collected as part of the study.

During the familiarization stage, you can also take notes and write down anything that comes to your mind that can help you to analyze the data as you continue reading. As noted before, this process is known as memoing (see Chapter 17). When doing these, it would be helpful to consider the research questions, the research design, the participants, and the data collection tools and methods. This will help your analysis to be in line with your research design and the context in which the data have been collected. It is also important to be neutral at this stage and approach the task with an open mind, without imposing your own biases or making any assumptions or presumption, about the data. These considerations will help with the accuracy of the coding, interpretations, and the conclusion drawn from the data. Altogether, the goal of the familiarization stage is to gain a general grasp of the data and to lay the groundwork for a meaningful analysis later on.

Data familiarization, also known as data immersion, refers to the process of gaining a general understanding of the data for a meaningful analysis later on.

POINTS TO PONDER

What challenges might you face when coding and categorizing qualitative data, and how do these challenges impact the overall quality of the analysis?

Coding

After the data have been transcribed, you can start coding the data. Coding is an important component of qualitative data analysis as it changes the data into a form that can be analyzed and interpreted. Codes are labels assigned to the chunk of text to capture its meaning. It can be a shorthand notation or a descriptive label that includes words or phrases to represent specific concepts within the data. Coding helps you to further identify patterns and themes in the data, enabling you to systematically organize and categorize the information. This process also helps reduce large amounts of data into manageable and organized units, making it easier to understand the raw data and analyze and interpret them in a meaningful way.

Coding refers to the process of reading and rereading the transcribed text and assigning labels (codes) to segments of text in order to categorize and organize the information for analysis.

The coding process can be performed manually or with the help of computer software.

Codes, Categories, and Themes

Codes are specific labels or identifiers that are assigned to pieces of information, often used in a systematic and standardized way. For example, in qualitative research on motivation, the code "enjoyment" may be used to code instances where the participant describes being motivated by their enjoyment of doing a language task or activity.

While codes are specific, categories are broader and are used to group information or codes that are similar or share common characteristics. For example, in the study mentioned above about motivation, you may categorize the codes into two broader categories: intrinsic motivation and extrinsic motivation. Each of these categories represents a different type of motivation that the participants may experience.

Themes refer to underlying patterns that emerge from data. They can refer to a recurring pattern or idea that emerges from the data and runs through a set of data. In that sense, a theme is a higher-level concept that represents a summary of the information gathered from the categories in the data. Themes are more abstract than codes and categories and reflect a higher-level understanding of the data. Example 16.1 presents a hypothetical scenario.

EXAMPLE 16.1

Suppose you are conducting a study on students' motivation, and you have collected the following data from a learner, which you want to code.

> I started learning French because most of my friends were taking French courses. Also, I decided to start learning French because I heard that it would look good on my resume and I can have an advantage in the job market. I know that speaking another language is also becoming more important in this world and helps you move up in your career.

In this example, the participant is expressing a specific reason that has influenced their motivation to learn French. The quote highlights the impact that peers can have on someone's motivation to learn a new language. So, it could be coded as "peer pressure." Of course, other labels may also be used, and they are all fine as long as they accurately capture the meaning underlying that segment.

The learner is also expressing the desire to learn French to increase their chances of getting a job or to make themselves more marketable for potential employers. Therefore, the code "job opportunities" can be used to capture those ideas.

The participant is also expressing how his desire to advance his career has motivated his decision to learn French. Therefore, the code "career advancement" can be used to capture the idea.

In the above example, "peer pressure," "job opportunities," and "career advancement" are specific codes assigned to that hypothetical piece of data gathered through an interview. These codes try to capture the specific reason why the learner is motivated to learn a language. These codes could be grouped into a category called "extrinsic motivation," because they all refer to motivation that comes from outside the learner. Then these codes and the category can be taken to be related to a theme like "social influence" as it highlights how external factors, such as societal or cultural norms, can impact a learner's motivation.

The theme of "social influence" represents a higher-level abstract concept that emerges from the data and summarizes the key findings from that segment, as shown in Figure 16.1. Of course, in this hypothetical example, the data might be too short to arrive at a theme, as a theme is an idea that runs through many segments or all of the data.

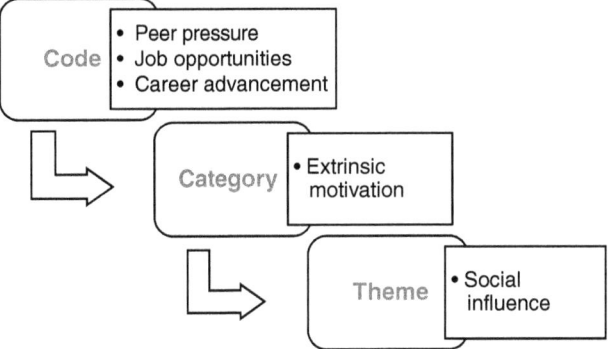

Figure 16.1 The relationship between code, category, and theme in Example 16.1

POINTS TO PONDER

What are the most common types of coding used in qualitative data analysis, and what are some strategies that you can use to ensure the quality of your coding?

Types of Coding

As noted above, coding is a data analysis technique in qualitative research that is used to identify the relevant information in the text and categorize the data into patterns and themes. There are a few layers of coding that researchers use when coding the data, each serving a specific purpose. These stages are open coding, axial coding, and selective coding (Figure 16.2). These three coding techniques are used particularly in grounded theory.

Open coding refers to the initial stage of breaking down the data into smaller segments. This process also involves reviewing these segments a number of times

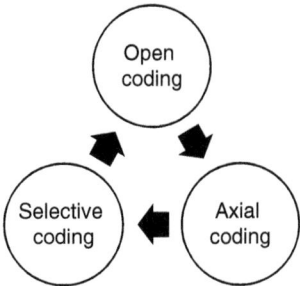

Figure 16.2 Types of coding

and generating initial codes so as to capture the essence of the segment. Axial coding refers to the process whereby the open codes generated are connected with each other to create higher-level relationships between them. This process involves grouping similar codes and organizing them into categories and exploring the connections between categories. Selective coding refers to the process of focusing on some key categories and codes that are most relevant to the research question and that capture the essence of the data. This process involves further refinement of the categories and codes and exploring in depth their higher-order relationships to identify the central themes and patterns running through the data.

Open coding is the initial stage of coding where data are segmented into smaller chunks and codes are assigned; **axial coding** connects codes and organizes them into categories; and **selective coding** is the final stage of coding where the most relevant codes and categories are used to identify overall themes and patterns.

Take Example 16.1 about motivation for language learning. In this example, all three stages of open coding, axial coding, and selective coding could be seen to be used. For example, in the open coding stage, we identified an individual quote (or passage) related to motivation and assigned codes to it: "peer pressure," "job opportunities," and "career advancement." In the axial coding stage, we then grouped and organize these codes into categories based on similarities or relationships between them. In this case we, identified "extrinsic motivation" as the best category to capture the relationship among the three specific codes. Finally, in the selective coding stage, we focused on the most relevant categories and codes, such as "extrinsic motivation," "career advancement," and "peer "pressure" and explored their relationships. This helped us to identify a central theme related to motivation running through that data. We called that theme "social influence."

It should be noted that the use of open coding, axial coding, and selective coding in the above example, which contains a small segment of data, is only for the purpose of illustration. However, in a qualitative study, these methods are used to analyze and organize data collected from the entire interview or dataset, leading to the development of a theory in grounded theory research. We will explain each of the three types of coding in more detail below.

Open Coding As noted above, coding is a data-driven descriptive process, involving segmenting the data into smaller, more manageable chunks and assigning codes or labels to each chunk. According to Strauss and Corbin (1998, p. 101), it is "the analytic process through which concepts are identified and their properties and dimensions are discovered in data." Open coding involves the following steps:

1. **Familiarization:** In this initial phase, you read through the data to familiarize yourself with the content. You recognize similarities, differences, and emerging concepts, gaining insights into potential patterns, themes, and relationships. Approach this task with an open mind to avoid preconceived notions, making notes of observed concepts or summaries for future reference during coding.

2. **Identifying segments**: The second step in open coding is to identify and break down data into smaller segments or chunks. The goal here is to make the data more manageable, which can then facilitate the coding process. When the data are broken down into smaller segments, it is easier to identify patterns and themes within each segment and assign codes to them. What size the segments should be depends on the nature of the data and the purpose of the research. For example, depending on the amount of data you have and their kind, you might decide to code the data line by line so that the segment can consist of individual sentences, or it could be a few sentences or even a paragraph. Sometimes the segment could even be individual words or phrases.

3. **Generating initial codes**: In this step, you assign descriptive codes to each data segment based on observed meanings. You categorize the data, identifying key concepts as you read through each segment multiple times. Note that initial codes may evolve and change during the coding and analysis process.

4. **Refining initial codes**: Step 4 in the open coding process is refining the codes generated so far. For this, you revisit the codes generated in Step 3 and make any necessary modifications so that they accurately reflect the intention and themes of the data. This refining and redefining is a continual process, and you will keep doing it as you continue to code and analyze the data.

5. **Evaluating existing codes**: The next step is to review and evaluate the codes you have generated so far to determine if they are appropriate or if any further or additional modifications are needed to improve their accuracy. This evaluation process necessitates that you can compare the already generated codes to the data and assess their accuracy and specificity. To do this, you will also compare the codes to each other and consider whether there are still any codes that need to be combined or grouped together to create more concise and comprehensive categories. Through this process of continually refining and evaluating the codes, you will be able to build a robust and well-rounded framework for analyzing and interpreting your data.

Example 16.2 illustrates the above steps.

EXAMPLE 16.2

Suppose you have conducted a focus group interview with a group of second language learners to explore their motivation for learning French as an L2. The discussion question you have asked them is:

"Can you describe your motivation to learn French?"

You have recorded the discussion and you have transcribed it.

The first step will be to read through the transcript to familiarize yourself with the data. Then you will start to divide the data into manageable segments. For example, suppose one of the segments you have identified is the following paragraph from one of the learners.

Well, I really enjoy learning French and I find it really satisfying when I gain new knowledge and skills in a new language. I also like the challenge of learning a new language. It is not an easy task, but it is a positive experience, and also enjoyable when you find ways to understand people. Also, I am learning it because I want to be able to communicate with my friends who live abroad and speak French. I have many of them and would like to be able to talk to them. I am also interested in learning about French culture and want to be able to travel to French-speaking countries and learn about their traditions.

You will then read this segment (a few times, if necessary) and then start assigning initial codes to the concepts you identify. Suppose on your initial reading of the first statement of this segment, you code it into "enjoying learning French." You may then refine it to capture the perspectives of the second language learners more accurately. Upon reading that paragraph, you may realize that the theme of that segment seems to be about learning language in general. So, you might refine the code to "enjoyment of learning." You continue coding, through which you generate the following codes for that segment:

- enjoyment of learning
- satisfaction from gaining new skills
- challenge of learning a new language
- communication with friends
- interest in culture
- traveling
- learning about traditions.

You will then evaluate and combine codes as needed so that they are comprehensive enough. For example, you might decide to combine the following two codes "enjoyment of learning" and "satisfaction from gaining new skills" into "learner enjoyment and satisfaction." You will recode "challenge of learning a new language" into "challenge seeking and personal development" (as the learner suggested that the challenges are a good thing), and also combine "communication with friends" and "interest in culture" into "interpersonal communication and cultural interest." You will combine "traveling" and "learning about traditions" into "cultural exposure and exploration." So, the final codes derived for that segment would be:

- learner enjoyment and satisfaction
- challenge seeking and personal development
- interpersonal communication and cultural interest
- cultural exposure and exploration.

These codes help to organize and simplify the data, making it easier to understand the experiences and motivations of the participants. The grouping can also help you to see how the different motivations are related, and how they may interact with each other.

As noted earlier, the final stage of open coding is refinement of codes. Here you will review and refine the codes to make sure that they accurately reflect the participants' motivations. So, during this stage, you might decide to recode "challenge seeking and personal development" to "cognitive growth." You might feel that one of these two better captures the participant's meaning and could be a better label for the theme of a learner who is motivated by the challenges of learning a new language. You may also recode "cultural interest" to "cultural immersion" as this seems to better capture the motivation of a learner who is interested in learning about the culture and tradition of a group.

Through using open coding, in Example 16.2, we have gained some insights into the perspectives of this second language learner's motivation for language learning.

Axial Coding Axial coding is the next step after the open coding, and its purpose is to develop relationships between the initial codes and categories that emerge during the open coding, in order to capture the essence of the data at a higher and more abstract level. During the open coding phase, the data are segmented into discrete parts, which are closely examined to identify concepts by using specific codes and then combining them into some respective categories. In axial coding, we move up one step and attempt to reorganise the already specified open coded data into more abstract conceptual categories. This involves relating codes to each other and linking the codes generated from open coding to create connections between them in order to form a higher-level conceptual framework. The reason this stage is called axial coding is that it is a systematic categorization of data along specific dimensions or categories (referred to as "axes") and the assignment of codes or labels to the data based on these categories. Thus, axial coding is a method of categorizing and identifying patterns in the data being analyzed.

Axial coding is an important concept in grounded theory, a qualitative research method that involves creating theories from data by inductively identifying themes and constantly comparing them within the data in order to build a theoretical framework from the data. As Strauss (1998, p. 109) noted, in this theory, "[a]xial coding identifies relationships between open codes, for the purpose of developing core codes. Major (core) codes emerge as aggregates of the most closely interrelated (or overlapping) open codes for which supporting evidence is strong." This process can also be used in other qualitative research whose aim is develop a conceptual and thematic understanding of the data.

Selective Coding Selective coding is the next phase in the data coding after the axial coding. It is also a coding method used in grounded theory, but this phase is also used in many other types of qualitative data analysis, particularly thematic analysis. It involves the process of selecting, focusing, and categorizing data in a systematic manner to identify higher-order patterns and themes. Axial coding, which was discussed earlier, concerns linking concepts and categories identified through open coding, helping to see how the different codes and concepts identified in the data relate to one another, and how they contribute to the development of categories. Selective coding is the process of categorizing data into yet higher-level themes based on recurring patterns and relationships among categories. It continues the process of axial coding "at a higher level of abstraction through actions that lead to an elaboration or formulation of the story of the case" (Flick, 2009, p. 310). A theme here refers to the overarching idea or concept that runs throughout the data. Themes capture the essence of the data and represent the underlying structure of the information in a given study. Themes are often more abstract and broader than categories. A category is a more specific way of organizing the data and is a way of grouping similar data elements or codes together. In qualitative data analysis, themes and categories can represent different levels of abstraction in the data analysis. Themes capture the overarching concepts, while categories provide a more specific way of grouping and organizing the data.

Selective coding, as described above, is a specific method used in grounded theory to identify and categorize data into concepts and themes in a systematic manner. The aim of selective coding is to develop a theory from the collected data and to identify the core concepts and themes that provide insights into the research question. In a thematic analysis, the process might stop here, but in the grounded theory, this phase eventually leads to development of theories from the collected data. In grounded theory, selective coding involves the selection of the most relevant data and the formation of a core theme, which becomes the focus of further analysis. Thus, selective coding allows you to bring coherence to the data, providing structure for your analysis and facilitating insights into the research question.

Figure 16.3 shows the relationships between the three levels or phases of coding.

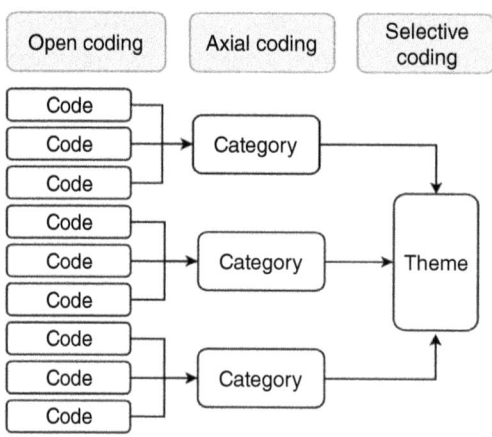

Figure 16.3 The relationships between the three levels of coding

Example 16.3 is a hypothetical scenario involving open coding, followed by axial and selective coding, as illustrated in Figure 16.4.

EXAMPLE 16.3

Suppose you are conducting a study with a group of English L2 learners. The participants were interviewed about their reasons for learning English. Their motivations were diverse and are reported in the interview transcripts, which have been analyzed using open, axial, and selective coding. Brackets indicate the codes assigned to specific segment of their transcripts during the open coding (see also Table 16.1).

In my opinion, learning English is not just about acquiring a new language, it's about gaining access to new opportunities [new prospects]. I've always seen it as a way to expand my experiences, both personally and professionally [self-improvement]. For example, I want to be able to travel to English-speaking countries [travel] and communicate with ease [communication skills] and learn about their cultures and tradition [cultural exposure]. I want to be able to communicate with people from all over the world [global connection]. And I want to improve my career by working with people from all over the world, so being able to speak English fluently is a must [career progress]. I also hope to study abroad in an English-speaking country one day [educational opportunities] and work for an international company [work opportunities].

Table 16.1 Segments and their associated codes in Example 16.3

Segment	Codes
In my opinion, learning English is not just about acquiring a new language, it's about gaining access to new opportunities.	New prospects
I've always seen it as a way to expand my experiences, both personally and professionally.	Self-improvement
For example, I want to be able to travel to English-speaking countries	Travel
and communicate with ease	Communication skills
and learn about their cultures and tradition.	Cultural exposure
I want to be able to communicate with people from all over the world.	Global connection
And I want to improve my career by working with people from all over the world, so being able to speak English fluently is a must.	Career progress
I also hope to study abroad in an English-speaking country one day	Educational opportunities
and work for an international company.	Work opportunities

Axial coding organizes initial codes into categories based on similarities, differences, and relationships. From the open codes above, the following categories can be derived:

- **Cultural and educational opportunities**: Includes "cultural exposure," "education opportunities," and "travel," highlighting opportunities that enhance cultural understanding and intellectual growth.

- **Personal growth:** Includes "self-improvement," "communication skills," and "global connections," focusing on individual development and social networks.
- **Professional aspirations:** Includes "work opportunities," "career progress," and "new prospects," emphasizing professional advancement.

Selective coding identifies the overarching theme: **Personal and professional growth.** This theme reflects how exposure to cultural, educational, and work-related opportunities fosters both personal development and career advancement.

All of this is depicted in Figure 16.4, which shows the relationships between the codes, categories, and the central theme derived from Example 16.3.

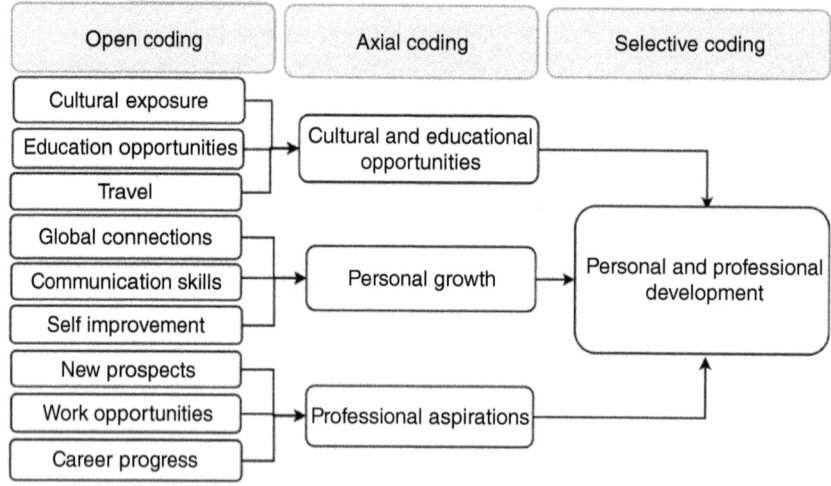

Figure 16.4 The relationship between codes, categories, and themes in Example 16.3

The Use of a Codebook

When coding, it might be helpful to have a codebook, which can be used to list and define the codes or categories that you come up with when coding and categorizing the data. A codebook can be a very useful tool in helping with the quality and accuracy of the data analysis, providing a systematic approach that helps improve the consistency of the coding. It also allows you to trace your decisions and the reasoning behind them. In addition, it also helps others do the analysis or use it for future analysis.

A codebook is a tool to list and define the codes or categories that you come up with when coding and categorizing the data.

A codebook can include the kind of information shown in Table 16.2, which is illustrated with examples.

Data-Driven versus Theory-Driven Coding

There are generally two approaches to coding the data in qualitative data analysis: data-driven and theory-driven coding. Data-driven coding is a process of coding

Table 16.2 Components of a codebook

Information	Definition	Example
Code name	The descriptive label used to code the data	"Positive feedback"
Code definition	A clear and concise definition of the code, including any relevant contextual information that can help understand its meaning	Statements made by the teachers indicating their satisfaction the students' work
Examples	Examples of the type of data that was coded using this code	"This essay is very well done! I am very happy with how it has been written."
Notes	Any relevant information that can help with using the code, such as when to use it or how to distinguish it from similar or overlapping codes.	Since the data segment shows praise for what has been written, it was coded as "positive feedback."

based on the concepts that emerge from the data rather than predefined categories. This approach is iterative, involving reading and rereading the data, and identifying themes and patterns as they emerge from the data. In this approach the data drive the analysis, hence data-driven. Data-driven coding is also a cyclical and flexible process in which you continuously refine the analysis to gain a deeper insight of the data. Because data-driven coding begins with the data, it is often considered a bottom-up approach. In a bottom-up approach, the analysis begins with the data and works its way up to the development of higher-level concepts and interpretations.

Theory-driven coding, also known as concept-driven or predetermined coding, is a method of coding in which the codes or categories are established prior to the data analysis. In this approach, the concepts or themes are preexisting; they may come from previous research, some theoretical framework, or prior knowledge and experience, and they are imposed on the data. Therefore, this approach is top-down. In this approach, you have a clear idea of what you are looking for in the data, and thus search the data for those pieces of information. The aim is often to test specific hypotheses or compare results to previous studies.

Data-driven coding is a process of coding based on the concepts that emerge from the data rather than predefined categories. **Theory-driven coding,** also known as concept-driven or pre-determined coding, is a method of coding in which the codes or categories are established prior to the data analysis.

Both the data-driven and theory-driven approaches have their own strengths and limitations, and the choice of which one to use will depend on the research question, goals, and the nature of the data. The advantages of the data-driven approach include the following:

- It helps discover new insights.
- It is flexible, allowing you to constantly refine the analysis of the data to gain a deeper understanding of the data.
- It produces less biased results because in this approach the data drive the analysis, rather than predefined categories, frameworks, or the researcher's perspectives steering the analysis.

Some limitations include the following:

- It is time-consuming.
- It is unstructured, which can make coding challenging and comparisons across studies difficult.
- It relies on the researcher's interpretation, and because of this, different researchers may interpret the data differently, and this can make drawing conclusions and the comparison of the results with other studies more difficult.

The theory-driven approach also has some advantages and limitations. Some of the advantages are as follows:

- It is consistent as the data are analyzed using the same codes and categories.
- It is efficient as the codes are preexisting; this reduces the time required to analyze the data.
- It makes the comparison across studies using the same codes easy and possible.

Some of the limitations include the following:

- It is inflexible, which may then reduce the ability to code all the data, as it does not allow for the emergence of new themes or insights.
- It can introduce bias. The predetermined categories may be influenced by the researcher's biases or assumptions in selecting the codes and categories, potentially leading to a biased interpretation of the data.

Quantification of Qualitative Data

Quantification of qualitative data refers to the process of converting qualitative nonnumerical data into numerical form. This process is often used in order to analyze and compare the data using statistical techniques. Example 16.4 presents a hypothetical situation.

EXAMPLE 16.4

Suppose you have conducted a questionnaire study to gather learners' opinions on a certain corrective feedback strategy. In that questionnaire, you have asked them the following open-ended question: "How useful do you find direct error correction in which the teacher provides you with the correct language form?" Possible responses include:

A. Not useful at all
B. Slightly useful
C. Moderately useful
D. Useful
E. Very useful
F. Exceptionally useful

To quantify this qualitative data, you could assign numerical values to each response, such as

Not useful at all = 1
Slightly useful = 2
Moderately useful = 3
Useful = 4
Very useful = 5
Exceptionally useful = 6

Now that you have converted these text-type responses to numerical values, you can perform various statistical analyses on the data. You can, for example, calculate the mean or median and compare the results across different groups of participants. You can create tables and graphs to visually present the data.

Inter- and Intracoder Reliability in Qualitative Data Analysis

As discussed in Chapter 11, interrater or intercoder reliability, measures the consistency and agreement between different raters or coders. It is a numerical measure of the consistency and agreement between raters or coders.

At least two coders are needed for intercoder reliability, and while having more can enhance robustness, practical considerations such as resources, time, and training complexities should be considered. The number of coders, therefore. Depends on the available resources as well as the specific research qoals.

To assess intercoder reliability, it is not always necessary for coders to code all the data. Selecting a sample sometimes suffices. A common question often asked here is what percentage of the data should be chosen for the purpose of intercoder reliability. The percentage of data chosen varies, and there is no set standard. Some researchers may consider recoding 10–30 percent of the data, while others may recode a larger sample. The size of the sample of data selected depends on various factors including the amount of the data itself, the complexity of the coding, and the level of agreement desired.

In qualitative research, intercoder reliability is not the only method for evaluating the reliability of the coding. Another method, as noted before, is intracoder reliability, which evaluates the consistency of a single coder's classification of the data. In this method, the reliability is assessed by having the same coder code the whole or a sample of the data twice, with an appropriate time interval between the two codings. The level of agreement between the two codings is then assessed to determine the intracoder reliability.

Both intercoder and intracoder reliability can be assessed through several methods, including percentage agreement and Cohen's kappa (see Chapter 11).

Intercoder versus Interrater Reliability

Intercoder reliability and interrater reliability are two important concepts in qualitative research that are often used interchangeably. But it is important to note these two are not exactly the same. Interrater reliability refers to the process of calculating reliability among raters, whereas intercoder reliability refers to the process of calculating the reliability among coders. Although rating and coding are related concepts, they are different in that rating concerns assigning numerical values to data based on a set of predetermined criteria, whereas coding concerns categorizing and labeling qualitative nonnumerical data, such as text, into concepts and themes. Rating is often used when the raters rate their level of agreement with a statement on certain scales. Coding is used in more open-ended qualitative studies, such as those involving interviews and focus groups, where you have transcribed the data and then code and categorize them into certain emerging themes and concepts. Most qualitative analyses involve coding, and therefore intercoder reliability is the more common approach used in qualitative research.

Caveats

Intercoder reliability in qualitative research is a subject of debate, with varying perspectives on its necessity and the acceptable level of agreement among coders. Some argue for its importance in ensuring coding robustness, while others contend that it can affect creativity and flexibility. Critics question its suitability for qualitative research, which values subjective experiences and an interpretive perspective.

The level of agreement between coders is another point of contention. While some advocate for high agreement levels, others suggest that a certain degree of discrepancy is acceptable and even desirable, reflecting the inherent complexity and diverse perspectives present in qualitative data.

These debates highlight the subjective nature of qualitative research and the difficulties in establishing definitive standards for reliability and validity. Despite controversies, intercoder reliability remains a widely used tool in applied linguistics research, particularly when we want to make sure that the findings are not solely dependent on the subjective judgment or interpretation of an individual coder or the researcher.

POINTS TO PONDER

What is content analysis, and how is it different from thematic analysis? Can you provide examples of situations or research questions where content analysis might be particularly suitable?

Common Methods of Qualitative Data Analysis

All qualitative studies involve qualitative data that should be analyzed. There are different methods or approaches to qualitative data analysis. Some common methods include content analysis, thematic analysis, conversation analysis, and grounded theory. In terms of coding the data, there are some differences among these methods. To understand the differences, it can be useful to think of them on a continuum, with some methods being more structured and others being more open-ended (Figure 16.5).

For example, content analysis can be considered to be the most structured of methods of analysis; it involves categorizing and coding the data into specific categories and then quantifying them for the purpose of knowing the frequency or their relationship. Thematic analysis and grounded theory, on the other hand, can be considered to be more open-ended and inductive, as they involve inducing patterns and themes from the data, and eventually grounded theory will often lead to constructing a theory from the data. Conversation analysis can fall somewhere between content analysis and thematic and grounded theory as it includes a combination of both the inductive process of coding naturalistic data into emerging categories and themes and also sometimes converting the qualitative data into quantitative data for the purpose of comparison.

It is important to note, however, that in practice these methods are not very distinct and mutually exclusive. They can also be used in combination. For example, you may start with a more structured method such as content analysis and then move towards a more open-ended approach such as discourse analysis as the analysis progresses. We will explain each in more detail below.

Content Analysis

Content analysis is a method of qualitative data analysis that is used to identify patterns and meanings in any textual data. The focus is on analyzing the content of any written and spoken text or any visual material. Content analysis typically involves a more structured approach to coding and categorizing than other qualitative data analysis approaches. An important distinguishing feature of content analysis is the quantification of the qualitative data, and calculating and tabulating the frequency of occurrence of the features, categories, or any other content-related aspects of the text that have been analyzed. The analysis can be on any written or spoken text or document including essays, articles, textbooks, newspapers, TV news, speeches, website, advertisements, or social-media posts. It involves coding and categorizing various elements of the text and interpreting patterns and trends in the data. Content analysis involves the following steps:

1. **Selecting the content to be analyzed:** This includes decisions about the type of content to be analyzed, such as essays, news articles, social-media posts, or

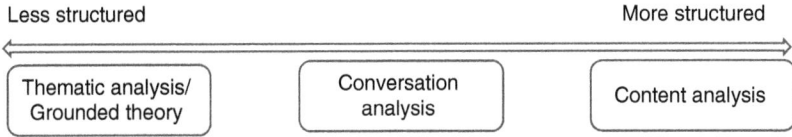

Figure 16.5 Methods of qualitative data analysis

textbooks, and also the sample of content to be analyzed. The sample can be either a purposive sample or a random sample. At this stage, decisions should also be made about transcribing any audio or video content and making the content ready for analysis. Before analyzing the content, it is also important to make sure that the content is of good quality and relevant to the research question.

2. **Defining the unit of analysis or segments of the text to be coded:** This involves breaking the text into smaller units for analysis The unit of analysis is the smallest section of text that can be meaningfully analyzed. This selection often depends on the research question and the type of content. For example, if the goal is to analyze the reaction of students to specific classroom instruction in social-media posts, the unit of analysis might be the students' individual post. However, if the goal is to analyze the representation of a certain language structure in students' essays, the unit of analysis might be the sentence or paragraph. Segmenting the text into smaller chunks makes it easier to apply the coding scheme and to analyze the content in a more systematic and reliable manner.

3. **Developing a coding scheme or system for coding the data:** The coding scheme or categories should be directly related to the purpose of the study and the goal of the analysis. For example, if the purpose is to examine the use and representation of specific cultures in a language textbook, the coding categories should include those cultures. At this stage, a decision should also be made about how to code the content: whether the manner of coding will be data-driven or theory-driven. If it is theory-driven, it would be helpful to make sure that the coding can be reliably used. A helpful strategy would be to code a small sample of the data and check for the consistency of the coding. You can then make any changes to the coding system based on this testing.

4. **Coding the content:** At this stage, you start coding the data by applying the coding scheme developed in the previous step. You code the content by reading the content and making judgments about which code or categories should be assigned to each piece of content.

5. **Checking the reliability of the coding:** This step is important to make sure that the results of the coding and the analysis are reliable. This can be done by checking the intercoder or intracoder reliability of the coding. The intercoder reliability can be done by having a second coder independently code a sample of the content and check for consistency and agreement using measures such as Cohen's kappa, and the intracoder reliability can be done by the same coder coding a sample of the data at another time (see the previous section and Chapter 11).

6. **Recording the results:** This step concerns recording the results of the coding in a structured manner; for example, by using a spreadsheet or database to facilitate further analysis and interpretation.

7. **Analyzing the results of the coding to draw conclusions:** At this stage, you will summarize the results of the coding; for example, by calculating the frequency

or percentage of each category, identifying any patterns and trends, and interpreting the results in light of the research question.

8. **Reporting the results:** Finally, you will write a report of the content analysis, describing the research question, the methods used, the results of the coding, any patterns and trends identified, and the conclusions drawn from the analysis. The purpose of this step is to communicate the results to a wider community or audience including researchers, practitioners, or any other stakeholders.

It is important to note that the exact procedures involved in content analysis depend on the specific goals and methodologies of the content analysis, but the above steps can provide a general overview of the procedure. Example 16.5 presents a hypothetical scenario that illustrates the application of content analysis.

EXAMPLE 16.5

Suppose you are conducting a study on the use of certain grammatical structures, such as passive and active sentences, in students' academic essays. You may collect a sample of academic essays written by students on a specific topic and use the content analysis techniques to identify patterns in the use of those structures. This could include coding and counting the number of instances of passive and active constructions as they occur in the essay, analyzing their frequency, and identifying the various contexts in which they have been used. You may then compare the use and distribution of those structures across different essays written by different students, showing them using graphs and tables. Depending on the purpose of the study, you could also analyze when and where the students have used these constructions accurately or erroneously. The results of such content analysis could provide insight into when and how students use a specific language structure in their writing, identifying their strengths and weaknesses in this area. The findings of such a study could provide important implications for written language instruction and research.

Advantages and Limitations of Content Analysis

One advantage of content analysis is that collection of data can be relatively simple and straightforward, especially if the data already exist in a written or oral form. Another advantage is that the analysis can be considered highly objective as it relies on systematic coding, categorization, and identification of data. The clarity of the coding and the possibility of conducting intercoder reliability can also reduce the potential for subjective interpretation. Compared to other types of qualitative analysis, content analysis is fairly straightforward, allowing you to analyze a large amount of data. The findings of content analysis are often generalizable only to the specific data analyzed and cannot be automatically applied to other contexts. Content analysis provides an overview of the data and hence may not provide a detailed and in-depth understanding of the meaning and context in which the data occurred.

Thematic Analysis

Thematic analysis is another widely used qualitative research method. This approach to data analysis concerns the identification and analysis of patterns or themes in data, typically from interviews, focus groups, or written texts. The approach is inductive and much less structured than content analysis. It is called thematic because the data are analyzed by theme.

An important difference between content analysis and thematic analysis is that content analysis does not go beyond specific codes and categories. In terms of the levels of coding involved, content analysis may involve the open coding and axial coding levels only. In thematic analysis, selective coding is an important layer of coding, which involves the process of identifying the most important and relevant themes in the data. Also, in content analysis, the data are often coded into categories based on predetermined coding schemes, and the frequency of each category is counted.

Content analysis, as just noted, does not involve selective coding as thematic analysis, as the focus is more on counting and categorizing the data rather than identifying and interpreting the underlying themes and perspectives of participants. In thematic analysis, the coding does not come from outside, and it is not imposed upon the data. Content analysis can involve both a data-driven manner of coding and a concept-driven approach, where the codes and categories can come from the literature. In thematic analysis, the themes and patterns are derived from the data, and the data collection and analysis take place simultaneously. That is why thematic analysis is more open-ended and qualitative in nature. Table 16.3 shows the main differences between thematic analysis and content analysis:

Table 16.3 Differences between thematic analysis and content analysis

Thematic analysis	Content analysis
Focuses on inductively identifying and interpreting themes and patterns regarding the participants' experiences and perspectives	Focuses on the frequency and patterns related to various textual and nontextual elements in a specific content
Can be used on a variety of qualitative data sources, such as interviews, focus group discussions, and field notes	Is typically used to analyze written or oral texts, such as articles, reports, or advertisements, news, etc.
Involves coding the data, identifying the relationships between and among codes, organizing them into categories and then into overarching themes	Involves coding the data, identifying the relationships between and among codes and organizing them into categories and counting the frequency of codes and categories
Provides an in-depth qualitative understanding and insights into the participants' experiences and opinions	Provides a quantitative analysis of patterns of specific categories in the data

Conversation Analysis

Conversation analysis, as discussed in Chapter 14, is a qualitative research method that focuses on the examination of the structure and organization of talk in interaction through identifying and understanding the conversational practices and routines that people use to accomplish their communicative goals. This method is used to analyze recorded or transcribed talking in its natural setting to discover its underlying rules and patterns. The steps used in conversation analysis are similar to those for other qualitative research, but there are also differences as to the nature of the data to be analyzed. For example, the transcription used for the purpose of conversation analysis should be detailed and verbatim, including all the elements that relate to interaction including pauses, overlapping speech, and other features of the interaction. Referred to as "micro-level features," these elements of the interaction are sometimes important to be captured in the transcription as they provide valuable information about the structure and organization of the talk or conversation. Pauses, for example, can indicate uncertainty, hesitation, or a change in the direction of the conversation. Overlapping speech can show how turns are negotiated. They can reveal important information about the timing and ordering of the interaction and how they are used to exchange information.

The data analysis in conversation analysis is highly systematic and structured and relies on detailed examination of the interaction patterns and communication strategies used by the participants. As far as its place on the continuum of qualitative data analysis is concerned, conversation analysis falls towards the middle of the spectrum.

Advantages and Limitations of Conversation Analysis

The data analysis in conversation analysis is fairly systematic and structured and relies on detailed examination of the interaction patterns and communication strategies used by the participants. It may therefore involve quantification of the data: for example, counting the number of turns by participants, measuring the duration of specific speech elements, or analyzing the frequency of specific conversational features. One limitation is that it requires specialized skills, including a strong understanding of conversation analysis techniques and a thorough knowledge of the data, particularly the conversational features being analyzed.

Grounded Theory

Grounded theory is another qualitative research method that is widely used in applied linguistics research. As discussed in Chapter 14, the goal of grounded theory is to develop a theory that is grounded in the data. The theory is developed inductively from the data through a process of constant comparison, where patterns and relationships are identified and refined as the analysis progresses. It is achieved by iteratively collecting data, coding it, and using the codes to develop categories and concepts that capture the underlying patterns and relationships in the data. The ultimate aim is thus to produce a theoretical explanation that is grounded in the participants' experiences and understandings rather than imposed from outside.

The three layers of coding discussed earlier (open coding, axial coding, and selective coding) are all important stages in the process of developing grounded theory. The theory is developed from these three stages, generating an explanation that is grounded in and consistent with the data.

Conclusion

Qualitative data analysis is a step in the qualitative research process. Its effective application requires a systematic examination and interpretation of nonnumerical data, such as interview transcripts, field notes, and audio recordings. In this chapter, we have provided an overview of qualitative data analysis, including its definition, purpose, and methods. We have discussed the important topic of data preparation in qualitative research and have also covered issues related to data transcription and how it can be done. The chapter also discussed different types of coding, including open, axial, and selective coding, as well as the quantification of qualitative data. Finally, the chapter covered coding in common methods of qualitative data analysis, such as content analysis, thematic analysis, conversation analysis, and grounded theory. Altogether, the chapter has provided a through discussion and description of the various processes and steps in analyzing qualitative data. In Part V, we focus on quantitative data analysis, starting with descriptive statistics and then moving onto inferential statistics and the various concepts and issues associated with such analyses. However, before that, the next chapter will explore reliability and validity in qualitative research.

DISCUSSION AND ACTIVITY QUESTIONS

Discussion Questions

1. How do personal biases and preconceptions impact the process of qualitative data analysis in applied linguistics?
2. What challenges might arise when trying to balance the subjective nature of qualitative analysis with the need for rigor and reliability?
3. In your opinion, what is the significance of data familiarization? How can it impact the quality of the results?
4. When should you start analyzing your qualitative data, and what are some factors you need to consider when making this decision?
5. How would you distinguish between open coding, axial coding, and selective coding? How are these coding methods typically used in qualitative data analysis?
6. How does the choice of coding method (e.g., data-driven vs. theory-driven) affect the depth and flexibility of the data analysis? What are the trade-offs between these two approaches?
7. What are the key characteristics of content analysis, and in what research contexts would this method be most effective?
8. What is conversation analysis, and how is it different from grounded theory?

Activity Questions

1. Choose a qualitative research article in applied linguistics and identify the types of coding used in the study. Compare and contrast the advantages and disadvantages of the coding types.

2. In a group of two or three, discuss the importance of data preparation and transcription in qualitative data analysis. Identify some of the key challenges you may face during these processes and brainstorm potential solutions.

3. Transcribe a five-minute segment of an audio or video file provided to you by your instructor or to which you have access. Identify any challenges or difficulties you encountered during the transcription process and discuss how you addressed them. Finally, reflect on what you learned from this practice and how it contributed to your understanding of the processes and challenges involved in transcribing the data.

4. Select a qualitative research study in applied linguistics that includes some form of quantification in the data analysis process, such as frequency counts or coding schemes. Identify and discuss the benefits and limitations of the approach used. What strategies did the study use to confirm that the quantification of qualitative data is accurate and reliable? Present your analysis to the class, focusing on the data analysis section of the article and what you learned from this analysis.

5. Choose two qualitative research articles in applied linguistics that include different forms of data analysis: content analysis and thematic analysis. Analyze and compare the approaches and discuss how each contributes to the overall analysis process and our understanding of the research question. Also identify any limitations you encountered in the analysis and discuss strategies that you would use to overcome these limitations. Finally, present your analysis and findings to the class.

17 Understanding and Establishing Reliability and Validity in Qualitative Research

CHAPTER OBJECTIVES

After completing this chapter, you should be able to

- Explain the importance of reliability and validity in qualitative research.
- Understand the differences between reliability and validity in qualitative research compared to quantitative research.
- Assess credibility, transferability, dependability, and confirmability as measures of reliability in qualitative research.
- Identify techniques for ensuring reliability and validity in qualitative research, such as member checking, prolonged engagement, and triangulation.

Introduction

In Chapters 11 and 12, we discussed the role of reliability and validity in quantitative research. The aim of this chapter is to provide an overview of the notions of reliability and validity in qualitative research. As noted in Chapter 12, in quantitative research, reliability refers to the consistency of a measurement or the study. For example, if a test is reliable, it should give the same results if it is administered multiple times to the same group of people. In contrast, validity refers to the extent to which a measure accurately measures what it is supposed to measure. In qualitative research, reliability and validity take on different meanings. Reliability refers to the consistency of the researcher's observations and interpretations, while validity refers to the credibility and trustworthiness of the data. In this chapter, we will discuss the role and importance of these concepts in qualitative research and also explore various techniques that you can use to enhance the reliability and validity of your qualitative studies. Throughout the chapter, we will also provide examples to illustrate how these concepts can be used and interpreted.

POINTS TO PONDER

Why is it important to consider both reliability and validity in qualitative research? How do you distinguish between reliability and validity in qualitative research? In determining reliability and validity in qualitative applied linguistics research, what specific obstacles or constraints do you think researchers might encounter, and how might these challenges be addressed?

The Issue of Reliability and Validity in Qualitative Research

As discussed earlier, qualitative research can be broadly defined as a kind of inquiry that is naturalistic and deals with nonnumerical data. It seeks to understand and explore rather than to explain and manipulate variables. It is contextualized and interpretive, emphasizing the process or patterns of development rather than the product or outcome of the research. Similar to quantitative research, good qualitative research is also robust, well informed, and thoroughly validated. Although naturalistic and interpretive, qualitative research is also systematic, involving a careful process of identifying the problem, collecting, analyzing, explaining, evaluating, and interpreting the data. Thus, when doing qualitative research, it is essential to maintain its rigor and quality as well as its reliability and validity.

Similar to quantitative research, **good qualitative research** is also robust, well informed, and thoroughly validated.

As noted earlier, in quantitative research, reliability is defined as a measure to assess the consistency of results over time, and validity refers to the degree to which a study measures what it claims to measure. However, the notions of reliability and validity in qualitative research can be both contentious and challenging issues. In quantitative research, it can be said that it is easier to establish validity because quantitative research relies on arguably objective measurements and statistical analysis, which can be more easily replicated and verified. Additionally, the methods used in quantitative research are more standardized, making it easier for the study to be conducted in a consistent manner.

In qualitative research, however, establishing reliability and validity can be more complex and challenging because of a number of reasons. First the methods used in qualitative research, such as observation and interviews, are open-ended and subjective, and they are not as standardized as quantitative methods. The subjective nature of qualitative data can make it difficult to establish the credibility and trustworthiness of the findings. Determining validity in qualitative research can also be challenging because it often relies on an insider perspective; that is, the researcher's interpretation and understanding of the data. This can lead to multiple perspectives and interpretations of the same data, making it difficult to establish a clear and consistent understanding of the findings. Researchers' own biases can also affect the interpretation of the data. Qualitative and quantitative research are also based on different epistemological assumptions about what knowledge is and how it can be defined. Because of such differences between qualitative and quantitative research and the complexities involved in the former, some researchers have disagreed on using the notions used in quantitative research to describe validity and reliability in qualitative research.

However, despite challenges, similar to quantitative research, reliability and validity are key aspects of the qualitative research design and analysis. Since qualitative research is based on subjective data and open to interpretation, it is essential to ensure that findings are credible and accurately reflect participants' experiences and perspectives. Given that such research often addresses sensitive and complex issues, attention to reliability and validity becomes particularly important. As a result, numerous strategies have been proposed to establish the trustworthiness of findings in qualitative research.

Because of the differences in the aims and methods of the research, reliability and validity in qualitative research are not defined in the same way as those in quantitative research. For example, in qualitative research, the goal is often to understand the subjective ideas and perspectives of participants, and thus validity means demonstrating that the findings accurately represent those realities. In quantitative research, the goal is often to test hypotheses or generalize about a population, thus validity is considered to be established by demonstrating that a study measures what it claims to measure. For the same reasons, the methods and criteria proposed to establish reliability and validity are different in the two types of research. And for those reasons, researchers have proposed other terms to use when discussing these notions in qualitative research (Lincoln and Guba, 1985; Onwuegbuzie & Johnson, 2006). Lincoln and Guba (1985), for example, while emphasizing "trustworthiness" as an important aspect of qualitative research, argued that this term should replace the notions of validity and reliability in quantitative research.

As noted earlier, the notions of reliability and validity in quantitative research have always been used in relation to consistency and accuracy of tests or measurements used. Lincoln and Guba stated that in qualitative research, these notions should be used to address the question of "How can an inquirer persuade his or her audiences that the research findings of an inquiry are worth paying attention to?" (1985, p. 290). Lincoln and Guba discussed four such trustworthiness principles, which have been accepted and considered important by many qualitative researchers. These include credibility, transferability, dependability, and confirmability, which have been considered parallel substitutions for the conventional notions of internal validity, external validity, reliability, and objectivity used in quantitative research (Figure 17.1). I will briefly discuss these principles below.

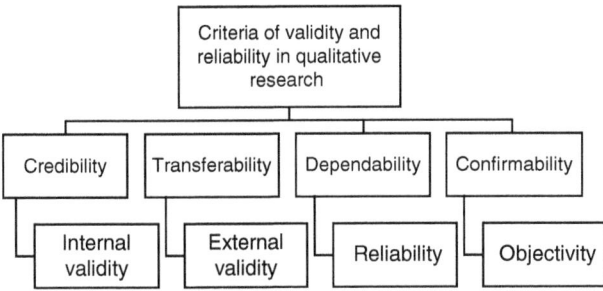

Figure 17.1 Validity and reliability in qualitative research

Credibility

The principle of credibility in qualitative research concerns the extent to which the research findings and conclusions can be viewed to be believable. In other words, it concerns the truthfulness and believability of the research findings and is similar to the concept of internal validity in quantitative research.

There are a number of strategies that can be used to enhance credibility, which will be discussed in detail below.

Credibility in qualitative research concerns the extent to which the research findings and conclusions can be viewed to be believable.

Transferability

Transferability concerns the extent to which the researchers' interpretation or conclusions are transferable to other similar contexts. This requires thorough and rich description of the research activities and assumptions. Transferability looks analogous to generalizability in quantitative research. However, since qualitative research is interpretive and the participants are often small in number and not representative of the population, the findings cannot be generalizable in the sense used in quantitative research. Thus, as Lincoln and Guba (1985) noted, transferability does not mean that the researcher can make generalizable claims but instead that they should provide sufficient details to make transfer possible in case readers should wish to do so. Transferability can be achieved through detailed descriptions of the participants, contexts, and methods of data collection and analysis used in the study.

Transferability concerns the extent to which the researchers' interpretation or conclusions are transferable to other similar contexts.

Dependability

Dependability is an alternative notion to reliability in quantitative research. In quantitative research, reliability refers to the consistency of data collection tools or measures. In qualitative research, this principle indicates that the study should be reported in such a way that others can understand the study process accurately and arrive at similar interpretations if they review the data. This can be enhanced by carefully and thoroughly documenting and describing all the aspects of the research, the research processes, activities, research contexts, participants, the various decisions made during the research, or any changes that occur as the research evolves. Such documentations can then be reviewed by an outside researcher to examine their accuracy and the extent to which the conclusions are grounded in the data.

Dependability is an alternative notion to reliability in quantitative research and indicates that the study should be reported in such a way that others can understand the study process accurately and arrive at similar interpretations if they review the data.

Confirmability

Confirmability concerns the extent to which the findings are rooted in the experiences of the participants and to which others can confirm the researcher's interpretations and conclusions. This standard is considered to be parallel to objectivity in quantitative research. While quantitative research seeks objectivity by dissociating the researcher from the research process, qualitative research emphasizes the researcher's active role and engagement in the research. In qualitative research, confirmability can be established by describing the data and the findings in such a way that their accuracy can be confirmed by others. One strategy is careful checking and rechecking of the data throughout the data collection and data analysis to confirm that the results are accurate and can be verified by others. Another useful strategy is an audit trail, where you record and rationalize all the steps taken and the decisions made regarding the data coding and analysis. Reflexivity is a further strategy that can support the confirmability of the research (see below). These records are then made available for any further evaluation and confirmation.

Confirmability is considered to be parallel to objectivity in quantitative research and concerns the extent to which the findings are rooted in the experiences of the participants and to which others can confirm the researcher's interpretations and conclusions.

POINTS TO PONDER

In the following section, we will discuss different types of validity. How do these various types contribute to the overall methodological rigor and credibility of qualitative research? Which of them is/are particularly challenging to address in applied linguistics qualitative studies, and why?

Types of Validity in Qualitative Research

The notions of credibility and transferability have been discussed as two important criteria for establishing validity in qualitative research. They have also been considered as parallel to the concepts of internal and external validity in quantitative research. However, they are not the same as internal and external validity as understood in quantitative research. This is because the issues of whether the study measures what it purports to measure or whether the assessment tool assesses a construct consistently over time are not very relevant to qualitative research. After all, the assumptions, aim, methods, and context in which qualitative research is conducted are different from those of quantitative research. Thus, the positivist perspective of validity and reliability that emphasize objectivity and repeatable findings used in quantitative research are not applicable to qualitative research. To better appreciate the role of validity in qualitative research, Maxwell (1992) suggested five types of validity: descriptive validity, interpretive validity, theoretical validity, generalization validity, and evaluative validity.

Descriptive Validity

This refers to the factual accuracy and completeness of an account and to what extent the description of situations, behaviors, and people reported by the researcher matches what has happened in the research. The notion of descriptive validity is very close to the notion of credibility discussed earlier. For a qualitative study to be descriptively valid, the researcher's account should not be selective or distorted. This means that you should not select part of the data to support your preconceived ideas but instead should present all the relevant information in a neutral and honest manner as heard or seen in the research. A selective or distorted account can undermine the validity of qualitative research and harm its credibility.

Descriptive validity is an important aspect of qualitative research because accurate and comprehensive description of the experiences, behaviors, and perspectives of the participants is a major goal of qualitative research. Description helps to provide a detailed and in-depth understanding of the phenomenon under investigation and is important in establishing the credibility and trustworthiness of the findings. Thus, descriptive validity is enhanced through the use of rich and detailed data. This idea of descriptive validity seems to be comparable to internal validity in quantitative research but refers to the researcher's account rather than a test or assessment tool.

Descriptive validity refers to the factual accuracy and completeness of an account and to what extent the description of situations, behaviors, and people reported by the researcher matches what has happened in the research.

Interpretive Validity

Interpretive validity in qualitative research refers to the accuracy of the interpretation made by the researcher of the data collected and the degree to which the interpretation accurately captures and reflects the perspectives and experiences of the participants being studied. The goal is to make sure that the interpretation is trustworthy and that there is rigor and transparency in the interpretation process. One way to enhance interpretive validity is through using multiple sources of data, triangulating the findings, and involving participants in understanding and interpreting the data.

An example of interpretive validity could be seen in a study exploring the language learning experiences of a group of English language learners. You may conduct focus group interviews with the participants and then transcribe the interview and analyze it through a thematic analysis to identify themes and patterns in the data. To achieve interpretive validity, you may engage the participants in the interpretation process by going back to them to verify that your interpretations accurately reflect their experiences. For example, if, during an interview, the participant bangs the desk, it may have been to emphasize a point or have been done in anger. For you to ensure an accurate evaluation of the act, you have to look for clues in the transcript (the participant may later refer to it as an act of anger or frustration) or in body language (the participant may have a smile or be laughing).

Interpretive validity refers to the accuracy and credibility of the interpretation made by the researcher of the data collected, and the degree to which the interpretation accurately captures and reflects the perspectives and experiences of the participants being studied.

Theoretical Validity

This type of validity goes beyond descriptive and interpretive validity and concerns the degree to which the understandings, explanations, or theory generated through the research are valid and come from the data. Thus, it is about whether the theories, concepts, categories, and the proposed relationships developed in the study are grounded in the data. Since the goal of qualitative research is to gain a deeper understanding of the issues studied, theoretical validity is particularly important in this kind of research. A study with high theoretical validity can also have clear theoretical implications and can lead to concepts or theories that can guide future research questions, data collection methods, and data analysis.

It is important to differentiate between the use and role of theory in qualitative and quantitative research. In quantitative research, the focus is often on testing and verifying theories or hypotheses, whereas in qualitative research, the focus is on understanding the experiences, meanings, and perspectives of the participants rather than testing and verifying theories. In qualitative research, the process in inductive, with the meanings, theories, and explanation starting with the data and developing from it, whereas in most quantitative research, this process in deductive. Thus, in qualitative research, theoretical validity is established through rich, detailed, and accurate description of the phenomena being studied rather than though hypothesis testing or the use of tests of significance.

Theoretical validity concerns the degree to which the understandings, explanations, or theory generated through the research are valid and come from the data.

Generalization Validity

This type of validity has to do with the extension of the research to similar contexts or situations. In particular, it concerns the degree to which the understandings, explanations, or theory generated or constructed through the research can be applied to understanding similar contexts, situations, or research participants. This is what was discussed before as transferability.

Here it would be helpful to consider the difference between generalization in quantitative and qualitative research. In quantitative research, generalization refers to and is achieved mainly through statistical generalization using a large and representative sample size. It is concerned with the extent to which the findings can be generalized to other participants, settings, or times beyond the specific individuals or events investigated. However, in qualitative research, generalization refers to and is achieved through theoretical or conceptual generalization, that is through generating concepts, theories, or frameworks that can be applied to other similar situations. Therefore, instead of using a large sample size and intending to make generalizations to a wider population, qualitative researchers aim to generate theories, categories, or concepts that can be applied to understanding the research problem in other situations.

For example, you may conduct a qualitative study of students' motivations for language learning. The study would be conducted with small groups of ESL students using interviews, focus groups, and observation. Through your analysis of the data, you derive a theory of the various social, cultural, and personal factors that influence the motivation of these language learners. Even though this study involves a small group of participants, these theoretical understandings can then be used to explore students' motivation for language learning in other similar, or even different, situations or contexts.

In understanding the notion of generalizability in qualitative research, Maxwell (1992) made a distinction between two types of generalizability: internal generalizability and external generalizability. Internal generalizability is context-specific and relates to the extent to which the conclusions derived from the research are applicable to the same group or setting. So, it is a within-study generalizability. External generalizability is the extent to which concepts can be applied beyond the specific context of the study. This is because theories derived from qualitative data can have two levels: an abstract level and a specific-to-the-situation level (Auerbach & Silverman, 2003). At the situation-specific level, a theory is unique and applicable only to the situation being studied, but at the more abstract and holistic level, it can be applied to situations beyond the context of the study. Qualitative research is more concerned with specific-to-situation theories, or internal generalizability, but there are cases, such as the study on motivation mentioned above, where the study can have external generalizability (or validity). However, as noted earlier, this generalizability is different from generalizability in quantitative research as it concerns the extension of the theory generated through the research beyond its context, rather than extending the results to a larger population.

Generalization validity concerns the degree to which the understandings, explanations, or theory generated or constructed through the research can be applied to understanding similar contexts, situations, or research participants.

Evaluative Validity

This type of validity concerns the researchers' evaluation of the conclusions made. It refers to the extent to which an evaluation process can be applied to the research and the research findings. Evaluative validity can also be seen as the ability to look critically at the conclusions one has drawn from the research to evaluate the accuracy of the interpretations. This process can also be used as a way of refining the concepts or ideas developed through the research.

Strategies to Achieve Validity and Reliability in Qualitative Research

As previously discussed, validity and reliability are important aspects of qualitative research in determining the accuracy and trustworthiness of the research findings. In this section, we will discuss strategies that can be used to enhance validity and reliability in qualitative research.

The strategies discussed include:

- triangulation
- member checking
- audit-trail
- prolonged engagement
- reflexivity
- negative case analysis
- thick description
- peer debriefing
- memoing.

POINTS TO PONDER

Reflect on the concept of triangulation in qualitative data analysis. How can combining multiple sources and methods strengthen the overall validity of research findings? What are some examples of triangulation techniques, and how can they be used in applied linguistics research?

Triangulation

Triangulation is a method of establishing the validity of qualitative research by using multiple sources of data, methods, or theory which helps reduce the influence of a single perspective or bias. The term comes from geometry and refers to the process of finding a location by forming a triangle using multiple points of reference. In its current sense in qualitative research, the term was initially used by psychologist Donald Campbell in social science research in the 1970s and has since become a widely used method of validity in qualitative research. Campbell argued that using multiple methods and sources of data is essential in qualitative research as they provide a more comprehensive understanding of the research issue and potentially a different perspective. Since then, the term has become widely used in qualitative research as an important tool for ensuring the robustness and validity of research findings.

Triangulation is a method of establishing the validity of qualitative research by using multiple sources of data, methods, or theory, which helps reduce the influence of a single perspective or bias.

Triangulation in qualitative research provides a number of benefits, including the following:

- Helping to increase the validity of research findings by providing multiple perspectives on a phenomenon and in doing so reducing the risk of bias and increasing the accuracy of the findings.

- Improving reliability of the findings by allowing the researcher to compare and cross-check multiple sources of data.
- Enhancing a more nuanced understanding. When multiple methods or sources of data are used, a more detailed understanding of the phenomenon can be achieved.
- Facilitating the identification of patterns and themes that may not be evident when a single method or source of data is used.
- Helping to address the limitations of single methods or sources of data. Each research method has its own strengths and limitations, and triangulation can address those limitations by providing a more complete picture.

Example 17.1 illustrates a hypothetical scenario for triangulation.

EXAMPLE 17.1

Suppose you are conducting a study investigating the classroom English learning experiences of adult immigrants in an ESL school. You might conduct interviews with a group of adult immigrants who are currently learning a new language, in order to understand their experiences, perspectives, and challenges in learning a new language. To triangulate the data, in addition to the interview, you might also include observations of the participants in their language classes or collect written or oral samples of their language (such as essays, emails, or texts). This will expand the data sources which will, in turn, increase the validity of the study. You might also give the participants a questionnaire including open-ended questions about their background, motivation for learning a new language, the strategies they use to learn it, and any difficulties or challenges they have encountered.

In Example 17.1, you as the researcher have used multiple sources of data and by doing so you can triangulate the data to gain a more complete and accurate understanding of the effectiveness of the new teaching method. By using multiple data sources, you can cross-check and compare the data to gain a more comprehensive understanding of the effectiveness of the new teaching method. For example, if the observation data show that the students are not participating in the classroom as expected, you can use the interview data to explore why this has occurred. The interview data may reveal that while the new teaching method is effective at increasing participation, it may not be focused enough on language development.

Different Types of Triangulation
Triangulation can be achieved in a variety of ways, including by collecting data from different sources, such as interviews, surveys, and observation, or from different types of participants; by using different data analysis; and also by interpreting or explaining the data using different perspectives or multiple theoretical

frameworks. Four types of triangulation have been distinguished in the literature (Figure 17.2): data-source triangulation, methodological triangulation, theoretical triangulation, and investigator triangulation (Denzin, 1978) as shown in Figure 17.2.

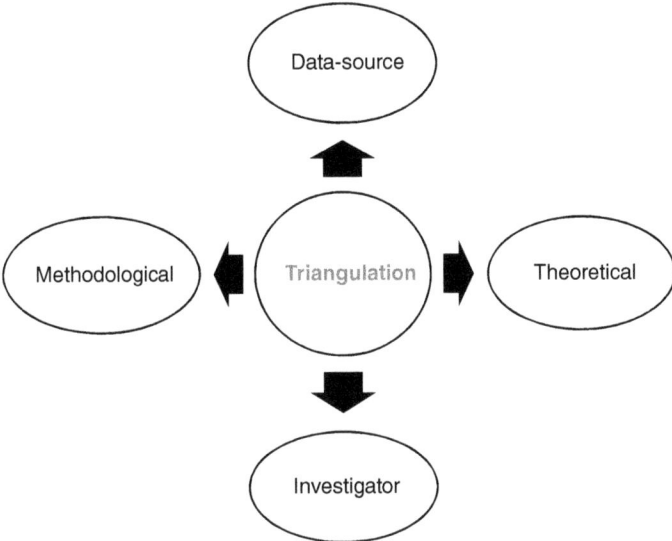

Figure 17.2 Types of triangulation

Data-Source Triangulation   Data-source triangulation refers to using data from multiple sources to gather information on the topic or phenomenon in order to compare and cross-check the data to confirm its validity and credibility. This includes collecting data from different participants, in different places, and using different sources, such as questionnaires, interviews, and observations. This approach helps to reduce bias and increase confidence in the results by allowing the comparison of different types of data. When the data from multiple sources converge to support a major theme or pattern in the data, this can lend credibility to the study findings.

Data-source triangulation refers to using data from multiple sources to gather information on the topic or phenomenon in order to compare and cross-check the data to confirm its validity and credibility.

Methodological Triangulation   Methodological triangulation refers to using multiple methods of research to investigate an issue or to analyze the data. It is similar to data-source triangulation. However, the key difference is that methodological triangulation focuses on using different methods, such as qualitative and quantitative methods, to study the same phenomenon, whereas data-source triangulation involves using multiple sources to collect data on the same topic. By using different methods to collect and analyze the data, you can cross-check and compare the findings to gain a more comprehensive understanding of the phenomenon under investigation. When the cross validation of the data across different methods converges or provides consistent findings, this can enhance the validity and the credibility of the study.

Methodological triangulation refers to using multiple methods of research to investigate an issue or to analyze the data.

Example 17.2 presents a hypothetical scenario.

EXAMPLE 17.2

Suppose you aim to conduct a study to examine the language learning strategies used by adult English as a second language (ESL) learners. To explore this topic, you could employ a combination of qualitative and quantitative methods. For instance, you might use a questionnaire to gather quantitative data on the strategies used by the learners. At the same time, you might use qualitative interviews with the learners to gather more in-depth information about the strategies they use and why. Finally, you could also conduct **classroom observations** to gather qualitative data on how these strategies are used by the learners in a naturalistic setting. By combining both quantitative and qualitative methods, you can use methodological triangulation to gain a more complete and more accurate picture of the language learning strategies used by the adult ESL learners being studied.

Theoretical Triangulation   Theoretical triangulation refers to using multiple theories or perspectives to interpret, understand, or explain the phenomenon being studied. This can involve using different theories from both within and outside the discipline. Using multiple theories provides you with different lenses through which different aspects or dimensions of the research problem can be explored, resulting in a more comprehensive understanding of the research issue. This type of triangulation is particularly helpful in examining complex problems that do not fit easily into a single theoretical viewpoint or perspective. Of course, using different theoretical perspectives may also lead to different explanations or interpretations, which may not always be congruent. Despite this, theoretical triangulation can provide insights into the complexity of the issue being examined.

Theoretical triangulation refers to using multiple theories or perspectives to interpret, understand, or explain the phenomenon being studied.

Example 17.3 provides a hypothetical scenario for theoretical triangulation.

EXAMPLE 17.3

Suppose you are conducting a study that investigates the benefits of translanguaging in an L2 classroom setting. Translanguaging refers to the use of students' L1 or other languages to support their learning of a second language. You might use three different theoretical frameworks to guide the study: (a) the code-switching model of Gumperz (1982), which argues that code-switching, which is an aspect of translanguaging, is a strategic tool used by L2 speakers to convey their meaning; (b) Norton's (2000) theoretical model of identity, which argues that language and identity are closely connected and that language use is a way for individuals to assert their cultural identities; and (c) the Vygotskian sociocultural theory (SCT), which emphasizes the role of social interactions and mediation in language development. SCT posits that cognitive development is mediated by social interactions and that individuals learn through participation in social practices and cultural tools. The use of L1 in the classroom can be considered and understood as a mediation tool to facilitate learning. By triangulating these three different theoretical frameworks, you can examine how translanguaging is related to the students' ability to communicate effectively, how it is related to their cultural identities, and how it can be used as a strategic and mediational tool to convey social meaning. Such a theoretical triangulation allows you to gain a deeper understanding of the complex phenomenon of translanguaging in a classroom setting.

It is important to keep the following in mind when doing theoretical triangulation:

- **Compatibility of the theories:** It is important to use theories that are compatible and can be integrated in a meaningful way. The theories chosen for triangulation should be able to complement and supplement each other, rather than contradicting or competing with each other. For example, if you are studying the impact of social interaction on L2 development, you may choose to use a social theory of L2 development and a theory of interaction. These theories are compatible because they can be integrated to provide a comprehensive understanding of how interaction affects L2 development. Compatibility also means that the theories should be able to address different aspects of the phenomenon being studied but in a complementary way. For instance, one theory may focus on the micro-level interactions, and another theory may focus on the macro-level cognitive factors; together they can provide a holistic understanding of the research issue investigated.
- **The limitations of each theoretical perspective:** Each theoretical perspective may have its own limitations. So, it is important to be aware of these when using them in triangulation. Being aware of the limitations can also help identify any inconsistencies or contradictions in the data. For example, a theory that focuses on internal mental processes may tend to overlook the role social context or the learners' emotions play in shaping their behavior. Many theories may

focus on specific aspects of a phenomenon and exclude others. Moreover, certain theories may have certain limitations in terms of the population they are developed for and tested on. This can limit the generalizability of the theory to other populations. In short, it is important to be aware of the assumptions and limitations of each theoretical perspective used.

- **Transparency about the process:** When reporting the findings of a study that has used theoretical triangulation, it is important to be transparent about the theoretical perspectives used, and how they are integrated. This can include information about how decisions were made, who was involved, and what data or evidence was used to support those decisions. Transparency helps to build trust and accountability and allows stakeholders to understand and evaluate the process. Additionally, transparency can promote collaboration and participation and can help to identify potential issues or areas for improvement.

- **Openness to new theoretical perspectives:** Theoretical triangulation is an ongoing process, and new theoretical perspectives may emerge as the research progresses. So, it is important to be open to incorporating new perspectives, as they may provide new insights into the issue being studied.

Investigator Triangulation Investigator triangulation is a method of triangulation in which multiple researchers collect and analyze the data to increase the validity and reliability of the research findings. This helps to reduce bias and increase the trustworthiness of the results by providing multiple perspectives on the same phenomenon. This can be done by having different researchers collect different types of data (e.g., one researcher conducting interviews, another conducting observations) and then comparing their findings. This type of triangulation can help compare and integrate the data collected by different investigators to identify patterns and discrepancies, and to enhance the overall rigor of the research.

Investigator triangulation is a method of triangulation in which multiple researchers collect and analyze the data to increase the validity and reliability of the research findings.

The following criteria should be kept in mind when using investigator triangulation:

- **Training, experience, and expertise:** It is important that investigators have adequate training and experience in the research method being used. They should also have a clear understanding of the purpose of the study and be similarly motivated to conduct the research. This is different from hiring someone to collect and analyze the data.

- **Collaboration and communication:** The researchers should ideally be research partners who participate and collaborate in all phases of the study, including the data collection and the interpretation of the results. Also, clear and regular communication among investigators is essential for increased consistency and coherence in data collection and analysis.

- **Diversity of background**: When conducting investigator triangulation, it is important to have investigators with different backgrounds, expertise, and perspectives to increase the reliability and validity of the research findings. By using multiple investigators with different backgrounds, expertise, and perspectives, the research can benefit from a wider range of viewpoints, which can lead to a more comprehensive understanding of the research topic.

- **Reflection**: The researchers should reflect on their role as investigators and how it has shaped the research process and outcome. In doing so, they should consider how their perspectives and experiences may have influenced the findings. Reflection can also be used to identify and address potential sources of the researchers' bias, preconceptions, or assumptions that may have affected the research design or data interpretation. By reflecting on their own perspectives, beliefs, and experiences, investigators can become more aware of their own preconceptions and take steps to minimize their effects on the research. Reflection also allows them to consider how the research may have influenced the participants, and how their relationships with the participants may have influenced the data collected. For example, if you have a strong rapport with participants, you may have more access to sensitive information, but this rapport may also affect the participants' willingness to disclose information that might be considered sensitive. Reflection can also be beneficial in identifying areas where the research may have limitations in terms of the researcher's lack of expertise or knowledge. This can help to identify potential areas where you can collaborate with other researchers with different expertise. Altogether, reflection is an important consideration when conducting investigator triangulation because it allows you to examine how your own beliefs and assumptions may have influenced the research findings. It allows you to identify and address potential biases.

POINTS TO PONDER

How might member checking contribute to the credibility and trustworthiness of qualitative research findings? Are there specific challenges when conducting member checking in applied linguistics research? If so, how can you address these challenges effectively?

Member Checking

Member checking (or respondent/participant validation) is a strategy for establishing the credibility of qualitative research findings through seeking feedback from the study participants on the interpretations and conclusions that you have drawn from the data. The process entails presenting the findings to the participants, such as transcripts of interviews or observation findings, and asking them to review and comment on them. Researchers may ask participants to clarify any statements they made during the study or to provide additional information if they feel anything is missing. The purpose of member checking is to make sure that your understanding of the data is in line with the participants' perspective and to identify any discrepancies or misunderstandings. This can enhance the credibility and trustworthiness of the research because the participants have had an opportunity to review and validate your understanding and interpretations. It also helps to establish trust in the participants since it shows them that their perspectives and experiences are important and that you are committed to the accurate representation of their views.

Member checking is a strategy for establishing the credibility of qualitative research findings through seeking feedback from the study participants on the interpretations and conclusions drawn from the data.

Member checking can be done in a number of ways, such as meeting face-to-face with the participants or asking them to participate in a phone conversation or to provide written comments. The participants can also be invited to attend a presentation of the study findings and provide feedback.

It is important to note that member checking is not always possible or appropriate in all research studies, but when it is feasible, it can be a valuable tool for increasing the validity and trustworthiness of qualitative research. Example 17.4 presents a hypothetical scenario.

EXAMPLE 17.4

Suppose you are conducting a study investigating the language needs of ESL undergraduate university students. You conduct a focus group with a group of participants and then transcribe the data. You then provide the transcript of the interview to each participant for review. The participants would then be asked to confirm that the transcript accurately represents their views and experiences, and to point out any errors or discrepancies. This process helps to make the data collected valid and reliable, and your interpretation an accurate reflection of the participants' perspectives.

When conducting member checking, the following factors should be considered:

- **Participants' availability and willingness:** You need to make sure that participants are willing and able to review the research findings and provide feedback.
- **Data sensitivity:** This is an important consideration in member checking. Member checking involves sharing the findings with participants. However, sometimes it is not appropriate to do so. For example, if the research deals

with sensitive or confidential topics, member checking would not be an appropriate step.

- **Ethical considerations:** You should also be sure that participants' feedback and validation is voluntary and that there is no harm for the participants as a result of the member checking process.
- **Purpose of the research:** You should also take into account the purpose of the research because depending on the type and purpose of the research, member checking may be more or less appropriate. For example, member checking might be more appropriate for exploratory and interpretive research, whose purpose is to understand the thoughts and experiences of participants, rather than for confirmatory or explanatory research, where the researcher is going to explain hypotheses.

Audit Trail

An audit trail is a validity strategy in qualitative research that refers to a process of maintaining an audit of the whole research process through documenting all the steps, decisions, and activities used so that an auditor (someone external to the research) can check them and verify their accuracy. It is a process of keeping a record of what happened, when it happened, and why. Thus, an audit trail necessitates maintaining detailed and systematic records of the research steps and process, including the methods used, data collected, and any choices made during the analysis. It also entails keeping the raw data collected throughout the study, including those obtained in the interviews, focus groups, and observations, and also documenting the decisions regarding how the interviewees were selected or how the observations were made and the rationale behind them.

Audit trail refers to a process of maintaining an audit of the whole research process through documenting all the steps, decisions, and activities used so that an auditor (someone external to the research) can check them and verify their accuracy.

The purpose of an audit trail is to provide accountability and transparency for the data and to show that the research has been conducted in an unbiased and rigorous manner. The audit trail allows an external auditor to review, examine, and verify the accuracy of the data and the conclusions drawn from it; in this way, it can contribute to the overall credibility and trustworthiness of the study. When conducting an audit trail, the following should be considered:

- **Detailed documentation:** This means keeping detailed records of all aspects of the research process, including data collection methods, data analysis procedures, and any decisions made during the analysis.
- **Transparency:** You should be transparent about the research process and your potential biases, documenting not only what was done but also how your views could have affected the results.

- **Data management:** You should establish a clear system for managing and storing data, including the use of appropriate software tools.
- **Keeping track of the time:** It is important to record and keep track of the time. The time should be recorded when each step is taken in the research process so that it can be traced back in case of any questions or doubts.

Example 17.5 presents a hypothetical scenario for an audit trail.

EXAMPLE 17.5

Suppose you are exploring the experiences and attitudes of L2 learners toward a task-based language teaching method in an L2 classroom. You first conduct observations of the classroom in which the task-based language instruction was implemented; then conduct semistructured interviews with the teacher and students; and collect classroom materials, such as lesson plans and student work samples, and also students' stories about their lessons. You use a discourse analytic approach to examine the classroom interactions and narrative analysis to examine the students' stories. You also use a thematic analysis to analyze the transcriptions of the interviews to identify patterns and themes in the learner's experiences and attitudes. Using an audit trail as a strategy for validity, during the study you record all the steps and the decisions made. For example, you record the steps taken to conduct the interviews, including the recruitment of the participants and the steps in preparing the transcriptions of the interview for analysis. You document the whole coding procedure, including how the codes were developed and any decisions made during the coding process, such as which data to include or exclude, and how to interpret the data. You record the process of identifying themes in the data, such as grouping similar codes together and assigning labels to the themes; you also record any decisions made during the theme-identification process, such as which themes to include or exclude, and how to interpret the themes. You also record all the steps taken to interpret the data, such as relating the themes to the research questions and explaining the significance of the themes. Also, you record the time when each step is taken and how long it took to complete. For example, "The observation was conducted for a period of four weeks and the interview took one hour for each participant." Finally, you can provide this documentation to an auditor to examine and confirm its credibility. By keeping detailed documentation of the research process so that an auditor can examine it, you can enhance the credibility of the findings.

Prolonged Engagement

Prolonged engagement is a validity strategy in qualitative research, which means that you should spend an extended period of time with participants in the study. It is indeed an important feature of any ethnographic study. The aim is to understand the reality of the participants, their context, and culture accurately and fully, which can then increase the credibility of the research. This is achieved by spending a significant amount of time in their natural setting, building rapport and engaging with them in various activities, and gathering rich and detailed data. Spending time in the field allows a deeper understanding of the research participants and their context.

Prolonged engagement means that you should spend an extended period of time with participants in the study to understand their reality, their context, and their culture accurately and fully.

The following are the benefits of prolonged engagement in qualitative research:

- gaining deeper understanding
- building rapport and trust with participants
- collection of rich and detailed data
- increased opportunities for data verification and triangulation
- increased opportunities for reflection
- increased opportunities to explore complexities
- improved data saturation.

Reflexivity

Reflexivity is a validity-check process through which researchers reflect on and reveal their own background, assumptions, beliefs, perspectives, and biases and how these may have affected their research. In qualitative research, reflexivity is considered as an important strategy for validity as it helps enhance the transparency and credibility of the research by acknowledging what you have brought to the task. This reveals the subjective nature of the research process and hence reduces the potential for researcher bias. Reflexivity can also acknowledge the power dynamic between research participants and the researchers and its potential impact on the research process and findings. By examining and documenting these issues, reflexivity can contribute to transparency, credibility, and rigor of qualitative research.

Reflexivity is a validity-check process through which researchers reflect on and reveal their own background, assumptions, beliefs, perspectives, and biases and how they may have affected their research.

Example 17.6 presents a hypothetical scenario for reflexivity.

EXAMPLE 17.6

Suppose you are examining the socialization of a group of immigrant language learners in a particular language school. You reflect on your own assumptions, background, and experiences as a L1 English speaker and realize that this may influence the research process and the manner in which the data collected might be interpreted. In order to address this, you actively attempt to understand the students' thoughts and perspectives through in-depth interviews and observations, and at the same time document your own subjective interpretations and any potential biases you may have brought to the data analysis and conclusion. This allows you to be transparent by acknowledging the potential impact of your own beliefs and attempting to minimize their effect on your understanding of the students' views and experiences.

Negative Case Analysis

Negative case analysis is a validity strategy in qualitative research where you look for and examine cases that contradict or challenge the emerging results. Once these inconsistences are located, you can reflect on how they can be explained. This might demand the consideration of multiple perspectives, viewpoints, and explanations for the findings, which can then strengthen the overall trustworthiness of the research. It requires you to be attentive to disconfirming evidence and to be reflexive in your analysis and interpretation of the data.

When conducting negative case analysis, the following should be taken into account:

- **Its purpose:** You should clearly articulate the purpose of such an analysis and why it is conducted.
- **Looking for cases:** You should actively look for and choose cases that challenge or contradict the emerging findings.
- **Rigor:** You should carefully and critically examine the data related to the negative cases, looking for patterns, trends, and explanations that may challenge the findings.
- **Potential for new insights:** You should make sure that such analysis has the potential to provide new insights and highlight alternative perspectives.
- **Communication:** You should clearly communicate the results of negative case analysis and its implications for the overall findings and conclusions from the study.
- **Temptation for bias:** One issue with conducting negative case analysis is that it is often hard to resist our temptation to confirm existing findings. This can lead to selective attention, where only findings that align with our beliefs or assumptions may be considered, at the expense of those that contradict our beliefs. This can then have a significant impact on the quality and validity of the research; thus, it is important to avoid such temptations.

Example 17.7 provides a hypothetical illustration of negative case analysis.

EXAMPLE 17.7

Suppose you are conducting a study on the factors affecting learner motivation in language classrooms. In this study, you have conducted in-depth interviews with language learners to explore the factors contributing to their motivation. The emerging results suggest that a primary factor in motivating the learners is a supportive classroom environment. To evaluate the robustness of these findings, you conduct negative case analysis by looking for and examining cases of classroom environments that are not supportive but students report a high level of motivation. You carefully consider the data pertaining to these negative cases to identify any possible patterns or trends that may contradict the initial findings. Such negative case analysis enables you to identify alternative explanations for language learning motivation, which can then strengthen the trustworthiness of the findings. Negative case analysis also helps increase transparency and hence can lead to a more well-rounded understanding of the factors affecting language learning motivation.

Thick Description

Another strategy to enhance credibility in qualitative research is rich and thick description, which refers to providing detailed and rich accounts of the research partici-pants, context, background, themes, and behavior, including their thoughts, feelings, and perspectives. The term thick description was initially introduced by philosopher Gilbert Ryle and was then used with its current meaning by Clifford Geertz, an anthropologist known for his interpretive approach to anthropology, which examines and emphasizes the importance of understanding the meaning and significance of cultures, cultural practices, and beliefs within particular cultural contexts. In his influential essay, "Thick Description: Toward an Interpretive Theory of Culture" (1973), Geertz argued against simple description as a method for cultural analysis; he advocated and emphasized instead the need for rich and detailed information that provides a full picture of the cultural context and the practices within that culture, which he called "thick description." The term has now been used more broadly in qualitative research to refer to a detailed account of the phenomenon that is being studied and includes an understanding of the context and meaning of the experiences under investigation.

Thick description refers to providing detailed and rich accounts of the research participants, context, background, themes, and behavior, including their thoughts, feelings, and perspectives.

The aim of thick description is to provide an in-depth report to capture the situational and cultural context in which the study is taking place and to understand the full meanings and experiences of the participants being studied in such a way that others can understand the study's findings in context.

There are a number of benefits of thick and detailed description. First it provides a deeper understanding of the topic being studied, enabling you to understand it fully and from multiple perspectives. It can prevent oversimplification and provide a more thorough understanding of the issues being studied. By including a wide range of details and perspectives, this strategy enables you to take into account multiple factors, characteristics, and complexities that may not be evident in a more simplified view. It encourages completeness and attention to detail, which can enhance the reliability and validity of the research findings. It can also allow the reader to understand the research context very well, making the phenomenon more vivid and encouraging deeper engagement. Here are some of the main characteristics of a thick description:

- **It is concrete:** A thick description focuses on the concrete and specific details rather than general concepts.
- **It is detailed:** It offers a thorough and in-depth analysis of an event or action with all its relevant details.
- **It is contextual and holistic:** A thick description provides a complete account of an event or phenomenon within its historical, cultural, and social context with all its various components, relationships, and their significance.
- **It is interpretive:** A thick description goes beyond factual description and also includes thick interpretation of the meaning and significance of an event or an action.
- **It is emic:** It provides the account from the perspective of those being studied, including their cultural beliefs and understandings.
- **It is reflexive:** A thick description is reflexive, considering the researcher's own perspective, biases and assumptions, and the ways in which these may have affected the research and its findings.

Peer Debriefing (Peer Review)

Peer debriefing is another strategy used in qualitative research to validate findings and promote rigor. It refers to having a group of researchers or peers, with similar expertise and training, who review, critically evaluate, and comment on the research. This can include reviewing and evaluating the research design, data collection methods, analysis, and the interpretation of the findings. This process helps identify potential shortcomings and inconsistencies in the research and research findings, leading to more accurate and more credible results.

When doing peer debriefing, the following should be considered:

- **Research questions and design:** Evaluate the research questions and the design to make sure that they align with the overall qualitative research methodology used.
- **Data collection methods:** Review and evaluate the methods used to collect and analyze the data to make sure that they are appropriate.
- **Results and interpretations:** Critically evaluate the results and interpretation, looking for accuracy and consistency with the data.
- **Trustworthiness:** Consider and evaluate the strategies used to establish the trustworthiness of the study in terms of its credibility, dependability, and transferability to confirm that the study is conducted in a rigorous manner.
- **Ethics:** Pay attention to ethical considerations and their implications and make sure that the study is conducted in a responsible and respectful manner.

By examining the above aspects of the research, peer debriefing can augment the quality and credibility of qualitative research. Here is a summary of the benefits of peer debriefing:

- Increasing the credibility of the findings and confirming that the data have been collected and analyzed in an accurate and reliable manner.
- Identifying potential preconceptions that may have affected the research and the research process.
- Enhancing the rigor of the analysis by identifying any limitations or weaknesses in the research methods and analysis.
- Facilitating the interpretation of the data by allowing different viewpoints to be heard about the data.

Overall, peer review can improve the trustworthiness of the research and hence is an important step in improving the validity of qualitative research.

Memoing

Memoing in qualitative research is a process through which you record and reflect on your observations and thoughts during the study. It is a tool for keeping track of your ideas and observations, which can help in the analysis and interpretation of the data collected. Thus, it captures your evolving understanding of the data. Memos can be in the form of notes, journal entries, or other written forms, and can be revisited and revised as the research progresses. Memoing can be done during the various stages of the research, including data collection, coding, and analysis. It contributes to the rigor and transparency of the research process, thereby enhancing the validity and credibility of the research. For example, you can write memos while reading or reviewing the raw data (e.g., transcripts or field notes) for the first time. These memos capture initial impressions, observations, or questions about the data. Memos can also be written during data collection, such as when conducting interviews or observing participants, to capture your reflections on the process. Also, you might use memos to track your personal thoughts or reactions to the research topic over time. Example 17.8 illustrates how you can use memos to document your observations during data collection.

EXAMPLE 17.8

Suppose you are conducting an interview with a group of L2 participants about their experiences learning English as a second language. As you start the interview you may notice that one of the participants is very excited about sharing his experiences. Therefore, you may want to write a memo capturing this initial impression:

Memo 1: The participant seemed to be excited about the interview and sharing his language learning experiences.

You start the interview and ask the first question.

The first question: "Can you tell me about your first experience learning a new language?"

Participant response: "I started learning French in high school and it was really difficult for me. I took a few courses, but I was unable to talk because I wasn't exposed to it outside the classroom. I then had a chance to participate in a study abroad program in France for one semester and that made a huge difference. It really helped me improve my speaking and communication skills."

Memo 2: During the interview, the participant mentioned the importance of study abroad and its impact on his learning. This is a significant point as it highlights the importance of immersion. This particular participant seems to have a strong appreciation for immersion experiences in language learning, and I should pay attention to this issue as I interview others.

Conclusion

This chapter has focused on the issue of reliability and validity in qualitative research. It began by discussing the importance of and the differences between reliability and validity in qualitative research compared to quantitative research, as well as the techniques used to enhance reliability and validity in qualitative research. It discussed measures of credibility, transferability, dependability, and confirmability, which are considered as parallel to the traditional measures of internal validity, external validity, reliability, and objectivity in quantitative research. Techniques for achieving these kinds of reliability and validity were discussed along with hypothetical examples in applied linguistics research. Altogether, the chapter has provided a detailed overview of the key issues related to reliability and validity in qualitative research and has offered practical suggestions on how to enhance the trustworthiness of qualitative data. In subsequent chapters, we will move on to discussing data analysis techniques commonly used in quantitative research.

DISCUSSION AND ACTIVITY QUESTIONS

Discussion Questions

1. In what ways do the concepts of reliability and validity differ between qualitative and quantitative research? Can you provide examples of how these differences impact research design and analysis?
2. What are some common misconceptions about reliability and validity in qualitative research? How can these misconceptions be addressed in practice?
3. How are measures such as credibility, transferability, dependability, and confirmability relevant to qualitative research in applied linguistics? What are some of the techniques that you will use for achieving these measures in qualitative applied linguistics research?

4. What are some limitations of using reliability and validity measures in qualitative research? Are there alternative ways of assessing the trustworthiness of qualitative data?
5. What is the difference between credibility and transferability, and how do they relate to traditional measures of internal validity, external validity, reliability, and objectivity in quantitative research?
6. How does transferability differ from generalizability, and why is transferability emphasized in qualitative research instead of generalizability?
7. Discuss the role of confirmability in qualitative research. How can you make sure that your findings are confirmable by others?
8. How can you balance the trade-offs between reliability and validity in qualitative research? Why is it important to consider both measures in the overall design and analysis of a study?
9. Reflecting on your experience or knowledge, which of the techniques for ensuring reliability and validity in qualitative research do you find most challenging to implement, and why? How might these challenges be overcome?

Activity Questions

1. Choose a research question that you are interested in and design a study using qualitative research methods. Identify the types of triangulation strategies that you would use to enhance the reliability and validity of your findings.
2. Find an example of a qualitative research study in applied linguistics and identify the techniques used to enhance the credibility, transferability, dependability, and confirmability of the data. Discuss the effectiveness of these techniques in improving the trustworthiness of the findings.
3. Choose a research article that reports a qualitative study in applied linguistics. Evaluate the credibility, transferability, dependability, and confirmability of the study, and consider whether alternative measures of trustworthiness could have been used. Discuss the implications of the study's trustworthiness for its broader significance.
4. After completing the activity in question 3, reflect on how you would apply the concepts of credibility, transferability, dependability, and confirmability to your own research. Consider how you can use techniques such as triangulation, prolonged engagement, and member checking to enhance the trustworthiness of your data.
5. Locate a study that has used both qualitative and quantitative research methods. Identify the techniques used to establish validity in the two types of research methods. Then, evaluate the strengths and limitations of these validity measures in both methods.

PART V
Quantitative Research: Data Analysis and Interpretation

18 Analyzing Quantitative Data: Descriptive Statistics

CHAPTER OBJECTIVES

After completing this chapter, you should be able to

- Define and explain the importance of descriptive statistics for analyzing numerical data.
- Identify and apply the most appropriate descriptive statistics for a given dataset and interpret its meaning.
- Describe data distribution and how it can be used.
- Describe different ways of visualizing data, using different graphical representations, such as histograms, bar charts, boxplots, and scatter plots.
- Explain measures of central tendency, including mean, median, and mode, and where and how they can be used.
- Explain measures of dispersion, including range, variance, and standard deviation, and how and when they can be used.
- Understand percentiles, quartiles, and interquartile range and how they can be used.
- Describe confidence intervals for the population mean and proportion.

Introduction

As discussed earlier, quantitative data refer to data that are numerical and can be measured and quantified. In research, once the data are collected, they need to be analysed. Quantitative data analysis often involves two main stages: descriptive statistics and inferential statistics. In this chapter, we will focus on descriptive statistics and in the next chapters, we will discuss inferential statistics.

Descriptive statistics is a type of statistics that deals with describing and summarizing quantitative data. It provides the tools and techniques for organizing, summarizing, and visualizing data in a way that makes them easier to understand and interpret. The goal of descriptive statistics is to provide a concise and informative representation of a dataset that can be used to better understand the underlying patterns and relationships within the data.

However, before doing any descriptive statistics, we need to make sure that the data that are to be analyzed are reliable and valid (see Chapter 12). In this chapter, we will continue to build upon that discussion by exploring the tools and techniques that can be used to summarize and describe the main features of the sample data.

POINTS TO PONDER

Before reading the next sections, how do you define descriptive statistics, and what is its importance in quantitative research? Can you share specific examples from your work where the application of descriptive statistics has provided meaningful insights or highlighted key trends in the data?

Definition and Importance of Descriptive Statistics

Descriptive statistics is conducted on numerical data with the purpose of providing a concise and meaningful summary of the main characteristics of the data. This will be done by providing measures of central tendency (such as the mean or averages, median, and mode), measures of dispersion or variability (such as range, variance, and standard deviation), producing frequency distribution and providing information about the shape of the distribution (such as skewness and kurtosis). The importance of descriptive statistics lies in its power to provide a simple and straightforward representation of a considerable and complicated set of data. Through summarizing the data in a meaningful way, descriptive statistics can help identify patterns, trends, or relationships in the data and also inform further analysis, such as inferential statistics, which can be used for testing hypotheses, making predictions about the relationship of variables, or making generalizations about the population based on the data.

Descriptive statistics is a type of statistics that deals with describing and summarizing quantitative data. It provides the tools and techniques for organizing, summarizing, and visualizing data in a way that makes them easier to understand and interpret.

Another important advantage of descriptive statistics is that it can help identify missing data, errors, outliers, or unusual cases in data. Outliers, for example, are data points that are very different from the rest of the data and can arise from various sources, such as measurement errors, data entry errors, unusual cases, sampling issues or errors in the data collection process. Descriptive statistics can play an important role in identifying such cases in the data, which can have a significant impact on the results. When such errors or others are identified, the data can be cleaned to be accurate and ready for further analysis. In short, descriptive statistics have the following benefits:

- offering an easy way to explore the data
- creating visual representations of the data
- reducing a large amount of data into a more manageable form
- helping identify patterns and relationships in the data
- helping identify unusual cases and errors in the data
- making comparison possible
- providing a foundation for inferential statistics
- enhancing communication.

Frequency Distribution

A very useful and common first step in analyzing numerical data is examining its frequency distribution. Frequency distribution is a descriptive statistical tool used to analyze the data by counting how many times a particular value has occurred. Frequency distribution makes interpretation easy and helps identify patterns, trends, and also outliers. There are several ways to show frequency distribution. These include frequency tables and graphical representation of the data, such as bar graphs, pie charts, line graphs, box and whisker plots, scatter plots, and histograms.

Frequency Tables
A frequency table is a table that displays the frequency of each value or range of values in the data. It is a simple and useful way to summarize large amounts of data. To create a frequency table, we would first determine the range of values used, and then count the number of times each value appears in the dataset. The counts are then organized into a table that lists each value along with its corresponding frequency or count. Example 18.1 illustrates the use of a frequency table.

EXAMPLE 18.1

Consider a dataset of thirty students' scores on a test out of 50. To create a frequency table for this, we would count the number of students who scored a particular mark on the test and record those frequencies in the table. The resulting frequency table for such data might look like Table 18.1

Table 18.1 Frequency table for the data in Example 18.1

Data	Frequency	Percentage	Cumulative percentage
29.00	2	6.7	6.7
31.00	1	3.3	10.0
35.00	4	13.3	23.3
41.00	4	13.3	36.7
43.00	19	63.3	100.0
Total	30	100.0*	

*The percentages do not total 100 precisely due to rounding.

In the frequency table above, the most common mark is 43, received by 19 students. The table also includes percentage and cumulative percentage distributions. Percentage distribution calculates the percentage of values by dividing the frequency of each value by the total number of observations and multiplying the result by 100. For instance, if the frequency of "29" is 2 in a total of 30 observations, the percentage is 6.7%. Cumulative percentage distribution shows the percentage of observations equal to or below a certain value. For example, the 10 in the second row shows that 10% of the students have got a score equal to 31 or less than 31. To create it, you should arrange the data in ascending order, and as you go down the list, you will add up the percentages to get the cumulative percentage for each value, with the final cumulative percentage representing the total percentage of observations in the data.

POINTS TO PONDER

What are some of the challenges that you may encounter when working with large datasets, and how can descriptive statistics address these challenges?

Graphical Representation of Data

Data can be displayed graphically using various types of charts and graphs, such as bar graphs, pie charts, line graphs, scatter plots, and histograms. The choice of which graphical representation to use depends on the type of data and the kind of information we would like to convey. There are software tools available, such as Excel and SPSS, that can help in creating graphical representations of data.

Bar Graphs

A bar graph, or what is also known as a bar chart, is a type of data visualization used to display categorical data. Categorical data is a type of data that represents variables that can be divided into categories. They are used as labels that represent a variable or a characteristic. Examples of categorical data include type of language background (e.g., Chinese, Japanese, Korean) and levels of language proficiency (e.g., beginner, intermediate, advanced). Categorical data are often analyzed using frequency tables, contingency tables (also known as cross-tabulation tables, which display the relationship between two or more categorical variables), or bar graphs.

A bar graph, or what is also known as a bar chart, is a type of data visualization used to display categorical data.

Graphically, a bar graph consists of a series of bars, each of which represents a category, with the height of the bar representing the frequency of the category. Bar graphs are useful tools for comparing frequencies of different categories. They can be shown either vertically or horizontally. To create a bar graph, we would first list the categories on the x-axis and the frequency of each on the y-axis. We would then draw a bar for each category, with the height of the bar proportional to the frequency of that category. However, although they can be created manually, it is much easier to use a computer program such as SPSS or R. To create the bar graph in SPSS, you can follow the procedure in SPSS Steps 18.1.

SPSS STEPS 18.1
- Open the data file in SPSS.
- Go to "Graphs" > "Bar."
- Select bar graph type (Simple, Clustered, Stacked). Choose "Simple".
- Tick "Summaries for groups of cases" > "Define."
- Move X-axis variable from "Variables" to "Category Axis." Under "Bars Represent," choose "N of cases."
- Click "OK."

Once the graph is created in SPSS, it can be further customized by editing the title, font, color, and other features. Example 18.2 illustrates the use of a bar graph.

EXAMPLE 18.2

An illustration of a bar graph can be seen in the context of a study examining the nationalities of participants. The x-axis depicts various nationalities, such as Chinese, Japanese, and Korean, while the y-axis represents the frequency of each nationality. Each nationality is represented by a bar, with the height of each bar indicating the frequency of that specific nationality. To exemplify this, let's consider data from a study involving 12 participants and their respective nationalities as shown in Table 18.2.

The bar graph, created using the SPSS steps mentioned earlier, is presented in Figure 18.1.

Table 18.2 The nationalities of participants in Example 18.2	
Participants	Nationality
1	Chinese
2	Chinese
3	Chinese
4	Chinese
5	Japanese
6	Japanese
7	Japanese
8	Japanese
9	Japanese
10	Japanese
11	Korean
12	Korean

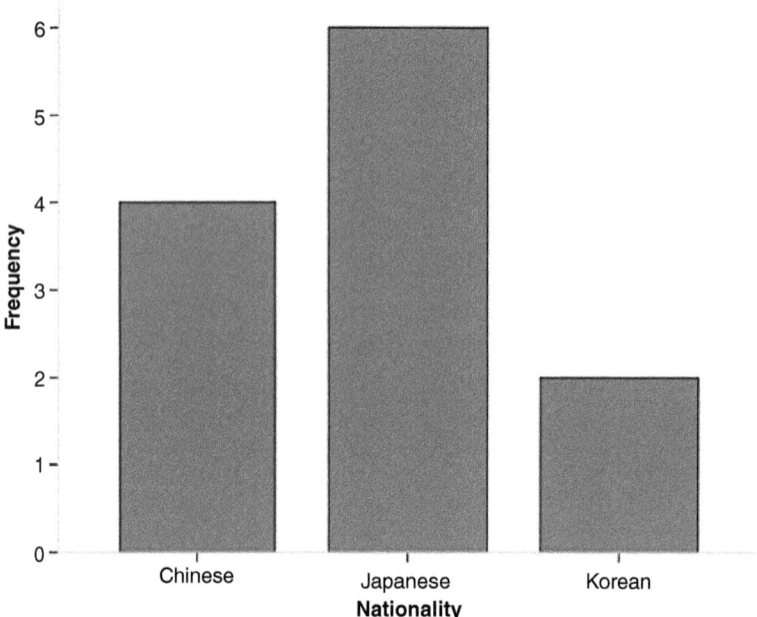

Figure 18.1 The bar graph for Example 18.2

In this bar graph, we can see that Japanese students were the most frequent, followed by Chinese and then Korean.

Bar graphs can also be used to visualize the relative frequencies or percentages of different categories and subcategories by using grouped (clustered) or stacked bar graph format. In a grouped bar graph, multiple bars are displayed side-by-side with each bar representing a distinct category or subgroup. This type of bar graph is useful for comparing different categories or subgroups not related to each other. Stacked bar graphs show multiple bars stacked on top of each other with each bar representing a subcategory of a larger category. This type of graph is useful for comparing the proportions of different subcategories within a larger category.

To create a clustered bar graph in SPSS, you can follow the procedure in SPSS Steps 18.2.

SPSS STEPS 18.2

- Open the data file in SPSS
- Select "Graphs" > "Bar."
- Choose "Clustered" in "Type of Bar Chart," check "Summaries for groups of cases," and click "Define."
- Move x-axis variable from the list to "Category Axis" box.
- Move y-axis variable(s) to "Define Clusters by" box.
- Under "Bars Represent," choose "N of cases."
- Click "OK."

Example 18.3 illustrates the use of a clustered or grouped bar graph.

EXAMPLE 18.3

An example of using clustered or grouped bar graphs could be for analyzing the distribution of different types of errors made by language learners in a different writing task: Task A and Task B. For instance, you may have collected the following data (Table 18.3) on the frequency of spelling, lexical, and grammatical errors made by a group of 20 English language learners.

Table 18.3 The frequency of types of errors in Example 18.3

Writing task	Types of error	Frequency
Task A	Grammatical errors	32
Task B	Grammatical errors	28
Task A	Lexical errors	21
Task B	Lexical errors	18
Task A	Spelling errors	4
Task B	Spelling errors	7

You can use a clustered or grouped bar graph to visually represent the relative frequencies or percentages of each error type. List task categories such as "Task A" and "Task B" on the horizontal axis, with the vertical axis representing error frequencies. Each bar shows an error type, and its height indicates frequency. Figure 18.2 shows an example of an SPSS-generated grouped bar graph with task categories on the horizontal axis and error frequencies on the vertical axis. It reveals that grammatical errors are most frequent, followed by lexical and spelling errors in both Task A and Task B.

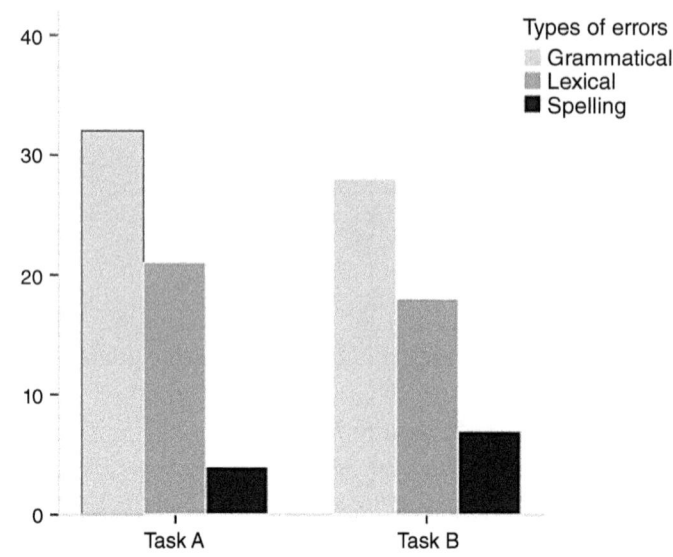

Figure 18.2 A grouped bar graph for Example 18.3

Pie Charts

A pie chart is another way of graphically representing data. A pie chart is a circular data visualization that displays the proportional parts of a whole. It is divided into slices, with each slice representing a proportion of the total. Pie charts are useful tools for showing how the different parts of the data compare to each other in terms of proportion. One limitation of a pie chart is that it becomes difficult to read it if there are too many categories. Like bar graphs, pie charts can be made by using statistical programs such as SPSS and R. To create pie charts in SPSS, you can follow the procedure in SPSS Steps 18.3.

SPSS STEPS 18.3

- Open the data file in SPSS.
- Go to the "Graphs" > "Pie", tick "Summaries for groups of cases," > "Define."
- In the "Pie" dialog box, select the variable for the slices of the pie chart and move it to the "Define Slices By" box.
- Under "Slices Represent choose "% of cases."
- Click "OK."

Table 18.4 displays the frequency and Figure 18.3 shows a pie chart of the nationalities of participants presented earlier in Example 18.2.

Table 18.4 Participant nationalities distribution from Example 18.2

Nationality	Frequency	Percentage
Chinese	4	33.3
Japanese	6	50.0
Korean	2	16.7
Total	12	100

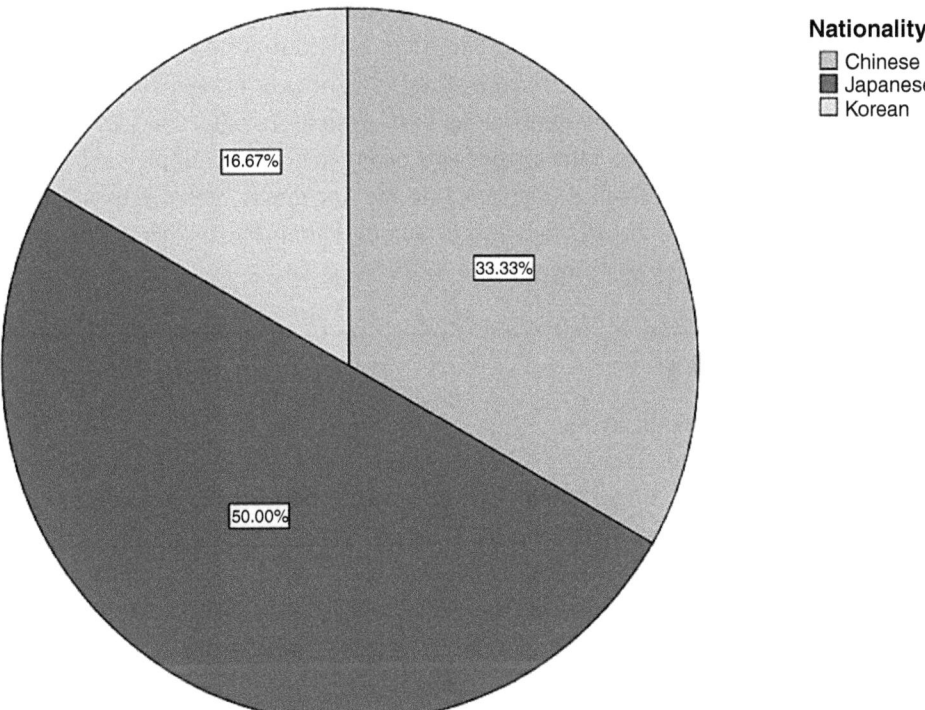

Nationality
- Chinese
- Japanese
- Korean

Figure 18.3 A pie chart of participant nationalities from Example 18.2

Line Graphs

A line graph is a chart that displays data using a series of points connected by a line. A line graph is usually used to show the trend of a continuous variable over time or across different conditions or variables. Line graphs are thus often used to track changes in a variable over time or to compare the relationship between two or more variables, such as the relationship between a teaching method and students' test scores on a language proficiency measure, for example. When there is a dependent and independent variable, such as in the example just given, in a line graph, the horizontal axis represents the independent variable (e.g., the language teaching method) and the vertical axis represents the dependent variable (students' test scores).

A line graph is a chart that displays data using a series of points connected by a line. A line graph is usually used to show the trend of a continuous variable over time or across different conditions or variables.

As noted above, line graphs are useful when you want to examine changes in values over time or for changes in one variable compared to another. They are also useful for time-series designs or for the prediction of future trends or patterns based on the data. The main difference between a bar graph and a line graph is the type of data that they are used to represent. A bar graph is used to display categorical data, which are data that can be divided into distinct categories or groups. However, a line graph is often used to display continuous data, which are data that can take any value within a given range. Line graphs can be created with multiple variables, in which case multiple lines will be displayed on the line graph. This can be useful for comparing the trend or changes between or among variables. To create a line graph in SPSS, you can follow the procedure in SPSS Steps 18.4.

SPSS STEPS 18.4

- Open the data file in SPSS.
- Go to "Graphs" > "Line."
- Select "multiple" under "Line Charts," check "Summaries for groups of cases," click "Define."
- In "Lines represent" box, click "Other Statistic."
- Choose x-axis variable and move it to "Category Axis" box.
- Select y-axis variable(s) and move it to "Define Lines by" box.
- Click "OK."

Example 18.4 illustrates the use of a line graph.

EXAMPLE 18.4

An example of a line graph could be a graph showing the growth in grammatical knowledge over the course of a year for language learners. Suppose you are conducting a study with two groups: Beginner-level and more advanced-level students. The x-axis would represent different time points, such as months, and the y-axis would represent the learners' knowledge of grammar using a grammatical judgment test. A different line could be used to represent the grammatical knowledge growth for the two groups of learners. The line would show the trend of increase in knowledge over time. The hypothetical data are shown in Table 18.5 followed by the line graph performed on SPSS in Figure 18.4.

Time	Score on grammatical judgment test	
Table 18.5 The data for Example 18.4		
	Beginner level	More advanced
Month 1	50	70
Month 2	55	75
Month 3	60	78
Month 4	65	80
Month 5	68	82
Month 6	70	84
Month 7	72	86
Month 8	75	88
Month 9	78	90
Month 10	80	92
Month 11	82	94
Month 12	86	98

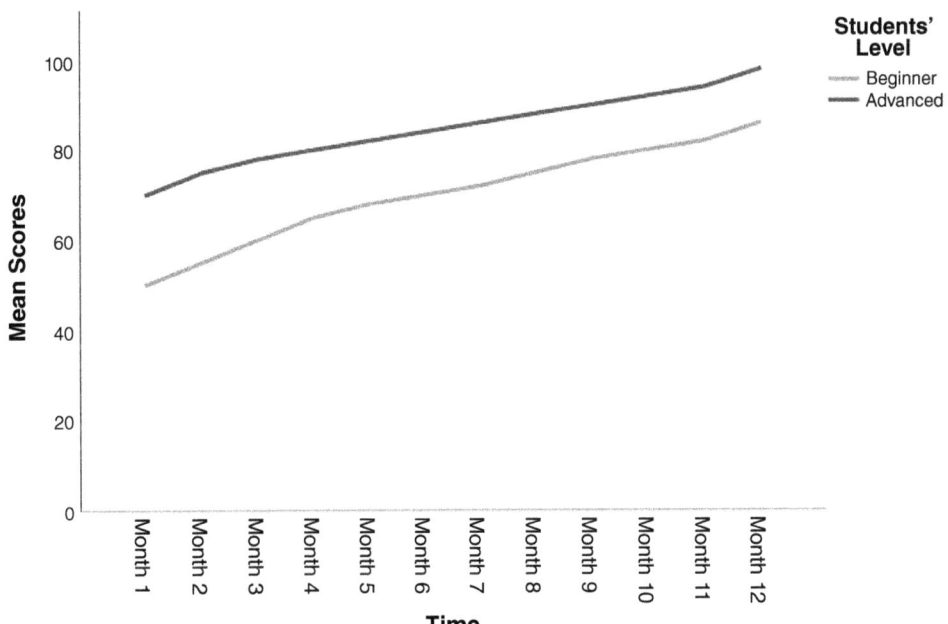

Figure 18.4 Line graph for the data in Example 18.4

Line graphs have several advantages, including ease of interpretation and effectiveness in conveying information. They efficiently display trends over time or across variables, aiding in pattern identification. Line graphs are suitable for comparing multiple datasets, simplifying variable comparisons. However, they work best for continuous data and may not be ideal for discrete or categorical data. Additionally, line graphs are limited to displaying one variable on the horizontal axis, making them less suitable for complex relationships involving multiple variables.

Box and Whisker Plots (or Boxplots)

A box and whisker plot (or a boxplot) is a visual representation that shows the distribution of the data, including the median, the upper and lower quartiles, and outliers. The box displays the middle 50% of the data (represented by the median) and the whiskers extend it to the minimum and maximum values. Any data points outside the whiskers are considered outliers. Thus, the median is the middle value in the dataset. The quartiles divide the data into four equal parts. The first quartile (Q1) is the value that is 25% of the way through the dataset, and the third quartile (Q3) is the value that is 75% of the way through the dataset. The range is the difference between the minimum and maximum values in the dataset. Outliers are shown as individual points outside the whiskers (i.e., the lines extending from the box that represent the minimum and maximum values).

A boxplot is particularly useful for comparing the distribution of two or more datasets and identifying any extreme or unusual observations, such as outliers or skewed data. Boxplots can help identify any differences in the central tendency (i.e., the median), the spread of the values, or the presence of any outliers for the two datasets.

A box and whisker plot (or a boxplot) is a visual representation that shows the distribution of the data, including the median, the upper and lower quartiles, and outliers.

There are different ways of creating a boxplot in SPSS. One way is to use the "Graph" menu. To create the boxplot, you can follow the procedure in SPSS Steps 18.5.

SPSS STEPS 18.5

- Open the data file in SPSS.
- Click on "Graphs" in the top menu, then "Boxplot."
- Select "Simple" and "Summaries for groups of cases."
- Click "Define"
- In the "Boxplots" dialog box, select the grouping variable and move it to the "Category Axis" box and the variable you want to plot to the "Variable" box.
- Click "OK."

Please note that in SPSS, the format of your data depends on your specific analysis and how you want to create your boxplot. Long format is typically used when you want to create boxplots to compare multiple groups or categories based on a single variable. In this format, you have one column for the grouping or categorical variable and another column for the numeric variable you want to visualize in the boxplot.

In applied linguistics research, boxplots can be used to visualize the distribution of various linguistic variables, such as language proficiency scores, lexical knowledge, or speaking skills, and so on. Example 18.5 illustrates the use of boxplots.

EXAMPLE 18.5

Suppose you want to investigate the effect of a specific feedback type on ESL students' grammatical accuracy. You administer pre and posttests and compare score distributions. You then create boxplots for both tests. A posttest boxplot with a higher median and a narrower distribution suggests improved performance. Conversely, a posttest boxplot with a similar or wider distribution may suggest no significant performance changes. For example, consider the dataset of test scores shown in Table 18.6.

To create a boxplot for the dataset, we first need to find the median, quartiles, and range of the dataset. To find the median and quartiles for the pretest data, you first need to sort the data in ascending order: 66, 71, 71, 73, 81, 82, 84, 86, 89, 90. The median is the middle value of the sorted data. Since there are an even number of values, the median is the average of the two middle values: Median = (81 + 82) / 2 = 81.5. To find the first quartile (Q1), you take the median of the lower half of the data: Q1 = Median of {66, 71, 71, 73, 81} = 71. To find the third quartile (Q3), you take the median of the upper half of the data: Q3 = Median of {82, 84, 86, 89, 90} = 86. To find the range of the data, you subtract the smallest value from the largest value. The smallest value is 66 and the largest value is 90.

We will follow the same steps for the posttest and that gives the following Median = 89.5, Q1 = 84, Q3 = 92, Range = 19. The smaller posttest range (19) compared to the pretest range (24) suggests a relatively smaller spread in the posttest scores. Figure 18.5 shows the boxplot of the data created by SPSS.

Table 18.6 Dataset for Example 18.5

Participants	Test score	
	Pretest	Posttest
Student 1	73	90
Student 2	81	84
Student 3	84	95
Student 4	71	82
Student 5	89	91
Student 6	66	76
Student 7	71	84
Student 8	82	89
Student 9	90	92
Student 10	86	93

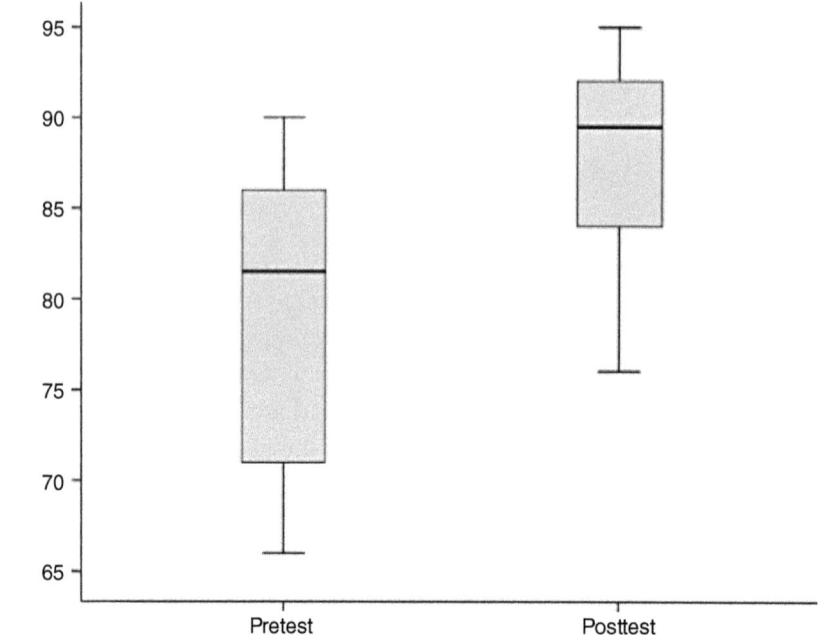

Figure 18.5 Boxplot for the data in Example 18.5

In the boxplot, each box represents the middle 50% of the data. The median for the pretest (81.5) and posttest (89.5) are shown as lines inside the respective boxes. Whiskers extend from the box to the minimum (66, 76) and maximum (90, 95) values for pretest and posttest, respectively. Q1 for pretest (71) and posttest (84) indicates the value below which 25% of the data lie. Q3 for pretest (86) and posttest (92) indicates the value below which 75% of the data lie, with 25% above. Overall, the following observations can be made for the pretest and posttest boxplots:

- Boxplots show different distributions for pretest and posttest scores. The posttest plot, which is relatively short, suggests a smaller overall data spread compared to the pretest.
- The posttest median is higher than the pretest median, indicating improvement from pretest to posttest.
- No outliers are observed in either dataset.

Advantages and Limitations of Boxplots

One of the advantages of a boxplot is that it provides a quick visual summary of the data distribution, including the median, variability, and skewness of the data. It also displays outliers and unusual cases, helping to identify anomalies in the data. The limitations include its inability to provide a detailed view of the distribution. For example, it does not show the shape or frequency of the data and may not be useful for small datasets. Its interpretation may also be difficult for those who are not familiar with the concepts used in interpreting boxplots, such as quartiles and percentiles.

Stem and Leaf Plots

A stem and leaf plot is a graphical representation that shows the distribution of numerical data while including the original data values. It consists of two parts: the stem and the leaf. The stem shows the leftmost digit or digits of the data values, and the leaf shows the rightmost digits. Stems are listed vertically, and the leaves for each stem are listed horizontally next to that stem. This allows for a quick and easy way to see not only the data but its distribution, including the range, shape, and outliers. Stem and leaf plots are particularly useful for small to medium-sized datasets and for when we want to display the distribution of the dataset in a compact format while including the individual data values. Stem and leaf plots can quickly identify the range of values, central tendency, and variability of the data, as well as any outliers or unusual patterns. This graphical representation can be used with both continuous and discrete numerical data. However, it is more suitable for continuous data, which can be grouped into intervals or groups. Other types of graphs such as bar graphs or pie charts are usually more appropriate for categorical data.

A stem and leaf plot is a graphical representation that shows the distribution of numerical data while including the original data values. It consists of two parts: the stem and the leaf. The stem shows the leftmost digit or digits of the data values, and the leaf shows the rightmost digits.

To create a stem and leaf plot in SPSS, follow the procedure in SPSS Steps 18.6.

SPSS STEPS 18.6

- Open the data file in SPSS.
- Select "Analyze" > "Descriptive Statistics" > "Explore."
- Move the variable you want to plot into the "Dependent List" box.
- Click "Plots."
- Select "Stem-and-leaf."
- Under "Boxplots" select "None" for "Boxplots."
- Click "Continue."
- Under "Display" select "Plots."
- Click "OK."

EXAMPLE 18.6

In applied linguistics research, stem and leaf plots can be used to graphically represent the distribution of various linguistic data. Take for example the study presented earlier that intended to investigate the effect of a particular type of feedback on students' accuracy of test scores in an ESL classroom. The data for the pretest is shown in Table 18.7.

Table 18.7 The data for Example 18.6

Participants	Pretest score
Student 1	73
Student 2	81
Student 3	84
Student 4	71
Student 5	89
Student 6	66
Student 7	71
Student 8	82
Student 9	90
Student 10	86

The distribution of the data for the pretest can be visually shown with a stem and leaf plot. To create a stem and leaf plot, we will first choose the stems. One common method is to use the tens digit as the stem and the units digit as the leaf. In the case of our example, the stems would be 6, 7, 8, and 9.

The stems are listed vertically on the left side, while the corresponding "leaves" (the units digits) are listed horizontally on the right side. This allows us to visualize the distribution of the data and quickly identify any patterns or outliers.

```
6 | 6
7 | 1 1 3
8 | 1 2 4 6 9
9 | 0
```

6 is for the number 66
7 is for the numbers 71, 71, 73
8 is for the numbers 81, 82, 84, 86, and 89
9 is for the number 90

Advantages and Limitations of Stem and Leaf Plots

One of the advantages of stem and leaf plots is that they provide a quick visual summary of a dataset while including the individual data values, allowing for easy identification of specific values. They also allow for easy comparisons between groups or subgroups of data. A limitation would be that they may not be suitable for large datasets with many values.

Scatter Plots

A scatter plot visually represents the relationship between two continuous variables. It displays dots on a two-dimensional plane, with one variable on the x-axis and the other on the y-axis. Each dot represents an individual data point, positioned based on the values of the corresponding variables. The arrangement of the dots indicates the nature and strength of the relationship. For instance, closely arranged points around a straight line suggest a strong linear relationship, while widely scattered points indicate a weaker or no relationship. Scatter plots in applied linguistics help explore variable relationships, identify outliers, and can include a line or curve to show the degree of linearity (see Figure 18.6).

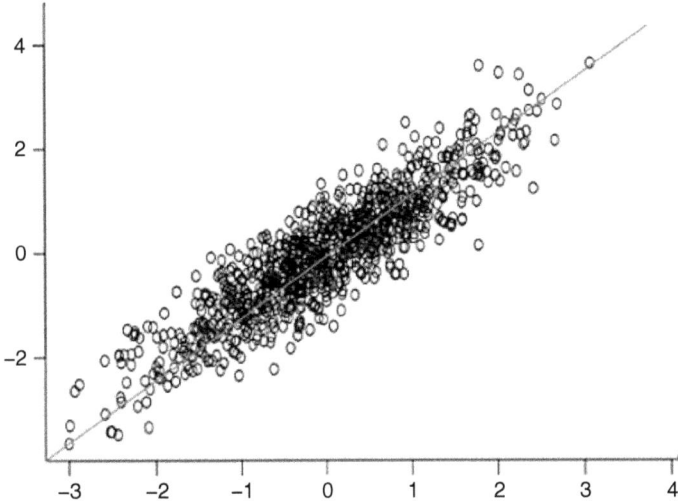

Figure 18.6 An example of a scatter plot

A scatter plot is type of visual representation that is used to graphically represent the relationship between two continuous variables.

A scatter plot can display different types of relationships between two variables. These include the following:

- **Positive linear relationship:** As one variable increases, the other tends to increase, with points on the upward-sloping scatter plot forming a straight line from left to right.
- **Negative linear relationship:** As one variable increases, the other tends to decrease, with points on the downward-sloping scatter plot forming a straight line from left to right.
- **Nonlinear relationship:** The relationship is not linear, and points on the scatter plot follow a curved or irregular pattern.
- **No relationship:** There is no clear relationship between variables, and points on the scatter plot are scattered randomly.
- **Curvilinear relationship:** The relationship is not linear, and as one variable changes, the other does not change at a constant rate, resulting in a curved pattern on the graph.

These relationships are depicted in Figure 18.7
You can create a scatter plot in SPSS by following the procedure in SPSS Steps 18.7.

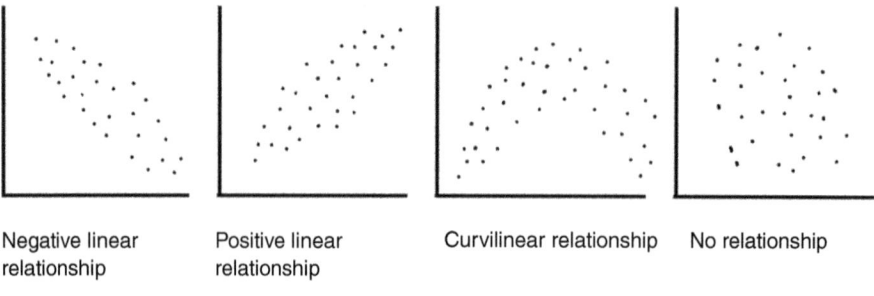

Negative linear   Positive linear   Curvilinear relationship   No relationship
relationship   relationship

Figure 18.7 Different types of relationships

SPSS STEPS 18.7

- Open the data file in SPSS.
- Click on "Graphs."
- Click "Scatter/Dot."
- Select "Simple Scatter."
- Click "Define."
- Move one of the variables to the "Y Axis" box, and the other to the "X Axis" box.
- Click "OK."

Histograms

A histogram is a type of bar graph used to display the distribution of a continuous variable. It is different from a typical bar graph, which is a chart that represents categorical data. A histogram provides a visual representation of continuous data and its distribution. It is a graphical representation, consisting of rectangular bars to show the frequency of the data points that fall within a specified range of values. The height of each rectangle is proportional to the number of data points that fall within that area. The shape of the entire histogram represents the total number of the data points. The difference between a histogram and a bar graph is that a histogram shows the distribution of a continuous variable whereas a bar graph is often used to display categorical data.

A histogram is a type of bar graph used to display the distribution of a continuous variable.

A histogram offers insights into data distribution, revealing variability, symmetry, skewness, multimodality, and outliers. Outliers, significantly differing from most data points, can impact statistical analyses, affecting measures such as the mean or median and the overall distribution shape. Identifying and understanding outliers is crucial for accurate data conclusions. Histograms also facilitate comparisons between datasets or variables, such as vocabulary test scores for different classes. The shape of a histogram can guide us in choosing the most appropriate measure of central tendency (such as the mean, median, or mode) and variability (such as the range or standard deviation) depending on the distribution of the data. For example, if the data are symmetric, the mean and standard deviation may be suitable, while for skewed data, the median and interquartile range might be more appropriate (see below).

The histogram shape can vary depending on the distribution of the data it represents. Three common shapes are bell-shaped (normal) distribution, skewed distribution, and bimodal distribution.

Bell-shaped or normal distribution: A bell-shaped histogram has a normal distribution with a peak in the middle, narrowing off symmetrically on either side, forming a bell shape (see Figure 18.8). This type of histogram shows that the distribution of the data is normal, with a high degree of symmetry.

Skewed distribution: A skewed histogram represents a distribution which is not normal and has a long tail in one direction. A skewed distribution can be either positively skewed or negatively skewed. A positively skewed histogram has a long tail to the right (see Figure 18.10), and a negatively skewed histogram has a long tail to the left (see Figure 18.9).

Bimodal distribution: A bimodal histogram (see Figure 18.11) represents a distribution that has two peaks. It is called bimodal because this kind of distribution has two distinct modes or data concentration centers. A bimodal distribution may indicate that data come from two distinct populations or groups.

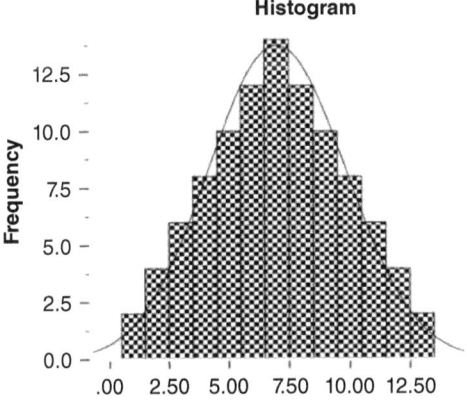

Figure 18.8 A bell-shaped histogram showing a normal distribution

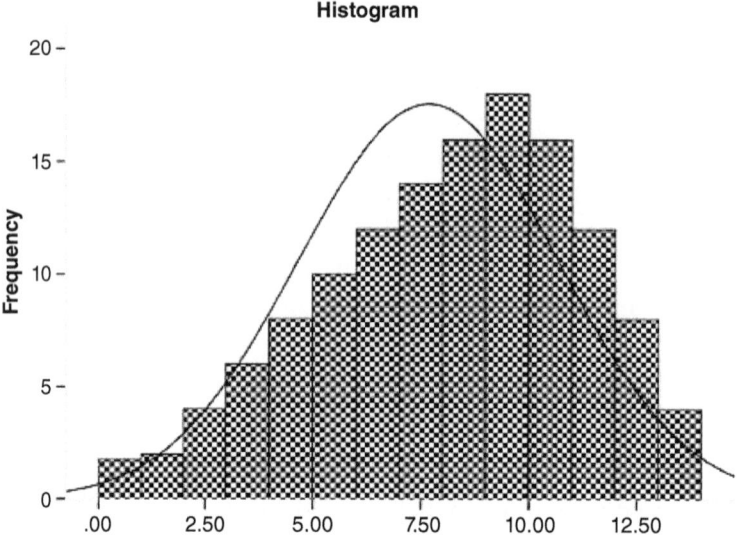

Figure 18.9 A histogram with a negatively skewed distribution

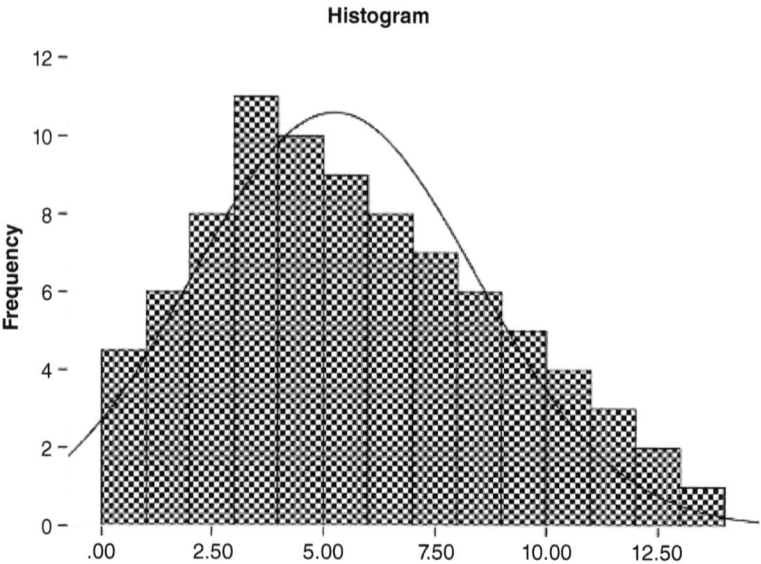

Figure 18.10 A histogram with a positively skewed distribution

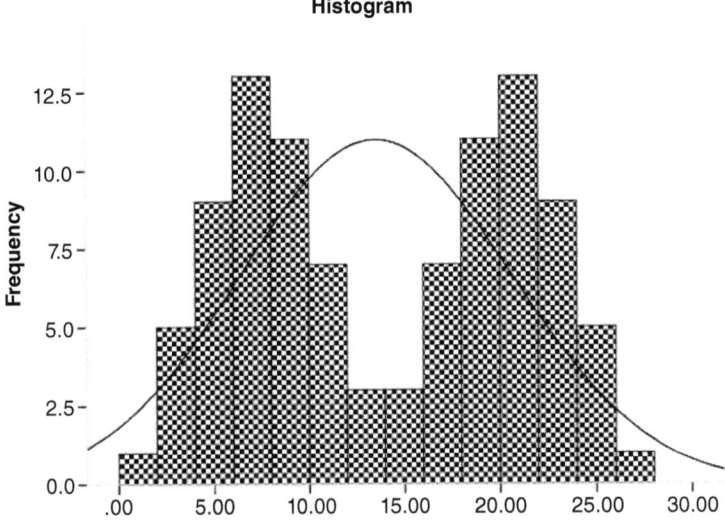

Figure 18.11 A histogram showing a bimodal distribution

POINTS TO PONDER

Before reading the next section, what are the different types of measure of central tendency, and could you provide examples of situations where a specific measure of central tendency might be more appropriate than others? What considerations should be taken into account when choosing the most suitable measure for a given dataset or scenario?

Measures of Central Tendency

After visually inspecting the data, the next step is to summarize the data using summary statistics. Measures of central tendency are statistical measures that summarize a set of numerical data by finding and describing the center of the database. They calculate a single value, and by doing so, they provide a quick and easy way to describe the dataset. Such measures are very helpful when we are dealing with large datasets that would be difficult to describe in detail. The three most commonly used measures of central tendency are the mean, the median, and the mode.

Measures of central tendency are statistical measures that summarize a set of numerical data by finding and describing the center of the database.

Mean

The mean is the average and is calculated by taking the sum of all the values in a dataset and dividing it by the number of values. The formula for the mean is

Mean = $(\Sigma x) / n$.

Suppose we have the following five test scores (out of 50): 40, 30, 35, 27, 48. We add up all the values divided by the number of values:

(40 + 30 + 35 + 27 + 48) / 5 = 180 / 5 = 36.

So, the mean or the average of this dataset is 36.

The mean is used for continuous and interval data, which are types of numerical data that represent the magnitude or difference between two values but do not have a true zero point. An example of continuous data is test scores. The mean is the most commonly used measure of central tendency, but it is important to note that the mean is sensitive to outliers or extreme values in the data. In cases where there are outliers or the distribution of the data is heavily skewed, the median (see below) is a more appropriate measure of central tendency. Also, the mean is not appropriate for categorical or nominal data (such as first language background), because they are not numerical and cannot be converted to an average. In these cases, the mode may be a more appropriate measure of central tendency.

Median

The median is the middle point of a dataset when the values in the dataset are arranged by magnitude. The median is the middle value with the dataset having an odd number of values. If the dataset has an even number of values, the median is the average of the two middle values (see Example 18.7). So, to calculate the median, you can follow these steps:

- Order the data values from the smallest value to the largest value.
- For an odd number, the median of the data would be the middle value.
- For an even number, the median of the data would the average (mean) of the two middle values.

EXAMPLE 18.7

Here is an example to show how the calculation of the median is conducted when there are an odd number of values. The dataset is: 4, 8, 6, 12, 9. We order the dataset from smallest to largest: 4, 6, 8, 9, 12. Since the number of values is five, the dataset has an odd number of values. Therefore, the median would be the middle value: 8.

Here is an example of when there are an even number of values. The dataset is: 5, 7, 9, 6. We order the data from smallest to largest: 5, 6, 7, 9. We take the average of the two middle values: (6 + 7) / 2 = 6.5. So, the median of the dataset is 6.5.

Mode

The mode is the most frequently occurring value in a dataset, applicable to categorical or nominal data. A dataset may have one mode, multiple modes, or none. The mean, median, and mode offer different insights into data. The mean is sensitive to outliers. The median is not sensitive to outliers but provides less information than the mean. The mode identifies the most common value but lacks information about overall data distribution.

Which Measure of Central Tendency Should We Use, and When?

Choosing between the mean, median, or mode as a measure of central tendency depends on the nature of the data and the information needed. As discussed before, there are four measurement scales: nominal, ordinal, interval, and ratio. The mean is suitable for interval and ratio data and is best when the data are normally distributed. However, as noted earlier, it is sensitive to outliers or skewed data. In such cases, the median is a better choice as it is not influenced by extreme values, representing the middle value when data are ordered. For example, in a proficiency test with some students scoring exceptionally high, the median is less affected, providing a more accurate reflection of typical scores. In symmetrical data, the mean, median, and mode are all the same, but in nonnormal distributions, they can differ.

Example 18.8 illustrates normally distributed data. Example 18.9 illustrates data that are not normally distributed.

EXAMPLE 18.8

Normally distributed data: 10, 12, 12, 14, 14, 14, 14, 16, 16, 18
    In this dataset, the mean, median, and mode will be the same:

The mean is 14: $(10 + 12 + 12 + 14 + 14 + 14 + 14 + 16 + 16 + 18)/ 10 = 14$
The median (middle value) is 14, which is the fifth and sixth value in the
    ordered dataset.
The mode is also 14 as it is the most popular score.

EXAMPLE 18.9

Nonnormally distributed data: 10, 12, 12, 12, 14, 16, 20, 26, 26, 30.
    In this dataset, the mean, median, and mode will be different.

The mean is 17.8 $(10 + 12 + 12 + 12 + 14 + 16 + 20 + 26 + 26 + 30)/ 10 = 17.8$
The median (middle value) is 15, which is the average of the fifth and sixth values
    in the ordered dataset.
The mode is 12 as it is the most popular score.

Measures of Dispersion

Measures of dispersion are descriptive statistics tools that describe the extent to which data are spread around the central tendency, such as the mean or the median. Three widely used measures of dispersion are the range, variance, and standard deviation.

Range
The range is a measure of dispersion that represents the difference between the minimum (the smallest) and the maximum (the largest) values or scores in a dataset.

It is a very basic and simple measure that tells us about the spread of the data. It is calculated by subtracting the smallest value or score from the largest value or score (see Example 18.10):

Range = maximum value − minimum value.

EXAMPLE 18.10

Suppose we have a dataset of the following scores on an exam from ten students: 44, 45, 45, 46, 46, 47 49, 52, 58, 62.

The range for this dataset is calculated as follows:

Range = 62 − 44 = 18
Range = 18

Therefore our example data have a range of 18. This means that the difference between the smallest and the largest value is 18 points. In other words, the spread of the data is over a range of 18 units, from 44 to 62.

While easy to calculate, the range can be misleading when outliers are present, leading to an inflated sense of data variability. The range can significantly change with the addition of outliers, providing a distorted view. For instance, suppose the dataset of the exam scores above included one additional value of 200. This additional value would change the range dramatically. In this case, the range would be 136: (200−44), which is much larger than the actual variability of most of the data. This large range is because of the value of 200, which is an outlier. As range only considers the difference between the highest and lowest values, it is a crude measure of variability. For more accurate representations, measures such as variance and standard deviation can be used.

Interquartile Range (IQR)

Another measure of variability that is less affected by outliers is the interquartile range (IQR). This statistic provides a measure of the spread of the middle 50% of the data. It is calculated as the difference between the first quartile (Q1) and the third quartile (Q3) of a dataset. As noted before, quartiles are values that divide a dataset into four equal parts, such that Q1 represents the lower 25% of the data (25th percentile) and Q3 represents the upper 25% of the data (75th percentile). The IQR is the area between the 25th and 75th percentile (75−25), which is where there is 50% of the data (see Example 18.11). The IQR is a more robust measure of spread than range because it is less sensitive to outliers than other measures, such as the range, variance, or standard deviation (see below). Additionally, the IQR can be used to define the upper and lower bounds for outliers, which are typically defined as data points that are more than 1.5 times the IQR away from the nearest quartile.

EXAMPLE 18.11

Suppose we have the following database of a set of exam scores for a class of nineteen students (Table 18.8).

The IQR is found to be 20 points. The first quartile (Q1) is 63, and the third quartile (Q3) is 83.

IQR = 83−63, which is 20 points.

Table 18.8 The data for Example 18.11

51	56	59	61	63	65	67	69	71	73	75	77	78	81	83	85	90	95	100
				Q1					Q2					Q3				
								Median										

To identify any potential outliers, we can use the IQR to define the upper and lower bounds.

The lower bound is calculated as $Q1 - 1.5 \times IQR$, which is $63 - (1.5 \times 20) = 33$.
The upper bound is calculated as $Q3 + 1.5 \times IQR$, which is $83 + (1.5 \times 20) = 113$.

Thus, any data values that fall below 33 or above 113 can be considered potential outliers. For example, if there were a score of 114 in the database, it would be considered a potential outlier since it is greater than the upper bound of 113. Similarly, a score of 34 would be considered a potential outlier since it is less than 33.

To calculate the IQR in SPSS, follow the procedure in SPSS Steps 18.8.

SPSS STEPS 18.8

- Open the data file in SPSS.
- Select "Analyze" > "Descriptive Statistics."
- In the "Descriptive Statistics" menu, select "Explore."
- In the "Explore" dialog box, select the variable(s) for which you want to calculate the IQR.
- Under "Statistics," check the box for "Quartiles" to calculate the quartiles of your selected variable(s).
- Under "Display" select "Both" to create a boxplot and the statistics.
- Click "OK."

In the output, the IQR will be listed in the Descriptive Statistics table.

Variance

Variance is another measure of variability. It is a quantified measure of how much individual values or scores in a database deviate from the mean. Therefore, it measures the degree of variability of data values around the mean. A high variance means that the data are spread out widely, whereas a low variance indicates that the data points are clustered closely around the mean. The variance is the average of the squared deviations of each value from the mean. Variance differs from range in that it considers the distribution of all data points within a dataset, whereas range only takes into account the difference between the highest and lowest values.

Variance is a quantified measure of how much individual values or scores in a database deviate from the mean.

The formula to calculate variance is shown in Equation 18.1.

Equation 18.1
$$S^2 = \frac{\Sigma(xi - \bar{x})^2}{n - 1}$$

Where:

S^2 = sample variance
Σ is the summation symbol
xi is the individual values or scores in the data
$\bar{x}$ is the mean of the sample
n is the sample size or the number of data values in the sample.

We first calculate the differences between each individual value or score (xi) and the mean of the data ($\bar{x}$) : (xi − $\bar{x}$), This calculation shows how far each individual data value is from the mean. We will then square the difference: $(xi - \bar{x})^2$. This makes all the values positive and also provides more weight to larger differences, which can help to identify extreme values in the data. In the next step, we will take the sum of the squared differences between each data point and the sample mean: $\sum(xi - \bar{x})^2$. This provides a measure of how much all the data points vary from the sample mean. We will finally divide the sum of the squared differences by the sample size minus one to provide an average measure of the amount of variability in the data.

EXAMPLE 18.12

To illustrate variance with an example, consider the following dataset of four numbers: 2, 5, 8, and 9. The mean is (2 + 5 + 8 + 9)/4 = 6. The variance can be calculated as follows:

$$S^2 = ((2-6)^2 + (5-6)^2 + (8-6)^2 + (9-6)^2)/4 - 1 = (16 + 1 + 4 + 9)/4 - 1 = 10$$

So, the sample variance of this dataset is 10. This means that the individual data points are spread out over a wide range of 10 values, relative to the mean.

It is important to note that although variance can be calculated manually, most researchers nowadays use software programs as calculating variance by hand is not only a time-consuming process but is also prone to errors, particularly when we are dealing with large databases. Many spreadsheet programs, such as Excel, have built-in functions that can easily calculate variance, and there are also statistical software programs, such as R or SPSS, which can do such analyses and are commonly used by researchers. The method for calculating variance in SPSS is given in SPSS Steps 18.9.

SPSS STEPS 18.9

- Open the data file in SPSS.
- Select "Analyze" > "Descriptive Statistics" > "Descriptives."
- In the "Descriptives" dialogue, choose the variable(s).
- Click "Options," select "Variance" under "Dispersion".
- Choose other options if needed.
- Click "Continue" > "OK."

Although, as noted earlier, statistical software can calculate variance for us, it is always useful to know and understand what its calculation involves. This knowledge can help us understand and interpret our results more effectively.

Standard Deviation

Standard deviation is another statistical measure of variability that is widely used in applied linguistics research. Similar to variance it indicates how much the individual data values deviate from the mean of the data. Therefore, both of them measure the degree of spread around the mean. The difference between the two is that variance is the average of the squared deviations of each data point from the mean, whereas the standard deviation is the square root of the variance. Because the standard deviation is the square root of the variance, it is often a preferred way of showing variability in the data as it provides a measure of data spread in the same units as in the original data. The variance is the units squared, which can be more difficult to understand intuitively. For example, if in a study the data points represent the number of errors produced by learners, the standard deviation will also be the number of errors, while the variance will be the number of errors squared. Therefore, standard deviation is easier to interpret and hence is more commonly used as a measure of data variability. Second, variance gives weight to outliers when it squares the data. Thus, if the data have many outliers, variance may not be appropriate as it is heavily affected by those extreme values. In cases where a dataset has a significant number of outliers, it may be more appropriate to use a different measure of spread such as the interquartile range (IQR), which is less affected by extreme values.

Standard deviation measures data variability by calculating the square root of the variance, thus showing how the data are dispersed around the mean.

The formula for standard deviation is shown in Equation 18.2.

Equation 18.2
$$S = \sqrt{\frac{\Sigma(xi - \bar{x})^2}{n - 1}}$$

As before, Σ is the summation symbol, xi is the individual values or scores in the data, $\bar{x}$ is the mean of the sample, and n is the sample size or the number of data values in the sample (see Example 18.13).

EXAMPLE 18.13

Let's assume that we are conducting a study on the effect of written corrective feedback on students' revision accuracy. We have collected data from ten participants, and we want to calculate the standard deviation of the data. To this end, we will first calculate the variance of the data and then take the square root of the variance. Let's assume that we have collected the following data on the number of errors corrected by ten participants.

46, 56, 46, 61, 52, 57, 55, 55, 48, 54

To calculate the standard deviation, we first need to find the mean of the data. We can do this by adding up all the data points and dividing by the total number of participants.

Mean = (46 + 56 + 46 + 61 + 52 + 57 + 55 + 55 + 48 + 54)/10 = 53

The mean number of corrections is 53.

Next, we need to calculate the deviation of each data point from the mean. To do this, we subtract the mean from each data point. Then, we square each deviation. We add up all the squared deviations and the result by the number of participants minus one. To save space, we will not do these calculations as you have learned how to do them in the previous section on variance. If we follow the procedures, the result will be the variance of the data, in which case it will be 24.66 (or 25). Finally, we take the square root of the variance to find the standard deviation:

$$\sqrt{(24.66)} = 4.96 \ (or \ 5)$$

Although we can calculate the standard deviation manually, it is much more efficient to use statistical software such as SPSS to do so. The method for calculating standard deviation in SPSS is shown in SPSS Steps 18.10.

SPSS STEPS 18.10

- Open the data file in SPSS.
- Select "Analyze" > "Descriptive Statistics" > "Descriptives."
- In the "Descriptives" dialogue box, select the variable(s) for which you want to calculate the standard deviation.
- Click on the "Options" button and select "Std. deviation" under the "Dispersion."
- Click "Continue" > "OK."

In general, the standard deviation estimates the percentage of data values that fall within a certain range around the mean. The common interpretation of the standard deviation is based on the following rule: 68–95–99.7. According to this rule, for a normally distributed dataset (i.e., a bell-shaped curve), approximately:

- 68% of the data fall within one standard deviation from the mean (34% below and 34% above the mean).
- 95% of the data fall within two standard deviations from the mean (below and above the mean).
- 99.7% of the data fall within three standard deviations from the mean (both below and above the mean).

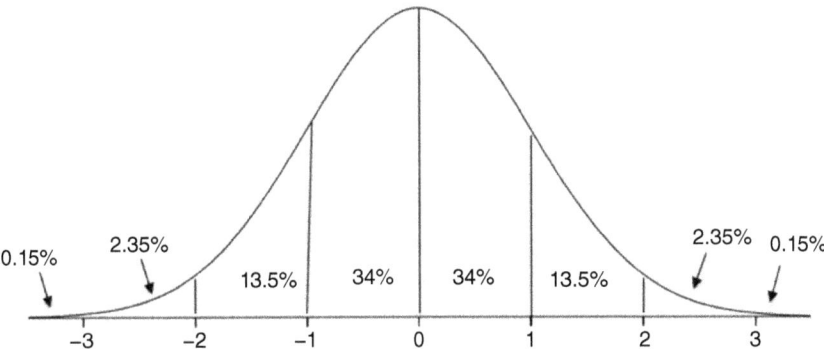

Figure 18.12 The percentage of data values around the mean in normally distributed data

We can use the rule mentioned earlier and the percentages shown in Figure 18.12 to estimate the percentage of data variability around the mean in Example 18.13. The mean of the data was 53 and the standard deviation was 5. Therefore:

- About 68% of the corrections fall between 48 and 58 (1 standard deviation from the mean, both below and above).
- About 95% of the corrections fall between 43 to 63 (2 standard deviations from the mean, 47.5% below and 47.5% above).
- About 99.7% of the corrections fall between 38 to 68 (3 standard deviations from the mean, 49.85% below and 49.85% above).

It is important to note that the rule is an approximation and is also based on the assumption of normality of distribution. Therefore, although very useful and widely used, standard deviation may not similarly apply to all datasets, particularly if the data are not normally distributed. Standard deviation is preferred over variance due to its easier interpretation and unit consistency with the data. Comparing standard deviations between datasets is straightforward since they share the same units, whereas variance, expressed in squared units, can be challenging to compare directly. For instance, a standard deviation of 5 in the context of a study on the number of corrections means that 68% of the data fall within 5 corrections of the mean. On the other hand, the variance expressed in squared units (e.g., 25 corrections squared) makes direct interpretation challenging. However, variance remains useful for comparing data variability across studies using the same measures.

Z Scores and Standardized Data

Z scores are a statistical measure used to standardize data by converting individual data points into standardized scores that can be compared more easily. The z score shows how many standard deviations a particular observation or score is away from the mean. It is useful because it allows for the comparison of data points measured on different scales or having different units of measurement.

Statistically, a z score and a standard deviation are related but distinct concepts. While standard deviation provides a measure of the degree of variation around the mean, a z score indicates how many standard deviations an individual data point or score is away from the mean. For example, a z score of 1 for a particular score indicates that the data value or score is one standard deviation away from the mean, whereas a standard deviation of 1 means that if the dataset has a mean value of 4, 68% of the data fall between 3 and 5 (one standard deviation below and one standard deviation above the mean).

Z scores are a statistical measure used to standardize data by converting individual data points into standardized scores that can be compared more easily. It shows how many standard deviations a particular observation or score is away from the mean.

A positive z score indicates that the data point is above the mean and a negative z score shows that the data point is below the mean. A z score of 0 indicates that the data point is at the mean or the same as the mean. Z scores are used in research when the intention is to compare observations from different distributions, to identify outliers in a dataset, and to standardize data for analysis. A z score is calculated by subtracting the mean of the data from the observation (or the raw score) and dividing the result by the standard deviation. Thus, the formula for calculating the z score is:

Equation 18.3 $$z = \frac{(x - \mu)}{\sigma}$$

where

x is a particular score
μ is the mean of the population
σ is the standard deviation of the population.

The above z score is for the population. We can use the formula given in Equation 18.4 for the sample, which is the same as Equation 18.3 with the difference that instead of μ (the population mean), $\bar{x}$ (the sample mean) is used, and instead of σ (the population standard deviation), S (the sample standard deviation) is used.

Equation 18.4 $$z = \frac{(x - \bar{x})}{S}$$

EXAMPLE 18.14

Suppose you have a dataset of writing scores of a class of thirty students and you want to know how well a particular student did compared to the rest of the class. Suppose the student has received 50 on the test. This does not tell you much about how well the student has done on the test compared to others. If everyone else has received above 50, this student has not performed well. However, if everyone else has received below 50, this student's performance has been outstanding compared to others. Now, to see how well that student has done, we need both the mean and the standard deviation of the test. Suppose the mean is 30 and the standard deviation is 10; to find their z score, we can use the formula given in Equation 18.4.

where:

x is the student's score (50 in this case)
$\bar{x}$ is the mean test score for the class (30)
S is the standard deviation of the test scores (10)

Plugging the values into the formula, we will get

$$z = (50 - 30)/10 = 2$$

Assuming a normal distribution, this means that the student's score is 2 standard deviations above the mean of the class. In other words, the student has performed better than approximately 97.5% of their classmates (see Figure 18.13).

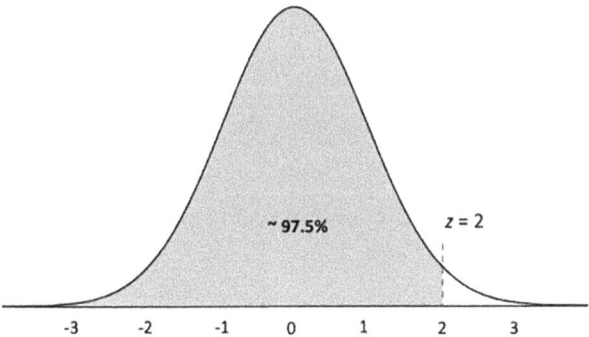

Figure 18.13 Z score and its relationship with standard deviation

To calculate z scores in SPSS, follow the procedure set out in SPSS Steps 18.11.

SPSS STEPS 18.11

- Open the data file in SPSS.
- Select "Analyze" > "Descriptive Statistics" > "Descriptives."
- In the "Descriptives" dialogue box, select the variable(s) and move them to the "Variable(s)" box.
- Select the "Save standardized values as variables" option.
- Click "OK."

Percentiles and Quartiles

Percentiles and quartiles are descriptive statistics used to depict data distribution. Percentiles divide scores into 100 equal parts, representing the percentage of data below a specific value. Commonly used percentiles include the 25th, 50th (median), and 75th percentiles. They help understand data distribution and identify extreme values. For example, the 50th percentile is the value below which 50% of the data fall and above which the other 50% fall. Comparing percentiles between groups can highlight differences. Quartiles divide data into four equal parts, with each part representing 25% of the data. The interpretation is the same for percentiles. The first quartile (Q1) is the value below which 25% of the data fall, the second quartile (Q2) is the value below which 50% of the data fall (also known as the median), and the third quartile (Q3) is the value below which 75% of the data fall. As discussed earlier, the difference between the third and first quartiles (Q3−Q1) is known as the interquartile range (IQR), which is a measure of the spread of the data.

Both percentiles and quartiles are valuable for nonnormally distributed data, aiding in outlier identification and providing a comprehensive view when used with mean and standard deviation.

Percentiles divide the distribution of a set of scores into 100 equal parts, with each part representing 1 percent of the data. **Quartiles** divide a distribution into four equal parts, with each part representing 25% of the data.

POINTS TO PONDER

Before reading the next section about confidence intervals, how would you define a confidence interval? How does the use of confidence intervals contribute to a more accurate interpretation of the findings?

Confidence Intervals for Population Mean

A confidence interval is a statistical measure that provides an estimate of the value of a population parameter, such as a population mean or proportion, based on a sample of data (see also Chapter 19). They are a range within which the true value of a population characteristic such as the mean is estimated to lie with a certain degree of confidence. The level of confidence in the confidence interval shows the probability that the true population characteristic (such as the mean) falls within that confidence interval. Levels of confidence commonly used in statistical analysis are 90% or 95%. For example, 95% confidence for a population mean shows that if the same study using the same sampling process and size is repeated multiple times, we are 95% confident that the mean will fall within the range given by the confidence interval.

The steps to calculate confidence intervals using SPSS are shown in SPSS Steps 18.12.

SPSS STEPS 18.12

- Open the data file in SPSS.
- Select "Analyze" > "Descriptive Statistics" > "Explore."
- In the "Explore" dialog box, select the variable and move it to the "Dependent List" box.
- Under "Display" check "Statistics".
- Click "Statistics" and check the "Descriptives" box.
- Click "Continue" > "OK."

Once the analysis is complete, the output window will display the sample mean, the confidence interval, and other statistics such as the standard deviation, median, range, etc. (see Example 18.15).

A confidence interval is a statistical measure that provides an estimate of the value of a population parameter, such as a population mean or proportion, based on a sample of data. It represents a range within which the true value of a population characteristic such as the mean is estimated to lie with a certain degree of confidence.

EXAMPLE 18.15

Suppose we have conducted a study of the effect of a particular language program on university students' English language proficiency. Our sample contains the scores of twenty students who were tested after they went through the program. The hypothetical data for these students' test scores are as follows:

Students' test scores: 85, 78, 92, 68, 88, 76, 95, 70, 89, 75, 91, 74, 94, 86, 67, 90, 72, 77, 87, 93

The mean of the data is 82.35, and now we want to estimate the population mean for all the students who go through such a program with 95% confidence. To this end, we calculate the 95% confidence interval for the population mean of English proficiency score. To do so, we use SPSS using the steps given in SPSS Steps 18.12. The output shown in SPSS Output 18.1 includes the mean and the confidence interval of the data.

SPSS OUTPUT 18.1

Descriptives			Statistic	Std. Error
Language Proficiency	Mean		82.35	2.094
	95% Confidence Interval for Mean	Lower Bound	77.97	
		Upper Bound	86.73	

As we can see, the mean of language proficiency in our sample is 82.35 and the 95% confidence interval shows a range: 77.97 (Lower Bound) to 86.73 (Upper Bound). In SPSS outputs, the upper and lower bounds refer to the two endpoints of the interval, or the lowest and the highest possible values for the population mean. The confidence intervals shown in this table (77.97 to 86.73) mean that we are 95% confident that the true mean of English proficiency scores of all the students going through this program at the university falls between 77.97 and 86.73. This information can be useful when we are assessing the effectiveness of this particular language program. Here are a few important things to know about confidence intervals:

- A confidence interval is a range of values within which the true value of a population parameter (e.g., mean) is expected to fall with a certain level of confidence. It is usually indicated as a percentage, such as 95% or 99%.
- The size of the confidence interval depends on the nature of the sample, including its size and the variability of the data. A larger sample size or lower variability can produce a narrower interval, whereas a higher level of confidence can produce a wider interval.
- A confidence interval is specific to the sample being used to calculate it. It is not a definite measure but rather an estimate of the range where the population parameter is likely to fall based on the sample.
- The wider the confidence interval the greater the uncertainty in the estimate of the population parameter. Conversely, the narrower the confidence interval, the greater accuracy and confidence there is in the estimate.
- The interpretation of a confidence interval depends on the size of the sample and the extent to which it represents the population.

Altogether, the confidence interval is a useful tool, and it is important to use it appropriately in the context of the research question.

Conclusion

This chapter on descriptive statistics has provided an overview of the fundamental concepts and techniques used in descriptive data analysis. Descriptive statistics is an essential tool in quantitative data analysis as it provides a useful way of summarizing and describing the data. The chapter began by discussing the importance of descriptive statistics, followed by an exploration of frequency distributions and the use of graphical representations, such as bar graphs, pie charts, line graphs, box and whisker plots, scatter plots, and histograms. It then introduced different types of descriptive statistics, including measures of central tendency and variability of a dataset, such as mean, median, mode, range, variance, and standard deviation, with examples to help you understand and apply these concepts in applied linguistics research. The chapter also addressed issues related to percentiles, quartiles, and interquartile range and their applications and interpretation. Altogether, the chapter aimed to provide a thorough introduction to the topic of descriptive statistics and its applications and interpretation in quantitative data analysis.

It is important to note that descriptive statistics only describes and summarizes the data and cannot be used to make predictions or inferences about the larger population. In order to draw inferences about the data, we need to go further and conduct inferential statistics. This topic will be covered in some detail in the next four chapters.

DISCUSSION AND ACTIVITY QUESTIONS

Discussion Questions

1. What is the purpose of descriptive statistics, and how does it contribute to the initial stages of data analysis?
2. Why is it important to select the most appropriate descriptive statistics for a dataset? How might misinterpretation occur if the wrong one is used?
3. What is a histogram, and how is it different from a boxplot? How do these graphical representations help you identify patterns and trends in your data?
4. How can measures of dispersion, such as range and standard deviation, contribute to a more comprehensive understanding of language data?
5. When analyzing data, how do you decide whether to use the mean, median, or mode? What are the potential pitfalls of relying on only one measure of central tendency?
6. What are outliers? How do they affect the data, and how do you deal with them in your quantitative data analysis?
7. How can the characteristics of data distributions (e.g., skewness, kurtosis) affect the interpretation of the findings? Can you give an example from your work or research?
8. What insights can percentiles, quartiles, and interquartile ranges offer about the spread of data? Provide an example where these measures add value to an analysis.
9. How does the width of a confidence interval affect the interpretation of results, and what factors can influence the width? When interpreting results, is a narrower or wider confidence interval preferred, and why?

Activity Questions

1. Collect some quantitative data of your choice, for example, the number of hours you spend studying a second language each day or the number of words you learn in a week. Calculate the mean, median, and mode of the data and compare them using a statistical program or by hand. What do the different measures tell you about the data?

2. Find some quantitative data from a published study in applied linguistics and create a frequency distribution table and a histogram using a statistical program such as SPSS. Describe the shape of the distribution and interpret what it tells you about the data.

3. Collect some quantitative data such as test scores from a group of language learners and calculate the variance and standard deviation of the scores using a statistical program such as SPSS. How would you interpret these measures, and what do they tell you about the data?

4. Find a published study in applied linguistics that has used descriptive statistics. Evaluate the appropriateness of the methods used. Were any graphical representations used? If so, what were they, and how useful were they in summarizing the data?

5. Collect some data through a survey or a questionnaire and use descriptive statistics to analyze the results. What measures of central tendency would you use and why?

6. Working in groups of four or five, collect some quantitative data on a particular issue that you are interested in through a survey. Analyze the data using measures of central tendency (e.g., mean, median, mode) and measures of dispersion (e.g., variance, standard deviation), using a statistical program such as SPSS. Also use appropriate graphical representations to illustrate the patterns in the data. Discuss the results within the group and draw some conclusions about your findings. Then write a brief report summarizing them and present them to the class.

19 Analyzing Quantitative Data: Exploring Key Concepts in Inferential Statistics

---

CHAPTER OBJECTIVES

After completing this chapter, you should be able to

- Define inferential statistics, its importance, and purpose in statistical analysis.
- Explain probability distributions and the central limit theorem, and their relevance in statistical inference.
- Define point estimation and interval estimation.
- Calculate confidence intervals, and the difference between one-tailed and two-tailed intervals.
- Explain the difference between one-tailed and two-tailed tests, and how to choose the appropriate test based on the research question and the data.
- Explain hypothesis testing and its importance.
- Understand the concepts of Type I and Type II errors, the factors that lead to these errors, and how they can be avoided.

Introduction

In the previous chapter, we discussed descriptive statistics, introducing key concepts such as data distributions (normal, skewed, bimodal), visual representations (histograms, boxplots, scatter plots), and central tendency measures (mean, median, mode) alongside variability measures (range, variance, standard deviation). This laid the groundwork for understanding data before conducting inferential statistics. Inferential statistics is vital in applied linguistics research and extends beyond data description to drawing conclusions about a larger population based on a sample. This chapter will discuss key inferential statistics concepts, including their definition, importance, and purpose. We will explore concepts such as random sampling, probability distributions, and the central limit theorem, highlighting their relevance in statistical inference. The chapter will address confidence intervals, detailing their calculation and distinguishing between one-tailed and two-tailed tests, as well as Type I and Type II errors. Throughout, we will provide examples to illustrate these concepts and their significance in analysis and interpretation.

POINTS TO PONDER

How does inferential statistics differ from descriptive statistics, and why is it considered an important step in statistical analysis? Can you provide examples of situations where inferential statistics might be more valuable than descriptive statistics?

Inferential Statistics: Its Definition, Importance, and Purpose

Inferential statistics is a branch of statistics that uses the data from a sample to make inferences about a larger population from which the sample has been selected. In other words, it is used to analyze the data and draw conclusions about the characteristics of a population based on the data from a sample of that population. It is called inferential statistics because it involves the use of statistical methods to draw inferences about the population from the data collected from the sample.

For instance, when comparing the effect of a new instructional approach on language proficiency in L2 learners with a traditional approach, inferential statistics (e.g., *t*-tests or ANOVA) help determine significant differences. Descriptive statistics alone cannot provide such information due to sampling error and variability. Inferential statistics, relying on probability theory and statistical methods, estimate the likelihood that observed sample data reflect the characteristics of the broader population. This is important for researchers in fields such as applied linguistics to enable them to make informed predictions. In the following sections, we will provide an overview of some key concepts in inferential statistics, including probability distributions and the central limit theorem. These concepts are fundamental for understanding and applying methods used to make inferences about a population based on a sample of data.

Probability Distributions and the Central Limit Theorem

In statistics, inferential statistics involves drawing inferences about the population based on sample data, using probability laws to estimate population characteristics. Valid statistical estimations rely on a representative sample obtained through probability sampling. Sampling, as explained in Chapter 8, is the process of selecting a subgroup, called a sample, from a larger population to make inferences. Sampling is practical, as studying the entire population is often unfeasible or time-consuming. To have valid inferences, the samples must be representative of the population.

Probability sampling ensures each population member has an equal chance of inclusion in the sample, minimizing bias. Probability sampling methods, such as simple random sampling, systematic sampling, stratified sampling, and cluster sampling, were discussed in Chapter 8.

In statistics, characteristics of the sample data are called sample statistics (or just statistics). This includes properties such as the sample mean, sample variance, sample standard deviation, or sample proportion. The corresponding properties in the population are called parameters, which include the population mean, population variance, population standard deviation, or population proportion. Sample statistics and population parameters are typically expressed using the symbols shown in Table 19.1.

Table 19.1 Sample statistics and population parameters

	Mean	Variance	Standard deviation	Proportion
Sample statistic	$\bar{x}$	s^2	s	$\hat{p}$
Population parameter	μ	σ^2	σ	p

Note that the symbols for the sample mean and proportion have often a bar or hat on top, respectively, while the symbols for population parameters do not.

Sample statistics (or statistics) refers to the characteristics of the sample, including properties such as the sample mean, sample variance, sample standard deviation, or sample proportion. The corresponding properties in the population are called **parameters**.

Parameters are typically unknown and need to be estimated from the statistics of the sample data. When conducting research that aims to draw conclusions about a larger population based on sample data, sample statistics are calculated from the data, and these statistics are then used to estimate the corresponding population parameters. In this process the sampling distribution plays a key role by providing a framework for understanding how sample statistics are likely to vary across different samples drawn from the same population.

The distribution of the sample statistics is called the sampling distribution. The sampling distribution is thus the probability distribution of a statistic, such as the mean of a random sample. In other words, it is the distribution of a statistic that we would anticipate to get if we selected many random samples from the population and calculated the statistic (or the mean of that sample).

It might be helpful here to distinguish between sample distribution and sampling distribution. Sample distribution refers to the distribution of a particular variable in a single study. This is the notion we covered in Chapter 18 on descriptive statistics. For example, if you take a random sample of fifty students from a population and measure vocabulary size, the distribution of the vocabulary size in the sample in that study is the sample distribution. On the other hand, the sampling distribution refers to the distribution of sample statistics (such as the mean, standard deviation, etc.) calculated from multiple random samples of the same size from a population. For example, if you take fifty random samples of fifty students from a population and calculate the mean of their vocabulary size in each sample, the distribution of these sample means is called the sampling distribution of means. In other words, the sample distribution refers to the distribution of a variable in a single sample, whereas the sampling distribution refers to the distribution of the statistic of interest (such as the mean) across multiple samples. By analyzing the sampling distribution, you can make probabilistic statements about the accuracy and precision of their estimates and draw inferences about the larger population based on the characteristics of the sample.

Sample distribution refers to the distribution of a particular variable in a single study. The sampling distribution refers to the distribution of the statistic of interest (such as the mean) across multiple samples.

The sampling distribution of a sample statistic can be different for different samples taken from a population. However, there is a theory in statistics called the central limit theorem (CLT), which states that the sampling distribution of a statistic tends to be approximately normal, regardless of the differences in the sample statistics, as long as the sample size is sufficiently large.

This means that if we repeatedly take random samples of the same size from a population and calculate the mean of each sample, the distribution of those means will approach normality. This principle allows us to use the sampling distribution of means to estimate the population mean with confidence. The CLT is foundational in statistics because it enables us to make inferences and test hypotheses about a population based on the properties of a normal distribution derived from representative subsets of data through random sampling and probability sampling distributions.

POINTS TO PONDER

How do probability distributions and the central limit theorem relate to statistical inferences, and why is it important to understand these concepts? Could you discuss the advantages and limitations of using point estimates in statistical analysis?

Point Estimation and Interval Estimation

In the previous section, we explained the concepts of sampling, probability, and sampling distributions, which are the foundation of inferential statistics. We also discussed the central limit theorem, which states that the distribution of sample means approaches a normal distribution as the sample size increases. We also explained what a parameter is and how it differs from a statistic.

In this section we cover two other fundamental concepts in inferential statistics: point estimation and interval estimation. In many real-world situations, it is not feasible or practical to study an entire population, so we always collect data from a sample, which we will then use to make inferences about the population parameters. This process through which quantitative values from the sample are found for the unknown population parameters is called estimation and is considered an important process in inferential statistics.

Point estimation and interval estimation are procedures used to estimate population parameters from the sample data and quantify the uncertainty or probability associated with those estimates. Point estimation involves using a single value, or what is called "point estimate," to estimate the unknown population parameter (see Example 19.1).

EXAMPLE 19.1

Suppose you randomly select 100 high school L2 English learners in a specific country to assess their vocabulary knowledge. After administering a standardized test, the calculated sample mean score is 90 out of 100. This can serve as a point estimate for the population mean score (μ). This point estimate (90) allows you to infer that high school L2 English learners in that country possess a relatively high level of English vocabulary knowledge.

Interval estimation, on the other hand involves a range of values within which the population parameter falls. The sample mean is the most common point estimate used to estimate the population mean. The point estimate includes the sample proportion and the sample variance. These two are also typically used to estimate the population proportion and the population variance.

Point estimation involves using a single value, or what is called the "point estimate," to estimate the unknown population parameter. **Interval estimation**, on the other hand involves a range of values within which the population parameter falls.

Point estimation is a simple and straightforward method, offering a single, easily interpretable value. However, it lacks information on the validity and accuracy of the estimate. Its reliance on assumptions of normality and justification for large sample sizes limit its applicability. A single point estimate from one sample may not precisely represent the population parameter due to sampling errors and biases. To address this, other statistical procedures such as calculating a margin of error or confidence interval are necessary to account for variability and to assess accuracy.

Interval estimation involves computing an interval or a range of values for estimating the unknown parameter of the population. In statistics this interval is called a confidence interval. A confidence interval is constructed based on the point estimate and a measure of the variability of the estimate, such as the standard error. Thus, this measure takes into account the variability of the data.

For instance, in Example 19.1 above, if you wanted to estimate the mean of all the high school students on the vocabulary test in the country, you could use an interval estimate to give an idea of the range of possible values for the population mean. For example, you might find that the true mean of the population would be between 75 and 85. This is called an estimate or confidence interval (see also Chapter 18).

A confidence interval does not only provide a range of values within which the true value of a population parameter such as the mean may fall, but it also provides information about the precision of the estimate. It provides a range of values that is likely to include the true value of the parameter with a certain level of confidence. The level of confidence in the interval confidence is called the confidence level and shows the probability that the true population parameter falls within that confidence interval.

Levels of confidence commonly used in statistical analysis are 90% or 95%. For example, a 95% confidence level for a population mean shows that if the same study using the same sampling process and size is repeated multiple times, we are 95% confident that the mean falls within the range given by the confidence interval. The rest of the level of confidence is the significance level or what is represented by α (alpha). If the level of confidence is 95%, then the significance level is 0.05. In other words, if the level of confidence is 95%, then the remaining probability (100% − 95% = 5%) is the significance level (α) because they are complementary probabilities. Both together comprise 100% of the data distribution.

The level of confidence shows the probability that the true value of the population parameter lies approximately within the calculated confidence interval. For example, if we calculate a 95% confidence interval for the mean of a population, we are saying that we are 95% confident that the true population mean falls within the calculated interval.

For a 95% confidence interval using a standard normal distribution, the critical values are approximately ± 1.96. This is the value that separates the middle 95% of the distribution from the tails. This means that 95% of the area under the curve falls within ± 1.96 standard deviations of the mean. This value is also referred to as the "z score" for a 95% confidence level. The remaining 5% falls in either tail, each tail being 2.5%. In a normal distribution, approximately 90% of the data fall within 1.645 standard deviations of the mean. Similarly, for a 99% confidence interval, the critical value is approximately 2.576. In a normal distribution, approximately 99% of the data fall within 2.576 standard deviations of the mean. Therefore, for a 99% confidence interval, the critical value is taken to be 2.576. See Figure 19.1.

In the graphs shown in Figure 19.1, the shaded areas in the tails of the distribution are the critical region. In hypothesis testing, the critical region is a range of values where, if the test statistic falls within it, the null hypothesis is rejected. The critical

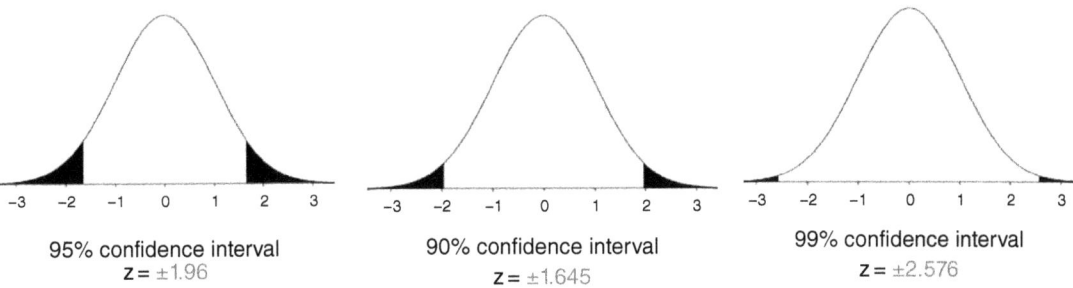

Figure 19.1 Confidence intervals and critical values

value(s) are the value(s) that define the boundaries of that range. If the test statistic falls beyond the critical value(s), then the null hypothesis is rejected in favor of the alternative hypothesis (see the following section). The boundary of the critical region is determined by a critical value, which is calculated based on the sample size and the level of confidence. Thus, the critical value is the point on the distribution beyond which we reject the null hypothesis.

It is important to note that the critical value depends on both the level of confidence and the underlying distribution of the data. The above values could be used when the sample size is large. However, if the sample size is small, the critical value can be calculated using the t distribution instead of the normal distribution, in which case, the critical value would depend on both the level of confidence and the degrees of freedom associated with the t distribution. Therefore, when using the critical value, it is important to use the appropriate value, taking into account the sample size and the underlying data distribution.

POINTS TO PONDER

Do you know the process for calculating a confidence interval? Can you provide an example where understanding confidence intervals plays a role in interpreting statistical results or making decisions based on the data?

Calculating Confidence Intervals

We introduced the notion of the confidence interval in Chapter 18. As we noted, confidence intervals are an important statistical procedure that enables us to estimate with a certain level of confidence the range of values within which a population parameter is likely to fall. This calculation is based on the sample data while taking into account the sample size, sample mean, and sample standard deviation. We provided an example in Chapter 18 (Example 18.15), and as mentioned, statistical software can calculate confidence intervals quickly and accurately, but it is still important to understand the underlying steps and concepts involved in calculating confidence intervals. Therefore, in Example 19.2 we provide a further example to show how they can be calculated manually.

EXAMPLE 19.2

Suppose you have conducted a study on the effect of a particular language program on university students' English writing skills. You have randomly selected forty students and tested their writing skills after they went through the program. Their scores are shown in Table 19.2.

Table 19.2 Dataset for Example 19.2

Students' scores			
70	86	78	82
83	69	73	80
68	80	81	75
91	88	89	86
79	75	82	88
80	72	76	78
76	87	85	84
81	89	77	73
92	90	93	90
77	84	69	80

We have calculated the mean (80.90) and standard deviation (6.88) for our sample of forty university students who underwent the language program to improve their English writing skills. Now, we aim to estimate the population mean with a 95% confidence interval. To do so, we can use the following formula:

Equation 19.1 $$CI = \bar{x} \pm t \times \frac{s}{\sqrt{n}}$$

where

$\bar{x}$ is the sample mean
n is the sample size
t is the critical value from the t distribution corresponding to the desired confidence level

Since the sample size is 40, we have 39 degrees of freedom ($n-1 = 40-1$). For a 95% confidence interval and 39 degrees of freedom, the critical t value is approximately 2.021. Please note that if the sample size is large (usually $n \geq 30$) and we know the population standard deviation, we could use the z value instead of the t value. The z value is approximately 1.96 for a 95% confidence interval. However, in the case of our example, the t distribution is more appropriate because although the sample size is larger than 30, the population standard deviation is unknown.

To calculate the CI, we use the following procedure:

Step 1: We calculate the sample mean and sample standard deviation: Sample mean ($\bar{x} = 80.90$) and sample standard deviation ($s = 6.88$).

Step 2: We determine the critical value of t for the desired level of confidence and degrees of freedom. Critical value of t for a 95% confidence interval with 39 degrees of freedom is 2.021.

This critical value of 2.021 can be obtained from a t distribution table in a statistics book or by using statistical software such as Microsoft Excel, SPSS, or R. Alternatively, the TINV function in Excel, with the formula TINV (0.05, 39), provides the t value for a 95% confidence interval with 39 degrees of freedom, where 0.05 represents the probability level associated with the two-tailed t-distribution.

Step 3: We calculate the confidence interval.

$$CI = \bar{x} \pm t \times \frac{s}{\sqrt{n}}$$

$$CI = 80.90 \pm [2.021 \times (6.88/\sqrt{40})] = 80.90 \pm 2.2$$

Lower limit $= 80.90 - 2.2 = 78.70$

Upper limit $= 80.90 + 2.2 = 83.10$

Therefore, the 95% confidence interval for the mean of the writing scores is (78.70, 83.10), indicating that we are 95% confident the true population mean falls within this range.

As noted before, statistical software, such as SPSS, can also calculate confidence intervals, using the steps mentioned in Chapter 18 (SPSS Steps 18.12). SPSS Output 19.1 shows the confidence interval calculated for the data in Example 19.2.

SPSS OUTPUT 19.1

Descriptives

			Statistic	Std. Error
score	Mean		80.90	1.08
	95% Confidence Interval for Mean	Lower Bound	78.70	
		Upper Bound	83.10	

One-Tailed versus Two-Tailed Confidence Intervals

In the above section, we explained the concept point estimation and how it is different from a confidence interval; in this section we will explain the difference between one-tailed and two-tailed intervals.

A one-tailed interval is an interval that is used to estimate the range of values for a population parameter based on a sample with a focus on only one of the directions of the distribution: either the upper or the lower tail, depending on the hypothesis being tested.

One-tailed confidence intervals are usually used when we have previous knowledge or a hypothesis that suggests that the true value of the parameter is likely to fall within a certain range. Example 19.3 demonstrates how a one-tailed confidence interval can be used.

EXAMPLE 19.3

Suppose you are interested in examining what scores on average international students who have gone through a new writing program get on a writing proficiency test. Based on previous literature and your knowledge of the students, you hypothesize that the average score for the students would be at least 80 out of 100. Now you want to test this with 95% confidence. You would collect data from a random sample of 100 international students in your university and calculate the sample mean and the standard deviation. Suppose the sample mean is 75 and the standard deviation is 7. To create an estimate at a 95% confidence level for the population mean being at least 80, you calculate the lower bound using the formula:

Equation 19.2 $$CI = \bar{x} - t \times \frac{s}{\sqrt{n}}$$

Assuming a one-tailed alpha level of 0.05, the critical t value for 99 degrees of freedom (df) is approximately 1.660. The df is calculated as $n-1$, which is $100 - 1 = 99$. While the z score for a normal distribution at this significance level is 1.645, the t value for 99 degrees of freedom is slightly higher because the t distribution accounts for additional variability due to the sample size. Using the formula, the one-tailed interval estimate is:

Lower bound $= 75- [1.660 \times 7 /10] = 73.84$

Upper bound of confidence interval $= \infty$ (since the directional hypothesis is "at least").

Therefore, the one-tailed interval estimate for the true population mean score is at least 73.84 out of 100, with 95% confidence. This suggests that the true population mean score is likely to be greater than or equal to 73.84, with 95% confidence. This does not provide evidence in support of the hypothesis that the average score for the population who go through the program is at least 80. Since the lower bound of the confidence interval is 73.84, this does not provide strong evidence that the population mean is at least 80. In fact, it suggests that the population mean could be below 80, which contradicts the hypothesis.

As noted earlier, we will use z scores to calculate the confidence interval when the population standard deviation (σ) is known and when the sample size is large. Tables 19.3 and 19.4 show the z scores for one-tailed and two-tailed confidence intervals at different significance levels (α) and their corresponding confidence levels.

In Table 19.4, α represents the total probability in both tails of the distribution. This total α is divided by 2 to allocate the probability to each tail.

Table 19.3 Z scores for one-tailed confidence intervals at different confidence and significance levels (α)

Confidence level	α for one-tailed CI	z score (positive tail)	z score (negative tail)
90%	0.10	1.28	−1.28
95%	0.05	1.645	−1.645
99%	0.01	2.33	−2.33

Table 19.4 Z scores for two-tailed confidence intervals at different confidence and significance levels (α)

Confidence level	α for two-tailed CI	z score
90%	0.10	1.645
95%	0.05	1.96
99%	0.01	2.576

In Example 19.3, we calculated the confidence interval for one mean coming from only one sample. However, in many cases in applied linguistics research, we are interested in comparing the means of two groups, to see whether there is a difference between them. In such cases, we can calculate a confidence interval for the difference between the means of the two groups instead of one mean. This will help us define the range of values within which the true difference between the two-group means is likely to fall with a certain degree of confidence. Example 19.4 presents a scenario for a two-tailed mean difference CI.

EXAMPLE 19.4

Suppose you aim to evaluate the effectiveness of a new vocabulary learning strategy, such as using flashcards. You select sixty L2 learners, dividing them randomly into two groups: a flashcard group ($n = 30$) and a no-flashcard group ($n = 30$). Measuring their vocabulary knowledge through a test, you anticipate a positive effect from flashcards based on prior research. Your hypothesis posits that the mean score of the flashcard group will be at least 5 points higher than the mean score of the no-flashcard group. To test this with 95% confidence, you construct a 95% one-tailed confidence interval. However, although the scenario suggests a one-tailed confidence interval, let's calculate a two-tailed confidence interval first to illustrate its calculation. Since you are comparing two groups, the confidence intervals will be for the difference between the two means. Suppose the data from the two groups are as shown in Table 19.5.

Table 19.5 Data for Example 19.4

Flashcard group	$n_1 = 30$	$\bar{x}_1 = 78$	$S_1 = 7$
No-flashcard group	$n_2 = 30$	$\bar{x}_2 = 70$	$S_2 = 6$

Here is the formula.

Equation 19.3
$$CI = (\bar{x}_1 - \bar{x}_2) \pm t \times \sqrt{\frac{s_1}{n_1} + \frac{s_2}{n_2}}$$

where

$\bar{x}_1$ and $\bar{x}_2$ are the sample means for the Flashcard and No-flashcard groups, respectively

S_1 and S_2 are the sample standard deviations for the groups

n_1 and n_2 are the sample sizes for the two groups

t is the critical t value from the t distribution corresponding to the desired confidence level (95%) based on the df

Since we have two independent groups, the df for the t distribution is calculated as: $n_1 + n_2 - 2 = 58$. Since we are calculating a two-tailed 95% confidence interval, the associated t value will be approximately 2.

Here are the calculation and the result.

$$CI = (78 - 70) \pm 2 \times \sqrt{\frac{7^2}{30} + \frac{6^2}{30}}$$

$$CI = (78 - 70) \pm 2 \times 1.683$$

$$CI = 8 \pm 3.366$$

$$CI = 4.6 - 11.37$$

The above calculation suggests that, with a 95% confidence, the true difference in means between the two groups in the study falls between 4.6 and 11.37.

Now let us calculate a one-tailed 95% confidence interval for the mean difference in test scores as originally suggested. At this time, all the 5% of alpha would fall in one of the tails, and the t value for that will be about 1.671. When using a one-tailed test with a 95% confidence level, the critical value is -1.671 for the lower tail, which corresponds to the 5% area to the left of the mean in the standard normal distribution.

You would like to see whether the difference in the mean score of the two groups will be at least 5 points with 95% confidence. Thus, you would focus on the lower bound of the confidence interval, looking for evidence that the mean score of the treatment is at least 5 points greater than the mean of comprehension without the treatment. So you calculate the confidence interval but this time only for the lower bound. This process is laid out in Example 19.5.

EXAMPLE 19.5

Here is the formula.

Equation 19.4 $$\mathrm{CI} = (\bar{x}_1 - \bar{x}_2) - t \times \sqrt{\frac{s_1}{n_1} + \frac{s_2}{n_2}}$$

Here are the calculation and the result.

Lower end of confidence interval: $\mathrm{CI} = (78 - 70) - 1.671 \times \sqrt{\frac{7^2}{30} + \frac{6^2}{30}}$

Lower end of confidence interval: $\mathrm{CI} = (78 - 70) - 1.671 \times 1.68$

Lower end of confidence interval: $\mathrm{CI} = 8 - 2.80$

Lower end of confidence interval: $\mathrm{CI} = 5.19$

Upper end of confidence interval $= \infty$

This means that you are 95% confident that the true mean difference of the test score is greater than or equal to 5.19. Since the lower bound of the confidence interval is more than 5 points, it provides evidence in favor of your hypothesis that the treatment students would on average score at least 5 points higher.

It is important to note that although the confidence interval may provide information about the strength of our hypothesis, we do not reject the null hypothesis simply based on the confidence interval. In the following section, we will discuss issues related to hypothesis testing and how it can be applied in research, including the formulation of null and alternative hypotheses, computing a test statistic and a p value, selecting a significance level, and interpreting the results.

POINTS TO PONDER

What is hypothesis testing, and why is it important in scientific research? Can you explain the key steps involved in hypothesis testing?

Hypothesis Testing

In the previous section, we covered the concept of the confidence interval and learned that a confidence interval provides a range of values that may include the true population parameter with a certain degree of confidence. We also discussed how to calculate confidence intervals for different types of data and how to interpret the results. In statistical analysis, confidence intervals and hypothesis testing are two powerful tools used to draw conclusions about a population based on a sample of data. Although confidence intervals may provide information about our hypothesis, they do not directly test its validity. In other words, they are not a hypothesis-testing procedure. Hypothesis testing is a procedure that allows us to determine whether a certain statement about the population is supported by the data or not.

The Importance of Hypothesis Testing

Hypothesis testing is a statistical procedure in quantitative research to determine the strength of evidence in support of a certain claim or hypothesis about a population by analyzing data from a sample. It is a formal procedure for making inferences and is widely used in various fields, including the field of applied linguistics. Hypothesis testing is important for several reasons. First, it provides a systematic framework for making inferences about the data so that the conclusions drawn are based on a sound and verifiable statistical analysis, rather than subjective evidence. By testing hypotheses, you can determine whether a certain claim, assumption, or theory is supported by the available data and hence it plays an important role in scientific research. Hypothesis testing is also essential for the replicability of research findings. By providing a clear and transparent statistical analysis, it helps you to make sure that your results are replicable and can be independently verified.

Hypothesis testing is a statistical procedure in quantitative research to determine the strength of evidence in support of a certain claim or hypothesis about a population by analyzing data from a sample.

The Process of Hypothesis Testing

Hypothesis testing assesses the credibility of a proposed hypothesis, usually by comparing it against a null hypothesis. This involves collecting and analyzing data to determine whether the evidence supports or refutes the hypothesis being tested. The process typically involves the following steps:

1. Formulating a null hypothesis.
2. Formulating an alternative hypothesis.
3. Collecting and analyzing the data.
4. Choosing an appropriate statistical significance test.
5. Calculating the test statistic.
6. Deciding on a p value to determine the level of significance of the results.
7. Interpreting the results.

Formulating a Null Hypothesis

The first step in the hypothesis-testing process is the formulation of a null hypothesis. The null hypothesis is the hypothesis that you want to reject. It is a default hypothesis, representing a neutral position, and is usually denoted as H^O.

There are different forms of a null hypotheses, depending on the research question and the variables being examined. One form is formulating it in terms of the difference between groups or variables, such as "There is no significant difference in vocabulary scores between students who study with a dictionary and those who study without a dictionary." Another form is expressing it in terms of relationships, hypothesizing no significant relationship between two variables, such as "There is no significant relationship between first language background and language learning." A null hypothesis can also be formulated in terms of the effects, hypothesizing no effect from a treatment or an intervention, such as "There is no significant effect of corrective feedback on second language grammar acquisition."

The null hypothesis is the hypothesis that you want to reject. It is a default hypothesis, representing a neutral position and is usually denoted as H^0.

The reason a study often begins with a null hypothesis and then attempts to reject it is that it is easier to formulate and test a null hypothesis. Also, it is not possible to prove the alternative hypothesis; therefore, first, a null hypothesis is formulated and then tested against the data. This approach is also consistent with the principles of statistical inference and scientific inquiry and also the process of discovering knowledge and testing a theory. If the null hypothesis is rejected, it suggests that there is evidence to support the alternative hypothesis or the theory. However, if the null hypothesis cannot be rejected, it suggests that the result of the study does not provide enough evidence to support the alternative hypothesis or theory.

It is important to keep in mind that failure to reject the null hypothesis does not prove the truth of the null hypothesis. It simply suggests that that there is not enough evidence from the current study to reject it. Therefore, additional research may be needed to further investigate the issue.

Formulating the Alternative Hypothesis

The second step in the hypothesis-testing process is the formulation of the alternative hypothesis. The alternative hypothesis is the one that the researcher is interested in providing evidence for, and it is the one being tested against the null hypothesis. It is usually denoted as H_a or H_1, and it can be either directional (one-tailed) or nondirectional (two-tailed), depending on whether the research question is directional or not.

A one-tailed or directional alternative hypothesis is one that predicts the direction of the effect, relationship, or the difference between or among groups or variables. In other words, it specifies that the effect will be in a particular direction. A one-tailed hypothesis is also sometimes called a one-sided hypothesis.

For example, a one-tailed alternative hypothesis might be "Students who use dictionaries to study will perform better on a vocabulary test than students who do not use a dictionary." In contrast, a two-tailed alternative or nondirectional hypothesis predicts that there will be a significant effect or difference between two groups or variables, but it does not specify the direction of the effect. For instance, in the above example, a two-tailed alternative hypothesis might be "There is a significant difference in vocabulary scores between students who study with a dictionary and students who study without a dictionary."

Whether we should choose a one-tailed or two-tailed alternative hypothesis depends on the research question and the nature of the variables being investigated. A one-tailed hypothesis is appropriate in situations where there is a clear directional prediction based on previous research or theory, whereas a two-tailed hypothesis is appropriate when the relationship between the variables is not clear or when there is not enough prior theoretical or empirical knowledge to predict a specific direction for the effect or the relationship. For example, a study examining the effects of extensive reading for the development of vocabulary knowledge may use a directional hypothesis predicting that extensive reading will lead to an increase in learners' vocabulary knowledge. However, in many cases, the alternative hypothesis is nondirectional because the research question or theoretical framework does not specify a particular direction of the effect. For example, a study examining the relationship between language proficiency and the effectiveness of corrective feedback may use a nondirectional alternative hypothesis that simply predicts the presence of a relationship without specifying that higher language proficiency enhances the effectiveness of corrective feedback.

Collecting and Analyzing Data

The next step in hypothesis testing involves gathering relevant data using valid instruments for the variables in question. The aim is to collect data from a representative sample, balancing reliability and manageability. The sample should be of sufficient size for reliable estimates of population parameters to be made, while minimizing bias and errors (see Chapter 8).

Once the data are collected, the dataset is organized and analyzed to determine whether the results from the study support or refute the null hypothesis. This is generally done by comparing the observed results with what we expect under the null hypothesis. If the observed results are consistent with the null hypothesis, we fail to reject the null hypothesis, but if the observed results are inconsistent with the null hypothesis, we reject it and accept the alternative hypothesis.

Choosing an Appropriate Statistical Significance Test

When analyzing the data, an important step is using an appropriate statistical significance test. Statistical significance tests are routinely used in research in applied linguistics. They are mathematical techniques used to establish the likelihood of specific results observed in the sample data, given the assumption that the data were drawn from a larger population. These are the tests that are used to reject the null hypothesis, which proposes no relationships or effects of interest in the population. In other words, the null hypothesis means that what we see in the sample does not exist in the population and has occurred as a result of sampling error. Since it is not possible to prove the alternative hypothesis, first a null hypothesis is formulated and then a significance test is performed to determine whether it is possible to reject it.

Statistical significance tests are mathematical techniques used to establish the likelihood of specific results being observed in the sample data, given the assumption that the data were drawn from a larger population.

Maintaining the null hypothesis suggests nonsignificant results, indicating that the observed relationship in the sample is likely due to chance. Rejecting the null hypothesis implies a systematic relationship or effect existing in the population. Various statistical significance tests, such as *t*-tests, ANOVA, correlation, regression, and chi-square, are employed in applied linguistics research based on the research question and data type. Choosing an appropriate test requires understanding the study's data and variables, and also ensuring that the underlying assumptions of the statistical test are met. Further explanation on the choice of significance tests will be provided in the next chapters.

Computing a Test Statistic and a *P* Value

In statistical testing it is not possible to determine the truth of a null hypothesis in absolute terms, as hypothesis testing results are based on probabilities and do not provide definitive proofs. Therefore, the analysis should involve the use of probabilities. Significance tests assess the probability of the data based on the assumed truth of the null hypothesis. To test the null hypothesis, the significance test first computes a test statistic, which is a numerical value, calculated from the sample data based on a known sampling distribution. This is a value that is calculated from the data and is used to test the null hypothesis. The choice of the test statistic depends on the type of data being analyzed and the research question being asked. Common test statistics include *t*-statistics, chi-square statistics, and *F* statistics. For example, in a two-sample *t*-test (which is a statistical test used to determine if there is a significant difference between the means of two groups), the test statistic is the *t* value, and it is calculated from the difference between the means of the two samples in the study, divided by an estimate of the standard error.

Significance tests assess the probability of the data based on the assumed truth of the null hypothesis. To test the null hypothesis, the significance test first computes a test statistic, which is a numerical value, calculated from the sample data based on a known sampling distribution.

The significance test also calculates a corresponding *p* value for the test statistic. This value is the probability of getting a test statistic as large as the one obtained, under the assumption that the null hypothesis is true. Thus, the p value indicates how likely it is that the observed test statistic is due to sampling errors.

The p value is the probability of getting a test statistic as large as the one obtained, under the assumption that the null hypothesis is true.

These days statistical packages such as SPSS, R, or SAS can perform these various statistical tests easily. These packages can provide all kinds of statistical analyses, making doing statistics very efficient and comprehensive. Therefore, there is no need to calculate them by hand, and we just need to be able to interpret the output generated by these programs. For example, SPSS Output 19.2 shows the t value (t statistic) and the p value calculated for an independent t-test.

SPSS OUTPUT 19.2

Independent Samples Test

		Levene's Test for Equality of Variances		t-test for Equality of Means		Significance			
		F	Sig.	t	df	One-Sided p	Two-Sided p	Mean Difference	Std. Error Difference
Vocabulary scores	Equal variances assumed	.11	.73	2.89	38	.00	.01	1.20	.42
	Equal variances not assumed			2.89	37.38	.00	.01	1.20	.42

You now need to judge whether the observed p value is small enough to justify the rejection of the null hypothesis, which will be done based on our selected significance level.

Selecting a Significance Level

To assess the plausibility of the null hypothesis, we use a threshold level called the significance level (α, alpha). The significance level is often set at 0.05 in social sciences, including applied linguistics research. The significance level is closely related to the confidence level we discussed earlier. If you remember, the confidence interval is a range of values that may contain the true population parameter such as the mean or proportion with a certain level of confidence. For example, a 95% confidence level indicates that if we repeat the sampling process many times, 95%

of the resulting intervals would contain the true population mean whereas 5% of the intervals would not. The significance level and confidence level are related in that a 95% confidence level corresponds to a 5% significance level (see the previous section). This means that if we reject the null hypothesis at a 5% significance level, we have sufficient evidence to conclude that the true population parameter likely differs from the hypothesized value.

To assess the plausibility α of the null hypothesis, we use a threshold level called **the significance level (α, alpha),** which is often set at 0.05 in social sciences, including applied linguistics research.

Interpreting the Results

This step involves comparing the calculated p value to our set significance level and deciding on whether to accept or reject the null hypothesis. If the p value is lower than or equal to this cut-off significance level, the null hypothesis is rejected, and the results are considered to be statistically significant. In other words, the p value is the level of risk you are willing to accept when rejecting the null hypothesis. We said that the common significance level is 0.05, which means that there is a 5% chance of incorrectly rejecting the null hypothesis when it is actually true. However, it can also be set to other values depending on the specific context and level of risk that is acceptable.

To interpret our results, we compare the calculated **p value** to our set **significance level**. If the p value is lower than or equal to the cut-off significance level, the null hypothesis is rejected, and the results are considered to be statistically significant.

In the following section, we will explain two types of errors that we may commit when addressing or rejecting the null hypothesis. These are known as Type I and Type II errors. We will briefly discuss these two concepts and also explain the factors that may lead to these errors and how they can be avoided. We will also explore the difference between one-tailed and two-tailed tests and describe how to choose the appropriate test based on the research question that we have and the nature of our data.

Type I and Type II Errors

Two important notions related to hypothesis testing and statistical analysis are the notions of Type I and Type II errors.

A Type I error occurs when the null hypothesis is rejected even though it should not have been. In other words, it is rejected by our study, but it is actually true. For example, the result of our statistical analysis suggests that there is a significant difference between two groups when actually there is no difference. In other words, our study has erroneously rejected the null hypothesis and has erroneously concluded that there is a significant effect or relationship when in reality there is no significant effect or relationship. A Type I error is also known as a false positive because a statistical test has falsely detected a positive result. In other words, it is a positive result, but it is false or incorrect. This kind of error is important to be aware of because it can lead to incorrect conclusions.

A Type II error occurs when the null hypothesis is accepted even though it is false and should have been rejected. For example, the result of our statistical analysis suggests that there is no significant difference between two groups, but in fact there is a difference. A Type II error is also known as a false negative because a statistical test has falsely detected a negative result. In other words, the study has produced a negative result (e.g., no significant relationship) that is false. This kind of error is also important to be aware of because it can lead to wrong conclusions and can make you think that there is no difference between groups when actually there is a difference. The probability of making a Type I error and a Type II error is inversely related; decreasing the probability of one type often increases the chances of the other type. Thus, it is important to control and minimize both types of errors in statistical analysis.

A **Type I error** occurs when the null hypothesis is rejected even though it is actually true. A **Type II** error occurs when the null hypothesis is accepted even though it is false.

Factors Leading to Type I and Type II Errors

Type I and Type II errors can occur for various reasons, including the following:

- **Inappropriate significance level:** Setting the significance level too high, such as at 0.10, increases the risk of a Type I error, leading to incorrect rejection of the null hypothesis. Conversely, setting it too low, such as at 0.01, raises the probability of a Type II error, where a true effect may be missed due to stringent criteria. Choosing an appropriate significance level is essential to strike a balance between the two types of errors, considering factors such as research context, sample size, and statistical power.
- **Inappropriate statistical test:** Selecting an unsuitable statistical test, for example using a *t*-test on ordinal data, can result in erroneous conclusions. It may lead to a Type I error if the assumptions are not met. Additionally, opting for a test insensitive to small differences between groups increases the risk of a Type II error.
- **Weak or poor research design:** Weak research design, lacking control over extraneous variables or improper sample selection, introduces confounding

factors. Confounding variables can distort results, causing both Type I and Type II errors by either incorrectly suggesting or missing a significant effect. A robust research design that addresses potential confounds is important to minimize these errors.

- **Small sample size:** A small sample size lowers statistical power, making it challenging to detect small differences between groups. This increases the likelihood of a Type II error, where a meaningful effect may go unnoticed. Adequate sample size is essential to enhance the reliability of statistical tests and decrease the risk of a Type II error.

- **Sample size that is too large:** While a large sample size can provide precision, it can also increase the chance of a Type I error. Under similar circumstances, as the sample size increases, the p value decreases, potentially leading to the rejection of the null hypothesis when it may be true. Conducting a power analysis can guide you in determining an optimal sample size to maintain an appropriate balance between Type I and Type II errors (see Chapter 8).

POINTS TO PONDER

Discuss the differences between one-tailed and two-tailed tests. When might it be appropriate to use one over the other? How does the choice between one-tailed and two-tailed tests affect the results of the study?

One-Tailed and Two-Tailed Tests

Previously, we discussed one-tailed and two-tailed confidence intervals. In this section we explain one-tailed and two-tailed statistical tests. A one- or two-tailed test and a one- or two-tailed confidence interval are two distinct concepts. As noted earlier, a confidence interval is used to estimate the range within which the true population parameter lies with a certain level of confidence. In this case, "one-tailed," for example, means that the interval is constructed in a way that it extends only in one direction. This could be useful in cases where you are interested in establishing a lower or upper boundary for a population parameter (such as the mean). A one-tailed or two-tailed test is a type of statistical test in which the critical region of a distribution is either one-sided (meaning it is either on the left or the right) or two-sided. Thus, the key difference between a one- or two-tailed test and a one- or two-tailed confidence interval is that the former is used for hypothesis testing, while the latter refers to the construction of a confidence interval (e.g., for a mean).

As discussed earlier, hypothesis testing is the process of defining a null hypothesis (which is a prediction about the outcome of the study), and then collecting data from a sample selected from a population to test the plausibility of that hypothesis. To this end, we use statistical tests, which calculate a test statistic based on the data. The test statistic provides a measurement of how far the sample estimate is from the proposed null hypothesis. We then compare the test statistic to a predetermined level of significance to judge whether the data provides evidence to reject or to accept the null hypothesis. The significance level is the probability of rejecting the null hypothesis when it is actually true. Therefore, it is the maximum allowable probability of making a Type I error (false positive, or wrongly rejecting the null hypothesis). This is typically set at 5%, which means that if we reject the null hypothesis, there is a 5% chance that we have made an error.

A one-tailed test tests the hypothesis in only one direction. Therefore, in this kind of analysis all of the 5% significance level is concentrated in one tail of the distribution. This means that the critical region is in either the upper or lower tail, depending on the specific alternative hypothesis being tested. A one-tailed test is appropriate when you specify a direction for the research hypothesis based on previous research and expect that the results are either positive or negative. In other words, you have a strong a priori reason to expect an effect in just one direction. For example, if you are interested in whether corrective feedback assists language acquisition in general, and past research has often shown a positive effect, you might use a one-tailed test to test the hypothesis that corrective feedback contributes to language learning. In this case, the level of significance is set in a way to decrease the probability of making a Type II error focusing on only one specified direction.

A two-tailed test, on the other hand, is a nondirectional test and examines the research hypothesis in both directions. In other words, it tests the hypothesis regardless of its direction. This type of test is appropriate when you have no prior expectation of the results being positive or negative. In other words, you are not formally anticipating the direction of the effect. In a two-tailed test, the significance level (e.g., the 5%) is divided between the two tails of the distribution. For example, with a 5% significance level, the critical region is divided equally, allocating 2.5% in the upper tail and 2.5% in the lower tail (see Figure 19.2). This implies that you could reject the null hypothesis if your test statistic falls in either the upper or lower tail of the distribution, depending on the nature of your alternative hypothesis. Thus, a two-tailed test is more stringent than a one-tailed test. This increases the probability of making a Type II error as it makes it more difficult to detect a true effect. In such cases, there is a need for stronger evidence to reject the null hypothesis.

A one-tailed test tests a hypothesis in just one direction, concentrating the 5% significance level in one tail of the distribution. **A two-tailed test** is nondirectional, examining the research hypothesis in both directions, dividing the 5% significance level equally between the upper and lower tails of the distribution.

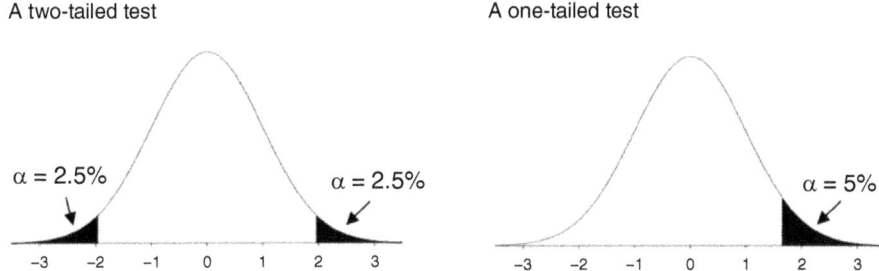

Figure 19.2 Significance level (α) in one-tailed and two-tailed tests

In short, if the hypothesis is directional and you have a strong a priori reason to expect an effect in just one direction, a one-tailed test may be appropriate, and the level of significance is applied to one tail, which decreases the probability of Type II error. However, if the hypothesis is nondirectional and you have no prior expectation of the direction of the effect, a two-tailed test may be appropriate, and the level of significance is split between the two tails. This decreases the risk of making a Type I error and increases the risk of making a Type II error. As noted earlier, the relationship between Type I and Type II errors depends on the level of significance. As the level of significance decreases, the probability of committing a Type I error decreases and vice versa.

In hypothesis testing, even when a directional hypothesis is formulated based on previous knowledge, the study always starts with a null hypothesis, serving as a baseline for comparison. Statistical methods are then employed to assess whether the observed results significantly differ from the null hypothesis. If they do, the null hypothesis is rejected in favor of the alternative hypothesis. In the case of a directional hypothesis, a one-tailed test is used to detect a significant difference in a specific direction. For a nondirectional hypothesis, a two-tailed test is employed to detect any significant difference, regardless of direction. The choice between one-tailed and two-tailed tests should align with the research question and study design to maintain the statistical validity and reliability of inferences.

Conclusion

Inferential statistics is a powerful statistical tool used to draw inferences about populations based on sample data. In this chapter, we have explored some of the key concepts and principles of inferential statistics, including random sampling, probability distributions, the central limit theorem, point estimation, interval estimation, hypothesis testing, and Type I and Type II errors, and looked at some examples. Understanding these concepts is important in inferential statistics and for how they work in research. Hypothesis testing is a fundamental concept, and the understanding of how to formulate null and alternative hypotheses, choose appropriate significance tests, and interpret the results is essential for making appropriate decisions based on statistical analyses. Altogether, the chapter aimed to provide a detailed discussion of issues related to inferential statistics, which are helpful to know when we want to conduct statistical analyses. In the next three chapters, we will explore commonly used inferential statistics in applied linguistics research, and how to apply them to analyze and interpret data.

DISCUSSION AND ACTIVITY QUESTIONS

Discussion Questions

1. What is inferential statistics and how does it differ from descriptive statistics? Why is inferential statistics important in research?
2. What is the central limit theorem, and why is it fundamental to statistical inference? How does it enable us to make conclusions about the population parameters based on sample data?
3. What are the key differences between point estimation and interval estimation? How can interval estimation provide more useful information than point estimation?
4. Can you give an example of a null hypothesis and an alternative hypothesis, and explain how they are different and how they are used in hypothesis testing?
5. What are Type I and Type II errors, and how can you avoid them in statistical analyses?
6. When performing hypothesis testing, how do you determine whether to use a one-tailed or a two-tailed test? How does the research question influence this decision?
7. What are the implications of using a 90% versus a 99% confidence level when calculating a confidence interval, and how does this choice impact the likelihood of making a Type I error?

Activity Questions

1. Read a research article in applied linguistics and analyze the statistical analyses used to test their hypotheses. What null and alternative hypotheses did the authors formulate, and how did they choose an appropriate statistical test?
2. Choose a research study in applied linguistics that has used confidence intervals and explain how it was used and why. How useful did you find it in assisting you to understand the results?
3. In groups of three or four, choose a research question in applied linguistics that you are interested in. Together, generate at least two hypotheses (a null and an alternative hypothesis) about the research question. Consider and write down the criteria that you would use when formulating your hypotheses. Then present your results to the rest of the class, explaining your rationale for each hypothesis and how it relates to the research question. Finally, revise your hypotheses based on the feedback you received from your peers and present your revised hypotheses to the rest of the class.

4. Choose a research study that used a one-tailed or two-tailed test to test a hypothesis, and explain how the test was used to evaluate the evidence against the null hypothesis. How was it interpreted in light of the research question?
5. Analyze the potential sources of error in a research study in applied linguistics. What factors could have contributed to Type I or Type II errors in the study? How could you minimize the risk of those errors in the study design and statistical analysis?

Commonly Used Inferential Statistics Tests in Applied Linguistics Research: Parametric Tests

CHAPTER OBJECTIVES

After completing this chapter, you should be able to

- Understand the concept of parametric tests and distinguish them from nonparametric tests.
- Explain how parametric tests work and when it is appropriate to use them.
- Discuss the assumptions of such tests, learn how to test the assumptions, and what to do if the assumptions are violated.
- Use common parametric tests in applied linguistics research, such as *t*-tests, ANOVA, and regression analysis, and know how to apply and interpret the results.
- Use SPSS to conduct parametric tests and know how to interpret the output.

Introduction

There are numerous inferential statistical tests available to applied linguistics researchers, each with its own specific purpose, assumptions, and applications. These tests provide important information about the significance and the degree of the relationships between variables under study or the effect of one on another. In this chapter, we will discuss some of the most commonly used inferential statistical tests in applied linguistics research, including their purpose, assumptions, and interpretation.

In the field of statistics, statistical tests are classified into two broad categories: parametric tests and nonparametric tests. We will begin with parametric tests in this chapter, discussing their significance and appropriate use. While doing so, we provide hypothetical examples of applied linguistics research and research questions that can be answered using each test, along with instructions for conducting them in SPSS.

How do you distinguish parametric from nonparametric tests? What are the key assumptions associated with parametric tests, and in what situations is it most appropriate to use them?

Parametric Tests

Two broad categories of statistical tests that we need to know about are parametric and nonparametric tests. Parametric tests are those that make certain assumptions about the data and the population, such as normality of distribution and equal variances. If these assumptions are violated, parametric tests can lead to incorrect conclusions. Examples of parametric tests include the t-test, one-way analysis of variance (ANOVA), Pearson correlation, and regression analysis. Parametric tests are different from nonparametric tests, which are those that do not make the above assumptions about data distribution. Nonparametric tests are often used when the data are not normally distributed or when sample sizes are small. In the following sections, we will discuss parametric tests and their types in more detail.

Parametric tests are those that make certain assumptions about the data and the population, such as normality of distribution and equal variances.

Assumptions of Parametric Tests and Strategies for Checking Them

To use statistical tests appropriately, it is important to understand their underlying assumptions because it is only when those assumptions are met that the findings of the analysis are valid and meaningful. In the following section, we will discuss the assumptions of parametric tests, including normality, independence, homogeneity of variances, and the absence of extreme outliers. We will also show how to check these assumptions and what to do if they are violated.

Normality of Distribution

One of the assumptions underlying parametric tests is that the data come from a normally distributed population. Parametric tests require the assumption of normality because the process of testing the null hypothesis relies on this assumption. A normal distribution is a bell-shaped symmetrical curve with a specific set of characteristics, such as a mean and standard deviation. Many statistical tests, such as t-tests and ANOVA (see the next section for a discussion of these tests), assume that the data are normally distributed. If the data are normally distributed, we can assume that they come from a normally distributed population. Therefore, before using such tests, it is important for the data to meet the normality assumption.

One of the **assumptions** underlying parametric tests is that the data come from a normally distributed population.

How to Check the Normality Assumption

The normality of the distribution of a dataset can be checked in a number of ways, including visual inspection, statistical tests, and checking skewness and kurtosis.

Visual Inspection One approach to check the distribution of the data is by visually inspecting our data through creating histograms, normal probability plot (or a Q-Q plot), or boxplot. Visual inspection can always provide a helpful indication of normality (see Chapter 18 for how to use these tools). If the data appear to be heavily skewed, you may want to consider using a nonparametric test instead of a parametric test.

Statistical Tests You can also check the normality assumption using statistical tests such as the Shapiro–Wilk test and the Kolmogorov–Smirnov test. The Shapiro–Wilk test is a statistical test to check whether a dataset is normally distributed by calculating a W statistic and comparing it to a critical value. If the calculated W statistic is smaller than the critical value, the null hypothesis is rejected. The null hypothesis is that the data are normally distributed. Now if the p value is less than the significance level (usually set at 0.05), the null hypothesis is rejected, meaning that the data are not normally distributed. However, if the p value is greater than or equal to the significance level, the null hypothesis is maintained, and the data are considered to be normally distributed. Similarly, the Kolmogorov–Smirnov test is a statistical test that can be used to test whether a dataset follows a specified distribution. The test calculates a test statistic and compares it to a critical value. If the calculated test statistic is greater than the critical value, the null hypothesis (that the data follow the specified distribution) is rejected. We can use statistical programs to conduct the Shapiro–Wilk test and Kolmogorov–Smirnov test (see SPSS Steps 20.1).

SPSS STEPS 20.1

- Open the data file in SPSS.
- Select "Analyze" > "Descriptive Statistics" > "Explore."
- Move variable(s) to the "Dependent List" box.
- Under "Display," choose "Both."
- Click "Plots" > "Normality plots with tests."
- Click "Continue" > "OK."

SPSS will generate a table showing the results of the Shapiro–Wilk test and the Kolmogorov–Smirnov test as well as normality plots. SPSS Output 20.1 is an example of such a table.

SPSS OUTPUT 20.1

Tests of Normality

	Kolmogorov–Smirnov[a]			Shapiro–Wilk		
	Statistic	df	Sig.	Statistic	df	Sig.
Language proficiency scores	.067	41	.200*	.982	41	.740

*. This is a lower bound of the true significance.
a. Lilliefors Significance Correction

The "Sig" in the table for both tests shows the p value. The p values shown under both are bigger than 0.05, suggesting that the data have met the assumption of normality.

One may wonder what the difference is between the Kolmogorov–Smirnov and Shapiro–Wilk tests. Both have been designed to test for normality. However, although in most situations either can be used, the Shapiro–Wilk test is generally considered more powerful than the Kolmogorov–Smirnov test, particularly for small-to-moderate sample sizes (less than 50). For larger sample sizes, both tests are typically powerful enough to detect deviations from normality. So overall, Shapiro–Wilk is an appropriate test for most situations. However, ultimately, the choice of test depends on the research question and the kind of analysis being used. For example, if we are testing the normality assumption for using t-tests or ANOVAs, the Shapiro–Wilk test may be more appropriate since it explicitly tests for normality under the assumption of a specific mean and variance.

Checking Skewness and Kurtosis Skewness provides a statistical measure of the symmetry of a probability distribution by showing the degree to which the data are skewed to the right or left of the mean. Kurtosis measures the degree to which the distribution has a heavy peak as compared to the normal distribution. Both measures can be obtained in SPSS by using the procedure shown in SPSS Steps 20.2.

SPSS STEPS 20.2

- Open the data file in SPSS.
- Select "Analyze" > "Descriptive Statistics," "Descriptives."
- In the "Descriptives" dialog box, select variable(s) and move it to the "Variables" box.
- Click on "Options," select "Kurtosis" and "Skewness" under "Distribution."
- Click "Continue" > "OK."

SPSS will generate a table showing skewness and kurtosis values (SPSS Output 20.2).

SPSS OUTPUT 20.2

	Descriptive Statistics				
	N	Skewness		Kurtosis	
	Statistic	Statistic	Std. Error	Statistic	Std. Error
Language proficiency scores	41	−.185	.369	−.607	.724
Valid N (listwise)	41				

The normality of the distribution of a dataset can be checked in a number of ways, including the following: visual inspection, statistical tests, checking skewness and kurtosis.

A positive skewness value indicates a positively skewed distribution, which has a longer right tail and most of the values on the left side of the distribution. A negative skewness value indicates a negatively skewed distribution, which has a longer left tail and most of the values on the right side of the distribution. A zero skewness value indicates perfect symmetrical distribution. There are different rules about interpreting the degree of skewness and when to decide that our data do not meet the normality assumption. Common guidelines are as follows:

- If the skewness coefficient is between −0.5 and 0.5, the data are relatively symmetrical.
- If the skewness coefficient is between −1 and −0.5 (i.e., negatively skewed) or between 0.5 and 1 (i.e., positively skewed), the data are moderately skewed.
- If the skewness coefficient is less than −1 (i.e., negatively skewed) or greater than 1 (i.e., positively skewed), the data are highly skewed. For example, if you are analyzing your data, and you find that the skewness is −1.5 or 1.5, it indicates a high degree of skewness. Some consider that when the skewness value is ±2, the distribution is considered highly skewed, and parametric tests may not be appropriate.

As noted above, while skewness provides a measure of the symmetry of the data distribution, kurtosis is a measure of data peakedness or flatness. There are three general types of kurtosis distributions leptokurtic distribution, platykurtic distribution, and mesokurtic distribution (see Figure 20.1).

- A distribution with a sharp peak and a narrow range of values is called leptokurtic. This has a positive kurtosis coefficient.

- A distribution that is flatter and has a wider range of values is called platykurtic. This has a negative kurtosis coefficient.
- A distribution that is between these two extremes is mesokurtic. This kind of kurtosis has a kurtosis coefficient of zero, which is characteristic of normal distribution.

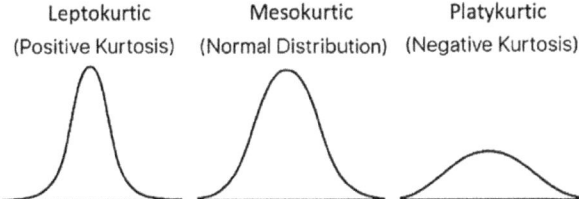

Figure 20.1 Different types of kurtosis

There are two types of kurtosis values: excess kurtosis and standard kurtosis. Standard kurtosis, which is also known as Pearson's kurtosis, measures the degree of peakedness or flatness of a distribution compared to the normal distribution. The kurtosis of a normal distribution is 3. Therefore, a distribution with a kurtosis value larger than 3 is leptokurtic or has a higher peak, whereas a distribution with a kurtosis value below 3 is platykurtic or is flatter. Excess kurtosis is the standard kurtosis minus 3 and provides a measure of the kurtosis of a distribution compared to the kurtosis of the normal distribution. Both types of kurtosis values are commonly used in statistics and can provide important information about the shape of a distribution. However, the Kurtosis value provided by SPSS is an "excess kurtosis." A normal distribution has an excess kurtosis of 0, so a positive kurtosis value indicates a distribution with a higher peak and heavier tails, and a negative kurtosis value indicates a distribution with a flatter peak and lighter tails.

In the SPSS table generated above (SPSS Output 20.2), the data are shown to have a negative kurtosis value, indicating a flatter peak than a normal distribution. When it comes to the actual interpretation, there is no absolute rule, but there are some guidelines:

- If the excess kurtosis value is between -1 and 1, the distribution can be considered to be approximately normal.
- If the excess kurtosis value is less than -1 or greater than 1, it can be considered to be moderately to highly nonnormal, depending on the size of the kurtosis value.

A normal distribution has an excess kurtosis of 0, so a **positive kurtosis** value indicates a distribution with a higher peak and heavier tails, and a **negative kurtosis** value indicates a distribution with a flatter peak and lighter tails.

However, to be more accurate, and also to be able to compare the data across different datasets and variables with different scales or units of measurement, the skewness and kurtosis values can be transformed to standardized values by performing a z test. This can be done by dividing the skewness or excess kurtosis values by their standard errors (SE):

- z = Skewness value/SE of skewness
- z = Excess kurtosis value/SE of excess kurtosis

These z scores measure how many standard errors the observed skewness or kurtosis deviates from zero (the expected value under normality). Both the skewness value and the excess kurtosis values are given in the SPSS output. The calculation gives us a critical value for rejecting the null hypothesis at 0.05 (i.e., concluding that the distribution is nonnormal). But this critical value differs for different sample sizes. Since the standard error changes depending on the sample size, to interpret the z score (Kim, 2013) suggests the following:

- For small samples (smaller than 50), a z score larger than 1.96 suggests nonnormal distribution (this corresponds to $\alpha = 0.05$).
- For sample sizes greater than 50 but below 300, a z score above 3.29 suggests nonnormal distribution (still at $\alpha = 0.05$).
- For sample sizes greater than 300, use the histograms and the absolute values of skewness. An absolute skewness value greater than 2, or an absolute kurtosis value larger than 7 suggests substantial nonnormality. Here z scores are no longer reliable because even small deviations from normality can yield significant z scores due to the large sample size.

Please note that the above z scores differ from the z scores used for individual data points that measure how many standard deviations a single data point is from the mean of a distribution. Z scores for skewness and kurtosis assess whether the observed skewness or kurtosis significantly deviates from what is expected in a normal distribution. They are used to determine if a distribution is nonnormal based on critical thresholds (e.g., ± 1.96 or ± 3.29), depending on the sample size.

Although skewness and kurtosis provide useful information about the distribution, their values should always be interpreted in conjunction with other descriptive statistics, such as the mean, median, and standard deviation, to fully understand the nature of the distribution. Also, they should be considered in combination with other methods discussed above such as visual inspection through graphic tools (e.g., a histogram or Q-Q plot), and the use of formal statistical tests such as the Shapiro–Wilk and Kolmogorov–Smirnov tests.

The Independence of the Data

Parametric tests generally require that the data or observations be independent of each other. This means that the value of one observation or piece of data should not influence the value of another observation. In other words, each data point should represent an independent measurement. For dependent data, such as paired measurements (e.g., pre- and posttest scores from the same individuals), pairs themselves are related because they come from the same participants. In such cases, parametric tests designed for dependent data, such as a paired-samples *t*-test, can be used if the assumptions of normality and other assumptions are met. Otherwise, nonparametric tests may be required (see Chapter 21).

Parametric tests generally require that the data or observations be **independent** of each other. In other words, the value of one observation or piece of data should not influence the value of another observation.

There are some ways in which we can check the assumption of independence in our data, including random selection and time independence.

Random Selection
One important way in which independence can be achieved is through random selection of the participants. If the data are obtained from randomly selected participants, and if the data collected from one participant does not affect the data from another participant, then the assumption of independence is normally met.

Time Independence
If we are collecting data over time, we need to make sure that the different sets of data are collected at distinct points in time in such a way that one is not influencing the other. As noted earlier, when a study involves repeated-measures, that is, when multiple pieces of data are collected from the same participant or group (such as in pretest–posttest designs), the measurements can be said to be not independent, because they come from the same participants. In such cases, we should use statistical tests that take into account the data dependency, such as paired-samples *t*-tests or repeated-measures ANOVAs. It is important to note that even paired-samples *t*-tests or repeated-measures ANOVAs assume that the data meet the assumption of independence of observations. Specifically, the differences between paired measurements in a paired-samples *t*-test should be independent across participants, and the residuals in repeated-measures ANOVAs should not exhibit systematic dependencies (e.g., autocorrelation). If these assumptions are violated, nonparametric tests like the Wilcoxon Signed-Rank Test or the Friedman Test may be more appropriate (see Chapter 21).

Equality (Homogeneity) of Variances
Parametric tests often assume that the variances of the populations being compared are homogeneous or equal. It means that the degree of variability of the data in one

population in the study is similar to that of the other population. In other words, the spread of data or variance in each population from which our sample has been drawn is similar. This assumption is important in many parametric tests, such as the independent samples *t*-test and ANOVA, because unequal variances can affect the reliability of the test results.

There are a few ways to check for equality of variances, including visual inspection and Levene's test.

Visual Inspection

One way of checking the equality or homogeneity of variances is through checking the data visually. For example, we can plot the data for each group in a boxplot or a histogram and compare the spread of the data. If the shape and sizes of the histograms or boxplots are similar, we can then assume that the variance is likely to be similar. Otherwise, the variance may be different.

Levene's Test

Levene's test assesses whether the variances are equal across different groups. The null hypothesis of Levene's test is that the variances are equal, and therefore, if the hypothesis is rejected, it means that the assumption of equality of variances has not been met. In other words, if the p value of Levene's test is greater than 0.05, then the variances are considered equal. Otherwise, the variances are considered unequal.

In SPSS, Levene's test can be found in the output of statistical tests such as ANOVA and the independent samples *t*-test. SPSS Steps 20.3 shows the steps to conduct a Levene's test in SPSS when doing an independent samples *t*-test.

SPSS STEPS 20.3

- Open the data file in SPSS.
- Select "Analyze" > "Compare Means and Proportions" > "Independent-Samples T Test."
- In the dialog box, choose the variable to anlayze and move it to the "Test Variable(s)" box.
- Select "Grouping Variable," and define the groups by specifying the grouping variable's values (e.g., 1 for Group 1, 2 for Group 2).
- Click "OK."

The output (SPSS Output 20.3) generated by SPSS for an independent samples *t*-test shows the results of the Levene's test. The p value of the Levene's test result under "Sig" is greater than 0.05. This means that the data meet the assumption of equality of variances.

SPSS OUTPUT 20.3

Independent Samples Test

		Levene's Test for Equality of Variances		t-test for Equality of Means			
						Significance	
		F	Sig.	t	df	One-Sided p	Two-Sided p
Vocabulary scores	Equal variances assumed	.11	.73	2.8	38	.003	.006
	Equal variances not assumed			2.8	37.3	.003	.006

If the assumption of equal variances is violated in the independent samples *t*-test, you can use the *t*-test results calculated in the second row, "Equal variances not assumed." However, if the sample sizes are small and/or the deviations from equal variances are large, it may be more appropriate to use a nonparametric test, such as the Mann–Whitney *U* test for independent samples, which does not require the assumption of equal variances.

For one-way ANOVA, you can follow the steps in SPSS Steps 20.4 to get the Levene's test.

SPSS STEPS 20.4

- Open the data file in SPSS.
- Select "Analyze" > "Compare Means and Proportions" > "One-Way ANOVA."
- In the dialog box, move dependent variable to the "Dependent List" box.
- Move the independent variable to the "Factor" box.
- Click "Options" > "Homogeneity of variance test."
- Click "Continue" > "OK."

SPSS will generate an output table such as SPSS Output 20.4 that includes the results of Levene's test for equality of variances.

SPSS OUTPUT 20.4

Tests of Homogeneity of Variances

		Levene Statistic	df1	df2	Sig.
Writing score	Based on Mean	.45	2	87	.63
	Based on Median	.33	2	87	.71
	Based on Median and with adjusted df	.33	2	70.06	.71
	Based on trimmed mean	.34	2	87	.71

In the above case, the result of the Levene's test is not significant, so the assumption of homogeneity of variances has been met. If the assumption is violated, you can use Welch's t-test for comparing two groups, particularly if the sample sizes are different. For more than two groups, Welch's ANOVA, a modified version of the one-way ANOVA that does not assume equal variances, can be used. Another option is to use the nonparametric version of one-way ANOVA which is the Kruskal–Wallis test. The third option is to transform your data to achieve equal variances, particularly if the data distribution is approximately normally distributed. Common transformations include logarithmic, square root, or reciprocal transformations. You can transform the data in SPSS using the "Transform" menu.

Absence of Extreme Outliers

Outliers are data points that differ significantly from the rest of the data. Outliers, particularly extreme ones, can distort statistical analyses; therefore, it is important to check for them when conducting parametric tests. To identify outliers, you can use visual methods like boxplots, histograms, and scatter plots, as well as statistical methods such as z scores (values above 3 or below -3) (see Chapter 19). If significant outliers are found, you can first investigate their cause, as they may result from data entry errors or they may represent real values. Depending on the situation, you may remove them, apply a transformation to reduce their impact, or use appropriate statistical methods to minimize their influence.

Types of Parametric Tests

As noted earlier, parametric tests are a group of statistical tests that assume certain assumptions about the data and the population. In the following sections, we will discuss some of the most commonly used parametric tests in applied linguistics. These include:

- one-sample t-test
- independent samples t-test

- paired-samples *t*-test
- one-way ANOVA
- two-way ANOVA
- Pearson correlation
- regression analysis
    - multiple regression
    - hierarchical multiple regression
    - logistic regression
        - binary logistic regression
        - multinomial logistic regression
        - ordinal logistic regression.

One-Sample *t*-Test

A one-sample *t*-test is a statistical test used to determine whether the mean of a single sample of data is significantly different from a hypothetical population mean. This statistical test is used with continuous data and only when we have collected data from one sample on one variable with no intention of making any comparison across groups. The aim is to know whether the mean of the data we have collected is similar or different from a known population mean. The one-sample *t*-test is a parametric test that has specific assumptions regarding the data, as discussed earlier. Therefore, to perform this test, the data must meet those assumptions.

A one-sample *t*-test is a statistical test that is used to determine whether the mean of a single sample of data is significantly different from a hypothetical population mean.

Table 20.1 summarizes the characteristics of the one-sample *t*-test.

Table 20.1 Characteristics of the one-sample *t*-test

Characteristics	Description
Test	One-sample *t*-test
Type of test	Parametric
Assumptions	Normality, independence of observations (values are not influenced by one another or each data point is independent of the others)
Purpose	To determine if the sample mean differs significantly from the population mean
Number of groups	One
Type of Data	Continuous (e.g., test scores)

Example 20.1 provides a hypothetical scenario.

EXAMPLE 20.1

Suppose you want to assess whether the mean language proficiency score of 100 ESL students on the TOEFL test differs significantly from the population mean (e.g., 85). You use a one-sample t-test to see if there is a significant difference.

SPSS Steps 20.5 outlines the steps in performing a one-sample t-test in SPSS.

SPSS STEPS 20.5

- Open the data file in SPSS.
- Select "Analyze" > "Compare Means and Proportions" > "One-Sample T Test."
- In the dialog box, select the variable and move it to the "Test Variable(s)" box.
- Enter known/hypothesized population mean in the "Test Value" box (e.g., 85).
- Click "OK."

SPSS generates the output, including the t-statistic, degrees of freedom, p values (for both one-tailed and two-tailed tests), and confidence interval. SPSS Output 20.5 is an example of an output table generated by SPSS for the example data given above.

SPSS OUTPUT 20.5

One-Sample Test

Test Value = 85

	t	df	Significance One-Sided p	Significance Two-Sided p	Mean Difference	95% Confidence Interval of the Difference Lower	95% Confidence Interval of the Difference Upper
TOEFL score	-23.47	99	.000	.000	-35.94	-38.97	-32.90

The one-sample t-test rejects the null hypothesis that the mean of the language proficiency scores of the 100 ESL students tested on the TOEFL test is equal to the population mean of 85. The p value for the t-test is less than 0.05 ($p < .001$). Since the mean score of students (M = 49.06) is lower than the population mean, we can conclude that the students' scores are significantly below the mean of the population.

POINTS TO PONDER

Do you know where t-tests and ANOVA can be used? Give examples of specific research questions or situations where each of these tests is most suitable?

Independent Samples t-Test

An independent samples t-test is a statistical test that is used to compare the mean data from two groups to determine whether they are significantly different. These tests are commonly used in applied linguistics research to analyze data and to compare the means of two independent groups. The independent samples t-test is a parametric test that assumes that the two groups of data are independent, have approximately equal variances, and their data distributions are approximately normal. The type of data used is continuous, such as test scores.

An independent samples t-test is a statistical test that is used to compare the mean data from two independent groups to determine whether they are significantly different.

Table 20.2 summarizes the characteristics of the independent samples t-test.

Table 20.2 Characteristics of the independent samples t-test

Characteristics	Description
Test	Independent samples t-test
Type of test	Parametric
Assumptions	Normality, independence, homogeneity of variances, no significant outliers
Purpose	To determine if means of two groups differ significantly
Number of groups	Two
Type of Data	Continuous (e.g., test scores)

Here are some examples of research questions that could be addressed using an independent samples t-test:

- Are there any significant differences in the vocabulary knowledge of those ESL learners who have been exposed to extensive versus intensive reading?

- Do L2 students who receive explicit instruction in grammar perform better on a grammaticality judgment test than those who do not receive implicit instruction?
- Is there any differential effect of corrective feedback on the writing accuracy of those English L2 learners who are more proficient in English than those who are less proficient?
- Do students who receive corrective feedback on their written errors perform better on subsequent writing assessments than those who do not receive such feedback?

In each of these research questions, an independent samples *t*-test could be used because we need to compare the means of two groups and determine if there is a significant difference between them.

Example 20.2 presents a hypothetical scenario.

EXAMPLE 20.2

Suppose you aim to compare the effectiveness of explicit and implicit vocabulary teaching methods on learning vocabulary. You randomly assign forty ESL participants to two groups: explicit method (experimental) and implicit method (comparison). After the intervention, you will conduct an independent samples *t*-test to assess if the mean score of the experimental group significantly surpasses that of the comparison group. You should make sure that the normality assumptions are met; if not, you should use the Mann–Whitney *U* test as a nonparametric alternative (see Chapter 21).

SPSS Steps 20.6 outlines the steps for conducting an independent samples *t*-test in SPSS.

SPSS STEPS 20.6

- Open the data file in SPSS.
- Select "Analyze" > "Compare Means and Proportions" > "Independent-Samples T Test."
- In the "Independent-Samples T Test" dialog box, move dependent variable to "Test Variable(s)" box.
- Move variable identifying groups to the "Grouping Variable" box, and define groups.
- Click "Continue."
- In the "Independent-Samples T Test" dialog box, click "Options" to adjust confidence intervals (optional).
- Click "Continue," > "OK."

SPSS will generate the results, including a descriptive statistics table (showing the means and standard deviations of the groups), and an "Independent Samples Test" table that includes the t value as well as the p value, confidence interval and the Levene's test for equality of variances. The "Independent Samples Test" table is shown in SPSS Output 20.6 and the descriptive statistics table is shown in SPSS Output 20.7. When interpreting SPSS Output 20.6, it is important to use the appropriate t statistic, depending on whether the assumption of equal variances has been met. If the assumption is met, choose the t value in the row for "Equal variances assumed." If not, choose the t value in the row for "Equal variances not assumed."

SPSS OUTPUT 20.6

Independent Samples Test

		Levene's Test for Equality of Variances		t-test for Equality of Means					
						Significance			
						One-Sided p	Two-Sided p	Mean Difference	Std. Error Difference
		F	Sig.	t	df				
Vocabulary scores	Equal variances assumed	.11	.73	2.8	38	.003	.006	1.20	.415
	Equal variances not assumed			2.8	37.3	.003	.006	1.20	.415

The independent samples t-test in SPSS Output 20.6 rejects the null hypothesis that the mean of the vocabulary proficiency scores of the two groups are equal by producing a p value that is less than 0.05 ($p = .006$). A comparison of the means of the two groups (SPSS Output 20.7) shows that the explicit method has been more effective ($M = 12.15$) than the implicit method ($M = 10.95$). The result of Levene's test for equality of variances (denoted by "Sig.") in SPSS Output 20.6 is also nonsignificant ($p = .73$), suggesting that the data meet the assumption of the equality of variances needed for parametric tests.

SPSS OUTPUT 20.7

Group Statistics

	Vocabulary teaching methods	N	Mean	Std. Deviation	Std. Error Mean
Vocabulary scores	Explicit	20	12.15	1.2258	.274
	Implicit	20	10.95	1.3945	.311

Paired-Samples *t*-Test

A paired-samples *t*-test is used when we want to compare the means of two related samples. By related samples, we mean that two sets of observations or data come from the same group of participants. An example of that would be when we measure the same participants at two different times (such as a pretest and a posttest) or under two different conditions (e.g., small group and dyadic conditions). This provides within-subjects or repeated-measures data, which refers to data where multiple measurements are taken from the same participants. A paired-samples *t*-test is thus a within-subjects or repeated-measures test that is used to test repeated-measures data.

A paired-samples *t*-test is used when we want to compare the means of two related samples, which refers to two sets of observations or data coming from the same group of participants.

Table 20.3 summarizes the characteristics of the paired-samples *t*-test.

Table 20.3 Characteristics of the paired-samples *t*-test

Characteristics	Description
Test	Paired-samples *t*-test (within-subjects/repeated-measures)
Type of test	Parametric
Assumptions	Normality, independence of observations (i.e., Measurements or responses of one participant are not influenced by the measurements or responses of another participant), no significant outliers
Purpose	To compare means of related samples (e.g., same participants at two times/ conditions)
Number of groups	One
Type of Data	Continuous (e.g., test scores)

Example 20.3 presents a hypothetical scenario.

EXAMPLE 20.3

Suppose you want to examine the effect of extensive reading on the reading comprehension of intermediate ESL Learners. The research question is "Can intensive reading enhance the reading comprehension of these learners?" Employing a classroom-based design, participants engage in a three-week extensive reading program, spending 30 minutes daily on graded readers and maintaining a reading log. The study evaluates reading comprehension before and after the program, using a standardized test. You will use a paired-samples *t*-test to compare the mean scores before and after the extensive reading intervention.

SPSS Steps 20.7 outlines the steps in performing a paired-samples t-test in SPSS.

SPSS STEPS 20.7

- Open the data file in SPSS.
- Select "Analyze" > "Compare Means and Proportions" > "Paired-Samples T Test."
- In the "Paired-Samples T Test" dialog box, select the variables you want to compare and move them to the "Paired Variables" box.
- Click "OK."

SPSS will generate the results depending on what has been requested. In the case of our sample data, two of the tables generated by SPSS are shown below. The first includes the means and the standard deviations (SPSS Output 20.8), and the second includes the result of the t-test (SPSS Output 20.9).

SPSS OUTPUT 20.8

Paired Samples Statistics

		Mean	N	Std. Deviation	Std. Error Mean
Pair 1	Pretest	42.96	30	3.178	.580
	Posttest	44.60	30	2.954	.539

SPSS OUTPUT 20.9

Paired Samples Test

	Paired Differences							Significance	
				95% Confidence Interval of the Difference					
	Mean	Std. Deviation	Std. Error Mean	Lower	Upper	t	df	One-Sided p	Two-Sided p
Pair 1 Pretest – Posttest	−1.63	1.49	.27	−2.19	−1.07	−5.97	29	.000	.000

The mean difference in the SPSS Output 20.9 (−1.63) is the difference between the paired means. If the mean difference is negative, it means that the second mean (e.g., the posttest) is higher than the first mean (e.g., the pretest). The p value

($p < .001$) is smaller than 0.05. This means that the difference between the pretest and the posttest scores is significant.

Analysis of Variance (ANOVA)

ANOVA is an acronym for "Analysis of Variance." It is a statistical test that is used to compare the means of three or more groups or sets of data. It is a parametric test, which assumes that the groups are independent, the variances among the data are equal, and the data are normally distributed; it is used with continuous data.

ANOVA is commonly used in applied linguistics research to compare the effectiveness of different teaching methods, examine the effect of various factors on language learners' performance, or explore how diverse variables influence language acquisition and instructional outcomes. There are several types of ANOVA, including one-way ANOVA, one-way repeated-measures ANOVA, two-way ANOVA, two-way repeated-measures ANOVA, and so on.

ANOVA is an acronym for "Analysis of Variance." It is a statistical test that is used to compare the means of three or more groups or sets of data.

POINTS TO PONDER

In what situations can you use a two-way ANOVA? Explain the concept of interaction effects in a two-way ANOVA.

One-Way and Two-Way (Factorial) ANOVA

One-way ANOVA compares the means of three or more groups for a single independent variable. In other words, it is used when there is only one independent variable or factor that divides the groups, and the aim is to investigate if that independent variable has any effect on one dependent variable. Two-way ANOVA involves two independent variables. There are various research questions in applied linguistics that can be examined via one-way ANOVA. Some examples include the following:

- Does the use of different instructional strategies (e.g., task-based, traditional, project-based learning) have a differential effect on L2 learners' speaking fluency?
- Is there a significant difference in the writing skills of English language learners across different proficiency levels (e.g., beginner, intermediate, advanced)?
- Does the use of different types of language outcome measures (free production, grammaticality judgment, oral elicitation tasks) have a significant effect on the test scores of English language learners (repeated-measures)?

These research questions can be addressed by comparing the means of continuous data across different groups or levels of the independent variable.

One-way ANOVA compares the means of three or more groups for a single independent variable,

---

Table 20.4 summarizes the characteristics of one-way and two-way ANOVA.

Table 20.4 Characteristics of one-way and two-way ANOVA

Characteristics	One-way ANOVA	Two-way ANOVA
Type of test	Parametric	Parametric
Assumptions	Normality, independence, equal variance for each group, no significant outliers	Normality, independence, equal variance for each group, no significant outliers
Independent variable	One categorical variable	Two categorical variables
Dependent variable	Continuous variable	Continuous variable
Number of groups	Three or more	Multiple groups defined by two factors
Purpose	To test for differences between means of groups	To test for differences between means based on two independent variables and their interaction effect

Example 20.4 provides a hypothetical scenario for one-way ANOVA.

EXAMPLE 20.4

Suppose you want to investigate the effect of different types of written corrective feedback on the writing performance of intermediate-level English L2 learners. Your research question is "Does the writing performance of English L2 learners differ significantly with three feedback types: direct correction, indirect correction, and metalinguistic feedback?". To answer this question, you will conduct an experimental study where sixty intermediate-level L2 learners are randomly assigned to one of three groups, each receiving a different type of feedback on their short essays. The three types of feedback are direct correction, indirect correction, and metalinguistic feedback. After receiving the feedback, the learners' essays will be assessed using a standardized rubric, resulting in continuous data (writing scores). To determine whether there are significant differences in writing performance among the three groups, you will use Analysis of Variance (ANOVA). The writing scores will serve as the dependent variable, while the type of feedback received will be the independent variable.

SPSS Steps 20.8 outlines the steps to perform a one-way ANOVA in SPSS.

SPSS STEPS 20.8

- Open the data file in SPSS.
- Select "Analyze" > "Compare Means and Proportions" > "One-Way ANOVA."
- In the "One-Way ANOVA" dialog box, select the variable and move it to the "Dependent List."
- Choose grouping variable and move it to the "Factor" box, and define the range of values or categories that represent the groups.
- Click "Options" for additional options (e.g., descriptive statistics and homogeneity of variance test).
- Click "Continue," then click "Post Hoc" to select the type of post hoc tests, if needed.
- Click "Continue" > "OK."

SPSS will generate the results depending on what has been requested. SPSS Outputs 20.10–20.12 show the hypothetical results for Example 20.4. These include a descriptive statistics table (SPSS Output 20.10), showing the means, standard deviations, and sample sizes for each group; a table showing the results of tests of homogeneity of variances (SPSS Output 20.11); and an ANOVA table (SPSS Output 20.12), showing the between- and within-groups variations, sum of squares, degrees of freedom, mean squares, F value, and the p value for the analysis.

SPSS OUTPUT 20.10

Descriptives

Writing score

	N	Mean	Std. Deviation	Std. Error	95% Confidence Interval for Mean Lower Bound	95% Confidence Interval for Mean Upper Bound
Direct correction	30	7.50	2.42	.44	6.60	8.40
Indirect correction	30	13.60	3.25	.59	12.38	14.82
Metalinguistic feedback	30	18.50	2.52	.46	17.56	19.44
Total	90	13.20	5.28	.56	12.09	14.31

SPSS OUTPUT 20.11

Tests of Homogeneity of Variances

		Levene Statistic	df1	df2	Sig.
Writing score	Based on Mean	.45	2	87	.63
	Based on Median	.33	2	87	.71
	Based on Median and with adjusted df	.33	2	70.06	.71
	Based on trimmed mean	.34	2	87	.71

SPSS OUTPUT 20.12

ANOVA

Writing score

	Sum of Squares	df	Mean Square	F	Sig.
Between Groups	1822.20	2	911.10	120.06	.000
Within Groups	660.20	87	7.59		
Total	2482.40	89			

The result of the test of homogeneity of variances are nonsignificant (denoted by "Sig.") in SPSS Output 20.11, meaning that this assumption of ANOVA has been met.

The ANOVA table (SPSS Output 20.12) shows that the difference among the groups is statistically significant ($p < .001$; under "Sig.").

If requested, the SPSS output also generates a post-hoc test table, showing the results of the post-hoc test, such as Tukey's HSD or Bonferroni, which helps understand which groups are significantly different from each other. For the hypothetical example, we have chosen the Tukey's HSD, the results of which are shown in SPSS Output 20.13.

SPSS OUTPUT 20.13

		Multiple Comparisons				
		Dependent Variable: Writing score				
		Tukey HSD				
					95% Confidence Interval	
(I) Group	(J) Group	Mean Difference (I-J)	Std. Error	Sig.	Lower Bound	Upper Bound
Direct correction	Indirect correction	−6.10*	.71	.000	−7.80	−4.40
	Metalinguistic feedback	−11.00*	.71	.000	−12.70	−9.30
Indirect correction	Direct correction	6.10*	.71	.000	4.40	7.80
	Metalinguistic feedback	−4.90*	.71	.000	−6.60	−3.20
Metalinguistic feedback	Direct correction	11.00*	.71	.000	9.30	12.70
	Indirect correction	4.90*	.71	.000	3.20	6.60

*. The mean difference is significant at the .05 level.

The multiple comparisons table shows the mean difference between each pair of groups, using the Tukey test. It also shows the lower and upper bounds of the confidence interval for the mean difference, and the p value for each comparison. As the table shows all the pairwise comparisons in our example data are significant ($p < .001$; under "Sig.").

The Difference between Different Post Hoc Tests ANOVA simply shows whether there are any differences among the groups without specifying where the difference lies. If any significant difference is found, post-hoc tests could be conducted to determine which group has a significantly higher mean score.

In SPSS, there are several options for post-hoc tests after performing a one-way ANOVA, the choice of which depends on the research question and the tolerance for Type I error. Here are some of the most common options:

Bonferroni: This is a conservative type of test and involves conducting a series of t-tests between pairs while adjusting the p values of the pairwise comparisons. The adjustment is to control for the increased risk of a Type I error due to multiple testing and is made by dividing the significance level α by the number of comparisons, thereby setting a more stringent significance threshold for each individual comparison. It is more conservative compared to the Tukey HSD test and can be more powerful when the number of comparisons is small.

Tukey HSD (honestly significant difference): Similar to Bonferroni, this test also controls for the Type I error rate, but it does so by adjusting the critical value or the test statistics used to evaluate the pairwise comparisons. It is a more powerful test than the Bonferroni when there are a large number of pairs, and it is one of the most commonly used tests. However, for a small number of pairwise comparisons, the Bonferroni correction may be more powerful.

Scheffé: This is another popular test that also controls the overall Type I error rate. It does so by adjusting the test statistics but in a different way from the Tukey test. It is more conservation than the Tukey test in that it makes it less likely to commit a Type I error (rejecting the null hypothesis). But it also has less power to detect true effects. Tukey's HSD test provides a narrower confidence interval than the Scheffé test, which means that it is more likely to detect a significant difference between groups if that exists.

If the assumption of homogeneity of variances is not met, SPSS provides a number of options for post hoc comparison. These include:

Games–Howell: This test assumes that there are unequal variances between groups and therefore can be used when the assumption of homogeneity of variances has not been met. The Games–Howell test takes into account unequal sample sizes, and it is a powerful procedure with large sample sizes, which means that it is more likely to find significant differences, but it is more conservative with small sample sizes.

Dunnett's T3: Similar to Games–Howell, this test does not assume homogeneity of variances between groups and also takes into account unequal sample sizes. Dunnett's T3 is thus commonly recommended for use when the sample sizes are small, typically less than 50 per group.

Dunnett's C: This test assumes equal variances between groups and adjusts for unequal sample sizes. Dunnett's C may be less powerful than Dunnett's T3. Both Dunnett's T3 and Dunnett's C are designed to examine the differences between the treatment groups and the control groups separately, while adjusting for multiple comparisons. Therefore, if you want to find the differences between the control group and treatment groups, these tests would be suitable to use.

Tamhane's T2: This test does not assume homogeneity of variances or equal sample sizes. But it is less powerful than Games–Howell and Dunnett's T3 procedures. It is recommended when sample sizes are different.

If the assumption of **homogeneity of variances** is not met, SPSS provides a number of options for post-hoc comparison, including Games-Howell, Dunnett's T3, Dunnett's C, and Tamhane's T2.

Example 20.5 provides a hypothetical study for a two-way ANOVA.

EXAMPLE 20.5

Suppose you want to investigate the effect of language proficiency and oral feedback methods (recasts, elicitation, explicit correction) on L2 learners' speaking accuracy. You recruit ninety participants from low- and high-proficiency levels, assigning them to six groups based on feedback methods. After treatment, you will examine participants' speaking accuracy in a recorded task using a rubric. The research questions for the study are as follows:

- Does oral feedback significantly affect learners' speaking accuracy?
- Does language proficiency have a significant impact on learners' speaking accuracy?
- Is there a significant interaction effect between feedback methods and language proficiency on learners' speaking accuracy?

For the above example, you can use a two-way ANOVA to determine whether oral feedback and language proficiency have a significant impact on speaking accuracy. SPSS Steps 20.9 outlines the steps for conducting a two-way ANOVA using SPSS.

SPSS STEPS 20.9

- Open the data file in SPSS.
- Select "Analyze" > "General Linear Model" > "Univariate."
- In the "Univariate" dialog box move the dependent variable to the "Dependent Variable" Box.
- Move the two independent variables (the factors) to the "Fixed Factor(s)" box.
- Click "Options," select "Descriptive Statistics" and check "Homogeneity tests." Click "Continue."
- Click "Post Hoc" if you want to conduct post hoc comparisons. Select the independent variable(s) for the post hoc tests and move them to the "Post Hoc Tests for" box.
- Choose the test (e.g., Tukey, Bonferroni).
- Click "Continue" > "OK."

Once the analysis is complete, SPSS will display the results. The descriptive statistics table (SPSS Output 20.14) provides a summary of the data for each combination of the levels of the two factors. This table typically includes the mean values of the dependent variable for each combination of the levels of the two factors, the standard deviations, and the sample size (N).

SPSS OUTPUT 20.14

Descriptive Statistics

Dependent Variable: Speaking accuracy scores

Feedback Group	Language proficiency	Mean	Std. Deviation	N
Recasts	Low	11.87	2.60	16.00
	High	14.14	2.41	14.00
	Total	12.93	2.73	30.00
Elicitation	Low	15.38	2.19	16.00
	High	15.43	2.24	14.00
	Total	15.40	2.18	30.00
Explicit correction	Low	18.50	3.29	16.00
	High	17.79	2.08	14.00
	Total	18.17	2.77	30.00
Total	Low	15.25	3.82	48.00
	High	15.79	2.67	42.00
	Total	15.50	3.33	90.00

The Levene's test table (SPSS 20.15) shows the Levene's test statistic (based on the mean and the median), degrees of freedom, and the p value associated with the Levene's test statistic. For the hypothetical example in Example 20.5, the Levene's test of equality of variances is nonsignificant ($p = .36$), meaning that the equality of variances assumption has been met.

SPSS OUTPUT 20.15

Levene's Test of Equality of Error Variances[a,b]

		Levene Statistic	df1	df2	Sig.
Speaking accuracy scores	Based on Mean	1.11	5	84.00	.36
	Based on Median	1.12	5	84.00	.36
	Based on Median and with adjusted df	1.12	5	75.03	.36
	Based on trimmed mean	1.13	5	84.00	.35

Tests the null hypothesis that the error variance of the dependent variable is equal across groups.

a. Dependent variable: Speaking accuracy scores

b. Design: Intercept + feedback + Proficiency + feedback * Proficiency

The table for tests of between-subjects effects (SPSS Output 20.16) provides information on the main effects of each factor and the interaction between the factors. It includes the source of variance, the Type III sum of squares (which is a method for partitioning the total sum of squares into components that are independent of the order of variables in the model), the degrees of freedom associated with each source of variance, the mean square, the F values, and the p values. For our hypothetical example (Example 20.5), the p value for the main effect of feedback is less than 0.05 ($p < .001$), meaning that the effect is significant. The p values of the main effect of language proficiency and the interaction effect of language proficiency and feedback are nonsignificant.

SPSS OUTPUT 20.16

Tests of Between-Subjects Effects

Dependent Variable: Speaking accuracy scores

Source	Type III Sum of Squares	df	Mean Square	F	Sig.
Corrected Model	453.50[a]	5	90.70	14.29	.000
Intercept	21576.03	1	21576.03	3400.35	.000
Feedback	394.20	2	197.10	31.06	.000
Proficiency	6.43	1	6.43	1.01	.32
Feedback * Proficiency	35.80	2	17.90	2.82	.07
Error	533.00	84	6.35		
Total	22609.00	90			
Corrected Total	986.50	89			

a. R Squared = .460 (Adjusted R Squared = .428)

The multiple comparisons table (SPSS Output 20.17) provides the following information: pairwise comparisons, mean difference, standard error, p value, and the 95% confidence interval. For our hypothetical example, we have conducted a Tukey post-hoc test, and the p values for all pairwise comparisons are significant (denoted by "Sig.").

SPSS OUTPUT 20.17

Multiple Comparisons

Dependent Variable: Speaking accuracy scores

Tukey HSD

(I) Feedback Group	(J) Feedback Group	Mean Difference (I-J)	Std. Error	Sig.	95% Confidence Interval	
					Lower Bound	Upper Bound
Recasts	Elicitation	−2.47*	.65	.00	−4.02	−.91
	Explicit correction	−5.23*	.65	.00	−6.79	−3.68
Elicitation	Recasts	2.47*	.65	.00	.91	4.02
	Explicit correction	−2.77*	.65	.00	−4.32	−1.21
Explicit correction	Recasts	5.23*	.65	.00	3.68	6.79
	Elicitation	2.77*	.65	.00	1.21	4.32

Based on observed means.
The error term is Mean Square (Error) = 6.345.
*. The mean difference is significant at the .05 level.

Why Use ANOVA and Not Multiple *t*-Tests? One may wonder why we need ANOVA and what the problem is with using multiple *t*-tests as a tool to compare means of three or more groups in a pairwise manner. For example, if we have groups A, B, and C, cannot we just use three *t*-tests and compare A and B, B and C, and A and C?

Of course, one way to compare the means of three or more groups could be by using multiple *t*-tests. However, while this is possible, this approach has at least two drawbacks.

Drawback 1 (increasing Type I error): One of the problems with conducting multiple *t*-tests is that doing so increases the probability of committing a Type I error (i.e., rejecting the null hypothesis when it is actually true). This is important to consider because a Type I error can lead to incorrect conclusions.

The reason why multiple tests increase the risk of a Type I error is that the probability of making a Type I error increases with the number of tests performed. Suppose you are conducting a study and have set the significance level at 0.05. For each test that you perform, there is a 5% chance of making a Type I error. Now, if you conduct three *t*-tests to compare the means of three groups with each test having a 5% chance of error, the overall probability of making a Type I error across all the tests is about 15%, which is greater than 5%.

There is a formula that can calculate the probability of making a Type I error in such situations:

p (at least one Type I error) $= 1 - p$ (no Type I error).

This formula means that the probability of making at least one Type I error in multiple tests is equal to 1 minus the probability of making no Type I error at all. To use the formula we need to first calculate the probability of making "no Type I error." This is always 1 minus the probability of making a Type I error (note the p of Type I error is the significance level). Now, in a t-test with $\alpha = 0.05$, the probability of not making a Type I error in rejecting the null hypothesis (or getting a significant result) is 1 minus $0.05 = 0.95$. Now if we perform three t-tests, and if for each the probability of not making a Type I error is 0.95, for all three, that probability will be:

p (no Type I error) $= 0.95 \times 0.95 \times 0.95 = 0.8574$.

To obtain the probability of making at least one Type I error across all three tests, we can subtract this value from 1:

p (at least one Type I error) $= 1 - p$ (no Type I error) $= 1 - 0.857 = 0.143$.

Therefore, the probability of making at least one Type I error in three t-tests with a significance level of 0.05 is 0.143, or approximately 14.3%.

One mechanism that can be used to control this overall Type I error rate is to adjust the significance level for each t-test in such a way that, overall, the Type I error across all tests becomes 5%. One commonly used method is the Bonferroni correction. This technique adjusts the level of significance based on the number of tests being performed by dividing the original significance level by the number of tests performed. For example, if we have performed three t-tests, the Bonferroni correction would adjust the significance level to $0.05/3 = 0.0167$ for each test. This adjustment keeps the overall Type I error rate across all three tests at 5%.

Drawback 2: The second drawback of using multiple t-tests is that multiple t-tests do not provide an overall assessment of significance to assess the difference between all groups at the same time. This is because when we perform multiple t-tests, we are comparing two groups at a time. Therefore, we cannot obtain a comprehensive picture of the overall significance of the differences among the three groups. For example, if we have three groups (A, B, and C) and if we perform three t-tests between A and B, B and C, and A and C, we will obtain three p values. But these three p values do not provide a comprehensive index for the overall significance of the differences among all three groups.

For the above reasons, it is always advised not to use multiple t-tests for comparing the means of three groups or more. A much-preferred approach is to use ANOVA, which is a test that assesses the differences between all groups simultaneously while controlling for the overall level of significance. ANOVA can also allow us to perform post-hoc pairwise comparisons, using Tukey, Scheffé, or

Bonferroni tests to determine whether there is a significant difference between each pair of data. Therefore, ANOVA is a more appropriate test than t-tests when it comes to comparing three or more groups.

One drawback of conducting multiple t-tests is that doing so increases the probability of committing a Type I error. The **second drawback** is that multiple t-tests do not provide an overall assessment of significance to assess the difference between all groups at the same time.

One-Way Repeated-Measures ANOVA

One-way repeated-measures ANOVA is used to compare the means of three or more repeated measurements from one group of participants. It is called "one-way" because there is only one independent variable with three or more levels measured repeatedly over time. The reason it is called "repeated-measures" is that the same group of participants is tested multiple times under each of the levels of the independent variable. The purpose is to determine whether there are significant differences among the means. Similar to one-way ANOVA, If there are significant differences among the means, the next step would be to conduct post-hoc tests to identify which pairs of means are different. As noted before, there are several post-hoc tests that can be used, such as the Bonferroni test, Tukey's honestly significant difference (HSD) test, and the Scheffé test. These tests are different in their power and can be used depending on the nature of the research.

Since one-way repeated-measures ANOVA is a parametric test, there are several assumptions that should be met before performing such a test. These include:

- Normality: This can be checked using visual inspection of histograms or by using statistical tests such as the Shapiro–Wilk test.
- Sphericity: This assumes that the variances of the differences between pairs of data (means) are equal. Sphericity can be tested using the Mauchly's test, which is provided in SPSS.
- Independence of observations: Although repeated-measures designs involve correlated observations from the same participants, the measurements themselves should still be independent of each other within the same condition.
- No significant outliers: The data should be free of extreme values that could skew the analysis.

If any of these assumptions are violated, the results of the one-way repeated-measures ANOVA may not be accurate, and instead nonparametric tests may be used that do not require these assumptions.

Table 20.5 summarizes the characteristics of one-way repeated-measures ANOVA.

Table 20.5 Characteristics of one-way repeated-measures ANOVA

Characteristics	Descriptions
Name of the test	One-way repeated-measures ANOVA
Type of test	Parametric
Assumptions	Normality, sphericity, independence of observations, no significant outliers
Independent variables	One categorical variable
Dependent variable	One continuous variable
Number of groups	One group
Purpose	To test for significant differences among three or more means from the same participants
Type of data	Continuous/interval (e.g., test scores)

Example 20.6 presents a hypothetical study.

EXAMPLE 20.6

Suppose you aim to explore the effect of different vocabulary exercises (games, flashcards, and word association) on vocabulary improvement in EFL students. You use a sample of thirty intermediate EFL students and employ a within-subjects design in which participants complete each exercise type in a randomized order over three sessions, focusing on ten target words each time. They then take a fill-in-the-blank vocabulary test. You test whether there is any significant difference in the means of the vocabulary scores for the three types of exercises.

In the above example, there is one continuous dependent variable, which is the participants' vocabulary score, and one independent variable, which is the type of vocabulary exercise with three levels (vocabulary games, flash cards, and word-association exercises). Since we are examining one group of participants measured three times under the three different conditions, we can conduct one-way repeated-measures ANOVA to determine whether there is a significant difference in the learner's vocabulary learning across the three types of exercise. If a difference is found, post-hoc tests (e.g., Bonferroni) can be used to identify where the specific differences are.

SPSS Steps 20.10 outlines the steps in conducting a one-way repeated-measures ANOVA in SPSS.

SPSS STEPS 20.10

- Open the data file in SPSS.
- Select "Analyze" > "General Linear Model" > "Repeated Measures."
- In the "Repeated Measures" dialog box, name the within-subjects factor(s), enter the number of levels (e.g., 3 for three time points).

SPSS STEPS 20.10 (cont.)

- Click "Add."
- Click "Define." In the next dialog box, move the appropriate variables to the "Within-Subject Variables" box.
- Click "Options" for output options (e.g., descriptive statistics), click "Continue."
- Click "EM Means," move the variables to the "Display Means For" box.
- Check "Compare main effects," select "Bonferroni" (or another method).
- Click "Continue" > "OK."

When running the repeated-measures ANOVA in SPSS using the above steps, the program generates a number of outputs including descriptive statistics, multivariate tests, Mauchly's test of sphericity, tests of within-subjects effects, tests of between-subjects effects, and pairwise comparison. Each of these will be explained below with respect to the hypothetical study.

SPSS Output 20.18 shows the descriptive statistics for the hypothetical study. This output provides information about the mean, standard deviation, and sample size for each of the variables in our example study.

SPSS OUTPUT 20.18

Descriptive Statistics

	Mean	Std. Deviation	N
Vocabulary games	16.23	2.90	30.00
Word association	16.67	2.78	30.00
Flash cards	17.03	2.43	30.00

To examine whether there are differences among the means, SPSS generates a few other tables, one of which shows the results of the multivariate tests, and the other, the results of univariate test (within-subjects effects; see below). Both compare the means of the group across different levels of the independent variable. In other words, both can show us if there are significant differences among the means. One difference is that the within-subjects univariate test assumes a criterion called sphericity, whereas the multivariate test does not. In cases where the assumption of sphericity is met, the univariate within-subjects test is more powerful than the multivariate test. That is why most often researchers report the results of the within-subjects test rather than the multivariate tests.

SPSS OUTPUT 20.19

	Multivariate Tests[a]					
Effect		Value	F	Hypothesis df	Error df	Sig.
Vocabulary exercises	Pillai's Trace	.09	1.36[b]	2.00	28.00	.27
	Wilks's Lambda	.91	1.36[b]	2.00	28.00	.27
	Hotelling's Trace	.10	1.36[b]	2.00	28.00	.27
	Roy's Largest Root	.10	1.36[b]	2.00	28.00	.27

a. Design: Intercept
Within-Subjects Design: Vocabulary exercises
b. Exact statistic

The multivariate tests examine the overall multivariate effect of the independent variable on the dependent variable. The table in SPSS Output 20.19 includes four multivariate test statistics, including Pillai's Trace, Wilks's Lambda, Hotelling's Trace, and Roy's Largest Root with their associated p values. It also includes the degrees of freedom for each test.

The four multivariate test statistics test the null hypothesis that there are no significant differences between the means of the conditions. Of the four tests, the most commonly used one is Wilks's Lambda, and the first three usually provide similar results when there is one dependent variable in the analysis. However, there are some differences among them in terms of their power. Pillai's Trace provides a measure of the overall effect, and it ranges from 0 to 1 with a larger value indicating a larger effect of the independent variable(s). It is a powerful test and is a good option when the data do not meet the assumption of homogeneity of variance–covariance or when the sample sizes are uneven and small.

Wilks's Lambda also measures the overall effect of the independent variable(s) and also ranges from 0 to 1. Hotelling's Trace measures the effect of the independent variable(s) on a linear combination of the dependent variables, and Roy's Largest Root provides a measure of the largest effect of the independent variable(s) on any linear combination of the dependent variables.

For our hypothetical study example, the p values of the multivariate tests (denoted by "Sig.") are all more than 0.05 ($p = .27$), indicating no significant differences among the three types of exercise.

The output also includes Mauchly's test of sphericity. This output provides information about whether the assumption of sphericity has been met (SPSS

Output 20.20). Sphericity is an important assumption for repeated-measures ANOVA and refers to the assumption that the variances of the differences between all possible pairs of related groups (or levels or conditions) are equal. This assumption is important because, if violated, the results of the repeated-measures ANOVA may be inaccurate as the violation of the sphericity assumption can lead to an increased risk of a Type I error (the likelihood of rejecting the null hypothesis when it is actually true).

When conducting a repeated-measures ANOVA in SPSS, the "Tests of Sphericity" table is generated as part of the output. This output provides the results of Mauchly's test of sphericity, which tests whether that assumption has been met. If Mauchly's test is significant, then the assumption of sphericity is violated. In this case, when interpreting the results of the within-subjects effects (SPSS Output 20.21), you can use the Greenhouse–Geisser or Huynh–Feldt correction to adjust the degrees of freedom to account for this violation. In the case of our hypothetical study, the p value (denoted by "Sig.") is 0.18, which means that this assumption has been met.

SPSS OUTPUT 20.20

Mauchly's Test of Sphericity[a]

Measure: MEASURE_1

Within Subjects Effect	Mauchly's W	Approx. Chi-Square	df	Sig.	Epsilon[b]		
					Greenhouse-Geisser	Huynh-Feldt	Lower-bound
Vocabulary exercises	.89	3.39	2	.18	.90	.95	.50

Tests the null hypothesis that the error covariance matrix of the orthonormalized transformed dependent variables is proportional to an identity matrix.

a. Design: Intercept

Within-Subjects Design: Vocabulary exercises

b. May be used to adjust the degrees of freedom for the averaged tests of significance. Corrected tests are displayed in the Tests of Within-Subjects Effects table (SSPS Output 20.21).

Tests of within-subjects effects provides information about the effects of the within-subjects factors on the dependent variable. This includes statistics such as Type III sum of square, degrees of freedom, mean square, F values, and p values (under Sig."). In the case of our hypothetical study from Example 20.6, it shows the main effect of exercises to be statistically nonsignificant, suggesting no difference among the three types of exercises.

SPSS OUTPUT 20.21

Tests of Within-Subjects Effects

Measure: MEASURE_1

Source		Type III Sum of Squares	df	Mean Square	F	Sig.
Vocabulary exercises	Sphericity Assumed	9.62	2	4.81	.97	.38
	Greenhouse-Geisser	9.62	1.80	5.36	.97	.38
	Huynh-Feldt	9.62	1.91	5.05	.97	.38
	Lower-bound	9.62	1	9.62	.97	.33
Error (Vocabulary exercises)	Sphericity Assumed	287.04	58	4.95		
	Greenhouse-Geisser	287.04	52.07	5.51		
	Huynh-Feldt	287.04	55.28	5.19		
	Lower-bound	287.04	29	9.90		

In our hypothetical example, the result of Mauchly's test was not significant. Therefore, the assumption of sphericity was met, and thus we use the results shown for "Sphericity Assumed" in the table shown in SPSS Output 20.21. However, as noted earlier, if the Mauchly's test was significant, then the assumption of sphericity was violated, in which case, you could use the Greenhouse–Geisser or Huynh–Feldt correction (as shown in SPSS Output 20.21) to adjust the degrees of freedom to account for this violation.

As to whether we should use the Greenhouse–Geisser or Huynh–Feldt correction, we can look at the Greenhouse–Geisser and Huynh–Feldt epsilon estimates which are provided in the Tests of Sphericity table (SPSS Output 2020). These values provide the estimated values of epsilon (ϵ), which are used to adjust the degrees of freedom for the within-subjects effect(s) in the ANOVA. The epsilon values produced by each method provide an indication of the degree to which the assumption of sphericity has been violated. The epsilon values range from 0 to 1, with 1 indicating perfect sphericity and smaller values indicating greater departures from sphericity. The Greenhouse–Geisser and Huynh–Feldt epsilon values can be used to select the appropriate correction method for the F tests. In general, the choice between Greenhouse–Geisser and Huynh–Feldt correction should be based on the degree of sphericity violation. The Huynh–Feldt correction is more powerful than the Greenhouse-Geisser correction and can be a better choice when the assumption of sphericity is violated and the effect sizes are large. However, if the sphericity assumption is violated minimally and the Greenhouse-Geisser epsilon value is greater than 0.75, either correction can be used. If Greenhouse-Geisser epsilon is below 0.75 and we want for our test to have more power, it is recommended to use the Greenhouse-Geisser correction results in the within-subjects test table.

SPSS also generates tables showing the results of pairwise comparisons (the post-hoc analyses; e.g., SPSS Output 20.22). The pairwise comparison table includes information such as the mean differences, the standard error of the difference, the p value (under "Sig"), and the confidence interval for the difference between means. The p value shows whether the difference between pairs is significant. If the p value is less than the alpha level (typically 0.05), the difference is considered statistically significant. In the case of our example, none of the pairwise differences are significant as the p values are greater than 0.05 (in the table, the numbers 1, 2, and 3 denote vocabulary exercise types). This is not surprising as there was no overall significant difference among the three types of exercises in the first place.

SPSS OUTPUT 20.22

Pairwise Comparisons

Measure: MEASURE_1

(I) Vocabulary exercises	(J) Vocabulary exercises	Mean Difference (I-J)	Std. Error	Sig.[a]	95% Confidence Interval for Difference[a] Lower Bound	Upper Bound
1	2	−.43	.56	1.00	−1.86	.99
	3	−.80	.49	.34	−2.05	.45
2	1	.43	.56	1.00	−.99	1.86
	3	−.37	.66	1.00	−2.04	1.31
3	1	.80	.49	.34	−.45	2.05
	2	.37	.66	1.00	−1.31	2.04

Based on estimated marginal means

a. Adjustment for multiple comparisons: Bonferroni.

Two-Way Mixed-Design ANOVA

As explained above, two-way ANOVA involves two independent variables, and the aim is to determine how an outcome (a dependent variable) is affected by each of the two variables. In the example given earlier (Example 20.5), the level of language proficiency and methods of oral feedback were the two independent variables. Both of them were between-subjects variables, that is, they were used to compare differences between groups.

A two-way mixed-design ANOVA also tests the effect of two independent variables. However, one of the independent variables is repeated, which means that the same group of participants is measured two or more than two times under different levels of the same independent variable. In statistics, the term "repeated-measures" is used when the same participants receive different tests or when they participate in all conditions of the study. In a two-way mixed-design ANOVA, one of the variables is a between-subjects variable and the other one is a within-subjects variable.

The between-subjects variable is the one that is varied between different groups, and the within-subjects variable is the one that is varied within each participant or is repeated within participants. For example, in a study that involves a pretest and a posttest, the testing time is a within-subjects (or repeated-measures) variable as the same participants are tested twice. The within-subjects designs control for individual differences between participants, and thus allows for a more precise analysis of the effects of the independent variable on the dependent variable. However, it might be subject to practice or test effect as participants are tested on the same variable multiple times.

A two-way mixed-design ANOVA tests the effect of two independent variables: a between-subjects variable and a within-subjects variable.

Table 20.6 summarizes the characteristics of two-way mixed-design ANOVA.

Table 20.6 Characteristics of two-way mixed-design ANOVA

Characteristics	Description
Test	Two-way mixed-design ANOVA
Type of test	Parametric
Independent variables	Two: one between-subjects variable and one within-subjects variable
Dependent variable	Continuous data
Assumptions	Normality, homogeneity of variances, sphericity, no significant outliers
Purpose	To examine effects of both between-subjects and within-subjects variables on a dependent variable and their interaction
Number of groups	Two or more groups

Example 20.7 presents a hypothetical scenario.

EXAMPLE 20.7

Suppose you aim to compare the effect of oral corrective feedback methods (peer, teacher, and peer + teacher) on L2 learners' speaking fluency in a pretest, posttest, delayed posttest design. The two independent variables include feedback method (between-subjects) and testing time (within-subjects), with the dependent variable being learners' scores on speaking fluency tests. Sixty intermediate-level L2 participants are randomly assigned to three groups. The research questions examine differences in fluency among feedback types, changes in fluency over time, and interaction effects between method and testing time.

To address the questions in the above study, you can use a two-way mixed-design ANOVA, with feedback method as the between-subjects factor and testing time as a within-subjects factor. SPSS Steps 20.11 outlines the steps for conducting a two-way mixed-design ANOVA in SPSS.

SPSS STEPS 20.11
- Open the data file in SPSS
- Select "Analyze" > "General Linear Model" > "Repeated Measures."
- In the "Repeated Measures" dialog box, under "Within-Subject Factor Name," enter the name of the within-subjects factor(s), specify levels, click "Add."
- Click "Define", move variables to "Within-Subjects Variables."
- Move the between-subjects variable to "Between-Subjects Factor(s).
- Click "Options" for output options (e.g., descriptive statistics, homogeneity tests).
- Click "Continue".
- Click "EM Means," move variables to the "Display Means for" box, check "Compare main effects," select e.g., "Bonferroni."
- Click "Continue."
- Click "Post Hoc," move variables to the "Post Hoc Test for" box, choose the appropriate post hoc test.
- Click "Continue" > "OK."

SPSS generates several outputs, including main effects and interaction effects between the two independent variables and post-hoc tests to compare differences between and across groups and conditions, if they exist. The post-hoc tests include Bonferroni, Tukey, Scheffé, and the Least Significant Difference (LSD) test. We have explained the differences among the first three before. The LSD test examines the difference between pairs of means without making any adjustments to the p values. It is generally considered to be the least conservative test.

We run the two-way mixed-design ANOVA in SPSS on the data for the hypothetical study mentioned in Example 20.7, and the program generates a number of outputs: descriptive statistics, Box's test of equality of covariance matrices, multivariate tests, Mauchly's test of sphericity, tests of within-subjects effects, Levene's test of equality of error variances, tests of between-subjects effects, and pairwise comparisons. Each of these will be explained below.

SPSS Output 20.23 shows the descriptive statistics for our hypothetical study. This output provides descriptive information about the data, including the mean, standard deviation, and sample size for each of the variables.

SPSS OUTPUT 20.23

Descriptive Statistics

	Feedback Group	Mean	Std. Deviation	N
Pretest	Peer feedback	9.70	1.64	30.00
	Teacher feedback	13.03	1.61	30.00
	Peer + teacher feedback	14.03	2.17	30.00
	Total	12.26	2.59	90.00
Posttest	Peer feedback	12.50	3.05	30.00
	Teacher feedback	15.57	2.67	30.00
	Peer + teacher feedback	18.17	2.77	30.00
	Total	15.41	3.64	90.00
Delayed Posttest	Peer feedback	8.67	2.47	30.00
	Teacher feedback	13.83	2.76	30.00
	Peer + teacher feedback	18.10	3.36	30.00
	Total	13.53	4.81	90.00

Box's test of equality of covariance matrices (SPSS Output 20.24) contains several statistics, such as the Box's statistic, the degrees of freedom, and the p value. Box's test is a multivariate statistic test examining whether the covariance matrices of the repeated-measures variables are equal across the between-subjects factor group. The assumption of homogeneity of covariance is an important assumption in many statistical analyses, including repeated-measures ANOVA, multivariate analysis of variance (MANOVA), and multiple regression analysis. This test also assumes that the data in each group are normally distributed, and therefore, it is sensitive to the violation of normality and should not be used if the data do not meet this assumption. In addition, sample size can impact the results of Box's test in that as the sample size increases, the power of the test to detect differences in covariance matrices increases. If the sample size is too small, the test may not have enough power to detect differences in the covariance matrices even if they exist. Therefore, the test may not provide valid results for small sample sizes. On the other hand, if the sample size is too large, the test may reveal small differences which may not be practically significant. In such cases and in fact in general, a smaller significance level of 0.001 is recommended to be used, rather than 0.05 for this test. The above issue suggests the importance of carefully considering the sample size when using this test. If the p value is less than 0.001, the assumption of homogeneity of covariance matrices has been violated. In our example, as can be seen below, the p value (under "Sig.") is greater than 0.001, so this assumption of homogeneity of covariance matrices has been met.

SPSS OUTPUT 20.24

Box's Test of Equality of Covariance Matrices[a]	
Box's M	19.88
F	1.57
df1	12
df2	36680.53
Sig.	.091

SPSS also generates a table called "Multivariate Tests" (SPSS Output 20.25), which presents the results of a multivariate analysis for comparing the means of two or more groups across different levels of the dependent variable. (The multivariate test measures the overall effect of the independent variable(s) on the dependent variable.) The multivariate test table also includes the degrees of freedom, and the p value for each test.

As was seen in the analysis of the two-way ANOVA presented before (SPSS Output 20.19), the multivariate test table includes four multivariate test statistics including the Pillai's Trace, Wilks's Lambda, Hotelling's Trace, and Roy's Largest Root, with their associated p values. The four multivariate test statistics test the null hypothesis that there are no differences between the means of the groups or conditions on the dependent variables. As noted earlier, of the four test statistics, the first three usually provide similar results when there is one dependent variable in the analysis. The Pillai's Trace provides a measure of the overall effect, and it ranges from 0 to 1 with a larger value indicating a larger effect of the independent variable(s). It is a powerful test and is a good option when the data do not meet the assumption of homogeneity of variance–covariance or when the sample sizes are uneven and small. Wilks's Lambda also measures the overall effect of the independent variable(s) and it, too, ranges from 0 to 1. Hotelling's Trace measures the effect of the independent variable(s) on a linear combination of the dependent variables, and Roy's Largest Root provides a measure of the largest effect of the independent variable(s) on any linear combination of the dependent variables. For our hypothetical study, all the multivariate tests are significant for the effect of testing time and the interaction between testing time and feedback.

SPSS OUTPUT 20.25

Multivariate Tests[a]

Effect		Value	F	Hypothesis df	Error df	Sig.
Time	Pillai's Trace	.54	50.60[b]	2	86.00	.00
	Wilks's Lambda	.46	50.60[b]	2	86.00	.00
	Hotelling's Trace	1.18	50.60[b]	2	86.00	.00
	Roy's Largest Root	1.18	50.60[b]	2	86.00	.00
Time * Feedback	Pillai's Trace	.37	9.92	4	174.00	.00
	Wilks's Lambda	.63	10.97[b]	4	172.00	.00
	Hotelling's Trace	.57	12.02	4	170.00	.00
	Roy's Largest Root	.55	23.81[c]	2	87.00	.00

a. Design: Intercept + Feedback
Within-Subjects Design: Time
b. Exact statistic
c. The statistic is an upper bound on F that yields a lower bound on the significance level.

The Mauchly's test of sphericity (SPSS Output 20.26) provides information about whether the assumption of sphericity has been met. Sphericity is another important assumption for repeated-measures ANOVA and refers to the assumption that the variances of the differences between all possible pairs of related groups (or levels or conditions) are equal. This assumption is important because, if violated, the results of the repeated-measures ANOVA may be inaccurate as the violation may lead to increasing the Type I error rate (the likelihood of rejecting the null hypothesis when it is actually true).

To assess sphericity, If the p value of the Mauchly's test is less than the significance level (usually set at 0.05), then the assumption of sphericity has been violated. In this case, when interpreting the results of the within-subjects effects (SPSS Output 20.27), you can use the Greenhouse–Geisser or Huynh–Feldt correction to adjust the degrees of freedom to account for this violation. In the case of our hypothetical study, the p value (denoted by "Sig.") is 0.317, which means that this assumption has been met.

SPSS OUTPUT 20.26

Mauchly's Test of Sphericity[a]

Measure: MEASURE_1

Within Subjects Effect	Mauchly's W	Approx. Chi-Square	df	Sig.	Epsilon[b]		
					Greenhouse-Geisser	Huynh-Feldt	Lower-bound
Time	.974	2.296	2	.317	.974	1.000	.500

Tests the null hypothesis that the error covariance matrix of the orthonormalized transformed dependent variables is proportional to an identity matrix.

a. Design: Intercept + Feedback
Within-Subjects Design: Time

b. May be used to adjust the degrees of freedom for the averaged tests of significance. Corrected tests are displayed in the Tests of Within-Subjects Effects table.

SPSS Output 20.27 provides information about the effects of the within-subjects factors on the dependent variable. It includes statistics such as F values, degrees of freedom, and p values. In the case of our hypothetical study (Example 20.7), it shows the main effect of testing time and the interaction effect of testing time by feedback are both significant.

SPSS OUTPUT 20.27

Tests of Within-Subjects Effects

Measure: MEASURE_1

Source		Type III Sum of Squares	df	Mean Square	F	Sig.
Time	Sphericity Assumed	453.49	2	226.74	50.99	.000
	Greenhouse-Geisser	453.49	1.95	232.72	50.99	.000

SPSS OUTPUT 20.27 (cont.)

(cont.)

Tests of Within-Subjects Effects

Measure: MEASURE_1

Source		Type III Sum of Squares	df	Mean Square	F	Sig.
Time * Feedback	Huynh-Feldt	453.49	2	226.74	50.99	.000
	Lower-bound	453.49	1	453.49	50.99	.000
	Sphericity Assumed	219.42	4	54.86	12.34	.000
	Greenhouse-Geisser	219.42	3.90	56.30	12.34	.000
	Huynh-Feldt	219.42	4	54.86	12.34	.000
	Lower-bound	219.42	2	109.71	12.34	.000
Error (Time)	Sphericity Assumed	773.76	174.00	4.45		
	Greenhouse-Geisser	773.76	169.53	4.56		
	Huynh-Feldt	773.76	174	4.45		
	Lower-bound	773.76	87	8.89		

In the output of the repeated-measures ANOVA, we can also see the results of the Levene's tests (SPSS Output 20.28). Both Box's test, mentioned earlier, and Levene's test are used to examine equality of variances, but Levene's test is a univariate test of homogeneity of variances and examines the equality of variances for each of the dependent variables separately as happens in one-way ANOVA. However, as noted above, Box's test assumes that the variances being compared are normally distributed and is also used when the sample sizes are equal or approximately equal. If Levene's test is not significant but Box's test is significant, providing the sample sizes are equal, the Box's test result can be ignored, and we can use Pillai's Trace instead of Wilks's Lambda to test the overall significance of our data. In the case of our hypothetical study, the Levene's test is not significant for any of the dependent variables. Therefore, the assumption of homogeneity of variances has been met.

SPSS OUTPUT 20.28

		Levene's Test of Equality of Error Variances[a]			
		Levene Statistic	df1	df2	Sig.
Pretest	Based on Mean	1.73	2	87	.18
	Based on Median	1.63	2	87	.20
	Based on Median and with adjusted df	1.63	2	77.69	.20
	Based on trimmed mean	1.75	2	87	.18
Posttest	Based on Mean	2.43	2	87	.09
	Based on Median	2.46	2	87	.09
	Based on Median and with adjusted df	2.46	2	78.07	.09
	Based on trimmed mean	2.46	2	87	.09
Delayed Posttest	Based on Mean	1.04	2	87	.36
	Based on Median	1.03	2	87	.36
	Based on Median and with adjusted df	1.03	2	82.30	.36
	Based on trimmed mean	1.074	2	87	.35

Tests the null hypothesis that the error variance of the dependent variable is equal across groups.

a. Design: Intercept + Feedback

Within-Subjects Design: Time

Tests of between-subjects effects (SPSS Output 20.29) provides information about the effects of the between-subjects factor (the independent variable) on the dependent variable. It includes statistics such as F values, degrees of freedom, and p values. In the case of our example study, the effect of feedback type has been shown to be significant ($p < .001$).

SPSS OUTPUT 20.29

Tests of Between-Subjects Effects

Measure: MEASURE_1

Transformed Variable: Average

Source	Type III Sum of Squares	df	Mean Square	F	Sig.
Intercept	50923.20	1	50923.20	4717.90	.000
Feedback	1911.09	2	955.54	88.53	.000
Error	939.04	87	10.79		

SPSS also generates tables showing the results of pairwise comparisons (the post-hoc analyses) between the levels of the the independent variable (e.g., SPSS Output 20.30). The pairwise comparison table includes information such as the mean differences, the standard error of the difference, the p value, and the confidence interval for the difference between means. The p value shows whether the difference is significant. In the case of our example, all the differences between the groups (feedback types) are significant as the p values are smaller than 0.05.

SPSS OUTPUT 20.30

Pairwise Comparisons

Measure: MEASURE_1

(I) Feedback Group	(J) Feedback Group	Mean Difference (I-J)	Std. Error	Sig.[b]	95% Confidence Interval for Difference[b]	
					Lower Bound	Upper Bound
Peer feedback	Teacher feedback	−3.856[*]	.490	.000	−4.83	−2.88
	Peer + teacher feedback	−6.478[*]	.490	.000	−7.45	−5.50
Teacher feedback	Peer feedback	3.856[*]	.490	.000	2.88	4.83
	Peer + teacher feedback	−2.622[*]	.490	.000	−3.60	−1.65
Peer + teacher feedback	Peer feedback	6.478[*]	.490	.000	5.50	7.45
	Teacher feedback	2.622[*]	.490	.000	1.65	3.60

Based on estimated marginal means

*. The mean difference is significant at the .05 level.

b. Adjustment for multiple comparisons: Least Significant Difference (equivalent to no adjustments).

POINTS TO PONDER

When is the Pearson correlation used and what does a correlation coefficient reveal about the relationship between two variables? Can you provide examples of studies where the Pearson correlation can be suitable?

Pearson Correlation

The Pearson correlation is a statistical test that measures the degree and direction of the linear relationship between two continuous variables (such as test scores). It is a method commonly used in applied linguistics research to determine the degree of association between two variables. The Pearson correlation coefficient ranges from -1 to 1, with -1 representing a perfect negative correlation, 0 representing no correlation, and 1 representing a perfect positive correlation. A positive correlation means that as one variable increases, the other variable tends to increase as well, while a negative correlation means that as one variable increases, the other variable tends to decrease.

The Pearson correlation is a parametric test, and therefore it assumes that the variables are normally distributed and the relationship between them is linear. If the data do not meet these assumptions, nonparametric correlation tests such as the Spearman correlation or Kendall's tau correlation can be used, which do not assume normality of distribution and linearity of data (see Chaper 21).

The Pearson correlation is a parametric test that measures the degree and direction of the linear relationship between two continuous variables.

To check the assumption of linearity, a scatter plot can be used that provides a visual representation of the two variables. In the case of a linear relationship, the points on the scatter plot will form an almost straight line.

Table 20.7 summarizes the characteristics of the Pearson correlation.

Table 20.7 Characteristics of the Pearson correlation

Characteristic	Description
Test	Pearson correlation test
Type of test	Parametric
Assumptions	Linearity, normal distribution, no significant outliers
Purpose	To test relationship between two continuous variables
Type of data	Continuous interval data
Test statistics	Pearson correlation coefficient

EXAMPLE 20.8

Suppose you are interested in examining the relationship between L2 proficiency and language anxiety among ESL intermediate learners. The research question is "Is there a relationship between ESL learners' language proficiency and language anxiety?". Thirty intermediate ESL learners are recruited from an English language program, and their L2 proficiency is measured using a standardized language proficiency test. Language anxiety is measured using the Foreign Language Classroom Anxiety Scale (FLCAS). The null hypothesis is that there is no significant correlation between L2 proficiency and language anxiety among intermediate ESL learners.

Pearson correlation analysis can be used to examine the degree and direction of the relationship between L2 proficiency and language anxiety in the above example. For the data, first a scatter plot was created to check the assumption of linearity of relationship (see Figure 20.2).

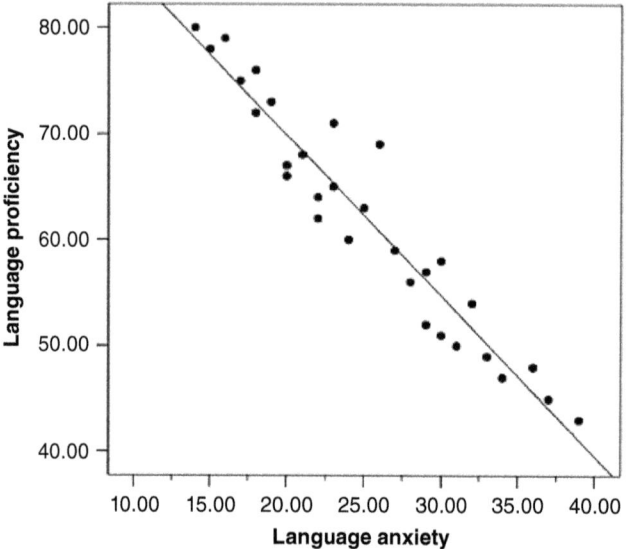

Figure 20.2 The scatter plot of language proficiency and language anxiety

As can be seen, there is a linear relationship between the variables in this dataset as shown by points that are closely clustered around a straight line that runs through the middle of the points. Based on this scatter plot we can conclude that the assumption on linearity of relationship has been met. It also shows a negative relationship, with the learners who have higher levels of L2 proficiency having lower levels of language anxiety.

A Pearson correlation can now be conducted to determine whether this relationship is statistically significant. SPSS Steps 20.12 outlines the steps to calculate the Pearson correlation coefficient (Pearson's *r*) in SPSS.

SPSS STEPS 20.12

- Open the data file in SPSS.
- Select "Analyze" > "Correlate" > "Bivariate."
- In the "Bivariate Correlations" dialog box, select the variables and move them to the "Variables" box.
- Choose "Pearson" under "Correlation Coefficients."
- Click "Options" for additional settings.
- Click "Continue" > "OK."

The SPSS generates a correlation table that provides the Pearson's *r* and their associated *p* values (see SPSS Output 20.31). As noted earlier, the Pearson correlation coefficient ranges from −1 to 1, with −1 representing a perfect negative correlation, 0 representing no correlation, and 1 representing a perfect positive correlation. The table also shows the p value associated with the Pearson correlation coefficient, which, if it is less than 0.05, suggests that the correlation is statistically significant. In the case of our hypothetical study, the correlation coefficient for the relationship between L2 proficiency and language anxiety is -0.960 (this is hypothetical and may not reflect real-world complexity), and the p value is less than 0.05, suggesting an almost perfect correlation between the two.

SPSS OUTPUT 20.31

Correlations		Language proficiency	Language anxiety
Language proficiency	Pearson Correlation	1	$-.960^{**}$
	Sig. (2-tailed)		.000
	N	30	30
Language anxiety	Pearson Correlation	$-.960^{**}$	1
	Sig. (2-tailed)	.000	
	N	30	30

**. Correlation is significant at the 0.01 level (2-tailed).

Please note that a significant correlation does not imply causation, and it simply shows that two factors or variables are related, without showing which one causes the other. When it comes to interpreting the correlation coefficient, there are some general guidelines that can be used:

- A correlation coefficient of 0 indicates no linear relationship between the two variables.
- A correlation coefficient between 0.1 and 0.39 (or -0.1 and -0.39) represents a weak correlation.
- A correlation coefficient between 0.4 and 0.69 (or -0.4 and -0.69) represents a moderate correlation.
- A correlation coefficient between 0.7 and 0.99 (or -0.7 and -0.99) represents a strong correlation.

However, it is important to note that the strength of Pearson's r should always be interpreted in the context of the research question and nature of the study.

POINTS TO PONDER

What distinguishes regression analysis from correlation analysis, and why might you choose one over the other? In what situations is multiple regression suitable?

Regression Analysis

Regression analysis is a statistical method used to examine and model the relationship between a dependent variable and one or more independent variables. It is a commonly used statistical analysis in applied linguistics research, with the main purpose of understanding how changes in an independent variable can predict changes in the dependent variables. Both correlation and regression analysis examine the relationship between variables. However, correlation examines the degree of the association between two variables, while regression examines the extent to which the value of a dependent variable can be predicted by the value of one or more independent variables. Another way of explaining the purpose of regression analysis is to say that it seeks to determine to what extent one or more independent variables can account for or explain the variance in a dependent variable.

Regression analysis examines the extent to which the value of a dependent variable can be predicted by the value of one or more independent variables.

In regression analysis, the dependent variable is also referred to as the criterion, outcome, or response variable because it is the variable that the regression analysis is trying to predict. The independent variables are also known as the predictor or explanatory variables because they are used to predict or explain the variance within the dependent variable. There are different categories of regression analysis, including simple linear regression and multiple linear regression. Simple linear regression involves only one independent and one dependent variable, whereas multiple regression involves one dependent variable and more than one independent variables. Some examples of questions in applied linguistics that can be addressed using regression analysis are as follows:

- To what extent do L2 learners' scores on a vocabulary test and grammar test predict their writing proficiency?
- Can vocabulary size be used to predict reading comprehension?
- To what extent do language learning strategies account for the variance in speaking ability among second language learners?
- Does the frequency of correct use of a particular language feature in written production predict its accurate use in oral production?
- What is the contribution of phonological awareness to L2 spelling ability?
- To what extent does L2 learners' phonological and orthographic knowledge explain differences in L2 reading comprehension?

There are both parametric and nonparametric regression methods. However the most commonly used regression techniques in applied linguistics research tend to be parametric, including simple linear regression, logistic regression, and multiple regression. Most parametric regression methods rely on certain assumptions that should be met, including linearity of relationship, independence, homoscedasticity, normality, and absence of multicollinearity.

- **Linearity of relationship:** This assumption requires the relationship between the dependent variable and the independent variables to be linear. Non-linear relationships can lead to poor model fit and inaccurate predictions.
- **Independence:** This assumes that the observations are independent of each other in that the value of one observation does not influence the value of another observation.
- **Homoscedasticity:** This refers to the assumption that the error variances are the same across values of the independent variables. It is similar to homogeneity of variances in ANOVA. If the degree of the error term or the spread of residuals differs across values of an independent variable, this assumption has been violated.
- **Normality of residuals:** This assumption means that the errors or residuals are normally distributed or should follow a normal distribution. Residuals refer to the differences between the observed and predicted values, which should follow a normal distribution.
- **Absence of multicollinearity:** According to this assumption, the independent variables should not be highly correlated with each other. Multicollinearity can lead to inaccurate and unreliable results.

Violations of the above assumptions can affect the accuracy and reliability of the regression results. Therefore, it is important to check the assumptions and take appropriate steps to address violations when necessary.

Please note that the assumptions listed above may not equally apply to all types of parametric regressions, as certain types may have slightly different assumptions. For example, logistic regression does not require normality of residuals because it deals with a binary (or categorical) dependent variable. Simple linear regression does not require the absence of multicollinearity, as this assumption applies when there are multiple independent variables. In simple linear regression, with only one independent variable, multicollinearity is not a concern.

Simple Linear Regression

Simple linear regression is one of the most widely used regression methods in applied linguistics research. This type of regression aims to examine the relationship between a dependent variable and one single independent variable. Both variables are continuous, but the independent variable can also be categorical if it is converted into a numerical dummy variable. Dummy variables are binary variables that show the presence or absence of a certain category. For example, if we have a categorical variable such as "language learning environment" with two categories of "classroom" and "online," we can create a dummy variable, coding "classroom" into 0 and "online" into 1 or vice versa.

Simple linear regression analysis examines the extent to which the value of a dependent variable can be predicted by the value of one independent variable.

Simple linear regression is a parametric test that assumes a linear relationship between the two variables. It is a predictive model that is used to make predictions about the dependent variable, based on the values of the independent variable, and test hypotheses about this relationship. The use of simple linear regression requires that the assumptions mentioned earlier be met about the data, including linearity, independence, normality, and homoscedasticity. Table 20.8 summarizes the characteristics of simple linear regression.

Table 20.8 Characteristics of simple linear regression

Characteristic	Description
Test	Simple linear regression
Type of test	Parametric
Assumptions	Linearity, independence, normality of residuals, homoscedasticity
Purpose	To predict the dependent variable based on the independent variable
Independent variable	One continuous or binary/categorical (coded as dummy variable)
Dependent variable	One continuous variable

EXAMPLE 20.9

Suppose you want to investigate the impact of vocabulary knowledge depth on reading comprehension in ESL learners. The question is whether vocabulary knowledge significantly contributes to reading comprehension ability. Forty intermediate-level ESL learners from a language school take a vocabulary knowledge test and the TOEFL Reading Section. Their scores on both tests are collected. The study uses a simple linear regression analysis to explore whether depth of vocabulary knowledge predicts reading comprehension scores.

SPSS Steps 20.13 outlines the steps to run a simple linear regression analysis in SPSS.

SPSS STEPS 20.13

- Open the data file in SPSS.
- Select "Analyze" > "Regression" > "Linear."
- In the "Linear Regression" dialog box, select the dependent variable and move it to "Dependent" box. Select the independent variable and move it to the box for the independent variable.

SPSS STEPS 20.13 (cont.)

- "Click "Statistics" for desired statistics. "Estimates" and "Model fit" are selected by default.
- Click "Continue" > "OK."

SPSS generates the results including several tables, such as the descriptive statistics table, a correlation table, a model summary table, an ANOVA table, and a coefficients table.

The descriptive statistics table (SPSS Output 20.32) shows the mean, standard deviation, and the number of participants.

SPSS OUTPUT 20.32

Descriptive Statistics			
	Mean	Std. Deviation	N
Reading comprehension	79.15	9.41	40
Vocabulary score	75.72	8.43	40

The correlations table (SPSS Output 20.33) shows the Pearson correlation coefficient between the dependent and independent variables. In the case of our example study, the correlation between the dependent and the independent variable is 0.888, which is statistically significant ($p < .05$).

SPSS OUTPUT 20.33

Correlations		Reading comprehension	Vocabulary score
Pearson Correlation	Reading comprehension	1.000	.888
	Vocabulary score	.888	1.000
Sig. (1-tailed)	Reading comprehension	.	.000
	Vocabulary score	.000	.
N	Reading comprehension	40	40
	Vocabulary score	40	40

The model summary table (SPSS Output 20.34) provides several important pieces of information, including the R, the R-squared (R^2) value, the adjusted R^2 value, and the standard error of the estimate. The R is the simple correlation, which in the case of our hypothetical study is 0.888. The R^2 is the squared R and represents the proportion of variance in the dependent variable explained by the independent variable, which is 0.788 in the case of our hypothetical study. The adjusted R^2 value takes into account the number of predictor variables in the analysis, and in the case of our study it is 0.783. It is the proportion of the variance in the dependent variable explained by the independent variables when the value is adjusted for the number of independent variables that are not significant in the analysis. Adjusted R^2 becomes a more relevant concept in multiple regression when there are multiple independent variables and in the cases of simple regression where there is only one independent variable, the two values are almost the same (as can be seen below). The standard error of the estimate (SEE) is a measure of the variability of data around the regression line.

SPSS OUTPUT 20.34

Model Summary				
Model	R	R Square	Adjusted R Square	Std. Error of the Estimate
1	.888[a]	.788	.783	4.387

a. Predictors: (Constant), Vocabulary score

The ANOVA table (SPSS Output 20.35) shows the results of the analysis of variance (ANOVA) test and presents information about the sources of variance and the associated sum of squares, degrees of freedom, and mean squares. This table can be used to determine whether the regression model is statistically significant overall, including all the variables. If we check the p value in the following table, we will see that the p value is less than 0.05, indicating that the regression model is statistically significant overall.

SPSS OUTPUT 20.35

ANOVA[a]					
Model	Sum of Squares	df	Mean Square	F	Sig.
1 Regression	2723.56	1	2723.56	141.47	.000[b]
Residual	731.54	38	19.25		
Total	3455.10	39			

a. Dependent Variable: Reading comprehension
b. Predictors: (Constant), Vocabulary score

The coefficients table (SPSS Output 20.36) is another table which shows several important pieces of information, including the unstandardized coefficient (B) for intercept (constant) and the regression slope for the dependent variable along with their standard errors, t values, p value and 95% confidence interval. The constant coefficient shows the value of the dependent variable when the predictor (independent) variable is equal to zero. The regression slope coefficient shows the change in the dependent variable for a one-unit increase in the predictor (or independent variable). The table also shows the standard error for the unstandardized B, which shows the standard deviation of the sampling distribution of the coefficient estimate and is similar to the standard deviation for a mean. The larger this value is, the more deviated the points are from the regression line. The standardized beta (β) is the same as the correlation coefficient in simple linear regression. The coefficients table also shows the p value, which indicates whether the independent variable is a significant predictor of the dependent variable.

SPSS OUTPUT 20.36

Coefficients[a]

Model		B	Std. Error	Beta	T	Sig.
		Unstandardized Coefficients		Standardized Coefficients		
1	(Constant)	4.12	6.35		.65	.520
	Vocabulary score	.99	.08	.89	11.89	.000

a. Dependent Variable: Reading comprehension

In the case of our study, the intercept coefficient is 4.12, which means that the expected value of the reading comprehension score when the vocabulary score is zero would be 4.12. In other words, a student is expected to score 4.12 when their score on the vocabulary tests is zero. The regression slope coefficient (B) for the vocabulary score is 0.99 which means that a one-unit increase in the vocabulary score would result in a 0.99-unit increase in the reading comprehension score. The value of Beta (β) under standardized coefficients (0.89) in the simple regression analysis is the same as the value of Pearson correlation. The p value indicates whether the predictor variable significantly predicts the dependent variable. In the case of our study, it is less than 0.05 ($p < .001$), which means that the predictor variable (vocabulary) is a significant predicator of reading comprehension.

Multiple Linear Regression
Multiple linear regression is another widely used statistical method in applied linguistics research, which can be used to understand the contributions of multiple

independent variables to a dependent variable. As noted earlier, simple linear regression involves only one independent variable and one dependent variable. Multiple linear regression is an extension of simple regression and examines the relationship between one dependent variable and two or more independent variables. The goal is to determine to what extent each independent variable contributes to the variance in the dependent variable. Table 20.9 summarizes the characteristics of multiple linear regression.

Table 20.9 Characteristics of multiple linear regression

Characteristic	Description
Test	Multiple linear regression
Type of test	Parametric
Assumptions	Linearity, independence, normality, homoscedasticity, lack of multicollinearity
Purpose	To predict the dependent variable based on two or more independent variables
Independent variable	Two or more continuous or binary/categorical variables (coded as dummy variables)
Dependent variable	One continuous variable

Multiple linear regression tests the extent to which the value of a dependent variable can be predicted by the value of two or more independent variables.

Example 20.10 presents a hypothetical scenario.

EXAMPLE 20.10

Suppose you aim to examine the predictors of L2 reading comprehension among ESL university students, including vocabulary depth, vocabulary size, age, and working memory. Eighty-two participants complete tests measuring reading comprehension, depth of vocabulary knowledge, vocabulary size, and working memory.

For the above example, a multiple linear regression analysis can be conducted to examine the contributions of the three independent variables (vocabulary size, vocabulary depth, age, and working memory) to the dependent variable (reading comprehension).

SPSS Steps 20.14 outlines the steps to conduct a multiple regression analysis in SPSS.

SPSS STEPS 20.14

- Open the data file in SPSS.
- Select "Analyze" > "Regression" > "Linear."
- In the "Linear Regression" dialog box, select the dependent variable and move it to the "Dependent" box.
- Select independent variables and move them to the box for independent variables.
- Click "Method" for variable inclusion (e.g., Enter).
- Click "Statistics" for desired statistics. "Estimates" and "Model fit" are selected by default. Choose additional options as needed (e.g., "Descriptives," "Part and partial correlations," Collinearity diagnostics," "R square change").
- Click "Continue" > "OK."

For our study in Example 20.10, SPSS generates a few outputs, including a descriptive statistics table, a correlation table, a model summary table, an ANOVA table, and a coefficients table.

As before, the descriptive statistics table shows the mean, standard deviation, and the number of participants, similar to what we had in the simple regression output.

SPSS OUTPUT 20.37

Descriptive Statistics			
	Mean	Std. Deviation	N
Reading comprehension	81.01	10.45	82
Depth of vocabulary	87.83	18.98	82
Size of vocabulary	98.54	32.16	82
Working memory	6.72	2.49	82
Age	20.65	1.84	82

The correlation table (SPSS Output 20.38) shows the Pearson correlation coefficient between the dependent and independent variables and their p values.

SPSS OUTPUT 20.38

Correlations		Reading comprehension	Depth of vocabulary	Size of vocabulary	Working memory	Age
Pearson Correlation	Reading comprehension	1.00	.79	.64	.49	.09

SPSS OUTPUT 20.38 (cont.)

(cont.)						
		Correlations				
		Reading comprehension	Depth of vocabulary	Size of vocabulary	Working memory	Age
	Depth of vocabulary	.79	1.00	.53	.41	−.02
	Size of vocabulary	.64	.53	1.00	.42	.12
	Working memory	.49	.41	.42	1.00	.03
	Age	.09	−.02	.12	.03	1.00
Sig. (1-tailed)	Reading comprehension	.	.000	.000	.000	.204
	Depth of vocabulary	.000	.	.000	.000	.413
	Size of vocabulary	.000	.000	.	.000	.136
	Working memory	.000	.000	.000	.	.406
	Age	.204	.413	.136	.406	.
N	Reading comprehension	82	82	82	82	82
	Depth of vocabulary	82	82	82	82	82
	Size of vocabulary	82	82	82	82	82
	Working memory	82	82	82	82	82
	Age	82	82	82	82	82

The Model summary table (SPSS Output 20.39) provides the R, the R squared (R^2) value, the adjusted R^2 value, and the standard error of the estimate. As noted earlier, the R is the simple correlation, which in the case of multiple regression, would be the correlation of the all the independent variables as a set. In the case of our hypothetical study, it is 0.84. The R square shows the proportion of variance explained by all the independent variables in the model (again as a whole set) in the dependent variable, which is 0.71 in the case of our hypothetical study. This means that 71% of the variance in the dependent variable is explained by the independent variables. As noted earlier, the adjusted R^2 value takes into account the number of predictor variables in the analysis. If we compare this value to the R^2 value and it is lower, it means that additional independent variables which were nonsignificant did not add to the predictive power.

When some predictors are not significant in the model, they still increase the value of R^2 but will lower the adjusted R^2. A lower adjusted R^2 means that adding nonsignificant predictors to the model does not contribute significantly to the model's predictive power. In such cases, we should use the adjusted R^2. In the case of our study, the adjusted R^2 is 0.69 which is the proportion of the variance in the dependent variable explained by the independent variables, when the value is adjusted for the number of independent variables in the analysis. Here is the formula for adjusted R^2:

Equation 20.1 $$\text{Adjusted } R^2 = 1 - \frac{(1 - R^2)(n - 1)}{n - p - 1}$$

Where:

R^2 is the sample R^2
n is the sample size
p is the number of predictors in the model

The next piece of information in the table is the standard error of the estimate (*SEE*), which is a measure of the variability of data around the regression line.

SPSS OUTPUT 20.39

			Model Summary	
Model	R	R Square	Adjusted R Square	Std. Error of the Estimate
1	.84[a]	.71	.69	5.82

a. Predictors: (Constant), Age, Depth of vocabulary, Working memory, Size of vocabulary

The ANOVA table (SPSS Output 20.40) shows whether the regression model or the R^2 is statistically significant. The p value in the following table is less than 0.05, indicating that the regression model is statistically significant overall. In other words, the result shows that the combination of vocabulary size, depth of vocabulary, working memory, and age significantly predicts reading comprehension.

SPSS OUTPUT 20.40

				ANOVA[a]		
Model		Sum of Squares	df	Mean Square	F	Sig.
1	Regression	6240.07	4	1560.02	46.04	.000[b]
	Residual	2608.92	77	33.88		
	Total	8848.99	81			

a. Dependent Variable: Reading comprehension
b. Predictors: (Constant), Age, Depth of vocabulary, Working memory, Size of vocabulary

The coefficients table (SPSS Output 20.41) shows the extent to which each of the independent variables contributes to the dependent variable. In other words, it shows which of the variables is a significant predictor of the dependent variable by showing a t statistic and a p value. The table also shows several other important pieces of information including the unstandardized regression coefficients (B) for the intercept (constant) and each predictor variable, along with their standard errors (Std. Error). (See the section on simple regression for how to interpret these.) The p value indicates what predictor variable significantly predicts the dependent variable. In the case of our example study, the p values for depth of vocabulary knowledge, size of vocabulary knowledge, and working memory are less than .05 and the p value for age is higher than .05. This means that except for age, all other variables were significant predictors of reading comprehension.

SPSS OUTPUT 20.41

							Coefficients[a]	
		Unstandardized Coefficients		Standardized Coefficients			Collinearity Statistics	
Model		B	Std. Error	Beta	t	Sig.	Tolerance	VIF
1	(Constant)	31.63	7.99		3.96	.000		
	Depth of vocabulary	.33	.04	.59	7.86	.000	.67	1.49
	Size of vocabulary	.08	.02	.25	3.30	.001	.65	1.53
	Working memory	.60	.29	.14	2.05	.044	.78	1.29
	Age	.41	.36	.07	1.16	.251	.97	1.03

a. Dependent Variable: Reading comprehension

The intercept (constant) coefficient is 31.63, which means that the predicted value of reading comprehension score when the value of all the other variables is zero would be 31.63. The regression slope coefficient (B) for the depth of vocabulary score is 0.33, which means that a one-unit increase in the vocabulary score would result in a 0.33-unit increase in the reading comprehension score. This is 0.08 and 0.60 for size of vocabulary knowledge and working memory respectively.

The standardized coefficient (β) represents the effect size on the dependent variable, independent of measurement scales. It is expressed in standard deviation units, indicating the change in the dependent variable associated with a one standard deviation increase in the independent variable, while other variables are held constant. For instance, in our study, the β for depth of vocabulary knowledge is

0.59, showing a 0.59 standard deviation increase in reading comprehension with a one standard deviation change in vocabulary depth. Larger β values denote a stronger effect of the independent variable on the dependent variable.

The coefficient table in multiple regression analysis includes important information about the relationship between independent variables, particularly regarding multicollinearity measured by the variance inflation factor (VIF). VIF measures the extent of multicollinearity, calculated as 1/tolerance. Multicollinearity arises from high correlations among independent variables, negatively impacting regression results. A VIF value of 1 implies no correlation, while values above 1 indicate varying degrees of correlation. A VIF of 5 or higher suggests multicollinearity, with values exceeding 10 indicating serious multicollinearity, leading to unreliable coefficients. In our study, all VIFs are below 5, indicating no multicollinearity in our sample data.

In the presence of multicollinearity, examination of the next table helps identify sources. If only two VIF values exceed 5 or 10, it indicates collinearity between those variables, and further investigation is unnecessary. However, with more than two predictors having large VIF (e.g., above 10), the collinearity diagnostics table (SPSS Output 20.42) becomes important. The table includes two important pieces of information that can help identify the sources of collinearity: condition index and variance proportion.

A condition index of above 15 suggests the presence of collinearity, and an index of greater than 30 suggests that there may be significant collinearity in the model. To identify the exact source, we first look at the condition index column to see if there are any values above 15. If there are, we then check the variance propositions for those independent variables. If there are pairs or sets of independent variables with values higher than 0.90, that suggests a collinearity problem between those predictors (one value higher than 0.90 does not indicate a problem). If there is a condition index value higher than 15 and no value of proportion variance above 0.90, we can look for values such as 0.80 or 0.70 as those values are still high and can suggest collinearity.

In our data, there is only one condition index value greater that 30 (age = 36.600). But when we check the variance proportions column, we see only one value over 0.90 (age = 0.94). Since there are not two values for two independent variables, we conclude that there is no collinearity problem.

SPSS OUTPUT 20.42

Collinearity Diagnostics[a]

					Variance Proportions			
Model	Dimension	Eigenvalue	Condition Index	(Constant)	Depth of vocabulary	Size of vocabulary	Working memory	Age
1	1	4.83	1.00	.00	.00	.00	.00	.00
	2	.08	7.59	.01	.00	.02	.69	.02
	3	.06	9.09	.01	.01	.73	.28	.01

SPSS OUTPUT 20.42 (cont.)

(cont.)

Collinearity Diagnostics[a]

Model	Dimension	Eigenvalue	Condition Index	(Constant)	Depth of vocabulary	Size of vocabulary	Working memory	Age
	4	.02	13.93	.01	.91	.23	.03	.03
	5	.00	36.60	.97	.08	.02	.00	.94

a. Dependent Variable: Reading comprehension

Different Approaches to Variable Selection in Multiple Regression Analysis
Multiple regression involves multiple independent variables. When dealing with several independent variables, we often need to select the most important variables to include in the model. This is known as variable selection, and it can help improve the fit of the regression model. There are several approaches to variable selection in regression analysis, including the "enter," "stepwise," "remove," "backward," and "forward" methods, which are also provided by SPSS and can be chosen when we are entering our predictors (i.e., independent variables) into the regression model. Here we will provide a brief overview of these different approaches or methods to variable selection.

Enter method: This method is the simplest and most commonly used method for multiple regression analysis. The enter method is also known as the "full" or the "standard" method of regression and is distinguished from other approaches in which the predictors are entered in specific steps. In the enter method, all the predictors are entered into the model at the same time and in one step. It is a useful method when there are variables that are theoretically important and we want to know their contribution to the dependent variable and their level of significance. However, the enter method can also become problematic if we enter many variables at the same time and the sample size is not large enough to support them or if there are highly correlated independent variables in the model. In such cases, the enter method may lead to inaccurate predictive accuracy.

Stepwise method: This method is a combination of both forward and backward methods. It begins by selecting the best subset of independent variables that can predict the dependent variable and adding or removing variables (based on a certain F value or p value). This method is a particular type of hierarchical regression that builds a regression model in a stepwise fashion with the one most correlated with the dependent variable being entered first until there are no more variables to add. Then, variables with the least statistical significance are removed from the model one-by-one until there are no more variables to remove. This process continues until the final model is obtained. Stepwise is a useful method when we have many independent variables, and the model is used to narrow them down to those that are significant. For example, if we have three independent variables and have set the entry criterion for variable selection at a p value of 0.05, the variable with the highest correlation with the dependent variable that meets the p value criterion of 0.05 will be entered into the model first, followed by the variables with the second and third highest correlation and a statistically significant effect in the second and third steps.

Remove method: This method cannot be used by itself, and if it is used, SPSS gives a warning that this is an invalid method and that remove cannot be used as the first method. If we use it, regression uses enter as the first method and removes all the variables entered first as the second method, which is not very useful. To use the remove method appropriately, we can use the enter method first with all the variables in the model, and then as a second regression, try to remove those which you think are less significant, to see if their removal changes the model significantly.

Backward method: This method starts with all variables included in the model and then removes, one by one, the variable contributing the least, until only the significant variables remain. At each step, the variable with the highest p value is removed until all variables have p values below the particular threshold level defined.

Forward method: This method starts with a model containing no independent variables and then adds one variable at a time, based on their significance, until no more significant variables can be added.

Hierarchical Multiple Regression

Hierarchical multiple regression is a statistical technique also used to examine the relationship between a dependent variable and one or more independent variables. In hierarchical multiple regression, however, the independent variables are entered into the regression equation in a specific order or hierarchy. In the above section, we discussed the enter model where the program automatically selects variables by adding or removing them from the regression model. Hierarchical regression involves adding independent variables to the model in a predetermined order based on their theoretical or practical importance. This method is used when you decide what variable to enter first in the regression model, based on some theoretical framework or previous research. In this type of regression, we begin by entering the variable that we think is the best predictor and then add to the model the next variable, to see if the next one would account for any additional variance. Compared to the enter method, the hierarchical method is more appropriate when there are a large number of potential independent variables to consider or when you have a strong theoretical or practical basis for the order in which the variables are added to the model. More specifically, a hierarchical approach can be used when you want to control for the contribution of other variables in the model or to determine the unique contribution of a particular variable after accounting for the effects of other variables. This can be done by entering the variables of interest last in the model. This allows you to isolate the effect of that variable while controlling for the effects of previous variable.

Hierarchical regression is a method that involves adding independent variables to the model in a predetermined order, based on their theoretical or practical importance.

To illustrate, let's consider Example 20.10, where you were interested in examining the contribution of depth of vocabulary knowledge, size of vocabulary knowledge, working memory, and age to ESL reading comprehension. As we saw, our multiple regression analysis of the data showed that the first three variables were all significant predictors of reading comprehension. Now suppose that in this research, you are also interested to determine whether depth of vocabulary knowledge contributes to reading comprehension while the contribution of other variables has been controlled. To address this question, you can use a hierarchical approach, in which these variables are added in a predetermined order in two different blocks:

Regression block 1: A regression model with size of vocabulary knowledge, working memory, and age as predictors.

Regression block 2: A regression model with size of vocabulary knowledge, working memory, age, and depth of vocabulary knowledge as predictors.

SPSS Steps 20.15 outlines the steps for doing such a hierarchical regression analysis in SPSS.

SPSS STEPS 20.15

- Open the data file in SPSS.
- Select "Analyze" > "Regression" > "Linear."
- In the "Linear Regression" dialog box, select the dependent variable and move it to the "Dependent" box.
- Select the predictors to be included in the first step and move them to the box for independent variables.
- Click "Method" tab and choose "Enter."
- Click "Next" and add the variable in the next step as the predictor(s).
- Click "Statistics" for desired statistics (e.g., R squared change).
- Click "Continue" > "OK."

By controlling for the effects of size of vocabulary knowledge, working memory, and age in the first block, we are now able to examine the unique contribution of depth of vocabulary knowledge to the variance in reading comprehension in the second block. To this end, we can check the model summary table in SPSS (see SPSS Output 20.43) for that information.

As can be seen (and as noted earlier), the table provides a number of pieces of information including R square (R^2) and R^2 change (if you recall, we asked the regression model to provide us with R^2 change under "Statistics"). The initial R^2

value (in Model 1) is 0.47. This indicates that size of vocabulary knowledge, working memory, and age explained 47% of the variance in reading comprehension. The R^2 in Model 2 shows that, after adding depth of vocabulary knowledge as a predictor variable, the R^2 value increased to 0.71. The value under R^2 change shows the amount of increase, which is 0.24 and the p value is significant. This suggests that the inclusion of the predictor variable (depth of vocabulary knowledge) in the model has resulted in a significant increase in the proportion of variance in the dependent variable (reading comprehension), after controlling for size of vocabulary knowledge, working memory, and age. So, we can conclude that depth of vocabulary knowledge alone explained an additional unique 24% of the variance in reading comprehension over and above what was accounted for by the other variables in the model. The fact that the change in the R^2 is significant suggests that depth of vocabulary makes a statistically significant unique contribution to the prediction of reading comprehension, after controlling for the effect of size of vocabulary knowledge, working memory, and age.

SPSS OUTPUT 20.43

Model Summary

Model	R	R Square	Adjusted R Square	Std. Error of the Estimate	Change Statistics				
					R Square Change	F Change	df1	df2	Sig. F Change
1	.68[a]	.47	.45	7.76	.47	22.96	3	78	.000
2	.84[b]	.71	.69	5.82	.24	61.71	1	77	.000

a. Predictors: (Constant), Age, Working memory, Size of vocabulary
b. Predictors: (Constant), Age, Working memory, Size of vocabulary, Depth of vocabulary

POINTS TO PONDER

What is binary logistic regression? Provide an example of research questions that could be addressed using binary logistic regression.

Logistic Regression

Logistic regression is a particular type of regression analysis that is widely used in the field of applied linguistics. The aim is to predict the values of a dependent variable based on one or more predictor variable(s) while the dependent variable is categorical. The independent variables are often continuous; however, they can also be categorical if coded appropriately, by converting them to dummy variables coded as 0 or 1, where 0 represents one category and 1 represents the other.

Logistic regression is used to predict the values of a dependent variable based on one or more predictor variables when the dependent variable is categorical.

Depending on the type of the dependent variable, the three most commonly used logistic regressions are binary logistic regression, multinomial regression, and ordinal logistic regression.

Binary regression: This is the most common type of logistic regression and is used when the dependent variable is binary (has two possible outcomes, usually coded as 0 and 1). For example, the dependent variable might represent whether the research participant is an L1 speaker of English (e.g., coded as 1 or 0) or an L2 speaker of English (coded as 1 or 0). Examples of other binary variables include language proficiency (e.g., low/high), task outcome (e.g., successful/unsuccessful), and feedback mode (e.g., oral/written).

Multinomial logistic regression: This type of logistic regression is used when the dependent variable is nominal and has more than two unordered levels. For example, you can use a multinomial logistic regression to predict learners' use of various types of strategies, such as cognitive strategies, metacognitive strategies, and social/affective strategies based on some predictor variables such as age, language proficiency, and motivation.

Ordinal logistic regression: This type of logistic regression is used when the dependent variable is ordinal with three or more ordered categories. This means that the categories have a natural order, such as "low," "medium," and "high," or "agree," "neutral," and "disagree." Ordinal logistic regression can be used in applied linguistics research to analyze data from surveys or questionnaires that ask participants to rate their level of agreement with a statement on a Likert scale. For example, you might use ordinal logistic regression to determine how factors such as age, language proficiency, and years of schooling can predict learners' self-reported foreign language classroom anxiety when they respond to a questionnaire using a 4- or 5-point Likert scale ranging from "strongly disagree" to "strongly agree."

The choice of logistic regression model depends on the research question and the nature of the data. In the following section, we will discuss this in more detail and provide an example of how to conduct and interpret the results of a binary logistic regression analysis as this is the most commonly used regression analysis in applied linguistics research. Table 20.10 describes the different types of logistic regression and the types of variables used in each.

Table 20.10 Types of logistic regression

Type of Logistic Regression	Type of Dependent Variable	Type of Independent Variable
Binary logistic regression	Binary	Continuous or categorical
Multinomial logistic regression	Nominal with more than two levels	Continuous or categorical
Ordinal logistic regression	Ordinal	Continuous or categorical

Binary Logistic Regression As noted above, this type of regression examines which predictor variables can predict the probability of the occurrence of a binary (dichotomous) outcome or dependent variable. Logistic regression does not need some of the assumptions of the linear regression, such as linearity, normality, or homoscedasticity. However, it has several other assumptions that should be met:

Binary dependent variable: The dependent variable must be binary or dichotomous with only two possible values.

Independence of observations: Logistic regression requires that each observation should be independent of other observations. In other words, one observation should not affect the other, or the observations should not be in the form of repeated-measures coming from the same participants.

No multicollinearity: This assumption requires that the independent variables should not be highly correlated with each other. This assumption can be checked via correlation coefficients or variance inflation factors (*VIF*s) discussed earlier.

Adequate sample size: An adequate sample size is needed to obtain accurate results. As a rule of thumb, it is suggested to have at least ten to twenty cases per independent variable.

It is important to check for these assumptions before running or interpreting the results of a binary logistic regression analysis. Table 20.11 summarizes the characteristics of binary logistic regression.

Table 20.11 Characteristics of binary logistic regression

Characteristic	Description
Test	Binary logistic regression
Type of test	Parametric
Assumptions	Independence of observations, no multicollinearity, adequate sample size, no significant outliers
Purpose	To predict a binary outcome or dependent variable based on the values of independent variables.
Dependent variable	Binary or dichotomous (e.g., "0" and "1")
Independent variables	Continuous, categorical or a mix of both

EXAMPLE 20.11

Suppose you want to explore the link between language proficiency and intrinsic/extrinsic motivation among eighty ESL learners in Canada. You measure motivation with a self-report questionnaire and language proficiency with a standardized test. You analyze the data using binary logistic regression, treating motivation as the dependent variable (binary) and language proficiency as the independent variable.

SPSS Steps 20.16 outlines the steps to conduct a binary logistic regression analysis in SPSS.

SPSS STEPS 20.16

- Open the data file in SPSS.
- Select "Analyze" > "Regression" > "Binary Logistic."
- In the "Binary Logistic Regression" dialog box, select the dependent variable and move it to the "Dependent" box.
- Select the independent variable(s) and move it to the "Covariates" box.
- If the independent variable is a categorical variable, click "Categorical," and enter the variable, and click "Continue."
- Click "Options" for additional output (e.g., Hosmer–Lemeshow, CI).
- Click "Continue" > "OK."

The analysis generates several tables. One is the omnibus test of model coefficients (SPSS Output 20.44) which is a chi-square table and assesses the overall fit of the model relative to the null model. A good model fit indicates that the model can be used to make accurate predictions about the relationship between the predictor variables and the dependent variable, with the predicted values matching well with the observed values. The table includes "chi-square" values with their associated degrees of freedom (df) and p values (Sig.). If the results are significant, this shows that there is a significant improvement in fit of the model compared to the null model. In other words, it evaluates whether the model as a whole, with all predictor variables included, significantly predicts the outcome variable better than a model without any predictor variables. For our example study, the test is significant ($p = .009$), which suggests the model with the independent variable significantly predicts the dependent variable better than a model that includes only the intercept (null model).

SPSS OUTPUT 20.44

Omnibus Tests of Model Coefficients

		Chi-square	df	Sig.
Step 1	Step	6.80	1.00	.009
	Block	6.80	1.00	.009
	Model	6.80	1.00	.009

The output also includes another important table called "Model Summary" (SPSS Output 20.45), which contains information about the explained variance in the dependent variable explained by the independent variable. There are two values, the "Cox & Snell R Square" and "Nagelkerke R Square" values (these are different methods of calculating an R^2 for logistic regression). In terms of interpretation, they are similar to (but not exactly the same as) the R^2 in linear regression and show the amount of variance explained in the dependent variable although they have lower values than R square in linear regression. As shown in SPSS Output 20.45, this ranges from 14.9% to 19.9% for our example data, depending on whether we use the Cox & Snell R Square or Nagelkerke R Square. Nagelkerke R Square is a modification of Cox & Snell R Square adjusted for the maximum possible value of the likelihood function, and therefore it is suggested to provide a more accurate measure of the proportion of the variance in the dependent variable explained.

SPSS OUTPUT 20.45

	Model Summary		
Step	-2 Log likelihood	Cox & Snell R Square	Nagelkerke R Square
1	51.42[a]	.149	.199

a. Estimation terminated at iteration number 4 because parameter estimates changed by less than 0.001.

The Hosmer–Lemeshow Test (SPSS Output 20.46) is another chi-square test and is used to evaluate the goodness-of-fit of the model by comparing predicted probabilities to observed outcomes. The interpretation is a bit different from the previous chi-square table (SPSS Output 20.44). To interpret this table, we would look at the chi-square statistic and its associated p value. If the p value is greater than 0.05 (or if there is a nonsignificant result), it suggests that the model fits the data well. Thus, in this test, a statistically significant result would indicate that the model does not fit the data perfectly.

SPSS OUTPUT 20.46

	Hosmer–Lemeshow Test		
Step	Chi-square	df	Sig.
1	32.55	8	.000

Then there is the contingency table for the Hosmer–Lemeshow test (SPSS Output 20.47), which is a table that compares the observed and expected frequencies of events. The table is typically divided into several bins or groups based on the predicted probabilities. The observed frequencies and the expected frequencies for each bin are compared to evaluate the model's goodness of fit. Interpreting the contingency table in the Hosmer–Lemeshow test involves examining the differences between the observed and expected frequencies in each bin or subgroup. A closer match between the observed and expected frequencies suggests a better fit of the model, while significant differences might indicate issues with the model's calibration and the need for further adjustments or improvements.

SPSS OUTPUT 20.47

		Intrinsic vs extrinsic motivation = Intrinsic		Intrinsic vs extrinsic motivation = Extrinsic		
		Observed	Expected	Observed	Expected	Total
Step 1	1	4	3.187	0	.813	4
	2	4	3.054	0	.946	4
	3	2	2.761	2	1.239	4
	4	0	2.440	4	1.560	4
	5	0	2.241	4	1.759	4
	6	3	1.821	1	2.179	4
	7	4	1.584	0	2.416	4
	8	4	1.404	0	2.596	4
	9	0	1.113	4	2.887	4
	10	0	1.396	6	4.604	6

Contingency Table for Hosmer and Lemeshow Test

For our example study, the observed and the expected values for intrinsic motivation are relatively similar. The two values are also relatively similar for the extrinsic motivation. However, the values are closer for the extrinsic category, suggesting a better fit. Despite this, the actual test was significant because of some discrepancies in the data.

The classification table (SPSS Output 20.48) displays the accuracy of the model in predicting the dependent variable based on the independent variables. It shows the number and percentage of cases correctly and incorrectly classified. In our example, the total number of learners that were identified with intrinsic motivation was 21. Of these 10 were accurately classified as having intrinsic motivation, and 11 were classified as having extrinsic motivation. Therefore, 47.6% of those with intrinsic motivation were predicted accurately by the model to have intrinsic motivation. The same was true with extrinsic motivation, that is 47.6% of those with extrinsic motivation were also predicted accurately by the model to have extrinsic motivation. A higher percentage of cases correctly classified indicates more accurate model performance, while a lower percentage suggests that the model may need to be improved or evaluated further.

SPSS OUTPUT 20.48

Classification Table[a]

			Predicted		
			Intrinsic vs extrinsic motivation		Percentage Correct
	Observed		Intrinsic	Extrinsic	
Step 1	Intrinsic vs extrinsic motivation	Intrinsic	10	11	47.6
		Extrinsic	11	10	47.6
	Overall Percentage				47.6

a. The cut value is 0.500

An important table in the binary logistic regression is the "Variables in the Equation" table (SPSS Output 20.49), which shows the estimated coefficients (B) (the regression slope) for the independent variable, standard errors, Wald statistics, and significance levels for each independent variable in the model and Exp(B). The estimated coefficient (B) shows the expected change in the log odds of the dependent variable for a one-unit increase in the independent variable when all other variables are constant. The magnitude of the B coefficient indicates the strength of the association between the independent variable and the dependent variable. A larger magnitude of the B coefficient indicates a stronger association between the two variables. Also, a positive B coefficient indicates that an increase in the independent variable is associated with an increase in the log odds of the dependent variable, and a negative B coefficient indicates that an increase in the independent variable is associated with a decrease in the log odds of the dependent variable.

So, in our sample study, the B coefficient for language proficiency is positive, which means that an increase in language proficiency is associated with an increase in the log odds of having extrinsic motivation (compared to intrinsic motivation) (or an increase in language proficiency is positively associated with a greater likelihood of falling into the target group. The target group is the extrinsic group coded as 1). More specifically, the B coefficient of 0.048 for language proficiency means that a one-unit increase in language proficiency is associated with a 0.048 increase in the log odds of having extrinsic motivation compared to intrinsic motivation. Although all this seems a bit technical, the key takeaway is that a positive B coefficient indicates a positive association between the dependent and independent variables and a negative B coefficient indicates a negative association. In our example, this positive B suggests that language proficiency can positively predict the likelihood of having extrinsic motivation over intrinsic motivation.

The standard error of the coefficient estimate shows the accuracy of the estimated coefficient, with smaller standard errors indicating greater accuracy. The Wald statistic for the coefficient tests whether there is a relationship between the independent and the dependent variable, and the p value of less than 0.05 indicates a statistically significant relationship. Therefore, in our example study, the p value of 0.016 shows that language proficiency is a statistically significant predictor of types of motivation.

There is another piece of information, which is the "Exp(B)," which is actually the odds ratio of the dependent variable. The odds ratio is calculated by taking the exponential function of the coefficient estimate (B), so Exp(B) represents the odds of the dependent variable as having the outcome of interest for a one-unit increase in the corresponding independent variable. An odds ratio of 1 indicates no association between the independent variable and the dependent variable. An odds ratio greater than 1 indicates that an increase in the independent variable is associated with an increased odds of the dependent variable being a success, while an odds ratio less than 1 indicates that an increase in the independent variable is associated with decreased odds of the dependent variable being a success. In the case of our example (Example 20.11), the odds ratio is 1.05 for language proficiency, which means that for a one-unit increase in language proficiency, the odds of having extrinsic motivation (compared to intrinsic motivation) increases by a factor of 1.05. In other words, learners with higher language proficiency have 1.05 times greater odds of having extrinsic motivation compared to intrinsic motivation, relative to individuals with lower language proficiency.

SPSS OUTPUT 20.49

Variables in the Equation

		B	S.E.	Wald	df	Sig.	Exp(B)
Step 1[a]	Language proficiency	.048	.020	5.852	1	.016	1.050
	Constant	−3.227	1.381	5.462	1	.019	.040

a. Variable(s) entered on step 1: Language proficiency.

Conclusion

In this chapter, we have discussed the most commonly used techniques in inferential statistics used in applied linguistics, with a focus on parametric tests. We began by defining parametric tests, and their assumptions and differences from nonparametric tests. We then explained the most commonly used parametric tests in applied linguistics research, such as t-tests, ANOVAs, and regression analysis, and explained how to use them and interpret their results. Throughout the chapter we provided hypothetical examples to illustrate how each test can be conducted and how it can be interpreted.

We also described how to perform these statistical tests using SPSS and provided detailed explanations about how to interpret the outputs. By demonstrating the practical application of inferential statistics in applied linguistics research and providing step-by-step guidance on how to perform and interpret their results, we hope to have equipped you with a deeper understanding of this important topic.

It is important to note that while we have focused on the most commonly used techniques, there are many other statistical approaches that can be applied, depending on the specific research question or dataset. Due to space and scope constraints, we have not been able to explain all of them here, but we have provided a foundation in the most commonly used methods. Thus, you are encouraged to continue exploring this area to gain a more comprehensive understanding of the various statistical methods available to you as a researcher.

DISCUSSION AND ACTIVITY QUESTIONS

Discussion Questions

1. What are the key differences between parametric and nonparametric tests, and why are these differences important in research?
2. In what types of applied linguistics studies would parametric tests be most appropriate, and why?
3. What are the major assumptions underlying parametric tests, and how can these assumptions influence the validity of research findings?

4. How can you test the assumptions of parametric tests, such as normality, homogeneity of variances, and independence?
5. What steps should be taken if the assumptions of a parametric test are violated? Can you provide specific examples?
6. What are the main differences between *t*-tests and ANOVA, and how can you determine which test is more appropriate for your data?
7. What are post-hoc tests, and when and why should they be used?
8. What are the potential drawbacks associated with conducting multiple independent *t*-tests instead of using a one-way ANOVA, and how do these drawbacks impact the overall validity of the study?
9. What is multiple regression, and where is it used? What factors should be considered when selecting predictors for a multiple regression analysis, and why are these choices important?

Activity Questions

1. Find a dataset from a previous study in applied linguistics. Then conduct a one-way ANOVA to test for differences between three or more groups. Interpret and report the results of the test to your classmates, and discuss the implications of your findings.
2. Select a research question in applied linguistics that could be answered using a paired-samples *t*-test. Create a hypothetical dataset, conduct the *t*-test using SPSS, and interpret and report the results. Discuss the advantages and limitations of using a paired-samples *t*-test in this context.
3. Using SPSS, conduct a correlation analysis between two variables of interest. Interpret and report the results to the class. Discuss how this type of test differs from parametric tests such as ANOVA or *t*-tests.
4. Work in groups to create a hypothetical research question that could be answered using a multiple regression analysis. Identify relevant predictor and outcome variables and conduct a multiple regression analysis using SPSS. Interpret and report the results of the analysis to the class and discuss the implications of the findings for the research question.
5. Find a study in applied linguistics that has used a parametric test to analyze the data. Read the study carefully and identify the specific parametric test used. Then consider the following questions and finally write a short report summarizing your analysis of the study and present it to the class.
   a) Was the test appropriate for the type of data analyzed and the research question investigated?
   b) Were the assumptions of the test met? If not, how this could have impacted the results?
   c) Did the study report any significant difference, and if so, were any post-hoc tests used to find where the differences were?
   d) Were the results reported accurately and clearly? Were the implications of the findings discussed?

21 | Commonly Used Inferential Statistics Tests in Applied Linguistics Research: Nonparametric Tests

---

CHAPTER OBJECTIVES

After completing this chapter, you should be able to

- Define nonparametric tests and their use and importance.
- Explain why nonparametric tests are useful in applied linguistics research.
- Identify the most commonly used nonparametric tests in applied linguistics research.
- Describe the assumptions underlying each nonparametric test, and how to assess whether these assumptions are met.
- Understand the appropriate use and application of nonparametric tests in different research scenarios.
- Conduct nonparametric tests in SPSS and know how to interpret the output.

Introduction

Nonparametric tests are statistical tests that do not rely on assumptions about data distribution or population parameters, such as normality and equality of variances. Therefore, nonparametric tests are often used when the data do not meet the assumptions of parametric tests. Nonparametric tests are widely used in applied linguistics research and are often preferred over parametric tests when the data do not meet assumptions about the underlying distribution of the data. In this chapter, we will discuss the most commonly used nonparametric tests in applied linguistics research, the assumptions underlying such tests, their appropriate use and application, and how to interpret their results. We will also address some of the limitations and challenges associated with nonparametric tests, including their reduced power and precision compared to parametric tests. While doing so, we provide hypothetical examples and research questions that can be answered using each type of test along with instructions for conducting the analyses in SPSS.

POINTS TO PONDER

Have you encountered or used any nonparametric tests, and if so, which ones? How do these tests differ from parametric alternatives, and what advantages do they bring to the research? Can you identify instances where nonparametric tests are particularly suitable, and explain why?

Types of Nonparametric Tests

Some of the most commonly used nonparametric tests used in applied linguistics research include:

- Wilcoxon signed-rank test
- Sign test
- Mann–Whitney U test
- Friedman test
- Kruskal–Wallis test
- Chi-square goodness-of-fit test
- Spearman's rho correlation.

One-Sample and Related-Samples Wilcoxon Signed-Rank Tests

The Wilcoxon signed-rank test is a nonparametric version of the one-sample and paired-samples t-tests discussed in the previous chapter (see Table 21.1 for key characteristics). When used as a one-sample test, it examines whether the median of a sample is significantly different from a known or a hypothesized value. When used as a related-samples test, which is conceptually similar to a paired-samples t-test in parametric statistics, it evaluates whether there are significant differences between paired data. Paired data refers to two sets of data that are taken from the same individuals or participants. This can be either at different times or under different conditions.

As a related-samples test, the Wilcoxon signed-rank test examines the median of the differences between two related samples, with reference to a hypothesized zero. For example, in an interventional study, you may measure the performance of a group of learners before and after the treatment by using a pretest and a posttest. In this case, the paired data are the pretest and the posttest data as they come from the same participants before and after the treatment. If you want to assess whether there is a significant difference between the pretest and the posttest, you can use the Wilcoxon signed-rank test if the data do not meet the assumptions of parametric tests.

The Wilcoxon signed-rank test is a nonparametric version of the one-sample and paired-samples t-tests.

Table 21.1 Characteristics of the Wilcoxon signed-rank test

Characteristics	Description
Test	The Wilcoxon signed-rank test
Type of test	Nonparametric
Assumptions	No assumption of normality of distribution. The data are either paired or a single set coming from the same sample
Purpose	To test whether the median of the sample (or a group) is significantly different from the hypothesized population median or whether the median of the differences between paired data is zero
Number of groups	One group (with one set of data or two sets of related data)
Type of Data	Metric (interval) data that are not normally distributed or ranked data (e.g., measured on an ordinal scale)

Example 21.1 provides a hypothetical scenario for a one-sample Wilcoxon signed-rank test. Please note that there is also the one-sample Kolmogorov-Smirnov (K-S) test, which is used to determine whether the sample data are consistent with a specific theoretical distribution. The test asseses the null hypothesis that the sample data come from a specified continuous distribution, such as a normal, uniform, or exponential distribution.

EXAMPLE 21.1

Suppose you want to examine whether there is a significant difference between the scores of a group of language learners on a vocabulary test and a hypothesized median score of 60. You recruit a group of thirty language learners and administer a vocabulary test to them. The scores on the test are not normally distributed. A one-sample Wilcoxon signed-rank test can be used to compare the median score of the group (which is 62.5) to the hypothesized median score of 60. (The median of the score of the group can be calculated under "Descriptive Statistics" then "Explore".)

Here are the steps for conducting a one-sample Wilcoxon signed-rank test in SPSS:

SPSS STEPS 21.1

- Open the data file in SPSS.
- Select "Analyze" > "Nonparametric Tests" > "One-Sample."
- On the Objective tab, check "Customize analysis."
- On the Fields tab, choose the desired variable(s) and move it to the "Test Fields."
- On the Settings tab, check "Customize tests," then check the box for "Compare median to hypothesized (Wilcoxon signed-rank test)," and enter the hypothesized median value (insert 60 for the above example).
- Click "Run."

SPSS will generate outputs showing the results of the one-sample Wilcoxon signed-rank test (SPSS Output 21.1).

SPSS OUTPUT 21.1

Hypothesis Test Summary

	Null Hypothesis	Test	Sig.[a,b]	Decision
1	The median of Vocabulary test equals 60.00.	One-Sample Wilcoxon Signed Rank Test	.057	Retain the null hypothesis.

a. The significance level is .050.
b. Asymptotic significance is displayed.

SPSS OUTPUT 21.2

One-Sample Wilcoxon Signed Rank Test Summary

Total N	30
Test Statistic	232.00
Standard Error	36.47
Standardized Test Statistic	1.90
Asymptotic Sig. (2-sided test)	.057

The one-sample Wilcoxon signed-rank test shows no significant difference ($p = .057$) between the median score of the group (median = 62.5) and the hypothesized median score of 60, indicating that the group's median score was not significantly higher than 60. The p value of 0.057 suggests that the result is not significant at the conventional $p < .05$ threshold, although it is close to significance.

Example 21.2 presents a hypothetical scenario for the use of a related-samples Wilcoxon signed-rank test.

EXAMPLE 21.2

Suppose you want to test whether there is a significant change in the speaking proficiency levels of ESL learners before and after a pronunciation teaching program. You recruit a group of twenty ESL learners who take a speaking proficiency test before and after completing a ten-week pronunciation program. The speaking proficiency test scores are on an ordinal scale from 1 (low) to 5 (high). The data collected do not meet the assumption of normality of distribution. The median of the speaking proficiency score before the course was 4.5, and the median score after the course is 5.5. A related-samples Wilcoxon signed-rank test can be conducted to determine whether there is a significant difference between the before and after scores.

SPSS Steps 21.2 shows the steps for conducting the Wilcoxon signed-rank test for the above scenario in SPSS.

SPSS STEPS 21.2

- Open the data file in SPSS.
- Select "Analyze" > "Nonparametric Tests" > "Legacy Dialogs" > "2 Related Samples."
- In the "Two Related Samples Test" dialog box, select the variables from the list of variables.
- Select "Wilcoxon" from the "Test Type" options.
- Click "OK."

The output will include a "Ranks" table (SPSS Output 21.3), which shows the rank assigned to each observation in the sample, and a "Test Statistics" table, which provides the test statistic (z), and the significance value (p value).

SPSS OUTPUT 21.3

Ranks		N	Mean Rank	Sum of Ranks
Speaking after – Speaking before	Negative Ranks	17[a]	11.82	201.00
	Positive Ranks	3[b]	3.00	9.00
	Ties	0[c]		
	Total	20		

a. Speaking after < Speaking before
b. Speaking after > Speaking before
c. Speaking after = Speaking before

SPSS OUTPUT 21.4

Test Statistics[a]

	Speaking after – Speaking before
Z	-3.591^{b}
Asymp. Sig. (2-tailed)	.000

a. Wilcoxon Signed Ranks Test
b. Based on positive ranks.

As can be seen in SPSS Output 21.4, the results show that the pronunciation program had a significant effect on the speaking proficiency levels of the ESL learners, as shown by the p value of the z test ($p < .001$).

One-Sample and Related-Samples Sign Tests

Another nonparametric test similar to the Wilcoxon signed-rank test is the Sign test, which can be used as a one-sample or related-samples nonparametric test to test whether the median of a sample is equal to a specified value or whether the median difference between two related samples is equal to zero. The Sign test has a lower statistical power than the Wilcoxon signed-rank test, especially when the sample size is small or the differences between the paired observations are large. The Wilcoxon test is more powerful than the Sign test when the sample size is moderate to large. However, as a related-samples test, the Wilcoxon test assumes that the differences between the two related data are symmetrically distributed, and the distribution of the differences is the same for both sets of data.

The Sign test involves comparing the observed values to a hypothesized median and determining whether the number of observations with positive differences is statistically significant. The Sign test can be used as a related-samples test too, to compare two related samples when the data are ordinal or interval data that do not meet the assumption of normality. In this case, the Sign test is used to test whether the median difference between the two related samples is equal to zero Characteristics of the sign test are shown in Table 21.2.

Table 21.2 Characteristics of the Sign test

Characteristics	Description
Test	Sign test
Type of test	Nonparametric
Assumptions	No assumptions regarding the distribution of the data
Purpose	To test whether the median of a sample is equal to a specified value or whether the median difference between two related samples is equal to zero
Number of groups	One group (with one set of data or two related sets of data)
Type of Data	Continuous (metric) nonnormally distributed data or ordinal data

The Sign test can be used as a one-sample and a related-samples nonparametric test to test whether the median of a sample is equal to a specified value or whether the median difference between two related samples is equal to zero.

To use the Sign test as a paired- or related-samples test, the differences between the paired observations are first calculated, and the signs of these differences are determined (positive if the first observation is greater than the second, negative if the second observation is greater than the first, and zero if they are equal). The test then involves comparing the number of positive differences to the number of negative differences using a binomial distribution.

Example 21.3 provides a hypothetical scenario of a one-sample Sign test.

EXAMPLE 21.3

Suppose you want to examine whether the grammar test scores for a newly registered group of ESL students in a grammar class differ significantly from a hypothesized median score of 50. You recruit a group of thirty language learners and administer a grammar test to them after one month of task-based instruction. The scores on the test are not normally distributed. A one-sample Sign test can be used to compare the median score of the group to the hypothesized median score of 50. Please note that to run this analysis on SPSS, you need to create two variables, one that is the students' test scores and the other that shows the median score for each student.

Please note that SPSS does not have an option for a one-sample Sign test. To conduct such a test, we can first create a variable with the value equal to the hypothesized test value (in the case of our example study, it is 50), and then run a nonparametric two-related-samples test.

SPSS Steps 21.3 shows you how to conduct the Sign test for the above scenario.

SPSS STEPS 21.3

- Open the data file in SPSS.
- Select "Analyze" > "Nonparametric Tests" > "Legacy Dialogs" > "2 Related Samples."
- In the "Two- Related-Samples Tests" dialog box, select the variables from the list of the variables.
- Select "Sign" from the "Test Type" options.
- Click "OK."

The outputs generated for the above example study are presented in SPSS Output 21.5 and 21.6.

SPSS OUTPUT 21.5

	Frequencies		N
Median score – Grammar scores	Negative Differences[a]		23
	Positive Differences[b]		0
	Ties[c]		7
	Total		30

a. Median score < Grammar scores
b. Median score > Grammar scores
c. Median score = Grammar scores

SPSS OUTPUT 21.6

Test Statistics[a]	Median score – Grammar scores
Exact Sig. (2-tailed)	.000[b]

a. Sign Test
b. Binomial distribution used.

As can be seen in SPSS Output 21.6, the Sign test shows a significant difference between the grammar test score and the hypothesized median of 50 ($p < .001$).

Example 21.4 provides a hypothetical scenario of a paired-samples Sign test.

EXAMPLE 21.4

Suppose you want to examine whether there is a significant difference in the reading speed of ESL learners before and after a reading comprehension program. You recruit a group of twenty ESL students to participate in the study for one semester. The reading speed of the participants is measured in terms of the number of words per minute before and after the program. The data collected do not meet the assumption of normality of distribution. A related-samples Sign test can be used to analyze the data since the data are not normally distributed and because the sample size is small. The null hypothesis for the test is that there is no significance difference in the median of the reading speed of the participants before and after the reading program.

SPSS Steps 21.4 shows the procedure for conducting the Sign test for the above scenario.

SPSS STEPS 21.4

- Open the data file in SPSS.
- Select "Analyze" > "Nonparametric Tests" > "Legacy Dialogs" > "2 Related Samples."
- In the "Two-Related Samples Test" dialog box, choose the variables.
- Select "Sign test" under "Test Type."
- Click "OK."

SPSS Output 21.7 and 21.8 show the outputs generated for the study in Example 21.4.

SPSS OUTPUT 21.7

Frequencies		N
Post program – pre program	Negative Differences[a]	0
	Positive Differences[b]	20
	Ties[c]	0
	Total	20

a. Post program < pre program
b. Post program > pre program
c. Post program = pre program

SPSS OUTPUT 21.8

Test Statistics[a]	
	Post program – pre program
Exact Sig. (2-tailed)	.000[b]

a. Sign Test
b. Binomial distribution used.

As can be seen, the related-samples Sign test shows a significant difference between the median of reading speed before and after the reading program (p < .001), indicating that the reading program had a positive effect on the reading speed of the ESL learners.

POINTS TO PONDER

Can you provide an example where the Mann–Whitney U test could be used? What considerations would be important in such a scenario?

Mann–Whitney U test

The Mann-Whitney U test is a nonparametric version of the independent-samples t-test and is used to determine whether there are differences between two sets of data when the data do not meet the assumptions of parametric tests. For example, if you have two groups of participants and want to compare their scores on nonnormally distributed data about their attitudes, or you have two groups of participants and want to compare their performance on datasets that involve ordinal data, such as Likert scale data, you can use the Mann–Whitney U test. The Mann–Whitney U test is also an appropriate test for when the sample size is small, in which case it is often preferred over the parametric t-test as it can still provide robust results even when the sample size is small. In the Mann–Whitney U test, the data for each group are ranked, and the analysis is based on the sum of the ranks.

The Mann–Whitney U test is a nonparametric version of the independent-samples t-test and is used to determine whether there are differences between two sets of data when the data do not meet the assumptions of parametric tests.

The Mann-Whitney U test is often used in applied linguistics research to compare the effects of different treatments or interventions. Table 21.3 summarizes the characteristics of the Mann-Whitney U test.

Table 21.3 Characteristics of the Mann–Whitney U test

Characteristics	Description
Test	The Mann-Whitney U test
Type of test	Nonparametric
Assumptions	Independent samples, no significant outliers
Purpose	To compare two independent groups on a continuous or ordinal dependent variable
Number of groups	Two groups
Type of Data	Continuous (metric) or ordinal data

Example 21.5 provides a hypothetical scenario for a Mann–Whitney U test.

EXAMPLE 21.5

Suppose you want to investigate the effectiveness of input enhancement on ESL learners' vocabulary learning. You randomly assign thirty intermediate-level participants to two groups: one with typographical enhancement and one without. Each group reads a 600-word text with ten highlighted target words, differing only in typographic treatment. After a fifteen-minute reading period, both groups take a vocabulary test. The research question assesses whether there's a significant difference in vocabulary learning between the two groups. Due to a small sample size and nonnormal data, the Mann–Whitney U test is chosen for analysis.

To perform a Mann–Whitney U test in SPSS, you can follow the steps shown in SPSS Steps 21.5.

SPSS STEPS 21.5

- Open the data file in SPSS.
- Select "Analyze" > "Nonparametric Tests" > "Legacy dialogs" > "2 Independent Samples."
- In the "Two-Independent-Samples Tests" dialog box, select the dependent variable and move it to the "Test Variable List" Box.
- Choose the variable identifying the independent groups and move it to the "Grouping Variable" box and define groups.
- Under "Test Type," choose "Mann–Whitney U."
- Click "Options" > "Descriptive statistics" > "Continue."
- Click "OK."

The output will provide you with the results of the Mann–Whitney U test, including a descriptive statistics table (SPSS Output 21.9), which displays the means and standard deviations of the groups; a ranks table (SPSS Output 21.10), which displays the mean ranks and the sum of ranks for the two groups; and a test statistics table (SPSS Output 21.11), which displays the Mann–Whitney U statistic, the z score, and the p value. If the p value is less than or equal to your chosen alpha level (usually 0.05), you can conclude that there is a significant difference between the two groups.

SPSS OUTPUT 21.9

Descriptive Statistics

	N	Mean	Std. Deviation	Minimum	Maximum
Vocabulary scores	30	6.07	2.74	1.00	10.00
Text	30	1.53	.51	1.00	2.00

SPSS OUTPUT 21.10

Ranks

	Text	N	Mean Rank	Sum of Ranks
Vocabulary scores	Unenhanced	14	11.32	158.50
	Enhanced	16	19.16	306.50
	Total	30		

SPSS OUTPUT 21.11

Test Statistics[a]

	Vocabulary scores
Mann-Whitney U	53.50
Wilcoxon W	158.50
Z	−2.44
Asymp. Sig. (2-tailed)	.014
Exact Sig. [2*(1-tailed Sig.)]	.013[b]

a. Grouping Variable: Text
b. Not corrected for ties.

The Mann–Whitney U test ranks table (SPSS Output 21.10) shows the distribution of ranks between the two groups. The "Test Statistics" table (SPSS Output 21.11) shows the Mann–Whitney U test statistics, which measures the difference in ranks between the two groups. This table shows whether there is a significant difference between the groups. In the SPSS output, you can see two p values, one under

"Asymp. Sig. (2-tailed)" and the other under Exact Sig." The former refers to the asymptotic significance level, and the p value is calculated using the t-test statistic asymptotic distribution. The latter, "Exact Sig." refers to the exact significance level, and the p value is calculated based on the exact distribution of the test statistic. The "2-tailed" indicates that the p value is based on a two-tailed test. It tests a nondirectional alternative hypothesis. The table shows a small p value (less than 0.05), for both significance levels, which suggests that there is a significant difference between the groups.

Friedman Test

The Friedman test is the nonparametric version of one-way repeated measures ANOVA and is used when the assumptions of the parametric ANOVA are not met. The Friedman test is used to determine whether there are any significant differences between three or more related means or the means coming from the same participants. Like the repeated measures ANOVA, it tests the null hypothesis that there are no differences between the three repeated measures means. If the result of the test is significant, then we reject the null hypothesis and conclude that there are significant differences among the means. If we find a significant difference, similar to the repeated measures ANOVA, the, post-hoc tests can be used to determine which mean differs significantly from the others.

The Friedman test is the nonparametric version of one-way repeated measures ANOVA and is used when the assumptions of the parametric ANOVA are not met.

Table 21.4 summarizes the characteristics, assumptions, purpose, example, and type of data for the Friedman test.

Table 21.4 Characteristics of the Friedman test

Characteristics	Description
Name of the test	The Friedman test
Type of test	Nonparametric
Assumptions	Related samples, independence of observations within groups
Independent variables	One categorical variable
Number of groups	One group measured repeatedly over time or under different conditions
Purpose	To determine whether there is any significant difference among three or more medians coming from the same participants
Hypotheses	Null hypothesis: All the medians are equal
Type of data	Continuous or interval (e.g., test scores) or ordinal
Dependent variable	There is one dependent variable being measured repeatedly on the same group of participants

Example 21.6 presents a hypothetical scenario for the use of the Friedman test.

EXAMPLE 21.6

Suppose you want to explore the perception of a group of bilingual speakers of English and French about the quality of the translation of Google Translate across three different types of sentences that differ in their complexity (e.g., simple, complex, and idiomatic sentences).

You recruit a group of thirty bilingual speakers of English and French. They are presented with ten English sentences from each sentence type, each of which has been translated into French using Google Translate. The sentences for each type are presented in a randomized order, and participants are asked to rate their translation quality on a 5-point scale, where 1 indicates "very poor" and 5 indicates "excellent." The research question examines differences in perception across sentence types. A Friedman test is used to examine significant differences in participants' perceptions of translation quality.

There are two ways in which the Friedman test can be carried out in SPSS. One is through the legacy dialogs option, which is an easy route but lacks the option of pairwise comparison. The other is through the "Nonparametric tests > Related samples" option, which provides pairwise comparisons. SPSS Steps 21.6 shows the procedure for the first route.

SPSS STEPS 21.6

- Open the data file in SPSS.
- Select "Analyze" > "Nonparametric Tests" > "Legacy Dialogs" > "K Related Samples."
- In the variables section, move the test variables to the "Test Variables" box.
- In Test Type, select "Friedman."
- Click on "Statistics" > "Descriptive" > "Quartiles."
- Click "Continue" > "OK."

SPSS generates outputs, including a descriptive statistics table, ranks table, and test statistics table. The descriptive statistics table (SPSS Output 21.12) displays observations and ranks for each condition. It also provides quartile information useful for understanding rank distribution and identifying potential outliers. In our example for simple sentences, 25% of the participants rate the quality of translation at or below 2.00, 50% at or below 3.00, and 75% at or below 4.00. The "Ranks" table (SPSS Output 21.13) shows mean ranks for the related data, while the "Test Statistics" table (SPSS Output 21.14) assesses significant differences in median scores by comparing sum of ranks. For our example, the Friedman test's chi-square value (15.46) and the p value ($< .05$) indicate a significant difference in participants' ratings for the three sentence types.

SPSS OUTPUT 21.12

Descriptive Statistics

	N	Mean	Std. Deviation	Minimum	Maximum	25th	50th (Median)	75th
							Percentiles	
Simple sentences	30	3.13	.937	2.00	5.00	2.00	3.00	4.00
Complex sentences	30	3.03	.964	1.00	5.00	2.00	3.00	4.00
Idiomatic sentences	30	2.63	1.06	1.00	5.00	2.00	3.00	3.00

SPSS OUTPUT 21.13

Ranks

	Mean Rank
Simple sentences	2.25
Complex sentences	2.20
Idiomatic sentences	1.55

SPSS OUTPUT 21.14

Test Statistics[a]

N	30
Chi-Square	15.465
df	2
Asymp. Sig.	.000

a. Friedman Test

When using legacy dialogs for the Friedman test, pairwise comparisons are not included. To address this, after detecting a significant difference, perform Wilcoxon tests for pairwise comparisons. For multiple comparisons, adjust p values by dividing them by the number of comparisons. This provides a Bonferroni correction. Alternatively, you can perform the Friedman test through "Nonparametric Tests > Related samples" for a more direct route. SPSS Steps 21.7 shows the steps for the second route.

SPSS STEPS 21.7

- Open the data file in SPSS.
- Select "Analyze" > "Nonparametric Tests" > "Related samples."
- Go to "Objective" > "Customize analysis."
- On the Fields tab, move variables of interest from "Fields" to "Test Fields."
- On the Settings tab, choose "Customize tests," check "Friedman's 2-way ANOVA by ranks (k samples)."
- Under "Multiple comparisons", select "All pairwise."
- Click "Run."

The output includes tables and graphs, such as a hypothesis test summary (SPSS Output 21.15) and a "related-samples Friedman's two-way analysis of variance by ranks summary," displaying the Friedman test p value (SPSS Output 21.16). In our example, the p value is smaller than 0 .05, indicating a significant difference in participants' ratings of sentence types.

The pairwise comparisons table (SPSS Output 21.17) and accompanying figure (SPSS Output 21.18) reveal significant differences. For instance, idiomatic sentences (mean rank = 1.55) are rated significantly less positively than complex sentences (mean rank = 2.20). Similarly, idiomatic sentences are rated significantly less positively than simple sentences (mean rank = 2.25). No significant difference is observed between complex and simple sentences. SPSS Output 21.17 provides two p values: one indicating simple differences in mean ranks and the other, an adjusted p value using a Bonferroni correction for multiple comparisons.

SPSS OUTPUT 21.15

	Hypothesis Test Summary			
	Null Hypothesis	Test	Sig.[a,b]	Decision
1	The distributions of Simple sentences, Complex sentences and Idiomatic sentences are the same.	Related-Samples Friedman's Two-Way Analysis of Variance by Ranks	.000	Reject the null hypothesis.

a. The significance level is .050.
b. Asymptotic significance is displayed.

SPSS OUTPUT 21.16

Related-Samples Friedman's Two-Way Analysis of Variance by Ranks Summary	
Total N	30
Test Statistic	15.46
Degree Of Freedom	2
Asymptotic Sig.(2-sided test)	.000

SPSS OUTPUT 21.17

Pairwise Comparisons					
Sample 1-Sample 2	Test Statistic	Std. Error	Std. Test Statistic	Sig.	Adj. Sig.[a]
Idiomatic sentences-Complex sentences	.65	.25	2.51	.01	.035
Idiomatic sentences-Simple sentences	.70	.25	2.71	.007	.020
Complex sentences-Simple sentences	.05	.25	.19	.84	1.00

Each row tests the null hypothesis that the Sample 1 and Sample 2 distributions are the same.
Asymptotic significances (2-sided tests) are displayed. The significance level is .050.
a. Significance values have been adjusted by the Bonferroni correction for multiple tests.

SPSS OUTPUT 21.18

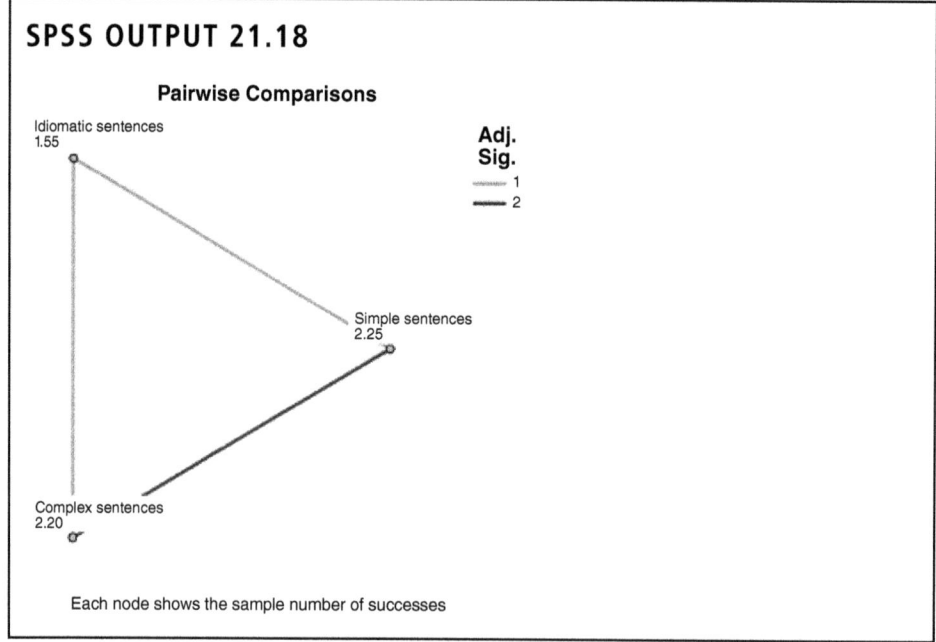

Each node shows the sample number of successes

POINTS TO PONDER

Provide an example of where a Kruskal–Wallis test could be used and explain why.

Kruskal–Wallis Test

The Kruskal-Wallis test is a nonparametric statistical test used to compare the median of three or more independent groups. It is a nonparametric version of the one-way ANOVA and is used when the assumptions of ANOVA such as normality of distribution or equal variances are not met, or when the data are ordinal. It is also used when the sample size is too small for a parametric test.

The Kruskal-Wallis test is similar to the Mann–Whitney U test in that it is performed by ranking the data from all the groups and then calculating the sum of ranks for each group. The test statistic is then calculated as the ratio of the sum of squares of the ranks to the total sample size, and it follows a chi-square distribution with degrees of freedom equal to the number of groups minus one. The Kruskal-Wallis test is used to compare three or more independent groups, whereas the Mann–Whitney U test is used to compare two independent groups.

The **Kruskal–Wallis** test compares the median of three or more independent groups. It is a nonparametric version of the one-way ANOVA test, and it is used when the assumptions of ANOVA such as normality of distribution or equal variances are not met.

Table 21.5 summarizes the characteristics of the Kruskal–Wallis test.

Table 21.5 Characteristics of the Kruskal–Wallis test

Characteristics	Description
Test	The Kruskal–Wallis Test
Type of test	Nonparametric
Assumptions	Independent samples, no significant outliers
Purpose	To compare three or more independent groups on a continuous or ordinal dependent variable
Number of groups	Three or more groups
Type of data	Continuous or ordinal data

Example 21.7 presents a hypothetical scenario for the use of the Kruskal–Wallis test.

EXAMPLE 21.7

Suppose you want to investigate the perspectives of three groups of ESL learners from different levels of language proficiency on peer feedback on L2 writing. The research question is: what are the perspectives of L2 learners with different levels of language proficiency on peer feedback on L2 writing? You recruit sixty participants from which three proficiency groups are formed: Group A (high proficiency), Group B (intermediate proficiency), and Group C (low proficiency), each comprising twenty learners. Participants are asked to indicate their opinion using a six-point Likert scale (1= Not useful at all, 2 = Slightly useful, 3= Somewhat useful, 4 = Moderately useful, 5 = Very useful, 6 = Extremely useful). The ordinal nature of the data necessitates the use of the Kruskal–Wallis test to compare responses among the three proficiency groups.

Similar to the Friedman test, there are two ways in which the Kruskal–Wallis test can be carried out in SPSS. One is through the legacy dialogs option and the other is through "Nonparametric tests > Independent samples." The former lacks the option of pairwise comparisons, but the latter provides pairwise comparisons.

SPSS Steps 21.8 shows the steps for the first route.

SPSS STEPS 21.8

- Open the data file in SPSS.
- Select "Analyze" > "Nonparametric Tests" > "Legacy Dialogs" > "K Independent Samples."
- In the variables section, move the test variables to the "Test Variable List" box.
- In "Test Type," choose "Kruskal Wallis H."
- Move the grouping variable into the "Grouping Variable" box.
- Click on "Define Range" and define the range of the grouping variable.
- Click on "Options," then select "Descriptive" and "Quartiles."
- Click "Continue" > "OK."

SPSS generates outputs, including a descriptive statistics table, a ranks table, and a test statistics table. In the descriptive statistics table (SPSS Output 21.19), for our sixty participants, 25% rate the degree of usefulness at or below 3.00 (Somewhat useful), 50% at or below 5.00 (Very useful), and 75% at or below 6.00 (Extremely useful). The ranks table (SPSS Output 21.20) displays mean ranks for related groups. The test statistics table (SPSS Output 21.21), using the chi-square test for the Kruskal–Wallis test, indicates a significant difference among participants ($p < .05$).

SPSS OUTPUT 21.19

Descriptive Statistics

	N	Mean	Std. Deviation	Minimum	Maximum	25th	Percentiles 50th (Median)	75th
Degree of usefulness	60	4.37	1.49	1	6	3.00	5.00	6.00
Groups	60	2.00	.823	1.00	3.00	1.00	2.00	3.00

SPSS OUTPUT 21.20

Ranks

	Groups	N	Mean Rank
Degree of usefulness	Beginner	20	25.25
	Intermediate	20	27.53
	Advanced	20	38.73
	Total	60	

SPSS OUTPUT 21.21

Test Statistics[a,b]

	Degree of usefulness
Kruskal–Wallis H	7.184
df	2
Asymp. Sig.	.028

a. Kruskal–Wallis Test
b. Grouping Variable: Groups

The legacy dialogs route for the Kruskal–Wallis test lacks post-hoc pairwise comparisons. In the case of a significant difference, use Mann–Whitney U tests for pairs and adjust the p values by dividing them by the number of comparisons for a Bonferroni correction. Alternatively, the second route automatically includes pairwise post-hoc comparisons. SPSS Steps 21.9 shows how to conduct the Kruskal–Wallis test through the second route.

SPSS STEPS 21.9

- Open the data file in SPSS.
- Select "Analyze" > "Nonparametric Tests" > "Independent Samples."
- On the Objective tab, choose "Customize analysis."
- In Fields, select the dependent variable and move it to the "Test Fields," and choose the variable for groups and move it to the "Groups" box.
- Click "Setting" > "Customize tests", and select "Kruskal–Wallis 1-way ANOVA (k samples)."
- Under "Multiple comparisons," select "All pairwise."
- Click "Run."

SPSS produces the Kruskal–Wallis test results, including a hypothesis test summary table and an "independent-samples Kruskal–Wallis test summary" table indicating a p value. In our example, the p value is smaller than .05 (SPSS Outputs 21.22 and 21.23), indicating a significant difference among participants' ratings for the three sentence types.

The pairwise comparisons table (SPSS Output 21.24) and the associated figure (SPSS Output 21.25) highlight significant differences. In our example study, based on the adjusted p values, there is a significant difference between beginner- (mean rank = 25.25) and advanced-level learners (mean rank = 38.73) in rating peer feedback usefulness, with advanced learners rating it more highly (adj $p = .037$). No significant difference is observed between beginner- and intermediate-level learners (adj $p = 1.000$) and between intermediate- and advanced-level learners (adj $p = .112$). As can be seen, the table (SPSS Output 21.24) provides two p values: one showing simple differences in mean ranks from the Kruskal–Wallis test, and the other showing an adjusted p value using a Bonferroni correction for multiple comparisons. The adjusted p value accounts for the increased risk of Type I error when conducting multiple pairwise comparisons. Thus, this is a preferred approach when we need to identify specific group differences after finding a main effect.

SPSS OUTPUT 21.22

	Hypothesis Test Summary			
	Null Hypothesis	Test	Sig.[a,b]	Decision
1	The distribution of Degree of usefulness is the same across categories of Groups.	Independent-Samples Kruskal–Wallis Test	.028	Reject the null hypothesis.
2	The distribution of Degree of usefulness is the same across categories of Groups.	Independent-Samples Jonckheere–Terpstra Test for Ordered Alternatives	.012	Reject the null hypothesis.

a. The significance level is .050.
b. Asymptotic significance is displayed.

SPSS OUTPUT 21.23

Independent-Samples Kruskal–Wallis Test Summary

Total N	60
Test Statistic	7.184[a]
Degree of Freedom	2
Asymptotic Sig. (2-sided test)	.028

a. The test statistic is adjusted for ties.

SPSS OUTPUT 21.24

Pairwise Comparisons of Groups

Sample 1-Sample 2	Test Statistic	Std. Error	Std. Test Statistic	Sig.	Adj. Sig.[a]
Beginner-Intermediate	−2.27	5.38	−.42	.673	1.000
Beginner-Advanced	−13.47	5.38	−2.50	.012	.037
Intermediate-Advanced	−11.20	5.38	−2.08	.037	.112

Each row tests the null hypothesis that the Sample 1 and Sample 2 distributions are the same.
Asymptotic significances (2-sided tests) are displayed. The significance level is .050.

a. Significance values have been adjusted by the Bonferroni correction for multiple tests.

SPSS OUTPUT 21.25

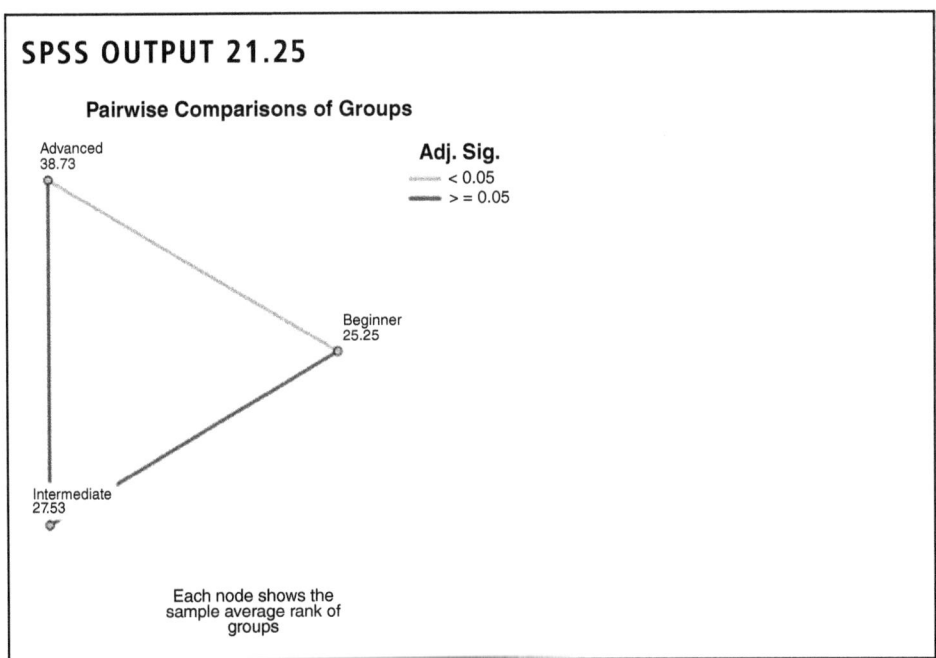

Pairwise Comparisons of Groups

Advanced
38.73

Beginner
25.25

Intermediate
27.53

Adj. Sig.
< 0.05
> = 0.05

Each node shows the
sample average rank of
groups

Chi-Square Test

Another commonly used test in applied linguistics research is the chi-square test, which is a statistical test to determine whether there is any significant relationship between two categorical variables. As noted earlier, categorical variables are those that categorize participants or conditions into categories. Examples include nationality, first language background, and so on. These variables have no numerical values and instead they are represented by labels or names that represent the category to which the data belong.

The chi-square test is a statistical test to determine whether there is any significant association or relationship between two categorical variables.

The chi-square test does not rely on the assumptions that are usually considered for parametric tests such normality of distribution. However, there are two other assumptions that should be met before performing any chi-square tests. These include the following:

Independence of observations: According to this assumption, the observations used in the chi-square test must be independent of each other. This means that the values of one observation in the study should not be influenced by the values of any other observations.

Expected frequency counts equal to or higher than 5: The expected frequency counts for each cell in the contingency table should be 5 or higher. If the sample size is small, the expected counts in each of the cells in the contingency table are smaller than 5. If this assumption of the chi-square test is not met, the Fisher's exact test can be used. The Fisher's exact test is a variation of the chi-square test and is appropriate for analyzing the association between two or more categorical variables when the expected frequency assumption of the chi-square test is not met.

Table 21.6 summarizes the characteristics of the chi-square test.

Table 21.6 Characteristics of the chi-square test	
Characteristics	Description
Test	Chi-square test
Type of test	Nonparametric
Assumptions	Independence of observations, expected frequency counts ≥ 5
Purpose	To test the relationship between two categorical variables
Type of data	Categorical
Null hypothesis	There is no significant relationship between the variables

Example 21.8 presents a hypothetical scenario for the use a chi-square test.

EXAMPLE 21.8

Suppose you are interested in examining the use of different types of corrective feedback by two groups of experienced and less experienced language teachers in second language classrooms. The study compares two teachers (one experienced, one less experienced). Data collection involves recordings of five hours of classroom interactions for each of the teachers. The data are transcribed and coded for instances of corrective feedback types provided to students. The types of corrective feedback identified are recasts, explicit correction, and metalinguistic feedback, which are then tallied and compared between the two teachers. The study involves two categorical variables, type of feedback and type of teacher, and therefore the chi-square test is a suitable test to examine the relationship between the two.

SPSS Steps 21.10 shows how to conduct a chi-square test in SPSS.

SPSS STEPS 21.10

- Open the data file in SPSS.
- Select "Analyze" > "Descriptive Statistics" > "Crosstabs."
- In the Crosstabs dialog box, select the variables and move one of them to the "Row(s)" and the other to the "Column (s)" boxes.
- Click on "Statistics" > "Chi-square." Choose additional options (e.g., Phi and Cramer's V) if you want.
- Click on "Continue."
- Click on "Cells" > "Percentages" and choose "Row" or "Column."
- Click "Continue" > "OK."

The SPSS output consists of tables and charts, including a crosstabulation table displaying the frequency distribution of analyzed variables; a chi-square test statistics table with the chi-square statistic, degrees of freedom, and p value; and a table with association measures such as phi and Cramer's V coefficients. In our hypothetical study, the case processing summary table (SPSS Output 21.26) shows the total observations, and the crosstabulation table (SPSS Output 21.27) illustrates the distribution of variables with frequencies and percentages. For this study, the experienced teacher shows a higher percentage of metalinguistic feedback (37%) and a lower percentage of explicit correction (9%) compared to the less experienced teacher, indicating a difference in their use of feedback types.

SPSS OUTPUT 21.26

Case Processing Summary

	Cases					
	Valid		Missing		Total	
	N	Percent	N	Percent	N	Percent
Teachers * Feedback Types	207	100.0%	0	0.0%	207	100.0%

SPSS OUTPUT 21.27

Teachers * Feedback Types Crosstabulation

			Feedback Types			
			Recasts	Explicit correction	Metalinguistic feedback	Total
Teachers	Less experienced	Count	52	30	18	100
		% within Teachers	52.0%	30.0%	18.0%	100.0%
	Experienced	Count	57	10	40	107
		% within Teachers	53.3%	9.3%	37.4%	100.0%
Total		Count	109	40	58	207
		% within Teachers	52.7%	19.3%	28.0%	100.0%

The next table (SPSS Output 21.28) is the chi-square table, which shows whether the difference is significant. It shows two tests of significance, including the Pearson chi-square test statistics and the likelihood ratio test, with their values, degrees of freedom, and p values. Both the Pearson chi-square and likelihood ratio chi-square tests are used to analyze the association between categorical variables in a contingency table, but the likelihood ratio test has fewer assumptions about the data and is more appropriate when the sample size is small or the expected frequencies are low. The interpretation of the results of the two tests differs slightly too. While the Pearson chi-square test is often used to examine the presence of statistically significant differences between the observed and expected frequencies, the likelihood ratio test examines whether there is a significant association between the variables by determining the likelihood of the observed data under the null hypothesis of no association between variables, and the alternative hypothesis of some association between variables. Regarding our hypothetical data, both tests are significant (p value smaller than 0.05).

The note under the table tells us that the assumption of the chi-square test with respect to the expected counts per cell has been met. Otherwise, we could have used other tests, including the Fisher's exact test. In particular, it is often recommended that if more than 20 percent of cells have expected frequencies of less than 5, we should use Fisher's exact test otherwise the results would be inaccurate.

SPSS OUTPUT 21.28

Chi-Square Tests

	Value	df	Asymptotic Significance (2-sided)
Pearson Chi-Square	18.358[a]	2	.000
Likelihood Ratio	19.015	2	.000
Linear-by-Linear Association	2.262	1	.133
N of Valid Cases	207		

a. 0 cells (0.0%) have expected count less than 5. The minimum expected count is 19.32.

The next output (SPSS Output 21.29) shows the phi and Cramer's V coefficients. These provide the effect sizes, or strength of the association between the two variables. They range from 0 to 1 with the higher values indicating a stronger association between the two variables. SPSS produces both coefficients, but phi is used more often with a 2×2 contingency table. In our hypothetical study we have a 2×3 contingency table (2 rows, three columns); therefore, a more appropriate measure is Cramer's V (see Chapter 23 for more details).

SPSS OUTPUT 21.29

Symmetric Measures

		Value	Approximate Significance
Nominal by Nominal	Phi	.298	.000
	Cramer's V	.298	.000
N of Valid Cases		207	

The value of Cramer's V is often interpreted based on the degree of freedom. Therefore, in the context of our example study, the value of 0.298 for 2 degrees of freedom suggests that there is some degree of association, but it is not strong (see Table 21.7 for the interpretation of Cramer's V values).

Table 21.7 The interpretation of the value of Cramer's *V*

Degrees of freedom	Small	Medium	Large
1	0.10	0.30	0.50
2	0.07	0.21	0.35
3	0.06	0.17	0.29
4	0.05	0.15	0.25
5	0.04	0.13	0.22

POINTS TO PONDER

Provide an example from applied linguistics research where the Spearman's rho test would be more suitable.

Spearman's Rho Test

The Spearman's rho test, also known as Spearman's rank test or the Spearman test, is a statistical test that assesses the strength and direction of the relationship between two variables. It is a nonparametric test of correlation, meaning that it does not rely on the assumptions about the distribution of the data such as normality of distribution. It is an alternative to the Pearson correlation coefficient, which assumes that the data should be normally distributed and that there is a linear relationship between the two variables being compared. Unlike the Pearson correlation, which measures the linear relationship between two variables, the Spearman's rho correlation measures the monotonic relationship between two variables, which means that it examines the degree to which the two variables change together, but not necessarily at a constant rate. The Spearman's rho test is widely used in the field of applied linguistics to analyze the relationship between variables when the assumptions of parametric tests are not met, such as when the data are not normally distributed or when there are outliers. Another alternative to the Pearson correlation, in addition to the Spearman's rho test, is the Kendall's tau correlation, which is another nonparametric correlation test used when the assumptions of Pearson correlations are not met.

The Spearman's rho test assesses the strength and direction of the relationship between two variables. It is a nonparametric test of correlation and does not rely on the assumptions about the distribution of the data.

The Spearman's rho correlation coefficient is calculated by assigning ranks to each observation for each variable, and then calculating the correlation between the ranks. The correlation coefficient ranges from -1 to 1, where -1 indicates a perfect negative correlation, 0 indicates no correlation, and 1 indicates a perfect positive correlation as shown in Table 21.8.

Table 21.8 Characteristics of the Spearman's rho correlation test

Characteristics	Description
Test	The Spearman's rho (Spearman's rank) correlation test
Type of test	Nonparametric test of correlation
Assumptions	No assumptions about normality of distribution of the data
Purpose	To test the relationship between two variables.
Type of data	Ordinal or ranked data
Interpretation	−1 indicates a perfect negative correlation, 0 indicates no correlation, and 1 indicates a perfect positive correlation

Example 21.9 presents a hypothetical scenario for the use of the Spearman's rho test.

EXAMPLE 21.9

Suppose you want to investigate the relationship between learners' attitudes towards the English language and their motivation to learn English. You collect data from a group of thirty ESL learners using a survey with Likert-scale questions: one about attitudes towards English (ranging from 1 = strongly disagree to 5 = strongly agree) and another about motivation to learn English (ranging from 1 = not at all motivated to 5 = very motivated). The data collected are ordinal in nature and not normally distributed. In addition, the relationship between the two variables may not be linear, which would violate the assumptions of parametric tests such as the Pearson correlation. Therefore, to analyze the relationship between the two variables, the Spearman's rho (Spearman's rank) correlation can be used. The Spearman's rho correlation converts the raw scores for each variable into ranks, and by doing so it avoids any issues related to nonnormality and outliers in the data.

SPSS Steps 21.11 shows the procedure for conducting the Spearman's rank correlation coefficient test.

SPSS STEPS 21.11

- Open the data file in SPSS.
- Select "Analyze" > "Correlate" > "Bivariate."
- In the "Bivariate Correlations" dialog box, select the two variables to be analyzed and move them to the "Variable" box.
- Under the "Correlation Coefficients" select "Spearman."
- Click "OK."

SPSS will then generate the output for the results of the Spearman's rho correlation test, including the correlation coefficient value (r), the p value, and the number of cases used in the analysis (SPSS Output 21.30).

SPSS OUTPUT 21.30

		Correlations	Attitude	Motivation
Spearman's rho	Attitude	Correlation Coefficient	1.000	.884[**]
		Sig. (2-tailed)	.	.000
		N	30	30
	Motivation	Correlation Coefficient	.884[**]	1.000
		Sig. (2-tailed)	.000	.
		N	30	30

[**]. Correlation is significant at the 0.01 level (2-tailed).

The analysis shows a significant positive correlation between attitude towards learning English and motivation, with a Spearman's rho correlation coefficient of 0.884 ($p < .001$). This indicates a positive and strong correlation between the two variables.

Limitations of Nonparametric Tests

Nonparametric tests are valuable tools for analyzing data that do not meet the assumptions of parametric tests. However, they have certain limitations that we should be aware of. First, they have less power than parametric tests. Power in statistics refers to the ability of a statistical test to detect an effect or difference when it actually exists. A test with higher power is more likely to correctly detect an effect as statistically significant, while a test with lower power is less likely to do so. Second, nonparametric tests are often based on ranking the data rather than the actual values. This can result in a loss of information compared to when the full range of data is considered. For example, when participants are ranked, they can be shown to have the same rank, whereas the ranking may not reflect the differences that may actually exist in the data. Nonparametric tests are also limited in their application as they are not suitable for all types of data. They are designed for specific situations and may not be able to handle complex analyses of data. Additionally, nonparametric tests are not as popular as parametric tests, and therefore people may be less aware of their application, which can potentially lead to problems in correctly interpreting and reporting their results. To address some of these limitations, there are strategies that you could use. One strategy is to increase the sample size when using nonparametric tests. Since nonparametric tests are generally less powerful than parametric tests, the power decreases even more with small sample sizes. Therefore, increasing the sample size can help to improve the power of the tests. Another strategy would be transforming the data. If the data do not meet the assumptions of a parametric test, it may be useful to transform the data to meet the assumptions of a parametric test. For example, log transformation or square root transformation can be used to normalize the data.

Alternatively, for more complex data scenarios, generalized linear models (GLMs) and generalized linear mixed models (GLMMs) can be valuable options, as they handle certain limitations of nonparametric tests by allowing for flexible modeling of nonnormal data distributions and accommodating random effects. These models provide a robust framework for analyzing a broader range of data types, potentially preserving more information and increasing power. The next chapter will explore GLMs and GLMMs, highlighting how they can be applied effectively in various research contexts.

Conclusion

In this chapter, we have discussed nonparametric tests, which are statistical procedures used to analyze data when the assumptions of parametric tests, such as normality of distribution, are not met or when the sample size is small. Since these tests do not require the same specific assumptions about the data as parametric tests, they are often used to analyze ordinal or nominal data. In this chapter, we have covered the fundamentals of nonparametric tests in applied linguistics research and also discussed some of the most commonly used nonparametric tests, including the Wilcoxon signed-rank test, the Mann–Whitney U test, the Kruskal–Wallis test, and the Friedman test, as well as their underlying assumptions, appropriate use, and interpretation. The chapter also provided hypothetical examples of research questions that can be addressed using nonparametric tests, along with instructions for conducting such tests using SPSS. We hope that the chapter has provided you with a good understanding of what nonparametric tests are and their role and use in applied linguistics research.

DISCUSSION AND ACTIVITY QUESTIONS

Discussion Questions

1. In what types of applied linguistics research situations might nonparametric tests be more appropriate than parametric tests? Can you provide specific examples?
2. What assumptions do nonparametric tests make about the data, and why is it important to assess whether these assumptions are met before applying them?
3. What are some limitations or potential drawbacks of nonparametric tests, and how can you address them?

4. How does the Kruskal–Wallis test differ from the Wilcoxon signed-rank test? Can you give some specific examples of research questions that can be addressed using each of them?

5. In what situations would you use the Friedman test, and why? How does this test differ from other nonparametric tests, such as the Mann–Whitney U test and the Kruskal–Wallis test?

6. How does the chi-square test differ from the t-test and ANOVA in terms of the types of data they analyze, their assumptions, and the research questions they address?

7. What are some alternatives to the Pearson correlation in applied linguistics research? What are the advantages and disadvantages of using nonparametric correlation to analyze your data?

Activity Questions

1. Consider a research question that can be addressed using a nonparametric test. Which nonparametric test would you use for your research question, and why?

2. Conduct a literature search to find two examples of applied linguistics research that have used two different types of nonparametric tests. Identify the types of test and discuss why the studies have used them and why.

3. Create a fictitious dataset with two independent groups, then practice conducting a Mann–Whitney U test using your sample dataset in SPSS. Report the findings to the class.

4. Compare and contrast the results obtained from a nonparametric test (e.g., the related-samples Wilcoxon signed-rank test) and the equivalent parametric test (e.g., a paired-samples t-test) using a sample dataset that you may have, using SPSS. Are the results different? If so, what are the implications of these differences for interpreting the results?

5. Use a sample dataset and conduct a correlation analysis using the Spearman's rank correlation in SPSS. Do the same analysis using the Pearson correlation. Are the results different? If so, what are the implications of these differences for interpreting the results?

6. Analyze a research article in applied linguistics that has used a nonparametric test. What were the research questions, why was that test used, and were the results interpreted and reported accurately and clearly?

Advanced Statistical Models: GLMs, Mixed Models, and Multivariate Analysis

Introduction

In our discussion so far, we have explored traditional parametric and nonparametric tests. As noted earlier, parametric tests make specific assumptions about the parameters of the population distribution from which the samples are drawn. These tests, such as *t*-tests, ANOVA, and regression models, are powerful tools when their assumptions, normality and homogeneity of variances, for example, are met. However, in real-world data, these assumptions are not always satisfied. Violations of these assumptions can lead to inaccurate results and compromised validity of the findings.

To address the limitations of parametric tests, researchers may turn to nonparametric tests, such as the Mann–Whitney U test, the Wilcoxon signed-rank test, the Kruskal–Wallis test, and the Spearman's rank correlation. Nonparametric tests do not assume a specific population distribution, making them more flexible and robust in the face of assumption violations. They are particularly useful when dealing with ordinal data, small sample sizes, or data that are skewed or have outliers.

However, this flexibility comes with its own set of drawbacks. As previously mentioned, nonparametric tests often have less statistical power compared to their parametric counterparts, meaning they may be less likely to detect true effects when they exist. Additionally, nonparametric tests can be less informative, providing fewer insights into the nature and strength of the relationships between variables. Moreover, nonparametric tests may struggle to handle complex data structures, such as those involving multiple predictors, interactions, or hierarchical nesting. They generally do not allow for the inclusion of random effects, which limits their ability to model data with grouped or clustered structures effectively.

This chapter discusses advanced statistical methods that go beyond the limitations of traditional parametric and nonparametric tests. It introduces generalized linear models (GLMs) and mixed effects models, including generalized linear mixed models (GLMMs), which are powerful tools for analyzing data with complex structures. GLMMs broaden the scope of parametric analysis by incorporating both fixed and random effects, allowing us to account for both the fixed effects of predictors and the random effects of grouping factors, such as subjects or items. This makes GLMMs particularly useful for dealing with complex hierarchical data structures commonly found in applied linguistics research.

In addition, the chapter briefly introduces advanced multivariate tests, such as factor analysis, path analysis, and structural equation modeling (SEM), as well as the Bayesian approach. However, we will only provide a brief overview to highlight their potential applications and significance in applied linguistics research without going into detail about these methods.

POINTS TO PONDER

As we move beyond traditional parametric tests such as *t*-tests and ANOVAs, are you familiar with generalized linear models (GLMs)? Can you explain what they are, and why they might be useful in applied linguistics research?

Generalized Linear Models (GLMs)

The generalized linear model (GLM) is an extension of the general linear model that includes univariate tests such as ANOVA as well as multivariate and repeated measures tests.

ANOVA, for example, falls under the broader category of general linear models (not to be confused with generalized linear models). As noted earlier, ANOVA is limited to normally distributed response variables with equal variances. GLMs, however, can handle situations where the assumptions of ANOVA are not met, such as when the data are skewed or variances are unequal across groups. They can also be used with other data types, allowing us to use different link functions to model nonlinear relationships between predictors and response variables. For example, we could use a logistic regression model for binary data (e.g., pass/fail) or a Poisson regression model for count data (e.g., the number of errors). Furthermore, GLMs enable the inclusion of multiple covariates and interaction terms, offering a more comprehensive analysis of the factors influencing writing performance (see Table 22.1 for the GLMs characteristics).

Table 22.1 Characteristics of generalized linear models

Characteristic	Description
Test	Generalized linear model
Type of test	Parametric
Assumptions	Linearity of the link function, independence
Purpose	To predict a dependent variable based on independent variable(s)
Dependent variable	One or more continuous or categorical variables
Independent variables	Can be continuous, binary, count, or categorical, depending on the link function used

Generalized linear models (GLMs) are statistical models that can handle various types of data, including data that do not follow a normal distribution.

Commonly used statistical models within the GLM framework include:

- linear regression for outcomes that follow a normal distribution
- logistic regression for binary outcomes (yes/no responses)
- loglinear models for count data (how many times something happens).

EXAMPLE 22.1

Suppose you aim to investigate the factors that influence the writing scores of ESL students. You collect data from a sample of forty students, including their writing scores and various predictors such as the number of hours spent on writing practice per week, the type of feedback received (direct, indirect, or metalinguistic), the students' first language, and their motivation levels. The research question is which factors contribute the most to ESL students' writing scores.

For the above scenario, let's assume the writing scores are positively skewed. In this case a GLM with a gamma distribution and a log link function would be appropriate for modeling the writing scores. SPSS Steps 22.1 shows the procedure to perform the analysis in SPSS. The variables used are Writing Score (dependent variable), Feedback Types and First Language (factors), and Hours of Practice and Motivation Level (covariates).

SPSS STEPS 22.1

- Open data in SPSS.
- Select "Analyze" > "Generalized Linear Models" > "Generalized Linear Models."
- In the dialog box, choose "Type of Model" and select "Gamma with log link" as the distribution and link function.
- Under the "Response" tab, Choose the dependent variable (e.g., Writing Score).
- Under the "Predictors" tab, specify "Factors" (e.g., Feedback Type and First Language) and "Covariates" (e.g., Hours of Practice and Motivation Level).
- Under the "Model" tap, move all the specified variables (Factors and Covariates) to the "Model" box and choose "Factorial" as the model type.
- Click on the "ES Means" tap, select the relevant variables and move them to the "Display Means for" box. Choose "Pairwise" under "Contrast".
- Click "Ok."

In the SPSS procedure, under the "Type of Model" tab, when selecting "Scale Response," choosing "Linear" assumes a normal distribution with the link function set to "Identity." Other scale responses can be selected depending on the data type. For example, selecting "Gamma with log link" specifies gamma as the distribution and log as the link function.

In the "Response" tab, if the dependent variable is binary (i.e., takes only two values), you can specify the reference category for parameter estimation. A binary response variable can be either string or numeric.

In the "Predictors" tab, you should select the factors and covariates that will be used to predict the dependent variable. Factors are categorical predictors, while covariates are numeric predictors.

In the "Model" tab, you can specify model effects involving the selected factors and covariates. Options include main effects, interaction, factorial, all 2-way, all 3-way, all 4-way, and all 5-way interactions.

There are also advanced options under additional tabs such as "Estimation," "Statistics," and "EM Means." For simplicity, we only used "EM Means" in our example and did not use the other options.

The analysis generates several tables, some of which are particularly important. For example, it generates a table including various measures of goodness-of-fit statistics (SPSS Output 22.1). In this table, "Deviance" refers to a measure of how well the model fits the data. A lower deviance value indicates a better fit. The value (5.526) divided by degrees of freedom (Value/df) is 0.173, which suggests a good fit

(Values less than 1 are usually considered indicative of a good fit). The Pearson chi-square statistic is another measure of goodness of fit. It measures the discrepancy between the observed and expected values. The value (6.214) divided by degrees of freedom (Value/df) is 0.194, indicating a good fit as it is less than 1. Overall, these statistics suggest that the model fits the data well, with minimal discrepancy between the model's predictions and the observed data.

SPSS OUTPUT 22.1

Goodness of Fit[a]

	Value	df	Value/df
Deviance	5.526	32	.173
Scaled Deviance	40.899	32	
Pearson Chi-Square	6.214	32	.194
Scaled Pearson Chi-Square	45.990	32	
Log Likelihood[b]	−104.884		
Akaike's Information Criterion (AIC)	227.767		
Finite Sample Corrected AIC (AICC)	233.767		
Bayesian Information Criterion (BIC)	242.967		
Consistent AIC (CAIC)	251.967		

Dependent Variable: Writing_Score

Model: (Intercept), Feedback_Type, First_Language, Hours_Practice, Motivation_Level

a. Information criteria are in smaller-is-better form.

b. The full log likelihood function is displayed and used in computing information criteria.

SPSS OUTPUT 22.2

Omnibus Test[a]

Likelihood Ratio Chi-Square	df	Sig.
14.789	7	.039

Dependent Variable: Writing_Score

Model: (Intercept), Feedback_Type, First_Language, Hours_Practice, Motivation_Level

a. Compares the fitted model against the intercept-only model.

The omnibus test table (SPSS Output 22.2) provides information about the overall fit of the model by comparing the fitted model to an intercept-only model. The significance level (p value) indicates the probability of observing a chi-square value as extreme as, or more extreme than, the value observed under the null hypothesis that the model with predictors does not provide a better fit than the intercept-only model. The p value is less than 0.05, indicating that the model with predictors (feedback type, first language, hours of practice, and motivation level) fits the data significantly better than the intercept-only model.

SPSS OUTPUT 22.3

	Tests of Model Effects		
		Type III	
Source	Wald Chi-Square	df	Sig.
(Intercept)	84.585	1	.000
Feedback_Type	6.642	2	.036
First_Language	8.617	3	.035
Hours_Practice	9.879	1	.002
Motivation_Level	2.071	1	.150

Dependent Variable: Writing_Score
Model: (Intercept), Feedback_Type, First_Language, Hours_Practice, Motivation_Level

---

The tests of model effects table (SPSS Output 22.3) provides information on the significance of each predictor variable in the model. The table indicates that feedback type, first language, and hours of practice are significant predictors of ESL students' writing scores, while motivation level is not.

The parameter estimates (SPSS Output 22.4) table provides detailed information about the regression coefficients for each predictor in the model, including their standard errors, confidence intervals, and significance levels. The intercept represents the expected value of the writing score when all predictors are at their reference levels. It is significant ($p < .001$), indicating that the baseline writing score is significantly different from zero.

The metalinguistic feedback is the reference category for feedback type, so its B value is set to zero and not directly estimated in the model. The coefficient for direct feedback is not statistically significant at the 0.05 level ($p = .083$). This suggests that direct feedback does not have a strong effect on writing score compared to the reference category (metalinguistic feedback). Compared to metalinguistic feedback (reference category), direct feedback is associated with a decrease in the writing score by 0.273 units.

The coefficient for indirect feedback is statistically significant ($p = .011$), indicating that indirect feedback is associated with a significantly lower writing score compared to metalinguistic feedback. The coefficient B value shows that compared to metalinguistic feedback, indirect feedback is associated with a decrease in the writing score by 0.400 units.

SPSS OUTPUT 22.4

			95% Wald Confidence Interval		Hypothesis Test		
Parameter	B	Std. Error	Lower	Upper	Wald Chi-Square	df	Sig.
(Intercept)	2.377	.2629	1.862	2.893	81.789	1	.000
[Feedback_Type =Direct]	−.273	.1574	−.581	.036	3.008	1	.083
[Feedback_Type =Indirect]	−.400	.1570	−.708	−.092	6.486	1	.011
[Feedback_Type =Metalinguistic]	0[a]	.	.	.	.	.	.
[First_Language=Arabic]	−.346	.1825	−.704	.011	3.607	1	.058
[First_Language=Chinese]	−.169	.2186	−.597	.260	.596	1	.440
[First_Language=Other]	.108	.1643	−.214	.430	.428	1	.513
[First_Language=Spanish]	0[a]	.	.	.	.	.	.
Hours_Practice	.077	.0246	.029	.126	9.879	1	.002
Motivation_Level	−.083	.0578	−.196	.030	2.071	1	.150
(Scale)	.135[b]	.0296	.088	.207			

Parameter Estimates

Dependent Variable: Writing_Score

Model: (Intercept), Feedback_Type, First_Language, Hours_Practice, Motivation_Level

a. Set to zero because this parameter is redundant.

b. Maximum likelihood estimate.

Spanish is the reference category for first language, so its coefficient value is set to zero and is not directly estimated in the model. Compared to Spanish (reference category), having Arabic as a first language is associated with a decrease in the writing score by 0.346 units. This effect is marginally significant ($p = .058$). The coefficient for Chinese as a first language is not statistically significant ($p = .440$), indicating no strong effect on writing score. Having Chinese as a first language is associated with a decrease in the writing score by 0.169 units. Having a first language other than Arabic, Chinese, or Spanish is associated with an increase in the writing score by 0.108 units. This effect is not statistically significant ($p = .513$).

The coefficient for hours of practice is positive and statistically significant ($p = .002$), indicating that more hours of practice are associated with higher writing scores. For each additional hour of practice, the writing score is expected to increase by 0.077 units.

For each one-unit increase in motivation level, the writing score is expected to decrease by 0.083 units. This effect is not statistically significant ($p = .150$).

Please note that when conducting a GLM in SPSS, the reference category for categorical variables is automatically assigned based on the variable's coding scheme, such as by alphabetical order or by the first/last category in the dataset. However, you can change the reference category by either recoding the variable or adjusting the settings within the GLM procedure. For example, when selecting your categorical predictor(s) under the "Predictors" tap, you can click "Options" and change the category order by selecting either "Ascending" or "Descending," which affects the default reference category.

SPSS OUTPUT 22.5

		Pairwise Comparisons						
		Mean Difference	Std.			95% Wald Confidence Interval for Difference	
(I) Feedback_Type	(J) Feedback_Type	(I-J)	Error	df	Sig.	Lower	Upper
Direct	Indirect	1.08	1.27	1	.397	−1.42	3.58
	Metalinguistic	−2.84	1.67	1	.089	−6.12	.44
Indirect	Direct	−1.08	1.27	1	.397	−3.58	1.42
	Metalinguistic	−3.92[a]	1.61	1	.015	−7.08	−.75
Metalinguistic	Direct	2.84	1.67	1	.089	−.44	6.12
	Indirect	3.92[a]	1.61	1	.015	.75	7.08

Pairwise comparisons of estimated marginal means based on the original scale of dependent variable Writing_Score

a. The mean difference is significant at the .05 level.

The pairwise comparisons table (SPSS Output 22.5) compares the mean of writing scores between different types of feedback. The table provides the mean differences, standard errors, significance levels (p values), and confidence intervals for these comparisons. The comparisons are as follows:

- Metalinguistic vs. indirect feedback: This is significant, with metalinguistic feedback leading to significantly higher writing scores.
- Direct vs. indirect feedback: This is not significant.
- Direct vs. metalinguistic feedback: This is marginally significant.

SPSS OUTPUT 22.6

Pairwise Comparisons

(I) First_Language	(J) First_Language	Mean Difference (I–J)	Std. Error	df	Sig.	95% Wald Confidence Interval for Difference	
						Lower	Upper
Arabic	Chinese	−1.45	1.71	1	.397	−4.79	1.90
	Other	−4.28[a]	1.52	1	.005	−7.25	−1.30
	Spanish	−3.08	1.70	1	.070	−6.42	.26
Chinese	Arabic	1.45	1.71	1	.397	−1.90	4.79
	Other	−2.83	1.89	1	.135	−6.54	.89
	Spanish	−1.63	2.10	1	.436	−5.74	2.48
Other	Arabic	4.28[a]	1.52	1	.005	1.30	7.25
	Chinese	2.83	1.89	1	.135	−.89	6.54
	Spanish	1.19	1.80	1	.507	−2.33	4.72
Spanish	Arabic	3.08	1.70	1	.070	−.26	6.42
	Chinese	1.63	2.10	1	.436	−2.48	5.74
	Other	−1.19	1.80	1	.507	−4.72	2.33

Pairwise comparisons of estimated marginal means based on the original scale of dependent variable Writing_Score

a. The mean difference is significant at the .05 level.

The pairwise comparisons table (SPSS Output 22.6) presents the differences in mean of writing scores between different first languages (Arabic, Chinese, other, and Spanish). Arabic vs. other is significant, with Arabic speakers having significantly lower writing scores compared to speakers of other languages. There are no statistically significant differences between Arabic and Chinese, Arabic and Spanish, Chinese and other, Chinese and Spanish, and Spanish and other.

Linear Mixed Models

In cases where the data have complex structures, such as repeated measures or hierarchical data, mixed models offer an advanced solution to GLMs. These models, which include both linear mixed models (LMMs) and generalized linear mixed models (GLMMs), extend GLMs by incorporating both fixed and random effects, allowing for more complex analyses.

The LMMs procedure extends the general linear models by letting the unpredictable parts of the data (the errors) and certain random factors vary, while handling both correlated and nonconstant variability. Correlated variability means that the variations or changes in one part of the data are related to variations in another part. For example, if the errors (unpredictable parts) in one set of observations are similar to the errors in another set, they are correlated. It is like saying that if one student does better on one test, they are likely to do better on another test as well. Nonconstant variability means that the amount of variation is not the same across all data points. In some parts of the data, the values might vary a lot, while in other parts, they might vary very little. For example, the performance of students might vary more at the beginning of the school year and less at the end.

Linear mixed models (LMMs) extend traditional linear models by including both fixed effects and random effects, making them suitable for analyzing data with complex structures.

LMMs are appropriate when the dependent variable is continuous, and the residuals from the model (the differences between the observed and predicted values) are normally distributed. However, although LMMs rely on the assumption of normally distributed residuals, they are also relatively robust to violations of normality when the sample sizes are large (see Table 22.2 for the characteristics of LMMs).

LMMs use both fixed-effects and random-effects factors. Therefore, they provide a more nuanced and flexible analysis of the data. Fixed-effects factors represent specific categories we are interested in and want to study directly. Hence, we measure them deliberately. For example, suppose you are interested in examining the effect of two teaching methods (grammar-translation method and communicative language teaching) on students' test scores. If you treat "teaching method" as a fixed effect, you are interested in the difference in test scores between these two specific methods, assuming that these methods represent the entire population of

Table 22.2 Characteristics of linear mixed models

Characteristic	Description
Test	Linear mixed model
Type of test	Parametric
Assumptions	Linearity, normality of residuals, independence of observations
Purpose	To examine the relationship between dependent and independent variables while accounting for both fixed and random effects
Dependent variable	One continuous variable
Independent variables	One or more continuous, binary, or categorical variables; includes both fixed and random effects

interest or are the only methods of concern for the study. Fixed effects are not intended to generalize beyond the levels included in the analysis. For example, when "teaching methods" are treated as "fixed effects," the goal is not to generalize findings to all possible teaching methods but rather to compare the effects of the specific methods under study (e.g., grammar translation and communicative language teaching). In this case, we are interested in the differences between these particular methods, and they are considered to fully represent the conditions we care about.

Random effects, on the other hand, represent broader categories with inherent random variability. They include levels that are just a sample from a larger population or are one of many possible levels that could exist. These effects are used when they are not of primary interest, but their influence needs to be controlled. For instance, if your study involves multiple classrooms or schools, and you believe differences between them are random and not the focus of your research, you will treat "classroom" or "school" as a random effect. This approach accounts for variability between classrooms or schools without emphasizing their specific differences. By treating these factors as random, the findings can generalize to other classrooms or schools beyond those included in the study.

Using linear models such as ANOVA, we might also infer general trends. However, the variability within the levels of the independent variable is not statistically modeled, and generalization is assumed rather than justified by the model. For instance, if you test two teaching methods across several classrooms in a simple ANOVA and one method leads to better test scores, you might infer that the method is effective more broadly. However, this generalization is based on the representativeness of the sample, not on the statistical model itself. In this situation, if the classrooms in your study happen to differ substantially in ways that are not representative of the broader population, generalizing the findings becomes problematic.

Fixed-effects factors represent specific categories we are interested in and want to study directly. **Random effects,** on the other hand, represent broader categories with inherent random variability. They are used when the specific levels are not of primary interest, but their influence needs to be controlled.

Example 22.2 gives a hypothetical scenario where a linear mixed model would be appropriate.

It is important to note that the assumption of normally distributed residuals is central to the validity of the linear mixed model. In our example study, it is assumed that the residuals from the model (the differences between observed and predicted values) follow a normal distribution.

EXAMPLE 22.2

Suppose you are studying the effect of different interactional contexts on the pragmatic performance of intermediate-level English L2 learners, with a particular focus on how learners perform in various settings such as formal meetings, casual conversations, and academic discussions. You are also interested in exploring whether exposure to the target language influences this relationship. To address these research questions, you employ a linear mixed model (LMM) to account for both fixed and random effects. To carry out this study, you recruit a sample of thirty-six intermediate-level English L2 learners from four different language schools. The sample includes an equal number of learners with different amounts of exposure to English: high-exposure (eighteen participants who have lived in an English-speaking country for over six months) and low exposure (eighteen participants who have little to no experience in English-speaking environments). The participants are then divided into three groups, with a balanced distribution of exposure to the target language within each group (six participants from each exposure group in every group). Each group is exposed to one type of interactional context: one group experiences formal meetings, another group engages in casual conversations, and the third group participates in academic discussions. The assessment is conducted through a series of role-play activities, resulting in one overall score for each student that reflects their pragmatic competence in the particular speech act in the given context.

By treating Interactional Context and Exposure Level as fixed effects, and Language School as random effects, the linear mixed model approach enables you to examine the overall effects of Interactional Context and Exposure Level on the dependent variable while accounting for the variability associated with differences among language schools.

To analyze the data, we can use an LMM, in which type of interactional context (formal meetings, casual conversations, academic discussions) and exposure levels (high, low) will be considered as fixed effects, and language schools will be considered as random. By including language schools as a random-effect factor, the LMM will account for the fact that student performance might vary from school to school due to factors unique to each school. The model provides estimates of the variance associated with this random factor, helping to explain why outcomes might differ across different groups beyond the fixed effects.

Please note that if your focus is solely on the specific four language schools you have chosen and you do not intend to extend your findings to other schools, you can treat "Language School" as a fixed effect. However, if your goal is to account for the variability among schools in general, rather than just the differences among these particular four schools, you can treat "Language School" as a random effect.

SPSS Steps 22.2 shows the procedure, using the following variables: Pragmatic Score (dependent variable), Exposure Level and Interactional Context (fixed factors), and Language School (random factor).

SPSS STEPS 22.2

- Open data file in SPSS.
- Select "Analyze" > "Mixed Models" > "Linear."
- Leave the subjects list box empty > "Continue," as we do not consider having any correlated random effects. Specify the random effects factors in the Random Effects dialog box.
- Select the dependent variable (e.g., Pragmatic Score) and move it to the "Dependent Variable" box.
- Select "Exposure level", "Language School" and "Interactional Context" and move them to the "Factor(s)" box.
- Click "Fixed" and select "Exposure Level" and "Interactional Context" from the "Factors and Covariates" list > "Add" > "Continue." We then choose "Main Effects" for simplicity.
- Click "Random," select "Language School" from the "Factors and Covariates list" > "Add" > "Continue."
- Click "Statistics," select "Parameter estimates for fixed effects", "Tests for covariance parameters," and "Covariances of random effects" > "Continue."
- Click "EM Means," select "Overall", "Exposure Level", and "Interactional Context" and move them to "Display Means for" box.
- Select "Compare main effects" > "Bonferroni" > "Continue" > "OK."

SPSS generates a number of outputs. Some of the most important ones are as follows.

SPSS OUTPUT 22.7

		Number of Levels	Covariance Structure	Number of Parameters
Fixed Effects	Intercept	1		1
	Exposure_Level	2		1
	Interactional_Context	3		2
Random Effects	Language_School	4	Variance Components	1
Residual				1
Total		10		6

Model Dimension[a]

a. Dependent Variable: Pragmatic Score.

SPSS Output 22.7 summarizes the chosen model. It details the number of levels and parameters for each effect in the model. For random effects, it also specifies the covariance structure.

SPSS OUTPUT 22.8

Type III Tests of Fixed Effects[a]				
Source	Numerator df	Denominator df	F	Sig.
Intercept	1	3.00	1618.53	.000
Exposure_Level	1	31.24	.37	.548
Interactional_Context	2	29.09	7.07	.003

a. Dependent Variable: Pragmatic Score.

SPSS Output 22.8 is an important table. It presents F tests for each fixed effect included in the model. Significance values below 0.05 suggest that the effect significantly contributes to the model. In our hypothetical data, the effect of interactional context is statistically significant, but that of exposure level is not.

SPSS OUTPUT 22.9

Estimates of Fixed Effects[a]						95% Confidence Interval	
Parameter	Estimate	Std. Error	df	t	Sig.	Lower Bound	Upper Bound
Intercept	79.26	2.79	12.25	28.46	.000	73.21	85.32
[Exposure_Level=High]	1.48	2.43	31.24	.61	.55	−3.48	6.44
Exposure_Level=Low	.00[b]	.00	.	.	.	.	.
[Interactional_Context= Academic Discussion]	−3.00	2.88	29.09	−1.04	.31	−8.88	2.88
[Interactional_Context= Casual Conversation]	−10.50	2.88	29.09	−3.65	.00	−16.38	−4.62
[Interactional_Context= Formal Meeting]	0[b]	0	.	.	.	.	.

a. Dependent Variable: Pragmatic Score.
b. This parameter is set to zero because it is redundant.

SPSS Output 22.9 provides estimates of the fixed effects and tests their significance. The estimate (79.26) is the baseline pragmatic score when all other predictors are at their reference levels (i.e., for low-exposure group in a formal meeting context). The significance level shows that the intercept is significant.

The table also represents the reference categories, which in this case includes the second level of "Exposure Level" (low) and the third level of "Interactional Context" (formal meeting). Consequently, the estimate for high exposure is compared to low exposure and the estimates for the first two levels of "Interactional Context" are compared to the third level (formal meeting). For exposure level, there is not a statistically significant difference between high- and low-exposure groups. High-exposure participants have a pragmatic score that is, on average, 1.48 points higher than low-exposure groups, holding all other factors constant. But the difference is not statistically significant.

For "Interactional Context," the estimates show that "Academic Discussion" and "Casual Conversation" have significantly different effects compared to "Formal Meeting." Participants in academic discussions scored 3.00 points lower on average compared to those in formal meetings (baseline). But this difference is not statistically significant ($p = .31$) Participants in the casual conversation group scored, on average, 10.5 points lower than those in a formal-meeting context, holding all other factors constant, and this difference is statistically significant ($p < .001$). Therefore, "formal meeting" appears to be the most favorable context for higher pragmatic scores, although academic discussions appear to be closer in effect, though not significantly different, compared to casual conversation, which is associated with significantly lower scores.

SPSS OUTPUT 22.10

Estimates of Covariance Parameters[a]

Parameter		Estimate	Std. Error	Wald Z	Sig.	95% Confidence Interval Lower Bound	95% Confidence Interval Upper Bound
Residual		49.64	13.02	3.81	.000	29.69	82.98
Language_School	Variance	8.57	11.59	.74	.46	.61	121.34

a. Dependent Variable: Pragmatic Score.

SPSS Output 22.10 presents the estimates for the random effects (covariance parameters) in the model, specifically focusing on the residual variance and the variance associated with language schools. The residual variance is 49.64 and is statistically significant (p < .001), This indicates a substantial amount of variability in scores not accounted for by the model. For the variance associated with language schools, the estimate is 8.57 with a wide confidence interval (0.61 to 121.34), reflecting considerable uncertainty. The p value indicates that the variance due to differences between language schools is not statistically significant, suggesting that the differences between schools are unlikely to explain the variability in pragmatic scores.

SPSS OUTPUT 22.11

Pairwise Comparisons[a]

(I) Exposure_ Level	(J) Exposure_ Level	Mean Difference (I-J)	Std. Error	df	Sig.[b]	95% Confidence Interval for Difference[b]	
						Lower Bound	Upper Bound
High	Low	1.48	2.43	31.24	.55	−3.48	6.44
Low	High	−1.48	2.43	31.24	.55	−6.44	3.48

Based on estimated marginal means.
a. Dependent Variable: Pragmatic Score.
b. Adjustment for multiple comparisons: Bonferroni.

SPSS Output 22.11 shows the pairwise comparison between high- and low-exposure participants, indicating that the difference is not statistically significant.

SPSS OUTPUT 22.12

Pairwise Comparisons[a]

(I) Interactional Context	(J) Interactional Context	Mean Difference (I-J)	Std. Error	df	Sig.[c]	95% Confidence Interval for Difference[c]	
						Lower Bound	Upper Bound
Academic Discussion	Casual Conversation	7.50*	2.88	29.09	.04	.19	14.81
	Formal Meeting	−3.00	2.88	29.09	.92	−10.31	4.31
Casual Conversation	Academic Discussion	−7.50*	2.88	29.09	.04	−14.81	−.19
	Formal Meeting	−10.50*	2.88	29.09	.00	−17.81	−3.19
Formal Meeting	Academic Discussion	3.00	2.88	29.09	.92	−4.31	10.31
	Casual Conversation	10.50*	2.88	29.09	.00	3.19	17.81

Based on estimated marginal means
*. The mean difference is significant at the .05 level.
a. Dependent Variable: Pragmatic Score.
c. Adjustment for multiple comparisons: Bonferroni.

SPSS Output 22.12 presents pairwise comparisons for different interactional contexts. It shows significant differences between "academic discussion" and "casual conversation" (with "academic discussion" having higher pragmatic scores than "casual conversation"), and between "casual conversation" and "formal meeting," (with "formal meeting" having higher pragmatic scores than "casual conversation," but no significant difference was found between "academic discussion" and "formal meeting."

POINTS TO PONDER

How confident are you in your ability to use GLMMs, which combine fixed and random effects?

Generalized Linear Mixed Model

Linear mixed models (LMMs), introduced earlier, are used when the response variable is continuous, and the residuals are assumed to be normally distributed. Generalized linear mixed models (GLMMs) are an extension of generalized linear models, which can handle continuous data, but they are also especially useful for response variables that follow other distributions, whether they are continuous or noncontinuous (see Table 22.3 for the characteristics of GLMMs).

A GLMM is a flexible statistical approach that extends the GLM by incorporating both fixed and random effects, allowing for the analysis of data with complex structures. Unlike traditional linear models, GLMMs can handle nonnormal response distributions (e.g., binary, count data) and account for correlations within grouped data, such as repeated measures or hierarchical data structures. This is achieved by including random effects, which introduce variability at different levels, such as individual differences or group-level variations, while fixed effects estimate the overall impact of predictor variables.

Another advantage of GLMMs is their ability to incorporate link functions, which provide a way to model relationships between the linear predictors and the expected value of the response variable, even when the relationship is not linear. For example, the logit link function is commonly used in logistic regression to model binary outcomes.

GLMMs are particularly useful in fields such as applied linguistics where researchers often deal with nested data and seek to understand how various factors interact and influence outcomes while accounting for inherent randomness and subject-specific variations. This versatility makes GLMMs a powerful tool for investigating complex research questions and drawing more generalized and robust conclusions from empirical data.

A generalized linear mixed model (GLMM) extends generalized linear models by incorporating both fixed and random effects, enabling the analysis of nonnormal data with complex, hierarchical, or nested structures.

Table 22.3 Characteristics of generalized linear mixed models

Characteristic	Description
Test	Generalized linear mixed model
Type of test	Parametric (can also include nonparametric elements depending on the model)
Assumptions	Distribution of the dependent variable (e.g., normal, binomial, Poisson), linearity of the link function, independence of observations
Purpose	To examine the relationship between dependent and independent variables while accounting for both fixed and random effects, with flexibility for different distributions for the dependent variable
Dependent variable	Can be continuous, binary, count, or categorical, depending on the chosen distribution and link function
Independent variables	Can be continuous, binary, count, or categorical; includes both fixed and random effects
Link function	A function that links the linear predictor to the distribution of the dependent variable (e.g., logit, log, identity)
Random effects	Used to account for variability between groups or subjects, providing a way to model nested or hierarchical data structures

EXAMPLE 22.3

Suppose you want to investigate how different types of pronunciation training (e.g., segmental vs. suprasegmental) affect the intelligibility of L2 learners over time, accounting for the variability due to individual differences and native language backgrounds. Participants are thirty L2 learners from various native language backgrounds. They are divided into three groups based on the type of pronunciation training received: segmental training group, suprasegmental training group, and control group (no specific pronunciation training). Intelligibility scores are measured using a standardized intelligibility test at three time points: pretest: before any training; posttest: immediately after training; delayed posttest: three months after training. Participants come from diverse native language backgrounds, which will be treated as a random effect to account for variability.

SPSS Steps 22.3 shows the procedure to follow. The variables are Participant ID, Time (repeated measure), Intelligibility Test Score (dependent variable), Group (fixed effect) and Native Language (random effect).

SPSS STEPS 22.3
- Open data file in SPSS.
- Select "Analyze" > "Mixed Models" > "Generalized Linear Mixed Models."
- Under "Data Structure," drag "Participant ID" to "Subjects" and "Time" to "Repeated Measures."

SPSS STEPS 22.3 (cont.)

- Under "Fields & Effects," use "Intelligibility Test Score" as the "Target" (dependent variable) and choose "Linear model" for Target distribution.
- Click "Fixed Effects" and drag "Group" and "Time" to the Fixed "Effect builder" box.
- Click "Random Effects, and then "Add Block." Then drag "Participant ID" and "Native Language" to the "Effect builder" box, and click "OK."
- Under "Build Options," if needed check "Use robust estimation if concerned about violations of model assumptions." Otherwise, leave the default setting as is.
- Under "Model Options," check "Estimate Means" for "Group" and "Time," and under "Contrast Type," select "Pairwise."
- Click "Run."

In our example, since we have repeated measures for each participant (pretest, posttest, delayed posttest), it is essential to account for within-subject correlation. This means that measurements from the same participant are likely to be more similar to each other than measurements from different participants. Therefore, we will include participant ID as a random effect to model this within-subject variability and obtain more accurate estimates of the fixed effects. Additionally, we suspect that there might be variability in intelligibility scores based on the native language of the participants, so we will include native language as a random effect. This will account for the potential influence of native language on intelligibility scores.

In the SPSS procedure, the "Target" refers to the dependent variable, which is the outcome or response variable you are trying to predict.

For target distribution, the following options are available:

- Linear model: Uses a normal distribution with an identity link, ideal for predicting outcomes with linear regression or ANOVA.
- Gamma regression: Uses a Gamma distribution with a log link, suited for predicting positive, skewed data.
- Loglinear: Uses a Poisson distribution with a log link, best for counting occurrences over a fixed time period.
- Negative binomial regression: Uses a negative binomial distribution with a log link, ideal for modeling overdispersed count data (where the variance exceeds the mean).
- Multinomial logistic regression: Uses a multinomial distribution, for predicting multicategory outcomes with cumulative logit (for ordinal) or generalized logit (for nominal) links.
- Binary logistic regression: Uses a binomial distribution with a logit link, for predicting binary outcomes in logistic regression.

- Binary probit: Uses a binomial distribution with a probit link, for binary outcomes with an underlying normal distribution.
- Interval censored survival: Uses survival distributions (e.g., Weibull, log-normal) with a complementary log–log link, useful for survival analysis when some data points have not yet experienced the event by the end of the study (right censoring).

For our analysis, given that the intelligibility test scores are continuous and likely to be normally distributed, we choose the "Linear" model. If a test of normality indicates that the intelligibility scores are not normally distributed and the scores are positive and skewed, we could use gamma regression instead.

The "Model Options" tab allows you to display the estimated marginal means for factor levels and their interactions.

SPSS generates a number of tables; some of the most important ones are shown in SPSS Outputs 22.13–22.19.

SPSS OUTPUT 22.13

Source	F	df1	df2	Sig.
Corrected Model	9.11	4	85	.000
Group	1.02	2	85	.366
Time	17.21	2	85	.000

Fixed Effects[a]

Probability distribution: Normal
Link function: Identity
a. Target: Intelligibility Score

The SPSS Output 22.13 presents the results of a fixed effects analysis for the data. The F value for the connected model is 9.11 ($p < 001$. This indicates that the overall model is statistically significant, meaning that the combination of factors (group and time) explains a significant portion of the variance in the intelligibility test scores. The F value for group is 1.02 with a p value of 0.366. This suggests that there is no significant difference between the groups in terms of intelligibility test scores. The F value for time is 17.21 ($p < .001$). This indicates a significant effect of time on intelligibility test scores, suggesting that scores change significantly over the different time points.

SPSS Output 22.14 shows these relationships schematically. The thicker line for time shows a greater effect of time than group.

SPSS OUTPUT 22.14

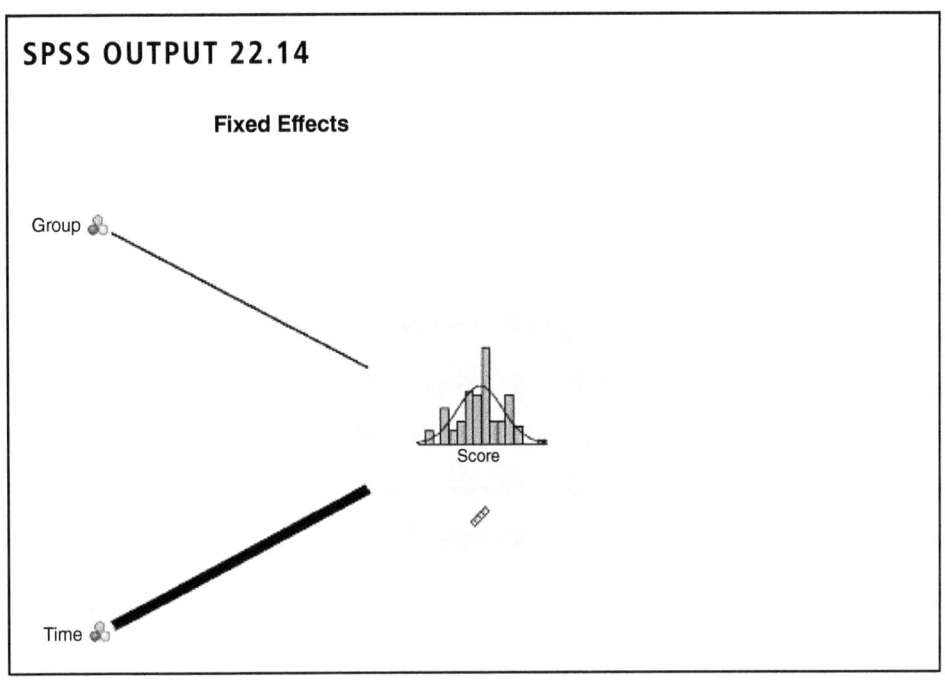

SPSS OUTPUT 22.15

Fixed Coefficients[a]						
					95% Confidence Interval	
Model Term	Coefficient	Std. Error	T	Sig.	Lower	Upper
Intercept	57.127	2.5851	22.099	.000	51.987	62.267
Group=1	2.818	2.8755	.980	.330	−2.899	8.535
Group=2	−.885	3.0189	−.293	.770	−6.887	5.117
Group=3	0[b]	.	.	.	.	.
Time=1	−7.394	1.5672	−4.718	.000	−10.510	−4.278
Time=2	−1.419	1.3109	−1.082	.282	−4.025	1.188
Time=3	0[b]	.	.	.	.	.

Probability distribution: Normal
Link function: Identity
a. Target: Intelligibility Score
b. This coefficient is set to zero because it is redundant.

SPSS Output 22.15 presents the results of the fixed effects analysis for group and time on the outcome variable, which is the intelligibility score, while controlling for the random effects (e.g., participant ID, and native language).

The intercept value (57.127) in the model represents the expected value of the dependent variable (intelligibility score) when all predictors are at their reference levels. The p value indicates that this is statistically significant ($p < .001$), meaning that the baseline level of the dependent variable (in this case, the intelligibility score) is significantly different from zero when all other predictors are at their reference levels.

Group 3 (segmental group) and Time 3 (delayed posttest) are the reference categories, so their coefficients are set to zero by definition. They serve as the baseline against which other group and time effects are compared.

The coefficient of being in the suprasegmental group (Group 1), compared to the reference group is 2.818. This indicates that Group 1's intelligibility score is 2.818 points higher than Group 3's, but the p value of 0.330 shows that this difference is not statistically significant.

The coefficient of Group 2 (Control group) is −0.885. This indicates that Group 2's intelligibility score is 0.885 points lower than Group 3's, but the p value of 0.770 shows that this difference is not statistically significant.

The coefficient of time = 1 (pretest), compared to the reference time point (time = 3 delayed posttest) is −7.394. This indicates that at Time 1, the intelligibility score is 7.394 points lower than at Time 3. The p value shows that this difference is statistically significant.

This coefficient of Time 2 (delayed posttest) is −1.419, indicating that at Time 2, the intelligibility score is 1.419 points lower than at Time 3, but the p value of 0.282 shows that the effect of Time = 2 compared to the reference time point (Time = 3, delayed posttest) is not significant. SPSS Output 22.16 shows the above relationships schematically.

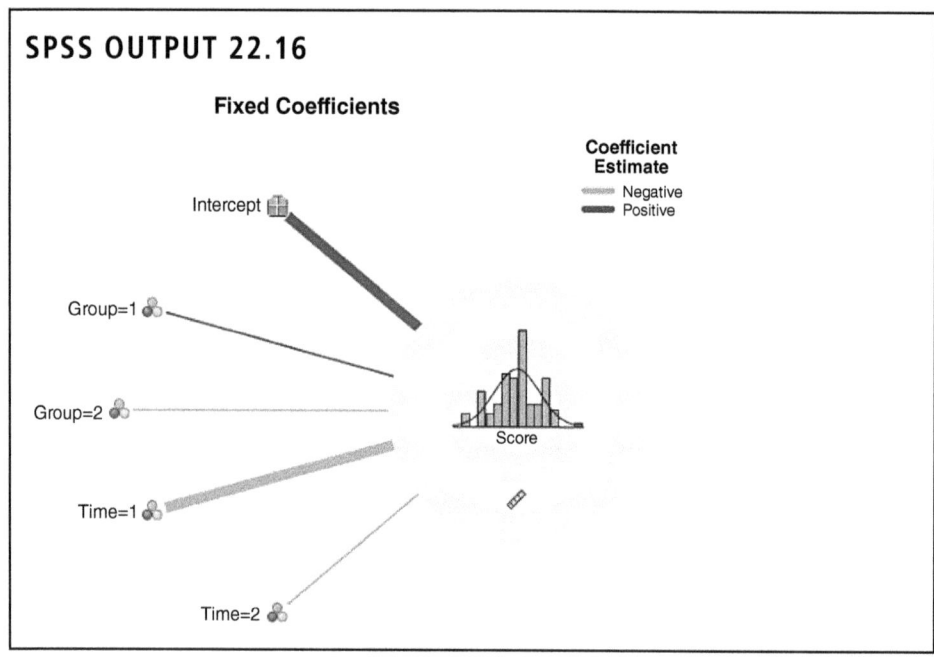

SPSS OUTPUT 22.16

Fixed Coefficients

SPSS OUTPUT 22.17

	Random Effect					
					95% Confidence Interval	
Random Effect Covariance	Estimate	Std. Error	Z	Sig.	Lower	Upper
Var (Participant ID)	34.057	11.149	3.055	.002	17.929	64.692
Var (Native)	1.834	5.677	.323	.747	.004	791.351

Covariance Structure: Variance components
Subject Specification: (None)

SPSS Output 22.17 presents the results of the random effects. Random effects account for variations that are not explained by the fixed effects, often representing subject-specific deviations.

The estimate for "Var (Participant ID)" is 34.057, indicating variability in intelligibility scores attributable to differences among participants. The standard error is 11.149, and the z value of 3.055 with a p value of 0.002 suggests that this variability is statistically significant. The confidence interval (17.929 to 64.692) shows that we can be 95% confident that the true variance lies within this range. Thus, some of the variance in the intelligibility scores can be attributed to differences among participants. The "Var (Native)" shows the variance attributed to the variable "native language." The nonsignificant p value (0.747), suggests that this source of variance is not statistically significant. In other words, the variance due to the "native language" variable does not contribute much to the overall variability in intelligibility scores.

SPSS OUTPUT 22.18

	Pairwise Contrasts						
						95% Confidence Interval	
Group Pairwise Contrasts	Contrast Estimate	Std. Error	t	df	Adj. Sig.	Lower	Upper
Suprasegmental - Control	3.704	2.736	1.354	85	.179	−1.737	9.145
Suprasegmental - Segmental	2.818	2.875	.980	85	.330	−2.898	8.534
Control - Suprasegmental	−3.704	2.736	−1.354	85	.179	−9.145	1.737
Control - Segmental	−.885	3.018	−.293	85	.770	−6.886	5.115
Segmental - Suprasegmental	−2.818	2.875	−.980	85	.330	−8.534	2.898
Segmental - Control	.886	3.018	.293	85	.770	−5.115	6.886

The least significant difference adjusted significance level is .05.

SPSS Output 22.18 presents the results of pairwise contrasts comparing the means of different groups. The comparisons are made between the control, segmental, and suprasegmental groups, with adjusted significance levels to account for multiple comparisons. As can be seen, none of the pairwise contrasts between the groups are statistically significant at the adjusted significance level of 0.05.

SPSS OUTPUT 22.19

Pairwise Contrasts

Time Pairwise Contrasts	Contrast Estimate	Std. Error	t	df	Adj. Sig.	95% Confidence Interval	
						Lower	Upper
1.00 – 2.00	−5.976	1.079	−5.537	85	.000	−8.121	−3.830
1.00 – 3.00	−7.394	1.567	−4.718	85	.000	−10.510	−4.278
2.00 – 1.00	5.976	1.079	5.537	85	.000	3.830	8.121
2.00 – 3.00	−1.419	1.311	−1.082	85	.282	−4.025	1.188
3.00 – 1.00	7.394	1.567	4.718	85	.000	4.278	10.510
3.00 – 2.00	1.419	1.311	1.082	85	.282	−1.188	4.025

The least significant difference adjusted significance level is .05.

SPSS Output 22.19 presents the results of pairwise contrasts comparing the means at different times. The comparisons are made between three time points (1 = pretest, 2 = posttest, and 3 = delayed posttest) with adjusted significance levels to account for multiple comparisons. Time 1 scores are significantly lower than both Time 2 and Time 3 scores. Time 2 scores are significantly higher than Time 1 scores. Time 3 scores are significantly higher than Time 1 scores.

POINTS TO PONDER

Do you know what factor analysis, path analysis, and structural equation modeling (SEM) are, and how they each contribute to analyzing complex relationships and structures in linguistic data?

Advanced Multivariate Techniques

Following our discussion of mixed effects models and generalized linear models, it is also important to know about techniques that allow for the examination of complex relationships among multiple variables simultaneously. Three of these advanced multivariate techniques are factor analysis, structural equation modeling

(SEM), and path analysis. These methods, which build upon the foundational concepts of correlation and regression analysis discussed earlier, offer powerful tools for understanding and modeling the underlying structures in your data. In this section, we will describe these methods very briefly; due to space limitations, we will not be able to show how to conduct these analyses. Readers are thus encouraged to consult other guides or resources available for learning how to do so. In this respect, some useful recourses include Tabachnick & Fidell (2018), Kline (2016), and Streiner (2005).

Factor Analysis

Factor analysis is a statistical method used to identify underlying relationships between variables. By examining the correlations among a set of observed variables, factor analysis seeks to uncover latent constructs, or factors, that explain these correlations. There are two types of factor analysis: exploratory factor analysis (EFA) and confirmatory factor analysis (CFA). EFA is used when the researcher does not have a priori hypotheses about the structure or number of factors. It helps identify the underlying factor structure by grouping correlated variables. CFA is employed when the researcher has specific hypotheses about the number of factors and their relationships with the observed variables. It is used to test the fit of the hypothesized factor structure to the observed data (see Example 22.4).

EXAMPLE 22.4

Suppose you want to understand the different dimensions of language learning motivation among university students. You collect survey data with various items measuring intrinsic motivation, extrinsic motivation, and language anxiety. Factor analysis is used to identify whether these survey items cluster into distinct factors that represent different aspects of motivation. The analysis might reveal that the items load onto factors corresponding to intrinsic motivation, extrinsic motivation, and anxiety, providing insights into the structure of language learning motivation.

Structural Equation Modeling (SEM)

Structural equation modeling (SEM) is a versatile statistical method used to simultaneously analyze relationships among multiple variables. Unlike single procedures, SEM is a family of techniques that combines principles of regression and factor analysis to examine both measurement properties and interrelationships. You can use SEM to test theoretical models by proposing relationships among variables and checking whether observed data support these hypotheses. It allows you to model multiple independent and dependent variables, error terms, interactions, and correlations, offering more robustness and flexibility than, for example, multiple regression. SEM begins with a theory where you intend to test the relationship among constructs of interest in the study. These relationships are modeled into a theoretical framework represented by a schematic diagram, which presents the hypotheses of interest to be tested in the study.

EXAMPLE 22.5

Suppose you hypothesize that language learning strategies, such as metacognitive and cognitive strategies, influence language proficiency through their effects on language use and engagement. You collect data on students' use of learning strategies, their language use patterns, and their language proficiency. Using SEM, you test a theoretical model where learning strategies directly affect language use, which in turn affects language proficiency. SEM allows you to assess the overall fit of the model and the strength of each path in the proposed relationships.

Path Analysis

Path analysis is a statistical technique used to examine the directed dependencies among a set of variables. It is an extension of multiple regression analysis and is part of the broader family of SEM. Path analysis allows you to specify and test complex models that involve multiple predictors and outcomes, including direct and indirect effects (see Example 22.6). While both path analysis and factor analysis are multivariate statistical techniques used in research to understand relationships among variables, they serve different purposes and have distinct methodological approaches. Path analysis is used to specify and test causal models, examining the direct and indirect relationships among a set of observed variables. Factor analysis is used to identify underlying latent variables (factors) that explain the patterns of correlations among observed variables. It reduces the dimensionality of the data by grouping related variables together.

EXAMPLE 22.6

Suppose you want to explore how classroom environment factors influence students' language acquisition. You hypothesize that classroom environment factors such as teacher support, classroom climate, and peer interactions have direct effects on students' language skills, and that these effects are mediated by students' engagement and participation. The proposed path model includes direct paths from teacher support, classroom climate, and peer interactions to students' language skills; and indirect paths, where teacher support, classroom climate, and peer interactions affect students' engagement and participation, which in turn influence language skills. Using path analysis, you specify and test this model to evaluate the direct and indirect effects of the classroom environment factors on language acquisition. The analysis provides insights into how different aspects of the classroom environment contribute to language learning outcomes, both directly and through their impact on student engagement.

POINTS TO PONDER

How could adopting Bayesian statistics change our approach to data interpretation in applied linguistics, and what advantages might this method offer in managing uncertainty and making inferences from complex datasets?

Bayesian Statistics

So far, we have covered the fundamental concepts and applications of parametric and nonparametric tests within the traditional frequentist framework. We explored various parametric tests, such as t-tests, ANOVA, and regression analysis, examining their assumptions, computations, and interpretations. Nonparametric tests, such as the Kruskal–Wallis test, were also discussed as part of the frequentist approach, offering alternatives for situations where parametric assumptions may not hold, such as with ordinal data or nonnormal distributions. Additionally, we provided a brief introduction to GLMs, LMMs, and GLMMs, all of which are commonly used within the frequentist approach. As noted, these models extend the traditional linear model framework and some of them handle a wider range of data types and structures, such as binary or count data, and account for hierarchical or nested data through random effects.

However, we have not yet discussed Bayesian statistics, despite its powerful and flexible tools for statistical inference. There are several reasons for this choice. Our goal has been establishing a solid foundation in common statistical tests, central to many applied linguistics analyses. Introducing both frequentist and Bayesian approaches in depth would extend beyond the scope of this book. Bayesian methods often require a deeper understanding of probability theory and can often be computationally intensive, which might overwhelm readers who are new to statistical analysis. Frequentist methods are more widely used and understood in various fields of applied research and thus provide a practical starting point for learners.

However, due to its importance, we briefly explain that Bayesian statistics is a branch of statistics where probability represents a degree of belief in an event. This approach incorporates prior knowledge or beliefs, along with new evidence or data, to update the probability of a hypothesis being true. The core idea is summarized by Bayes' theorem, which mathematically combines prior probability and likelihood to produce a posterior probability. Frequentist statistics, however, focuses on the frequency or proportion of data. Probabilities are long-run frequencies of events. Hypotheses are tested using data alone, without incorporating prior beliefs. Bayesian statistics uses probability to represent uncertainty in hypotheses.

Bayesian statistics differs from frequentist methods by incorporating prior beliefs and updating them with data, offering a more flexible approach to statistical inference.

In frequentist statistics, a p value represents the probability of obtaining results as extreme as those observed, assuming that the null hypothesis is true. Confidence intervals provide a range within which the parameter lies with a certain confidence level. In Bayesian statistics, posterior probabilities provide a direct measure of the likelihood of hypotheses. Credible intervals represent the range within which the parameter lies with a certain probability, given the data and prior knowledge. Frequentist statistics is generally simpler to apply and interpret, and widely used in traditional statistical testing. Bayesian statistics is more flexible and allows the incorporation of prior knowledge, but it is often computationally intensive and can be complex to apply. Readers interested in Bayesian statistics are encouraged to explore dedicated resources and advanced courses that specifically address Bayesian methods and their applications. Some useful resources include Gelman et al. (2013); Kruschke (2015), and Kurt (2019).

Conclusion

In this chapter, we have expanded our understanding of statistical models beyond the traditional parametric and nonparametric tests, exploring the flexibility and robustness of generalized linear models (GLMs) in applied linguistics research. We began by revisiting the assumptions and limitations of parametric and nonparametric tests, and how nonparametric alternatives, while useful, also come with their own constraints. As noted, GLMs provide a powerful solution to these challenges, allowing the analysis of data that do not adhere to the assumptions of those models. Additionally, we introduced linear mixed models (LMMs), which are used to analyze data involving both fixed and random effects. We also discussed generalized linear mixed models (GLMMs), which extend both GLMs and LMMs by allowing for a wider range of response variable distributions and link functions, thus accommodating nonnormal data and providing greater flexibility in modeling complex relationships. To this end, and to support practical application, we provided examples and step-by-step instructions for using SPSS to conduct such analyses. Finally, we touched upon more advanced multivariate tests, such as factor analysis, path analysis, and structural equation modeling (SEM), as well as the Bayesian approach. While we highlighted their potential applications and significance, due to space limitations, we did not cover them in detail. We encourage readers to explore these topics further through additional reading and study to fully grasp their complexities and applications.

DISCUSSION AND ACTIVITY QUESTIONS

Discussion Questions

1. What are the key differences between traditional parametric tests and generalized linear models (GLMs)?
2. Can you provide examples of research scenarios in applied linguistics where GLMs would be more appropriate than traditional regression models?

3. What are the primary purposes of factor analysis, path analysis, and structural equation modeling (SEM) in applied linguistics research?
4. How do these advanced multivariate tests differ from GLMs and generalized linear mixed models (GLMMs) in terms of their application and objectives?
5. Discuss an applied linguistics research example where each of these advanced multivariate tests (factor analysis, path analysis, SEM) would be appropriate.
6. What are the fundamental differences between Bayesian statistics and traditional (frequentist) statistics?
7. Suppose you are conducting research on the impact of task-based language teaching (TBLT) on students' speaking proficiency and anxiety levels. Your study involves multiple classrooms across different schools, where you measure students' speaking proficiency and anxiety at three different points in time: before, during, and after the TBLT intervention. Additionally, you have collected data on various learner characteristics (e.g., age, motivation, language proficiency) and classroom-level factors (e.g., teacher experience, class size) that might influence the outcomes. You hypothesize that anxiety might mediate the relationship between the TBLT intervention and speaking proficiency, and that the effect of the intervention might differ across schools due to varying classroom-level factors. Given this scenario:
   a) Which of the following approaches would be most appropriate for analyzing your data: GLMM, factor analysis, or SEM?
   b) Explain your choice by considering the nature of the data, the research questions, and the relationships you want to investigate.

Activity Questions

1. Review a published applied linguistics study that uses a GLM or a GLMM. Summarize the study and critically evaluate the study in terms of the following questions:
   a) What were the main research questions and hypotheses of the study?
   b) How did the authors apply a GLM or a GLMM?
   c) What strengths and weaknesses can you identify in their approach and conclusions?
2. Analyze a hierarchical dataset (e.g., students nested within classrooms) using a GLMM in SPSS. Include both fixed and random effects in your model.
   a) What fixed and random effects did you include in your GLMM? Why?
   b) How does the inclusion of random effects impact the interpretation of your model?
   c) What conclusions can you draw about the hierarchical structure of your data from the GLMM results?
3. Using a provided dataset with a mix of continuous and categorical variables, perform three different types of analyses: a traditional linear regression, a GLM, and a GLMM. Compare the results and interpretations from each model.
   a) What were the main findings from each of the three models (linear regression, GLM, GLMM)?

        b) How did the choice of model affect the significance and interpretation of the predictors?

        c) Discuss the strengths and limitations of each modeling approach in the context of your dataset.

        d) Based on your results, which model do you believe is the most appropriate for your data and why?

4. Work in small groups to design a survey with thirty items that measure different aspects of language learning strategies (e.g., cognitive, metacognitive, social, affective) among ESL learners. Administer the survey to at least twenty participants (e.g., classmates or language learners) and organize the collected data into a well-labeled spreadsheet. Then, under your instructor's guidance, use factor analysis to identify underlying factors in the data. Then, examine the output and interpret the identified factors. Discuss how these factors align with existing theories of language learning strategies and explore their potential implications for teaching practices.

23 Effect Sizes: Types, Calculations, and Interpretation

> **CHAPTER OBJECTIVES**
>
> After completing this chapter, you should be able to
>
> - Understand the importance of effect sizes in applied linguistics research.
> - Identify and differentiate between different types of effect sizes commonly used in applied linguistics research, including Cohen's *d*, eta-squared, partial eta-squared.
> - Calculate and interpret different effect sizes.
> - Understand the use of odds and risk ratio as effect sizes in analyzing categorical data and learning how to calculate and interpret them.
> - Understand different correlation coefficients, including the Pearson product moment correlation coefficient, Spearman's rank correlation coefficient, Kendall's tau correlation coefficient, and the point-biserial correlation coefficient, and how to calculate and interpret them.

Introduction

In recent years, the importance of effect sizes has become increasingly recognized in the field of applied linguistics and second language research. The Publication Manual of the American Psychological Association (APA) has consistently emphasized the importance of the inclusion of effect sizes in quantitative research alongside significance levels, and consequently, many journals that publish applied linguistics and second language research now require or recommend that authors report them.

In this chapter, we will discuss the concept of effect sizes and their importance in quantitative research. We will explore different types of effect sizes commonly used in applied linguistics research, such as Cohen's *d*, Hedges's *g*, Glass's delta, eta-squared, partial eta-squared, the odds and risk ratios, the phi coefficient, and Cramer's *V*. We will also discuss the calculation and interpretation of these effect sizes. We will also discuss correlational effect sizes, such as the Pearson product moment correlation coefficient, Spearman's rank correlation coefficient, Kendall's tau correlation coefficient, the point-biserial correlation coefficient, and the coefficient of determination (R^2). We will present hypothetical examples to illustrate their application.

The Concept of Effect Size

Effect size is a statistical tool that provides a measure of the magnitude of an effect or relationship between variables. It shows the strength or the size of the effect of an experimental intervention or treatment. It is a standardized measure that provides an important piece of information in addition to the p value. Thus, it is an important measure as it allows researchers to determine if the difference or relationship is meaningful and has practical importance, rather than just being statistically significant.

Effect sizes are often used in combination with statistical significance, which is a measure of the probability that an effect or difference is not due to chance, and is usually determined by comparing the resulting p value of a statistical test to a preset significance level (e.g., 0.05). If the p value is equal to or less than the set significance level, the result is considered to be statistically significant. However, statistical significance does not tell us anything about how important the results are or what the size of the effect is. It simply tells us whether there is a difference or an effect, but not how large it is. Effect size is an index that shows the size of the effect or the magnitude of the relationship between variables.

For instance, a study comparing two types of instruction might find that one has a statistically significant effect. However, if the effect size is small, it suggests that the strength of the effect is weak. Although the difference is statistically significant, it is not strong enough to be meaningful or impactful in practical settings.

Furthermore, statistical significance is a function of the sample size. With a very large sample size, even small effects can become statistically significant. Therefore, the notion of p value or statistical significance alone can be misleading. Effect sizes, however, provide standardised measures, and therefore they allow us to compare the results of different studies, irrespective of the sample size or the measurement scale used.

Effect size refers to the magnitude of an effect or relationship between variables.

POINTS TO PONDER

Have you used or encountered situations where effect sizes have been used? If so, how did this enhance your understanding of the research results?

Types of Effect Sizes

As noted above, effect sizes are essential tools in research as they help quantify the magnitude of a relationship or difference, making results more interpretable and comparable across studies. Understanding different types of effect sizes is important as it allows you to choose the appropriate effect-size measure in your analysis.

Effect sizes can be broadly classified into three categories: those used for comparing means (typically involving continuous variables, such as Cohen's *d*), those for examining relationships between categorical variables (such as odds ratios or chi-square effect sizes), and those for examining relationships between continuous variables (such as correlation coefficients or regression coefficients).

In the following sections, we will discuss the most common types of effect sizes, along with how to calculate them and how to interpret their magnitude.

POINTS TO PONDER

Are you familiar with any effect sizes? If so, can you describe their applications and interpretation?

Effect Sizes for Comparing Means

Effect sizes for comparing means are used to determine the magnitude of differences between the means of two or more groups, typically involving continuous variables. They can also be used for comparing within-group means, such as in the case of pre-post measurements or within-subject designs. In the following sections, we will discuss some of the most commonly used effect sizes for comparing means such as Cohen's *d*, Hedges's *g*, Glass's delta, eta-squared, partial eta-squared, and Cohen's *f*.

Cohen's *d*

Cohen's *d* is a statistical tool that measures the strength of an effect by calculating the difference between two means in terms of standard deviations. It indicates by how many standard deviations the means differ from each other. For example, a Cohen's *d* of 1 indicates that the means of the two groups differ by one standard deviation. Cohen's *d* is commonly used in applied linguistics research to assess the effect size of an intervention or treatment. It provides a standardized measure used in *t*-tests including the independent samples *t*-test and the paired-samples *t*-test. The higher the value of the measure, the bigger the difference between the means of the two groups or conditions.

Cohen's *d* measures the strength of an effect of two means by calculating the difference between two means in terms of standard deviations.

Calculation and Interpretation of Cohen's d Although statistical software such as SPSS can automatically calculate various effect sizes for statistical tests, it is still helpful to understand the formula and how they are calculated. Knowing the underlying formulas and calculations behind effect sizes can help you better understand the logic behind each and interpret and communicate the results more effectively. Therefore, in this and the sections that follow, we will provide the formulas for the common effect-size measures discussed, and we will also explain how SPSS can be used to calculate them.

As for Cohen's d, it can be calculated by dividing the difference between the means by the pooled standard deviation, which is the square root of the average of the variances of the two groups (Equation 23.1). The pooled standard deviation is more appropriate when the two groups have similar (i.e., not very different) standard deviations.

Equation 23.1
$$d = \frac{\bar{x}_1 - \bar{x}_2}{S_{pooled}}$$

In the formula, $\bar{x}_1$ and $\bar{x}_2$ are the means of sample 1 and sample 2, respectively; S_{pooled} is the pooled standard deviation. It takes into account the variability within each group and thus provides a more accurate estimate of the population standard deviation when the sample sizes and variances of the two groups are not equal. The formula is presented in Equation 23.2, in which n_1 and n_2 are the sample sizes for group 1 and group 2, and S_1 and S_2 are standard deviations for group 1 and group 2.

Equation 23.2
$$S_{pooled} = \sqrt{\frac{(n_1 - 1)S_1^2 + (n_2 - 1)S_2^2}{n_1 + n_2 - 2}}$$

EXAMPLE 23.1

Suppose we have the following data that are taken from Example 20.2 and SPSS Output 20.7 (Chapter 20).

Group 1

$\bar{x}_1 = 12.15$
$n_1 = 20$
$S_1 = 1.2258$

Group 2

$\bar{x}_1 = 10.95$
$n_2 = 20$
$S_2 = 1.3945$

The pooled standard deviation for the two groups will be:

$$S_{pooled} = \sqrt{\frac{(20 - 1)1.2258^2 + (20 - 1)1.3945^2}{20 + 20 - 2}}$$

$$S_{pooled} = \sqrt{\frac{28.5475 + 36.9474}{38}}$$

$$S_{pooled} = 1.3128$$

So, the pooled standard deviation of the two groups is 1.3128. We plug the value into the following formula and you will get a Cohen's d effect size.

$$d = \frac{\bar{x}_1 - \bar{x}_2}{S_{pooled}}$$

$$d = \frac{12.15 - 10.95}{1.3128} = 0.914$$

However, although effect sizes such as Cohen's d can be calculated manually, such calculations can be time-consuming and error-prone, especially for complex analyses or large datasets. Therefore, it might be better to use statistical software or programs. These days, most statistical software packages, including SPSS, automatically calculate effect sizes as part of their output, making it easier and more accurate for researchers to interpret their results. SPSS, for example, provides several types of effect-size measures depending on the type of analysis you conduct. For example, you can request effect size measures when performing an independent-samples t-test. We described the steps in calculating an independent samples t-test in Chapter 20 (SPSS Steps 20.6 related to Example 20.2). After specifying your variables, in the "Independent-Samples T Test" dialog box, check the box for "Estimate effect sizes" to request effect size measures. SPSS then generates an output like SPSS Output 23.1, showing the effect sizes.

SPSS OUTPUT 23.1

Independent Samples Effect Sizes

		Standardizer[a]	Point Estimate	95% Confidence Interval Lower	95% Confidence Interval Upper
Vocabulary scores	Cohen's d	1.31	.914	.256	1.561
	Hedges's correction	1.33	.896	.251	1.530
	Glass's delta	1.39	.860	.174	1.528

a. The denominator used in estimating the effect sizes.

Cohen's d uses the pooled standard deviation.

Hedges's correction uses the pooled standard deviation, plus a correction factor.

Glass's delta uses the sample standard deviation of the control group.

In SPSS Output 23.1, you will see terms such as "standardizer" and "point estimate." The point estimate refers to the actual calculated value of the effect size (e.g., Cohen's d). It is the specific numeric result representing the magnitude of the effect. The standardizer is the value used to standardize the effect size measure. For Cohen's d, the standardizer is the pooled standard deviation. SPSS Output 23.1 shows the Cohen's d effect size under "Point Estimate," which is 0.914 and is the same as the one we calculated before. The value under "Standardizer" is the same as the pooled standard deviation calculated earlier.

The interpretation of Cohen's d is based on its magnitude, with larger values indicating larger effect sizes. Here are some general guidelines for interpreting Cohen's d:

- A value of $d = 0.20$ is considered a small effect size.
- A value of $d = 0.50$ is considered a medium effect size.
- A value of $d = 0.80$ or higher is considered a large effect size.

Cohen's d values can be larger than 1 too, as this effect size quantifies the difference between two groups, calculated by dividing that difference by the pooled standard deviation. If the difference between the means is greater than one standard deviation, then Cohen's d will be larger than 1. This means that the interpretation of Cohen's d depends on the context and design of the study, the research question, and also the specific field in which it is used. It is also important to consider previous studies in a specific area to see where the result can be situated with reference to the other studies in the field. As Cohen himself suggested, we need to be careful when interpreting the Cohen's d values, as the terms "small" and "large" are relative, and their interpretations can differ across areas. For example, what can be considered a large effect size in one discipline can be a small effect size in another.

As for the field of applied linguistics, based on empirical evidence from a review of the literature, Plonsky and Oswald (2014) argued that Cohen's (1988) guideline for Cohen's d such as small ($d = 0.2$), medium ($d = 0.5$), and large ($d = 0.8$) underestimates the range and degree of effects usually observed in L2 research and therefore they should not be applied to interpreting the results of L2 research. They instead suggested the following field-specific guideline for Cohen's d in applied linguistics and L2 research:

- $d = 0.40$ (small)
- $d = 0.70$ (medium)
- $d = 1.00$ (large)

When you request effect size measures for t-tests in SPSS, SPSS generates two other effect sizes, which can be seen in SPSS Output 23.1: Hedges's correction (which is Hedges's g) and Glass's delta, which we will explain below.

Hedges's g
Hedges's g is a correction or modification to Cohen's d effect size that addresses potential biases in small sample sizes. It is particularly useful when dealing with

small sample sizes, where Cohen's d might overestimate the population effect size.

Both Cohen's d and Hedges's g measures are used to estimate the magnitude of an effect. The difference between the two is in how they are calculated. Cohen's d is calculated by dividing the difference between two means by the pooled standard deviation, whereas Hedges's g is calculated by dividing the difference between two means by a modified estimate of the standard deviation that takes into account the sample sizes and variances of the two groups being compared. The formula for Hedges's g is given in Equation 23.3.

Equation 23.3
$$\text{Hedges's } g = d \times \left(1 - \frac{3}{4\,(df_1 + df_2 - 1)} \right)$$

The df is the degree of freedom. In Example 23.1, Cohen's d was 0.914. We can now convert Cohen's d to Hedges's g using the formula in Equation 23.3. Given that we have two groups with $n = 20$ in each group, the degrees of freedom for each group would be $20 - 1 = 19$. Therefore:

$$\text{Hedges's } g = 0.914 \times \left(1 - \frac{3}{4\,(19 + 19 - 1)} \right)$$

Hedges's $g = 0.914 \times (1 - 0.02027)$
Hedges's $g = 0.914 \times 0.97973$
Hedges's $g = 0.896$

This is the value that we can see in SPSS Output 23.1 for Hedges's correction.

Hedges's g is usually considered to be a more precise measure of effect size when sample sizes are small or unequal, as it provides a more accurate estimate of the true population effect size. In contrast, Cohen's d is more commonly used when sample sizes are large, and variances are assumed to be equal between groups.

The general guidelines for interpreting Hedges's g are similar to those of Cohen's d explained above.

Hedges's g is a correction or modification to Cohen's d effect size that addresses potential biases in small sample sizes.

Glass's Delta

Glass's delta (or Glass's Δ) is another effect-size measure that is similar to Cohen's d but uses only the standard deviation of the control group in the denominator, making it more straightforward. As noted earlier, the pooled standard deviation is more appropriate when the two groups have similar standard deviations. When the variance of the two groups is different, it would be better to replace the pooled standard deviation by the standard deviation of one of the groups, preferably the control group (as the standard deviation of the control group can be considered to be more representative of the standard deviation of the population). The resulting effect size will be what is called Glass's delta (Equation 23.4).

Equation 23.4 $$\text{Glass's } \Delta = \frac{\bar{x}_1 - \bar{x}_2}{SD_{control}}$$

Now we can calculate Glass's delta (Δ) for the data we discussed above (shown again below).

Group 1

- $\bar{x}_1 = 12.15$
- $n_1 = 20$
- $S_1 = 1.2258$

Group 2

- $\bar{x}_1 = 10.95$
- $n_2 = 20$
- $S_2 = 1.3945$

$$\text{Glass's } \Delta = \frac{12.15 - 10.95}{1.3945}$$

$$\text{Glass's } \Delta = \frac{1.2}{1.3945}$$

$$\text{Glass's } \Delta = 0.860$$

So, the calculated Glass's delta for the given data is approximately 0.860, as can be seen in SPSS Output 23.1. The general guidelines for interpreting Glass's delta are similar to those for Hedges's g and Cohen's d.

Glass's delta is another effect-size measure that is similar to Cohen's d but uses only the standard deviation of the control group in the denominator, making it more straightforward.

Eta-Squared and Partial Eta-Squared

Eta-squared and partial eta-squared are effect-size measures used when comparing the means of more than two groups, such as in the analysis of variance (ANOVA), and show the proportion of the total variance in the dependent variable explained by one or more independent variables. Eta-squared indicates the proportion of the variance in the dependent variable accounted for by the independent variable. It is usually suitable when there is one dependent and one independent variable. Partial eta-squared indicates the proportion of variance in the dependent variable that is explained by the independent variable while controlling for the effects of other independent variables in the statistical analysis. Therefore, partial eta-squared can be a more suitable measure when there is more than one independent variable in the statistical analysis. Eta-squared, denoted by η^2 and partial eta-squared denoted by η_p^2 can be calculated from the data in the ANOVA table in the SPSS output. Eta-squared (η^2) can be calculated by dividing the sum of squares (SS) for the effect by the total of the sum of squares (Equation 23.5), and partial eta-squared (η_p^2) is calculated by dividing the sum of squares of the effect of the independent variable by the sum of squares of the effect of the independent variable plus the error term (Equation 23.6). Since the value of η_p^2 is adjusted for the effects of other independent variables in the model, it tends to provide a more conservative estimate of the effect size than eta-squared.

Equation 23.5
$$\eta^2 = \frac{SS_{effect}}{SS_{Total}}$$

Equation 23.6
$$\eta_p^2 = \frac{SS_{effect}}{SS_{effect} + SS_{error}}$$

Please note that in the context of a one-way ANOVA with a single independent variable, the total variance is partitioned into two components: the variance between groups $(SS$ Between) and the variance within groups $(SS$ Within). In this type of ANOVA, the total variance is simply the sum of the variance between groups and the variance within groups. To measure the proportion of variance explained by the independent variable in one-way ANOVA, we usually calculate eta-squared (η^2). Alternatively, we can calculate partial eta-squared (η_p^2). However, eta-squared (η^2) and partial eta-squared (η_p^2) are equivalent in one-way ANOVA because the total variance is fully partitioned into these two components. Therefore, the formula is as shown in Equation 23.7.

Equation 23.7
$$\eta^2 = \eta_p^2 = \frac{SS_{Between}}{SS_{Between} + SS_{Within}}$$

Eta-squared indicates the proportion of the variance in the dependent variable accounted for by the independent variable and is used when there is one dependent and one independent variable. **Partial eta-squared** indicates the proportion of variance in the dependent variable explained by the independent variable while controlling for the effects of other independent variables in the statistical analysis.

SPSS Output 23.2 presents the ANOVA table, which was previously shown in SPSS Output 20.12 in Chapter 20 (Example 20.4), examining the effect of

SPSS OUTPUT 23.2

ANOVA

Writing score

	Sum of Squares	df	Mean Square	F	Sig.
Between Groups	1822.20	2	911.10	120.06	.000
Within Groups	660.20	87	7.59		
Total	2482.40	89			

written corrective feedback on the writing performance of intermediate English L2 learners.

In the ANOVA table:

- *SS* Between = 1822.20
- *SS* Within = 660.20
- *SS* Total = 2482.40

The sum of squares for the effect is represented by the Between Groups sum of squares (*SS*_Between). Let's now calculate η^2.

$$\eta^2 = \frac{1822.20}{2482.40}$$

$$\eta^2 = 0.734$$

This result indicates that approximately 73% of the total variance in the dependent variable is explained by the differences between the groups, reflecting the effect of the independent variable.

While manual calculations are possible, using software such as SPSS is faster and reduces errors, especially for complex analyses or large datasets. The steps for calculating a one-way ANOVA were presented in Chapter 20 (SPSS Steps 20.8). Effect sizes for one-way ANOVA can be requested in SPSS by selecting "Estimate effect size for overall tests" in the ANOVA dialog box. We have calculated the effect size using SPSS, and the eta-squared (η^2) obtained is 0.734 (see SPSS Output 23.3), which matches the effect size we calculated manually before.

SPSS OUTPUT 23.3

ANOVA Effect Sizes[a]

		Point Estimate	95% Confidence Interval	
			Lower	Upper
Writing score	Eta-squared	.734	.631	.791
	Epsilon-squared	.728	.623	.786
	Omega-squared Fixed-effect	.726	.620	.785
	Omega-squared Random-effect	.570	.450	.645

a. Eta-squared and Epsilon-squared are estimated based on the fixed-effect model.

As noted earlier, both eta-squared and partial eta-squared (η_p^2) are the same for one-way ANOVA and the values are 0.734, as can be seen in the following calculation.

$$\eta_p^2 = \frac{1822.20}{1822.20 + 660.2}$$

$$\eta_p^2 = 0.734$$

In more complex experimental designs with multiple independent variables, the values for the two can be different.

Let's calculate η_p^2 for data involving two independent variables, using the data from Example 20.5 in Chapter 20, which examined the effects of language proficiency and oral feedback methods on L2 learners' speaking accuracy. To calculate η_p^2, use the formula provided in Equation 23.6. Begin by locating SS_{effect} (for the independent variable) and SS_{error} in the ANOVA output (see SPSS Output 23.4). These values are in the "Type III Sum of Squares" column of the output. For the independent variable "Feedback," the SS_{effect} and SS_{error} are 394.20 and 533.00, respectively. Therefore, η_p^2 will be:

$$\eta_p^2 = \frac{394.205}{394.20 + 533.00}$$

$$\eta_p^2 = 0.425$$

Such effect sizes can also be requested in SPSS. The steps for conducting a two-way ANOVA were presented in Chapter 20 (SPSS Steps 20.9). To include effect size estimates, click "Options" in the main "Univariate" dialog box and select "Estimates of effect size" under "Display."

We calculated this effect size for "Feedback" using SPSS as shown in SPSS Output 23.4. The value is 0.425, which corresponds to the effect size calculated manually above.

For a repeated-measures ANOVA, the process is similar. To calculate partial eta-squared (η_p^2) manually, follow the procedure and formula outlined earlier (Equation 23.6). The steps for performing a one-way repeated-measures ANOVA were described in Chapter 20 (SPSS Steps, 20.10). To include effect sizes, open the repeated-measures dialog box, click "Options," and select "Estimates of effect size." The output will then displays the partial eta-squared (η_p^2) values.

SPSS OUTPUT 23.4

Tests of Between-Subjects Effects

Dependent Variable: Speaking accuracy scores

Source	Type III Sum of Squares	df	Mean Square	F	Sig.	Partial Eta Squared
Corrected Model	453.50[a]	5	90.70	14.29	.000	.460
Intercept	21576.03	1	21576.03	3400.35	.000	.976
Feedback	394.20	2	197.10	31.06	.000	.425
Proficiency	6.43	1	6.43	1.01	.32	.012
feedback * Proficiency	35.80	2	17.90	2.82	.07	.063
Error	533.00	84	6.35			
Total	22609.00	90				
Corrected Total	986.50	89				

a. R Squared = .460 (Adjusted R Squared = .428)

As far the interpretation is considered, the higher the values, the stronger the effect of the independent variable on the dependent variable. While there are no strict rules for interpreting the values, Cohen (1988) has suggested the following rough guideline for the interpretation of eta-squared and partial eta-squared:

- 0.01 indicates a small effect.
- 0.06 indicates a medium effect.
- 0.14 indicates a large effect.

Although the same guideline can be applied to both types of effect sizes, there are a few things that should be considered. As noted earlier, when there is only one independent variable, partial eta-squared and eta-squared are the same. However, if there is more than one independent variable, the partial eta-squared is more appropriate. Again, it is important to bear in mind that the interpretation of effect size measures, such as eta-squared and partial eta-squared, depends on the specific research question, the context of the study, and what is considered appropriate in a certain field.

Cohen's f

There is another effect size measure used in ANOVA called Cohen's f, which shows the strength of the differences between means across three or more groups. SPSS does not provide this measure directly but it can be calculated indirectly using the eta-squared (η^2) value provided in the ANOVA output, applying the formula shown in Equation 23.8. Cohen's f is a measure of the ratio of the variance explained by the independent variable to the residual variance and is calculated as follows:

Equation 23.8
$$f = \sqrt{\frac{\eta_p^2}{1 - \eta_p^2}}$$

In general, a Cohen's f of 0.10 indicates a small effect size, 0.25 indicates a medium effect size, and 0.40 or greater indicates a large value. It is important to note that although Cohen's f is a useful effect size measure in ANOVA, this measure is more appropriate when the assumptions about the normality of the data and homogeneity of variances are met. The effect size measure used in G*Power is Cohen's f.

POINTS TO PONDER

How can you measure and interpret effect sizes in the context of categorical data analysis, and what are the different types of such measures?

Effect Sizes for Categorical Data

When we compare groups, the data are either continuous or dichotomous. So far, the measures of effect size used have involved continuous variables. The risk ratio (RR) and odds ratio (OR) are measures that involve categorical variables. When we compare categorical variables (such as low proficiency versus high proficiency), the comparison is based on the probability of one group belonging to a certain category more than another category. Risk ratio and odds ratio are both measures of effect sizes.

The risk ratio (RR) and **odds ratio (OR)** are measures that involve categorical variables.

Risk Ratio

The risk ratio (RR) is a measure of the probability of an event occurring in one group or category compared to another group. This measure is calculated by dividing the percentage of occurrence of an event in one group by the percentage of the same event in another group. Take, for example, the contingency table (Table 23.1) that compares the occurrence of Event A and Event B in Group A and Group B.

Table 23.1 Contingency table for risk ratio

	Event A	Event B
Group A	a	b
Group B	c	d

To calculate the risk ratio for Event A occurring in Group A compared to Group B, we use the formula in Equation 23.9:

Equation 23.9
$$RR = \frac{(a/(a+b))}{(c/(c+d))}$$

where

a   is the number of Events A in Group A
b   is the number of Events B in Group A
c   is the number of Events A in Group B
d   is the number of Events B in Group B

So, the *RR* is the proportion of *a* divided by the proportion of *c*.

EXAMPLE 23.2

Suppose you want to compare the occurrence of written versus oral corrective feedback in a beginner-level class compared to an intermediate-level class. You conduct a study in which you document the occurrences of these two types of feedback in the two classes. Suppose you find altogether 200 instances of feedback in both classes (120 instances of oral feedback and 80 instances of written feedback). Out of 120 instances of oral feedback 85 have occurred in the beginner-level class and 35 in the intermediate level. Out of the total instances of written feedback, 15 have occurred in the beginner-level class and 65 in the intermediate-level class. Table 23.2 shows a cross tabulation of the data across classes and types of feedback. We can use the data in Table 23.2 to calculate the risk ratio.

Table 23.2 Data used to calculate risk ratio

	Oral	Written	Total
Beginner	85	15	100
Intermediate	35	65	100
Total	120	80	200

To calculate the risk ratio, we first calculate the percentage of occurrence of feedback in each class by dividing the number of instances of each feedback type by the total number of instances of that feedback type in that class. For example, the percentage of oral feedback in the beginner-level class is 85/100 = 0.85, while the percentage of the same feedback in the intermediate-level class is 35/100 = 0.35. The risk ratio for oral feedback is then calculated by dividing the percentage of oral feedback in the beginner-level class by the percentage of oral feedback in the intermediate-level class:

$$\text{Risk ratio} = (\% \text{ of oral feedback in the beginner level})/$$
$$(\% \text{ of oral feedback in the intermediate level}) = 0.85/0.35 = 2.42.$$

This means that oral feedback is 2.42 times more likely to happen in the beginner-level class than in the intermediate-level class. A risk ratio of 1 would indicate that there is no difference in occurrence between the two groups. A risk ratio greater than 1 indicates a higher occurrence in one class than in another class, while a risk ratio of less than 1 indicates a lower occurrence in one class than in another class.

Odds Ratio

Similar to the risk ratio, the odds ratio (*OR*) is also a measure of how much more or less likely it is for an event to occur. However, while the risk ratio compares the proportion of events in one group compared to the proportion of the same event in another group, the odds ratio compares the odds of an event occurring in one group to the odds of it occurring in another group. Specifically, the odds are calculated as the ratio of those who experience the event to those who do not experience the event. This is different from a probability, which is the ratio of those who experience the event to the total number of individuals. An *OR* greater than 1 suggests a positive association between the two variables.

The *RR* is generally preferred to *OR* for evaluating the effect of a factor or an intervention in observational studies because it compares the probability of an event occurring in one group relative to another, which is more intuitive and easier to interpret. In contrast, the *OR*, which compares the odds of an event occurring between two groups, requires a more complex interpretation.

Table 23.3 Contingency table for odds ratio

	Event A	Event B
Group A	a	b
Group B	c	d

Take for example the contingency table in Table 23.3, which displays the value for Event A and Event B across Groups A and B. The odds ratio can be calculated using the formula in Equation 23.10.

Equation 23.10
$$OR = \frac{a/b}{c/d}$$

where

a is the number of Events A in Group A
b is the number of Events B in Group A

c is the number of Events A in Group B
d is the number of Events B in Group B

Using the data given in Table 23.2, we can calculate the odds ratio (OR) for oral feedback in the beginner-level class.

$$OR = (a/b)/(c/d) = (85/15)/(35/65) = 10.52$$

The odds ratio for oral feedback relative to written feedback between the beginner and intermediate class is 10.52. This means that the likelihood of receiving oral feedback, as opposed to written feedback, is 10.52 times higher in the beginner-level class than in the intermediate-level class. This indicates a significant association between the type of feedback (oral vs, written) and class level, suggesting that teachers are much more likely to provide oral feedback in the beginner-level class than in the intermediate-level class.

As can be noted, both the odds ratio and risk ratio compare the likelihood of an event in different groups. However, while the odds ratio compares the odds, which is the ratio of the probability of an event occurring to the probability of it not occurring, the risk ratio compares the actual probabilities or risks of the event occurring in each group. For example, if the risk ratio of passing an exam is 2, it means that the probability of passing the exam is 2 times the probability of not passing. In other words, passing the exam is twice as likely as not passing. However, if the odds of passing an exam are 2, it means that the odds in favor of passing are 2 to 1. This can also be expressed as the probability of passing being 2 out of 3, and the probability of not passing being 1 out of 3. To summarize:

- A risk of 2 means the event is twice as likely to happen.
- An odds of 2 means the odds in favor of the event are 2 to 1.

Going back to the calculation process, although we explained how to calculate odds and risk ratios manually, SPSS can also calculate them as shown in SPSS Steps 23.1.

SPSS STEPS 23.1

- Open the data file in SPSS.
- Select "Analyze" > "Descriptive Statistics" > "Crosstabs."
- Move the Group variable to the "Rows" box and the outcome (event) variable to the "Columns" box.
- Click "Statistics" > "Risk."
- Click "Continue" > "OK."

SPSS Output 23.5 shows the output generated by SPSS for the data in Table 23.2 related to Example 23.2, presented earlier.

SPSS OUTPUT 23.5

Risk Estimate

	Value	95% Confidence Interval Lower	95% Confidence Interval Upper
Odds Ratio for Class (Beginner / Intermediate)	10.524	5.301	20.891
For cohort Feedback = Oral	2.429	1.836	3.212
For cohort Feedback = Written	.231	.142	.376
N of Valid Cases	200		

The output displays both the risk and odds ratio with their corresponding 95% confidence interval (CI). The odds ratio for oral feedback in the beginner-level class is 10.524, and the risk ratio is 2.429; these are the same as the ones we calculated before.

There is no specific rule for interpreting the values of the odds ratio, but the following can be used as a rough guideline for a 2×2 table:

- 1.5–2.0 = small
- 2.5–4.0 = medium
- 4.0–10 = large

Phi Coefficient (φ)

We have previously introduced the risk ratio (RR) and odds ratio (OR) as measures of association between categorical variables. Now, let's turn our attention to the phi coefficient, which is another important measure used to assess the strength of the relationship between two binary categorical variables. Unlike the odds and risk ratios, the phi coefficient, denoted by φ, is used to estimate the strength and direction of the association between two dichotomous and binary variables. It provides a correlation-like measure specifically for dichotomous data, ranging from −1 to 1, and is useful for understanding the association between two binary variables in a 2 × 2 contingency table. For example, if you want to examine the relationship between proficiency (low, high) and feedback preference (preferred, not preferred), you might use the phi coefficient. The phi coefficient can be interpreted as follows: A value of φ of −1 or 1 indicates a perfect negative or positive relationship between the two variables, while a value of 0 indicates no relationship.

The phi coefficient estimates the strength and direction of the association between two dichotomous and binary variables.

The phi coefficient is closely related to the chi-square test of significance as it provides a measure of the strength and direction of the association between two dichotomous (binary) variables. While both are measures of association between categorical variables, they serve different purposes. One difference between the two is that a chi-square test is used to determine whether there is any significant relationship between the two variables, whereas the phi coefficient quantifies the strength of that relationship. Therefore, it provides a measure of effect size for the chi-square test. Its calculation is based on the chi-square statistic, but it standardizes the chi-square statistic and also takes into account the sample size by taking the square root of the chi-square statistic divided by the total sample size. Since the phi coefficient ranges from -1 to 1, it is easy to interpret. The formula for the phi coefficient is provided in Equation 23.11.

Equation 23.11
$$\varphi = \sqrt{\frac{x^2}{N}}$$

where

- x^2 is the chi-square statistic
- N is the sample size or the number of observations.

For the data presented in Table 23.2, $x^2 = 52.08$ and the $N = 200$. Using this information, the phi coefficient is calculated below, using Equation 23.11, and the corresponding results are also presented in SPSS Output 23.6 (see SPSS Steps 23.2 for the SPSS procedure).

$$\varphi = \sqrt{\frac{52.08}{200}} = 0.510$$

SPSS OUTPUT 23.6

Symmetric Measures

		Value	Approximate Significance
Nominal by Nominal	Phi	.510	.000
	Cramer's V	.510	.000
N of Valid Cases		200	

The result shows that the phi coefficient for a chi-square value of 52.08 and a sample size of 200 is approximately 0.51.

As an effect size, the interpretation of phi coefficient can be guided by Cohen's general guidelines (0.1 = small effect, 0.3 = a medium effect, and 0.5 = a large effect) or our discipline-specific guideline (0.25 = small, 0.40 = medium, and 0.60 = large). These guidelines provide a framework for evaluating the strength of the relationship.

Cramer's V (φ_c)

Cramer's V is another estimate of effect size for categorical data. It is similar to, and an extension of, the phi effect size and provides a standardized measure of association, and also takes into account the sample size of the contingency table and the degree of freedom. Phi coefficient is appropriate for a 2×2 contingency table but if the table is greater than 2×2, then Cramer's V would be more appropriate. Cramer's V can handle tables of any size. The formula for Cramer's V is shown in Equation 23.12.

Equation 23.12
$$\varphi_c = \sqrt{\frac{x^2}{N \times min\ (k-1, r-1)}}$$

where

- x^2 is the chi-square statistic,
- N is the sample size or the total number of observations.
- k is the number of columns in the contingency table.
- r is the number of rows in the contingency table.
- $min\ (k-1, r-1)$ is the smaller of $(k-1)$ or $(r-1)$

Here is an example to illustrate how $min(k-1, r-1)$ works. Suppose we have a contingency table with:

- $k = 3$
- $r = 2$

Then $k-1 = 3-1 = 2$,
and $(r-1) = 2-1 = 1$
Take the smaller of the two values: $min(k-1, r-1) = min(2, 1) = 1$
Now let's calculate Cramer's V for the frequency data shown in Table 23.4 (Based on Example 21.8, Chapter 21). For these data, the chi-square value (χ^2) was 18.358.
Using the following information, Cramer's V is calculated below.

- $\chi^2 = 18.358$
- $N = 207$ (total of observations)
- $k = 3$ (number of columns)
- $r = 2$ (number of rows)
- $min(k-1, r-1) = min(2, 1) = 1$

Table 23.4 Data used to calculate Cramer's V

	Recasts	Explicit correction	Metalinguistic feedback	Total
Less experienced	52	30	18	52
Experienced	57	10	40	57
Total	109	40	58	109

$$\varphi_c = \sqrt{\frac{18.358}{207 \times min(3-1, 2-1)}}$$

$$\varphi_c = \sqrt{\frac{18.358}{207 \times 1}} = 0.298$$

The result shows that the Cramer's V value for the data is 0.298.

SPSS Steps 23.2 shows how to conduct the phi coefficient and Cramer's V in SPSS (along with the chi-square test).

SPSS STEPS 23.2

- Open the data file in SPSS.
- Select "Analyze" > "Descriptive Statistics" > "Crosstabs."
- Move the categorical variables you want to analyze into the "Row(s)" and "Column(s)" boxes.
- Click on the "Statistics" and check the "Chi-square" box and the box for "Phi and Cramer's V." under the "Nominal" section.
- Click "Continue" > "OK."

Using the data from Example 23.3, SPSS generates a crosstabulation (SPSS Output 23.7), the chi-square test results (SPSS Output 23.8), and the results for both the phi coefficient and Cramer's V (SPSS Output 23.9).

SPSS OUTPUT 23.7

Teachers * Feedback Types Crosstabulation

Count

		Feedback Types			
		Recasts	Explicit correction	Metalinguistic feedback	Total
Teachers	Less experienced	52	30	18	100
	Experienced	57	10	40	107
Total		109	40	58	207

SPSS OUTPUT 23.8

Chi-Square Tests

	Value	df	Asymptotic Significance (2-sided)
Pearson Chi-Square	18.358a	2	.000
Likelihood Ratio	19.015	2	.000
Linear-by-Linear Association	2.262	1	.133
N of Valid Cases	207		

a. 0 cells (0.0%) have expected count less than 5. The minimum expected count is 19.32.

The phi coefficient and Cramer's V shown in SPSS Output 23.9 are both 0.298. The Cramer's V value matches the one calculated manually earlier. Since the min(2, 1) = 1, the results for phi coefficient and Cramer's V are identical.

SPSS OUTPUT 23.9

Symmetric Measures

		Value	Approximate Significance
Nominal by Nominal	Phi	.298	.000
	Cramer's V	.298	.000
N of Valid Cases		207	

As noted earlier, like the phi coefficient, Cramer's V measures the strength of association between two categorical variables, with larger values indicating stronger association. A value of 0 indicates no association, while a value of 1 indicates a perfect association. Cohen's guidelines (0.1 = small effect, 0.3 = medium effect, and 0.5 = large effect) or our discipline-specific guideline (0.25 = small, 0.40 = medium, and 0.60 = large) can be used to interpret the strength of the values of the phi coefficient and Cramer's V, depending on the context of the study, when both represent a 2×2 contingency table. When the table is greater than 2×2, the guidelines in Table 21.7 (Chapter 21), which are based on the degree of freedom, can be used for Cramer's V.

Correlational Effect Sizes

Another group of effect sizes are those that are used in different types of correlation analyses and represent the strength and direction of the relationship between or among variables. They help determine the degree to which changes in one variable are associated with changes in another. As noted earlier, correlations coefficients range from −1 to +1, with +1 indicating a perfect positive correlation, −1 a perfect negative correlation, and 0 representing no correlation. As an effect size, the correlation coefficient indicates the magnitude of the relationship, with the larger value indicating a stronger relationship. As for its interpretation, Cohen's guidelines are commonly used in many disciplines; these guidelines are as follows:

- $r = 0.1$: small effect size
- $r = 0.3$: medium effect size
- $r = 0.5$: large effect size

However, it is important to note that these guidelines are general and may vary depending on the specific context of the study, research, questions, methodologies used, and the discipline. Based on their review of the literature, Plonsky and Oswald (2014) argued that such values underestimate what is usually observed in L2 research, and therefore they should not be applied to interpreting the results of L2 research. They instead suggested the following field-specific guidelines for the interpretation of r in applied linguistics and L2 research:

- $r = 0.25$ (small)
- $r = 0.40$ (medium)
- $r = 0.60$ (large).

Another group of effect sizes are those that are used in different types of **correlation analyses**; they represent the strength and direction of the relationship between or among variables.

There are several different types of correlation coefficients, each being used to measure different types of relationships between variables depending on the types of data. These include:

- the Pearson product moment correlation coefficient
- Spearman's rank correlation coefficient
- Kendall's tau correlation coefficient
- the point-biserial correlation coefficient.

Pearson Product Moment Correlation Coefficient

The Pearson product moment correlation coefficient (Pearson's r) is one of the most widely used correlation coefficients in many fields of study, including applied linguistics (see Chapter 20). It measures the linear relationship between variables and is used when both variables are continuous or measured on interval or ratio scales. Pearson correlation can also be used with dichotomous variables. However, for two dichotomous variables, the result is equivalent to the phi coefficient. As an effect size, the Pearson correlation coefficient can be interpreted using the field-specific guidelines proposed on page 710. The steps for conducting the Pearson correlation were presented in Chapter 20 (SPSS Steps 20.12).

Pearson's r is one of the most widely used correlation coefficients and measures the linear relationship between variables. It is used when both variables are continuous or measured on interval or ratio scales.

Spearman's Rank Correlation Coefficient

Denoted by ρ or rs, Spearman's rank correlation coefficient, also known as Spearman's rho (or rho), is a nonparametric measure of the strength of the relationship between two variables (see Chapter 21). It is used when both variables are ordinal or have used a ranked scale. It is also often used when the relationships are not linear or when the data are not normally distributed. The coefficient ranges from -1 to 1, with -1 indicating a perfect negative relationship, 0 no relationship, and 1 a perfect positive monotonic relationship. As an effect size, like Pearson's r, it can be interpreted using the guidelines for effect size proposed on page 710. However, since Spearman's rho measures different types of relationships, the same values may indicate a stronger relationship than Pearson's r, as the relationship between the two variables is nonlinear. Spearman's rho correlations are most robust to outliers that Pearson's r. The steps for conducting Spearman's rho in SPSS were presented in Chapter 21 (SPSS Steps 21.11).

Spearman's rho is a nonparametric measure of the strength of the relationship between two variables. It is used when both variables are ordinal or have used a ranked scale.

Kendall's Tau Correlation Coefficient

Kendall's tau correlation coefficient (usually denoted as τ) is also a nonparametric test and measures the strength and direction of the relationship between two variables. It is similar to Spearman's rank correlation coefficient in that it is used with ranked data, but it has some advantages over it in certain situations. It is even more robust than Spearman's rank correlation to outliers, does not assume that the data should be normally distributed, and is used when there are many tied ranks in the data (i.e., observations with the same value). The coefficient ranges from -1 to 1, with -1 indicating a perfect negative association, 0 no association, and 1 a perfect positive association. As an effect size, it can be interpreted using the guidelines for effect size proposed above. However, as with any statistical measure, it is important to consider the context of the study, the research question, and the assumptions of the analysis when interpreting the results. The steps for conducting Kendall's Tau in SPSS are the same as those for Pearson correlation and Spearman's rho. However, instead of selecting "Pearson" or "Spearman" under "Correlation Coefficients," you should choose "Kendall's Tau-b."

Kendall's tau correlation coefficient assesses the strength and direction of the relationship between two variables, akin to Spearman's rank correlation coefficient but with additional advantages, such as increased robustness to outliers, no assumption of normal distribution, and suitability for datasets with numerous tied ranks.

Point-Biserial Correlation Coefficient

The point-biserial correlation coefficient is used to estimate the strength and direction of the relationship between a binary dichotomous variable (such as yes/no) and a continuous metric variable. It is a special case of Pearson's correlation coefficient, but one of the variables is dichotomous. For example, if you are interested in examining the relationship between low- and high-proficiency and exam scores (a continuous variable), the point-biserial correlation coefficient can be used. There are also a few assumptions that should be met before carrying out this kind of correlation, such as the absence of any outliers in the continuous variable, the continuous variable being normally distributed, and having equal variances for the two categories of the dichotomous variable. Therefore, we need to check for these assumptions before using it. Like other correlation coefficients, the point-biserial correlation coefficient can be interpreted using guidelines for correlational effect sizes and the values also range from -1 or 1.

The point-biserial correlation coefficient estimates the strength and direction of the relationship between a binary dichotomous variable and a continuous metric variable.

Coefficient of Determination (R^2)

Another effect size related to correlational analysis is R^2 (r squared) or the coefficient of determination. This coefficient is a statistical measure that estimates the proportion of the variance in the dependent variable explained by the independent variable(s) in a regression model. As the name suggests, it is the square of the Pearson's r, and its value ranges between 0 and 1, with higher values indicating a larger proportion of the variance in the dependent variable being explained by the independent variable(s). For example, if the r of two variables is 0.4, the coefficient of determination is 0.16, which means that 16% of the variance of one of the variables is explained by the other. In other words, there is a 16% shared or common variance between the two. Since R^2 is r squared, the value is always positive, and therefore, it does not indicate any direction of the correlation.

R-squared is commonly used in the field of applied linguistics research to assess the strength of association between and among variables in regression analysis. Like other effect sizes, the interpretation of the strength of an R-squared effect size can depend on the context and the field of study. However, here is a general guideline for interpreting the strength of R-squared based on Cohen's effect size benchmarks:

- $R^2 = 0.01$: a weak effect size
- $R^2 = 0.09$: a medium effect size
- $R^2 = 0.25$ or higher: a strong effect size

As noted earlier, based on their review of the literature, Plonsky and Oswald (2014) suggest the following: $r = 0.25$ (small), $r = 0.40$ (medium), and $r = 0.60$ (large). Based on this, the field-specific values for R^2 in applied linguistics research should be:

- $R^2 = 0.06$ (small)
- $R^2 = 0.16$ (medium)
- $R^2 = 0.36$ or higher (strong)

A Summary of Effect Sizes

Table 23.5 shows the guidelines for interpreting all the effect sizes discussed so far.

Note that the interpretation of Cramer's V effect size depends on the degree of freedom (see Table 23.5), and what is given in Table 23.6 is most applicable to a degree of freedom of 1.

Table 23.5 Guidelines for interpreting effect sizes

	Cohen's benchmarks			Applied linguistics and L2 research guidelines		
	Small	Medium	Large	Small	Medium	Large
Cohen's d	0.2	0.5	0.8	0.4	0.7	1.0
Hedges's g	0.2	0.5	0.8	0.4	0.7	1.0
Glass's Delta	0.2	0.5	0.8	0.4	0.7	1.0
Eta-squared (η^2) and Partial Eta-squared (η_p^2)	0.01	0.06	0.14			
Cohen's f	0.10	0.25	0.40			
Odds/Risk Ratio	1.5 / 2.0	2.5 / 4.0	4.0 / 10.0			
Pearson's r	0.1	0.3	0.5	.25	.40	.60
Spearman's rho	0.1	0.3	0.5	.25	.40	.60
Kendall's tau	0.1	0.3	0.5	.25	.40	.60
Point-biserial r	0.1	0.3	0.5	.25	.40	.60
Phi coefficient	0.1	0.3	0.5	.25	.40	.60
Cramer's V	0.1	0.3	0.5			
R-squared	0.01	0.09	0.25	.06	.16	.36

It is important to note that the interpretations given for various effect sizes are all rough guidelines and should not be considered as fixed or rigid. While these guidelines can be helpful, it is important to recognize that they can vary depending on the specific research question and context. Thus, effect sizes should always be interpreted in the broader context of the study's methodology and the specific goals of the research, and considered alongside other relevant factors, such as practical significance and other design-related matters.

Conclusion

This chapter has discussed the notion of effect sizes and its importance in applied linguistics research. Effect sizes are statistical measures that quantify the size or magnitude of an effect or relationship. It is a standardized way of expressing the degree to which a treatment or independent variable has an impact on the dependent variable, or the extent to which two variables are related. The use of effect sizes is important in quantitative research as it provides a more precise picture of the results and their practical significance. In applied linguistics research, effect sizes are widely used to evaluate the effectiveness of different language teaching and learning strategies or to examine the relationships between variables. Therefore, as researchers, we need to understand effect sizes and how to calculate and interpret them correctly. In this chapter, we have explored various types of effect sizes and their respective calculations and interpretations, including those that are used for group comparisons such as Cohen's *d*, Hedges's *g,* and Glass's delta, eta-squared, partial eta-squared, as well as those that are used to measure relationship strengths, such as the Pearson product moment correlation coefficient, Spearman's rank correlation coefficient, Kendall's tau correlation coefficient, and the point-biserial correlation coefficient. The phi coefficient and Cramer's *V* were also explained. We hope that the chapter has allowed you to develop a good understanding of effect sizes and their significance in statistical analysis, which will assist you in making informed interpretations of your research findings and increasing the overall rigor of your work.

DISCUSSION AND ACTIVITY QUESTIONS

Discussion Questions

1. Why are effect sizes considered essential in applied linguistics research, and how do they complement significance testing?
2. How is the interpretation of effect sizes in applied linguistics different from other disciplines?
3. What are the key differences between Cohen's *d*, eta-squared (η^2), and partial eta-squared (η_p^2), and when would you use each in applied linguistics studies?
4. How would you interpret an effect size of 0.50 for Cohen's *d* in the context of L2 acquisition research?

5. Why is the interpretation of effect sizes dependent on the specific area of research, and how can the context of a study, such as language acquisition or language teaching, affect the meaning and relevance of different effect sizes?
6. What are the different types of categorical effect sizes, and how do they vary in their application to research in applied linguistics?
7. How do the Pearson correlation coefficient, Spearman's rank correlation coefficient, Kendall's tau, and the point-biserial correlation coefficient differ in their application, and how do you decide which one to use?
8. What are some of the challenges in calculating and interpreting effect sizes?

Activity Questions

1. Choose a research article in applied linguistics and identify the type of effect sizes reported. Are the effect sizes appropriate for the statistical analyses used? Are the effect sizes clearly reported and interpreted? What are some potential limitations of the effect sizes reported in this article?
2. Calculate Cohen's *d* for a study comparing two groups of language learners. Interpret the effect size and discuss the practical significance of the results.
3. Identify a study that reports eta-squared or partial eta-squared. Why and how were these effect sizes calculated, and how they were interpreted?
4. Choose a research study in applied linguistics in which eta-squared has been reported as an effect size. How is the effect size interpreted? Based on the size of the effect, do you think the result is practically significant? Why or why not? How might the interpretation of the study have changed if a different effect-size measure, such as partial eta-squared, had been used?
5. In groups of two or three, decide on a research question you are interested in, identify the appropriate inferential statistics to use, and calculate the effect size. What are the implications of the effect size for the research question?

PART VI
Carrying Out Mixed Methods Research

24 Mixed Methods Research: Integrating Qualitative and Quantitative Approaches

CHAPTER OBJECTIVES

After completing this chapter, you should be able to

- Describe mixed methods research, where it comes from and its philosophical orientation.
- Understand the different steps involved in conducting mixed methods research, including planning the study, collecting data, analyzing data, and integrating data across different sources.
- Identify the different types of mixed methods research designs and learn when and how each can be used.
- Analyze and integrate data across different data sources and develop strategies to effectively address challenges that may arise during the process.
- Explain the critical issue of validity in mixed methods research and identify strategies for ensuring the validity of mixed methods research findings.

Introduction

Mixed methods research is a type of research that combines quantitative and qualitative research methods to address complex research questions or problems. It is a complementary research method to the traditional single-method approach (i.e., either quantitative or qualitative). In mixed methods research, both quantitative and qualitative data are collected and analyzed using qualitative and quantitative techniques. Since this design integrates both types of data collection and analysis, it has become a popular research method in various disciplines, including the field of applied linguistics. This approach overcomes the limitations of using a single method. For example, while quantitative research provides numerical data that can be easily analyzed statistically, it may miss important contextual information that is better captured through qualitative data. On the other hand, qualitative research may provide rich contextual data, but it can be difficult to generalize findings beyond the specific sample or context. Therefore, combining both methods allows for using their individual strengths while addressing their limitations.

In this chapter, we will explore the origins and foundations of mixed methods research, outline the steps involved in conducting mixed methods research, and examine the various types of mixed methods research designs along with their key characteristics. We will also discuss the strengths and limitations of each design and provide examples of how these designs can be applied in applied linguistics research. Furthermore, we will address important considerations related to data collection, sampling, data analysis, and the integration of data from different sources. Finally, we will examine the challenges related to the validity of mixed methods research and explore ways to assess it, providing essential insights for conducting reliable and valid mixed methods studies.

Mixed methods research combines quantitative and qualitative research methods to address complex research questions or problems.

POINTS TO PONDER

What are the key philosophical orientations that underpin mixed methods research?

The Origin and Development of Mixed Methods Research

The idea of combining qualitative and quantitative research data has a long history. In fact, the purposeful utilization of both qualitative and quantitative approaches and methodologies and their combination, existed well before anyone had identified this as a distinct type of research. Maxwell (2015, p. 15) noted that "the combining of qualitative and quantitative approaches in the social sciences ... occurred much earlier than is often acknowledged," and the use of both modes of investigation can even be found in many studies on social issues conducted in the nineteenth and early twentieth centuries.

However, although many examples of mixed methods research can be found in very early studies, it wasn't until the late twentieth century that researchers started to use the term and recognized mixed methods research as a distinct approach.

The idea of **combining qualitative and quantitative research data** has a long history and existed well before anyone had identified this as a distinct type of research.

One of the earliest proponents of mixed methods research in the twentieth century, was the American sociologist Paul Lazarsfeld. Although he did not explicitly used the term "mixed methods," he was a strong proponent of combining qualitative and quantitative research methods. In the works that he conducted or led in the 1930s, 1940s, and 1950s, he developed a model of sociological research combining both methods by using a combination of surveys and interviews to study communication and social issues. One of the first team-based mixed methods projects led by Lazarsfeld and his colleagues was a study on unemployment in the Austrian town of Marienthal in the 1930s, which was used to understand the effects of unemployment on the residents of Marienthal. The research used and combined various types of data including numerical data, diaries and memoirs, interviews, observations, and surveys. Another two studies led by the same scholar, which also used mixed methods research, were the radio project, which examined the role of mass media in society, and the project on listening habits in the United States during the 1940s, which examined how people listened to the radio and what programs they preferred. Other studies in the early twentieth century that used qualitative and quantitative methods include the Hawthorne studies (Mayo, 1993; Roethlisberger & Dickson, 1939) and the Yankee City studies (Warner & Lunt, 1941).

The Hawthorne studies were a series of experiments conducted in the late 1920s and early 1930s at the Western Electric Hawthorne Works factory in Illinois. The studies were designed to investigate the effects of different working conditions on employee productivity, and to identify factors that could improve worker efficiency. Although the Hawthorne studies were not called mixed methods studies, they involved both quantitative experiments using quantitative measures and extensive qualitative interviews with and observation of employees. The Yankee City studies were a series of studies conducted by a team of social scientists, including William Lloyd Warner, in New England town in Connecticut in the 1930s. The studies focused on the social and economic factors that influenced the behavior of people in the community and were designed to provide insights into the broader social and economic issues of the time. Although this study was primarily ethnographic in nature, it used extensive qualitative interviews as well as quantitative surveys, therefore combining both methods of research.

Despite these early examples, the formalization of mixed methods research only gained momentum in the 1980s and 1990s. Scholars such as Tashakkori, Teddlie, Creswell, and Plano Clark played pivotal roles in advancing mixed methods research methodology. Tashakkori and Teddlie's comprehensive works (e.g., Tashakkori and Teddlie, 1998) introduced various designs and strategies, while Creswell and Plano Clark contributed influential books on research methodology such as *Research Design: Qualitative, Quantitative, and Mixed Methods Approaches* (Creswell, 2014), *A Concise Introduction to Mixed Methods Research* (Creswell, 2015), and *Designing and Conducting Mixed Methods Research* (Creswell & Plano Clark, 2018). Today, mixed methods research is widely utilized across disciplines, including applied linguistics. The approach is based on the belief that combining qualitative and quantitative methods provides a more comprehensive understanding of complex research phenomena than either method alone.

The Philosophical Orientations of Mixed Methods Research

In terms of its philosophical orientations, mixed methods research has been greatly influenced by both pragmatism and the postpositivist perspective. As discussed in Chapter 5, pragmatism is a philosophical approach that emphasizes the practical implications and utility of knowledge. It acknowledges that research questions are too complex to be addressed using a single method and that different research methods have their strengths and weaknesses. Because of that, when we use multiple methods, we can gain a more comprehensive understanding of the research question under investigation. Mixed methods research is based on the idea that different research questions may require different methods and that a combination of quantitative and qualitative methods may be needed to be fully able to address complex research problems.

The philosophical orientations of mixed methods research have been greatly influenced by both pragmatism and the postpositivist perspective.

Postpositivism recognizes that knowledge is relative and that there is no one objective reality that can be studied in the same manner. It recognizes that research findings are influenced by subjective experiences and assumptions, in contrast to positivism's emphasis on objectivity and verifiable quantitative data. As a weaker form of positivism, Postpositivism encourages the scientific approach but values the perspectives of both researchers and participants, advocating the use of multiple methods, including both quantitative (e.g., surveys, experiments) and qualitative (e.g., interviews, observations) approaches.

Mixed methods research has been influenced not only by postpositivism but also by constructivism. Constructivism contends that reality is constructed through human interaction with the world, emphasizing the social dimension. Rejecting the idea that one method suffices for research questions, constructivism supports the use of diverse methods in data collection and analysis.

Altogether, the philosophical orientations of mixed methods research is grounded in the notion that reality is complex and requires a flexible and iterative approach to research. Accordingly, mixed methods research emphasizes the integration of both quantitative and qualitative methods to effectively address complex research questions.

The Value of Mixed Methods Research

The use of mixed methods can enhance the validity of research in several ways: First of all, combining quantitative and qualitative methods can provide a more comprehensive understanding of the research question or problem. Each of these methods by itself has its own limitations, and in mixed methods research, the strengths of one method can complement the weaknesses of the other, resulting in a more complete and more accurate picture of the issue under investigation. Using multiple methods can also help triangulate the data by providing evidence from multiple sources, and in doing so it increases the validity of the research. If different methods produce results that consistently show the same conclusion, more confidence can be placed in the findings. Mixed methods research can also enable you to explore the different aspects of the question, hence leading to the expansion of the scope of the research. This helps with generating new research questions or hypotheses that can be explored in future research. Last but not least, mixed methods research can help you to cross-check the results across different sources of data which can then lead to greater assurance that the findings shown are more accurate.

Mixed methods research enhances the validity of research in several ways: It helps achieve a more comprehensive understanding of the research question, facilitates the triangulation of data, expands the research scope, and allows the cross-checking of results for greater accuracy,

POINTS TO PONDER

Can you provide a few examples of research questions or problems for which mixed-methods research might be well-suited?

Designing Mixed Methods Studies

Designing a mixed methods study requires careful planning and the consideration of a number of factors so that the study can be designed appropriately and the research questions can be addressed effectively. Many of the steps involved in designing a mixed methods study are similar to those used in any research design, including deciding on a topic, formulating a research question, conducting a literature review, choosing a research design, selecting the participants, and deciding on the data collection and analysis methods. (In Chapter 4, we outlined and described these steps in detail.) However, there are also specific steps that are unique to mixed methods research, such as integration, which involves combining and analyzing the qualitative and quantitative data collected in the study. We will briefly revisit these steps below, incorporating those related to mixed methods research.

1. **Determining what to investigate:** Before beginning your mixed methods research, it is essential to identify the research problem or issue you aim to investigate and the questions you want to answer. At this stage, the problem may be broad, indicating a general area of interest, which can later be refined into specific research questions.

2. **Reviewing the literature:** Conduct a literature review to identify gaps and refine research questions. While it does not need to be exhaustive at this stage, this review will help establish a solid theoretical foundation and guide the development of your research focus.

3. **Formulating research questions:** Develop clear and concise research questions suitable for a mixed methods approach. At this stage, you could also formulate your hypothesis if the quantitative component of the research is a hypothesis-testing study.

4. **Determining research design:** Select an appropriate mixed methods research design, considering both the overall design and the design for each qualitative and quantitative phase. This involves decisions on two levels. One is the overall mixed methods level. This means what type of mixed methods design should be used as there are a number of such designs that can be used (see below). The other decision relates to what type of design should be used in each of the qualitative or quantitative phases (see Chapters 9 and 14).

5. **Selecting participants:** Decide on sample size and selection methods, considering the research question and study design. Mixed methods research may involve using different sampling methods for the qualitative and quantitative components of the study or selecting a sample that can be used for both types of data (see Chapters 8 and 13).

6. **Collecting data:** Plan and implement data collection methods based on the research questions and the overall mixed methods design. Since mixed methods research involves both qualitative and quantitative data, the type of data collected and the timing of data collection may vary depending on the study's design. For example, both types of data may be collected simultaneously in some cases, while in others, one type may be collected before or after the other (see below).

7. **Processing and analyzing data:** Analyze both qualitative and quantitative data using suitable methods, ensuring integration is feasible. Quantitative data analysis involves statistical methods, including calculating means, medians, etc., or using inferential statistics to test hypotheses or compare groups (see Chapter 20). Qualitative data analysis, on the other hand, examines nonnumerical data such as text or images, utilizing coding techniques to identify patterns or themes (see Chapter 16). In a mixed methods study, the data analysis should be designed to integrate both qualitative and quantitative data.

8. **Integrating data:** An important step in a mixed methods study is integration. It involves combining quantitative and qualitative data to address the research question by synthesizing findings, comparing patterns across data types, and using one type of data to clarify, complement, or expand on the insights gained from the other.

9. **Interpreting and explaining results:** Interpret and explain the results from both data types. This involves considering the findings from both the qualitative and quantitative data to provide a detailed understanding of the research problem. Depending on the research design, this may involve comparing and contrasting the results to identify patterns, address discrepancies, and uncover insights that may not be apparent when each data type is considered separately.

10. **Writing the research report:** Communicate findings through a written report or presentation. This not only contributes to the existing body of knowledge in the field but also provides opportunities for replication and verification of the findings by others (see Chapter 25).

All in all, designing a mixed methods study involves careful consideration of the research question, the existing literature, the research design, the sampling strategy, the data collection methods, and the data analysis and integration strategies. It is important to note that the process is iterative and cyclical, not strictly linear.

The Aims of Mixed Methods Reseaech

When doing mixed methods research, you should have a clear idea about why you are using it. In Chapters 1 and 5, we categorized the aims of research into the following three main categories:

Descriptive: This aim involves describing a particular phenomenon or situation, such as stages of L2 acquisition, bilingual speech characteristics, or classroom discourse patterns.

Exploratory: This aim involves exploring a topic or issue in order to generate ideas or hypotheses for future research. This can involve collecting preliminary data, conducting literature reviews, or running pilot studies.

Explanatory: This aim involves explaining the relationship between different variables or factors, such as identifying the causes of a particular phenomenon or predicting future outcomes based on current data. This can involve using statistical analyses, experimental designs, or qualitative methods to understand the underlying mechanisms and processes involved.

In addition to the above aims, mixed methods research can also have other aims that can vary depending on the research question and the type of mixed methods design used. Some common aims include the following:

Complementary: This aim involves using both quantitative and qualitative methods to provide a more complete understanding of a research question than would be possible with either method alone. The aim is to use the strengths of each method to compensate for the weaknesses of the other, and to produce a more comprehensive understanding of the phenomenon under study.

Triangulation: This aim involves using multiple methods to cross-validate findings and improve the overall validity and reliability of the research. By using different methods to explore the same research question, you can compare and contrast findings, identify patterns, and address potential biases or limitations in the data.

Expansion: This aim involves using mixed methods research to generate new research questions or hypotheses that can be explored in future research. By using both quantitative and qualitative methods to explore a research question, you may uncover new avenues for exploration or identify gaps in existing knowledge that can be addressed in future research.

Overall, the aim of mixed methods research is to use multiple methods to gain a more refined and deeper understanding of a research question or phenomenon, and to produce findings that are more robust, reliable, and valid than would be possible with a single method alone, especially when the issue to be examined is complex.

Different Types of Mixed Methods Research

Although mixed methods research can be viewed as a research approach that combines both qualitative and quantitative methods, it is not a single method in and of itself. Rather, it is a complex research approach that involves the integration of multiple methods in various ways. Therefore, there are various types of mixed methods research that differ from one another in important ways. Within the academic literature, various taxonomies have been proposed, each structured around different criteria. In this section, we will discuss the most straightforward and common ones.

One way of categorizing mixed methods research designs will be based on the two factors of sequencing and emphasis. The first factor, sequence, refers to the order in which the quantitative and qualitative data are collected and analyzed. Depending on the order, the mixed methods may be sequential, concurrent, or a combination of the two. In sequential mixed methods, either the quantitative or the qualitative data are collected and analyzed first, followed by the collection and analysis of the other type of data. The results from each type of data are integrated at a later stage to draw overall conclusions. In concurrent mixed methods research, the quantitative and qualitative data are collected and analyzed simultaneously, and the results from each type of data are integrated throughout the research process to draw overall conclusions. The second factor, emphasis, refers to the priority given to either the qualitative or quantitative component or the degree of importance placed on each component in the research design. Depending on the emphasis, there could be three possibilities: quantitative methods being emphasized, qualitative methods being emphasized, and equal emphasis. Based on these two factors, sequence and emphasis, different types of mixed methods research have been identified and discussed in the literature (e.g., Creswell, 2014; Creswell & Plano Clark, 2018; Tashakkori & Teddlie, 1998; Tashakkori & Teddlie, 2003; Tashakkori, Teddlie, & Sines, 2012; Teddlie & Tashakkori, 2006). Creswell and Plano Clark (2018), for example, identified the following three core designs along with their variants:

- convergent design
- explanatory sequential design
- exploratory sequential design.

POINTS TO PONDER

In your academic experience, have you encountered the use of different mixed methods research designs, and if so, can you remember their names and primary characteristics? How did these designs combine qualitative and quantitative research, sequentially or simultaneously?

The Convergent Design

Convergent design is a design in which both quantitative and qualitative data are collected at the same time from the same participants, but they are analyzed separately, and then the results are merged to address the research question or problem. See Figure 24.1.

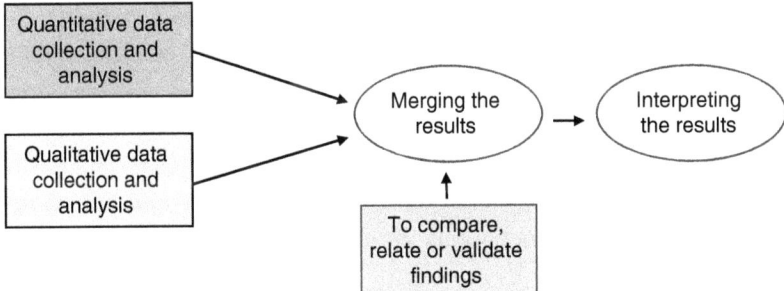

Figure 24.1 The convergent design

In most cases, in this type of mixed methods research, the researcher may put similar emphasis on both quantitative and qualitative data, considering them both as important sources of information. For example, interview data can be considered just as important as scores gathered from a test. The data that are collected quantitatively will be analyzed quantitatively, and the data collected qualitatively will be analyzed qualitatively. The results from both types of analysis are used to determine whether they support each other or not, and what additional insights the other type of data provides to the analysis. Thus, the main aim of the convergent mixed methods design is to triangulate the data from different sources and to provide a more comprehensive understanding of the research problem or question. In doing so, the researcher examines the two databases, looking for the extent to which they support each other.

Convergent design is a design in which both quantitative and qualitative data are collected at the same time but analyzed separately, and then the results are merged to provide a comprehensive understanding of the research question or problem.

Here are the steps in conducting a convergent mixed methods research study:

1. Begin with a research question requiring both quantitative and qualitative data.
2. Conduct qualitative data collection (interviews, focus groups, or observations) for an in-depth understanding (this step occurs alongside step 4).
3. Analyze qualitative data using methods such as thematic or content analysis to explore qualitative aspects of the research (this step occurs alongside step 5).
4. Gather quantitative data through surveys, experiments, or databases, focusing on numerical aspects.
5. Analyze quantitative data using statistical methods to quantify relationships and patterns.
6. Integrate qualitative and quantitative findings during interpretation, identifying patterns or contradictions.
7. Provide an overall interpretation, drawing conclusions based on integrated findings and discussing implications for theory, practice, and future research.

While mixed methods research offers opportunities to triangulate findings, the convergent design presents challenges, including time constraints, resource limitations, data integration, and complexity. Dealing with different sample sizes, merging data, and explaining contradictory results are additional hurdles. Strategies to address these challenges involve collecting sufficient qualitative samples, aligning concepts in quantitative and qualitative data, and sometimes gathering extra data to resolve contradictions. Example 24.1 provides a hypothetical convergent mixed methods study.

EXAMPLE 24.1

Suppose you want to investigate the effectiveness of a classroom instructional strategy designed to enhance cognitive processing in second language learners, specifically focusing on the use of metacognitive strategies such as self-regulation and reflection. You collect quantitative data through pre- and posttests to measure improvements in learners' language proficiency and cognitive skills related to language learning. Additionally, you collect qualitative data through interviews and classroom observations to explore the learners' perspectives, experiences, and cognitive engagement with the metacognitive strategies. For instance, interviews might reveal how students perceive the impact of self-regulation techniques on their language learning, while classroom observations could provide insights into how these strategies influence their cognitive processes during lessons. The quantitative and qualitative data are analyzed separately and then merged to provide a comprehensive understanding of the effectiveness of the instructional intervention. For example, the quantitative data might show improvements in language proficiency and cognitive skills, while the qualitative data could offer explanations for these improvements by uncovering insights into students' experiences, motivations, and engagement with the metacognitive strategies.

Variants of the Convergent Design

Creswell and Plano Clark (2018) discussed four types of variants for the convergent model that are commonly used in studies:

- the parallel-databases variant
- the data-transformation variant
- the questionnaire variant
- the fully integrated variant.

The Parallel-Databases Variant The parallel-databases variant occurs when two separate sets of data collected at the same time are analyzed separately and then merged during the interpretation.

EXAMPLE 24.2

Suppose you are interested in examining learners' beliefs about the use of code-switching in the classroom. You conduct in-depth interviews with a group of L2 learners to explore their personal attitudes and experiences with code-switching, asking questions about its impact on their learning and classroom dynamics. Concurrently, you distribute a closed-ended questionnaire to the same learners, which includes Likert-scale items to quantify their perceptions of code-switching's effectiveness and utility. After collecting the data, you analyze the questionnaire responses to identify general trends and use thematic analysis to interpret the interview transcripts, revealing insights into learners' beliefs. By integrating both sets of data, you gain a better understanding of how code-switching is perceived by learners and its role in their language-learning experience.

The Data-Transformation Variant The data-transformation variant refers to a research design in which two sets of data, such as quantitative data and qualitative data, are collected and then the qualitative data are analyzed quantitatively or transformed into quantitative data. The quantification of the qualitative data allows you to merge the two sets of data easily.

EXAMPLE 24.3

Suppose you are conducting a study to examine the students' and teachers' opinions about the effectiveness of translanguaging (the practice of using multiple languages in instruction to enhance learning) on the development of L2 grammar. You administer a quantitative survey to a group of students using multiple-choice questions or Likert scales to assess their opinions about the effectiveness of translanguaging. In addition to the survey, qualitative data are collected through interviews with a group of teachers. The qualitative data collected from the interviews are then analyzed quantitatively by coding the responses and categorizing them into themes. The frequency of each theme from the teachers' data is tallied and compared to the students' quantitative survey data to identify any patterns or discrepancies between the two sets of data.

The Questionnaire Variant The questionnaire variant refers to when you conduct a questionnaire study, and the questionnaire includes both closed-ended and open-ended questions. Closed-ended questions provide quantitative data by providing respondents with a set of predefined response options to choose from, while the open-ended questions provide qualitative data by asking participants to provide their own answers in their own words. Open-ended questions complement closed-ended questions by providing additional information and insights that can help to better explain participants' responses to closed-ended questions. Such questionnaires are widely used in applied linguistics because they allow you to collect both types of data at the same time; doing so gives participants the opportunity to express their views and opinions in their own words and can also provide insights that might not be possible through closed-ended questions.

The Fully Integrated Variant The fully integrated variant refers to the situation where the quantitative and qualitative data are collected when the study is being conducted, with one type of data collection informing the other. For example, if you are interested in examining teachers' cognition, you may interview teachers based on their responses to their questionnaire and vice versa.

Of course, sometimes, all the variants discussed above can be combined in different ways, with different emphasis given to each component, based on the purpose of the research and the research question, through a multi-phase design (see below). For example, a mixed methods study may combine the integrated variant and the questionnaire variant.

EXAMPLE 24.4

Suppose you are conducting a classroom-based study on the effectiveness of peer feedback in writing classes. You begin with a qualitative classroom observation where you visit several writing classes and observe the use of peer feedback during writing assignments. In the classroom observation, you take detailed notes on the use of peer feedback, including how the student pairs are structured, how the feedback is provided, and how students respond to the feedback. These notes are analyzed qualitatively, but they are then also used to inform the design of the survey administered to both the students and teachers who participated in the observed writing classrooms. The survey includes both closed-ended and open-ended questions. The data from the closed-ended survey are analyzed quantitatively, and those from the open-ended questions are analyzed qualitatively. The survey is then followed by other classroom observations to see to what extent what the students have indicated in the survey matches what they do in the classroom. In this study, the classroom observation, which is qualitative, is analyzed quantitatively, which would then add a data-transformation variant to the study.

Sequential Explanatory Design

Similar to the convergent design, the sequential explanatory design also combines qualitative and quantitative data collection and analysis methods, but it does so in two separate phases. Quantitative data are collected and analyzed first, followed by the collection and analysis of qualitative data to explain the quantitative findings. Therefore, an important factor distinguishing this design from the convergent design is that in this type of design, the research begins with a quantitative component and then, based on some of the results in the quantitative part, a subsequent qualitative study will be conducted to explain the findings of the quantitative component. Since the first phase is quantitative, the data collected will be numerical, using, for example, structured questionnaires or tests, which will be analyzed statistically. The aim of this phase is to identify any relationships between variables or to examine whether one variable affects another. Since the second phase is qualitative, you collect qualitative data using, for example, interviews, focus groups, or observations.

In **the sequential explanatory mixed methods design** quantitative data are collected and analyzed first, followed by the collection and analysis of qualitative data to explain the quantitative findings.

This design in called sequential explanatory design because the aim of the subsequent qualitative data collection phase is to help explain the results initially obtained through the first quantitative phase. For example, the qualitative phase can help to explain any unexpected or conflicting results from the quantitative phase and provide context to the data. This is the most popular type of mixed methods design in applied linguistics research. See Figure 24.2.

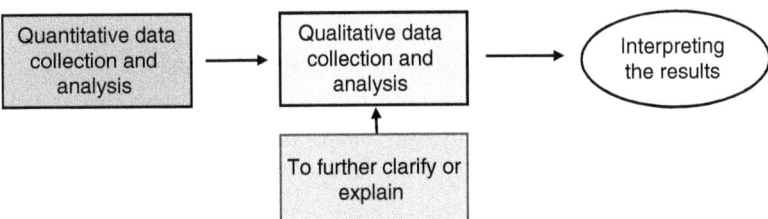

Figure 24.2 The sequential explanatory design

Here are the steps of an explanatory sequential mixed methods research design:

1. Start with a research question that requires quantitative data to answer.
2. Collect quantitative data through surveys, experiments, or other quantitative procedures.
3. Analyze the quantitative data quantitatively.
4. Identify the kind of findings from the quantitative phase that need further exploration and use those to guide the development of a qualitative phase. The qualitative phase should aim to explain the findings identified in the quantitative phase.
5. Conduct a qualitative phase to collect in-depth data through interviews, observations, or other methods, and analyze the data.
6. Integrate the results of the qualitative and quantitative phases to explain the research question. This integration can be done by comparing and contrasting the findings from the two sets to interpret and explain the quantitative data.
7. Use the findings to draw conclusions.

The sequential explanatory design is helpful because it allows for a deeper understanding of the research problem by combining the strengths of both quantitative and qualitative methods. The sequential nature of the design allows the data collected in each phase to inform subsequent phases, and the design can be tailored to suit the specific research question and context. The difference between the convergent method mentioned earlier and this one is that in this type of mixed methods research, in addition to collecting data at difference phases, the researcher often gives more importance to quantitative data collection and analysis by introducing it first and making it a major aspect of data collection. The qualitative component is usually smaller and comes after the quantitative one. The aim of the qualitative data is to provide more insight into the results obtained from the quantitative data by collecting more data from a subsample of the participants. According to Creswell and Plano Clark (2018, pp. 77–78), the explanatory sequential design is most useful in the following scenarios:

- The researcher and the research problem are more quantitatively oriented and thus it makes sense to start the procedures with a quantitative phase.
- The researcher knows the important variables and has access to quantitative instruments for measuring the constructs of primary interest.
- The researcher has the ability to return to the participants for a second round of qualitative data collection.
- The researcher has the time to conduct the research in two phases.
- The researcher has limited resources (perhaps the researcher is the sole investigator) and needs a design in which only one type of data is being collected and analyzed at a time.

EXAMPLE 24.5

Suppose you are interested in investigating how teachers perceive the use of the first language in their classrooms. In the first phase of the study, you use a survey to gather quantitative data on the use of first languages in the classroom. In the second phase, based on the findings in the first phase, more in-depth interviews are conducted with a smaller sample of teachers to provide a deeper insight into their perceptions and experiences with the use of L1 in the classroom. For example, two groups of teachers are identified in the first phase who have indicated high and low use of first language. Then from each group a few will be selected and interviewed using in-depth one-to-one interviews. The qualitative findings are then used to explain the quantitative results. For example, if the quantitative data has shown that some teachers reported using high levels of L1 use in the classroom, the qualitative data can examine their reasons and explain why they do so. Thus, the qualitative data can provide insights into why these teachers used or did not use the L1.

Variants of the Sequential Explanatory Design

Creswell and Plano Clark (2018) discussed two variants of the sequential explanatory design:

- the prototypical follow-up explanations variant
- the case-selection variant.

In the prototypical follow-up explanations variant, the priority is on the quantitative part, and the researcher uses the qualitative part to explain the results of the quantitative part. In the case-selection variant, the priority will be on the qualitative part, but the quantitative part is conducted first to identify the best cases for the subsequent in-depth qualitative study.

POINTS TO PONDER

What do you think are the characteristics and objectives of the sequential exploratory design. Can you provide an example of a research question or problem that you think could be addressed through sequential exploratory design?

Sequential Exploratory Design

The sequential exploratory design is the opposite of the sequential explanatory design in terms of the sequence of qualitative and quantitative methods. This design involves collecting and analyzing qualitative data first, followed by collecting quantitative data. The qualitative data are often collected through qualitative data collection tools, such as interviews, focus groups, or observations, and is often analyzed using qualitative data analysis methods, such as content analysis or thematic analysis. The aim of the first qualitative phase is to develop a preliminary understanding of the phenomenon under investigation. In the second phase, the findings from the qualitative phase are used to inform the design of a quantitative study. See Figure 24.3.

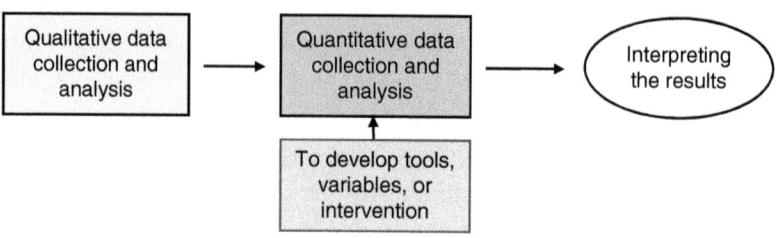

Figure 24.3 The sequential exploratory design

The sequential exploratory design is the opposite of the sequential explanatory design in terms of the sequence of qualitative and quantitative methods; it involves collecting and analyzing qualitative data first, followed by collecting quantitative data.

For example, the second phase may be conducted to test hypotheses generated in the qualitative phase or to provide a better understanding of the phenomenon being studied. In other cases, you may develop a quantitative data collection tool based on the result of the qualitative part and use that tool in the subsequent quantitative study. Based on the results of the first phase, the researchers may also test the effect of new variables or implement a new measure, such as a survey; they may develop and use a new intervention or experimental tasks, or develop new digital tools to be tested in the subsequent quantitative part (Creswell & Plano Clark, 2018).

The difference between the explanatory and the exploratory design, in addition to the difference in the sequence of qualitative and quantitative method, is that in an exploratory design, the research begins with more open-ended questions, and thus, in this type of research, the first intention of the study is to explore an area where little is known about a particular topic, and researchers want to explore it in depth to generate new insights and ideas. Therefore, the researcher may give more priority to qualitative data collection and analysis, by introducing it first and making it a major aspect of the data collection, and also providing a very detailed analysis of the qualitative findings. Because the exploratory design begins with qualitative data collection, the study often begins with data collected from a small group of individuals, followed by data collected from a larger sample.

In a sequential exploratory design, the intention is to use the quantitative data to refine and expand upon the initial qualitative findings by using, for example, an instrument or survey developed based on them. For instance, a study of an adult English language learners' literacy program might start with a qualitative exploration of learners' experiences. Thematic analysis identifies key themes. This is followed by a quantitative phase, assessing program effectiveness with language tests or surveys. The survey is informed by the qualitative insights. Integration of both qualitative and quantitative results provides a more holistic view of the program's effectiveness and associated factors.

The Variants of the Sequential Exploratory Design

Creswell and Plano Clark (2018) identified the following four variants for the sequential exploratory design:

- the new-variable development variant
- the survey-development variant
- the intervention-development variant
- the digital-tool-development variant.

The New-Variable Development Variant In the new-variable development variant, you follow a research approach that involves the identification of new variables. This process unfolds in two distinct phases: an initial qualitative phase and a subsequent quantitative phase. During the qualitative phase, you may conduct an in-depth qualitative study, employing methods such as interviews, focus groups, or observations to gather rich data. The primary goal is to uncover and understand aspects of the research topic that might not be fully captured by existing variables or frameworks. This phase is exploratory, allowing you to identify emergent themes, patterns, or variables that may not have been previously considered. Through the qualitative exploration, you identify new variables or a new conceptual or theoretical framework, the examination of which enhances your understanding of the subject matter. These insights can then be used to inform the subsequent quantitative phase.

EXAMPLE 24.6

Suppose you are conducting a mixed methods study examining language acquisition in a multicultural classroom. The initial qualitative phase involves interviews and classroom observations, through which you identify a previously unnoticed variable, such as the role of cultural identity in shaping language development. With the insights from the qualitative phase, you move on to the quantitative phase, which involves designing studies or experiments based on the newly identified variables. You might formulate quantitative research questions related to the impact of cultural identity on language acquisition. You then design surveys or experiments to collect quantitative data that can be statistically analyzed. The findings from the qualitative and quantitative phases are integrated to enable a fuller understanding of the research topic.

The Survey-Development Variant In the survey-development approach, you employ a two-step process, starting with a qualitative phase to inform the design of a survey instrument. The reason for conducting the first qualitative study is thus that the instruments or activities either do not yet exist, are unknown, have no guiding theoretical framework, or require the development of a measure specific to the participants in the study (Creswell & Plano Clark, 2018). Therefore, most often in such cases, the design involves a qualitative phase, a variable or instrument developmental phase, and a quantitative phase. To illustrate this, let's consider the study in Example 24.7.

EXAMPLE 24.7

Suppose you are conducting a study to examine students' perspectives on the effectiveness of using corpus-based materials for improving their writing skills. During the initial qualitative phase, you conduct in-depth qualitative focus group sessions to gain an understanding of participants' perspectives on corpus-based materials. Through these discussions, you identify key themes, concerns, and attitudes that might not have been apparent through quantitative methods alone. For example, participants may have expressed varying levels of confidence in using corpus tools and their perceived impact on their writing quality. Following the qualitative phase, you translate these qualitative insights into the development of a survey instrument. This instrument may include closed-ended questions, likely designed to capture binary responses, or Likert-scale ratings that could be analyzed quantitatively. The questions might reflect the identified themes and concerns from the qualitative phase, allowing for a more structured and broad assessment across a larger sample. Subsequently, in the quantitative phase, you administer the survey to a group of students. This allows you to quantify and analyze the prevalence of specific perspectives and attitudes identified during the qualitative phase.

The Intervention-Development Variant Building on the findings from a qualitative phase, researchers may choose to devise intervention activities for a second phase. For example, the qualitative data collection focuses on activities or the development of measures that could be used in the intervention. Interventions could be educational programs or activities aimed at addressing the specific concerns or issues revealed through the qualitative data.

EXAMPLE 24.8

Suppose you first conduct a qualitative study including interviews and focus groups with members of immigrant communities to understand their experiences and challenges in acquiring English language proficiency. Qualitative data may reveal common barriers such as limited access to language resources or cultural factors influencing language learning. You may also quantify the prevalence of identified challenges to gather insights into the language proficiency levels of the community members. Analysis of the qualitative data highlights specific concerns, such as a lack of accessible language resources, low confidence in language skills, and cultural factors impacting language learning outcomes. Based on the identified concerns, you design intervention activities aimed at addressing these issues. For instance, recognizing the need for accessible language resources, you could implement an intervention involving interactive English lessons with culturally tailored content. Activities may also include workshops or community events to boost confidence in language use and provide a supportive environment for practice. You may conduct additional quantitative data collection focused specifically on activities by using pre- and posttest measures related to the intervention to evaluate its effectiveness.

The intervention development can also involve piloting workshops, gathering participant feedback, and refining the intervention based on qualitative insights. The designed intervention in the above example is implemented within the immigrant community. Participants engage in the educational programs or activities tailored to address their specific needs and concerns. Qualitative data may include participant interviews, while quantitative measures could assess changes in language proficiency levels. You may adjust the intervention based on both qualitative narratives, highlighting areas of success or improvement, and quantitative data, providing statistical evidence of changes in language proficiency or confidence levels.

The Digital-Tool-Development Variant The digital-tool-development variant involves a design starting with qualitative exploration of the research questions. This qualitative insight is then used to shape the design of a digital tool, which is then tested in a subsequent study.

EXAMPLE 24.9

Suppose you are interested in enhancing language learning outcomes among English as a Second Language (ESL) students. You conduct a mixed methods study to develop and test a digital language learning application. Initially you conduct a qualitative study using qualitative interviews and focus groups with ESL students to understand their language learning preferences, challenges, and the types of activities that engage them effectively. Through these qualitative interactions, you identify themes such as the importance of interactive exercises, personalized content, and real-world language. Informed by the qualitative insights, you design a digital language learning application that incorporates interactive exercises, personalized content based on individual proficiency levels, and scenarios reflecting real-world language usage. The tool may include features such as multimedia lessons, interactive quizzes, and a chatbot for conversational practice. The developed digital tool is then tested with a group of ESL students in a real educational setting. Participants use the application for a set period, engaging with its various features and completing language exercises. You may then quantitatively assess the tool's impact by administering surveys to participants, collecting data on factors such as language proficiency improvement, user satisfaction, and perceived effectiveness of the digital tool.

Of course, there could be other variants as well, in addition to the four variants discussed here, depending on the aim of the subsequent phase. For example, if the aim is to test a hypothesis generated by the first study, in the second phase, another variant can also be called the testing-hypothesis variant.

POINTS TO PONDER

What is an embedded mixed methods research design? How does this design integrate qualitative and quantitative data, and what is its primary focus? Can you give examples of research questions or topics where an embedded design is particularly suitable?

In addition to the above core designs, Creswell (2014) discussed three additional mixed methods research designs: the embedded design, the transformative design, and the multiphase design.

The Embedded Design

The embedded design is a design whereby one method (qualitative or quantitative) is embedded within another method. In this approach, one type of data is considered as the primary data, while the other type is considered as secondary. In an embedded mixed methods design, the qualitative or quantitative data can be collected before, during, or after the other type of data, to support it. The specific timing and sequence depend on the research question and the overall design of the study. For example, if the primary research question is understanding the effectiveness of an instructional program, you may begin the study by collecting some qualitative data, such as conducting interviews in order to determine how to design the experimental study. Or you may first use a quantitative study to measure the outcome of the intervention, after which qualitative interviews with a subset of learners may be used to gain a deeper understanding of the factors contributing to its success. See Figure 24.4.

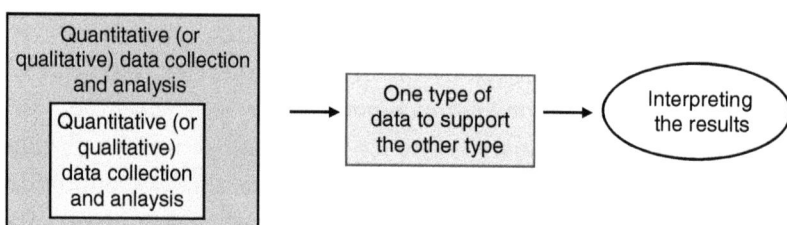

Figure 24.4 The embedded design

In **the embedded design**, qualitative or quantitative method is embedded within another method; the qualitative or quantitative data can be collected before, during, or after the other type of data to support it.

In some other cases, you may collect both quantitative and qualitative data simultaneously (i.e., collection of qualitative data during the collection of quantitative data) to supplement one type of data with the other. For instance, in a quantitative experimental study, you may want to understand not only whether the intervention is effective but also how the participants feel during the treatment. Overall, one difference between the embedded design and the other previous designs is that one form of data is used as a secondary source of data to provide support for the other type of data. The secondary data can be collected either before, during, or after the collection of primary data.

EXAMPLE 24.10

Suppose you are interested in investigating the effectiveness of two types of storytelling strategies for revitalizing an indigenous language: traditional oral storytelling and interactive digital storytelling. You conduct a quantitative experiment to compare the learning outcomes of students who receive instruction using traditional oral storytelling with those who receive instruction using interactive digital storytelling. The quantitative data are the major source of data and are collected through a pre- and posttest design assessing language proficiency.

To supplement this quantitative data, you collect qualitative data during the experiment to gain insights into students' experiences with the two storytelling methods. For example, you interview some of the students or give them a questionnaire during the study to explore their attitudes, perceptions, and experiences of traditional oral storytelling versus interactive digital storytelling. In this study, the qualitative data collection is embedded within the quantitative experiment, with the goal of providing a better understanding of the research question. By collecting both types of data, you can gain a deeper understanding of the effectiveness of the different storytelling methods. The qualitative data during the study can provide insights into the subjective experiences of students, which can be a valuable source of information in refining and improving the research design in subsequent studies.

Transformative Design

Similar to others, transformative mixed methods design also combines both quantitative and qualitative research methods to examine a particular research problem. It can use any of the designs mentioned above. However, it goes beyond simply describing or explaining a phenomenon, to attempting to transform the situation being studied by addressing power imbalances or promoting social change (hence it is called transformative). The transformative design emphasizes the importance of involving participants in the research process, giving them a voice, and recognizing their expertise. This approach can be used in various fields, such as education, social work, psychology, and applied linguistics, to address complex problems and promote transformation by using the results to inform action.

The transformative mixed methods design goes beyond simply describing or explaining a phenomenon, to attempting to transform the situation being studied by addressing power imbalances or promoting social change.

An example of a study with transformative mixed methods design can be an action research study using mixed methods design with the aim of bringing about social change. Action research is a research approach that aims to bring about change in a specific context, such as language teaching. It seeks to bring about transformative change with the aim of empowering research participants to address problems in their own context and to enable them to make positive changes beyond the result of the research project. In action research using a mixed methods design, both qualitative and quantitative data collection and analysis are used in combination with an iterative process of planning, reflection, evaluation, and action. The data collected through the qualitative and quantitative methods are used to inform the planning and implementation of actions, and to assess their outcomes and impacts.

Multiphase Design

A multiphase mixed methods design is a research design that includes the use of more than one mixed methods approach in a single study. It typically involves the combination and integration of two or more concurrent, sequential, or transformative designs, in order to answer different and complex research questions. This design is often used in large-scale research programs that consist of separate but at the same time related studies, each using a particular mixed methods approach.

A multiphase mixed methods design involves the combination and integration of two or more concurrent, sequential, or transformative designs, in order to answer different and complex research questions.

Overall, the purpose of a multiphase mixed methods design is to use a multiphase program of research that includes the strengths of different mixed methods designs while at the same time addressing the limitations of one single mixed methods design. The combination of various mixed methods designs can be done in different ways, depending on the research questions and the purpose of the study. For example, a program of research might use an embedded mixed methods design to explore the relationship between variables and the participants' experiences, a sequential explanatory mixed methods design to examine patterns and causal links, and a convergent mixed methods design to integrate qualitative and quantitative approaches to get further insights not only into learners' experiences but also into how variables affect one another.

The advantage of a multiphase mixed methods research design lies in using and combining multiple projects to gain a deeper understanding of an overarching research issue. It can also enhance the validity and reliability of the research as data are collected from various sources across time. It allows you to address multiple research questions, exploring different aspects of the research problem using different methods. However, one challenge is that it requires careful planning and coordination so that the different designs are integrated seamlessly with the research being focused on the research questions. Another one would be the ability to form a research team that can collaborate well despite their different method orientations, and to make sure that the different phases or studies are connected with all the studies contributing to the overall objective of the research program (Creswell, 2012).

Selecting Participants for Mixed Methods Research

In mixed methods research, sampling is important for both quantitative and qualitative phases, aiming to facilitate data integration. The choice of sampling methods should align with the research questions and study objectives. For the quantitative phase, if statistical analysis and population inference are the goals, large sample sizes following established procedures such as probability and nonprobability sampling are recommended. Probability methods include simple random sampling, systematic sampling, stratified sampling, cluster sampling, and multistage sampling, while nonprobability methods involve purposive, convenience, quota, snowball, or referral sampling.

Purposive sampling is commonly employed, particularly in qualitative research; it involves selecting participants based on specific criteria relevant to the research questions. However, it lacks random selection, limiting generalizability.

In mixed methods research, especially in sequential designs, participant selection can be sequential. For instance, if the initial phase is quantitative, participants for the qualitative phase are selected afterward, allowing findings from one phase to inform the other. In concurrent mixed methods, where both data types are collected simultaneously, participants can be selected concurrently for both phases.

Data Collection and Data Analysis Strategies in Mixed Methods Research

As noted earlier, mixed methods study involves both quantitative and qualitative data. Quantitative data consist of numerical information and can be gathered through tests and closed-ended surveys (see Chapter 10). Tests systematically assess individuals' knowledge, abilities, or skills, providing quantifiable scores (see Chapter 10 for types of measures and Part V for analysis methods). Qualitative data are nonnumerical in nature and include textual or visual information collected through tools such as interviews, focus groups, and observations. Interviews involve questioning participants about their opinions, conducted face-to-face or over the phone, and can be structured or unstructured (see Parts IV and V for details). Mixed methods researchers may also incorporate preexisting data from personal, academic, government, or organizational records to provide context or background, or to supplement data collected through other methods.

Within- and Between-Strategies Data Collection Procedures

The mixed methods data collection procedure can be done using several separate data collection instruments or sometimes only one instrument, through which both types of data can be collected. The former is called between-strategy data collection procedure, and the latter is called within-strategy data collection procedure. An example of within-strategy data collection procedure is when one instrument, such as a questionnaire, is used to collect both quantitative and qualitative data. A questionnaire, for example, can include both qualitative and quantitative data by incorporating different types of questions, such as closed-ended questions (e.g., multiple-choice questions, rating scales, and yes/no questions) and open-ended questions (e.g., short-answer questions and essay questions). There could also be mixed methods questions which include both closed-ended and open-ended components. For example, a question could ask respondents to rate their level of agreement with a statement on a scale of 1 to 5, and then ask them to explain their answer in a short paragraph. This type of question can provide both quantitative data (the numerical rating) and qualitative data (the explanation).

A **within-strategy** data collection procedure is a method in which both qualitative and quantitative data are collected through one instrument, and a **between-strategy** data collection procedure is a method in which both types of data are collected using several separate data collection instruments.

The same within-strategy technique can also be used in other data collection procedures, such as classroom observation. Classroom observation schemes can include both qualitative and quantitative data by using a combination of a rating scale or a checklist to collect specific data quantitatively, such as the number of times a teacher uses a certain instructional strategy, the amount of time spent on a particular task or topic, or the number of types of questions asked. Such data can be analyzed statistically to identify the frequency of the issues examined. The same classroom observation scheme can also incorporate qualitative data collection strategies, such as spaces for notetaking in which the researcher can comment on the nature of what has been observed. The teachers' notes collected during classroom observation can then be analyzed qualitatively, through coding the data into themes and categories, and identifying patterns and trends. It is important to note that any such data can also be analyzed quantitatively by, for example, calculating the frequency of certain themes or codes that represent certain instructional strategies or student behaviors.

POINTS TO PONDER

What are the different ways of integrating data across different sources in mixed methods research? What strategies would you use or what considerations would you take into account when merging qualitative and quantitative data?

Integration of Data in Mixed Methods Research

One of the key challenges in mixed methods research is integrating and analyzing data across different data sources. You must carefully consider how you will integrate the data so that the results and findings from both sources are synthesized in a valid and reliable manner. Integration involves the process of combining the qualitative and quantitative data collected in a study. Integration means analyzing and interpreting the data together in such a way that a more complete picture and understanding of the research question can be gained. The process of integration often involves comparing and contrasting the findings, looking for patterns and themes across both types of data, or using one type of data to further explain, support, or elaborate on the findings from the other type of data.

Integration means analyzing and interpreting the data together in such a way that a more complete picture and understanding of the research question can be gained.

Depending on the type and purpose of the research, the integration can take different forms. For example, in sequential studies where one type of data is collected and analyzed first followed by the other type, the findings from both can be integrated, with the second set of findings helping to explain, build upon, or validate the results from the first. For instance, you may conduct an experimental study to collect quantitative data and then conduct interviews to collect qualitative data. The findings from the qualitative data can be used to validate the findings from the quantitative data. In a concurrent design, both types of data are collected and analyzed at the same time. Therefore, the findings from both types of data are then combined during the interpretation phase. Integration of quantitative and qualitative data in a concurrent design can be done in different ways.

One way would be to show and discuss both types of data together in a single presentation. For example, a table or a graph can show the results of both. This concurrent display can be used to identify patterns, connections, or discrepancies between the findings from the two types of data. Another way would be to use a triangulation method. In this method you can compare and contrast the findings from the two types of data to identify areas of convergence or divergence. This approach can be useful for validating and confirming findings across both types of data.

Integration could also be done in a supplementary manner, in which the quantitative and qualitative data are used to answer different aspects of the research question. For example, in a study on corrective feedback, the quantitative data may be used to answer questions related to the effectiveness of corrective feedback, and the qualitative data may be used to answer questions related to the students' attitudes towards feedback.

Another method of integration is when one type of data is given priority over the other type. In this manner, typically a small set of data is collected from a subsample to support or explain aspects of the findings from the primary type of data. For example, you may use a large-scale survey to collect quantitative data about teachers' cognition, but conduct follow-up interviews with a small number of teachers to support the quantitative findings. In all of the above situations, the aim of the integration is to provide a more comprehensive understanding of the research question by combining and synthesizing both quantitative and qualitative data.

POINTS TO PONDER

What strategies would you use to ensure the validity of mixed methods research findings? How can you address potential threats to validity in a mixed methods study?

Validity and Reliability of Mixed Methods Research

In Chapters 12 and 17, we explored reliability and validity concepts in quantitative and qualitative research, emphasizing their application in both types of research. Reliability, an important concept particularly in quantitative research, pertains to the consistency and dependability of study findings and measurements. Quantitative validity concerns the accuracy of measuring what a study claims to measure, while in qualitative research, validity focuses on accurately representing subjective experiences and perspectives. As discussed in Chapter 17, criteria such as credibility, transferability, dependability, and confirmability assess the trustworthiness and quality of qualitative data. Detailed descriptions, a systematic approach to data, and transparency enhance these principles. Qualitative research also improves validity through prolonged engagement, member checking, and triangulation.

Quantitative research employs internal and external validity strategies. As discussed in Chapter 12, internal validity concerns causal relationships between independent and dependent variables, addressing factors such as study design and measurement issues. External validity concerns generalizability to other populations or settings, through factors such as careful sampling and consideration of population characteristics and context.

In addition to the validity and reliability issues, there are several other types of validity that are especially important in mixed methods research. Onwuegbuzie and Johnson (2006) discussed nine such types of mixed methods research validity, which they called types of "legitimation." These include:

- sample integration
- the inside–outside legitimation
- weakness minimization
- sequential legitimation
- conversion
- paradigmatic mixing
- commensurability
- multiple validities
- political validity.

Sample Integration
The first type of mixed methods research validity is what Onwuegbuzie and Johnson (2006) called sample integration. This emphasizes the importance of deriving meta-inferences from the combined analysis of both qualitative and quantitative data, making sure that inferences are based on the integration of findings from both approaches.

Inside–Outside Legitimation
Inside–outside legitimation refers to the researcher's effort to incorporate both the insider's and observer's perspectives in data presentation and analysis. By effectively integrating both viewpoints, the analysis and interpretation of data become robust, reflecting the complexities of the phenomenon under investigation and enhancing the validity of mixed methods research findings.

Weakness Minimization
The third type is weakness minimization, which refers to the degree to which the limitations or weaknesses of one research method can be compensated for by the strengths of another approach. For instance, the quantitative method may have limitations in terms of sample size or representativeness and thus rely primarily on data that may not be legitimate. In mixed methods research, this can be compensated for by the strengths of a qualitative approach, which provides in-depth data and hence increases the depth of understanding. Quantitative data may provide numerical data that are easy to understand and can show general trends, but they may be limited in their ability to capture the complexity of the issue being

investigated. They can be complemented by qualitative data that provide a better understanding of the experiences and perspectives of the participants.

Sequential Legitimation

Sequential legitimation has to do with the degree to which a mixed methods researcher has taken steps to minimize the risk that the order in which the quantitative and qualitative phases are conducted will influence the meta-inferences drawn from the study. For instance, in a study on instructional strategy effectiveness, collecting quantitative data first and then conducting qualitative interviews could potentially bias results based on method order. To mitigate this, you should make sure that the timing of phases does not unduly influence outcomes. Sandelowski (2003) describes a multiple wave design as one "in which the quantitative and qualitative data collection and data analysis phases oscillate multiple times" (cited in Onwuegbuzie & Johnson, 2006, p. 58).

Conversion

Conversion refers to the degree to which the process of quantitizing or qualitizing data produces high-quality inferences. Quantitizing refers to the process of converting qualitative data into numerical values, while qualitizing involves categorizing data based on nonnumerical characteristics. Conversion validity provides a measure of the effectiveness of this conversion process in generating quality meta-inferences. Therefore, when you use such conversion procedures or transform data into either quantitative or qualitative data during your analysis, you must attempt to make the quantitizing or qualitizing processes effective in producing high-quality meta-inferences or conclusions.

Paradigmatic Mixing

Paradigmatic mixing involves integrating the researcher's beliefs about knowledge, reality, values, methodology, and communication into a coherent framework. It includes epistemological, ontological, axiological, methodological, and rhetorical considerations. Epistemology concerns the researcher's understanding of knowledge and how it can be obtained. Ontology refers to the teachers' beliefs about the nature of reality or what exists. Axiology concerns the researcher's ethical values. Research also involves a methodology, which relates to the techniques and procedures used to gather and analyze data. We also have rhetoric, which has to do with the researcher's style of communication and presentation of the findings. Paradigmatic mixing thus refers to an effective and successful combination of all these components into a package that results in rigorous, coherent, and meaningful research.

Commensurability

Commensurability relates to the extent to which researchers' meta-inferences reflect a combined perspective through the cognitive processes of Gestalt switching and integration. Gestalt switching involves the ability to shift between various perspectives, recognizing the multiplicity of viewpoints on a problem. Gestalt integration is the skill of combining different pieces of information into a coherent whole.

Proficiency in these processes shows the researcher's capacity to think creatively and holistically about research data, drawing on multiple perspectives or theories in mixed methods research.

Multiple Validities

Multiple validities address the validity of a study by employing various validity types relevant to each approach in mixed methods research. In mixed methods research, both the quantitative and qualitative components must meet their respective validity criteria and those specific to mixed methods. Quantitative validity refers to the validity of quantitative data and analyses, while qualitative validity has to do with the credibility and trustworthiness of qualitative findings. These multiple validities help the integration of both the quantitative and qualitative components be sound and fit the overall purpose of the study.

Political Validity

The last type of validity is political validity, which relates to the degree of importance that the consumers of mixed methods research give to insights and conclusion drawn from both the quantitative and qualitative phases of the study. This is an important consideration because it can provide a measure of the significance of the study and the degree to which the meta-inferences made from the research contribute to the field.

Conclusion

This chapter has provided an overview of mixed methods research. Mixed methods research provides a powerful and flexible approach for studying complex research problems in applied linguistics that cannot be fully examined using only one single methodological approach. This chapter began by reviewing the foundations of mixed methods research and its philosophical assumptions. It then discussed the different types of mixed methods research and the steps involved in conducting them, including data collection, data analysis, and integration of data from multiple sources. We have also discussed issues associated with integrating and analyzing data across different datasets, and finally the issue of validity in mixed methods research. Validity is a critical issue in mixed methods research, and you must carefully consider the validity of your research at each stage of the research process. We hope the information presented here can serve as a valuable resource for you when using mixed methods research in your applied linguistics research projects.

DISCUSSION AND ACTIVITY QUESTIONS

Discussion Questions

1. How has your understanding of research design and methodology changed after reading this chapter and learning about mixed methods research?

2. How would you explain the philosophical orientation of mixed methods research to someone unfamiliar with it?

3. How might a researcher's personal philosophical stance influence the design and execution of a mixed methods study?

4. What are the most important considerations when planning a mixed methods study, and how do these considerations differ from those in a single-method study?

5. How would you decide on the timing and sequence of collecting qualitative and quantitative data in a mixed methods study?

6. How can researchers effectively triangulate findings from qualitative and quantitative analyses?

7. How does the integration of quantitative and qualitative data take place in convergent mixed methods research?

8. How can mixed methods researchers maintain the validity of their findings, and why is validity particularly challenging in this type of research?

Activity Questions

1. Design a research study using mixed methods research to investigate a research question that you are interested in. What kind of data would you collect for the quantitative phase, and what kind of data would you collect for the qualitative phase, and why? How would you analyze and integrate the two types of data to draw inferences and conclusions?

2. Choose a research study that has used mixed methods research. What kind of mixed methods research design has the study used? What are the strengths and limitations of the study? Does the author appropriately integrate the quantitative and qualitative data from the two phases of the study? What improvements would you suggest for the study design or methodology?

3. Choose a research study that has used a single method approach, either quantitative or qualitative. Why did the researcher use that method? Do you think the study could be improved by using a mixed methods approach? Explain how.

4. Think about a list of research questions in applied linguistics that could be addressed using mixed methods research. What types of research design would you use and why? What are the advantages of a mixed methods study compared to a single method study (either quantitative or qualitative) when addressing these research questions?

PART VII
Dissemination of Research Findings

25 Disseminating Research Findings: Writing Research Reports

CHAPTER OBJECTIVES

After completing this chapter, you should be able to

- Define the purpose and importance of preparing research reports and disseminating research findings.
- Identify and describe the components of a research report.
- Understand the purpose and importance of each component in a research report and how it contributes to the overall organization and structure of the document.
- Differentiate between different types of abstracts and explain the characteristics of a well-written informative abstract.
- Construct an effective introduction, literature review, and methods section, including the appropriate use of subsections to describe research design, participants, materials, procedures, and data analysis techniques.
- Report the results of commonly used statistical tests.
- Compose a well-structured discussion and conclusion section.
- Understand the importance of properly citing and referencing sources in a research report.

Introduction

Disseminating research findings is an essential phase in the research process. However, doing so effectively is not an easy task and can be particularly challenging for novice writers or students. It is challenging because it involves presenting complex information in a clear, accessible, and academic manner, while at the same time considering the backgrounds and interests of different audiences, such as researchers and practitioners. These challenges highlight the importance of developing effective communication and writing skills. Mastering these abilities not only facilitates the sharing of the findings but also creates opportunities to contribute meaningfully to the field.

There are different ways in which the findings of a research study can be communicated: in written form (such as written research reports, theses, dissertations, or research articles) or through oral presentations (at conferences, seminars, or other professional venues). This chapter focuses on written dissemination. Written reports vary in form. However, despite differences, similarities also exist. For example, all formal research reports require a clear, concise, and formal writing style along with a thorough understanding of the research methodology, analysis, and findings. In applied linguistics, reports such as theses, dissertations, and research articles involve critically evaluating existing literature, synthesizing key findings, identifying gaps in the research, reporting the study and its findings and exploring implications for future research and practice.

This chapter outlines the key steps for creating a document to communicate research findings in applied linguistics – be it a thesis, research report, or article – focusing on purpose, structure, and the effective communication of the findings. It discusses document format, including layout and organization, as well as the main sections and subsections typically found in research reports, such as the abstract, introduction, methodology, results, and conclusion. However, before doing this, we will discuss key principles of writing style and language that are fundamental to good writing and essential for effective communication. These principles apply to all components of the research report.

POINTS TO PONDER

What are the essential components of a research report, and what is the purpose and significance of each in effectively communicating research findings?

Writing Style and Language: Some Key Principles

To create an effective research report, it is important to emphasize the significance of writing style and language. The presentation of information strongly influences clarity, credibility, and overall impact. This section explores key aspects of writing style and language for a well-crafted report. Adhering to proper conventions and employing clear and concise language are fundamental to effective communication.

Let us now examine the key considerations for achieving a coherent and engaging writing style in the context of research reports.

Be Clear and Concise

Clarity and conciseness are two very important aspects of good writing. This means writing in a way that the meaning and intent of the text are easily understood by the reader without any unnecessary words or repetition. To achieve this, present information using language that is accessible to the reader, remove redundant or repetitive phrases, and eliminate filler words that do not contribute to the meaning of the sentence. We should use simple and straightforward language, which is free of jargon, unnecessary words, or complexity. Example 25.1 demonstrates the importance of using clear and concise language.

EXAMPLE 25.1

Unclear and wordy: "The findings were not commensurate with the projected outcomes, leading to incongruencies between the expected and actual results." Clear and concise: "The findings of this study did not align with the expected outcomes."

In this example, the first sentence uses complex language and words that are less commonly used such as "commensurate," "incongruencies," that may confuse the reader. The second sentence uses a simpler language and more common words, and therefore it is easier to understand.

Avoid Sentences That Are Too Long and Complex

When aiming for clarity, it is important to avoid sentences that are overly long or complex. While there is no strict rule on sentence length, shorter sentences are generally more concise and impactful. For complex ideas, breaking them down into simpler, more manageable sentences improves readability. Although longer sentences can be useful for expressing detailed explanations, it is essential to strike a balance. If a sentence becomes too long or convoluted, consider breaking it into shorter, more digestible parts.

Vary Sentence Length

Vary sentence lengths and structures to maintain reader engagement and prevent monotony. Use a mix of simple, compound, and complex sentences to convey information effectively. Using sentences of different lengths can enhance the overall readability and flow of the text. Too many long sentences without breaks can make the writing dense and challenging to follow. On the other hand, an abundance of short sentences can create a choppy rhythm and may not effectively convey more nuanced ideas.

Avoid Ambiguity

Try to remove ambiguity as much as possible. Ambiguous and vague statements or sentences can lead to confusion and misunderstanding. Clearly define any terms or concepts that may have multiple interpretations and avoid ambiguous pronouns, such as "this" or "that" with no clear reference, or vague words such as "some," "things," "stuff," and so on. Example 25.2 presents a sentence with vague words and shows how it can be improved.

EXAMPLE 25.2

Vague: "The data showed some correlation between the variables."
Clear: "The data revealed a moderate correlation coefficient of 0.45 between anxiety and classroom participation."

Check Your Grammar and Sentence Structure

Pay close attention to grammar and sentence structure in your writing to maintain accuracy, error-free content, and appropriateness. Error-free writing enhances your credibility and professionalism, as errors may convey carelessness or a lack of attention to detail. Proper sentence structures contribute to clarity, making your writing more understandable and less confusing. Grammatical accuracy can be achieved through attention to rules such as subject-verb agreement, correct word order, and appropriate punctuation usage. Avoid errors such as sentence fragments and run-on sentences. Choose precise and discipline-specific vocabulary that is also understandable to nonexperts.

Maintain Coherence

Effective writing is characterized by coherence and cohesion. Coherence involves presenting ideas logically, with a smooth flow between sentences and paragraphs. Cohesion, on the other hand, relies on linguistic and grammatical elements that connect different parts of the text. Indicate the connection between ideas and concepts by using transition words and phrases, acting as signposts for readers; examples include "in addition," "however," "on the other hand," "therefore," and "as a result." These aids guide readers through the logical progression of your ideas, making your writing more cohesive and comprehensible. Example 25.3 shows the importance of transition words.

EXAMPLE 25.3

Not well connected: "The study found a positive correlation between anxiety and classroom participation. Levels of anxiety increase. The level of classroom participation increases."
Better connected: "The study found a positive correlation between anxiety and classroom participation. This means that as the level of anxiety increases, so does the level of classroom participation."

Use Clear Headings and Subheadings

Organize your research report using clear and informative headings and subheadings. Headings and subheadings can indicate the relationship between sections, subtopics, or key points, allowing readers to navigate the document easily and understand the logical flow of your argument.

Use the Active Voice Whenever Possible

Use the active voice whenever possible for clarity and directness in your writing. Active voice starts with the subject followed by an action verb, making sentences easier to understand and more straightforward. It reduces ambiguity and promotes conciseness. For instance, "The study reveals significant trends in language acquisition" is often seen as clearer and more engaging than "Significant trends in language acquisition are revealed by the study." While the active voice is generally preferred, there may be specific instances where the passive voice is more appropriate, such as when the focus is on the action or the result or when the identity of the subject is less important. For example, in academic writing, it is common to see sentences like "An experiment was conducted to test the hypothesis," rather than "We conducted an experiment to test the hypothesis." This shift helps to emphasize the process and to avoid personalizing the research.

Proofread

Proofreading is the final step in the writing process; it involves carefully reading the text to identify and correct errors. This includes inaccuracies in grammar, punctuation, spelling, and formatting. Reading critically and objectively helps improve clarity and readability. Taking a break before proofreading provides a fresh perspective, making error detection easier. Seeking feedback from peers or colleagues is valuable, as they bring a new set of eyes to spot unclear areas or hard-to-detect errors that may have become familiar during prolonged immersion in the writing process.

The Components and Organization of a Research Report

No matter whether we are writing a research report for a thesis or dissertation, or preparing a peer-reviewed article for a journal, it is important to understand the key components of a research report so that we can communicate our work effectively. A well-written and well-structured report is important for effective communication of the findings. It not only enhances clarity by making it easier for readers to read the article but also helps present the information in an efficient and effective manner. In this section, we will explore the essential sections of a research report, including the title, abstract, introduction, literature review, methods, results, discussion, conclusion and implications, and references.

The essential elements of a research report include the title, abstract, introduction, literature review, methods, results, discussion, conclusion and implications, and references.

The structure of a research report is as follows:

1. Title
2. Abstract
3. Introduction

4. Literature review
5. Methods
6. Results
7. Discussion
8. Conclusion
9. References
10. Appendices (if applicable).

Title

The first component of a research report or article is a concise and clear title. The significance of a good title cannot be overstated, as it forms the first impression for potential readers and influences their decision to engage with the report. A well-constructed title not only informs the reader but also captures their attention. Consider the following tips when preparing your title:

- Make it concise.
- Make it clear.
- Make it engaging.
- Have the audience in mind.
- Use important key terms.

In addition to these tips, consulting with colleagues or peers is a valuable strategy when writing the title or even the entire manuscript. Feedback from others can help identify areas you may overlook, such as unclear phrasing, missing key elements, or gaps in coherence. It can also provide insights on how the report might be perceived by different audiences.

Example 25.4 gives some examples of poor and improved titles. The poor titles in examples 1–3 are too broad and do not provide specific information about the focus of the research. The improved titles are more specific, indicating the purpose of the study. The title in example 4 is too long and convoluted, and hence difficult to understand. The improved version is more concise and easier to understand.

EXAMPLE 25.4

Example 1

Poor title: "A study of the effect of corrective feedback on second language acquisition"

Improved title: "The effects of direct versus indirect corrective feedback on L2 writing accuracy."

Example 2

Poor title: An examination of language learning strategies in a university context

Improved title: The use of cognitive and meta-cognitive language learning strategies by university ESL students

Example 3
  Poor title: The role of task-based language teaching in language learning
  Improved title: The effectiveness of two-way versus one-way tasks in enhancing EFL learners' grammatical accuracy

Example 4
  Poor title: A comparative examination of the use of translanguaging among adult English language learners in diverse EFL classroom settings
  Improved title: The use of translanguaging in EFL classrooms: A comparative study

POINTS TO PONDER

What are the different types of abstracts, and what are their distinctive features? How can you write an informative abstract? What strategies would you use to write an effective abstract?

Abstract

After the title comes the abstract. An abstract is a short text that provides a brief summary of a research study and its purpose. It is used at the beginning of a research report or a research article to help the reader get the gist of the study's purpose. Abstracts may vary based on purpose, discipline, and audience, with different types being found in applied linguistics journals. Regardless, common features include conciseness, focused summarization, clarity, and accurate representation of the main points and significance of the research. Typically, abstracts are short, ranging from 150 to 250 words, though variations exist among journals, report type or discipline. Those written for theses and dissertations may be slightly longer, offering more detailed information about the study, methods, and findings. Despite appearing at the start of the report, abstracts are usually composed after the research is completed to provide an accurate and concise summary of the study and its findings.

An abstract is a short text that provides a brief summary of a research study and its purpose. It is used at the beginning of a research report or research article to help the reader get the gist of the study's purpose.

Types of Abstract

There are generally two main types of abstract: descriptive and informative. A descriptive abstract, of around 100 words, gives a brief overview of the study's main purpose without detailing research methods, results, or conclusions. Its aim is to help readers determine the study's relevance to their interests. In contrast, an informative abstract provides a more detailed summary, covering the research problem, methodology, main findings, and significance. Informative abstracts are common in applied linguistics and are crucial for empirical research as they offer insights into data collection, analysis techniques, results, and their implications for language learning or teaching.

Another less common type is the critical abstract, which provides an evaluation or critique of the study. These abstracts are usually longer and less common in applied linguistics. In applied linguistics research, informative abstracts are more common. Since much of applied linguistics research is empirical, involving collecting and analyzing data, informative abstracts are more useful as they provide information on the data collection methods and data analysis techniques used, as well as specific details on the results and their implications.

Example 25.5 is a hypothetical descriptive abstract.

EXAMPLE 25.5

Abstract

This study examines the role of student–teacher interaction in two adult intermediate-level English language classrooms. Drawing on Long's (1996) interaction hypothesis and using a mixed methods approach, the analyses reveal many instances of interaction and negotiation of meaning, including clarification requests, confirmation checks, and repetitions. The study also provides insights into how, when, and why teachers use these strategies in their classrooms.

In this example, the abstract provides a brief overview of the main focus of the study, including some information about the theoretical and the methodological approaches used. However, it does not provide specific details about the research methods, the results, and their significance.

Example 25.6 presents a hypothetical informative abstract.

EXAMPLE 25.6

Abstract

This study investigated the relationship between willingness to communicate (WTC) and student participation in adult ESL classrooms. Using a mixed methods research approach, the study collected data from 120 ESL students through closed-ended and open-ended questionnaire items measuring WTC and through students' self-reported participation. Results of correlation analysis revealed a strong positive relationship between WTC and the degree of student participation. Qualitative analysis of open-ended survey responses provided important insights into the factors that influenced students' WTC and participation, including anxiety, language proficiency, and the classroom setting. These findings highlight the important role of WTC in classroom interaction, suggesting that promoting it among L2 learners may be an effective strategy for increasing their participation in the classroom. Language teachers could thus consider incorporating activities and strategies that enhance WTC in their teaching, as these activities may increase students' participation and engagement in the classroom.

In Example 25.6, the abstract provides more detailed information than the one in Example 25.5. It provides a brief overview of the purpose of the research, the methodology, and the results of the study. It gives information about the participants and the tools used to collect data. The abstract also highlights the main findings of the study and their implications.

How to Write a Good Informative Abstract As noted earlier, there are different types of abstract. Also, different disciplines may have their own specific requirements for abstracts or expectations of them. For example, in some fields, abstracts may be shorter. In others, they may need to include more detail about the theory and methods used. In applied linguistics research, abstracts may also make reference to the theoretical and methodological framework used, leading to more detailed information about the research. Typically, a good informative abstract should include five main components:

1. **The background:** While not mandatory, introducing a brief description of the background or context helps readers to understand the study's purpose, motivation, and significance. The background statement should be focused on the specific research problem, followed by an explanation of the research aims. In the first few sentences, readers should quickly assess the study's significance and its contribution to existing knowledge.
2. **The research question or problem:** A good abstract should clearly state the problem or research question that the study aims to address.
3. **The research methodology:** This section of the abstract is important because it helps readers not only to understand how the study was conducted and how the data were collected and analyzed but also to assess the quality and rigor of the research.
4. **Major research findings:** A good abstract should also briefly present the main results of the study and describe any effects, relationships, patterns, or trends observed in the data.

5. **Conclusions and implications:** A good abstract should also highlight the potential theoretical and/or practical implications of the study. Writers should end their abstract by stating the answer to their research question. They might also mention implications or the need for further research.

The abstract from Egi (2010) quoted in Example 25.7 illustrates the key elements of a good informative abstract, including the background and aim, the research problem, the methodology, results, and conclusion and implications.

EXAMPLE 25.7

Uptake, Modified Output, and Learner Perceptions of Recasts:
Learner Responses as Language Awareness

Abstract

Recent research has shown that certain learners' responses to feedback, specifically repair and modified output, are predictive of subsequent second language (L2) development.	Background
Yet, little is understood about why these responses are associated with second language acquisition (SLA). The current study investigated this question by exploring the cognitive processes underlying learner responses.	Research problem
Learners of Japanese (n = 24) engaged in task-based interactions during which they received recasts of their errors. Each learner then watched video clips of the recast episodes and commented on them. The learners' stimulated recall reports were analyzed in relation to their responses to the recasts: uptake, repair, and modified output.	Research methodology
In recast episodes where they produced uptake, their reports indicated that they perceived the recasts as corrective feedback significantly more frequently compared to cases where they did not produce uptake. In episodes where learners correctly repaired their errors, they were significantly more likely to report not only recognizing corrective recasts but also noticing the interlanguage–L2 mismatch. Modified output was also significantly related both to learners' recognition of corrective recasts and to their noticing of the gap (Schmidt & Frota, 1986).	Major research findings
Given the developmental benefits commonly associated with noticing the gap, these findings may partly explain why repair and modified output have been found to be predictive of SLA. (Egi, 2010, p. 1)	Conclusion and implications

What is the purpose of the introduction in a research report? What strategies would you use to write an effective introduction?

Introduction

The introduction is an important section in a research report or article, distinct from the abstract. A good introduction sets the stage for the entire research. It provides readers with the necessary context to understand the topic and its significance, and it clearly outlines the research problem or question. It begins by providing the background and context, summarizing briefly key findings from prior research, and then narrows down to a specific research problem or gap, clearly explaining its importance. It would be good to end the introduction with the research question and/or hypothesis. Visualize the introduction as a cone, beginning broadly and gradually narrowing down to the specific research question. Keep it brief and concise, around one page for a research article and a few pages for a thesis or dissertation. In some cases, the introduction and literature review sections may be combined, offering a more streamlined narrative and avoiding redundancy, particularly in shorter articles or disciplines favoring concise formats. The key is to effectively introduce the research topic, provide context and background, and clearly state the research question.

A good introduction sets the stage for the entire research report or article. It provides readers with the necessary context to understand the topic and its significance, and it clearly outlines the research problem or question.

In the following section, we will discuss the most important elements of an effective introduction in more detail and provide some tips for writing an informative and engaging opening for your research report or article.

Components of an Effective Introduction

1. **Introduction to the topic/hook:** This part introduces the research problem, emphasizing its significance. Using a hook, it captures the reader's attention briefly. It will vary in length according to the type of publication.
2. **Theoretical and/or empirical background:** Focusing on recent research, this part reviews theoretical and empirical foundations concisely, supported by multiple references without getting into an exhaustive literature review.
3. **Identify gaps and justify the need:** Identifying gaps in prior research, this part justifies the study by explaining its unique contribution and importance. It may discuss anticipated impacts or implications.
4. **State the research issue, problem, questions, and/or hypotheses:** Transitioning logically, this segment explicitly states the research problem or

questions, with an emphasis on clarity and conciseness, preparing the reader for subsequent sections.

5. **Explain how the research issues or questions are addressed:** Optionally, this part hints at how the research questions will be addressed, offering a glimpse of expected outcomes or implications, without going into detail about the methods or results.

Example 25.8 presents an introduction from an applied linguistics study (Nassaji, 2007) to illustrate the key components we have discussed.

EXAMPLE 25.8

Elicitation and Reformulation and Their Relationship with Learner Repair in Dyadic Interaction

[Introduction]	Introduction to the topic
The role of interactional feedback in second language acquisition (SLA) has recently received considerable research attention. Interactional feedback is defined as feedback generated implicitly or explicitly through various negotiation and modification strategies (e.g., recasts, elicitations, clarification requests) that occur in the course of interaction to deal with communication problems (Gass, 1997; Long, 1981, 1983; Pica, 1987, 1994).	
Various arguments have been made for the value of such feedback and a growing body of observational and experimental research has addressed its role in communicative interaction and second language (L2) acquisition (e.g., Braidi, 2002; Doughty & Varela, 1998; Ellis, Basturkmen, & Loewen, 2001; Lyster, 1998b, 2001; Lyster & Ranta, 1997; Mackey, 1999; Mackey, Oliver, & Leeman, 2003; Mackey & Philp, 1998; Nabei & Swain, 2002; Oliver, 1995, 2000; Oliver & Mackey, 2003; Panova & Lyster, 2002; Philp, 2003; Pica, 2002). These studies have demonstrated that L2 learners might benefit from interactional feedback in general. However, many have also produced mixed results. For example, whereas some observational studies have demonstrated that recasts lead to a high amount of immediate uptake and repair of erroneous utterances (e.g., Ellis et al.; Mori, 2002; Sheen, 2004), others have shown that recasts lead to a limited amount of immediate repair (e.g., Lyster, 2004; Lyster & Ranta, 1997; Panova & Lyster, 2002).	Review of prior theory and research
These discrepancies indicate a need for further research into the role of such feedback in student–teacher interaction and the various factors that influence its effectiveness. Moreover, although recasts are considered as an implicit type of feedback, such feedback moves can take different forms in	Identifying the gaps and justifying the need

---

(cont.)

Elicitation and Reformulation and Their Relationship with
Learner Repair in Dyadic Interaction

---

the course of interaction that might vary in terms of the
degree of explicitness (Ellis & Sheen, 2006). A number of
studies have compared the relative usefulness of different
types of feedback, such as recasts, elicitations, or explicit
correction (e.g., Ellis et al. 2001; Ellis, Loewen, & Erlam, 2006;
Lyster & Ranta, 1997; Panova & Lyster, 2002). However, not
many have examined and compared the different forms of
the same feedback and their relationship with learner uptake
or acquisition (cf. Lyster, 1998b; Sheen, 2006).

The present research was conducted to investigate the above issue by exploring the role of two categories of interactional feedback that have been the focus of much SLA research and debate in student–teacher interaction: reformulations (recasts) and elicitations.	Stating the research issue (or aim)
Using a detailed set of coding categories, the study examined the different ways in which each feedback type was provided during interaction and its relationship with the learners' success in repairing their erroneous output. (Nassaji, 2007, pp. 511–512)	Explaining how the issues are addressed

---

While the above five components are generally essential for an effective introduction, their presentation and combination may vary based on factors such as the
research topic, the nature of the report, and/or the journal's requirements.
Introductions for theses or dissertations might include additional sections, such as
the theoretical framework, the research design, or key-term definitions. In contrast,
research articles follow a more condensed format. Despite variations, a well-written
introduction must consistently deliver a clear and engaging background, highlight
the study's significance, explain its rationale, and provide an overview of the
research question or hypothesis.

POINTS TO PONDER

What is the purpose of a literature review in a research report? What strategies and
techniques would you use to write an effective literature review?

Literature Review

The literature review is an important element in research reports or articles. The aim
is not just to summarize existing studies, but to establish the research context,
identify gaps in the current knowledge, argue for the study's necessity, and show the

author's expertise in the area. As the literature review progresses, it logically leads to formulating research questions or hypotheses, linking the existing body of knowledge to the study's specific focus. A literature review establishes the theoretical framework, informing the development of research questions or hypotheses. Moreover, it aids in selecting an appropriate research method by showing what approaches past research has used to address similar questions.

In theses and dissertations, the literature review and introduction are typically separate chapters. However, in research articles, the literature review might be part of an expanded introduction. Some articles may not explicitly use the heading "Literature Review" and instead use headings that align more closely with the focus of their research, such as "Theoretical Framework," "Previous Studies," or "Research Background." Decisions on structure and headings depend on a number of factors including the journal guidelines, field conventions, and overall focus and scope of the article.

Regardless of the chosen structure or headings, a literature review is essential for providing the background context, and demonstrating the significance of the research question or hypothesis. It identifies gaps in knowledge, justifying the need for the study and illustrating how the research contributes to the field.

Writing an Effective Literature Review

As noted earlier, the literature review is not simply a summary of previous work; it is a synthesis and evaluation of research findings that provides an argument and justification for the research question. The structure of the literature review is similar to that of the introduction but differs in that the section on background and prior research is expanded to offer a more detailed review of past theories and research. It should begin with an overview of the topic, setting the stage for the review, followed by a synthesis and analysis of the relevant body of knowledge. Depending on the purpose of the research, it may also describe the strategy used to identify and select the literature, including the databases and any inclusion and exclusion criteria. The cone shape concept discussed earlier applies here as well, starting with the most general information and narrowing it down to the research problem, question, or hypothesis. Overall, the literature review should provide background and context, highlight gaps in knowledge, justify the significance of the study, and illustrate its contribution to the field.

Types of Literature Review

In terms of structure and format, there are different ways the content can be organized. One is what I would call "bibliographic," and the other is thematic. The most effective type is thematic.

The Bibliographic Format A bibliographic format looks very much like an annotated bibliography. It simply provides a summary of each study with little evaluation and analysis of each source. It is very much like a "he said, she said" format in that it is simply a list of summarized studies, often with each source being reviewed in chronological order. This type of review is not uncommon and can even be seen in the literature review sections of some published articles. However, this is not a very effective way of constructing a literature review. One characteristic of this type of literature review is that each paragraph may begin with the name of the researcher(s) who conducted the study, rather than a theme, followed by how the research has been conducted and what it has shown. Also, in each paragraph we often see a single citation: the name of the researcher(s) whose research has been reviewed in that paragraph.

The Thematic Format A thematic literature review is organized around themes, ideas, or arguments, grouping relevant concepts together rather than isolating each source in a paragraph. In evaluating past research, it critically examines the relevance to the research question, analyzing findings and arguments from various sources to identify patterns, themes, gaps, and areas of (dis)agreement.

One characteristic of a thematic format is that each paragraph begins with a thesis statement containing the theme of that paragraph, instead of the name of an author. Also, since it groups ideas from various sources, the paragraph can include multiple citations instead of just one. In a thematic literature review, the reader can easily identify the main themes or topics covered in the document and can follow the argument more easily.

There are different ways in which a thematic literature review can be organized. One way, for example, is by concept or theoretical framework. Conceptual or theoretical themes refer to the main ideas, concepts, or theories that are used in a study to examine a particular topic. For example, if you are writing a literature review for a study on the effectiveness of recasts, you might organize the review by the themes, such as types of recasts (synthesizing and evaluating research that defines and describes different types of recasts), the effectiveness of recasts (synthesizing and evaluating research on the effectiveness of recasts in language learning, including studies that have compared recasts to other types of corrective feedback or those that have examined the effects of different types of recasts), factors affecting the impact of recasts (synthesizing and evaluating research on factors that can affect the effectiveness of recasts, such as proficiency level, learners' memory and language background), as well as factors related to the context of recasts, theoretical perspectives on recasts, and so on.

Another way to structure your literature review is by methodological approaches. A literature review organized around methodological themes focuses on the different methodological procedures used to study a particular problem, such the different research designs, different participants, or different outcome measures used in studies. To this end, the review can discuss and highlight the strengths and weaknesses of different research procedures, designs, and tools, and identify areas for improvement that will be addressed in the study for which the literature review is written. For example, a literature review for a study on the effectiveness of recasts might be organized around the following themes: types of research designs (e.g., descriptive or experimental research), types of participants (e.g., ESL versus EFL participants), the nature of task used (e.g., naturalist versus elicitation tasks), or different outcome measures (e.g., oral versus written tasks or free production tasks versus more controlled structure-based tasks such as error-correction or grammaticality-judgment tasks).

A literature review can also combine conceptual themes with methodological themes. Sometimes this might even be a more useful approach to take in order to provide a more nuanced understanding of the areas examined. For example, a literature review on the study of recasts can include theoretical themes, such as the different theoretical frameworks to explain the effectiveness of recasts, as well as methodological themes, such as research designs, types of participants, or assessment tools.

All in all, a thematic approach is more effective than a nonthematic one. When a literature review is organized around themes, it can help you to better see how different studies relate to one another; what the common themes, patterns, and trends are across studies; and how all these can be used to identify a gap and a justification for the research.

Methods

Another important section of a research report or article is the methods section. The methods section should provide a detailed description of how the study was conducted. It typically includes the following information and subsections.

Participants and Context

This section should include a detailed and clear description of the participants, including their number, characteristics (such as age, gender, language background, and proficiency level), and how they were recruited or selected, including any randomization techniques, as well as a description of the context in which the study was conducted, such as a classroom context, a lab context, an EFL or ESL context, and so on. The rationale for the choice of participants or context of the study should also be provided.

Study Design

This section should provide a description of the design of the study. For example, it should explain whether the design was experimental, observational/descriptive, cross-sectional, or longitudinal. If the study involves classroom research, or if it has used a particular interventional strategy, the intervention should be clearly and sufficiently described. The rationale for the choice of design should also be explained, with possible reference to past research that has used such a design. If the design is experimental, some key information can be provided, such as the number of groups, including the experimental and control groups, their characteristics, and how they were formed; the dependent and the independent variables and how they were measured; whether the participants were randomly selected or assigned to the groups; and any other relevant information about the study design. If the design is observational, information about the type of the design (e.g., naturalistic, participant, structured or unstructured observation) and justification for its selection should be provided. If the study is qualitative, the design – such as ethnography, grounded theory, case study, discourse analysis, or any other – should be described, as should the sampling strategies.

Data Collection Tools and Procedures

This section should provide a clear and detailed description of how the data were collected, including the kind of materials, tasks, instruments, tests, interviews, questionnaires, observation, and so on; how they were used; and how they addressed the research questions. The rationale for their use should be provided. Altogether, this section should provide a step-by-step account of what you and the participants did. It should provide sufficient information and be written in such a way as to allow other researchers to understand and replicate the study if they wish.

Data Analysis

This section should include information about how the data were analyzed, including a description of how the data were prepared; the scoring procedures; any statistical methods and, if applicable, software used, such as SPSS, SAS (in the case of quantitative studies); the procedures used to transcribe and code the data; and, if needed, the program used to code or analyze them, such as NVIVO (in the case of qualitative studies). In this section, information about validity and reliability of the data and the steps taken to measure or ensure validity and reliability can be described. If the study involves qualitative research methods, the data analysis might have been undertaken during and/or after the data collection. This process should be clearly and sufficiently described.

Results

The results section should provide a clear and concise presentation of the results of the study, including the results of any qualitative or quantitative/statistical analyses performed. The information should be sufficient and detailed, such that the reader can understand it easily. In the case of statistical analysis, this summary may include the results of descriptive statistics, such as the mean and the standard deviation, as well as inferential statistics and their types, such as t-tests, ANOVA, or regression analyses. The results of these tests should also be clearly reported. This can include the test statistic, degrees of freedom, p value, and confidence interval whenever applicable. For example, if a study is investigating the relationship between motivation and language learning using the Pearson correlation, the results section should report the correlation coefficient and the associated p value. Or, if it is comparing two groups using t-tests, it should report the results of the t-test including, if applicable, the t-values, significance level, and confidence intervals. The same should be done for other significance tests, such as ANOVA, which involves F tests. In the case of categorical data, frequencies, percentages, and the results of the chi-square test, if used, should be reported.

When reporting statistical results, such as the mean, the standard deviation, or other statistical values, it is common, for the sake of brevity, to use abbreviations when reporting them in tables (such as M for mean, SD for standard deviation, N for number, p for p value. For example, "The feedback group outperformed the control group ($M = 35$, $SD = 0.4$ vs $M = 20$, $SD = 0.5$)."

The *APA (American Psychological Association) Publication Manual* (American Psychological Association, 2020) is generally used when reporting research results in the social sciences, including applied linguistics. According to the APA guidelines (7th ed., 2020), symbols or abbreviations representing statistical values (e.g., M, SD, F, t, p, N, n, r) do not require definitions. However, it is important to define and explain other abbreviations when necessary. Also based on these guidelines, most statistical abbreviations are italicized in the tables or in parenthetical references in the text. For numbers, we use an uppercase N for the total sample (e.g., $N = 60$) and a lowercase n for subsamples ($n = 30$). Additionally, some journals or style guides may have specific guidelines on the use of acronyms and abbreviations, so it is a good idea to check the requirements of the journal you are submitting your research to or the style guide you are following.

When reporting p values, it is important to follow accepted conventions for presenting statistical significance. The most common significance level used in reports are $p = .05$, $p = .01$, or $p = .001$. Traditionally, there have been two ways of reporting p values, one is to use the selected alpha level (α) and the symbol for smaller than ($<$) or bigger than ($>$). Therefore, if the p value of a statistical test is 0.04, for example, it could be reported as $p < .05$. Another way is to report the exact p value produced by the statistical test. For example, if the p value reported was 0.03, it could be reported as $p = .03$. However, the seventh edition of the *APA Publication Manual* (APA, 2020, p. 180) gives the following guidance for reporting study results including p values:

> Report correlations, proportions, and inferential statistics such as t, F, and chi-square to two decimals. When reporting data measured on integer scales (as with many questionnaires), report means and standard deviations to one decimal place (as group measures, they are more stable than individual scores). Report exact p values (e.g., $p = .031$) to two or three decimal places. However, report p values less than .001 as $p < .001$. The tradition of reporting p values in the form of $p < .10$, $p < .05$, $p < .01$, and so forth was appropriate in a time when only limited tables of critical values were available. However, in tables the "$p <$" notation may be necessary for clarity.

Exact p values are helpful as they provide more precise information about the level of statistical significance than simply reporting that the result met a significance threshold (e.g., $p < .01$). This is particularly important when the p value is close to the threshold of statistical significance. This also helps other researchers to replicate and verify the findings.

Many journals now require the reporting of effect sizes in research articles. This is because effect sizes provide important information beyond just the statistical significance of the results. Statistical significance indicates whether the results are likely to be due to chance, without telling us about the strength of a relationship or an effect. Effect sizes, however, tell us the size or magnitude of an effect, which is an important piece of information when evaluating the practical significance of the finding (see Chapter 23). Therefore, it is important to report effect sizes when reporting p values. Because of their importance, the APA guidelines also state, "complete reporting of all tested hypotheses and estimates of appropriate effect sizes and confidence intervals are the minimum expectations for all APA journals." (APA, 2020, p. 87). The APA guidelines also recommend reporting confidence intervals when reporting the results of significance by putting the upper and lower limits within brackets: for example, 95% CI [5.21, 6.35].

When reporting confidence intervals, we can report them for either the mean difference or the effect size, depending on the research question and the statistical analysis used. Most often, if the research tests differences between groups, such as in a t-test or ANOVA, it is common to report confidence intervals for the mean difference or the effect size. This can provide information about the precision of the mean difference or the effect size measure. If the research tests associations or relationships between variables, such as in a correlation or in chi-square tests, the confidence intervals are usually reported for the effect size (e.g., correlation coefficient, regression coefficient, or odds ratio in chi-square tests).

When reporting the results, for ease of understanding, tables, graphs, and other visual aids can be used to illustrate the data. It is important to note that the information presented should primarily pertain to the results, and any interpretation or discussion of those results should be typically reserved for the discussion section. For example, if a study found no significant difference between two groups on a particular measure, the results section would report it, without necessarily making any judgments about its implications.

If the study is qualitative, the results section should describe the themes or categories that emerged from the data, with examples or quotations from the participants that illustrate and support each theme or category.

Reporting the Results of Commonly Used Statistical Tests

As noted earlier, in the data analysis section of our research report or article, we should also report the results of statistical tests. In doing so, the results should be reported based on the conventions accepted in the field. In applied linguistics, the convention for reporting statistical results is generally based on APA style guidelines. This style provides specific rules and the format for reporting statistical results. This section will discuss the key elements that we should include when reporting the results of some commonly used statistical tests in applied linguistics such as ANOVAs, t-tests, chi-square tests, correlations, and regression analyses.

One-Way ANOVA   For one-way ANOVA, we report two types of degrees of freedom, the between-groups degrees of freedom and the within-groups degrees of freedom separated by a comma, followed by the F statistic and significance level (see Example 25.9). We can also report the effect size and the confidence interval. SPSS Output 25.1 provides an example of some results generated by SPSS and Example 25.2 shows how to report them.

SPSS OUTPUT 25.1

ANOVA

Writing score

	Sum of Squares	df	Mean Square	F	Sig.
Between Groups	1822.20	2	911.10	120.06	.000
Within Groups	660.20	87	7.59		
Total	2482.40	89			

SPSS OUTPUT 25.2

ANOVA Effect Sizes[a]

		Point Estimate	95% Confidence Interval	
			Lower	Upper
Writing score	Eta-squared	.73	.63	.79
	Epsilon-squared	.73	.62	.79
	Omega-squared Fixed-effect	.73	.62	.78
	Omega-squared Random-effect	.57	.45	.65

a. Eta-squared and Epsilon-squared are estimated based on the fixed-effect model.

EXAMPLE 25.9

A one-way ANOVA was conducted to compare the mean scores of three groups on the dependent variable. The results showed a significant difference among the groups: $F (2, 87) = 120.06$, $p < .001$, $\eta^2 = .73$, 95% CI [0.63, 0.79].

In this example, the F statistic, degrees of freedom, and the p value are reported in the usual way for ANOVA results. The effect size estimate ($\eta^2 = .73$) is also reported to indicate the size of the effect, and the 95% confidence interval for the effect size (CI [0.631, 0.79]) is reported to indicate the precision of the estimate. Both the effect size estimate and the confidence intervals are usually reported to two decimal places. Here the effect size estimate ($\eta^2 = .73$) indicates that 73% of the variance in the dependent variable can be accounted for by independent variable. The 95% confidence interval for the effect size estimate (CI [0.631, 0.79]) indicates that with 95% confidence, the true effect size lies between 0.631 and 0.79.

Two-Way (Multiple-Way) ANOVA For two-way or multiple-way ANOVA, we report two types of degrees of freedom, the degrees of freedom of the independent variable whose effect we are reporting and the degrees of freedom of the error, separated by a comma, followed by the F statistic and the significance level. We can also report the effect size and the confidence interval. SPSS Output 25.3 provides an example of some results and Example 25.10 shows how to report them.

SPSS OUTPUT 25.3

Tests of Between-Subjects Effects

Dependent Variable: Speaking accuracy scores

Source	Type III Sum of Squares	df	Mean Square	F	Sig.	Partial Eta Squared
Corrected Model	453.50[a]	5	90.70	14.29	.000	.46
Intercept	21576.03	1	21576.03	3400.35	.000	.98
feedback	394.20	2	197.10	31.06	.000	.43
Proficiency	6.43	1	6.43	1.01	.32	.01
feedback * Proficiency	35.80	2	17.90	2.82	.06	.06
Error	533.00	84	6.35			
Total	22609.00	90				
Corrected Total	986.50	89				

a. R Squared = .460 (Adjusted R Squared = .428)

EXAMPLE 25.10

The results indicated a significant main effect for feedback, $F(2, 84) = 31.06$, $p < .001$, $\eta_p^2 = .43$; no significant main effect for language proficiency, $F(1, 84) = 1.01$, $p = .32$, $\eta_p^2 = .01$; and no significant interaction effect between feedback and language proficiency, $F(2, 84) = 2.82$, $p = .06$, $\eta_p^2 = .06$.

Chi-Square Test The results of chi-square tests are reported using the degrees of freedom and sample size in parentheses, which is then followed by the Pearson chi-square value ($\chi 2$) and the significance level. SPSS Output 25.4 provides an example of some results and Example 25.11 shows how to report them.

SPSS OUTPUT 25.4

Chi-Square Tests					
	Value	df	Asymptotic Significance (2–sided)	Exact Sig. (2–sided)	Exact Sig. (1–sided)
Pearson Chi-Square	52.08[a]	1	.000		
Continuity Correction[b]	50.02	1	.000		
Likelihood Ratio	55.17	1	.000		
Fisher's Exact Test				.000	.000
Linear-by-Linear Association	51.82	1	.000		
N of Valid Cases	200				

a. 0 cells (0.0%) have expected count less than 5. The minimum expected count is 40.00.
b. Computed only for a 2 × 2 table.

EXAMPLE 25.11

A chi-square test was conducted to examine the relationship between class level and feedback type in beginner- and intermediate-level classes. Results of the analysis revealed a significant association between the two variables, χ^2 (1, N=200) = 52.08, $p < .001$.

t-Tests   The results of *t*-tests are reported in the same way as those of chi-square tests with the difference that only the degrees of freedom are in parenthesis, followed by *t* statistic and the significance level. SPSS Outputs 25.5–6 present the results of a *t*-test analysis, while Example 25.12 shows how these results can be reported in APA format.

SPSS OUTPUT 25.5

Independent Samples Test								
		Levene's Test for Equality of Variances		t-test for Equality of Means				
						Significance		
						One-Sided	Two-Sided	Mean	Std. Error
		F	Sig.	t	df	p	p	Difference	Difference
Vocabulary scores	Equal variances assumed	.11	.73	2.8	38	.003	.006	1.20	.415
	Equal variances not assumed			2.8	37.3	.003	.006	1.20	.415

SPSS OUTPUT 25.6

Independent Samples Effect Sizes

		Standardizer[a]	Point Estimate	95% Confidence Interval	
				Lower	Upper
Vocabulary scores	Cohen's d	1.31	.91	.26	1.56
	Hedges's correction	1.33	.89	.25	1.53
	Glass's delta	1.39	.86	.17	1.53

a. The denominator used in estimating the effect sizes.
Cohen's d uses the pooled standard deviation.
Hedges's correction uses the pooled standard deviation, plus a correction factor.
Glass's delta uses the sample standard deviation of the control group.

EXAMPLE 25.12

A study was conducted to assess the efficacy of two distinct vocabulary teaching methods in enhancing learners' vocabulary knowledge. The comparison involved two groups, and an independent sample t-test was employed to analyze the test scores of both groups. The results showed a significant difference between the groups, $t(38) = 2.8$, $p = .006$, $d = .91$, 95% CI [0.26, 1.56].

In this example, the t-statistic, degrees of freedom, and p value are reported as they are typically reported for t-test results. The effect size estimate ($d = .91$) is also reported to indicate the size of the effect, and the 95% confidence interval for the effect size (CI [0.26, 1.56]) is also reported to indicate the precision of the effect size measure.

Correlations In the case of correlations, we report the degrees of freedom, which is N minus 2 in parentheses, followed by the significance level. SPSS Outputs 25.7–8 display the results of a correlation analysis, while Example 25.13 illustrates how to report these results.

SPSS OUTPUT 25.7

Correlations

		Language proficiency	Language anxiety
Language proficiency	Pearson Correlation	1	−.960[**]
	Sig. (2-tailed)		.000
	N	30	30

**. Correlation is significant at the 0.01 level (2-tailed).

SPSS OUTPUT 25.8

	Confidence Intervals			
	Pearson Correlation	Sig. (2-tailed)	95% Confidence Intervals (2-tailed)[a]	
			Lower	Upper
Language proficiency – Language anxiety	−.96	.000	−.98	−.92

a. Estimation is based on Fisher's r-to-z transformation.

EXAMPLE 25.13

A correlation analysis using Pearson correlation was conducted to examine the relationship between language anxiety and language proficiency. The results showed a significant negative correlation between the two variables, $r(28) = -0.96$, $p < .001$, 95% CI $[-0.98, -0.92]$.

Here, the correlation coefficient, degrees of freedom, and p value are reported as typically reported for correlation analyses. The correlation coefficient ($r = -.96$) indicates the strength and direction of the correlation, and the 95% confidence interval for the correlation coefficient (CI $[-0.98, -0.92]$) indicates the precision of the correlation estimate.

Linear Regression For the linear regression, we report the information presented in the ANOVA table of regression generated by SPSS (or other statistical software). We start by reporting the R-squared value, followed by the degrees of freedom of the regression and the degrees of freedom of the residual in parenthesis separated by a comma, followed by the F value, the p value, β (beta; the standardized regression coefficient), and the confidence interval. SPSS Outputs 25.9–11 provide examples of some results and Example 25.14 shows how to report the results.

SPSS OUTPUT 25.9

			Model Summary	
Model	R	R Square	Adjusted R Square	Std. Error of the Estimate
1	.89[a]	.79	.78	4.38

a. Predictors: (Constant), Vocabulary score

SPSS OUTPUT 25.10

ANOVA[a]

Model		Sum of Squares	df	Mean Square	F	Sig.
1	Regression	2723.55	1	2723.55	141.47	.000[b]
	Residual	731.54	38	19.25		
	Total	3455.10	39			

a. Dependent Variable: Reading comprehension
b. Predictors: (Constant), Vocabulary score

SPSS OUTPUT 25.11

Coefficients[a]

Model		B	Std. Error	Beta	t	Sig.	Lower Bound	Upper Bound
		Unstandardized Coefficients		Standardized Coefficients			95.0% Confidence Interval for B	
1	(Constant)	4.11	6.34		.64	.520	-8.73	16.96
	Vocabulary score	.99	.083	.89	11.89	.000	.82	1.16

a. Dependent Variable: Reading comprehension

EXAMPLE 25.14

A linear regression analysis was conducted to examine the relationship between a predictor variable and an outcome (dependent) variable. The results showed that the predictor variable significantly predicted the dependent variable, $R^2 = .79$, $F(1, 38) = 141.47$, $p < .001$, $\beta = .89$, 95% CI [−8.73, 16.96].

In this example, the R^2, the regression coefficients, degrees of freedom, and F value are reported. The p value is also reported to indicate the significance of the predictor variable. The effect size estimate ($\beta = 0.89$) is reported to indicate the strength and direction of the relationship between the predictor and the dependent variables, and the 95% confidence interval for the effect size (CI [−8.73, 16.96]) indicates the degree of the accuracy of the coefficient. The effect size estimate ($\beta = 0.89$) indicates a strong positive relationship between the predictor variable and the outcome variable, and the 95% confidence interval for the effect size (CI [−8.73,

16.96]) indicates that with 95% confidence, the true regression coefficient lies between −8.73 and 16.96. The R^2 value of the model was 0.79, indicating that approximately 79% of the variance in the dependent variable was accounted for by the predictor variable.

POINTS TO PONDER

What are the key components of a discussion and conclusion section? What strategies would you use to write an effective discussion section?

Discussion and Conclusion

The last substantive and very important sections of a research report are the discussion and conclusion sections. In theses and dissertations, often the discussion and the conclusion are two separate chapters, but in most research articles they are one section, two sections, or the conclusion will be a subsection within the discussion section. Sometimes, the discussion section does not receive the attention it deserves compared to other parts, particularly from novice researchers, despite being as important as the other sections.

The aim of the discussion section is to make sense of the findings and results of the study and explain what they mean. Its purpose is to interpret and provide an analysis of their significance in the broader context of the research question and the field. Therefore, it should include a thorough evaluation and analysis of the study's findings and their implications and limitations. The following elements are typically included in a discussion chapter.

Introduction: It would be helpful to begin the discussion section with an introduction, which can serve to remind the reader of the purpose and the significance of the study and transition from the results section to the discussion section.

Body: After the introduction, comes the body of the discussion where you provide a detailed explanation of the research findings and the evidence supporting them. The body should be organized in a logical and coherent manner, with clear and concise paragraphs that are well-structured and easy to follow. There are different ways that this section can be organized, depending on the nature of the research and the research question. However, two helpful ways to structure this section could be by research questions or hypotheses, and by themes.

Organizing the Discussion Section

When writing your discussion section, you have a variety of strategies for organizing it. The structure of this section plays an important role in how the findings are communicated and interpreted. Choosing the right approach helps to make sure that the results are clearly linked to the research questions and objectives. In the following sections, we will discuss two common organizational methods that will help you structure your discussion effectively.

Organization Based on the Research Questions   One way of organizing the discussion section is by the research questions or hypotheses. To do this, you can begin by restating the individual research questions or hypotheses of the study one by one, followed by a brief summary of the results related to that question or hypothesis. You can then provide an in-depth analysis of the results, discussing their significance and their relationship to previous research and highlighting similarities, differences, and discrepancies between the current study and previous studies.

When differences or similarities are found between the study's finding and previous findings, these should be explained. When similarities are found, it is still important to discuss how your study adds to the findings of previous research. This can be done, for example, by highlighting the unique aspects of the study, such as the research design, the context, the participants, or measurement tools, and discussing how these have contributed to advancing knowledge in the field.

In discussing the research findings, you could also discuss any unexpected findings or results and how these relate to the research question or hypothesis. You could also identify any potential confounding variables or alternative explanations for the results and discuss how these might impact the interpretation of the findings.

Overall, organizing the research section based on the research questions is a helpful way to discuss the findings of the study. This approach allows you to reintroduce and address each research question or hypothesis in detail, presenting a thorough analysis and explanation of the results and their contribution to the field.

Organization by Theme   Organizing the body of the discussion section by theme or topic is another effective way to structure the discussion section. In doing so, you can begin by identifying the key themes emerging from the data and then presenting the findings related to each theme. For example, if the study has examined the strategies that L2 learners use to write in an L2, you can identify several key strategies that emerged from the data (for example, cognitive, meta-cognitive, linguistic) and then present the findings related to each strategy, explaining them, and highlighting their significance.

A thematic presentation is appropriate for studies that address complex research questions or multiple variables that can be organized into themes. This approach is particularly useful for qualitative or mixed methods research. In qualitative research, data is frequently collected through interviews, observations, or other forms of unstructured or semistructured data collection methods. In such research, the data are often analyzed thematically, and therefore they can also be discussed thematically. Mixed methods research combines both qualitative and quantitative methods. This type of research also produces complex data integrated from various sources. Therefore, a discussion of the findings of this type of research may also benefit from a thematic presentation, as such a presentation can help to organize and synthesize these data into emerging themes.

Conclusion

The conclusion is often the final part of a research paper or report, typically following the discussion section. In the conclusion, you have an opportunity to summarize the main findings of the study and reiterate their significance, highlighting how the results of the study contribute to existing knowledge in the field. The conclusion can also include a discussion of the practical/pedagogical implications of the study, which may also be addressed in the discussion section.

When discussing the practical implications, you can offer specific recommendations for how practitioners or policymakers can use the study's findings to improve practice or policy. It is important to note that these recommendations should be tentative as one study may not be sufficient to draw definitive conclusions or to make far-reaching recommendations, particularly if the study is small in scale or has limited generalizability. Therefore, while it is possible to make recommendations, it is important to be cautious when doing so and to consider the limitations of the study. Finally, the conclusion can end with discussion and reflection on the limitations of the study.

When discussing limitations, it is important to identify and acknowledge possible weaknesses or shortcomings of the study, including any practical or logistical constraints that there were, and to consider their potential consequences for the study findings. A number of factors can be considered when discussing the limitations.

One is the issue of sample size and sample selection. For example, if the sample size of the study was small, you can discuss that and its implications, as it may be difficult to generalize the findings from a small sample size to the broader population. In such a case, you could not only acknowledge the limitations but also suggest how future research could address that issue. Similarly, if there were shortcomings about how the participants were selected, this could be acknowledged as well. For example, if the study selected participants using convenience sampling, the results may not be representative of the broader population, and hence the implications of this for the generalizability of the findings can be discussed. Or for example, if the study has used a specific group of learners in a specific context, there may be issues regarding the generalizability of the findings to other populations or settings, in which case, you could acknowledge these limitations and suggest how future research could address them.

Other issues to consider might relate to data collection and procedure. For example, if the data were collected using nonstandardized tests or researcher-made questionnaires or surveys, there may be concerns about the validity or the reliability of the data, which could be acknowledged. You could go on to explain how future research could revise the data collection tools or methods to increase the validity of the results.

Methodological issues could be another area to include in the discussion of limitations. If there are any such issue or concerns, these could be acknowledged. For example, if the study used a cross-sectional design, collecting data from participants at one point in time, you could acknowledge the potential limitations of this and explain that future research could use a more longitudinal study design to better examine the research question.

It should be noted that while discussing the methodological limitations, advantages could also be highlighted. While it is important to acknowledge and discuss the limitations of a study, it is also important to maintain a balanced perspective and not focus too much on them. Too much emphasis on limitations can reduce the credibility and importance of the study and may give the impression that the findings are not valuable.

References

The references section is typically the last major part of a research report or article following the conclusion, and contains all the cited sources (followed by appendices if needed). Primary sources, presenting original research, and secondary sources, created by other authors, should be included. However, unread primary sources should be cited in the text and secondary sources in the reference list (following APA guidelines). You should cross-check citations in the text with those in the reference list for consistency. You should make sure the reference list provides the bibliographic details, according to a consistent citation style. Popular styles, including APA, MLA, and Chicago exist, with APA style being commonly used in applied linguistics and second language research. APA style offers specific formatting guidelines for both in-text citations and the references section, ensuring uniformity in your report. Failing to properly cite sources and include references can lead to plagiarism or infringe intellectual property rights, which can have serious academic and legal consequences.

Appendices (if applicable)

Appendices provide supplementary material that is too detailed or lengthy to be included in the main body of the research report, including theses, dissertations, or articles. They are used to present additional data, tables, figures, questionnaires, interview transcripts, or technical details that support the research but are not essential for understanding the core arguments. They are placed after the references section at the end of the report. Including appendices allows readers to access detailed information without disrupting the flow of the main text. Each appendix should be clearly labeled and referenced in the body of the report to guide the reader to the relevant material. Properly organized appendices enhance the transparency of the research while maintaining the readability of the main report.

Conclusion

This chapter has discussed the various aspects and steps involved in preparing and writing a research report and disseminating the research findings. The dissemination of research findings is an important component of the research process. Writing a research report allows you to document and share your research and findings with a wider community; by doing so you contribute to the collective knowledge and advancement of the respective field. Research reports are also often a requirement for academic and scientific purposes, such as meeting funding or grant requirements or fulfilling the requirements of a graduate degree through the completion of a thesis or dissertation. In this chapter, we have discussed the format and structure of a research report, including its major sections and subsections: the title, abstract, introduction, literature review, methodology, results, discussion, and conclusion as well as the references, and appendices. Each section was explained in detail with strategies and tips about how to structure it effectively. Overall, the aim was to help you master the components and organization of an effective research report and provide you with knowledge that can contribute to the successful dissemination of your research findings.

DISCUSSION AND ACTIVITY QUESTIONS

Discussion Questions

1. Why is it important to share research findings, and how does this process contribute to the advancement of the field?
2. What are the key components of a research report, and how do they work together to create a cohesive document?
3. How does a good title contribute to an effective research report and what challenges do you face when writing one? Share any experiences you have with writing a title and how you made it effective.
4. What is the specific purpose of the introduction and of the literature review section in a research report, and why are these sections important?
5. How do you decide what findings from past research to include in your research report when synthesizing the literature?
6. What strategies do you use to write an effective literature review that not only synthesizes existing research but also provides a clear foundation for your study?
7. To what extent should statistical results be presented in a research report, and how do you determine the level of detail needed for clarity without overwhelming the reader?
8. Why is proper referencing and citation important in a research report? What citation format would you use in your research reports, and why?
9. How do you decide which materials or data to include or not to include in the appendices of a research report, and what criteria guide your decision?

Activity Questions

1. Locate the abstracts from a few research reports in applied linguistics. In small groups, analyze the abstracts, identify their type and discuss their effectiveness in summarizing the research study.
2. Find a research article in applied linguistics and evaluate its introduction section. In pairs or small groups, identify the research questions and objectives, and assess how well the significance of the study is justified.
3. Find a sample methods section in an applied linguistics research report that is not organized effectively. Work individually or in pairs to reorganize the subsections and improve the overall coherence of the section.

4. Find a list of references in an applied linguistics study. In pairs or individually, work to correct the references and make sure they adhere to the proper formatting style.
5. Find a research article in applied linguistics that includes statistical results and their interpretation. Read the article carefully, focusing specifically on the section where the statistical results are reported and discussed. Do the authors report the results properly and accurately? Do they provide sufficient information about the tests used, including their assumptions and rationale? Do the authors use particular statistical tests, and do they provide the results (including the means, standard deviations, and p values)? Are they reported properly? If you have identified any issues with the reporting, how would you address them?
6. Prepare and present a research report based on a topic that you are interested in. Organize your presentation following the components discussed in this chapter to communicate the research and its findings to your classmates.

References

Allen, P. B., Fröhlich, M., & Spada, N. (1984). The communicative orientation of language teaching: An observation scheme. In J. Handscombe, R. A. Orem, & B. Taylor (Eds.), *On TESOL '83: The question of control* (pp. 231–252). Washington, DC: TESOL.

Allwright, R. L. (1980). Turns, topics, and tasks: Patterns of participation in language learning and teaching. In D. Larsen-Freeman (Ed.), *Discourse analysis in second language research* (pp. 165–187). Rowley, MA: Newbury House.

American Association for Applied Linguistics (AAAL). (n.d.). AAAL ethics guidelines. Retrieved November 2, 2024 from www.aaal.org/ethics-guidelines.

American Educational Research Association (AERA). (1992). Ethical standards of the American Educational Research Association. *Educational Researcher, 21*, 23–26.

American Educational Research Association (AERA). (2006). Standards for reporting on empirical social science research in AERA publications. *Educational Researcher, 35*(6), 33–40.

American Educational Research Association (AERA). (2011). Code of ethics. *Educational Researcher, 40*(3), 145–146. https://doi.org/10.3102/0013189X11410403.

American Psychological Association (APA). (2017). Ethical principles of psychologists and code of conduct. Retrieved November 2, 2024 from www.apa.org/ethics/code.

American Psychological Association (APA). (2020). *Publication manual of the American Psychological Association* (7th ed.). Washington, DC: American Psychological Association.

Arnold, J., & Brown, D. (1999). A map of the terrain. In J. Arnold (Ed.), *Affect in language learning*. Cambridge: Cambridge University Press.

Auerbach, C. F, & Silverstein, L. B. (2003). *Qualitative data: An introduction to coding and analysis*. New York: New York University Press.

Austin, J. L. (1962). *How to do things with words*. Cambridge, MA: Harvard University Press.

Ayaå, R. (2015). Doing data: The status of transcripts in conversation analysis. *Discourse Studies, 17*(5), 505–528.

Barkhuizen, G. (2014). Narrative research in language teaching and learning. *Language Teaching, 47*(4), 450–466.

Baxter, J. (2010). Discourse-analytic approaches to text and talk. In L. Litosseliti (Ed.), *Research methods in linguistics* (pp. 117–137). New York: Continuum International Publishing Group.

Benson, P. (2014). Narrative inquiry in applied linguistics research. *Annual Review of Applied Linguistics, 34*, 154–170.

Berg, B., & Lune, H. (2012). *Qualitative research methods for the social sciences*. London: Pearson.

Billmyer, K., & Varghese, M. (2000). Investigating instrument-based pragmatic variability: Effects of enhancing discourse completion tests. *Applied Linguistics, 21*(4), 517–552.

Borg, S. (2009). English language teachers' conceptions of research. *Applied Linguistics, 30*(3), 358–388.

British Association for Applied Linguistics (BAAL). (1994). Recommendations on good practice in applied linguistics. Retrieved November 2, 2024 from https://bit.ly/3NIhRtt.

British Association for Applied Linguistics (BAAL). (2021). Recommendations on good practice in applied linguistics. Retrieved November 2, 2024 from https://bit.ly/40z6hZ6.

Brumfit, C. (1995). Teacher professionalism and research. In G. Cook and B. Seidlhofer (Eds.), *Principle and Practice in Applied Linguistics* (pp. 27–41). Oxford: Oxford University Press.

Canale, M., & Swain, M. (1980). Theoretical bases of communicative approaches to language teaching and testing. *Applied Linguistics, 1*(1), 1–47.

Carroll, J. (1981). Twenty-five years of research on foreign language aptitude. In K. Diller (Ed.), *Individual differences and universals in language learning aptitude* (pp. 83–118). Rowley, MA: Newbury House.

Carroll, J., & Sapon, S. (1959). *Modern language aptitude test (MLAT)*. New York: Psychology Corporation.

Celce-Murcia, M., & Olshtain, E. (2000). *Discourse and context in language teaching: A guide for language teachers.* Cambridge: Cambridge University Press.

Charmaz, K. (2000). Grounded Theory: Objectivist and Constructivist Methods. In N. Denzin & Y. Lincoln, (Eds.), *Handbook of qualitative research* (pp. 509–535). Thousand Oaks, CA: Sage.

Charmaz, K. (2006). *Constructing grounded theory: A practical guide through qualitative analysis.* London: Sage.

Chaudron, C. (1977). A descriptive model of discourse in the corrective treatment of learners' errors. *Language Learning, 27*(1), 29–46.

Chaudron, C. (1988). *Second language classrooms.* Cambridge: Cambridge University Press.

Clandinin, D. J., & Connelly, F. M. (2000). *Narrative inquiry: Experience and story in qualitative research.* San Francisco, CA: Jossey-Bass.

Cohen, J. (1960). A coefficient of agreement for nominal scales. *Educational and Psychological Measurement, 20*(1), 37–46.

Cohen, J. (1988). *Statistical power analysis for the behavioral sciences* (2nd ed.). Hillsdale, NJ: L. Erlbaum.

Cook, G. (2015). Birds out of dinosaurs: The death and life of applied linguistics. *Applied Linguistics, 36*(4), 425–433.

Cook, T. D., & Reichardt, C. S. (1979). *Qualitative and quantitative methods in evaluation research.* Beverly Hills, CA: Sage.

Cooper, H. M. (1988). Organizing knowledge syntheses: A taxonomy of literature reviews. *Knowledge in society, 1*(1), 104.

Corder, S. P. (1974). Error analysis. In J. P. B. Allen & S. P. Corder (Eds.), *The Edinburgh course in applied linguistics,* vol. 3, *Techniques in Applied Linguistics* (pp. 122–154). London: Oxford University Press.

Creswell, J. (2007). *Qualitative inquiry and research design: Choosing among five approaches* (2nd ed.). Thousand Oaks, CA: Sage.

Creswell, J. W. (2012). *Educational research: Planning, conducting, and evaluating quantitative and qualitative research.* Boston: Pearson Education.

Creswell, J. W. (2014). *Research design: Qualitative, quantitative and mixed methods approaches* (4th ed.). Thousand Oaks, CA: Sage.

Creswell, J. W. (2015). *A concise introduction to mixed methods research.* Thousand Oaks, CA: Sage.

Creswell, J. W., & Plano Clark, V. L. (2018). *Designing and conducting mixed methods research* (3rd ed.). Thousand Oaks, CA: Sage.

Cronbach, L. J. (1951). Coefficient alpha and the internal structure of tests. *Psychometrika, 16*, 297–334.

Czarniawska, B. (2004). *Narratives in social science research.* London: Sage.

Daneman, M., & Carpenter, P. A. (1980). Individual differences in working memory and reading. *Journal of verbal learning and verbal behavior, 19*(4), 450–466.

Denzin, N. K. (1978). *The research act: A theoretical introduction to sociological methods.* New York: McGraw-Hill.

Derwing, T. M. (1991). The Role of NS Personality and Experience in NS-NNS Interaction. *TESL Canada Journal, 9*(1), 9–28.

Dobbert, M. (1982). *Ethnographic research: Theory and application for modern schools and societies.* New York: Praeger.

Dörnyei, Z. (2005). *The psychology of the language learner: Individual differences in second language acquisition.* Mahwah, NJ: Lawrence Erlbaum Associates.

Dörnyei, Z. (2007). *Research methods in applied linguistics: Quantitative, qualitative, and mixed methodologies.* New York: Oxford University Press.

Doughty, C., & Varela, E. (1998). Communicative focus on form. In C. Doughty & J. Williams (Eds.), *Focus on form in classroom second language acquisition* (pp. 114–138). New York: Cambridge University Press.

Dulay, H., & Burt, M. (1973). Should we teach children syntax? *Language Learning, 23*(2), 245–258.

Dulay, H., & Burt, M. (1974). Natural sequences in child second language acquisition. *Language Learning, 24*, 37–53.

Egi, T. (2007). Interpreting recasts as linguistic evidence: The role of linguistic target, length, and degree of change. *Studies in Second Language Acquisition, 29*, 511–537.

Egi, T. (2010). Uptake, Modified Output, and Learner Perceptions of Recasts: Learner Responses as Language Awareness. *The Modern Language Journal, 94*(1), 1–21. https://doi.org/10.1111/j.1540-4781.2009.00980.x.

Ellis, R. (2004). The definition and measurement of L2 explicit knowledge. *Language Learning, 54*(2), 227–275.

Ellis, R. (2005). Measuring implicit and explicit knowledge of a second language – A psychometric study. *Studies in Second Language Acquisition, 27*(2), 141–172.

Ellis, R., & Barkhuizen, G. (2005). *Analysing learner language.* Oxford: Oxford University Press.

Ellis, R., Loewen, S., & Erlam, R. (2006). Implicit and explicit corrective feedback and the acquisition of L2 grammar. *Studies in Second Language Acquisition, 28*, 339–369.

Evans, A. N., & Rooney, B. J. (2008). *Methods in psychological research.* London: Sage Publications.

Fairclough, N. (2001). Critical discourse analysis as a method in social scientific research. In R. Wodak & M. Meyer (Eds.), *Methods of critical discourse analysis* (pp. 122–136). London: Sage.

Fairclough, N. (2012). Critical discourse analysis. In J. P. Gee & H. M. (Eds.), *The Routledge handbook of discourse analysis* (pp. 9–20). New York, NY: Routledge.

Fanselow, J. F. (1977a). Beyond Rashomon – conceptualizing and describing the teaching act. *TESOL Quarterly, 11,* 17–39.

Fanselow, J. F. (1977b). The treatment of error in oral work. *Foreign Language Annals, 10,* 583–593.

Feiman-Nemser, S. (2013). The role of experience in the education of teacher educators. In M. Ben-Peretz (Ed.), *Teacher educators as members of an evolving profession* (pp. 189–210). New York: Rowan & Littlefield.

Firestone, W. A. (1993). Alternative arguments for generalizing from data as applied to qualitative research. *Educational Researcher, 22*(4), 16–23.

Flanders, N. A. (1970). *Analyzing teaching behavior.* Reading, MA: Addison-Wesley Publishing Company.

Flick, U. (2009). *An introduction to qualitative research* (4th ed.). London: Sage Publications.

Fu, T., & Nassaji, H. (2016). Corrective feedback, learner uptake, and feedback perception in a Chinese as a foreign language classroom. *Studies in Second Language Learning and Teaching, 6,* 161–183.

Gall, M. D., Borg, W. R., & Gall, J. P. (2002). *Educational research: An introduction* (7th ed.). White Plains, NY: Pearson.

Gardner, R. C. (1985). *Social psychology and second language learning: The role of attitudes and motivation.* London: Edward Arnold.

Geertz, C. (1973). Thick description: Toward an interpretive history of culture. In C. Geertz (Ed.), *The Interpretation of Cultures* (pp. 3–30). New York: Basic Books.

Gelman, A., Carlin, J. B., Stern, H. S., Dunson, D. B., Vehtari, A., & Rubin, D. B. (2013). *Bayesian data analysis* (3rd ed.). New York: CRC Press.

Giles, D. (2002). *Advanced research methods in psychology.* London: Routledge.

Glaser, B. G. (1978). *Theoretical sensitivity: Advances in the methodology of grounded theory.* Mill Valley, CA: Sociology Press.

Glaser, B. (1992). *Basics of grounded theory analysis.* Mill Valley, CA: Sociology Press.

Glaser, B., & Strauss, A. (1967). *The discovery of grounded theory: Strategies for qualitative research.* Mill Valley, CA: Sociology Press.

Grabe, W. (2002). Applied linguistics: An emerging discipline for the twenty-first century. In R. B. Kaplan (Ed.), *The Oxford handbook of applied linguistics* (pp. 3–12). New York: Oxford University Press.

Grant, A., Gottardo, A., & Geva, E. (2011). Reading in English as a first or second language: The case of Grade 3 Spanish, Portuguese, and English speakers. *Learning Disabilities Research & Practice, 26*(2), 67–83. https://doi.org/10.1111/j.1540-5826.2011.00327.x.

Gregersen, T., & MacIntyre, P. D. (2014). *Capitalizing on language learners' individuality: From premise to practice.* Bristol: Multilingual Matters.

Gumperz, J. J. (1977). The sociolinguistic significance of conversational code-switching. *RELC Journal, 8*(2), 1–34.

Gumperz, J. J. (1982). *Discourse strategies.* Cambridge: Cambridge University Press.

Hammersley, M. (2003). Conversation analysis and discourse analysis: methods or paradigms? *Discourse & Society, 14*(6), 751–781.

Han, Y., & Hyland, F. (2015). Exploring learner engagement with written corrective feedback in a Chinese tertiary EFL classroom. *Journal of Second Language Writing, 30*, 31–44.

Hartshorn, K., Evans, N, Merril, P., Sudweeks, R., Stron-Krause, D., & Anderson, N. (2010). Effects of dynamic corrective feedback on ESL writing accuracy. *TESOL Quarterly, 44*, 84–109.

Hatch, E., & Lazaraton, A. (1991). *The research manual: Design and statistics for applied linguistics.* New York: Newbury House.

Hawkes, L., & Nassaji, H. (2016). The role of extensive recasts in error detection and correction by adult ESL students. *Studies in Second Language Learning and Teaching,* 6, 19–41.

Hessel, G. (2015). From vision to action: Inquiring into the conditions for the motivational capacity of ideal second language selves. *System,* **52**, 103–114.

Horwitz, E. K., Horwitz, M. B., & Cope, J. (1986). Foreign language classroom anxiety. *The Modern language journal,* *70*(2), 125–132.

Hutchby, I. & Wooffitt, R. (1998). *Conversation analysis: Principles, practices, and applications.* Cambridge: Polity Press.

Jakobovits, L. A. (1973). Freedom to teach and freedom to learn. *TESOL Quarterly,* 117–126.

Jefferson, G. (1984). Transcription notation. In J. Atkinson & J. Heritage (Eds.), *Structures of social interaction: Studies in conversation analysis.* Cambridge: Cambridge University Press.

John, O. P., Robins, R. W., & Pervin, L. A. (Eds.). (2008). *Handbook of personality: Theory and research* (3rd ed.). New York: The Guilford Press.

Johnson, B., & Christensen, L. (2014). *Educational research: Quantitative and qualitative approaches.* Thousand Oaks, CA: Sage.

Johnson, D. (1992). *Approaches to research in second language learning.* New York: Longman.

Kasper, G. (1985). Repair in foreign language teaching. *Studies in Second Language Acquisition, 7*(2), 200–215.

Kasper, G., & Wagner, J. (2014). Conversation analysis in applied linguistics. *Annual Review of Applied Linguistics, 34*, 171–212.

Kessler, C., & Idar, I. (1979). Acquisition of English by a Vietnamese mother and child. *Working Papers on Bilingualism, 18*, 66–79.

Kim, H. Y. (2013). Statistical notes for clinical researchers: assessing normal distribution (2) using skewness and kurtosis. *Restorative Dentistry and Endodontics, 38*(1), 52–54. https://doi.org/10.5395/rde.2013.38.1.52.

Kline, R. B. (2016). *Principles and Practice of Structural Equation Modeling* (4th ed.). New York: The Guilford Press.

Kramsch, C. (2015). Applied linguistics: A theory of the practice. *Applied linguistics, 36*(4), 454–465.

Krashen, S. (1982). *Principles and practice in second language acquisition.* Chicago, IL: Pergamon Press.

Krashen, S. (1985). *The input hypothesis: Issues and implications.* Chicago, IL: Pergamon Press.

Kruschke, J. K. (2015). *Doing Bayesian data analysis: A tutorial with R, JAGS, and*

Stan (2nd ed.). San Diego, CA: Academic Press.

Kuhn, T. S. (1962). *The structure of scientific revolutions.* Chicago: University of Chicago Press.

Kurt, W. (2019). *Bayesian statistics the fun way: Understanding statistics and probability with Star Wars, LEGO, and rubber ducks.* San Francisco, CA: No Starch Press.

Labov. (1972). *Sociolinguistic patterns.* Philadelphia: University of Pennsylvania Press.

Lazaraton, A. (2002). *A qualitative approach to the validation of oral language tests.* Cambridge: Cambridge University Press.

Leow, R. (1998). Toward operationalizing the process of attention in SLA: Evidence for Tomlin and Villa's (1994) fine-grained analysis of attention. *Applied Psycholinguistics, 19*(1), 133–159.

Lincoln, Y., & Guba, E. (1985). *Naturalistic inquiry.* Beverly Hills, CA: Sage.

Long, M. (1981). Input, interaction and second language acquisition. In H. Winitz (Ed.), *Native language and foreign language acquisition* (pp. 259–278). New York: New York Academy of Sciences.

Long, M. (1996). The role of the linguistic environment in second language acquisition. In W. Ritchie & T. Bhatia (Eds.), *Handbook of second language acquisition* (pp. 413–468). San Diego, CA: Academic Press.

Lyotard, J. F. (1984). *The postmodern condition: A report on knowledge*, vol. 10, *Theory and history of literature.* Minneapolis: University of Minnesota Press.

Lyster, R., & Ranta, L. (1997). Corrective feedback and learner uptake: Negotiation of form in communicative classrooms. *Studies in Second Language Acquisition, 19*(1), 37–66.

MacIntyre, P. (1999). Language anxiety: A review of literature for language teachers. In D. J. Young (Ed.), *Affect in foreign language and second language learning: A practical guide to creating a low-anxiety classroom atmosphere.* Toronto, Canada: McGraw-Hill.

MacIntyre, P. D., Clément, R., Dörnyei, Z., & Noels, K. A. (1998). Conceptualizing willingness to communicate in a L2: A situational model of L2 confidence and affiliation. *The Modern Language Journal, 82*(4), 545–562.

Mackey, A., Gass, S., & McDonough, K. (2000). How do learners perceive interactional feedback? *Studies in Second Language Acquisition, 22*(4), 471–497.

Mackey, A., & Oliver, R. (2002). Interactional feedback and children's L2 development. *System, 30*(4), 459–477.

Malterud, K., Siersma, V. D., & Guassora, A. D. (2016). Sample size in qualitative interview studies: Guided by information power. *Qualitative Health Research, 26*(13), 1753–1760.

Maoz, Z. (2002). Case study methodology in international studies. In F. P. Harvey & M. Brecher (Eds.), *Evaluating methodology in international studies: From storytelling to hypothesis testing* (pp. 161–186). Ann Arbor: University of Michigan Press.

Markee, N. (2000). *Conversation analysis.* Mahwah, NJ: Erlbaum.

Maxwell, J. (1992). Understanding and validity in qualitative research. *Harvard Educational Review, 62*(3), 279–301.

Maxwell, J. A. (2015). Expanding the history and range of mixed methods research. *Journal of Mixed Methods Research, 10*(1), 12–27.

Mayo, E. (1993). *The human problems of an industrial civilization*. New York: Macmillan.

McCarthy, T. M. (2018). Exploring inner speech as a psycho-educational resource for language learning advisors. *Applied Linguistics, 39*(2), 159–187.

McCroskey, J. C. (1992). Reliability and validity of the willingness to communicate scale. *Communication Quarterly, 40*, 16–25.

McCroskey, J. C., & Baer, J. E. (1985). Willingness to communicate: The construct and its measurement. Paper presented at the annual convention of the Speech Communication Association, Denver, Colorado.

McKay, S. L. (2006). *Researching second language classrooms*. New York: Routledge.

McKelvie, S. J. (1978). Graphic rating scales – How many categories? *British Journal of Psychology, 69*(2), 185–202.

Meara, P. (2005). *LLAMA language aptitude tests: The manual*. Swansea: Lognostics.

Miles, M. B., & Huberman, A. M. (1994). *Qualitative data analysis: An expanded source book* (2nd ed.). Thousand Oaks, CA: Sage.

Miles, M. B., Huberman, A. M., & Johnny, S. (1994). *Qualitative data analysis: An expanded sourcebook*. Thousand Oaks, CA: Sage.

Morse, J. M. (2008). Editorial: Confusing categories and themes. *Qualitative Health Research, 18*(6), 727–728.

Morse, J. M. (2015a). Analytic strategies and sample size. *Qualitative Health Research, 25*, 1317–1318.

Morse, J. M. (2015b). Critical analysis of strategies for determining rigor in qualitative inquiry. *Qualitative Health Research, 25*(9), 1212–1222.

Moskowitz, G. (1971). Interaction analysis: A new modern language for supervisors. *Foreign Language Annals, 5*(2), 211–221.

Moskowitz, G. (1976). The FLint system: An observational tool for the foreign language class. Mirrors for behavior. In A. Simon and E. G. Boyer, *Mirrors for behavior: An anthology of classroom observation instruments*. Section 15, 1–15. Philadelphia: Center for the Study of Teaching at Temple University.

Muljani, D., Koda, K., & Moates, D. (1998). The development of word recognition in a second language. *Applied Psycholinguistics, 19*(1), 99–113. https://doi.org/10.1017/s0142716400010602.

Mullet, D. R. (2018). A general critical discourse analysis framework for educational research. *Journal of Advanced Academics, 29*(2), 116–142.

Nassaji, H. (2007). Elicitation and reformulation and their relationship with learner repair in dyadic interaction. *Language Learning, 57*, 511–548.

Nassaji, H. (2009). Effects of recasts and elicitations in dyadic interaction and the role of feedback explicitness. *Language Learning, 59*, 411–452.

Nassaji, H., & Geva, E. (1999). The contribution of phonological and orthographic processing skills to adult ESL reading: Evidence from native speakers of Farsi. *Applied Psycholinguistics, 20*(2), 241–267.

Nassaji, H., & Wells, G. (2000). What's the use of 'triadic dialogue'?: An investigation of teacher–student interaction. *Applied Linguistics, 21*(3), 376–406.

Nipaspong, P., & Chinokul, S. (2010). The role of prompts and explicit feedback in raising EFL learners' pragmatic awareness. *University of Sydney Papers in TESOL, 5*(5).

Nixon, A., & Odoyo, C. O. (2020). Ethnography, its strengths, weaknesses and its application in information technology and communication as a research design. *Computer Science and Information Technology, 8*(2), 50–56.

Norton, B. (2000). *Identity and language learning: Gender, ethnicity and educational change.* Harlow: Pearson.

Nudzor, H. P. (2009). A critical commentary on combined methods approach to researching educational and social issues. *Issues in Educational Research, 19*(2), 114–127.

Omona, J. (2013). Sampling in qualitative research: Improving the quality of research outcomes in higher education. *Makerere Journal of Higher Education, 4*(2), 169–185.

Onwuegbuzie, A. J., & Johnson, R. B. (2006). The validity issue in mixed research. *Research in the Schools, 13*(1), 48–63.

Onwuegbuzie, A. J., & Leech, N. L. (2005). On becoming a pragmatic researcher: The importance of combining quantitative and qualitative research methodologies. *International Journal of Social Research Methodology, 8*(5), 375–387.

Onwuegbuzie, A. J., & Leech, N. L. (2007a). A call for qualitative power analyses. *Quality & Quantity, 41*(1), 105–121.

Onwuegbuzie, A. J., & Leech, N. L. (2007b). Sampling designs in qualitative research: Making the sampling process more public. *Qualitative Report, 12*(2), 238–254.

Ottó, I. (2002). Magyar Egységes Nyelvérzékmérő-Teszt [Uniform Hungarian Language Aptitude Test]. *Kaposvár, Hungary: Mottó-Logic.*

Paribakht, T. S., & Wesche, M. (1997). Vocabulary enhancement activities and reading for meaning in second language vocabulary acquisition. *Second Language Vocabulary Acquisition: A Rationale for Pedagogy, 55*(4), 174–200.

Patton, M. Q. (1990). *Qualitative evaluation and research methods.* Thousand Oaks, CA: Sage.

Patton, M. Q. (2015). *Qualitative research and evaluation methods* (4th ed.). Thousand Oaks, CA: Sage.

Pavlenko, A. (2007). Autobiographic narratives as data in applied linguistics. *Applied Linguistics, 28*(2), 163–188.

Pennycook, A. (2021). *Critical applied linguistics: A critical re-introduction.* Abingdon: Routledge.

Pervin, L. A., & John, O. P. (2021). *Personality: Theory and research.* New York: John Wiley & Sons.

Philp, J. (2003). Constraints on 'noticing the gap': Nonnative speakers' noticing of recasts in NS–NNS interaction. *Studies in Second Language Acquisition, 25*(1), 99–126.

Plonsky, L., & Oswald, F. L. (2014). How big is "big"? Interpreting effect sizes in L2 research. *Language Learning, 64*(4), 878–912.

Polit, D. F., & Beck, C. T. (2010). Generalization in quantitative and qualitative research: Myths and strategies. *International Journal of Nursing Studies, 47*(11), 1451–1458.

Polkinghorne, D. E. (1995). Narrative configuration in qualitative analysis. *International Journal of Qualitative Studies in Education, 8*(1), 5–23.

Popper, K. R. (1959). *The logic of scientific discovery.* New York: Basic Books.

Randolph, J. (2009). A guide to writing the dissertation literature review *Practical Assessment, Research, and Evaluation*

14(1): 13. https://doi.org/10.7275/b0az-8t74.

Richards, L., & Morse, J. M. (2007). *Readme first for a user's guide to qualitative methods* (2nd ed.). Thousand Oaks, CA: Sage Publications.

Roethlisberger, F. J., & Dickson, W. J. (1939). *Management and the worker.* Cambridge, MA: Harvard University Press.

Sacks, H. (1984a). Notes on methodology. In J. M. Atkinson & J. Heritage (Eds.), *Structures of social action: Studies in conversation analysis* (pp. 2–27). Cambridge: Cambridge University Press.

Sacks, H. (1984b). On doing "being ordinary". In J. M. Atkinson & J. Heritage (Eds.), *Structures of social action: Studies in conversation analysis* (pp. 413–429). Cambridge: Cambridge University Press.

Sakai, H. (2011). Do recasts promote noticing the gap in L2 learning? *The Asian EFL Journal Quarterly, 13*(1), 357–385.

Sandelowski, M. (2003) Tables or Tableaux? The challenges of writing mixed methods studies. In A Tashakkori & C. Teddlie (Eds.), *Handbook of mixed methods in social and behavioral research* (pp. 321–350). Thousand Oaks, CA: Sage.

Schegloff, E. (1982). Discourse as an interactional achievement: Some uses of 'uh huh' and other things that come between sentences. In D. Tannen (Ed.), *Analyzing discourse: Text and talk* (pp. 71–93). Washington, DC: Georgetown University Press.

Schegloff, E. (2000). When 'others' initiate repair. *Applied Linguistics, 21*(2), 205–243.

Schegloff, E., Jefferson, G. & Sacks, H. (1977). The preference for self-correction in the organization of repair in conversation. *Language, 53,* 361–382.

Schegloff, E. A., Sacks, H., & Jefferson, G. (1992). Lectures on conversation. Oxford, UK: Blackwell.

Schmidt, R. (1983). Interaction, acculturation, and the acquisition of communicative competence: A case study of an adult. In N. Wolfson & E. Judd (Eds.), *Sociolinguistics and language acquisition* (pp. 137–174). Rowley, MA: Newbury House.

Schmitt, N., & Celce-Murcia, M. (2002). An overview of applied linguistics. In N. Schmitt (Ed.), *An introduction to applied linguistics* (pp. 1–16). New York: Oxford University Press.

Schmidt, R., & Frota, S. (1986). Developing basic conversational ability in a second language. A case study of an adult learner of Portuguese. In R. Day (Ed.), *Talking to learn: Conversation in second language acquisition* (pp. 237–326). Rowley, MA: Newbury House.

Schumann, J. H. (1978). *The pidginization process: A model for second language acquisition.* Rowley, MA: Newbury House.

Scott, V. M., & de La Fuente, M. J. (2008). What's the problem? L2 learners' use of the L1 during consciousness-raising, form-focused tasks. *The Modern Language Journal, 92*(1), 100–113.

Searle, J. R. (1969). *Speech acts: An essay in the philosophy of language.* London: Cambridge University Press.

Sebastian, K. (2019). Distinguishing between the strains grounded theory: Classical, interpretive and constructivist. *Journal for Social Thought, 3*(1), 1–9.

Seedhouse, P. (1994). Linking the pedagogical purposes to linguistic patterns of interaction: The analysis of communication in the language classroom. *IRAL, 32*(4), 303–320.

Seedhouse, P. (2004). *The interactional architecture of the language classroom: A conversation analysis perspective.* Malden, MA: Blackwell.

Shadish, W., Cook, T. D., & Campbell, D. T. (2002). *Experimental and quasi-experimental designs for generalized causal inference.* Boston, MA: Houghton Mifflin.

Shapira, R. G. (1978). The non-learning of English: A case study of an adult. In E. M. Hatch (Ed.), *Second language acquisition.* Rowley, MA: Newbury House.

Sheen, Y. (2007). The effect of focused written corrective feedback and language aptitude on ESL learners' acquisition of articles. *TESOL Quarterly, 41*(2), 255–255.

Sheen, Y. (2008). Recasts, language anxiety, modified output, and L2 learning. *Language Learning, 58*(4), 835–874.

Spada, N., & Tomita, Y. (2010). Interactions between type of instruction and type of language feature: A meta analysis. *Language Learning, 60*(2), 263–308.

Spielberger, C. D. (1988). *Manual for the State-Trait Anger Expression Inventory.* Odessa, FL: Psychological Assessment Resources, Inc.

Stake, R. E. (1995). *The art of case study research.* Thousand Oaks, CA: Sage.

Stake, R. E. (2008). Qualitative case studies. In N. K. Denzin & Y. S. Lincoln (Eds.), *Strategies of qualitative inquiry* (pp. 19–149). Thousand Oaks, CA: Sage.

Stanovich, K. E., & West, R. F. (1989). Exposure to Print and Orthographic Processing. *Reading Research Quarterly, 24*(4), 402–433.

Starfield, S. (2018). Writing a research proposal. In A. Phakiti, P. De Costa, L. Plonsky, & S. Starfield (Eds.), *The Palgrave handbook of applied linguistics research methodology* (pp. 183–197). London: Palgrave.

Strauss, A. L. (1987). *Qualitative analysis for social scientists.* New York: Cambridge University Press.

Strauss, A. (1998). *Qualitative analysis for social scientists.* New York: Cambridge University Press.

Strauss, A., & Corbin, J. (1990). *Basics of qualitative research.* Beverly Hills, CA: Sage publications.

Strauss, A., & Corbin, J. (1998). *Basics of qualitative research: Techniques and procedures for developing grounded theory.* Thousand Oaks, CA: Sage.

Streiner, D. L. (2005). Finding Our Way: An Introduction to Path Analysis. *The Canadian Journal of Psychiatry, 50,* 115–122.

Sturman, A. (1997). Case study methods. In J. P. Keeves (Ed.), *Educational research methodology and measurement: an international handbook* (2nd ed., pp. 61–66). New York: Pergamon.

Tabachnick, B. G., & Fidell, L. S. (2018). *Using multivariate statistics* (7th ed.). New York: Pearson.

Taguchi, T., Magid, M., & Papi, M. (2009). The L2 motivational self system among Japanese, Chinese and Iranian learners of English: A comparative study. In Z. Dörnyei & E. Ushioda (Eds.), *Motivation, language identity and the L2 self* (pp. 66–97). Bristol: Multilingual Matters.

Tarone, E. (1980). Guidelines for ethical research in ESL. *TESOL Quarterly, 14*(3), 383–390.

Tarone, E. (2015). Second language acquisition in applied linguistics: 1925–2015 and beyond. *Applied Linguistics, 36*(4), 444–453.

Tashakkori, A., & Teddlie, C. (1998). *Mixed methodology: Combining qualitative and quantitative approaches.* Thousand Oaks, CA: Sage.

Tashakkori, A., & Teddlie, C. (Eds.). (2003). *Handbook of mixed methods research in social and behavioural research.* Thousand Oaks, CA: Sage.

Tashakkori, A., Teddlie, C., & Sines, M. C. (2012). Utilizing mixed methods in psychological research. In J. A. Schinka, W. F. Velicer, & I. B. Weiner (Eds.), *Handbook of psychology: Research methods in psychology* (2nd ed., pp. 428–450). John Wiley & Sons.

Teddlie, C., & Tashakkori, A. (2006). A general typology of research designs featuring mixed methods. *Research in the Schools, 13*(1), 12–28.

Teimouri, Y. (2017). L2 selves, emotions, and motivated behaviors. *Studies in Second Language Acquisition, 39,* 681–709.

Terrell, T. D. (1991). The role of grammar instruction in a communicative approach. *The Modern Language Journal, 75*(1), 52–63.

Tobin, G. A., & Begley, C. M. (2004). Methodological rigour within a qualitative framework. *Journal of Advanced Nursing, 48*(4), 388–396.

Tsui, A. B. (2007). Complexities of identity formation: A narrative inquiry of an EFL teacher. *TESOL Quarterly, 41*(4), 657–680.

Turner, J. E. (1993). Using Likert scales in L2 research. Another researcher comments. *TESOL Quarterly, 27*(4), 736–739.

Turner, M. L., & Engle, R. W. (1989). Is working memory capacity task dependent? *Journal of Memory and Language, 28*(2), 127–154.

Van Dijk, T. A. (1993). Principles of critical discourse analysis. *Discourse & Society, 4*(2), 249–283.

VanPatten, B. (1996). *Input processing and grammar instruction: Theory and research.* Norwood, NJ: Ablex.

VanPatten, B., & Cadierno, T. (1993). Explicit instruction and input processing. *Studies in Second Language Acquisition, 15,* 225–244.

Vogelzang, M., Thiel, C. M., Rosemann, S., Rieger, J. W., & Ruigendijk, E. (2020). Neural mechanisms underlying the processing of complex sentences: An fMRI study. *Neurobiology of Language, 1*(2), 226–248.

Warner, W. L., & Lunt, P. S. (1941). *The social life of a modern community.* New Haven, CT: Yale University Press.

Widdowson, H. G. (1984). *Explorations in applied linguistics.* New York: Oxford University Press.

Widdowson, H. G. (2000). On the limitations of linguistics applied. *Applied Linguistics, 21*(1), 3–25.

Woody, C. (1927). The values of educational research to the classroom teacher. *The Journal of Educational Research, 16*(3), 172–178.

Yang, Y., & Lyster, R. (2010). Effects of form-focused practice and feedback on Chinese EFL learners' acquisition of regular and irregular past tense forms. *Studies in Second Language Acquisition, 32*(02), 235–263.

Yilmaz, Y. (2011). Task effects on focus on form in synchronous computer-mediated communication. *The Modern Language Journal, 95*(1), 115–132.

Yin, R. (2003). Case study research: Design and methods (3rd ed.). Thousand Oaks, CA: Sage Publications.

Zheng, C. (2012). Understanding the learning process of peer feedback activity: An ethnographic study of exploratory practice. *Language Teaching Research, 16*(1), 109–126.

Index

For EU product safety concerns, contact us at Calle de José Abascal, 56–1°, 28003 Madrid, Spain or eugpsr@cambridge.org.

www.ingramcontent.com/pod-product-compliance
Ingram Content Group UK Ltd.
Pitfield, Milton Keynes, MK11 3LW, UK
UKHW052048081025
463757UK00014B/466